THE OXFORD BOOK OF WORK

THE OXFORD BOOK OF

WORK

Edited by
Keith Thomas

OXFORD
UNIVERSITY PRESS

OXFORD
UNIVERSITY PRESS

Oxford University Press, Great Clarendon Street, Oxford OX2 6DP

Oxford New York

Athens Auckland Bangkok Bogotá Buenos Aires Calcutta
Cape Town Chennai Dar es Salaam Delhi Florence Hong Kong Istanbul
Karachi Kuala Lumpur Madrid Melbourne Mexico City Mumbai
Nairobi Paris São Paulo Singapore Taipei Tokyo Toronto Warsaw
and associated companies in Berlin Ibadan

Oxford is a registered trade mark of Oxford University Press

British Library Cataloguing in Publication Data
Data available

Library of Congress Cataloging in Publication Data
The Oxford book of work / edited by Keith Thomas.
Includes bibliographical references and index.
1. Work. 2. Work. I. Keith Thomas, 1933– .
HD4901.093 1999 306.3'6—dc21 98–36795
ISBN 0–19–214217–8

1 3 5 7 9 10 8 6 4 2

Typeset in Hong Kong
by Best-set Typesetter Ltd.
Printed in Great Britain
on acid-free paper by
MPG Books Ltd.,
Bodmin, Cornwall

Preface

What a dreary subject! Though they were too polite to say so, that was obviously what most people thought when I told them that I was compiling *The Oxford Book of Work*. Dreary or not, work is a virtually inescapable part of the human condition. Many of us spend most of our waking hours engaged in it. It absorbs our energies and preoccupies our thoughts. It involves us in close relations with other people and gives us our sense of identity. It provides us with the means of subsistence, and it makes possible all the pleasures and achievements of civilization.

Yet, for all its centrality to human existence, work has never been a popular literary theme. By comparison with love or warfare, the business of getting a living has been relatively neglected by poets and novelists. For centuries the dominance of classical notions of decorum meant that the realistic treatment of mundane tasks was outlawed from Western literature. If agricultural life was depicted, then it was usually through the distorting lens of pastoral; and if labourers or craftsmen appeared, they were often comic or lumpen figures. The work of merchants, financiers, and bureaucrats was equally shunned. As George Crabbe wrote in *The Borough* (1810),

> 'Trades and Professions'—these are themes the Muse,
> Left to her freedom, would forbear to choose.

Even with the growth in nineteenth-century Europe and America of a mass reading public, much imaginative writing retained a predominantly escapist character; it sought to provide some relief from the humdrum realities of daily existence and to focus readers' minds on the heroic, the amusing, or the exceptional. As the novelist William Dean Howells wrote in 1911, 'The American public does not like to read about the life of toil. What we like to read about is the life of noblemen or millionaires . . . if our writers were to begin telling us on any extended scale how mill hands or miners or farmers or iron-puddlers really live, we should soon let them know that we do not care to meet with such vulgar and commonplace people.'[1] Of course, there were plenty of 'realistic' novelists who memorably depicted the life of labour. But, only too often, as with Émile Zola or George Gissing or Upton Sinclair, their vision was so bleak as to confirm the popular prejudice that writing about work was an inherently depressing business. In any case, work has never lent itself easily to literary treatment. Because it is a long, continuing process, rather than a dis-

[1] William Dean Howells, 'The Man of Letters as a Man of Business', *Literature and Life* (1911), p. 2.

crete act, it is harder to write about than other shorter and more intense forms of experience, in the same way that marriage is a more difficult subject for a novel than courtship or adultery.

Even those who have spent most of their lives working seldom say much about their work when they come to write about themselves. A modern social historian, who compiled an anthology of British working-class autobiographies of the nineteenth and twentieth centuries, discovered that workers wrote very little about their work: they preferred to discuss their personal triumphs and difficulties or their spiritual condition. 'Work, it seems, was not a central life-interest of the working-classes.'[2] Another distinguished historian has recently concluded that 'we know little enough of people's attitude to work at the best of times and have almost no accurate knowledge for the period before the 1930s'.[3]

Yet literary representations of work are everywhere if one looks for them. In novels and plays they are seldom central to the action, but they often form part of the essential backcloth to the emotional lives of the characters; and, in the poetry of the post-Romantic era, reflection upon the experience of work is increasingly frequent. This anthology draws heavily on such imaginative writing. It also includes extracts from the works of theologians, economists, and philosophers who have reflected upon work and its meaning; social investigators and journalists who have observed people at work, usually at a safe distance; and diarists, letter-writers, and autobiographers who have portrayed the experience of work as it affected their own lives.

I have followed the principle that, to qualify for inclusion, an excerpt must have some intrinsic literary value, that is to say it must be a piece that the reader would find it interesting to read more than once. The excerpt must also be fully intelligible on its own; many otherwise instructive passages, particularly from novels, have had to be left out because they would have presupposed too much prior knowledge of the context or the characters. Even so, some use has had to be made of that most brutally interventionist weapon in the anthologist's armoury, the three dots indicating that an unspecified number of words has been omitted. Moreover, like all anthologists, I have, for reasons of copyright and its associated costs, had to forgo some passages that I should much like to have included.

Subject to these constraints, I have chosen selections from a wide range of sources, most of them written in English by British or North American authors, but with a certain number drawn from other literatures in translation. Poetry has been juxtaposed with prose, fiction with fact, and the solemn with the absurd. I have tried to compile a selection that will be interesting and enjoyable, whether read straight through or dipped into at random. But my aim is not just to entertain. I also hope that this anthology will illuminate an

---

[2] John Burnett, *Useful Toil* (1971), p. 15.
[3] Ross McKibbin, *The Ideologies of Class* (1990), p. 148.

important but difficult subject. It is meant to show some of the ways in which the experience of work has changed over time and to illustrate the different modes in which people, whether the workers themselves or analytic observers, have responded to that experience. It also reveals something of the literary conventions and influences that have shaped the way in which writers have represented the subject. Above all, it attempts to illuminate the human dimensions of a topic that, if treated at all, is usually discussed in a somewhat abstract way. Like every anthology, this one is no more than a collection of quotations. But it is out of such quotations that history is written.

This is not the first anthology to have been compiled about work and associated topics, and I am inevitably indebted to my predecessors. I have been helped by such earlier works as Adrian Bell, *The Open Air* (1936), Anthony Bertram, *The Pleasures of Poverty* (1950), H. S. Salt, *Songs of Freedom* (1893), and Dorothy Wooldridge, *The Poetry of Toil* (1926), as well as by more recent anthologies like David Wright, *The Penguin Book of Everyday Verse* (1976), Marion Shaw, *Man Does, Woman Is: An Anthology of Work and Gender* (1995), and Jeremy Lewis, *The Chatto Book of Office Life* (1992). I owe a more general debt to the generations of historians, economists, and sociologists whose writings on work have shaped my thinking about the subject. I am also very grateful to friends and colleagues who have bombarded me with ideas as to where I might look for suitable material. Christina Colvin, John Gelsthorpe, and Brian Harrison have been particularly assiduous with their suggestions, but I also offer warm thanks for their help to Elisabeth Albanis, Kate Bucknell, Howard Colvin, Valentine Cunningham, Emily Gowers, Peter Hacker, Carol Howard, Anthony Kenny, Elizabeth Knowles, Colin Matthew, David Musson, and Edmund Thomas. Veronica Krailsheimer has uncomplainingly done a vast amount of photocopying and retyping. Donna Poppy, to whom I am indebted for her meticulous copy-editing, has provided a host of valuable suggestions. Judith Luna has been an exemplary editor, patient and encouraging. My wife, who has acted as the virtual co-editor of this book, has helped me most of all.

K. T.
Corpus Christi College
Oxford

Contents

Part Two: Kinds of Work

Part Three: The Reform of Work

Epilogue

Introduction

'Work' is harder to define than one might think. The *Concise Oxford Dictionary* tells us that it is 'expenditure of energy, striving, application of effort or exertion to a purpose'. Yet there are many ways of purposively expending energy that do not count as 'work'. In the late seventeenth century the scientist Robert Boyle remarked that 'tennis, which our gallants make a recreation, is much more toilsome than what many others make their work'. Two hundred years later the philosopher John Stuart Mill observed that 'many a day spent in killing game includes more muscular fatigue than a day's ploughing'. But, though tennis and killing game are both strenuous activities, neither can be classified as work, unless, of course, one happens to be a gillie or a professional tennis-player.

On the other hand, it is not enough to say that work is what we do in our paid employment. After all, many people have worked without being remunerated; and others have been remunerated without working. Paid employment itself is a relatively modern development in human history. In the past, including the recent past, a huge amount of the world's work was done by slaves and captives. This was the case in classical Greece and Rome, and it continued to be so in the age of European expansion, when millions of persons were forcibly transported from Africa to work as slaves in the Americas. In medieval Europe agricultural production was based on serfdom and compulsory labour services. In modern times there are still many people who, without being slaves, nevertheless work for little or no payment: for example, housewives, schoolchildren, the so-called 'unemployed', and the retired. For we know that housework and child-care are very exhausting, that schoolchildren, and not only Japanese ones, can work ferociously hard, that the 'unemployed' often engage in a variety of tiring activities, and that many academics look forward to their retirement because it will give them a chance to get on with what they call their 'own work'. It seems odd to regard a housepainter as working when he paints other people's houses for money, but not when he paints his own in his spare time; or to say that writers have ceased to work when they leave their word-processors and go to do some overdue digging in their gardens.

So how do we define work? The late Victorian economist Alfred Marshall said that labour was 'any exertion of mind or body undergone partly or wholly with a view to some good other than the pleasure derived directly from the work'. That definition is too wide; it would, for example, make physical exercise count as work if it were done for health rather than for pleasure. But it hints at ingredients that have to be included in any acceptable definition.

Work has an end beyond itself, being designed to produce or achieve something; it involves a degree of obligation or necessity, being a task that others set us or that we set ourselves; and it is arduous, involving effort and persistence beyond the point at which the task ceases to be wholly pleasurable.

This concept of 'work' as an undifferentiated abstraction comprehending an almost infinite variety of different activities is a relatively modern one. It could not emerge in the less complex societies of the remote past or the undeveloped world, where the whole of the population customarily engages in the business of procuring subsistence and where an individual's tasks are preordained by his or her social position. In such a world work is not easily separated from the rest of experience, but is inextricably confused with what we today would regard as non-work. The Dogons of Mali, for example, employ the same words to indicate both cultivating the ground and dancing at a religious ceremony, for they regard them as equally useful forms of activity. In this kind of simple society, work and leisure are not clearly distinguished from each other; instead, economic activities, like hunting or market-going, have their recreational dimensions, while agricultural work may be accompanied by singing or story-telling.

In medieval Europe it could be similarly difficult to tell where work ended and leisure began; for many pastimes were not so much recreations as the training rituals of a society organized for war: the tournament for the upper classes, archery for the people, riding, wrestling, and similar rehearsals for future conflict. Even chess was a war game. As late as the sixteenth century some Cornish stock-farmers used to let their beasts run wild and subsequently hunted them down with guns and crossbows. In this vanished world all the population, men and women, the young and the old, had some sort of economic role to play. Young children herded animals. Aristocratic ladies cooked and did embroidery. No firm line separated the 'employed' from the 'unemployed'; and work was less a separate domain than a dimension of all aspects of life.

Yet though everyone worked in one way or another, the modern undifferentiated abstraction, 'work', was slow to emerge. In the early Middle Ages 'labour' was thought of exclusively as physical labour. It was therefore conventional to say that there were three orders of society: one that fought, one that prayed, and one—only one—that worked, that is to say cultivated the soil. Only gradually did the concept of mental or intellectual labour develop and, with it, the acceptance of the idea—obvious enough to us—that all three orders of society worked, though in different ways.

By the early modern period economic writers had grown accustomed to conceptualizing work or labour in the abstract, rather than in the form of particular occupations. In 1535, for example, an unknown writer declared that 'the whole wealth of the realm riseth out of the labours and works of the common people'; in 1651 the political philosopher Thomas Hobbes wrote that 'a man's labour . . . is a commodity exchangeable for benefit as well as any other thing'; and in the later seventeenth century most commentators agreed that it was upon the labour of its inhabitants that a country's prosperity depended. Some even suggested that, from the economic point of view, the labour of the common people was more productive than that of their social superiors.

By this time it had become customary to accept that productive work was the basis of civilization. For example, the heraldic writer Edward Waterhouse claimed in 1663 that 'in the industry of man there is such a latent power and life of actuation that it comes near the verge of the miraculous'. He cited among the achievements of such industry not just building and metal-working, but 'arts, languages, sciences and professions'. In this celebration of human productive power we see the acceptance of the idea that 'work' or 'industry' was something common to an infinite range of different occupations. This notion was to be the foundation of what economists came to know as the labour theory of value.

For the most famous proponent of that theory, Karl Marx, as for many other nineteenth-century theorists, work was the defining feature of the human race. It was the purposive effort of men and women to ensure their survival and to meet their ever growing needs. This was said to be a uniquely human quality. Birds might build nests and bees gather honey, but they did so by following instinct rather than by acting in accordance with a conscious plan. Only mankind worked. Yet not all the efforts made by human beings to ensure their survival are regarded as work. The continuation of the human race requires not just that we should have food, clothing, and shelter, but also that we should reproduce ourselves. Yet sexual intercourse is not usually classified as work, save in the case of prostitutes and similar so-called 'sex workers'.

The development of capitalism over the last three hundred years has been accompanied by that of a free labour market. Typically, an employed person sells his or her labour for a defined period of time, and that labour is usually performed away from the worker's residence. This system makes possible a much clearer distinction between work and leisure, and between work and the home. It divides up the day into working time and leisure time; it provides a structure to the week, with half-days and weekends taking on their own special quality; and, through the device of the annual holiday, it gives a rhythm to the year. The system also draws a distinction between persons employed in this way and those who, like children, the retired, and the 'unemployed', supposedly do not work. The line is not always a clear one, as the case of the housewife demonstrates, but it makes it somewhat easier to determine which activities should or should not be counted as 'work'.

In the end, however, we have to recognize that the definition of work is not an objective matter. The term's different meanings embody different phases of historical development and different political viewpoints. Just as the male economists of the late nineteenth and early twentieth centuries were reluctant to accept that unpaid housework was really work, preferring to classify it as an 'unproductive' activity, so modern radicals are disinclined to accept that the Queen is working when she gives a garden party. In the era of the Reformation, Protestants denounced monks as idle parasites; for them, the contemplative life could not count as work. In North America the early English colonists lamented the idleness of the native Americans, who were warriors and hunters; as the English saw it, it was only the women who were engaged in real work, agriculture.

Business people and manual workers have always been sceptical about the existence of such a thing as intellectual work. When I was a schoolboy studying for examinations, my father, a farmer, understandably refused to concede that when I was sitting on a deckchair in the garden reading a book, rather than helping him in the cornfields with the harvest, I might be working as hard as he was. Basil Bunting has a wry little poem in which the Chairman tells Tom what he thinks of people who write poetry:

> Poetry? It's a hobby.
> I run model trains.
> Mr Shaw there breeds pigeons.
>
> It's not work. You dont sweat.
> Nobody pays for it . . .
>
> What you write is rot.
>
> Mr Hines says so, and he's a schoolteacher,
> he ought to know.
> Go and find *work*.

The raised feminist consciousness of recent times has rightly made us readier to classify unpaid housework and childcare as work— real work—than we used to be; and the Society of Authors would no doubt maintain that writing poetry was real work too. But is a businessman working when he takes a client to an expensive restaurant? Or when he plays golf in order to clinch a deal at the nineteenth hole? In today's world work and leisure are much more sharply segregated than they used to be, but the line is still not easy to draw.

In the absence of any single, universally acceptable definition of work, and in the knowledge that the large *Oxford English Dictionary* gives the noun 'work' no less than thirty-four different meanings and the verb thirty-nine, the compilation of this anthology has had to proceed pragmatically. Extracts have been assembled that relate either to paid employment or to those kinds of sustained physical or mental effort that have about them some form of necessity or constraint. Human industry takes so many different forms that it has been possible to represent only a small selection of occupations. But an attempt has been made to convey the huge variety of ways in which people have busied themselves, as well as the vast range of conflicting sensations that the experience of work can involve, from boredom, anger, and fatigue to delighted absorption. There is also a certain amount of material on rest, leisure, and idleness, since these states take their whole meaning from their implicit opposition to the activity of work.

In *David Copperfield* Dickens makes Uriah Heep complain that when he was at school ('the same school where I picked up so much 'umbleness'), he was taught 'from nine o-clock to eleven, that labour was a curse; and from eleven o-clock to one, that it was a blessing and a cheerfulness, and a dignity, and I don't know what all, eh'. The same inconsistency runs through this anthology. On the one hand, work has, since time immemorial, been seen as a curse, a result of the Fall and a punishment for sin. It was something that, it was assumed, everyone would naturally try to avoid, whether they were 'savages' lounging in the tropical sun, or European aristocrats, pursuing an existence of conspicuous leisure. The ideal society was a land of Cockaigne, where all things came by nature and the need to work had vanished.

On the other hand, work was widely admired as a divine activity, practised by God during the creation of the world and by Adam and Eve in Eden. It was a sacred duty and the source of all human comforts, creating wealth and making civilization possible. It was a cure for boredom and melancholy, and a remedy for vice. It was the only sure route to human happiness, bringing health, contentment, and personal fulfilment. It structured the day, gave opportunities for sociability and companionship, fostered pride in individual creativity, and created a sense of personal identity. Idleness could never make people happy; and the ideal society was one in which there was satisfying work available for everybody.

The classical economists took the first of these two views. Adam Smith agreed with Dr Johnson that every man was naturally an idler. It was axiomatic that human beings preferred leisure to work. Labour meant 'toil and trouble'. It was undertaken only for the sake of remuneration, what in North America is still revealingly called 'compensation'. The object of working was to acquire wealth; and the object of wealth was to avoid having to work. The labouring classes, it was said, worked only out of necessity: to avoid starvation, or to acquire additional goods that they coveted for their practical utility or as a means of keeping ahead of their neighbours. Without either stick or carrot, the inertial force of human indolence would be sure to reassert itself.

The native peoples in the overseas colonies were cited as further proof of this natural inclination to idleness. John Stuart Mill thought that the only way to 'civilize' such people, that is to say to make them take up a life of unrelenting toil, was to inculcate them 'with new wants and desires'. Otherwise, human nature being what it was, they would be idle. Mill's own upbringing (his father allowed him no holidays, 'lest the habit of work should be broken, and a taste for idleness acquired') had reflected this same belief that laziness was an innate and deep-seated urge, to which, without the most strenuous application, the human animal would invariably succumb.

This view of work as inherently repugnant went back to remote antiquity. The warrior societies of the past had, like the native Americans, thought fighting preferable to working, just as the classical moralists preferred *otium* to *negotium*. Physical labour was the business of slaves, women, and the subordinate classes. When the Benedictine monks of the early Middle Ages engaged in manual labour, they did so in a penitential spirit: work was an ascetic mortification of the flesh; the ideal life was one of piety and contemplation. The French word *travail* supposedly derived from *trepālium*, an instrument of torture; and the travails of childbirth recalled the curse that associated all forms of labour with pain.

In the twelfth and thirteenth centuries European theologians gave work a more positive status, stressing its social and moral benefits and repeating St Benedict's observation that idleness was the enemy of the soul. But they did not represent work as innately satisfying. Neither did the many proponents of the work ethic who emerged in the late medieval and early modern periods. For the Puritans in England and America, work was praiseworthy because St Paul had said that those who did not work should not eat; because work fostered a spirit of renunciation and was good for the character; because it made people healthier; and because society functioned more smoothly when everyone had a lawful calling. Above all, work was good because idleness was a dangerous state that led people into many vices and disorders, particularly those associated with drink, sex, and violence. The Puritans thus said very little about the intrinsic satisfactions that work might bring with it. For them, it was a divine command; and its main advantage was that it kept people out of mischief and enabled them to provide for themselves.

For all this emphasis on moral duty, there were plenty of people who demonstrably enjoyed the tasks they were paid to perform. But the conviction remained that, if labour were enjoyable, then it could not be counted as work. As Sir Dudley North (1641–91) put it: 'If it was agreeable to do anything called work, it was not really so but pleasure . . . It is incident to the true nature of work not to delight in it.'

Much of this anthology is taken up with similar negative reactions to work. They evoke the dreariness, discomfort, and tedium of repetitive factory work; the horrors of plantation slavery; the petty tyrannies of office life; and the major tyrannies of penal labour. The participants themselves have not left much of a literary record. But from the nineteenth century onwards it is possible to draw upon a rich tradition of realistic social observation. It confirms the inescapable fact that, through the centuries, the lot of most of the human race has been hard toil for small reward.

Utopian thinkers have speculated about a world in which the burden of work could be reduced by limiting human wants and sharing labour out among everyone. Communists have dignified manual labour and attempted to devise a social framework in which work becomes fulfilling because the worker owns the means of production. In the West the reaction of most social reformers has been to reduce the length of the working week, to increase the number of holidays, and to improve pay and conditions of labour. Others have looked to automation as the long-run means of eliminating dreary and laborious toil.

Meanwhile in the modern industrial world most people have continued to regard work as a tedious necessity. 'Why does the worker work?' asked Friedrich Engels in 1844. 'For love of work? From a natural impulse? Not at all! He works for money, for a thing which has nothing to do with the work itself.' This proposition is wholly consistent with the more recent findings of the sociologist John Goldthorpe, in a study of the car workers of Luton, Bedfordshire, in the 1960s.[1] He found that their attitude to work was instrumental: it was a means to an end, a temporary surrender of liberty for the sake of material reward. Among the managerial classes today there are many who find work stressful and view the workplace as a combative arena in which human beings strive aggressively for money and status. 'Oh, to get out of the rat-race,' they say. Nowadays millions of people speak of their work in this way. They only do it, they say, for the money; and they would give it up tomorrow if they could afford to do so. Meanwhile they look for their pleasures, their fulfilment, and their sense of identity to their private life and their recreations.

Yet it is well known that not all of those who come into an unexpected fortune immediately give up their jobs. On the contrary, they are usually advised not to do so, on the grounds that they would miss their work too much, just as persons who have to retire because of their age are known to do. In December 1996 the British tabloid newspapers reported the case of Linda Hill, who had won nearly £2 million in the national lottery but elected to continue with her £80-a-week job as a chambermaid at a Butlin's holiday camp ('I love my job, and life just wouldn't be the same without it').

This recognition that work can be a physical and emotional necessity for human beings, no less than an economic one, is not very conspicuous before the later seventeenth century, although it is implicit in much earlier moralistic writing about the miseries of idleness. Robert Burton, the Jacobean anatomist of melancholy, believed that, though the English nobility of his day had everything in abundance, they were disproportionately subject to melancholic gloom because they lived lives of idleness; counting it a disgrace to work, they suffered endless 'cares, griefs, false fears, discontents and suspicions'. In the nineteenth century Florence Nightingale would write of the sufferings and frustrations of middle-class women who were kept compulsorily idle: 'the accumulation of nervous energy, which has had nothing to do dur-

---

[1] *The Affluent Worker: Industrial Attitudes and Behaviour* (1968).

ing the day, makes them feel every night, when they go to bed, as if they were going mad; and they are obliged to lie long in bed in the morning to let it evaporate and keep it down'.

Medical writers had always urged the importance of physical exercise. Hence the philosopher John Locke's recommendation at the end of the seventeenth century that every scholar should spend three hours a day on manual labour, as well, of course, as nine hours on thinking and reading. But Locke also believed that, psychologically, 'men cannot be perfectly idle; they must be doing something. It was his eighteenth-century successor, David Hume, who did most to develop this insight. 'Every enjoyment,' he wrote, 'soon becomes insipid and distasteful, when not acquired by fatigue and industry.' There was no craving of the human mind more constant and insatiable than the desire for exercise and employment.

When Adam Smith declared that labour involved the worker only in 'toil and trouble', he was thinking primarily of manual work. Indeed he explicitly said that it was only what he called 'the inferior employments' that were performed solely for the sake of the money, thus conceding the possibility that other occupations could be rewarding in themselves. Nevertheless, Karl Marx had a point when he declared that Smith's view of labour as a curse and of tranquillity as the human ideal was psychologically misconceived. For the young Marx work was not just a way of securing a livelihood: it was potentially a liberating activity, leading to self-realization and freedom. Alfred Marshall also conceded that 'in a healthy state, pleasure predominates over pain in a great part even of the work that is done for hire'. He believed that 'as human nature is constituted, man rapidly degenerates unless he has some hard work to do, some difficulties to overcome'. Those who pursued success in business or science or the arts could hope to experience intense pleasure, alternating with periods of lassitude, whereas, for 'ordinary people', who had no strong ambitions, 'moderate and fairly steady work' offered 'the best opportunity for the growth of those habits of body, mind and spirit in which alone there is true happiness'.

Nevertheless, most of those who claimed to enjoy their work and to find life impossible without it were engaged not in manual toil but in relatively agreeable middle-class occupations. This did not inhibit a chorus of literary celebration of the supposed pleasures and joys of the labouring life. There is no shortage of sparkling milkmaids, laughing peasants, and healthy, long-lived labourers, happier in their cottages than the king in his castle. Think of James Thomson ('Better the toiling swain, oh happier far! / Perhaps the happiest of the sons of men'), Charles Churchill ('Labour his business and his pleasure too'), John Dyer ('cheerful are the labours of the loom'), William Cowper ('cheerful days and nights without a groan'), William Barnes ("Tis merry ov a summer's day, / When vo'k be out a-meaken hay'), Robert Bridges ("Tis merry winnowing') and even R. S. Thomas ('Ah, you should see Cynddylan on a tractor'). In Thomas Dekker's words:

Work apace, apace, apace, apace
Honest labour bears a lovely face;
Then hey nonny nonny, hey nonny nonny!

Was this long pastoral tradition a conspiracy to deceive the poor into thinking that they had the best of all possible worlds, and to reassure the rich that their comforts did not involve the exploitation of others? Did it show insensitivity to the hardships of the labouring poor? Or was it just another instance of the ubiquitous influence of classical literary models? Whatever the case, English poetry does not offer much in the way of a 'realistic' view of manual work until the appearance in the eighteenth century of the labourer–poet, Stephen Duck, with his unsentimental account, *The Thresher's Labour*, and the washerwoman Mary Collier, with her equally unsentimental riposte, *The Woman's Labour*. The early twentieth century saw a deluge of charming but wildly sentimental Georgian verse about old wagoners, dry-wallers, and mole-catchers, all perceived through the distorting mists of rural nostalgia. In the United States Walt Whitman had vigorously celebrated the realities of American labour, seeking to 'teach the average man the glory of daily walk and trade'. Yet his 'clean hair'd Yankee girl' working 'in the factory or mill' is far removed from the grim denizens of the West Virginia iron mills described by his younger contemporary, Rebecca Harding Davis.

Much writing about work is deficient because it expresses the external view of a comfortably placed observer, with an eye for the picturesque and a taste for the sight of the human body under strain. Yet there are also many persuasive accounts of the satisfactions of manual work, of pride in craftsmanship and of the self-esteem arising from achievement, even of the pleasures of work done for low wages in harsh surroundings. Alfred Williams was employed in the Swindon railway factory before the First World War and his account of conditions there is basically hostile; nevertheless, he evokes the delight of working until one sweats, in terms that will be familiar to any squash-player: 'every nerve and tissue seems to be aglow with intensest life; the blood courses through the body and limbs freely and vigorously, and produces a sense of unspeakable physical pleasure'. Even drudgery, it seems, can give pleasure to those who perform it, because some people like repetitive work. Vernon Scannell's poem 'The Old Books' marvellously evokes the satisfactions of low-grade clerking in the pre-computing age.

It seems that almost any form of work can be satisfying if it requires absolute concentration, to the extent of at least momentarily shutting out all distracting and painful thoughts. Those who praise work have always emphasized that it takes one's mind off other things and offers the best antidote for sorrow. Concentration on the task in hand allays anxiety and makes the time pass speedily. One can only speculate about the psychological roots of this long-persisting fear of being alone with oneself. Why has it been so universally agreed that any absorbing and distracting occupation is desirable because it keeps inner thoughts at bay?

This was the attribute of work that was praised by D. H. Lawrence, who wrote:

> There is no point in work
> unless it absorbs you
> like an absorbing game

W. H. Auden agreed:

> You need not see what someone is doing
> To know if it is his vocation,
>
> you have only to watch his eyes:
> a cook mixing his sauce, a surgeon
>
> making a primary incision,
> a clerk completing a bill of lading
>
> wear the same rapt expression,
> forgetting themselves in a function.
>
> How beautiful it is,
> that eye-on-the-object look.

Another notable celebration of utter concentration on the task in hand is James Kirkup's 'A Correct Compassion', a poem about an operation carried out by the celebrated heart surgeon Philip Allison, who, as it happens, used to be an Oxford neighbour of mine. Allison had an expensive Porsche and used to go shooting in Yorkshire on his weekends, but I have no doubt that, for him, work, as Noël Coward put it, was more fun than fun.

No account of the pleasures of work is adequate if it focuses only on the satisfactions afforded by the task itself. As often as not, the attraction lies not in the job but in the human relations involved. Samuel Pepys, who stayed late in the office so as to avoid coming home to quarrel with his wife, is one of an infinity of people who have found solace in the workplace for a frustrating life at home. I know of a porter in an Oxford college who is always very happy to be on duty on Christmas Day, because that is when his mother-in-law comes to visit.

More positively, the workplace is for most people their principal source of companionship. It provides them with a range of emotional necessities: gossip, repartee, intrigue, flirtation, practical jokes, and a sense of belonging. It is noticeable how much emphasis eighteenth-century accounts of women haymakers and weeders place on the chattering that invariably accompanied their labours. And who could write about modern workers on a building site without mentioning the way in which they greet young female passers-by? In his autobiography, *A Cab at the Door*, V. S. Pritchett deliciously evokes the constant sexual innuendo of the banter kept up by the male clerks in the leathersellers' office where he worked as a young man. What is modern office life if not a matter of birthday cards, anniversaries, and retirement parties, overheard telephone conversations and encounters at the photocopier? And where is there a more poignant evocation of the human relationships that can result than in Carol Rumens's 'Gifts And Loans'?

Much is said today about how new technology will make it possible for everyone to work from home. But I suspect that many people would miss the office too much for that ever to be the normal state. Indeed some actually prefer the orderliness, structure, and companionship of working life to the chaos of domesticity.

The term 'workaholic' was invented in the mid twentieth century, but the condition it describes was an ancient one. As the seventeenth-century bishop Gilbert Burnet declared: 'all men that are well suited in a profession that is agreeable to their genius and inclination are really the easier and the better pleased, the more they are employed in it'. By 1848 Mill could remark that 'the majority of Englishmen and Americans have no life but in their work; that alone stands between them and *ennui* . . . they are too deficient in senses to enjoy mere existence in repose; and scarcely any pleasure or amusement is pleasure or amusement to them'.

Today things may be about to change. The task of producing food has long ceased to occupy most of the population, while mechanization and automation have vastly reduced the demand for manual and clerical labour. It is a commonplace to say that work is much less central to people's existence than it used to be and that vast spaces of leisure and domesticity have opened up. We are told that work is only one of many possible forms of fulfilment and that full-time employment and the life-time career will become increasingly uncommon. In their place will emerge an economy of short-term contracts, part-time work and frequent retraining. If the trend to ever greater amounts of leisure continues, the basic human impulses towards activity and social involvement that were such a crucial feature in the working patterns of the past will have to be satisfied in other ways. The great economist J. M. Keynes wrote in 1930: 'there is no country and no people . . . who can look forward to the age of leisure and abundance without a dread'. His prescription was that we should try to share out what little work remained: three hours a day might be sufficient, he thought. In practice, however, it seems more likely that some of us will continue to be overworked, while others have no work at all.

But rather than speculating further about the future, it is more profitable to follow the advice of the old scholar, Martin, in Voltaire's *Candide*: 'Let's stop all this philosophizing and get down to work.'

Textual Note

This book makes no claim to any great textual authority. The excerpts that make it up have been drawn from a wide range of sources and types of edition; they consequently reflect a diversity of editorial practice on such matters as spelling, capitalization, and punctuation. When a medieval or early modern text seemed too archaic to be easily intelligible to the modern reader, it has been modernized. I have also silently corrected misprints. Omissions are indicated by an ellipsis or by an asterisk. Dates given are usually those of first publication, when known, or, in the case of most poems and essays, of first appearance in a published collection. Dates of authors are given in all cases where I have been able to discover them.

THE OXFORD BOOK OF WORK

Part One
The Nature of Work

I. THE PRIMAL CURSE

In the beginning there was no work, or so people liked to think. The ancient Greeks and Romans looked back to the Golden Age, when nature was bountiful and human beings lived a life of ease free from toil.

The race of men that the immortals who dwell on Olympus made first of all was of gold. They were in the time of Kronos, when he was king in heaven; and they lived like gods, with carefree heart, remote from toil and misery. Wretched old age did not affect them either, but with hands and feet ever unchanged they enjoyed themselves in feasting, beyond all ills, and they died as if overcome by sleep. All good things were theirs, and the grain-giving soil bore its fruits of its own accord in unstinted plenty, while they at their leisure harvested their fields in contentment amid abundance.

HESIOD (*fl. c.*700 BC), *Works and Days*, tr. M. L. West, 1988

> In firme content
> And harmless ease, their happy dayes were spent.
> The yet-free Earth did of her owne accord
> (Untorne with ploughs) all sorts of fruit afford.
> Content with Natures un-enforced food,
> They gather Wildings, Strawb' ries of the Wood,
> Sowre Cornels, what upon the Bramble growes,
> And Acorns, which *Ioue's* spreading Oke bestowes.
> 'Twas always Spring; warm *Zephyrus* sweetly blew
> On smiling Flowers, which without setting grew.
> Forth-with the Earth corne, unmanured, beares;
> And every yeare renews her golden Eares;
> With Milke and Nectar were the Rivers fill'd;
> And yellow Hony from greene Elms distill'd.

OVID (43 BC–AD 17), *Metamorphoses, ante* AD 8, tr. George Sandys, 1621–6

[Before the Flood] the said Earth . . . was yet generally much more fertile than ours is . . . The exterior *stratum* or surface of it consisted entirely of a kind of terrestrial matter proper for the nourishment and formation of plants

... Its soil was more luxuriant and teemed forth its productions in far greater plenty and abundance than the present earth does... requiring little or no care or culture, but yielding its increase freely, and without any considerable labour and toil, or assistance or human industry; by this means allowing mankind that time, which must otherwise have been spent in agriculture, ploughing, sowing and the like, to far and more divine and noble uses.

> JOHN WOODWARD (1665–1728), *An Essay toward a Natural History of the Earth*, 1695

After the Age of Gold came the Age of Iron; and after Eden the Fall of Man. In the Judaeo-Christian tradition, painful toil was God's curse, a punishment for Adam's disobedience. Work now involved fatigue and suffering, for nature had ceased to yield her fruits without the application of strenuous human effort. Yet it was widely assumed that human beings still inclined naturally to a state of idleness and would only labour when coerced or bribed into doing so.

Would that I were ... either dead earlier or born later! For now it is a race of iron; and they will never cease from toil and misery by day or night, in constant distress, and the gods will give them harsh troubles.

> HESIOD (*fl. c.*700 BC), *Works and Days*, tr. M. L. West, 1988

And unto Adam he said, Because thou hast hearkened unto the voice of thy wife, and hast eaten of the tree, of which I commanded thee, saying, Thou shalt not eat of it: cursed is the ground for thy sake; in sorrow shalt thou eat of it all the days of thy life;

Thorns also and thistles shall it bring forth to thee; and thou shalt eat the herb of the field;

In the sweat of thy face shalt thou eat bread, till thou return unto the ground; for out of it wast thou taken: for dust thou art, and unto dust shalt thou return.

> Genesis 3: 17–19

To get the whole world out of bed
And washed, and dressed, and warmed, and fed,
To work, and back to bed again,
Believe me, Saul, costs worlds of pain.

> JOHN MASEFIELD (1878–1967), *The Everlasting Mercy*, 1911

Who first invented work, and bound the free
And holy-day rejoicing spirit down
To the ever-haunting importunity
Of business, in the green fields and the town,
To plough, loom, anvil, spade; and oh, most sad,
To that dry drudgery at the desk's dead wood?
Who but the being unblest, alien from good,
Sabbathless Satan! he who his unglad
Task ever plies, 'mid rotatory burnings,
That round and round incalculably reel;
For wrath Divine hath made him like a wheel
In that red realm from which are no returnings;
Where, toiling and turmoiling, ever and aye,
He and his thoughts keep pensive worky-day.

CHARLES LAMB (1775–1834), letter to Bernard Barton, 11 Sept. 1822

In cases of extreme poverty my father took me to labour with him and made me a light flail for threshing, learning me betimes the hardship which Adam and Eve inflicted on their children by their inexperienced misdeeds, incurring the perpetual curse from God of labouring for a livelihood, which the teeming earth is said to have produced of itself before. But use is second nature, at least it learns us patience. I resigned myself willingly to the hardest toils and, though one of the weakest, was stubborn and stomachful and never flinched from the roughest labour. By that means I always secured the favour of my masters and escaped the ignominy that brands the name of idleness.

JOHN CLARE (1793–1864), *Sketches in the Life of John Clare*, 1821

Man . . . is by corruption of nature through sin so far degenerated and grown out of kind, that he taketh idleness to be no evil at all, but rather a commendable thing, seemly for those that be wealthy; and therefore is greedily imbraced of most part of men, as agreeable to their sensual affection, and all labour and travail is diligently avoided, as a thing painful and repugnant to the pleasure of the flesh.

ANON., perhaps John Jewel (1522–71), *An Homily against Idleness*, 1563

How vain the opinion is of some certain people of the East Indies, who think that apes and baboons, which are with them in great numbers, are indued with understanding, and that they can speak but will not, for fear they should be imployed and set to work.

ANTOINE LE GRAND (d. 1699), *An Entire Body of Philosophy*, tr. Richard Blome, 1694

The proneness of human Nature to a life of ease, of freedom from care and labour appears strongly in the little success that has hitherto attended every attempt to civilize our American Indians. In their present way of living, almost all their Wants are supplied by the spontaneous Productions of Nature, with the addition of very little labour, if hunting and fishing may indeed be called labour when Game is so plenty. They visit us frequently, and see the advantages that Arts, Sciences, and compact Society procure us. They are not deficient in natural understanding and yet they have never shewn any Inclination to change their manner of life for ours, or to learn any of our Arts; When an Indian Child has been brought up among us, taught our language and habituated to our Customs, yet if he goes to see his relations and make one Indian Ramble with them, there is no perswading him ever to return, and that this is not natural [to them] merely as Indians, but as men, is plain from this, that when white persons of either sex have been taken prisoners young by the Indians, and lived a while among them, tho' ransomed by their Friends, and treated with all imaginable tenderness to prevail with them to stay among the English, yet in a Short time they become disgusted with our manner of life, and the care and pains that are necessary to support it, and take the first good Opportunity of escaping again into the Woods, from whence there is no reclaiming them. One instance I remember to have heard, where the person was brought home to possess a good Estate; but finding some care necessary to keep it together, he relinquished it to a younger Brother, reserving to himself nothing but a gun and a match-Coat, with which he took his way again to the Wilderness.

BENJAMIN FRANKLIN (1706–90), letter to Peter Collinson, 9 May 1753

Every man is, or hopes to be, an Idler.

SAMUEL JOHNSON (1709–84), *The Idler*, 15 Apr. 1758

Equal quantities of labour at all times and places may be said to be of equal value to the labourer. In his ordinary state of health, strength and spirits; in the ordinary degree of his skill and dexterity, he must always lay down the same portion of his ease, his liberty, and his happiness. The price which he pays must always be the same, whatever may be the quantity of goods which he receives in return for it.

ADAM SMITH (1723–90), *An Inquiry into the Nature and Causes of the Wealth of Nations*, 1776

Work is the curse of the drinking classes.

OSCAR WILDE (1854–1900)

The exercise of the industrial faculty which is a delight for the free animals—the beavers, bees, wasps and ants—is a torment for man, who escapes it as soon as he acquires his freedom. Civilized man aspires only to inertia, and the supreme curse which the savage shouts at his enemy is this: 'May you be reduced to plowing a field!'. . .

Work is nonetheless a delight for many creatures such as the beavers, bees, wasps, and ants, who are perfectly free to lapse into a state of inertia. God has provided them with a social mechanism which attracts them to work and makes it a source of happiness for them. Why should he have failed to grant us a benefit which he bestows upon the animals? There is a huge difference between their work and ours! The Russians and the Algerians work out of fear of the whip or the cudgel; the English and the French work from fear of the hunger which besets their poor households. The liberty of the Greeks and Romans is much vaunted, but they had slaves who worked out of fear of being executed just like the Negroes in our colonies today. Such is the happiness of man in the absence of the *attractive industrial code*; such is the result of human laws and of the philosophical constitutions: they make humanity envy the lot of the industrious animals, for whom Attraction turns wearisome tasks into sources of pleasure.

> François Marie Charles Fourier (1772–1837), *La Théorie de l'Unité Universelle*, 2nd edn. 1841–3, tr. Jonathan Beecher and Richard Bienvenu, 1972

You are sitting under a tree, enjoying all the comfort and quiet of which you are capable; you see come from a narrow path a poor creature loaded with fagots. The unexpected and always surprising way in which this figure strikes you, instantly reminds you of the common and melancholy lot of humanity—weariness. It is always like the impression of La Fontaine's 'Wood-cutter,' in the fable:

> 'What pleasure has he had since the day of his birth?
> Who so poor as he in the whole wide earth?'

Sometimes, in places where the land is sterile, you see figures hoeing and digging. From time to time one raises himself and straightens his back, as they call it, wiping his forehead with the back of his hand. 'Thou shalt eat thy bread in the sweat of thy brow.' Is this the gay, jovial work some people would have us believe in? But, nevertheless, to me it is true humanity and great poetry!

> Jean François Millet (1814–75), quoted in Alfred Sensier (1815–77), *Jean François Millet: Peasant and Painter*, tr. Helena de Kay, 1881

I must pass, however, now to our third condition of separation, between the men who work with the hand, and those who work with the head.

And here we have at last an inevitable distinction. There *must* be work done by the arms, or none of us could live. There *must* be work done by the brains, or the life we get would not be worth having. And the same men cannot do both. There is rough work to be done, and rough men must do it; there is gentle work to be done, and gentlemen must do it; and it is physically impossible that one class should do, or divide, the work of the other. And it is of no use to try to conceal this sorrowful fact by fine words, and to talk to the workman about the honourableness of manual labour and the dignity of humanity. Rough work, honourable or not, takes the life out of us; and the man who has been heaving clay out of a ditch all day, or driving an express train against the north wind all night, or holding a collier's helm in a gale on a lee shore, or whirling white-hot iron at a furnace mouth, is not the same man at the end of his day, or night, as one who has been sitting in a quiet room, with everything comfortable about him, reading books, or classing butterflies, or painting pictures. If it is any comfort to you to be told that the rough work is the more honourable of the two, I should be sorry to take that much of consolation from you; and in some sense I need not. The rough work is at all events real, honest, and, generally, though not always, useful; while the fine work is, a great deal of it, foolish and false, as well as fine, and therefore dishonourable; but when both kinds are equally well and worthily done the head's is the noble work, and the hand's the ignoble. Therefore, of all hand work whatsoever, necessary for the maintenance of life, those old words, 'In the sweat of thy face thou shalt eat bread,' indicate that the inherent nature of it is one of calamity; and that the ground, cursed for our sake, casts also some shadow of degradation into our contest with its thorn and its thistle: so that all nations have held their days honourable, or 'holy,' and constituted them 'holydays,' or 'holidays,' by making them days of rest; and the promise, which, among all our distant hopes, seems to cast the chief brightness over death, is that blessing of the dead who die in the Lord, that 'they rest from their labours, and their works do follow them.'

JOHN RUSKIN (1819–1900), *The Crown of Wild Olive*, 1866

And yet as a path to happiness work is not valued very highly by men. They do not run after it as they do after other opportunities for gratification. The great majority work only when forced by necessity, and this natural human aversion to work gives rise to the most difficult social problems.

SIGMUND FREUD (1856–1939), *Civilization and Its Discontents*, 1930, tr. Joan Riviere

Attempts to define 'work' and to distinguish it from other strenuous activities concentrated upon this supposed unpleasantness.

We may define LABOUR as any exertion of mind or body undergone partly or wholly with a view to some good other than the pleasure derived from the work.

> ALFRED MARSHALL (1842–1924), *Principles of Economics*, 1890

I have heard him say, that work of itself was hard and taking care and pains fastidious; but if it was agreeable to do any thing called work it was not really so but pleasure; therefore it is incident to the true notion of work not to delight in it.

> ROGER NORTH (1651?–1734), on his brother Sir Dudley North (1641–91), *The Life of Sir Dudley North*, 1744

Tennis, which our gallants make a recreation, is much more toilsome than what many others make their work; and yet those delight in the one and these detest the other, because we do this out of necessity, and the other out of choice.

> ROBERT BOYLE (1627–91), 'The Aretology', wr. 1645–7, pub. 1991

Neither can tennis be a pastime, for it is too laborious for pastime, which is only a recreation, and there can be no recreation in sweaty labour; for it is laid as a curse upon men, that they shall live by the sweat of their brows.

> MARGARET CAVENDISH, MARCHIONESS OF NEWCASTLE (1623–73), *CCXI Sociable Letters*, 1664

I suppose the mind is as intensely employed in attending to an interesting play or novel, as at any time. Yet in that we can energise without much fatigue. 'As busy as a child at play' is a proverb, and a just one, which implies what I am now saying. But it is to be remarked, that what is play to one is hard work to another. I believe the mind of many would be more fatigued than even the body by field sports; and yet perhaps those very men would feel endless amusement in mathematics or other such pursuits, which to the generality are very fagging. The thing that most fatigues the mind, in short, seems to be that which is felt as a task; I mean that the latter circumstance is the cause of the former, not vice versâ. So at least it is with me, who often do the same thing with pleasure when voluntary, which fags me when I am compelled to it.

> RICHARD WHATELEY (1787–1863), commonplace book, June 1818

Tom . . . had discovered a great law of human action, without knowing it—namely, that in order to make a man or a boy covet a thing, it is only necessary to make the thing difficult to attain. If he had been a great and wise philosopher, like the writer of this book, he would now have comprehended that work consists of whatever a body is obliged to do. And this would help him to understand why constructing artificial flowers or performing on a treadmill is work, whilst rolling nine-pins or climbing Mont Blanc is only amusement. There are wealthy gentlemen in England who drive four-horse passenger-coaches twenty or thirty miles on a daily line in the summer, because the privilege costs them considerable money; but if they were offered wages for the service, that would turn it into work, and then they would resign.

MARK TWAIN (1835–1910), *The Adventures of Tom Sawyer*, 1876

Labour for labour['s] sake is against nature.

JOHN LOCKE (1632–1704), *Of the Conduct of the Understanding*, 1706

BOSWELL: 'But, Sir, the mind must be employed, and we grow weary when idle.' JOHNSON: 'That is, Sir, because, others being busy, we want company; but if we were all idle, there would be no growing weary; we should all entertain one another. There is, indeed, this in trade:—it gives men an opportunity of improving their situation. If there were no trade, many who are poor would always remain poor. But no man loves labour for itself.' BOSWELL: 'Yes, Sir, I know a person who does. He is a very laborious Judge, and he loves the labour.' JOHNSON: 'Sir, that is because he loves respect and distinction. Could he have them without labour, he would like it less.' BOSWELL: 'He tells me he likes it for itself.'—'Why, Sir, he fancies so, because he is not accustomed to abstract.'

JAMES BOSWELL (1740–95), *The Life of Samuel Johnson*, 20 Oct. 1769, pub. 1791

Meantime, as to *labour*, although the desire of it, of labour *simply*—desire of labour *for the sake of labour*—of labour considered in the character of an *end*, without any view to any thing else, is a sort of desire that seems scarcely to have place in the human breast; yet, if considered in the character of a *means*, scarce a desire can be found, to the gratification of which *labour*, and therein *the desire of labour*, is not continually rendered subservient. . . .

Aversion—not *desire*—is the emotion, the only emotion which *labour*, taken by itself, is qualified to produce. Of any such emotion as *love* or *desire*, *ease*, which is the *negative* or *absence* of labour, *ease*, not *labour*, is the object.

In so far as *labour* is taken in its proper sense, *love of labour* is a contradiction in terms.

JEREMY BENTHAM (1748–1832), Deontology, 1814–31

So far as the nature of the muscular or nervous effort is concerned, no distinction can be drawn between the agreeable and the irksome activities, or between those which are undertaken for pleasure and those which are undertaken for pay. Such severe physical labor, combined with hardship and exposure, as mountain climbing, is done for pleasure by tourists and for pay by guides. The pursuit of athletic sports is the most familiar of recreations and is also a familiar profession. A multitude of occupations ordinarily pursued for gain—woodworking, gardening, painting, acting— are also pursued by many persons for the satisfaction which the doing affords.

None the less it is true that the greatest part of the activity which men carry on in getting a living does not give pleasure. The chief reason seems to be that activity, in order to be effective toward getting a living, must be steady, unvaried, and long-continued; and it must be, in an important sense, not free. The characteristic of most activities that are sources of pleasure in themselves is the element of freshness or novelty, and the absence of compulsion. The guide who climbs mountains year after year, and knows the tracks by heart, soon finds the task a weary one; and this the more, because, in order to earn his living, he must follow his tracks regularly, regardless of his health or spirits at the moment. It is the zest of novelty and the sense of freedom and choice that cause pleasure in the summer's arduous vacation. Inactivity and idleness soon become irksome; but, with few exceptions, steady application to the same task also soon becomes irksome . . .

A fortunate minority may work at tasks which are in themselves pleasurable and are not performed chiefly for the return which they bring. But most work is now undertaken for reward, would not be done without reward, and is strenuous and well directed in proportion to the reward. It is doubtless true that the mass of mankind, though they find their labor irksome or repellent, are yet happier than they would be under complete idleness, or with only that fitful kind of exertion which attracts the savage. But labor is commonly felt to be a hardship, and the pay which it secures is the dominant motive for undertaking it. The fundamental problems that arise in economics are concerned with the relation between unwelcome exertion and the remuneration which induces that exertion.

F. W. TAUSSIG (1859–1940), Principles of Economics, 1911

Work and physical compulsion were inextricably linked. Over the centuries, slavery, serfdom, and indentured labour have been the lot of millions. People became slaves because they had fallen into debt, or were captured in war, or sold by their parents, or punished by their superiors, or born into slavery as the children of slaves. The great civilizations of antiquity were founded upon slavery, while the empires of modern times were nourished by the supply of indentured labourers from India and China. Plantation slavery can be traced back from the southern states of the USA of the ante-bellum era to the latifundia of the Roman Empire. Serfdom involving compulsory labour services was a normal feature of the feudal societies of the Middle Ages and later. Between 1492 and 1830 more than ten million black Africans were transported as slaves to the Americas. In modern times hard labour remained an accepted form of punishment, while in Nazi Germany and Soviet Russia the concentration camps and gulags imposed compulsory labour on their inhabitants. Arbeit Macht Frei ('Work will set you free') was the motto over the gates of Auschwitz.

'. . . But the pain I feel for the suffering to come is less for the people of Troy, less even for Hekabe and king Priam and my brothers, the many brave brothers who will fall in the dust at the hands of our enemies, than my pain for you, when one of the bronze-clad Achaians carries you away in tears and takes away the day of your freedom: and you will live in Argos, weaving at the loom at another woman's command, and carrying water from a foreign spring, from Messeïs or Hypereia, much against your will, but compulsion will lie harsh upon you. And someone seeing you with your tears falling will say: "This is the wife of Hektor, who was always the best warrior of the horse-taming Trojans, when they were fighting over Ilios." That is what they will say: and for you there will be renewed misery, that you have lost such a husband to protect you from the day of slavery. But may I be dead and the heaped earth cover me, before I hear your screams and the sound of you being dragged away.'

HOMER, *The Iliad*, c.750 BC, tr. Martin Hammond, 1987

'Slavery in Egypt'

And Vala, like a shadow, oft appear'd to Urizen.
The King of Light beheld her mourning among the Brick kilns, compell'd
To labour night & day among the fires: her lamenting voice
Is heard when silent night returns & the labourers take their rest:

'O Lord, wilt thou not look upon our sore afflictions,
Among these flames incessant labouring? our hard masters laugh
At all our sorrow. We are made to turn the wheel for water,
To carry the heavy basket on our scorchèd shoulders, to sift
The sand & ashes, & to mix the clay with tears & repentance.
The times are now return'd upon us: we have given ourselves

To scorn, and now are scornèd by the slaves of our enemies.
Our beauty is cover'd over with clay & ashes, & our backs
Furrow'd with whips, & our flesh bruisèd with the heavy basket.
Forgive us, O thou piteous one, whom we have offended: forgive
The weak remaining shadow of Vala, that returns in sorrow to thee.'

Thus she lamented day & night, compell'd to labour & sorrow.

WILLIAM BLAKE (1757–1827), *The Four Zoas*, 1795–1804

The slaves who are engaged in the working of them [the silver mines of Iberia] produce for their masters revenues in sums defying belief, but they themselves wear out their bodies both by day and night in the diggings under the earth, dying in large numbers because of the exceptional hardships they endure. For no respite or pause is granted them in their labours, but compelled beneath blows of the overseers to endure the severity of their plight, they throw away their lives in this wretched manner, although certain of them who can endure it, by virtue of their bodily strength and their persevering souls, suffer such hardships over a long period; indeed death in their eyes is more to be desired than life, because of the magnitude of the hardship they must bear.

DIODORUS SICULUS (*fl.* 1st c. BC), *The Library of History*, c.56 BC–30 BC, tr. C. H. Oldfather, 1939

Questions from a Worker who Reads

Who built Thebes of the seven gates?
In the books you will find the names of kings.
Did the kings haul up the lumps of rock?
And Babylon, many times demolished
Who raised it up so many times? In what houses
Of gold-glittering Lima did the builders live?
Where, the evening that the Wall of China was finished
Did the masons go? Great Rome
Is full of triumphal arches. Who erected them? Over whom
Did the Caesars triumph? Had Byzantium, much praised in song
Only palaces for its inhabitants? Even in fabled Atlantis
The night the ocean engulfed it
The drowning still bawled for their slaves.

The young Alexander conquered India.
Was he alone?
Caesar beat the Gauls.

Did he not have even a cook with him?
Philip of Spain wept when his armada
Went down. Was he the only one to weep?
Frederick the Second won the Seven Years War. Who
Else won it?

Every page a victory.
Who cooked the feast for the victors?
Every ten years a great man.
Who paid the bill?

So many reports.
So many questions.

BERTOLT BRECHT (1898–1956), 1935, tr. Michael Hamburger, 1976

When I think of antiquity, the detail that frightens me is that those hundreds of millions of slaves on whose backs civilization rested generation after generation have left behind them no record whatever. We do not even know their names. In the whole of Greek and Roman history, how many slaves' names are known to you? I can think of two, or possibly three. One is Spartacus and the other is Epictetus. Also, in the Roman room at the British Museum there is a glass jar with the maker's name inscribed on the bottom. '*Felix fecit*'. I have a vivid mental picture of poor Felix (a Gaul with red hair and a metal collar round his neck), but in fact he may not have been a slave; so there are only two slaves whose names I definitely know, and probably few people can remember more. The rest have gone down into utter silence.

GEORGE ORWELL (1903–50), 'Looking Back on the Spanish War', 1942

Teacher.   What have you to say, ploughman? How do you carry on your work?
Ploughman.   O master, I work very hard; I go out at dawn, drive the oxen to the field, and yoke them to the plough. There is no storm so severe that I dare to hide at home, for fear of my lord, but when the oxen are yoked, and the share and coulter have been fastened to the plough, I must plough a whole acre or more every day.
Teacher.   Have you any companion?
Ploughman.   I have a boy to urge on the oxen with a goad; he is now hoarse on account of the cold and his shouting.
Teacher.   What else do you do during the day?
Ploughman.   I do a good deal more. I must fill the bins of the oxen with hay, water them, and carry off their dung.

Teacher.   Oh! oh! the labour must be great!
Ploughman.   It is indeed great drudgery, because I am not free.
                       AELFRIC (*c.*955–*c.*1010), *Colloquy*, tr. Kevin Crossley-Holland, 1982

Yet my lord Yvain said nothing,
And went right on, and found
A great high hall, brand new,
With a walled courtyard in front of it,
And a wall of great sharpened stakes,
And inside, behind the stakes,
He saw three hundred girls
All sewing away, some working
With golden thread, some silk,
Working as hard as they could.
But their wretched poverty was such
That they sat there bareheaded, many
So poor that they wore no sash,
And their dresses were torn at the breast
And out at the elbows, and their shifts
Were dirty around the neck.
And their necks were thin, and their faces
Pale with hunger and misery.
He saw them, and they saw him,
And they bowed their heads, and they wept,
And for a long, long time did not move,
Knowing there was nothing to be done,
Unable to raise their eyes
From the ground, so bent with sorrow.

[One of the maids explains to Yvain that they are prisoners of demons, sent by their king as ransom for his release.]

None of us will ever leave.
We'll spend our days weaving
Silk, and wearing rags.
We'll spend our days poor
And naked and hungry and thirsty,
For they'll never pay us what we earn,
Let us buy better food.
We've only a bit of bread,
Some in the morning and less
At night. Our work doesn't pay

Any of us even as much
As four pennies in a single day.
And that's not enough to feed us
Or put clothes on our backs. Even
Earning twenty sous
A week, we're still miserable,
We never escape it. It's true:
There isn't one of us here
Who doesn't earn twenty or more—
And that's as rich as a duke!
And yet we're miserably poor,
And the ones we work for are rich
Because of what we produce.
We work most nights, and we work
All day, just to stay alive,
For they threaten to cut off our arms
And legs if we rest. No one
Dares to rest.

CHRÉTIEN DE TROYES (*fl.* 1170–90), *Yvain* (*c.*1177–81) tr. Burton Raffel,
1987

They import so many Negroes hither, that I fear this Colony will some time or
other be confirmed by the name of New Guinea. I am sensible of many bad
consequences of multiplying these Ethiopians amongst us. They blow up the
pride, and ruin the Industry of our White People, who seeing a Rank of poor
Creatures below them, detest work for fear it should make them look like
Slaves.

WILLIAM BYRD (1674–1744), writing from Virginia to Lord Egmont,
12 July 1736

And better in the untimely grave to rot,
The world and all its cruelties forgot,
Than drag'd once more beyond the western main,
To groan beneath some dastard planter's chain,
Where my poor countrymen in bondage wait
The slow enfranchisement of lingering fate.
Oh! my heart sinks, my dying eyes o'erflow,
When memory paints the picture of their woe!
For I have seen them, ere the dawn of day,

Rous'd by the lash, begin their cheerless way:
Greeting with groans unwelcome morn's return,
While rage and shame their gloomy bosoms burn:
And, chiding every hour the slow-pac'd sun,
Endure their toils till all his race was run;
No eye to mark their sufferings with a tear,
No friend to comfort, and no hope to cheer;
Then like the dull unpitied brutes repair
To stalls as wretched, and as coarse a fare;
Thank Heav'n, one day of misery was o'er,
And sink to sleep, and wish to wake no more.

THOMAS DAY (1748–89), *The Dying Negro*, 1773

God be thanked, all that is now at an end; and certainly, as far as I can as yet judge, if I were now standing on the banks of Virgil's Lethe, with a goblet of the waters of oblivion in my hand, and asked whether I chose to enter life anew as an English labourer or a Jamaica negro, I should have no hesitation in preferring the latter. For myself, it appears to me almost worth surrendering the luxuries and pleasures of Great Britain, for the single pleasure of being surrounded with beings who are always laughing and singing, and who seem to perform their work with so much *nonchalance*, taking up their baskets as if it were perfectly optional whether they took them up or left them there; sauntering along with their hands dangling; stopping to chat with every one they meet; or if they meet no one, standing still to look round, and examine whether there is nothing to be seen that can amuse them, so that I can hardly persuade myself that it is really *work* that they are about. The negro might well say, on his arrival in England—'Massa, in England every thing work!' for here nobody appears to work at all.

M. G. LEWIS (1775–1818), *Journal of a West India Proprietor*, 13 Jan. 1816, pub. 1834

In the latter part of August begins the cotton picking season. At this time each slave is presented with a sack. A strap is fastened to it, which goes over the neck, holding the mouth of the sack breast high, while the bottom reaches nearly to the ground. Each one is also presented with a large basket that will hold about two barrels. This is to put the cotton in when the sack is filled. The baskets are carried to the field and placed at the beginning of the rows.

When a new hand, one unaccustomed to the business, is sent for the first time into the field, he is whipped up smartly, and made for that day to pick as fast as he can possibly. At night it is weighed, so that his capability in cotton picking is known. He must bring in the same weight each night following. If it falls short, it is considered evidence that he has been laggard, and a greater or less number of lashes is the penalty.

An ordinary day's work is two hundred pounds. A slave who is accustomed to picking, is punished, if he or she brings in a less quantity than that. There is a great difference among them as regards this kind of labor. Some of them seem to have a natural knack, or quickness, which enables them to pick with great celerity, and with both hands, while others, with whatever practice or industry, are utterly unable to come up to the ordinary standard. Such hands are taken from the cotton field and employed in other business. Patsey, of whom I shall have more to say, was known as the most remarkable cotton picker on Bayou Bœuf. She picked with both hands and with such surprising rapidity, that five hundred pounds a day was not unusual for her.

Each one is tasked, therefore, according to his picking abilities, none, however, to come short of two hundred weight. I, being unskillful always in that business, would have satisfied my master by bringing in the latter quantity, while on the other hand, Patsey would surely have been beaten if she failed to produce twice as much.

*

The hands are required to be in the cotton field as soon as it is light in the morning, and, with the exception of ten or fifteen minutes, which is given them at noon to swallow their allowance of cold bacon, they are not permitted to be a moment idle until it is too dark to see, and when the moon is full, they often times labor till the middle of the night. They do not dare to stop even at dinner time, nor return to the quarters, however late it be, until the order to halt is given by the driver.

The day's work over in the field, the baskets are 'toted,' or in other words, carried to the gin-house, where the cotton is weighed. No matter how fatigued and weary he may be—no matter how much he longs for sleep and rest—a slave never approaches the gin-house with his basket of cotton but with fear. If it falls short in weight—if he has not performed the full task appointed him, he knows that he must suffer. And if he has exceeded it by ten or twenty pounds, in all probability his master will measure the next day's task accordingly. So, whether he has too little or too much, his approach to the gin-house is always with fear and trembling. Most frequently they have too little, and therefore it is they are not anxious to leave the field. After weighing, follow the whippings; and then the baskets are carried to the cotton house, and their contents stored away like hay, all hands being sent in to tramp it down. If the cotton is not dry, instead of taking it to the gin-house at once, it is laid upon platforms, two feet high, and some three times as wide, covered with boards or plank, with narrow walks running between them.

This done, the labor of the day is not yet ended, by any means. Each one must then attend to his respective chores. One feeds the mules, another the swine—another cuts the wood, and so forth; besides, the packing is all done by candle light. Finally, at a late hour, they reach the quarters, sleepy and over-come with the long day's toil. Then a fire must be kindled in the cabin, the corn ground in the small hand-mill, and supper, and dinner for the next day in the field, prepared . . .

An hour before day light the horn is blown. Then the slaves arouse, prepare their breakfast, fill a gourd with water, in another deposit their dinner of cold bacon and corn cake, and hurry to the field again. It is an offence invariably followed by a flogging, to be found at the quarters after daybreak. Then the fears and labors of another day begin; and until its close there is no such thing as rest. He fears he will be caught lagging through the day; he fears to approach the gin-house with his basket-load of cotton at night; he fears, when he lies down, that he will oversleep himself in the morning. Such is a true, faithful, unexaggerated picture and description of the slave's daily life, during the time of cotton-picking on the shores of Bayou Bœuf.

SOLOMON NORTHUP (*fl.* 1841–53), *Twelve Years a Slave*, 1853

I have often been utterly astonished, since I came to the north, to find persons who could speak of the singing, among slaves, as evidence of their content-ment and happiness. It is impossible to conceive of a greater mistake. Slaves sing most when they are most unhappy. The songs of the slave represent the sorrows of his heart; and he is relieved by them, only as an aching heart is relieved by its tears. At least, such is my experience. I have often sung to drown my sorrow, but seldom to express my happiness. Crying for joy, and singing for joy, were alike uncommon to me while in the jaws of slavery. The singing of a man cast away upon a desolate island might be as appropriately consid-ered as evidence of contentment and happiness, as the singing of a slave; the songs of the one and of the other are prompted by the same emotion.

FREDERICK DOUGLASS (1818–95), *Narrative of the Life of Frederick Douglass*, 1845

I was asked not long ago to tell something about the sports and pastimes that I engaged in during my youth. Until that question was asked it had never occurred to me that there was no period of my life that was devoted to play. From the time that I can remember anything, almost every day of my life has been occupied in some kind of labour; though I think I would now be a more useful man if I had had time for sports. During the period that I spent in slavery I was not large enough to be of much service, still I was occupied most of the time in cleaning the yards, carrying water to the men in the fields, or going to the mill, to which I used to take the corn, once a week, to be ground. The mill was about three miles from the plantation. This work I always dreaded. The heavy bag of corn would be thrown across the back of the horse, and the corn divided about evenly on each side; but in some way, almost without exception, on these trips, the corn would so shift as to become unbalanced and would fall off the horse, and often I would fall with it. As I was not strong enough to reload the corn upon the horse, I would have to wait, sometimes for many hours, till a chance passer-by came along who would help me out of my trouble. The hours while waiting for some one were usually spent in crying. The time consumed in this way made me late in reaching the mill, and by the time I got my corn ground and reached home it would be far into the night. The road was a lonely one, and often led through dense forests. I was always frightened. The woods were said to be full of soldiers who had deserted from the army, and I had been told that the first thing a deserter did to a Negro boy when he found him alone was to cut off his ears. Besides, when I was late in getting home I knew I would always get a severe scolding or a flogging.

BOOKER T. WASHINGTON (1856–1915), Up from Slavery, 1901

It is a truism to assert, that labour extorted by fear of punishment is inefficient and unproductive. It is true that in some circumstances, human beings can be driven by the lash to attempt, and even to accomplish, things which they would not have undertaken for any payment which it could have been worth while to an employer to offer them. And it is likely that productive operations which require much combination of labour, the production of sugar for example, would not have taken place so soon in the American colonies, if slavery had not existed to keep masses of labour together. There are also savage tribes so averse from regular industry, that industrial life is scarcely able to introduce itself among them until they are either conquered and made slaves of, or become conquerors and make others so. But after allowing the full value of these considerations, it remains certain that slavery is incompatible with any high state of the arts of life, and any great efficiency of labour. For all products which require much skill, slave countries are usually dependent on foreigners. Hopeless slavery effectually brutifies the intellect; and intelligence in the slaves, though often encouraged in the ancient world and in the East, is in a more advanced state of society a source of so much danger and an object of so much dread to the masters, that in some of the States of America it was a highly penal offence to teach a slave to read. All processes carried on by slave labour are conducted in the rudest and most unimproved manner. And even the animal strength of the slave is, on an average, not half exerted.

JOHN STUART MILL (1806–73), The Principles of Political Economy, 1848

I inspected the treadwheel at Northleach Bridewell, recently put up. The machinery still requires some alterations. The velocity with which the wheel revolved was too great so that the fatigue exceeded the strength of the prisoners. The revolutions should be limited to about 52 steps in a minute. A regulator must be applied to the machine in such a manner as to compensate for any difference in the weight of the gangs on the wheel, whether grown men or boys. The millwright was in attendance. It is intended to keep the machine going, should there at any time be a failure of corn to grind. Nine or ten prisoners were on the wheel at once, they worked each $4^1/_2$ or 5 minutes, one descending from the extremity of the wheel every half minute. A relay of prisoners is kept in an adjacent yard, walking in a circle.

REVEREND FRANCIS WITTS (1783–1864), *Diary*, 12 Oct. 1827

There are three distinct rooms where the prisoners pick oakum, one in the misdemeanour prison, and the two others in the felons' prison. We shall choose for our illustration and description the larger one in the felons' prison. It has lately been built on so vast a plan that it has seats for nearly 500 men. This immense room is situated to the west of the main or old prison, close to the schoolroom. It is almost as long as one of the sheds seen at a railway terminus where spare carriages are kept, and seems to have been built after the same style of architecture, for it has a corrugated iron roof, stayed with thin rods, spanning the entire erection. We were told that the extreme length is 90 feet, but that does not convey so good a notion of distance to the mind as the fact of the wall being pierced with eight large chapel windows, and the roof with six skylights. Again, an attendant informed us that there were eleven rows of forms; but all that we could see was a closely-packed mass of heads and pink faces, moving to and fro in every variety of motion, as though the wind was blowing them about, and they were set on stalks instead of necks.

On the side fitted with windows the dark forms of the warders are seen, each perched up on a raised stool. The bright light shines on the faces of the criminals, and the officer keeps his eye rapidly moving in all directions, almost as if it went by clockwork, so as to see that no talking takes place. If a man rest over his work for a moment and raise his head, he sees, hung up on the white walls before him, placards on which texts are printed. One is to the effect that IT IS GOOD FOR A MAN THAT HE BEAR THE YOKE IN HIS YOUTH; another tells the prisoners that GODLINESS WITH CONTENTMENT IS A GREAT GAIN; whilst a third counsels each of them to GO TO THE ANT, THOU SLUGGARD, CONSIDER HER WAYS, AND BE WISE.

We went to the wall where the warders were, and looked up the sloping floor at the dirty gray mass of life; the faces of the men seemed like the flesh showing through a tattered garment.

The building was full of men, and as silent as if it merely contained so many automata, for the only sound heard was like that of the rustling of a thicket, or, better, the ticking of clock-work—something resembling that heard in a Dutch clockmaker's shop, where hundreds of time-pieces are going together.

The utter absence of noise struck us as being absolutely terrible. The silence seemed, after a time, almost intense enough to hear a flake of snow fall. Perfect stillness is at all times more or less awful, and hence arises a great part of the solemnity of night as well as of death. To behold those whom we have seen full of life and emotion—some wondrous piece of breathing and speaking organism, reduced to the inanimateness of the statue, is assuredly the most appalling and depressing sight we can look upon. The stillness of the silent system, however, has, to our minds, even a more tragic cast about it; for not only is the silence as intense and impressive as that of death itself, but the movements of the workers seem as noiseless, and therefore unearthly, as spectres. Nor does the sense of our being surrounded by some five hundred criminals—men of the wildest passions, and almost brute instincts, all toiling in dumb show and without a single syllable escaping from their lips—in any way detract from the goblin character of the sight.

> HENRY MAYHEW (1812–87) and JOHN BINNY, *The Criminal Prisons of London*, 1862

'In the Soviet Labour Camp'

And the life of the natives consists of work, work, work; of starvation, cold, and cunning. This work, for those who are unable to push others out of the way and set themselves up in a soft spot, is that selfsame *general work* which raises socialism up out of the earth, and drives us down into the earth.

One cannot enumerate nor cover all the different aspects of this work, nor wrap your tongue about them. To push a wheelbarrow. ('Oh, the machine of the OSO, two handles and one wheel, so!') To carry hand barrows. To unload bricks barehanded (the skin quickly wears off the fingers). To haul bricks on one's own body by 'goat' (in a shoulder barrow). To break up stone and coal in quarry and mine, to dig clay and sand. To hack out eight cubic yards of gold-bearing ore with a pick and haul them to the screening apparatus. Yes, and just to dig in the earth, just to 'chew' up earth (flinty soil and in winter). To cut coal underground. And there are ores there too—lead and copper. Yes, and one can also . . . pulverize copper ore (a sweet taste in the mouth, and one waters at the nose). One can impregnate ties with creosote (and one's whole body at the same time too). One can carve out tunnels for railroads. And build roadbeds. One can dig peat in the bog, up to one's waist in the mud. One can smelt ores. One can cast metal. One can cut hay on hummocks in swampy meadows (sinking up to one's ankles in water). One can be a stableman or a drayman (yes, and steal oats from the horse's bag for one's own pot, but the horse is government-issue, the old grass-bag, and she'll last it out, most likely, but you can drop dead). Yes, and generally at the *selkhozy*—the Agricultural Camps—you can do every kind of peasant work (and there is no work better than that: you'll grab something from the ground for yourself).

But the father of all is our Russian forest with its genuinely golden tree trunks (gold is mined from them). And the oldest of all the kinds of work in the Archipelago is logging. It summons everyone to itself and has room for everyone, and it is not even out of bounds for cripples (they will send out a three-man gang of armless men to stamp down the foot-and-a-half snow). Snow comes up to your chest. You are a lumberjack. First you yourself stamp it down next to the tree trunk. You cut down the tree. Then, hardly able to make your way through the snow, you cut off all the branches (and you have to feel them out in the snow and get to them with your ax). Still dragging your way through the same loose snow, you have to carry off all the branches and make piles of them and burn them. (They smoke. They don't burn.) And now you have to saw up the wood to size and stack it. And the work norm for you and your brother for the day is six and a half cubic yards each, or thirteen cubic yards for two men working together. (In Burepolom the norm was nine cubic yards, but the thick pieces also had to be split into blocks.) By then your arms would not be capable of lifting an ax nor your feet of moving.

During the war years (on war rations), the camp inmates called three weeks at logging *dry execution*.

> ALEKSANDR SOLZHENITSYN (1918–), *The Gulag Archipelago*, 1973–5, tr. Thomas P. Whitney, 1975

Since feudal times, individuals in the West have not usually been made to work by the threat of physical force. The pressure has instead been economic. People worked because they had to secure the means of subsistence. Without that economic necessity, they would have chosen to be idle. Not surprisingly, many early economic commentators drew the moral that wages should be kept low in order to ensure that people would work continuously, rather than knocking off as soon as they had earned enough to buy themselves food, drink, and shelter.

Every one but an idiot knows that the lower classes must be kept poor, or they will never be industrious.

> ARTHUR YOUNG (1741–1820), *The Farmer's Tour through the East of England*, 1771

The old proverb is, wishers and woulders be no good householders. And if there were such plenty, farewell labour, art, learning, and obedience. But need is the prick and whip that causeth the ploughman to travail, the mariner to sail, the schoolmaster to teach, and, to conclude, every man to labour in his calling; through which labour and industry, the teaching of youth, the government of age, the building of cities, the maintenance of good laws, the rewarding of virtues, the punishment of vices, the defending of enemies, and rewarding of friends, and obedience to princes be maintained. Whereas through such abundance, all were cast away and every man would be a master. Everyone would disdain service, and so at length, all should be turned into slavery, and the harmony of the commonwealth should be changed into horror, whereas no order is. Example, if all the pipes in the organe were of tune of one degree, unpleasant were the music.

> WILLIAM BULLEIN (d. 1576), *Bulleins Bulwarke of Defence Against all Sicknesse,* 1579 edn.

I am an honest drunken fellow . . . and please your Worship, I work for nothing but money.

> DANIEL DEFOE (1660–1731), *The Great Law of Subordination Consider'd,* 1724

Sir D[udley] N[orth] used to Inferr, that to make Men rich was to force them upon shifting; for if you will out of Easyness, provide for them if they want, they will want to be provided for. And though it is Not fitt any one should starve, yet it is fitt Every one should fear starving, for Nothing stirs up men in Industry, Ingenuity and Thrift with Providence to lay up for themselves and their children more then utter despair of help from abroad . . .

> ROGER NORTH (1651?–1734)

This cannot be better illustrated, than by its contrary, which appears no where more than in *Ireland*; Where, by the largeness and plenty of the Soil, and scarcity of People, all things necessary to Life are so cheap, that an industrious Man, by two days labour, may gain enough to feed him the rest of the week; Which I take to be a very plain ground of the laziness attributed to the People . . .

> SIR WILLIAM TEMPLE (1628–99), *Observations upon the United Provinces of the Netherlands,* 1672

In the inferior employments, the sweets of labour consist altogether in the recompense of labour.

> ADAM SMITH (1723–90), *An Inquiry into the Nature and Causes of the Wealth of Nations,* 1776

There's many a one who would be idle if hunger didn't pinch him; but the stomach sets us to work.

GEORGE ELIOT (1819–80), *Felix Holt*, 1866

A man here who should write, and honestly confess that he wrote for bread, might as well send his manuscript to fire the baker's oven; not one creature will read him, all must be court bred poets, or pretend at least to be court bred, who can expect to please. Should the Caitiff fairly avow a design of emptying our pockets and filling his own, every reader would instantly forsake him; even those who write for bread themselves, would combine to worry him, perfectly sensible that his attempts only served to take the bread out of their mouths.

And yet this silly prepossession the more amazes me, when I consider, that almost all the excellent productions in wit that have appeared here, were purely the offspring of necessity; their Drydens, Butlers, Otways, and Farquhars, were all writers for bread. Believe me, my friend, hunger has a most amazing faculty of sharpening the genius; and he who with a full belly can think like a hero, after a course of fasting, shall rise to the sublimity of a demigod.

OLIVER GOLDSMITH (1730?–74), *The Citizen of the World*, 1762

They [his novels *Redburn* and *White-Jacket*] are two *jobs*, which I have done for money—being forced to it, as other men are to sawing wood.

HERMAN MELVILLE (1819–91), letter to Lemuel Shaw, 6 Oct. 1849

The following is a list of the books I have written, with the dates of publication and the sums I have received for them. The dates given are the years in which the works were published as a whole, most of them having appeared before in some serial form.

Names of Works	Date of Publication	Total Sums Received		
The Macdermots of Ballycloran, . .	1847	£48	6	9
The Kellys and the O'Kellys, . . .	1848	123	19	5
La Vendée, ...	1850	20	0	0
The Warden, ...	1855 }			
Barchester Towers, ...	1857 }	727	11	3
The Three Clerks, ...	1858	250	0	0
Doctor Thorne, ...	1858	400	0	0
The West Indies and the Spanish Main, ...	1859	250	0	0

The Bertrams, ...	1859	400	0	0
Castle Richmond, ...	1860	600	0	0
Framley Parsonage, ...	1861	1000	0	0
Tales of All Countries—1st Series .	1861 ⎫			
" " 2d " .	1863 ⎬	1830	0	0
" " 3d " .	1870 ⎭			
Orley Farm, ...	1862	3135	0	0
North America, ...	1862	1250	0	0
Rachel Ray, ...	1863	1645	0	0
The Small House at Allington, . . .	1864	3000	0	0
Can You Forgive Her?	1864	3525	0	0
Miss Mackenzie, ...	1865	1300	0	0
The Belton Estate, ...	1866	1757	0	0
The Claverings, ...	1867	2800	0	0
The Last Chronicle of Barset, . . .	1867	3000	0	0
Nina Balatka, ...	1867	450	0	0
Linda Tressel, ...	1868	450	0	0
Phineas Finn, ...	1869	3200	0	0
He Knew He Was Right, ...	1869	3200	0	0
Brown, Jones, and Robinson, . . .	1870	600	0	0
The Vicar of Bullhampton, . . .	1870	2500	0	0
An Editor's Tales, ...	1870	378	0	0
Cæsar (Ancient Classics),*	1870	0	0	0
Sir Harry Hotspur of Humblethwaite,	1871	750	0	0
Ralph the Heir, ...	1871	2500	0	0
The Golden Lion of Granpère, . . .	1872	550	0	0
The Eustace Diamonds, ...	1873	2500	0	0
Australia and New Zealand, . . .	1873	1300	0	0
Carry forward,		£45,439	17	5
Phineas Redux, ...	1874	2500	0	0
Harry Heathcote of Gangoil, . . .	1874	450	0	0
Lady Anna, ...	1874	1200	0	0
The Way We Live Now, ...	1875	3000	0	0
The Prime Minister, ...	1876	2500	0	0
The American Senator, ...	1877	1800	0	0
Is He Popenjoy?	1878	1600	0	0
South Africa, ...	1878	850	0	0
John Caldigate, ...	1879	1800	0	0
Sundries, ...		7800	0	0
		£68,939	17	5

* This was given by me as a present to my friend John Blackwood.

ANTHONY TROLLOPE (1815–82), *Autobiography*, wr. 1875–6, pub. 1883

Of course I had to face a prospect considerably changed by this great addition to my family. I had been obliged to work pretty hard before to meet all the too great expenses of the house. Now four people were added to it, very small two of them, but the others not inexpensive members of the house. I remember making a kind of pretence to myself that I had to think it over, to make a great decision, to give up what hopes I might have had of doing now my very best, and to set myself steadily to make as much money as I could, and do the best I could for the three boys.

*

I never did nor could, of course, hesitate for a moment as to what had to be done. It had to be done, and that was enough, and there is no doubt that it was much more congenial to me to drive on and keep everything going, with a certain scorn of the increased work, and metaphorical toss of my head, as if it mattered! than it ever would have been to labour with an artist's fervour and concentration to produce a masterpiece. One can't be two things or serve two masters. Which was God and which was mammon in that individual case it would be hard to say, perhaps; for once in a way mammon, meaning the money which fed my flock, was in a kind of a poor way God, so far as the necessities of that crisis went. And the wonder was that we did it, I can't tell now, economising, I fear, very little, never knowing quite at the beginning of the year how the ends would come together at Christmas, always with troublesome debts and forestalling of money earned, so that I had generally eaten up the price of a book before it was printed, but always—thank God for it!—so far successfully that, though always owing somebody, I never owed anybody to any unreasonable amount or for any unreasonable extent of time, but managed to pay everything and do everything, to stint nothing, to give them all that was happy and pleasant and of good report through all those dear and blessed boyish years. I confess that it was not done in the noblest way, with those strong efforts of self-control and economy which some people can exercise. I could not do that, or at least did not, but I could work. And I did work, joyfully, with pleasure in it and in my life, sometimes with awful moments when I did not know how I should ever pass some dreadful corner, where the way seemed to end and the rocks to close in: but the corner was always rounded, the road opened up again . . .

It was always a struggle to get safely through every year and make my ends meet. Indeed I fear they never did quite meet; there was always a tugging together, which cost me a great deal of work and much anxiety. The wonder was that the much was never too much. I always managed it somehow, thank God! very happy (and presuming a little on my privilege) when I saw the way tolerably clear before me, and knew at the beginning of the year where the year's income was to come from, but driving, ploughing on, when I was not at all sure of that all the same, and in

some miraculous way getting through. If I had not had unbroken health, and
a spirit almost criminally elastic, I could not have done it. I ought to have been
worn out by work, and crushed by care, half a hundred times by all rules, but
I never was so. Good day and ill day, they balanced each other, and I got on
through year after year.

MARGARET OLIPHANT (1828–97), *Autobiography*, 1899

While when we turn to Peter, he
The cause of this catastrophe,
There fell upon him such a fate
As makes me shudder to relate.
Just in its fifth and final year,
His University Career
Was blasted by the new and dread
Necessity of earning bread.
He was compelled to join a firm
Of Brokers—in the summer term!
And even now, at twenty-five,
He has to *work* to keep alive!
Yes! All day long from 10 till 4!
For half the year or even more;
With but an hour or two to spend
At luncheon with a city friend.

HILAIRE BELLOC (1870–1953), from 'Peter Goole, Who Ruined His Father
and Mother by Extravagance', 1930

PANDIT NEHRU: Why are you doing this work?
WORKER ON BHAKRA DAM: Sahib Bahadur, that man tells me to take those
stones over there. At the end of the work he gives me some money. That is why
I do it.

from SUNIL KHILNANI (1960–   ), *The Idea of India*, 1997

*Economists, however, soon spotted that most people were kept working not by the
need for mere subsistence but by the desire to satisfy an ever growing list of more
sophisticated wants.*

He used to say that the public profited exceedingly by luxury and vanity and that many good works moved from them . . . If you will allow a man his delights and he hath no other means but his labour to compass it, he will work like an horse.

> ROGER NORTH (1651?–1734), on his brother Sir Dudley North (1641–91), excised passage from *The Life of Sir Dudley North*, 1744

In former times . . . men were . . . forced to labour because they were slaves to others; men are now forced to labour because they are slaves to their own wants.

> SIR JAMES STEUART DENHAM (1713–80), *An Inquiry into the Principles of Political Oeconomy*, 1767

If men were contented to go naked, to lie under hedges, and, according to the fiction of the poets, to feed on acorns, there would be none to labour till the acorns were consumed. In general the industry of man bears proportion to his real or imaginary wants. Could the landlord be contented with the produce of his native soil, he would cultivate only what would be sufficient for the consumption of his family; or could the labourer be contented with what was barely sufficient to satisfy his hunger, when he no longer felt the cravings of his appetite, he would cease to labour. But as their wants are multiplied, the master is willing to employ more workmen, and the workman himself is reconciled to constant labour.

> JOSEPH TOWNSEND (1739–1816), *A Dissertation upon the Poor Laws*, 1786

Industry cannot exist without foresight and security. The indolence of the savage is well known; and the poor Egyptian or Abyssinian farmer without capital, who rents land which is let out yearly to the highest bidder, and who is constantly subject to the demands of his tyrannical masters, to the casual plunder of an enemy, and not unfrequently to the violation of his miserable contract, can have no heart to be industrious, and, if he had, could not exercise that industry with success. Even poverty itself, which appears to be the great spur to industry, when it has once passed certain limits, almost ceases to operate. The indigence which is hopeless destroys all vigorous exertion, and confines the efforts to what is sufficient for bare existence. It is the hope of bettering our condition, and the fear of want, rather than want itself, that is the best stimulus to industry; and its most constant and best directed efforts will almost invariably be found among a class of people above the class of the wretchedly poor.

> THOMAS ROBERT MALTHUS (1766–1834), *An Essay on the Principle of Population*, 1798

To civilize a savage, he must be inspired with new wants and desires, even if not of a very elevated kind, provided that their gratification can be a motive to steady and regular bodily and mental exertion. If the negroes of Jamaica and Demerara, after their emancipation, had contented themselves, as it was predicted they would do, with the necessaries of life, and abandoned all labour beyond the little which in a tropical climate, with a thin population and abundance of the richest land, is sufficient to support existence, they would have sunk into a condition more barbarous, though less unhappy, than their previous state of slavery. The motive which was most relied on for inducing them to work was their love of fine clothes and personal ornaments. No one will stand up for this taste as worthy of being cultivated, and in most societies its indulgence tends to impoverish rather than to enrich; but in the state of mind of the negroes it might have been the only incentive that could make them voluntarily undergo systematic labour, and so acquire or maintain habits of voluntary industry which may be converted to more valuable ends.

JOHN STUART MILL (1806–73), *The Principles of Political Economy*, 1848

Whether they worked for subsistence or in order to acquire more comforts, it was not obvious that those who sold their labour for money were necessarily much freer than those who were forced to work as slaves. Many wage-earners and salaried people continued to regard their work as inherently tedious. They engaged in it for the sake of the money with which they could enjoy their leisure or future retirement. The essential pleasures of life were to be found outside work.

Work is what you do so that some time you won't have to do it any more.

ALFRED POLGAR (1873–1955)

This spending of the best part of one's life earning money in order to enjoy a questionable liberty during the least valuable part of it reminds me of the Englishman who went to India to make a fortune first, in order that he might return to England and live the life of a poet. He should have gone up garret at once.

HENRY DAVID THOREAU (1817–62), *Walden, or Life in the Woods*, 1854

[An Egyptian father, who is placing his son in a school for scribes, contrasts the scribal career with the hardships of other occupations.]

I'll make you love scribedom more than your mother,
I'll make its beauties stand before you;
It's the greatest of all callings,
There's none like it in the land.

Barely grown, still a child,
He is greeted, sent on errands,
Hardly returned he wears a gown.
I never saw a sculptor as envoy,
Nor is a goldsmith ever sent;
But I have seen the smith at work
At the opening of his furnace;
With fingers like claws of a crocodile
He stinks more than fish roe.

The carpenter who wields an adze,
He is wearier than a field-laborer;
His field is the timber, his hoe the adze.
There is no end to his labor,
He does more than his arms can do,
Yet at night he kindles light.
The jewel-maker bores with his chisel
In hard stone of all kinds;
When he has finished the inlay of the eye,
His arms are spent, he's weary;
Sitting down when the sun goes down,
His knees and back are cramped.

The barber barbers till nightfall,
He betakes himself to town,
He sets himself up in his corner,
He moves from street to street,
Looking for someone to barber.
He strains his arms to fill his belly,
Like the bee that eats as it works.

The reed-cutter travels to the Delta to get arrows;
When he has done more than his arms can do,
Mosquitoes have slain him,
Gnats have slaughtered him,
He is quite worn out.

The potter is under the soil,
Though as yet among the living;
He grubs in the mud more than a pig,
In order to fire his pots.

His clothes are stiff with clay,
His girdle is in shreds;
If air enters his nose,
It comes straight from the fire.
He makes a pounding with his feet,
And is himself crushed;
He grubs the yard of every house
And roams the public places.

I'll describe to you also the mason:
His loins give him pain;
Though he is out in the wind,
He works without a cloak;
His loincloth is a twisted rope
And a string in the rear.
His arms are spent from exertion,
Having mixed all kinds of dirt;
When he eats bread [with] his fingers,
He has washed at the same time.

*

The gardener carries a yoke,
His shoulders are bent as with age;
There's a swelling on his neck
And it festers.
In the morning he waters vegetables,
The evening he spends with the herbs,
While at noon he has toiled in the orchard.
He works himself to death
More than all other professions.

*

The weaver in the workshop,
He is worse off than a woman;
With knees against his chest,
He cannot breathe air.
If he skips a day of weaving,
He is beaten fifty strokes;
He gives food to the doorkeeper,
To let him see the light of day.

*

The bird-catcher suffers much
As he watches out for birds;
When the swarms pass over him,
He keeps saying, 'Had I a net!'
But the god grants it not,
And he's angry with his lot.

I'll speak of the fisherman also,
His is the worst of all the jobs;
He labors on the river,
Mingling with crocodiles.
When the time of reckoning comes,
He is full of lamentations;
He does not say, 'There's a crocodile,'
Fear has made him blind.
Coming from the flowing water
He says, 'Mighty god!'

See, there's no profession without a boss,
Except for the scribe; he is the boss.
Hence if you know writing,
It will do better for you
Than those professions I've set before you,
Each more wretched than the other.

The Satire of the Trades, 14th c. BC, tr. from the Egyptian by Miriam
Lichtheim, 1976

Thus the three planes of the airmail service, from Patagonia, Chile, and
Paraguay, were converging from south, west, and north on Buenos Aires.
Their arrival with the mails would give the signal for the departure, about
midnight, of the Europe postal plane . . .

Then today's work would be over. Worn out, the crews would go to sleep,
fresh crews replace them. Rivière alone would have no respite; then, in its
turn, the Europe mail would weigh upon his mind. And so it would
always be. Always. For the first time in his life this veteran fighter caught
himself feeling tired. Never could an arrival of the planes mean for him
the victory that ends a war and preludes a spell of smiling peace. For
him it meant just one more step, with a thousand more to follow, along
a straight, unending road. Rivière felt as though for an eternity he had
been carrying a crushing load on his uplifted arms; an endless, hopeless effort.

'I'm ageing.' If he no longer found a solace in work and work alone, surely
he was growing old. He caught himself puzzling over problems which
hitherto he had ignored. There surged within his mind, like a lost ocean

murmuring regrets, all the gentler joys of life that he had thrust aside. 'Can it be coming on me—so soon?' He realized that he had always been postponing for his declining years, 'when I have time for it,' everything that makes life kind to men. As if it were ever possible to 'have time for it' one day and realize at life's end that dream of peace and happiness! No, peace there could be none; nor any victory, perhaps. Never could all the airmails land in one swoop once for all.

Rivière paused before Leroux; the old foreman was hard at work. Leroux, too, had forty years of work behind him. All his energies were for his work. When at ten o'clock or midnight Leroux went home it certainly was not to find a change of scene, escape into another world. When Rivière smiled towards him, he raised his heavy head and pointed at a burnt-out axle. 'Jammed it was, but I've fixed it up.' Rivière bent down to look; duty had regained its hold upon him. 'You should tell the shop to set them a bit looser.' He passed his finger over the trace of seizing, then glanced again at Leroux. As his eyes lingered on the stern old wrinkled face, an odd question hovered on his lips and made him smile.

'Ever had much to do with love, Leroux, in your time?'

'Love, sir? Well, you see——'

'Hadn't the time for it, I suppose—like me.'

'Not a great deal, sir.'

Rivière strained his ears to hear if there were any bitterness in the reply; no, not a trace of it. This man, looking back on life, felt the quiet satisfaction of a carpenter who has made a good job of planing down a board: 'There you are! *That's* done.'

'There you are,' thought Rivière. 'My life's done.'

Then, brushing aside the swarm of sombre thoughts his weariness had brought, he walked towards the hangar; for the Chile plane was droning down towards it.

> ANTOINE DE SAINT-EXUPÉRY (1900–44), *Night Flight*, 1931, tr. Stuart Gilbert, 1932

At present, in consequence of the existence of private property, a great many people are enabled to develop a certain very limited amount of Individualism. They are either under no necessity to work for their living, or are enabled to choose the sphere of activity that is really congenial to them, and gives them pleasure. These are the poets, the philosophers, the men of science, the men of culture—in a word, the real men, the men who have realised themselves, and in whom all Humanity gains a partial realisation. Upon the other hand, there are a great many people who, having no private property of their own, and being always on the brink of sheer starvation, are compelled to do the work of beasts of burden, to do work that is quite uncongenial to them, and to which they are forced by the peremptory, unreasonable, degrading Tyranny of want. These are the poor; and amongst them there is no grace of manner, or charm of speech, or civilisation or culture, or refinement in pleasures, or joy of life. From their collective force Humanity gains much in material prosperity. But it is only the material result that it gains, and the man who is poor is in himself absolutely of no importance. He is merely the infinitesimal atom of a force that, so far from regarding him, crushes him: indeed, prefers him crushed, as in that case he is far more obedient.

OSCAR WILDE (1854–1900), 'The Soul of Man under Socialism', 1891

Wages

The wages of work is cash.
The wages of cash is want more cash.
The wages of want more cash is vicious competition.
The wages of vicious competition is—the world we live in.

The work-cash-want circle is the viciousest circle
that ever turned men into fiends.

Earning a wage is a prison occupation
and a wage-earner is a sort of gaol-bird.

Earning a salary is a prison overseer's job
a gaoler instead of a gaol-bird.

Living on our income is strolling grandly outside the prison
in terror lest you have to go in. And since the work-prison covers
Almost every scrap of the living earth, you stroll up and down
on a narrow beat, about the same as a prisoner taking exercise.

This is called universal freedom.

D. H. LAWRENCE (1885–1930), 1929

All democratic theories, whether Socialistic or bourgeois, necessarily take in some concept of the dignity of labour. If the have-not were deprived of this delusion that his sufferings are somehow laudable and agreeable to God, there would be little left in his ego save a belly-ache. Nevertheless, a delusion is a delusion, and this is one of the worst. It arises out of confusing the pride of workmanship of the artist with the dogged, painful docility of the machine. The difference is important and enormous. If he got no reward whatever, the artist would go on working just the same; his actual reward, in fact, is often so little that he almost starves. But suppose a coal-miner got nothing for his labour: would he go on working just the same? Can one imagine him submitting voluntarily to hardship and sore want that he might express his soul in 200 more tons of coal?

H. L. MENCKEN (1880–1956), 'Types of Men', 1926

Hobbs

When Hobbs of the piston pace and the bowler hat
And the swinging case is catching his eight-fifteen,
Suburbia's eye at his bobbing by looks pat
To the mantel clock and checks machine with machine.

'I love this walk to the train, and the walk again
At the other end, to my desk and business drive,
Then both in reverse and none the worse for the rain',
Chirps Hobbs as his bowler bobs from the half-past-five.

Was he ever a boy who dreamed in hearth-rug joy
Of cities that shone in the fire, or mused on maps
That flickered and whispered of Trebizond and Troy,
And himself let loose? Perhaps, long ago, perhaps.

At least when the morning train is gone, and steam
Thins out from under the bridge, we may surmise,
Some wisp of Hobbs, some otherself of dream
Escapes in archipelagoes of clouds, and sighs.

GEOFFREY JOHNSON (1893–1966), 1968

That state is a state of slavery in which a man does what he likes to do in his spare time and in his working time that which is required of him.

ERIC GILL (1882–1940), 'Slavery and Freedom', 1918

Toads

Why should I let the toad *work*
   Squat on my life?
Can't I use my wit as a pitchfork
   And drive the brute off?

Six days of the week it soils
  With its sickening poison—
Just for paying a few bills!
  That's out of proportion.

Lots of folk live on their wits:
  Lecturers, lispers,
Losels, loblolly-men, louts—
  They don't end as paupers;

Lots of folk live up lanes
  With fires in a bucket,
Eat windfalls and tinned sardines—
  They seem to like it.

Their nippers have got bare feet,
  Their unspeakable wives
Are skinny as whippets—and yet
  No one actually *starves*.

Ah, were I courageous enough
  To shout *Stuff your pension!*
But I know, all too well, that's the stuff
  That dreams are made on:

For something sufficiently toad-like
  Squats in me, too;
Its hunkers are heavy as hard luck,
  And cold as snow,

And will never allow me to blarney
  My way to getting
The fame and the girl and the money
  All at one sitting.

I don't say, one bodies the other
  One's spiritual truth;
But I do say it's hard to lose either,
  When you have both.

PHILIP LARKIN (1922–85), 1955

Not surprisingly, the upper classes, who were in a position to choose, usually opted for a life of leisure. Immunity from labour, particularly manual labour, had always been the prerogative of social elites, many of whom made conspicuous idleness the proof of their superiority.

It is hard to say whether this is another thing that the Greeks have learnt from the Egyptians, for I know that among the Thracians, Scythians, Persians, Lydians, and well-nigh all foreign nations, men who learn trades and their descendants are held in less regard than other citizens, whilst any who need not work with their hands are considered noble, especially if they devote themselves to war.

HERODOTUS (*c*.480–*c*.425 BC), *Histories* (*c*.425 BC), tr. H. Carter, 1958

The citizens must not live the life of mechanics or shopkeepers, which is ignoble and inimical to goodness. Nor can those who are to be citizens engage in farming: leisure is a necessity, both for growth in goodness and for the pursuit of political activities.

ARISTOTLE (384–322 BC), *Politics*, *c*.335–322 BC, tr. Ernest Barker, rev. R. F. Stalley, 1995

This pervading sense of the indignity of the slightest manual labour is familiar to all civilised peoples, as well as to peoples of a less advanced pecuniary culture. In persons of delicate sensibility, who have long been habituated to gentle manners, the sense of the shamefulness of manual labour may become so strong that, at a critical juncture, it will even set aside the instinct of self-preservation. So, for instance, we are told of certain Polynesian chiefs, who, under the stress of good form, preferred to starve rather than carry their food to their mouths with their own hands. It is true, this conduct may have been due, at least in part, to an excessive sanctity or tabu attaching to the chief's person. The tabu would have been communicated by the contact of his hands, and so would have made anything touched by him unfit for human food. But the tabu is itself a derivative of the unworthiness or moral incompatibility of labour; so that even when construed in this sense the conduct of the Polynesian chiefs is truer to the canon of honorific leisure than would at first appear. A better illustration, or at least a more unmistakable one, is afforded by a certain king of France, who is said to have lost his life through an excess of moral stamina in the observance of good form. In the absence of the functionary whose office it was to shift his master's seat, the king sat uncomplaining before the fire and suffered his royal person to be toasted beyond recovery. But in so doing he saved his Most Christian Majesty from menial contamination.

THORSTEIN VEBLEN (1857–1929), *The Theory of the Leisure Class*, 1899

... the disdain of agricultural pursuits by the nobility [was] a fatal change, and one gradually bringing about the ruin of that nobility. It is expressed in the mediæval landscape by the eminently pleasurable and horticultural character of everything; by the fences, hedges, castle walls, and masses of useless, but lovely flowers, especially roses. The knights and ladies are represented always as singing, or making love, in these pleasant places. The idea of setting an old knight, like Laertes (whatever his state of fallen fortune), 'with thick gloves on to keep his hands from the thorns,' to prune a row of vines, would have been regarded as the most monstrous violation of the decencies of life; and a senator, once detected in the home employments of Cincinnatus, could, I suppose, thenceforward hardly have appeared in society.

JOHN RUSKIN (1819–1900), *Modern Painters*, 1843–60

But amongst us the badge of gentry is idlenesse: to be of no calling, not to labour, for that's derogatory to their birth, to be a meere spectator, a drone, *fruges consumere natus*, to have no necessary employment to busie himselfe about in Church and commonwealth (some few governers exempted) *but to rise to eat, &c.* to spend his dayes in hawking, hunting, &c. & such like disports and recreations (which our Casuists taxe) are the sole exercise almost and ordinary actions of our Nobility, and in which they are too immoderate. And thence it comes to passe that in Citty and Country so many grievances of body and minde, & this ferall disease of melancholy so frequently rageth, and now domineeres almost all over *Europe* amongst our great ones. They knowe not how to spend their times (disports excepted, which are all their businesse) what to doe or otherwise how to bestow themselves: like our moderne Frenchmen that had rather loose a pound of blood in a single combate, then a drop of sweat in any honest labour. Every man almost hath something or other to employ himselfe about, some vocation, some trade, but they doe all by ministers and servants, *ad otia duntaxat se natos existimant, immo ad sui ipsius plerumque & aliorum pernitiem*, as one freely taxeth such kinde of men, they are all for pastimes, tis all their study, all their invention tends to this alone to drive away time, as if they were borne some of them to no other ends.

ROBERT BURTON (1577–1640), *The Anatomy of Melancholy*, 1621

My Friend, Sir Andrew Freeport, as we were sitting in the Club last Night, gave us an Account of a sober Citizen, who died a few Days since. This honest Man being of greater Consequence in his own Thoughts, than in the Eye of the World, had for some Years past kept a Journal of his Life. Sir Andrew shewed us one Week of it. . . . I shall present my Reader with a faithful Copy of it; after having first informed him, that the Deceased Person had in his Youth been

fruges consumere natus] 'born only to consume his food'   *ad otia duntaxat . . . aliorum pernitiem*] 'they think themselves born only for idleness, indeed for their own and other people's ruin'

bred to Trade, but finding himself not so well turned for Business, he had for several Years last past lived altogether upon a moderate Annuity.

MONDAY, *Eight a Clock.* I put on my Cloaths and walked into the Parlour.

Nine a Clock, ditto. Tied my Knee-strings, and washed my Hands.

Hours Ten, Eleven and Twelve. Smoaked three Pipes of Virginia.
Read the *Supplement* and *Daily Courant.* Things go ill in the North. Mr Nisby's Opinion thereupon.

One a Clock in the Afternoon. Chid Ralph for mislaying my Tobacco-Box.

Two a Clock. Sat down to Dinner. *Mem.* Too many Plumbs, and no Sewet.

From Three to Four. Took my Afternoon's Nap.

From Four to Six. Walked into the Fields. Wind, S.S.E.

From Six to Ten. At the Club. Mr Nisby's Opinion about the Peace.

Ten a Clock. Went to Bed, slept sound.

TUESDAY, BEING HOLLIDAY, *Eight a Clock.* Rose as usual.

Nine a Clock. Washed Hands and Face, shaved, put on my double soaled Shoes.

Ten, Eleven, Twelve. Took a Walk to Islington.

One. Took a Pot of Mother Cob's Mild.

Between Two and Three. Returned, dined on a Knuckle of Veal and Bacon. *Mem.* Sprouts wanting.

Three. Nap as usual.

From Four to Six. Coffee-house. Read the News. A Dish of Twist. Grand Vizier strangled.

From Six to Ten. At the Club. Mr Nisby's Account of the great Turk.

Ten. Dream of the Grand Vizier. Broken Sleep.

WEDNESDAY, *Eight a Clock.* Tongue of my Shooe Buckle broke. Hands but not Face.

Nine. Paid off the Butchers Bill. *Mem.* To be allowed for the last Leg of Mutton.

Ten, Eleven. At the Coffee-house. More Work in the North. Stranger in a black Wigg asked me how Stocks went.

From Twelve to One. Walked in the Fields. Wind to the South.

From One to Two. Smoaked a Pipe and a half.

Two. Dined as usual. Stomach good.

Three. Nap broke by the falling of a Pewter Dish. *Mem.* Cook-maid in Love, and grown careless.

From Four to Six. At the Coffee-house. Advice from Smyrna, that the Grand Vizier was first of all strangled, and afterwards beheaded.

Six a Clock in the Evening. Was half an Hour in the Club before any Body else came. Mr Nisby of Opinion, that the Grand Vizier was not strangled the Sixth Instant.

Dish of Twist] a mixture of two ingredients, such as tea and coffee, or gin and brandy

Ten at Night. Went to Bed. Slept without waking till Nine next Morning.

THURSDAY, *Nine a Clock.* Staid within till Two a Clock for Sir Timothy. Who did not bring me my Annuity according to his Promise.

Two in the Afternoon. Sate down to Dinner. Loss of Appetite. Small Beer sowr. Beef overcorn'd.

Three. Could not take my Nap.

Four and Five. Gave Ralph a Box on the Ear. Turn'd off my Cook-maid. Sent a Message to Sir Timothy. *Mem.* I did not go to the Club to Night. Went to Bed at Nine a Clock.

FRIDAY. Pass'd the Morning in Meditation upon Sir Timothy, who was with me a Quarter before Twelve.

Twelve a Clock. Bought a new Head to my Cane, and a Tongue to my Buckle. Drank a Glass of Purl to recover Appetite.

Two and Three. Dined, and Slept well.

From Four to Six. Went to the Coffee-house. Met Mr Nisby there. Smoaked several Pipes. Mr Nisby of opinion that laced Coffee is bad for the Head.

Six a Clock. At the Club as Steward. Sat late.

Twelve a Clock. Went to Bed, dreamt that I drank Small-beer with the Grand Vizier.

SATURDAY. Waked at Eleven, walked in the Fields, Wind N.E.

Twelve. Caught in a Shower.

One in the Afternoon. Returned home, and dryed my self.

Two. Mr Nisby dined with me. First Course Marrow-bones, Second Ox Cheek, with a Bottle of Brooks and Hellier.

Three a Clock. Overslept my self.

Six. Went to the Club. Like to have faln into a Gutter. Grand Vizier certainly Dead.

JOSEPH ADDISON (1672–1719), *The Spectator*, 4 Mar. 1712

> Here languid Beauty kept her pale-fac'd Court:
> Bevies of dainty Dames, of high Degree,
> From every Quarter hither made Resort;
> Where, from gross mortal Care and Business free,
> They lay, pour'd out in Ease and Luxury.
> Or should they a vain Shew of Work assume,
> Alas! and well-a-day! what can it be?
> To knot, to twist, to range the vernal Bloom;
> But far is cast the Distaff, Spinning-Wheel, and Loom.

Purl] a mixture of hot beer and gin   *Hellier*] leading London wine-merchant of the time

Their only Labour was to kill the Time;
And Labour dire it is, and weary Woe.
They sit, they loll, turn o'er some idle Rhyme;
Then, rising sudden, to the Glass they go,
Or saunter forth, with tottering Step and slow:
This soon too rude an Exercise they find;
Strait on the Couch their Limbs again they throw,
Where Hours on Hours they sighing lie reclin'd,
And court the vapoury God soft-breathing in the Wind.

JAMES THOMSON (1700–48), *The Castle of Indolence,* 1748

[James Oglethorpe planned the colony of Georgia as a refuge for the well-to-do who had fallen on hard times and were incapable of earning a living.]

Let us in the mean Time cast our Eyes on the Multitude of unfortunate People in the Kingdom of reputable Families, and of liberal, or at least, [hon]est reputa[b]le Education: Some undone by Guardians, some by Law-Suits, some by Accidents in Commerce, some by Stocks and Bubbles, and some by Suretyship; But all agree [in thin]king in this one Circumstance, that they must either be Burthensome to their Relations, or betake themselves to little Shifts for Sustenance, which ('tis ten to one) do not answer their Purposes, and to which a well-educated Mind descends with the utmost Constraint. What various Misfortunes may reduce the Rich, the Industrious, to the Danger of a Prison, to a moral Certainty of Starving! These are the People that may relieve themselves and strengthen *Georgia,* by resorting thither, and Great *Britain* by their Departure.

I appeal to the Recollection of the Reader (tho' he be Opulent, tho' he be Noble) does not his own Sphere of Acquaintance? (I may venture to ask) Does not even his own Blood, his Set of near Relations furnish him with some Instances of such Persons as have been here describ'd? Must they Starve? What honest Mind can bear to think it? Must they be fed by the Contributions of Others? Certainly they must, rather than be suffered to perish. Are these Wealth to the Nation? Are they not a Burthen to themselves, a Burthen to their Kindred and Acquaintance? A Burthen to the whole Community?

I have heard it said (and 'tis easy to say so) let them learn to work; let them subdue their Pride, and descend to mean Employments, keep Ale-houses, or Coffee-houses, even sell Fruit, or clean Shoes for an honest Lively-hood. But alas! These Occupations, and many more like them, are overstock'd already by People who know better how to follow them, than do they whom we have been talking of. Half of those who are bred in low Life, and well versed in such Shifts and Expedients, find but a very narrow Maintenance by them. As for Labouring, I cou'd almost wish that the Gentleman, or Merchant who thinks that another Gentleman, or Merchant in want, can thresh, or dig, to the Value of Subsistence for his Family, or even for himself; I say I could wish the Person who thinks so, were obliged to make trial of it for a Week, or (not to be too severe) for only a Day: He would find himself to be less than the Fourth Part of a Labourer, and that the Fourth Part of a Labourer's Wages could not maintain him. I have heard it said, that a Man may learn to labour by Practice; 'tis admitted: But it must also be admitted that before he can learn, he may starve. Suppose a Gentleman were this Day to begin, and with grievous toil found himself able to earn Three Pence, how many Days, or Months, are necessary to form him that he may deserve a Shilling, *per diem*? Men, whose Wants are importunate, must try such Expedients as will give immediate Relief. 'Tis too late for them to begin to learn a Trade when their pressing Necessities call for the Exercise of it.

> JAMES EDWARD OGLETHORPE (1696–1785), *A New and Accurate Account of the Provinces of South-Carolina and Georgia,* 1732

There is another fault which is very apt to grow into a habit, and under which habit I have seen many of our countrymen suffer very grievously. This fault is *lounging,* which is a painful manner of letting time slip thro one's hands. Loungers are seen sauntering up and down a street, going into a coffee-house, not for the sake of company or reading the newspapers, but merely to fill up such a vacancy of time. The same persons are often found stretch'd out in an easy-chair in a corner of a room, without a book in their hands, without the least attention to the company they are in, without being either asleep or awake, and without any wish or desire, except that the clock would strike six when it strikes but five. The place in which these gentlemen shine most are the windows of White's. There you may see half a dozen of the same faces looking into the street every day from two till four, making dull remarks upon the people and coaches that pass by, and asking every ten minutes whether dinner is not ready, tho they declare at the same time that they are not hungry. I own the loungers are a set of men that I have not patience with. I have often wished that it were possible for me to buy at a good price that time that sits so heavily upon them, and to purchase the hours which they so lavishly squander. I was lucky enough to have an early taste for reading, and to that I owe my never having had time hang heavily upon my hands. If ever your Lordship finds yourself under any of the descriptions I have given you, I do prescribe two books, *viz., Gil Blas* and *Tom Jones,* and I beg every time you find the fit coming upon you to take a good dose of one of them.

> SIR CHARLES HANBURY-WILLIAMS (1708–59), letter to William, 4th Earl of Essex, Jan. 1751

A certain gentleman . . . who lived on his estate, issued forth to walk as the clock struck eleven. Every day he trod the same path, leading to an eminence which opened to a view of the sea. A rock on the summit was his seat, where, after resting an hour, he returned home at leisure. It is not a little singular, that this exercise was repeated day after day for forty-three years, without interruption for the last twenty years of the gentleman's life. And though he has been long dead, the impression of his heels in the sod remains visible to this day. Men by inaction degenerate into oysters.

> HENRY HOME, LORD KAMES (1696–1782), *Sketches of the History of Man,*
> 1774

'I think, Edward,' said Mrs Dashwood, as they were at breakfast the last morning, 'you would be a happier man if you had any profession to engage your time and give an interest to your plans and actions. Some inconvenience to your friends, indeed, might result from it—you would not be able to give them so much of your time. But (with a smile) you would be materially benefited in one particular at least—you would know where to go when you left them.'

'I do assure you,' he replied, 'that I have long thought on this point, as you think now. It has been, and is, and probably will always be a heavy misfortune to me, that I have had no necessary business to engage me, no profession to give me employment, or afford me any thing like independence. But unfortunately my own nicety, and the nicety of my friends, have made me what I am, an idle, helpless being. We never could agree in our choice of a profession. I always preferred the church, as I still do. But that was not smart enough for my family. They recommended the army. That was a great deal too smart for me. The law was allowed to be genteel enough; many young men, who had chambers in the Temple, made a very good appearance in the first circles, and drove about town in very knowing gigs. But I had no inclination for the law, even in this less abstruse study of it, which my family approved. As for the navy, it had fashion on its side, but I was too old when the subject was first started to enter it—and, at length, as there was no necessity for my having any profession at all, as I might be as dashing and expensive without a red coat on my back as with one, idleness was pronounced on the whole to be the most advantageous and honourable, and a young man of eighteen is not in general so earnestly bent on being busy as to resist the solicitations of his friends to do nothing. I was therefore entered at Oxford and have been properly idle ever since.'

> JANE AUSTEN (1775–1817), *Sense and Sensibility,* 1811

> From ten to eleven, ate a breakfast for seven;
> From eleven to noon, to begin 'twas too soon;
> From twelve to one, asked, 'What's to be done?'
> From one to two, found nothing to do;

From two to three began to foresee
That from three to four would be a damned bore.

THOMAS LOVE PEACOCK (1785–1866), 1875

Among a democratic people, where there is no hereditary wealth, every man works to earn a living, or has worked, or is born of parents who have worked. The notion of labor is therefore presented to the mind, on every side, as the necessary, natural, and honest condition of human existence. Not only is labor not dishonorable among such a people, but it is held in honor; the prejudice is not against it, but in its favor. In the United States a wealthy man thinks that he owes it to public opinion to devote his leisure to some kind of industrial or commercial pursuit or to public business. He would think himself in bad repute if he employed his life solely in living. It is for the purpose of escaping this obligation to work that so many rich Americans come to Europe, where they find some scattered remains of aristocratic society, among whom idleness is still held in honor.

ALEXIS DE TOCQUEVILLE (1805–59), *Democracy in America*, 1835–40, tr. Henry Reeve, rev. Francis Bowen, rev. Phillips Bradley, 1945

With the lower classes a gentleman is anyone who does not work for his living. The writer knew an old widow who worked for her subsistence in East Anglia, and who went by the name of Mistress Clarke. One day he found that she had changed her designation; her neighbours took to calling her The Lady Clarke, because, as they argued, rheumatism had invaded her hands, and prevented her from going out gleaning in the turnip-field, and she had been forced to go to the parish for half-a-crown a week, and to lay her hands on her lap and do nothing. Idleness ennobles, and this is the common idea among the working classes. 'I'm going to be a gentleman to-morrow and to take a holiday' is a common saying. That young ladies and gentlemen do lead very idle and unprofitable lives is true enough, but it is not the fact that they have nothing to do which constitutes them gentlefolk.

ANON. (Sabine Baring-Gould) (1834–1924), 'What is a Gentleman?', *Cornhill Magazine*, Nov. 1887

Lord Caversham. Good evening, Lady Chiltern! Has my good-for-nothing young son been here?
Lady Chiltern [*smiling*].   I don't think Lord Goring has arrived yet.
Mabel Chiltern [*coming up to Lord Caversham*].   Why do you call Lord Goring good-for-nothing?

Lord Caversham.   Because he leads such an idle life.

Mabel Chiltern.   How can you say such a thing? Why, he rides in the Row at ten o'clock in the morning, goes to the Opera three times a week, changes his clothes at least five times a day, and dines out every night of the season. You don't call that leading an idle life, do you?

OSCAR WILDE (1854–1900), An Ideal Husband, 1895

If, in addition to showing that the wearer can afford to consume freely and uneconomically, it can also be shown in the same stroke that he or she is not under the necessity of earning a livelihood, the evidence of social worth is enhanced in a very considerable degree. Our dress, therefore, in order to serve its purpose effectually, should not only be expensive, but it should also make plain to all observers that the wearer is not engaged in any kind of productive labour. In the evolutionary process by which our system of dress has been elaborated into its present admirably perfect adaptation to its purpose, this subsidiary line of evidence has received due attention. A detailed examination of what passes in popular apprehension for elegant apparel will show that it is contrived at every point to convey the impression that the wearer does not habitually put forth any useful effort. It goes without saying that no apparel can be considered elegant, or even decent, if it shows the effect of manual labour on the part of the wearer, in the way of soil or wear. The pleasing effect of neat and spotless garments is chiefly, if not altogether, due to their carrying the suggestion of leisure—exemption from personal contact with industrial processes of any kind. Much of the charm that invests the patent-leather shoe, the stainless linen, the lustrous cylindrical hat, and the walking-stick, which so greatly enhance the native dignity of a gentleman, comes of their pointedly suggesting that the wearer cannot when so attired bear a hand in any employment that is directly and immediately of any human use. Elegant dress serves its purpose of elegance not only in that it is expensive, but also because it is the insignia of leisure. It not only shows that the wearer is able to consume a relatively large value, but it argues at the same time that he consumes without producing.

The dress of women goes even farther than that of men in the way of demonstrating the wearer's abstinence from productive employment. It needs no argument to enforce the generalisation that the more elegant styles of feminine bonnets go even farther towards making work impossible than does the man's high hat. The woman's shoe adds the so-called French heel to the evidence of enforced leisure afforded by its polish; because this high heel obviously makes any, even the simplest and most necessary manual work extremely difficult. The like is true even in a higher degree of the skirt and the rest of the drapery which characterises woman's dress. The substantial reason for our tenacious attachment to the skirt is just this: it is expensive and it hampers the wearer at every turn and incapacitates her for all useful exertion. The like is true of the feminine custom of wearing the hair excessively long.

THORSTEIN VEBLEN (1857–1929), *The Theory of the Leisure Class,* 1899

Irina. When I woke up to-day and got up and dressed myself, I suddenly began to feel as if everything in this life was open to me, and that I knew how I must live. Dear Ivan Romanovitch, I know everything. A man must work, toil in the sweat of his brow, whoever he may be, for that is the meaning and object of his life, his happiness, his enthusiasm. How fine it is to be a workman who gets up at daybreak and breaks stones in the street, or a shepherd, or a schoolmaster, who teaches children, or an engine-driver on the railway . . . My God, let alone a man, it's better to be an ox, or just a horse, so long as it can work, than a young woman who wakes up at twelve o'clock, has her coffee in bed, and then spends two hours dressing . . . Oh it's awful! Sometimes when it's hot, your thirst can be just as tiresome as my need for work. And if I don't get up early in future and work, Ivan Romanovitch, then you may refuse me your friendship.

Chebutykin [*tenderly*]. I'll refuse, I'll refuse . . .

Olga. Father used to make us get up at seven. Now Irina wakes at seven and lies and meditates about something till nine at least. And she looks so serious! [*laughs*]

Irina. You're so used to seeing me as a little girl that it seems queer to you when my face is serious. I'm twenty!

Tuzenbach. How well I can understand that craving for work, oh God! I've never worked once in my life. I was born in Petersburg, a chilly, lazy place, in a family which never knew what work or worry meant. I remember that when I used to come home from my regiment, a footman used to have to pull off my boots while I fidgeted and my mother looked on in adoration and wondered why other people didn't see me in the same light. They shielded me from work; but only just in time! A new age is dawning, the people are marching on us all, a powerful, health-giving storm is gathering, it is drawing near, soon it will be upon us and it will drive away laziness, indifference, the prejudice against labour, and rotten dullness from our society. I shall work, and in twenty-five or thirty years, every man will have to work. Every one!

Chebutykin. Well, I shan't for one.

Tuzenbakh. You don't count.

Solyony. In twenty-five years you won't be here at all, thank God. In a couple of years or so you'll have a stroke and die or I'll lose my temper and put a bullet through your head, my good friend. [*Takes a bottle of scent from his pocket and sprinkles his chest and hands.*]

Chibutykin [*laughs*].   You know, I've never done a thing and that's a fact. Since I left the university I haven't lifted a finger, I've never even read a book. I've read nothing but newspapers.

> ANTON CHEKHOV (1860–1904), *Three Sisters*, 1901, tr. Ronald Hingley, 1980

[Herbert Pell (1884–1961) was a wealthy New Deal Democrat from an old family.]

When a niece of his joyfully told him how her husband had at last found a job, Uncle Bertie replied, 'Oh, my dear, I'm so sorry.'

> NELSON W. ALDRICH JR, *Old Money*, 1988

[Laura Ramsbotham is a country girl at a select Melbourne boarding school.]

Laura knew very well that good birth and an artistic appearance would not avail her, did the damaging fact leak out that Mother worked for her living. Work in itself was bad enough—how greatly to be envied were those whose fathers did nothing more active than live on their money! But the additional circumstance of Mother being a woman made things ten times worse: ladies did not work; someone always left them enough to live on, and if he didn't, well, then he, too, shared the ignominy. So Laura went in fear and trembling lest the truth should come to light—in that case she would be a pariah indeed.

> HENRY HANDEL RICHARDSON (Ethel Florence Lindesay Richardson) (1870–1946), *The Getting of Wisdom*, 1910

My dear Randolph,
. . . Your idle and lazy life is v[er]y offensive to me. You appear to be leading a perfectly useless existence. You do not value or profit by the opportunities wh[ich] Oxford offers for those who care for learning. You are not acquiring any habits of industry or concentration. Even in idleness you find it trying to pass the day.

> WINSTON CHURCHILL (1874–1965), letter to his son Randolph, 29 Dec. 1929

One of the most reassuring pockets of resistance to change was provided by my maternal cousins, the Limbury-Buses, a family consisting, in 1939, of old Mr and Mrs Limbury-Buse, in their mid-seventies, their son, Geoff, well on in his forties, and their daughter, Olive, in her early forties, and a well-starched maid in her seventies. The Limbury-Buses lived in a big Victorian house named Florian with a dank, dripping, overgrown garden, near a large gothic pinnacle in stone erected to the memory of Canon Edward Hoare, a noted nineteenth-century preacher and vicar of Holy Trinity Church, whose features in profile adorned one side of the monument. The house was on the road to Southborough and quite close to St John's church (which my cousins were never able to attend, owing to difficulties of time-table). They had occupied the house since the nineties. Though *aware* of the War—not that they ever read any newspapers, or listened to the wireless (the only one was in the kitchen), they made absolutely no concessions to it, maintaining the daily routines that had been gradually established over the previous twenty or thirty years, and that, by the time I came on the scene, had been frozen into a slow-moving ritual, prudent and solemn (Geoff and his father moved forward as if they had been royal heralds walking backwards, unhurried and stately) and fixed for ever. Old Mr Limbury-Buse had read Law at Cambridge with a view to 'taking articles' and practising as a solicitor. But, as he had been of delicate health, his parents had decided that he should not work, and he had moved to Tunbridge Wells in order to have a quiet time. In this, he had been entirely successful. He had never done a day's work since leaving Cambridge. Nor had he even been known to read, since that distant spurt of intellectual activity, unless the ability to distinguish between hearts, spades, diamonds and clubs, between ace, king, queen and jack, can be described as reading.

His son, Geoff, had followed his example, though he had failed to improve on it, having, after leaving Tonbridge, been caught up in the First World War, serving throughout it as an officer, and having then for a few years been involved in the film industry in Hollywood, though I do not know in what capacity. This spurt of energy had not been maintained; he had decided to stay at home, in the big house, so as to be near his parents. There had been no *need* for him to go on working, in any case, as the family enjoyed a steady income. Olive, however, did work, for a part of each year at least. In peacetime, she spent each autumn and winter in Switzerland, as an instructress in Winter Sports to English visitors. This period of activity was brought to an end, however, in September 1939, when she, too, settled down, apparently quite happily, to the slow tempo of Limbury-Buse family life.

Geoff, Olive and their parents had breakfast brought up in trays to their bedrooms at 9 o'clock. They were copious breakfasts, and remained so throughout the War. Geoff got up at midday. The old people and Olive had their lunches brought up in trays. Geoff had his alone, downstairs, handing down bits to a very old black dog who awoke briefly from his sleeping place under the table. Mrs Limbury-Buse got up at 3, in order to prepare for tea, a very splendid meal, involving a great deal of silver, and a variety of little trays.

*

Geoff went out every day at 2, carrying a shopping-bag, and dressed, like my father, in an oatmeal jacket and plus-fours. His route was invariable: past the Kent & Sussex Hospital, then along the edge of the Common, past Thackeray's house, a purchase at Romary's biscuit shop, thence to the Tunbridge Wells and Counties Club. As he moved with majestic slowness, he would not reach the club till 2.30. After playing a rubber or two of Bridge, he would have tea at the club, then a single sherry; home by the same route, for 6.30.

His father left the house at 3.30 after dressing with great care and deliberation between 2 and 3. He did not take Geoff's route, going down to the Five Ways, then down Mount Pleasant and Vale Road, rounding the Post Office, to reach the club, on the stroke of 4, in time for tea. He and Geoff sat at different tables, never played together, and never spoke to one another while at the club. The old man left the club at 6.30, to reach home, by the route on which he had come, by 7.

Supper was at 7.30 and was the only meal attended by the Limbury-Buse family. Everyone went to bed at 9. On Sundays, Geoff too had lunch in bed, but got up for a walk along Mount Ephraim, as far as the Wellington, dressed in a blue suit. He was back for tea, attended by his sister and parents, who had just dressed. Drinks at home at 6.30. Cold supper at 7.15. Bed, as other days, at 9.

Geoff was generally silent, his only sign of sociability being a slow, gentle smile and a shake of the head. Mrs Limbury-Buse was very talkative, coming out with such items of information as that she had not been to the ladies' Bridge club for twenty-five years, had not been as far as the Pantiles for fifteen, and had not taken a train since the age of 22. How nice it would be, she said, to see more of dear Dora (my mother, and her cousin), but it was much too far and Grove Hill was so steep; could not I persuade my mother to climb the hill and come and see them for tea, she was such a good walker, had always been?

*

Old Mr Limbury-Buse and Geoff also compelled my admiration for their total lack of *ambition*, as if they had never known the meaning of the word, or had long since forgotten it. In this sense, too, they lived outside the conventional time-scale imposed by education, achievement and promotion. The father had given up at 21, Geoff a bit later. But it was hard to know what had provoked this retreat from active life: it might have been the War, more likely, it could have been Hollywood. It was difficult to find out anything positive about him. It was impossible to say whether Geoff was bored or boring, he may have been both (though the combination would be most unusual); I think it much more likely that he had found a form of serenity by living at a very low key, and spending a lot of time, like the rest of the family, including the old maid and the untidy black dog, asleep. 'Poor Geoff,' my mother would say, 'he doesn't seem to get much *out* of life, he should *do* more.' My mother was an understanding woman in many ways, but total lack of ambition both puzzled her and shocked her, as flying in the face of some of her most cherished values. For she liked to be able to categorise people by achievement and promotion: an FRCS before he was 35, an LRCP at 40, a consultant at only 42 (a ladder that may also have been leaned in *my* direction; as one who took on his first salaried job at 38—I made rather nonsense of her cherished hurdles). In what category to place the passive, slow-moving Geoff?

RICHARD COBB (1917–96), *Still Life*, 1983

The inhabitants, particularly the male inhabitants, of economically unprogressive countries also appeared to prefer a life of idleness (though what contemporary observers took to be evidence of their congenital laziness modern economists might identify as symptoms of structural underemployment).

When the state has no war to manage, the German mind is sunk in sloth. The chase does not afford sufficient employment. The time is passed in sleep and gluttony. The intrepid warrior, who in the field braved every danger, becomes in time of peace a listless sluggard. The management of his house and lands he leaves to the women, to the old men, and the infirm part of his family. He himself lounges in stupid repose, by a wonderful diversity of nature exhibiting in the same man the most inert aversion to labour, and the fiercest principle of action.

TACITUS (AD c.56–c.118), *Germania*, AD 98, tr. Arthur Murphy, 1793

The inhabitants of *Naples* have been always very notorious for leading a life of laziness and pleasure, which I take to arise partly out of the wonderful plenty of their country, that does not make labour so necessary to them, and partly out of the temper of their climate, that relaxes the fibres of their bodies, and disposes the people to such an idle indolent humour.

JOSEPH ADDISON (1672–1719), *Remarks on Several Parts of Italy*, 1705

Surely there is no place in the world where the inhabitants live with less labor than in North Carolina. It approaches nearer to the description of Lubberland than any other, by the great felicity of the climate, the easiness of raising provisions, and the slothfulness of the people. Indian corn is of so great increase that a little pains will subsist a very large family with bread, and then they may have meat without any pains at all, by the help of the low grounds and the great variety of mast that grows on the high land. The men, for their parts, just like the Indians, impose all the work upon the poor women. They make their wives rise out of their beds early in the morning, at the same time that they lie and snore till the sun has risen one-third of his course and dispersed all the unwholesome damps. Then, after stretching and yawning for half an hour, they light their pipes, and, under the protection of a cloud of smoke, venture out into the open air; though if it happen to be never so little cold they quickly return shivering into the chimney corner. When the weather is mild, they stand leaning with both their arms upon the cornfield fence and gravely consider whether they had best go and take a small heat at the hoe but generally find reasons to put it off till another time. Thus they loiter away their lives, like Solomon's sluggard, with their arms across, and at the winding up of the year scarcely have bread to eat. To speak the truth, 'tis a thorough aversion to labor that makes people file off to North Carolina, where plenty and a warm sun confirm them in their disposition to laziness for their whole lives.

> WILLIAM BYRD (1674–1744), *History of the Dividing Line between Virginia and North Carolina Made in the Year of Our Lord 1728*, 1841

I have seen a large company of reasonable creatures, called Indians, sitting in a row on the side of a river, looking sometimes at one another, sometimes at the sky, and sometimes at the bubbles on the water. And so they sat (unless in time of war) for a great part of the year, from morning to night.

> JOHN WESLEY (1703–91), *An Earnest Appeal to Men of Reason and Religion*, 1743 edn.

It is universally found, that where bread can be obtained without care or labour, it leads through idleness and vice to poverty. Before they discovered the gold and silver mines of Peru and Mexico, the Spaniards were distinguished among the nations of Europe for their industry and arts, for their manufactures and their commerce. But what are they now? a lazy, poor, and miserable people. They have been ruined by their imaginary wealth.

> JOSEPH TOWNSEND (1739–1816), *A Dissertation on the Poor Laws*, 1786

They [the Irish] are by nature extremely given to idleness. The sea coasts and harbours abound with fish, but the fishermen must be beaten out before they will go to their boats. Theft is not infamous but rather commendable among them, so as the greatest men affect to have the best thieves to attend upon them; and if any man reprove them, they answer that they do as their fathers did, and it is infamy for gentlemen and swordsmen to live by labour and manual trades. Yea they will not be persuaded that theft displeaseth God, because he gives the prey into their hands, and if he be displeased, they say, yet he is merciful and will pardon them for using means to live. This idleness makes them also slovenly and sluttish in their houses and apparel, so as upon every hill they lie [de-]lousing themselves . . .

This idleness also makes them to love liberty above all things, and likewise naturally to delight in music, so as the Irish harpers are excellent, and their solemn music is much liked of strangers . . .

In my opinion this idleness hath been nourished by nothing more . . . than by the plenty of the land, and great housekeeping, drawing the people from trades, while they can be fed by others without labour. This experience hath showed of old as well in England, where the greatest robberies were commonly done by idle serving-men swarming in great houses.

FYNES MORYSON (1566–1630), *An Itinerary*, wr. 1617–20

Much hath been done; but whether it be from the heaviness of the climate, or from the Spanish or Scythian blood that runs in their veins, or whatever else may be the cause, there still remains in the natives of this island [Ireland] a remarkable antipathy to labour . . .

The house of an Irish peasant is the cave of poverty; within, you see a pot and a little straw; without, a heap of children tumbling on the dunghill. Their fields and gardens are a lively counterpart of Solomon's description in the Proverbs: 'I went (saith that wise king) by the field of the slothful, and by the vineyard of the man void of understanding, and lo! it was all grown over with thorns, and nettles had covered the face thereof, and the stone wall thereof was broken down.' In every road the ragged ensigns of poverty are displayed; you often meet caravans of poor, whole families in a drove, without clothes to cover, or bread to feed them, both which might be easily procured by moderate labour . . .

The Scythians were noted for wandering, and the Spaniards for sloth and pride; our Irish are behind neither of these nations, from which they descend, in their respective characteristics. 'Better is he that laboureth and aboundeth in all things, than he that boasteth himself and wanteth bread,' saith the son of Sirach; but so saith not the Irishman. In my own family a kitchen-wench refused to carry out cinders, because she was descended from an old Irish stock. Never was there a more monstrous conjunction than that of pride with beggary; and yet this prodigy is seen every day in almost every part of this kingdom. At the same time these proud people are more destitute than savages, and more abject than negroes. The negroes in our plantations have a saying, If negro was not negro, Irishman would be negro. And it may be affirmed with truth, that the very savages of America are better clad and better lodged than the Irish cottagers throughout the fine fertile counties of Limerick and Tipperary . . .

Mark an Irishman at work in the field; if a coach or horseman go by, he is sure to suspend his labour, and stand staring until they are out of sight. A neighbour of mine made it his remark in a journey from London to Bristol, that all the labourers, of whom he inquired the road, constantly answered without looking up, or interrupting their work, except one who stood staring and leaning on his spade, and him he found to be an Irishman.

> GEORGE BERKELEY (1685–1753), *A Word to the Wise, or an Exhortation to the Roman Catholic Clergy of Ireland*, 1749

'The Indolence of the Gauchos of La Plata'

At Mercedes I asked two men why they did not work. One gravely said the days were too long; the other that he was too poor.

> CHARLES DARWIN (1809–82), *A Naturalist's Voyage round the World in HMS* Beagle, 1839

Thieves, beggars, and vagabonds also kept clear of what the rest of society regarded as 'work'.

But when we dip down below the bourgeois and the regular working-classes which he has drilled in industry, we find a lower leisure class whose valuations and ways of living form a most instructive parody of the upper leisure class. Both in country and town life these types appear. They include 'gypsies', tramps, poachers and other vagabonds, who have never been enlisted in the army of industry, or have deserted in favour of a 'free' life of hazard, beggary and plunder. In towns natural proclivities or misfortune account for considerable groups of casual workers, professional or amateur thieves and prostitutes, street-sellers, corner-men, kept husbands, and other parasites who are a burden on the working-classes. Alike in country and in town, these men practise, so far as circumstances allow, the same habits and exhibit the same character as the leisure class at the top. The fighting, sporting, roving, generous, reckless, wasteful traits are all discernible, the same unaffected contempt for the worker, the same class camaraderie, often with a special code of honour, the same sex license and joviality of manners. Even their intelligence and humour, their very modes of speech, are the half-imitative, half-original replica of high life as it shows in the race-course, in the club smoke-room, or the flash music-hall. Often the parasites and hangers-on to upper-class sports and recreations, these form a large and growing class of our population, and their withdrawal from all industry that can be termed productive, coupled with the debased mode of consumption which they practise, count heavily in the aggregate of social waste.

J. A. HOBSON (1858–1940), *Work and Wealth*, 1914

All slothful persons, which will not travail for their livings; they do the will of the devil. God biddeth us to get our living with labour; they will not labour, but go rather about a begging, and spoil the very poor and needy. Therefore such valiant beggars are thieves before God. Some of these valiant lubbers, when they came to my house, I communed with them, burthening them with the transgression of God's laws. 'Is this not a great labour,' say they, 'to run from one town to another to get our meat? I think we labour as hard as other men do.' In such wise they go about to excuse their unlawful beggary and thievery. But such idle lubbers are much deceived; for they consider not that such labour is not allowed of God. We must labour so as may stand with godliness, according to his appointment; else thieves which rob in the night-time, do they not labour? Yea, sometimes they labour with great care, peril, and danger of their lives. Is it therefore godly, because it is a labour? No, no: we must labour as God hath appointed us, every man in his estate.

HUGH LATIMER (1492?–1555), 'The Fourth Sermon upon the Lord's Prayer', 1552

In these wylde deserts, where she now abode,
　　There dwelt a saluage nation, which did liue
　　Of stealth and spoile, and making nightly rode
　　Into their neighbours borders; ne did giue
　　Them selues to any trade, as for to driue
　　The painefull plough, or cattell for to breed,
　　Or by aduentrous marchandize to thriue;
　　But on the labours of poore men to feed,
And serue their owne necessities with others need.

EDMUND SPENSER (*c.*1552–99), *The Faerie Queene*, 1588–96

Right honourable and my very good Lord:

Having long observed the rapines and thefts committed within this county where I serve, and finding they multiply daily to the utter impoverishing of the poor husbandman that beareth the greatest burden of all services, and knowing your most honourable care of the preservation of the peace of this land, I do think it my bounden duty to present unto your honourable and grave consideration these calendars enclosed of the prisoners executed and delivered this year past in this County of Somerset, wherein your Lordship may behold 183 most wicked and desperate persons to be enlarged. And of these very few come to any good, for none will receive them into service, and in truth work they will not; neither can they without most extreme pain, by reason their sinews are so benumbed and stiff through idleness, as their limbs, being put to any hard labour, will grieve them above measure. So they will rather hazard their lives than work. And this I know to be true. For at such time as our houses of correction were up (which are put down in most parts in England, the more pity), I sent divers wandering suspicious persons to the house of correction and all in general would beseech me with bitter tears to send them rather to the gaol; and, denying that them, some confessed felonies unto me, by which they hazarded their lives, to the end they would not be sent to the house of correction where they should be enforced to work.

EDWARD HEXT, Somersetshire Justice of the Peace, 25 Sept. 1596

> Let the vile Slaves of business toil and strive,
> Who want the leisure or the wit to live:
> Whil'est we life's taedious journy shorter make,
> And reap those joys which they lack sence to take.

*

> Let others who such meannesses can brook,
> Strike Countenance to every Great man's Look:
> Let those that have a mind, turn slaves to eat,
> And live contented by another's Plate:
> I rate my Freedom higher, nor will I
> For Food and Rayment truck my Liberty.
> But, if I must to my last shifts be put,
> To fill a Bladder, and twelve yards of Gut:
> Rather with counterfeited wooden Leg,
> And my right Arm tied up, I'll chuse to beg:
> I'll rather chuse to starve at large, than be
> The gawdiest Vassal to Dependency.

JOHN OLDHAM (1653?–83), *A Dithyrambique on Drinking: Supposed to be Spoken by Rochester at the Guinny-Club*, 1677

There is one thing very remarkable in Bowness [Westmorland]; that most of the people are poor cottagers paying 15d a year to the king, yet will not betake themselves to any employment except begging. They inter-marry one with another and will spend all they have in the wedding week and then go begging, and bring up their children to the same trade, never permitting them to do a day's work for pay. There was only one man (as has been observed these forty years) that betook himself to an honest employment; he was sore exclaimed against for breaking their custom and his neighbours told him 'twas never a good world since Bowness people went to work.

THOMAS MACHELL (1647–98), *Journal,* wr. 1692

Some of our debtors, who after they have been for some time in a prison, and learn'd the way of living an idle life upon other folk's cost, tho' under confinement, they lose all sense of liberty, and never desire to subsist again upon the severe conditions of industry and labour.

FRANCIS FULLER (1670–1706), *Medicina Gymnastica,* 1704

[Statement by 'a beggar decently attired and with a simple and what some would call even a respectable look'.]

In wet weather, and when I couldn't chalk, as I couldn't afford to lose time, I used to dress tidy and very clean for the *'respectable broken-down tradesman or reduced gentleman'* caper. I wore a suit of black, generally, and a clean dickey, and sometimes old black kid gloves, and I used to stand with a paper before my face, as if ashamed:

TO A HUMANE PUBLIC—
I HAVE SEEN BETTER DAYS.

This is called standing pad with a fakement. It is a wet-weather dodge, and isn't so good as screeving, but I did middling, and can't bear being idle. After this I mixed with the street patterers (men who make speeches in the streets) on *the destitute mechanics' lurk.* We went in a school of six at first, all in clean aprons, and spoke every man in his turn. It won't do unless you're clean. Each man wanted a particular article of dress. One had no shirt—another no shoes—another no hat—and so on. No two wanted the same. We said:

' "Kind and benevolent Christians!—It is with feelings of deep regret, and sorrow and shame, that us unfortunate tradesmen are compelled to appear before you this day, to ask charity from the hands of strangers. We are brought to it from want—I may say, actual starvation." ' (We always had a good breakfast before we started, and some of us, sir, was full up to the brim of liquor.) ' "But what will not hunger and the cries of children compel men to do." ' (We were all single men.) ' "When we left our solitary

screeving] To draw on the pavement, as pavement artists do

and humble homes this morning our children were crying for food, but if a farthing would have saved their lives, we hadn't it to give them. I assure you, kind friends, me, my wife, and three children, would have been houseless wanderers all last night, but I sold the shirt from off my back as you may see (opening my jacket) to pay for a lodging. We are, kind friends, *English* mechanics. It is hard that you wont give your own countrymen a penny, when you give so much to *foreign* hurdy-gurdies and organ-grinders. Owing to the introduction of steam and machinery and foreign manufactures we have been brought to this degraded state. Fellow countrymen, there are at this moment 4,000 men like ourselves, able and willing to work, but can't get it, and forced to wander the streets. I hope and trust some humane Christian within the sound of my voice will stretch out a hand with a small trifle for us, be it ever so small, or a bit of dry bread or cold potato, or anything turned from your table, it would be of the greatest benefit to us and our poor children."' (Then we would whisper to one another, 'I hope they wont bring out any scran—only coppers').' "We have none of us tasted food this blessed day. We have been told to go to our parishes, but that we cannot brook; to be torn from our wives and families is heartrending to think of—may God save us all from the Bastile! (We always pattered hard at the overseers)."'

The next of the school that spoke would change the story somehow, and try to make it more heart-rending still . . .

I've been out on the *respectable family man* lurk. I was out with a woman and three kids the other day; her husband was on the pad in the country, as London was too hot to hold him. The kids draws, the younger, the better, for if you vex them, and they're oldish, they'll blow you. Liverpool Joe's boy did so at Bury St Edmund's, to a patterer that he was out with, and who spoke cross to him. The lad shouted out so as the people about might hear, 'Don't you jaw me, you're not my father; my father's at home playing cards.' They had to crack the pitch (discontinue) through that. The respectable family dodge did pretty well.

I've been on *the clean family* lurk too, with a woman and children. We dressed to give the notion that, however humble, at least we were clean in all our poverty. On this lurk we stand by the side of the pavement in silence, the wife in the perticler clean cap, and a milk-white apron. The kids have long clean pinafores, white as the driven snow; they're only used in clean lurk, and taken off directly they come home. The husband and father is in a white flannel jacket, an apron worn and clean, and polished shoes. To succeed in this caper there must be no rags, but plenty of darns. A pack of pawn-tickets is carried in the waistcoat pocket. (One man that I know stuck them in his hat like a carman's). That's to show that they've parted with their little all before they came to that. They are real pawn-tickets. I have known a man pay 2s 6d for the loan of a marriage certificate to go out on the clean lurk. If a question is asked I say: 'We've parted with everything, and can get no employment; to be sure, we have had a loaf from the parish, but what's that among my family?' That takes the start out of the people, because they say, why not go to the parish? Some persons say, 'Oh, poor folks, they're brought to this, and how clean they are—a darn is better than a patch any time.' The clean lurk is a bare living now—it was good—lots of togs came in, and often the whole family were taken into a house and supplied with flannel enough to make under clothing for them all; all this was pledged soon afterwards, and the tickets shown to prove what was parted with, through want.

Those are some of the leading lurks. There's others. 'Fits,' are bad now, and 'paralytics' are no better. *The lucifer lurk* seems getting up though. I don't mean the selling, but the dropping them in the street as if by accident. It's a great thing with the children; but no go with the old 'uns. I'll tell you of another lurk: a woman I knows sends out her child with $^1/_4$ oz. of tea and half a quarter of sugar, and the child sits on a door step crying, and saying, if questioned, that she was sent out for tea and sugar, and a boy snatched the change from her, and threw the tea and sugar in the gutter. The mother is there, like a stranger, and says to the child: 'And was that your poor mother's last shilling, and daren't you go home, poor thing?' Then there is a gathering—sometimes 18d in a morning; but it's almost getting stale, that is. I've done *the shivering dodge* too—gone out in the cold weather half naked. One man has practised it so much that he can't get off shivering now. Shaking Jemmy went on with his shivering so long that he couldn't help it at last. He shivered like a jelly—like a calf's foot with the ague—on the hottest day in summer. It's a good dodge in tidy inclement seasons. It's not so good a lurk, by two bob a day, as it once was. This is a single-handed job; for if one man shivers less than another he shows that it isn't so cold as the good shiverer makes it out—then it's no go.

HENRY MAYHEW (1812–87), *Morning Chronicle*, 31 Jan. 1850

The Docks

Rise early and watch the crowd at the St Katherine or the West and East India gates. The bell rings, the gate opens, and the struggling mass surge into the docks. The foremen and contractors stand behind the chain, or in the wooden boxes. The 'ticket men' pass through, and those constantly preferred are taken on without dispute. Then the struggle for the last tickets. To watch it one would think it was life and death to those concerned. But Jack having secured a ticket by savage fight, sells it to needier Tom for twopence, and goes off with the coppers to drink or to gamble. Or, if the flush of business forces the employers to 'clear the gates,' many of those who on a slack morning would be most desperate in their demand for work will 'book off' after they have earned sufficient for a pint of beer and pipe of tobacco and a night's lodging. Or take a day which offers no employment—watch the crowd as it disperses. The honest worker, not as yet attracted by the fascinations of East-end social life, will return to his home with a heavy heart: there he will mind the baby, while his wife seeks work; or, if not entirely hopeless, he trudges wearily along the streets searching in vain for permanent work. But the greater part of the crowd will lounge down the waterside and stand outside the wharf and dock gates. As the day draws on the more respectable element will disappear, while its place will be taken by the professional 'cadger' and dock lounger. These men would work at no price. They gain their livelihood by petty theft, by cadging the earnings of their working friends, through gambling or drink, and by charitable assistance. From all accounts I very much fear that these are the recipients of the free breakfasts with which the well-to-do West-end, in times of social panic, soothes its own conscience, and calms its own fears. But, apart from this semi-criminal class, the staple of the dock and waterside population subsisting by means of the extreme fluctuation and irregularity of employment is made up of those who are either mentally or physically unfit for worthful and persistent work. These men hang about for the 'odd hour' or work one day in the seven. They live on stimulants and tobacco, varied with bread and tea and salt fish. Their passion is gambling. Sections of them are hereditary casuals; a larger portion drift from other trades. They have a con- stitutional hatred to regularity and forethought, and a need for paltry excite- ment. They are late risers, sharp-witted talkers, and, above all, they have that agreeable tolerance for their own and each other's vices which seems charac- teristic of a purely leisure class, whether it lies at the top or the bottom of soci- ety. But if we compare them with their brothers and sisters in the London Club and West-end drawing-room we must admit that in one respect they are strikingly superior. The stern reality of ever-pressing starvation draws all together. Communism is a necessity of their life: they share all with one another, and as a class they are quixotically generous. It is this virtue and the courage with which they face privation that lend a charm to life among them. Socially they have their own peculiar attractiveness; economically they are worthless; and morally worse than worthless, for they drag others who live among them down to their own level. They are parasites eating the life out of the working class, demoralizing and discrediting it.

I venture to think that the existence, and I fear the growth, of this leisure class in our great cities, notably in London, is the gravest problem of the future.

> BEATRICE POTTER (later Webb) (1858–1943), 1887, in *Life and Labour of the People in London*, ed. Charles Booth, 1893
>
> [*See also* HENRY MAYHEW, pp. 193–5]

It is worth saying something about the social position of beggars, for when one has consorted with them, and found that they are ordinary human beings, one cannot help being struck by the curious attitude that society takes towards them. People seem to feel that there is some essential difference between beggars and ordinary 'working' men. They are a race apart— outcasts, like criminals and prostitutes. Working men 'work', beggars do not 'work'; they are parasites, worthless in their very nature. It is taken for granted that a beggar does not 'earn' his living, as a bricklayer or a literary critic 'earns' his. He is a mere social excrescence, tolerated because we live in a humane age, but essentially despicable.

Yet if one looks closely one sees that there is no *essential* difference between a beggar's livelihood and that of numberless respectable people. Beggars do not work, it is said; but, then, what is *work*? A navvy works by swinging a pick. An accountant works by adding up figures. A beggar works by standing out of doors in all weathers and getting varicose veins, chronic bronchitis, etc. It is a trade like any other; quite useless, of course—but, then, many reputable trades are quite useless. And as a social type a beggar compares well with scores of others. He is honest compared with the sellers of most patent medicines, high-minded compared with a Sunday newspaper proprietor, amiable compared with a hire-purchase tout—in short, a parasite, but a fairly harmless parasite. He seldom extracts more than a bare living from the community, and, what should justify him according to our ethical ideas, he pays for it over and over in suffering. I do not think there is anything about a beggar that sets him in a different class from other people, or gives most modern men the right to despise him.

Then the question arises, Why are beggars despised?—for they are despised, universally. I believe it is for the simple reason that they fail to earn a decent living. In practice nobody cares whether work is useful or useless, productive or parasitic; the sole thing demanded is that it shall be profitable. In all the modern talk about energy, efficiency, social service and the rest of it, what meaning is there except 'Get money, get it legally, and get a lot of it'? Money has become the grand test of virtue. By this test beggars fail, and for this they are despised. If one could earn even ten pounds a week at begging, it would become a respectable profession immediately. A beggar, looked at realistically, is simply a businessman, getting his living, like other businessmen, in the way that comes to hand. He has not, more than most modern people, sold his honour; he has merely made the mistake of choosing a trade at which it is impossible to grow rich.

GEORGE ORWELL (1903–50), *Down and Out in Paris and London*, 1933

> I see a column of slow-rising smoke
> O'ertop the lofty wood that skirts the wild.
> A vagabond and useless tribe there eat
> Their miserable meal. A kettle, slung
> Between two poles upon a stick transverse,
> Receives the morsel; flesh obscene of dog,
> Or vermin, or, at best, of cock purloined
> From his accustomed perch. Hard-faring race!

They pick their fuel out of every hedge,
Which, kindled with dry leaves, just saves unquenched
The spark of life. The sportive wind blows wide
Their fluttering rags, and shows a tawny skin,
The vellum of the pedigree they claim.
Great skill have they in palmistry, and more
To conjure clean away the gold they touch,
Conveying worthless dross into its place;
Loud when they beg, dumb only when they steal.
Strange! that a creature rational, and cast
In human mould, should brutalize by choice
His nature, and, though capable of arts
By which the world might profit and himself,
Self banished from society, prefer
Such squalid sloth to honourable toil!

WILLIAM COWPER (1731–1800), *The Task*, 1785

Even those who were in regular employment seemed careful to avoid over-doing it.

'The Elizabethan Working Man'

The labouring man will take his rest long in the morning; a good piece of the day is spent afore he comes at his work; then must he have his breakfast, though he have not earned it, at his accustomed hour, or else there is grudging and murmuring: when the clock smiteth, he will cast down his burden in the midway, and whatsoever he is in hand with, he will leave it as it is, though many times it is marred afore he come again; he may not lose his meat, what danger soever the work is in. At noon he must have his sleeping time, then his bever in the afternoon, which spendeth a great part of the day; and when his hour cometh at night, at the first stroke of the clock he casteth down his tools, leaveth his work, in what need or care soever the work standeth.

JAMES PILKINGTON, BISHOP OF DURHAM (1520?–76), *A Godlie Exposition upon Certeine Chapters of Nehemiah*, 1585

[Those pressed to do compulsory labour on the highways] work when they list, come and go at their pleasure, and spend most of their time in standing still and prating, and looking after their fellows, whom they send out from their work, most shamefully, to stop passengers for a largess.

WILLIAM MATHER (*fl.* 1695), *Of Repairing and Mending the Highways*, 1696

The Timetable

Ah, Doctor Piercemüller. Have you a second?

Not really, Maureen. Not really. Just popped in to collect the post. Got the nippers outside in the car. Anything that can wait?

Well, hardly, Doctor Piercemüller. It's your timetable for this term.

Next term. Good heavens. Is it here already? I've hardly had time to recharge my batteries since the last one.

Next Wednesday.

Ah well, I might have known there'd be something else. I've really got my hands full at the moment what with one thing and another. The car insurance to be renewed. Books to go back to the library. And to top it all Ilsa has gone and pranged her car so there's no one to ferry the young ones about.

I'll be as quick as possible.

All right then. Let's hear the worst.

Erm . . . first year 'Introduction to Behaviourism'. That's 10.15 on Tuesday morning.

Tuesday?

Yes.

Ten-fifteen?

There doesn't seem to be any other slot.

You know I'm not keen on early Tuesdays, Maureen. It's just far too close to the weekend. One hardly has time to unwind before one's back at the grindstone. Isn't there a mid-afternoon slot?

Only on Mondays.

That's out then. All right. Tuesday. 10.15.

And your 'Socialization and Language' option is on Wednesday morning at 11.15. And second year 'Experimental Methods' at 2.15 on Thursdays. Friday's clear as usual.

Tuesday-Wednesday-Thursday. Nasty. That means there's no real space mid-week. Any chance of getting 'Experimental Methods' into Wednesday. Then I'd have a clear run-up to the weekend.

Not really. We've got problems with joint degree students. Griffiths— Pol/Psych, and Spooner—Soc/Psych.

Spooner?

He's got to go somewhere.

No, I'm not having Spooner. I thought I'd made that quite clear. The man's a menace to any seminar. All that nonsense about epistemology. Upsets everybody. Can't you pop him into Group 4 with Doctor Stentonhoffer?

I'll try, But he's already got two American occasional students and that woman who insists on having the window wide open.

Oh well. Give me a ring and let me know. I'll be home most of tomorrow morning.

Not tomorrow, I'm afraid, Doctor Piercemüller. It's Saturday.

Oh yes. Sorry. Forget it then. Now must fly, or we'll be late for the matinee of Superman 2. *All the best for the new year.*

And you, sir.

You know something, Maureen? Sometimes I quite envy you.

Why's that, Doctor Piercemüller?

Oh, you know: the nice comfortable feeling of a nine-to-five job. Must be very relaxing.

Oh yes, sir. I always count my blessings.

That's the way. Must dash. Bye.

Hope you get everything done, Doctor Piercemüller.

We can but try, Maureen. We can but try.

LAURIE TAYLOR (1935–   ), *Professor Lapping Sends His Apologies* 1986

A man commonly saunters a little in turning his hand from one sort of employment to another. When he first begins the new work he is seldom very keen and hearty; his mind, as they say, does not go to it, and for some time he rather trifles than applies to good purpose. The habit of sauntering and of indolent careless application, which is naturally, or rather necessarily acquired by every country workman who is obliged to change his work and his tools every half hour, and to apply his hand in twenty different ways almost every day of his life; renders him almost always slothful and lazy, and incapable of any vigorous application even on the most pressing occasions.

ADAM SMITH (1723–90), *An Inquiry into the Nature and Causes of the Wealth of Nations*, 1776

Mr Pumblechook appeared to conduct his business by looking across the street at the saddler, who appeared to transact *his* business by keeping his eye on the coachmaker, who appeared to get on in life by putting his hands in his pockets and contemplating the baker, who in his turn folded his arms and stared at the grocer, who stood at his door and yawned at the chemist. The watchmaker, always poring over a little desk with a magnifying glass at his eye, and always inspected by a group in smock-frocks poring over him through the glass of his shop-window, seemed to be about the only person in the High-street whose trade engaged his attention.

CHARLES DICKENS (1812–70), *Great Expectations*, 1861

'Oh, here's a regular go,' said Scatterall. 'It's all up with Corkscrew, I believe.'
    'Why, what's the cheese now?'

'Oh! it's all about some pork chops, which Screwy had for supper last night.' Screwy was a name of love which among his brother navvies was given to Mr Corkscrew. 'Mr Snape seems to think they did not agree with him.'

'Pork chops in July!' exclaimed Charley.

'Poor Screwy forgot the time of year,' said another navvy; 'he ought to have called it lamb and grass.'

And then the story was told. On the preceding afternoon, Mr Corkscrew had been subjected to the dire temptation of a boating party to the Eel-pie Island for the following day, and a dinner thereon. There were to be at the feast no less than four-and-twenty jolly souls, and it was intimated to Mr Corkscrew that as no soul was esteemed to be more jolly than his own, the party would be considered as very imperfect unless he could join it. Asking for a day's leave Mr Corkscrew knew to be out of the question; he had already taken too many without asking. He was therefore driven to take another in the same way, and had to look about for some excuse which might support him in his difficulty. An excuse it must be, not only new, but very valid; one so strong that it could not be overset; one so well avouched that it could not be doubted. Accordingly, after mature consideration, he sat down after leaving his office, and wrote the following letter, before he started on an evening cruising expedition with some others of the party to prepare for the next day's festivities.

'Thursday morning,—July, 185–.

'MY DEAR SIR,

'I write from my bed where I am suffering a most tremendous indigges-tion, last night I eat a stunning supper off pork chopps and never remem-bered that pork chopps always does disagree with me, but I was very indiscrete and am now teetotally unable to rise my throbing head from off my pillar, I have took four blu pills and some salts and sena, plenty of that, and shall be the thing to-morrow morning no doubt, just at present I feel just as if I had a mill stone inside my stomac—Pray be so kind as to make it all right with Mr. Oldeschole and believe me to remain.

'Your faithful and obedient servant,

'VERAX CORKSCREW.

'Thomas Snape, Esq., &c.,
'Internal Navigation Office, Somerset House.'

Having composed this letter of excuse, and not intending to return to his lodgings that evening, he had to make provision for its safely reaching the hands of Mr Snape in due time on the following morning. This he did, by giving it to the boy who came to clean the lodging-house boots, with sundry injunctions that if he did not deliver it at the office by ten o'clock on the fol-lowing morning, the sixpence accruing to him would never be paid. Mr Corkscrew, however, said nothing as to the letter not being delivered before ten the next morning, and as other business took the boy along the Strand the same evening, he saw no reason why he should not then execute his commission. He accordingly did so, and duly delivered the letter into the hands of a servant girl, who was cleaning the passages of the office.

Fortune on this occasion was blind to the merits of Mr Corkscrew, and threw him over most unmercifully. It so happened that Mr Snape had been summoned to an evening conference with Mr Oldeschole and the other pundits of the office, to discuss with them, or rather to hear discussed, some measure which they began to think it necessary to introduce, for amending the discipline of the department.

'We are getting a bad name, whether we deserve it or not,' said Mr Oldeschole. 'That fellow Hardlines has put us into his blue-book, and now there's an article in the *Times!*'

Just at this moment, a messenger brought in to Mr Snape the unfortunate letter of which we have given a copy.

'What's that?' said Mr Oldeschole.

'A note from Mr Corkscrew, sir,' said Snape.

'He's the worst of the whole lot,' said Mr Oldeschole.

'He is very bad', said Snape; 'but I rather think that perhaps, sir, Mr Tudor is the worst of all.'

'Well, I don't know,' said the Secretary, muttering *sotto voce* to the Under-Secretary, while Mr Snape read the letter—'Tudor, at any rate, is a gentleman.'

Mr Snape read the letter, and his face grew very long. There was a sort of sneaking civility about Corkscrew, not prevalent indeed at all times, but which chiefly showed itself when he and Mr Snape were alone together, which somewhat endeared him to the elder clerk. He would have screened the sinner had he had either the necessary presence of mind or the necessary pluck. But he had neither. He did not know how to account for the letter but by the truth, and he feared to conceal so flagrant a breach of discipline at the moment of the present discussion.

Things at any rate so turned out that Mr Corkscrew's letter was read in full conclave in the board-room of the office, just as he was describing the excellence of his manœuvre with great glee to four or five other jolly souls at the 'Magpie and Stump.'

At first it was impossible to prevent a fit of laughter, in which even Mr Snape joined; but very shortly the laughter gave way to the serious considerations to which such an epistle was sure to give rise at such a moment. What if Sir Gregory Hardlines should get hold of it and put it into his blue-book! What if the *Times* should print it and send it over the whole world, accompanied by a few of its most venomous touches, to the eternal disgrace of the Internal Navigation, and probably utter annihilation of Mr Oldeschole's official career! An example must be made!

Yes, an example must be made. Messengers were sent off scouring the town for Mr Corkscrew, and about midnight he was found, still true to the 'Magpie and Stump,' but hardly in condition to understand the misfortune which had befallen him. So much as this, however, did make itself manifest to him, that he must by no means join his jolly-souled brethren at the Eel-pie Island, and that he must be at his office punctually at ten o'clock the next morning if he had any intention of saving himself from dismissal.

ANTHONY TROLLOPE (1815–82), *The Three Clerks*, 1857

Parkinson's Law

Work expands so as to fill the time available for its completion. General recognition of this fact is shown in the proverbial phrase 'It is the busiest man who has time to spare.' Thus, an elderly lady of leisure can spend the entire day in writing and dispatching a postcard to her niece at Bognor Regis. An hour will be spent in finding the postcard, another in hunting for spectacles, half an hour in a search for the address, an hour and a quarter in composition, and twenty minutes in deciding whether or not to take an umbrella when going to the pillar box in the next street. The total effort that would occupy a busy man for three minutes all told may in this fashion leave another person prostrate after a day of doubt, anxiety, and toil.

Granted that work (and especially paper-work) is thus elastic in its demands on time, it is manifest that there need be little or no relationship between the work to be done and the size of the staff to which it may be assigned. A lack of real activity does not, of necessity, result in leisure. A lack of occupation is not necessarily revealed by a manifest idleness. The thing to be done swells in importance and complexity in a direct ratio with the time to be spent. This fact is widely recognized, but less attention has been paid to its wider implications, more especially in the field of public administration. Politicians and taxpayers have assumed (with occasional phases of doubt) that a rising total in the number of civil servants must reflect a growing volume of work to be done. Cynics, in questioning this belief, have imagined that the multiplication of officials must have left some of them idle or all of them able to work for shorter hours. But this is a matter in which faith and doubt seem equally misplaced. The fact is that the number of the officials and the quantity of the work are not related to each other at all. The rise in the total of those employed is governed by Parkinson's Law and would be much the same whether the volume of the work were to increase, diminish, or even disappear. The importance of Parkinson's Law lies in the fact that it is a law of growth based upon an analysis of the factors by which that growth is controlled.

The validity of this recently discovered law must rest mainly on statistical proofs, which will follow. Of more interest to the general reader is the explanation of the factors underlying the general tendency to which this law gives definition. Omitting technicalities (which are numerous) we may distinguish at the outset two motive forces. They can be represented for the present purpose by two almost axiomatic statements, thus: (1) 'An official wants to multiply subordinates, not rivals' and (2) 'Officials make work for each other.'

To comprehend Factor 1, we must picture a civil servant, called A, who finds himself overworked. Whether this overwork is real or imaginary is immaterial, but we should observe, in passing, that A's sensation (or illusion) might easily result from his own decreasing energy: a normal symptom of middle age. For this real or imagined overwork there are, broadly speaking, three possible remedies. He may resign; he may ask to halve the work with a colleague called B; he may demand the assistance of two subordinates, to be called C and D. There is probably no instance, however, in history of A choosing any but the third alternative. By resignation he would lose his pension rights. By having B appointed, on his own level in the hierarchy, he would merely bring in a rival for promotion to W's vacancy when W (at long last) retires. So A would rather have C and D, junior men, below him. They will add to his consequence and, by dividing the work into two categories, as between C and D, he will have the merit of being the only man who comprehends them both. It is essential to realize at this point that C and D are, as it were, inseparable. To appoint C alone would have been impossible. Why? Because C, if by himself, would divide the work with A and so assume almost the equal status that has been refused in the first instance to B; a status the more emphasized if C is A's only possible successor. Subordinates must thus number two or more, each being thus kept in order by fear of the other's promotion. When C complains in turn of being overworked (as he certainly will) A will, with the concurrence of C, advise the appointment of two assistants to help C. But he can then avert internal friction only by advising the appointment of two more assistants to help D, whose position is much the same. With this recruitment of E, F, G, and H the promotion of A is now practically certain.

Seven officials are now doing what one did before. This is where Factor 2 comes into operation. For these seven make so much work for each other that all are fully occupied and A is actually working harder than ever. An incoming document may well come before each of them in turn. Official E decides that it falls within the province of F, who places a draft reply before C, who amends it drastically before consulting D, who asks G to deal with it. But G goes on leave at this point, handing the file over to H, who drafts a minute that is signed by D and returned to C, who revises his draft accordingly and lays the new version before A.

What does A do? He would have every excuse for signing the thing unread, for he has many other matters on his mind. Knowing now that he is to succeed W next year, he has to decide whether C or D should succeed to his own office. He had to agree to G's going on leave even if not yet strictly entitled to it. He is worried whether H should not have gone instead, for reasons of health. He has looked pale recently—partly but not solely because of his domestic troubles. Then there is the business of F's special increment of salary for the period of the conference and E's application for transfer to the Ministry of Pensions. A has heard that D is in love with a married typist and that G and F are no longer on speaking terms—no one seems to know why. So A might be tempted to sign C's draft and have done with it. But A is a conscientious man. Beset as he is with problems created by his colleagues for themselves and for him—created by the mere fact of these officials' existence—he is not the man to shirk his duty. He reads through the draft with care, deletes the fussy paragraphs added by C and H, and restores the thing to the form preferred in the first instance by the able (if quarrelsome) F. He corrects the English—none of these young men can write grammatically—and finally produces the same reply he would have written if officials C to H had never been born. Far more people have taken far longer to produce the same result. No one has been idle. All have done their best. And it is late in the evening before A finally quits his office and begins the return journey to Ealing. The last of the office lights are being turned off in the gathering dusk that marks the end of another day's administrative toil. Among the last to leave, A reflects with bowed shoulders and a wry smile that late hours, like grey hairs, are among the penalties of success.

> C. NORTHCOTE PARKINSON (1909–93), *Parkinson's Law, or the Pursuit of Progress*, 1958

And the Lord said unto Noah, Where is the ark, which I commanded thee to build?

And Noah said unto the Lord, Verily, I have had three carpenters off ill.

The gopher wood supplier hath let me down—yea, even though the gopher wood hath been on order for nigh upon twelve months. The damp-course specialist hath not turned up. What can I do, O lord?

And God said unto Noah, I want that ark finished even after seven days and seven nights.

And Noah said, It will be so.

And it was not so.

And the Lord said unto Noah, What seemeth to be the trouble this time?

And Noah said unto the Lord, Mine sub-contractor hath gone bankrupt. The pitch which Thou commandest me to put on the outside and on the inside of the ark hath not arrived. The plumber hath gone on strike.

Noah rent his garments and said, The glazier departeth on holiday to Majorca—yea, even though I offerest him double time. Shem, my son, who helpeth me on the ark side of the business, hath formed a pop group with his brothers Ham and Japheth. Lord, I am undone.

And God said in his wrath, Noah, do not thou mucketh me about.

The end of all flesh is come before me; for the Earth is filled with violence through them; and behold, I will destroy them with the Earth. How can I destroy them with the Earth if thou art incapable of completing the job that thou was contracted to do?

And Noah said, Lo, the contract will be fulfilled.

And Lo, it was not fulfilled.

And Noah said unto the Lord, The gopher wood is definitely in the warehouse. Verily, and the gopher wood supplier waiteth only upon his servant to find the invoices before he delivereth the gopher wood unto me.

And the Lord grew angry and said, Scrubbeth thou round the gopher wood. What about the animals?

Of fowls after their kind, and of cattle after their kind, of every creeping thing of the Earth after his kind, two of every sort have I ordered to come unto thee, to keep them alive.

Where for example, are the giraffes?

And Noah said unto the Lord, They are expected today.

And the Lord said unto Noah, And where are the clean beasts, the male and the female; to keep their seed alive upon the face of all the Earth?

And Noah said, The van cometh on Tuesday; yea and yea, it will be so.

And the Lord said unto Noah, How about the unicorns?

And Noah wrung his hands and wept, saying, Lord, Lord, they are a discontinued line. Thou canst not get unicorns for love nor money.

And God said, Come thou, Noah, I have left with thee a deposit, and thou hast signed a contract.

Where are the monkeys, and the bears, and the hippopotami, and the elephants, and the zebras and the hartebeests, two of each kind; and of fowls also of the air by sevens, the male and the female?

And Noah said unto the Lord, They have been delivered unto the wrong address, but should arriveth on Friday; all save the fowls of the air by sevens, for it hath just been told unto me that fowls of the air are sold only in half-dozens.

And God said unto Noah, Thou hast not made an ark of gopher wood, nor hast thou lined it with pitch within and without; and of every living thing of all flesh, two of every sort hast thou failed to bring into the ark. What sayest thou, Noah?

And Noah kissed the Earth and said, Lord, Lord, thou knowest in thy wisdom what it is like with delivery dates.

And the Lord in his wisdom said, Noah, my son, I knowest. Why else dost thou think I have caused a flood to descend upon the Earth?

KEITH WATERHOUSE (1929–   ), from 'How Long, O Lord . . .', 1985

At all times there were people who displayed a natural indolence and a conviction that there was more to life than work.

How long wilt thou sleep, O sluggard? when wilt thou arise out of thy
sleep?

   Yet a little sleep, a little slumber, a little folding of the hands to sleep.

Proverbs 6: 9–10

The Sluggard

'Tis the voice of the sluggard; I heard him complain,
'You have waked me too soon, I must slumber again.'
As the door on its hinges, so he on his bed,
Turns his sides and his shoulders and his heavy head.

'A little more sleep, and a little more slumber;'
Thus he wastes half his days and his hours without number;
And when he gets up, he sits folding his hands,
Or walks about saunt'ring, or trifling he stands.

I passed by his garden and saw the wild brier,
The thorn and the thistle grow broader and higher;
The clothes that hang on him are turning to rags;
And his money still wastes, till he starves or he begs.

I made him a visit, still hoping to find
He had took better care for improving his mind:
He told me his dreams, talked of eating and drinking;
But he scarce reads his Bible, and never loves thinking.

Said I then to my heart, 'Here's a lesson for me;
That man's but the picture of what I might be:
But thanks to my friends for their care in my breeding,
Who taught me betimes to love working and reading.'

ISAAC WATTS (1674–1748), 1715

Lazy Man's Song

I could have a job, but am too lazy to choose it;
I have got land, but am too lazy to farm it.
My house leaks; I am too lazy to mend it.
My clothes are torn; I am too lazy to darn them.
I have got wine, but I am too lazy to drink;
So it's just the same as if my cup were empty.
I have got a lute, but am too lazy to play;
So it's just the same as if it had no strings.

My family tells me there is no more steamed rice;
I want to cook, but am too lazy to grind.
My friends and relatives write me long letters;
I should like to read them, but they're such a bother to open.
I have always been told that Hsi Shu-yeh
Passed his whole life in absolute idleness.
But he played his lute and sometimes worked at his forge;
So even *he* was not so lazy as I.

Po Chü-I (AD 811), tr. Arthur Waley, 1919

Of the Slothful

He is a religious man, and wears the time in his cloister, and, as the cloak of his doing nothing, pleads contemplation; yet is he no whit the leaner for his thoughts, no whit learneder. He takes no less care how to spend time than others how to gain by the expense; and when business importunes him, is more troubled to forethink what he must do, than another to effect it. Summer is out of his favour for nothing but long days that make no haste to their even. He loves still to have the sun witness of his rising, and lies long, more for lothness to dress him than will to sleep; and after some streaking and yawning, calls for dinner unwashed, which having digested with a sleep in his chair, he walks forth to the bench in the market-place, and looks for companions. Whomsoever he meets he stays with idle questions, and lingering discourse; how the days are lengthened, how kindly the weather is, how false the clock, how forward the spring, and ends ever with, What shall we do? It pleases him no less to hinder others than not to work himself. When all the people are gone from church, he is left sleeping in his seat alone. He enters bonds, and forfeits them by forgetting the day; and asks his neighbour when his own field was fallowed, whether the next piece of ground belong not to himself. His care is either none or too late. When winter is come, after some sharp visitations, he looks on his pile of wood, and asks how much was cropped the last spring. Necessity drives him to every action, and what he cannot avoid he will yet defer. Every change troubles him, although to the better, and his dulness counterfeits a kind of contentment. When he is warned on a jury, he had rather pay the mulct than appear. All but that which Nature will not permit he doth by a deputy, and counts it troublesome to do nothing, but to do anything yet more. He is witty in nothing but framing excuses to sit still, which if the occasion yield not he coineth with ease. There is no work that is not either dangerous or thankless, and whereof he foresees not the inconvenience and gainlessness before he enters; which if it be verified in event, his next idleness

Hsi Shu-yeh] or Hsi K'ang (AD 223-62), Taoist philosopher and poet

hath found a reason to patronize it. He had rather freeze than fetch wood, and chooses rather to steal than work; to beg than take pains to steal, and in many things to want than beg. He is so loth to leave his neighbour's fire, that he is fain to walk home in the dark; and if he be not looked to, wears out the night in the chimney-corner, or if not that, lies down in his clothes, to save two labours. He eats and prays himself asleep, and dreams of no other torment but work. This man is a standing pool, and cannot choose but gather corruption. He is descried amongst a thousand neighbours by a dry and nasty hand, that still savours of the sheet, a beard uncut, unkempt, an eye and ear yellow with their excretions, a coat shaken on, ragged, unbrushed, by linen and face striving whether shall excel in uncleanness. For body, he hath a swollen leg, a dusky and swinish eye, a blown cheek, a drawling tongue, an heavy foot, and is nothing but a colder earth moulded with standing water. To conclude, is a man in nothing but in speech and shape.

JOSEPH HALL (1574–1656), *Characters,* 1608

The King [Pharaoh] when he saw them asked what they were of, taking it as certain that they had some trade: so unusual was it then for man to be idle. But had he asked many a man in our days, their answer peradventure would have been to seek, unless they should have answered that they used to walk from tavern to tavern, with a white rod in their hands to top daisies with.

GERVASE BABINGTON (1550?–1610), *Certaine Plaine, Briefe, and Comfortable Notes upon Everie Chapter of Genesis,* 1592

'A Difficult Question . . .'

Was God Almighty a drone? If not, what was He doing before He made the Earth?

WILLIAM SELBY (d. 1709), Rector of Elton, Nottinghamshire, Dec. 1708, quoted in J. D. Chambers, *Nottinghamshire in the Eighteenth Century,* 1966 edn.

'. . . Robustly Answered'

Thou scoffing Atheist that enquirest, what
Th'Almightie did before he framed that?
What waightie worke his mind was busied on
Eternally before this World begun
(Sith so deepe Wisedome and Omnipotence,
Nought worse beseemes, then sloath and negligence):

Know (bold blasphemer) that before, he built
A Hell to punish the presumptuous guilt
Of those ungodly, whose proud sence dares cite
And censure too, his wisedome infinite.

GUILLAUME DE SALLUSTE, SIEUR DU BARTAS (1544–90), *The Divine Weeks and Works,* (1563–1618), tr. Joshua Sylvester, 1592–1608

The great error in Rip's composition was an insuperable aversion to all kinds of profitable labor. It could not be from the want of assiduity or perseverance; for he would sit on a wet rock, with a rod as long and heavy as a Tartar's lance, and fish all day without a murmur, even though he should not be encouraged by a single nibble. He would carry a fowling-piece on his shoulder for hours together, trudging through woods and swamps, and up hill and down dale, to shoot a few squirrels or wild pigeons. He would never refuse to assist a neighbor even in the roughest toil, and was a foremost man at all country frolics for husking Indian corn, or building stone fences; the women of the village, too, used to employ him to run their errands, and to do such little odd jobs as their less obliging husbands would not do for them. In a word Rip was ready to attend to anybody's business but his own; but as to doing family duty, and keeping his farm in order, he found it impossible.

In fact, he declared it was of no use to work on his farm; it was the most pestilent little piece of ground in the whole country; everything about it went wrong, and would go wrong, in spite of him. His fences were continually falling to pieces; his cow would either go astray, or get among the cabbages; weeds were sure to grow quicker in his fields than anywhere else; the rain always made a point of setting in just as he had some out-door work to do; so that though his patrimonial estate had dwindled away under his management, acre by acre, until there was little more left than a mere patch of Indian corn and potatoes, yet it was the worst conditioned farm in the neighborhood . . .

Rip Van Winkle, however, was one of those happy mortals, of foolish, well-oiled dispositions, who take the world easy, eat white bread or brown, whichever can be got with least thought or trouble, and would rather starve on a penny than work for a pound. If left to himself, he would have whistled life away in perfect contentment; but his wife kept continually dinning in his ears about his idleness, his carelessness, and the ruin he was bringing on his family. Morning, noon, and night, her tongue was incessantly going, and everything he said or did was sure to produce a torrent of household eloquence. Rip had but one way of replying to all lectures of the kind, and that, by frequent use, had grown into a habit. He shrugged his shoulders, shook his head, cast up his eyes, but said nothing. This, however, always provoked a fresh volley from his wife; so that he was fain to draw off his forces, and take to the outside of the house—the only side which, in truth, belongs to a hen-pecked husband.

WASHINGTON IRVING (1783–1859), *Rip Van Winkle*, 1820

Mr Skimpole was as agreeable at breakfast, as he had been over-night. There was honey on the table, and it led him into a discourse about Bees. He had no objection to honey, he said (and I should think he had not, for he seemed to like it), but he protested against the overweening assumptions of Bees. He didn't at all see why the busy Bee should be proposed as a model to him; he supposed the Bee liked to make honey, or he wouldn't do it—nobody asked him. It was not necessary for the Bee to make such a merit of his tastes. If every confectioner went buzzing about the world, banging against everything that came in his way, and egotistically calling upon everybody to take notice that he was going to his work and must not be interrupted, the world would be quite an unsupportable place. Then, after all, it was a ridiculous position, to be smoked out of your fortune with brimstone, as soon as you had made it. You would have a very mean opinion of a Manchester man, if he spun cotton for no other purpose. He must say he thought a Drone the embodiment of a pleasanter and wiser idea. The Drone said, unaffectedly, 'You will excuse me; I really cannot attend to the shop! I find myself in a world in which there is so much to see, and so short a time to see it in, that I must take the liberty of looking about me, and begging to be provided for by somebody who doesn't want to look about him.' This appeared to Mr Skimpole to be the Drone philosophy, and he thought it a very good philosophy—always supposing the Drone to be willing to be on good terms with the Bee: which, so far as he knew, the easy fellow always was, if the consequential creature would only let him, and not be so conceited about his honey!

CHARLES DICKENS (1812–70), *Bleak House*, 1853

'Hallo, old chap; you got to work, hey?'

'Why, it's you, Ben! I warn't noticing.'

'Say, I'm going in a-swimming, I am. Don't you wish you could? But of course you'd druther work, wouldn't you? 'Course you would!'

Tom contemplated the boy a bit, and said:

'What do you call work?'

'Why, ain't that work?'

Tom resumed his whitewashing, and answered carelessly:

'Well, maybe it is, and maybe it ain't. All I know is, it suits Tom Sawyer.'

'Oh, come now, you don't mean to let on that you like it?'

The brush continued to move.

'Like it? Well, I don't see why I oughtn't to like it. Does a boy get a chance to whitewash a fence every day?'

That put the thing in a new light. Ben stopped nibbling his apple. Tom swept his brush daintily back and forth—stepped back to note the effect—added a touch here and there—criticized the effect again—Ben watching every move, and getting more and more interested, more and more absorbed. Presently he said:

'Say, Tom, let me whitewash a little.'

Tom considered—was about to consent; but he altered his mind: 'No, no; I reckon it wouldn't hardly do, Ben. You see, Aunt Polly's awful particular about this fence—right here on the street, you know—but if it was the back fence I wouldn't mind, and she wouldn't. Yes, she's awful particular about this fence; it's got to be done very careful; I reckon there ain't one boy in a thousand, maybe two thousand, that can do it the way it's got to be done.'

'No—is that so? Oh, come now; lemme just try, only just a little. I'd let you, if you was me, Tom.'

'Ben, I'd like to, honest injun; but Aunt Polly—well, Jim wanted to do it, but she wouldn't let him. Sid wanted to do it, and she wouldn't let Sid. Now, don't you see how I am fixed? If you was to tackle this fence, and anything was to happen to it——'

'Oh, shucks; I'll be just as careful. Now lemme try. Say—I'll give you the core of my apple.'

'Well, here. No, Ben; now don't; I'm afeard——'

'I'll give you all of it!'

Tom gave up the brush with reluctance in his face but alacrity in his heart. And while the late steamer *Big Missouri* worked and sweated in the sun, the retired artist sat on a barrel in the shade close by, dangled his legs, munched his apple, and planned the slaughter of more innocents. There was no lack of material; boys happened along every little while; they came to jeer, but remained to whitewash. By the time Ben was fagged out, Tom had traded the next chance to Billy Fisher for a kite, in good repair; and when he played out, Johnny Miller bought in for a dead rat and a string to swing it with; and so on, and so on, hour after hour. And when the middle of the afternoon came, from being a poor poverty-stricken boy in the morning, Tom was literally rolling in wealth. He had, besides the things I have mentioned, twelve marbles, part of a Jew's harp, a piece of blue bottle-glass to look through, a spool-cannon, a key that wouldn't unlock anything, a fragment of chalk, a glass stopper of a decanter, a tin soldier, a couple of tadpoles, six fire-crackers, a kitten with only one eye, a brass door-knob, a dog-collar—but no dog—the handle of a knife, four pieces of orange-peel, and a dilapidated old window-sash. He had had a nice, good, idle time all the while—plenty of company—and the fence had three coats of whitewash on it! If he hadn't run out of whitewash, he would have bankrupted every boy in the village.

MARK TWAIN (1835–1910), *The Adventures of Tom Sawyer*, 1876

We agreed that we would pull this morning, as a change from towing; and Harris thought the best arrangement would be that George and I should scull, and he steer. I did not chime in with this idea at all; I said I thought Harris would have been showing a more proper spirit if he had suggested that he and George should work, and let me rest a bit. It seemed to me that I was doing more than my fair share of the work on this trip, and I was beginning to feel strongly on the subject.

It always does seem to me that I am doing more work than I should do. It is not that I object to the work, mind you; I like work: it fascinates me. I can sit and look at it for hours. I love to keep it by me: the idea of getting rid of it nearly breaks my heart.

You cannot give me too much work; to accumulate work has almost become a passion with me: my study is so full of it now, that there is hardly an inch of room for any more. I shall have to throw out a wing soon.

And I am careful of my work, too. Why, some of the work that I have by me now has been in my possession for years and years, and there isn't a finger-mark on it. I take a great pride in my work; I take it down now and then and dust it. No man keeps his work in a better state of preservation than I do.

But, though I crave for work, I still like to be fair. I do not ask for more than my proper share.

But I get it without asking for it—at least, so it appears to me—and this worries me.

George says he does not think I need trouble myself on the subject. He thinks it is only my overscrupulous nature that makes me fear I am having more than my due; and that, as a matter of fact, I don't have half as much as I ought. But I expect he only says this to comfort me.

JEROME K. JEROME (1859–1927), *Three Men in a Boat*, 1889

II. COMPENSATIONS AND REWARDS

For all its unpopularity, work was the essential precondition of human society. Mankind's very survival depended upon the strenuous exertions that were necessary to secure food, shelter, and the means of subsistence. The comforts and pleasures of civilized life were equally the creation of human industry. Labour was accordingly recognized as an economic necessity, and the achievements of human productivity were a cause for celebration.

For of all things good and fair, the gods give nothing to man without toil and effort.

XENOPHON (*c.*430 BC–*c.*354 BC), *Memorabilia,* tr. E. C. Marchant, 1923

Labour is painful, but God doth sweeten it with the gain it bringeth.

PAUL BAYNES (d. 1617), *An Entire Commentary upon the Whole Epistle of the Apostle Paul to the Ephesians,* 1647

The labour process is the everlasting nature-imposed condition of human existence.

KARL MARX (1818–83), *Das Kapital,* 1867–94

Man's industry . . . brings impossible things to pass. This industry, oh, it can almost do anything. It has (as it were) removed mountains, or at least made ways through them: so did Caesar over the Alps, and Alexander in his voyage to the Indies. It has dried up and diverted seas and navigable torrents. It has erected hetacombs and pyramids from little atoms of principal materials. It has made glass malleable, instructed in all arts, languages, sciences, professions, found out the use of simples and their compositions, of metals and their digestion, of minerals and their use, of peace, war, justice, religion; nothing has been too hard for the industry of man to cope with and conquer. Yea, so far has it usurped upon God's peculiar, that it has found out many secrets; and if Archimedes did not delude himself, could move the centre of the earth if it might fix its engine.

Now, though I do not believe industry can do all that is boasted of it, yet I do advisedly conclude that in the industry of man there is such a latent power and life of actuation that it comes near the verge of miraculous.

EDWARD WATERHOUSE (1619–70), *Fortescutus Illustratus*, 1663

The whole wealth of the body of the realm riseth out of the labours and works of the common people.

ANON., 'How to Reform This Realm', 1535–6

For 'tis Labour indeed that puts the difference of value on every thing; and let any one consider, what the difference is between an Acre of Land planted with Tobacco, or Sugar, sown with Wheat or Barley; and an Acre of the same Land lying in common, without any Husbandry upon it, and he will find, that the improvement of labour makes the far greater part of the value. I think it will be but a very modest Computation to say, that of the Products of the Earth useful to the Life of Man $\frac{9}{10}$ are the effects of labour: nay, if we will rightly estimate things as they come to our use, and cast up the several Expences about them, what in them is purely owing to Nature, and what to labour, we shall find, that in most of them $\frac{99}{100}$ are wholly to be put on the account of labour.

There cannot be a clearer demonstration of any thing, than several Nations of the Americans are of this, who are rich in Land, and poor in all the Comforts of Life; whom Nature having furnished as liberally as any other people, with the materials of Plenty, i.e. a fruitful Soil, apt to produce in abundance, what might serve for food, rayment, and delight; yet for want of improving it by labour, have not one hundreth part of the Conveniencies we enjoy: And a King of a large and fruitful Territory there feeds, lodges, and is clad worse than a day Labourer in England.

JOHN LOCKE (1632–1704), *Second Treatise of Civil Government*, 1690

I think the first condition of a good education is that the child should know that all he uses does not fall from heaven ready-made, but is produced by other people's labour. To understand that all he lives on comes from the labour of other people who neither know nor love him, is too much for a child (God grant he may understand it when he is grown up); but to understand that the chamber-pot he uses is emptied and wiped, without any pleasure, by a nurse or a housemaid, and that the boots and goloshes he always puts on clean are cleaned in the same way—not out of love for him, but for some other reason quite unintelligible to him—is something he can and should understand, and of which he should be ashamed. If he is not ashamed and if he continues to use them, that is the very worst commencement of an education, and leaves the deepest traces for his whole life. To avoid that, however, is very simple, and is just what (to use poetic language), standing on the threshold of the grave, I beseech you to do for your children. Let them do all they can for themselves: carry out their own slops, fill their own jugs, wash up, arrange their rooms, clean their boots and clothes, lay the table, etc. Believe me that, unimportant as these things may seem, they are a hundred times more important for your children's happiness than a knowledge of French, or of history, etc.

LEV NIKOLAEVICH TOLSTOY (1828–1910), 'Letter on Education', 1902, tr. Aylmer Maude, 1903

Even Nature lives by toil:
Beast, bird, air, fire, the heavens, and rolling worlds,
All live by action: nothing lies at rest,
But death and ruin: man is born to care;
Fashioned, improved by labour. This of old,
Wise states observing, gave that happy law,
Which doomed the rich and needy, every rank,
To mutual occupation; and oft called
Their chieftains from the spade, or furrowing plough,
Or bleating sheepfold. Hence utility
Through all conditions; hence the joys of health;
Hence strength of arm, and clear judicious thought;
Hence corn, and wine, and oil, and all in life
Delectable. What simple Nature yields
(And Nature does her part) are only rude
Materials, cumbers on the thorny ground;
'Tis toil that makes them wealth;

JOHN DYER (1699–1757), *The Fleece*, 1757

A taste for cleanness is not equally distributed among all men; nor indeed is any branch of the moral sense equally distributed: and if, by nature, one person be more cleanly than another, a whole nation may be so. I judge that to be the case of the Japanese, so finically clean as to find fault even with the Dutch for dirtiness. Their inns are not an exception; nor their little-houses, in which water is always at hand for washing after the operation. I judged it also to be the case of the English, who, high and low, rich and poor, are remarkable for cleanness all the world over; and I have often amused myself with so singular a resemblance between islanders, removed at the greatest distance from each other. But I was forced to abandon the resemblance, upon a discovery that the English have not always been so clean as at present. Many centuries ago, as recorded in monkish history, one cause of the aversion the English had to the Danes was their cleanness: they combed their hair, and put on a clean shirt once a week. It was reputed an extraordinary effort in Thomas a Becket, that he had his parlour strewed every day with clean straw. The celebrated Erasmus, who visited England in the reign of Henry VIII, complains of the nastiness and slovenly habits of its people; ascribing to that cause the frequent plagues which infested them. 'Their floors,' says he, 'are commonly of clay, strewed with rushes, under which lies unmolested a collection of beer, grease, fragments, bones, spittle, excrements of dogs and cats, and of every thing that is nauseous.' And the strewing a floor with straw or rushes was common in Queen Elizabeth's time, not excepting even her presence-chamber. A change so extraordinary in the taste and manners of the English, rouses our curiosity; and I flatter myself that the following cause will be satisfactory. A savage, remarkably indolent at home, though not insensible of his dirtiness, cannot rouse up activity sufficient to attempt a serious purgation; and would be at a loss where to begin. The industrious, on the contrary, are improved in neatness and propriety, by the art or manufacture that constantly employs them: they are never reduced to purge the stable of Augeas; for being prone to action, they suffer not dirt to rest unmolested. Industrious nations, accordingly, all the world over, are the most cleanly. Arts and industry had long flourished in Holland, where Erasmus was born and educated: the people were clean above all their neighbours, because they were industrious above all their neighbours; and, upon that account, the dirtiness of England could not fail to strike a Hollander. At the period mentioned, industry was as great a stranger to England as cleanness: from which consideration, may it not fairly be inferred, that the English are indebted for their cleanliness to the great progress of industry among them in later times? If this inference hold, it places industry in an amiable light. The Spaniards, who are indolent to a degree, are to this day as dirty as the English were three centuries ago. Madrid, their capital, is nauseously nasty: heaps of unmolested dirt in every street, raise in that warm climate a pestiferous steam, which threatens to knock down every stranger. A purgation was lately set on foot by royal authority. But people habituated to dirt are not easily reclaimed: to promote industry is the only effectual remedy.

HENRY HOME, LORD KAMES (1696–1782), *Sketches of the History of Man*, 1774

'Manual Labour and the Victorian Economy'

Commercial progress depended quite largely on the physical adaptability of the worker, whether it involved crawling on all fours to gather the woad harvest, climbing up and down perpendicular ladders (in a Cornish tin mine the ascent would take an hour or more each day), or working, like boilermakers on repair jobs, upside down in tanks. The lungs of the glassblower, working as bellows, or those of the gas-fitter, soldering pipes, were not the least of the forces of production which 19th century capitalism summoned to its aid, nor were there any more important in the clothing trades than the needlewoman's fingers and thumbs. In the Potteries, dinner plates were shaped by dextrous jerks of the flat-presser's wrists, and surfaces varnished with the dipper's bare arms in a glaze tub (in 1861 Dr Greenhow estimated they were immersed for eight of a twelve hour day). Ironmaking depended on violent muscular exertion, and an ability to withstand white heat, engineering on precision of judgement and touch. In the metal-working trades no action was more highly valued than the ability to deliver well-directed blows with the hammer, while those engaged in press work were in almost perpetual motion with their arms and wrists: 'practised workers' in the metal button trade were said to make from 14,000 to 20,000 strokes a day, 'the whole strength of a woman' being needed on the heavier class of press.

Human beings were quite often used instead of horses for haulage, not only on the canals, but also on the brickfields, where the children who acted as 'off-bearers' or 'pushers-out', taking cart-loads of bricks from the moulder's table to the brick-setter's kiln, carried an average weight variously computed at between 12 and 25 tons a day. They were used as lifts in the lead factories, and as shunters in the docks. In the workshop trades, delivery boys were strapped to the heavier loads very much in the manner of Volga boatmen; so were some of the bakers' boys who went on 'rounds'. Men were also used like this in heavy industry, when there were plates to be drawn from the furnaces, or castings from their beds . . . Sturdy legs were essential for mould-runners in the potteries, carrying plates from the flat-pressers' wheels to the drying rooms; they were also much in demand at a glassworks, where a whole army of juvenile runners were kept on their feet all day: in a glass bottle factory of the 1860s it was calculated that they travelled the equivalent of between 13 and 17 miles a day. 'The smaller the articles . . . and the rougher the workmanship, the greater is the number of them turned out . . . and the greater also is the demand on a boy's exertion.'

Human beings were also used as balances and weights, whether to give motion to machinery, like the lathe-treaders, or to act as see-saws when there were heavy loads to hoist. In clay-treading they had to act as mangles, in baking as rotary knives. In the London fur trade grown men were employed in the 1890s to bring seal skins to plasticity by jumping on them. 'It is a curious sight, on entering a room, to see a row of . . . tubs each with its Jack in the-box bobbing up and down', wrote one of Booth's investigators. 'Every man is naked except for a vest, and a rough cloth which is tied round his waist and attached to the rim of his barrel. With hands resting on either ledge up and down he treads, and earns 20s to 25s piece-work. Skins cured by this process are said to be softer and silkier.'

In mid-Victorian England there were few parts of the economy which steam power and machinery had left untouched, but fewer still where it ruled unchallenged. At both top and bottom a mainly hand technology prevailed, at top because of the irreplaceability of human skill, at bottom because of the plentiful supply of drudges.

RAPHAEL SAMUEL (1934–96), 'The Workshop of the World', 1977

Caleb Garth often shook his head in meditation on the value, the indispensable might of that myriad-headed, myriad-handed labour by which the social body is fed, clothed, and housed. It had laid hold of his imagination in boyhood. The echoes of the great hammer where roof or keel were a-making, the signal-shouts of the workmen, the roar of the furnace, the thunder and plash of the engine, were a sublime music to him; the felling and lading of timber, and the huge trunk vibrating star-like in the distance along the highway, the crane at work on the wharf, the piled-up produce in warehouses, the precision and variety of muscular effort wherever exact work had to be turned out,—all these sights of his youth had acted on him as poetry without the aid of the poets, had made a philosophy for him without the aid of philosophers, a religion without the aid of theology. His early ambition had been to have as effective a share as possible in this sublime labour, which was peculiarly dignified by him with the name of 'business;' and though he had only been a short time under a surveyor, and had been chiefly his own teacher, he knew more of land, building, and mining than most of the special men in the county.

GEORGE ELIOT (1819–80), *Middlemarch*, 1871–2

House-building, measuring, sawing the boards,
Blacksmithing, glass-blowing, nail-making, coopering, tin-roofing, shingle-
    dressing,
Ship-joining, dock-building, fish-curing, flagging of sidewalks by flaggers,
The pump, the pile-driver, the great derrick, the coal-kiln and brick-kiln,

---

Booth] Charles Booth (1840–1916), shipowner and social reformer. His *Life and Labour of the People of London* (1889–1903) was the forerunner of the modern social survey.

Coal-mines and all that is down there, the lamps in the darkness, echoes, songs, what meditations, what vast native thoughts looking through smutch'd faces,

Iron-works, forge-fires in the mountains or by river-banks, men around feeling the melt with huge crowbars, lumps of ore, the due combining of ore, limestone, coal,

The blast-furnace and the puddling-furnace, the loup-lump at the bottom of the melt at last, the rolling-mill, the stumpy bars of pig-iron, the strong clean-shaped T-rail for rail-roads,

Oil-works, silk-works, white-lead-works, the sugar-house, steam-saws, the great mills and factories,

Stone-cutting, shapely trimmings for façades or window or door-lintels, the mallet, the tooth chisel, the jib to protect the thumb,

The calking-iron, the kettle of boiling vault-cement, and the fire under the kettle,

The cotton-bale, the stevedore's hook, the saw and buck of the sawyer, the mould of the moulder, the working-knife of the butcher, the ice-saw, and all the work with ice,

The work and tools of the rigger, grappler, sail-maker, block-maker,

Goods of gutta-percha, papier-maché, colors, brushes, brush-making, glazier's implements,

The veneer and glue-pot, the confectioner's ornaments, the decanter and glasses, the shears and flat-iron,

The awl and knee-strap, the pint measure and quart measure, the counter and stool, the writing-pen of quill or metal, the making of all sorts of edged tools,

The brewery, brewing, the malt, the vats, every thing that is done by brewers, wine-makers, vinegar-makers,

Leather-dressing, coach-making, boiler-making, rope-twisting, distilling, sign-painting, lime-burning, cotton-picking, electroplating, electrotyping, stereotyping,

Stave-machines, planing-machines, reaping-machines, ploughing-machines, thrashing-machines, steam wagons,

The cart of the carman, the omnibus, the ponderous dray,

Pyrotechny, letting off color'd fireworks at night, fancy figures and jets;

Beef on the butcher's stall, the slaughter-house of the butcher, the butcher in his killing-clothes,

The pens of live pork, the killing-hammer, the hog-hook, the scalder's tub, gutting, the cutter's cleaver, the packer's maul, and the plenteous winter-work of pork-packing,

Flour-works, grinding of wheat, rye, maize, rice, the barrels and the half and quarter barrels, the loaded barges, the high piles on wharves and levees,

The men and the work of the men on ferries, railroads, coasters, fish-boats, canals;

The hourly routine of your own or any man's life, the shop, yard, store, or
    factory,
These shows all near you by day and night—workman! whoever you are, your
    daily life!
In that and them the heft of the heaviest—in that and them far more than you
    estimated, (and far less also,)
In them realities for you and me, in them poems for you and me,
In them, not yourself—you and your soul enclose all things, regardless of
    estimation,
In them the development good—in them all themes, hints, possibilities.

I do not affirm that what you see beyond is futile, I do not advise you to stop,
I do not say leadings you thought great are not great,
But I say that none lead to greater than these lead to.

        WALT WHITMAN (1819–92), *A Song for Occupations*, 1881 edn.

The natural thing to do is to work—to recognise that prosperity and happiness can be obtained only through honest effort. Human ills flow largely from
attempting to escape from the natural course. I have no suggestion which goes
beyond accepting in its fullest this principle of nature. I take it for granted that
we must work. All that we have done comes as the result of a certain insistence
that since we must work it is better to work diligently and forehandedly; that
the better we do our work the better off we shall be. All of which I conceive to
be merely elemental common sense.

        HENRY FORD (1863–1947), in collaboration with Samuel Crowther, *My
        Life and Work*, 1922

The Moscow Workers Take Possession of the
Great Metro on April 27, 1935

We were told: 80,000 workers
Built the Metro, many after a day's work elsewhere
Sometimes all through the night. This past year
Young men and girls were always seen
Laughing as they climbed out of the tunnels, proudly flaunting
Their work clothes, mud-caked and drenched with sweat.
All obstacles—
Underground streams, pressure from multi-storey buildings
Massive cave-ins—were overcome. For the ornamentation
No pains were spared. The best marble
Was transported from afar, the finest woods
Worked with scrupulous care. The splendid trains
Ran almost soundlessly at last

Through tunnels light as day: for exacting clients
The best of everything.
Now that the railway was built in accordance with the most perfect plans
And the owners came to view it and
To ride on it, they were the selfsame people
Who had built it.
Thousands of them were there, walking about
Examining the giant halls, while in the trains
Great multitudes went riding past, their faces—
Men, women and children, greybeards as well—
Turned to the stations, beaming as if at the theatre, for the stations
Were all built differently, of different stone
In different styles; the light also
Came each time from a different source. Anyone getting aboard
Was shoved to the back in the cheerful crush
Since the seats up front were
Best for viewing the stations. At every station
The children were lifted up. As often as possible
The travellers rushed out and inspected
With eager, exacting eyes the finished job. They felt the pillars
And appraised their gloss. They scraped the soles of their shoes
Over the stone floors, to see if the slabs
Were smoothly fitted. Crowding back into the cars
They tested the wall surfaces and fingered
The glass. Men and women were continually
Pointing out—uncertain if they were the right ones—
Places where they had worked: the stone
Bore the imprint of their hands. Each face
Was distinctly visible, for there was much light
Many bulbs, more than in any railway I have seen.
The tunnels also were lighted, not one metre of labour
Went unlit. And all this
Had been built in a single year and by so many workmen
Unique among the railways of the world. And no
Other railway in the world had ever had so many owners.
For this wonder of construction was witnessing
What none of its predecessors in the cities of many centuries
Had witnessed: *the builders in the role of proprietors.*
Where would it ever have happened that the fruits of labour
Fell to those who had laboured? Where in all time
Were the people who had put up a building
Not always turned out of it?
When we saw them riding in their trains
The work of their own hands, we knew:

This is the grand picture that once upon a time
Rocked the classic writers who foresaw it.

BERTOLT BRECHT (1898–1956), 1935, tr. Edith Anderson, 1976

The spring is beautiful in California. Valleys in which the fruit blossoms are fragrant pink and white waters in a shallow sea. Then the first tendrils of the grapes, swelling from the old gnarled vines, cascade down to cover the trunks. The full green hills are round and soft as breasts. And on the level vegetable lands are the mile-long rows of pale green lettuce and the spindly little cauliflowers, the gray-green unearthly artichoke plants.

And then the leaves break out on the trees, and the petals drop from the fruit trees and carpet the earth with pink and white. The centers of the blossoms swell and grow and color: cherries and apples, peaches and pears, figs which close the flower in the fruit. All California quickens with produce, and the fruit grows heavy, and the limbs bend gradually under the fruit so that little crutches must be placed under them to support the weight.

Behind the fruitfulness are men of understanding and knowledge and skill, men who experiment with seed, endlessly developing the techniques for greater crops of plants whose roots will resist the million enemies of the earth: the moles, the insects, the rusts, the blights. These men work carefully and endlessly to perfect the seed, the roots. And there are the men of chemistry who spray the trees against pests, who sulfur the grapes, who cut out disease and rots, mildews and sicknesses. Doctors of preventive medicine, men at the borders who look for fruit flies, for Japanese beetle, men who quarantine the sick trees and root them out and burn them, men of knowledge. The men who graft the young trees, the little vines, are the cleverest of all, for theirs is a surgeon's job, as tender and delicate; and these men must have surgeons' hands and surgeons' hearts to slit the bark, to place the grafts, to bind the wounds and cover them from the air. These are great men.

Along the rows the cultivators move, tearing the spring grass and turning it under to make a fertile earth, breaking the ground to hold the water up near the surface, ridging the ground in little pools for the irrigation, destroying the weed roots that may drink the water away from the trees.

And all the time the fruit swells and the flowers break out in long clusters on the vines. And in the growing year the warmth grows and the leaves turn dark green. The prunes lengthen like little green birds' eggs, and the limbs sag down against the crutches under the weight. And the hard little pears take shape, and the beginning of the fuzz comes out on the peaches. Grape-blossoms shed their tiny petals and the hard little beads become green buttons, and the buttons grow heavy. The men who work in the fields, the owners of the little orchards, watch and calculate. The year is heavy with produce. And men are proud, for of their knowledge they can make the year heavy. They have transformed the world with their knowledge. The short, lean wheat has been made big and productive. Little sour apples have grown large and sweet, and that old grape that grew among the trees and fed the birds its tiny fruit has mothered a thousand varieties, red and black, green and pale pink, purple and yellow; and each variety with its own flavor. The men who work in the experimental farms have made new fruits: nectarines and forty kinds of plums, walnuts with paper shells. And always they work, selecting, grafting, changing, driving themselves, driving the earth to produce.

JOHN STEINBECK (1902–68), *The Grapes of Wrath*, 1939

In Victorian England the best-known artistic celebration of human industry was Ford Madox Brown's painting Work *(1852–63), now in the Manchester Art Gallery. Here are excerpts from the artist's explanation of his picture.*

This picture was begun in 1852 at Hampstead. The background, which represents the main street of that suburb not far from the Heath, was painted on the spot.

At that time extensive excavations were going on in the neighbourhood, and, seeing and studying daily as I did the British excavator, or *navvy*, as he designates himself, in the full swing of his activity (with his manly and picturesque costume, and with the rich glow of colour which exercise under a hot sun will impart), it appeared to me that he was at least as worthy of the powers of an English painter as the fisherman of the Adriatic, the peasant of the Campagna, or the Neapolitan lazzarone. Gradually this idea developed itself into that of *Work* as it now exists, with the British excavator for a central group, as the outward and visible type of *Work*. Here are presented the young navvy in the pride of manly health and beauty; the strong fully-developed navvy who does his work and loves his beer; the selfish old bachelor navvy, stout of limb, and perhaps a trifle tough in those regions where compassion is said to reside; the navvy of strong animal nature, who, but that he was when young *taught* to work at useful work, might even now be working at the *useless crank*. Then Paddy with his larry and his pipe in his mouth. The young navvy who occupies the place of hero in this group, and in the picture, stands on what is termed a landing-stage, a platform placed half-way down the trench; two men from beneath shovel the earth up to him as he shovels it on to the pile outside. Next in value of significance to these is the ragged wretch who has never been *taught* to *work*; with his restless, gleaming eyes he doubts and despairs of every one. But for a certain effeminate gentleness of disposition and a love of nature he might have been a burglar! He lives in Flower and Dean Street, where the policemen walk two and two, and the worst cut-throats surround him, but he is harmless; and before the dawn you may see him miles out in the country, collecting his wild weeds and singular plants to awaken interest, and perhaps find a purchaser in some sprouting botanist. When exhausted he will return to his den, his creel of flowers then rests in an open court-yard, the thoroughfare for the crowded inmates of this haunt of vice, and played in by mischievous boys, yet the basket rarely gets interfered with, unless through the unconscious lurch of some drunkard. The bread-winning implements are sacred with the very poor. In the very opposite scale from the man who can't work, at the further corner of the picture, are two men who appear as having nothing to do. These are the brain-workers, who, seeming to be idle, work, and are the cause of well-ordained work and happiness in others—sages, such as in ancient Greece published their opinions in the market square. Perhaps one of these may already, before he or others know it, have moulded a nation to his pattern, converted a hitherto combative race to obstinate passivity; with a word may have centupled the tide of emigration, with another, have quenched the political passions of both factions—may have reversed men's notions upon criminals, upon slavery, upon many things, and still be walking about little known to some. The other, in friendly communion with the philosopher, smiling perhaps at some of his wild sallies and cynical thrusts (for Socrates at times strangely disturbs the seriousness of his auditory by the mercilessness of his jokes—against vice and foolishness), is intended for a kindred and yet very dissimilar spirit. A clergy-man, such as the Church of England offers examples of—a priest without guile—a gentleman without pride, much in communion with the working classes, 'honouring all men,' 'never weary in well-doing.' Scholar, author, philosopher, and teacher, too, in his way, but not above practical efforts, if even for a small resulting good. Deeply penetrated as he is with the axiom that each unit of humanity feels as much as all the rest combined, and impulsive and hopeful in nature, so that the remedy suggests itself to him concurrently with the evil.

Next to these, on the shaded bank, are different characters out of work: haymakers in quest of employment; a Stoic from the Emerald Island, with hay stuffed in his hat to keep the draught out, and need for Stoicism just at present, being short of baccy; a young shoeless Irishman, with his wife, feeding their first-born with cold pap; an old sailor turned haymaker; and two young peasants in search of harvest work, reduced in strength, perhaps by fever—possibly by famine. Behind the Pariah, who never has learned to work, appears a group of a very different class, who, from an opposite cause, have not been sufficiently used to work either. These are the *rich*, who 'have no need to work'—not at least for bread—*the 'bread of life'* is neither here nor there. The pastrycook's tray, the symbol of superfluity, accompanies these . . .

Through this picture I have gained some experience of the navvy class, and I have usually found, that if you can break through the upper crust of *mauvaise honte* which surrounds them in common with most Englishmen, and which, in the case of the navvies, I believe to be the cause of much of their bad language, you will find them serious, intelligent men, and with much to interest in their conversation, which, moreover, contains about the same amount of morality and sentiment that is commonly found among men in the active and hazardous walks of life, for that their career is one of hazard and danger none should doubt. Many stories might be told of navvies' daring and endurance, were this the place for them . . .

I have only to observe, in conclusion, that the effect of hot July sunlight, attempted in this picture, has been introduced because it seems peculiarly fitted to display *work* in all its severity, and not from any predilection for this kind of light over any other.

> FORD H. MADOX HUEFFER (later Ford Madox Ford) (1873–1939), *The Life of Ford Madox Brown*, 1896

It was not surprising that some theorists held that it was the habit of purposive labour that had developed mankind's essential attributes and led to the distinction between human beings and animals. Those who did not work would regress into the animal state.

> These are thy Blessings, INDUSTRY! rough Power!
> Whom Labour still attends, and Sweat, and Pain;
> Yet the kind Source of every gentle Art,
> And all the soft Civility of Life:
> Raiser of Human Kind! by Nature cast,
> Naked, and helpless, out amid the Woods,
> And Wilds, to rude inclement Elements;
> With various Seeds of Art deep in the Mind
> Implanted, and profusely pour'd around
> Materials infinite; but idle all.
> Still unexerted, in th' unconscious Breast,
> Slept the lethargic Powers; Corruption still,
> Voracious, swallow'd what the liberal Hand
> Of Bounty scatter'd o'er the savage Year:
> And still the sad Barbarian, roving, mix'd
> With Beasts of Prey; or for his Acorn-Meal
> Fought the fierce tusky Boar; a shivering Wretch!
> Aghast, and comfortless, when the bleak North,
> With Winter charg'd, let the mix'd Tempest fly,
> Hail, Rain, and Snow, and bitter-breathing Frost:
> Then to the Shelter of the Hut he fled;
> And the wild Season, sordid, pin'd away.
> For Home he had not; Home is the Resort

Of Love, of Joy, of Peace and Plenty, where,
Supporting and supported, polish'd Friends,
And dear Relations mingle into Bliss.
But this the rugged Savage never felt,
Even desolate in Crouds; and thus his Days
Roll'd heavy, dark, and unenjoy'd along;
A Waste of Time! till INDUSTRY approach'd,
And rous'd him from his miserable Sloth:
His Faculties unfolded; pointed out,
Where lavish Nature the directing Hand
Of Art demanded; shew'd him how to raise
His feeble Force by the mechanic Powers,
To dig the Mineral from the vaulted Earth,
On what to turn the piercing Rage of Fire,
On what the Torrent, and the gather'd Blast;
Gave the tall antient Forest to his Ax;
Taught him to chip the Wood, and hew the Stone,
Till by Degrees the finish'd Fabric rose;
Tore from his Limbs the Blood-polluted Fur,
And wrapt them in the woolly Vestment warm,
Or bright in glossy Silk, and flowing Lawn;
With wholesome Viands fill'd his Table, pour'd
The generous Glass around, inspir'd to wake
The Life-refining Soul of decent Wit:
Nor stopp'd at barren bare Necessity;
But still advancing bolder, led him on,
To Pomp, to Pleasure, Elegance, and Grace;
And, breathing high Ambition thro' his Soul,
Set Science, Wisdom, Glory, in his View,
And bad him be the *Lord* of All below.

JAMES THOMSON (1700–48), from 'Autumn', *The Seasons*, 1726–30

Labour is the source of all wealth, the political economists assert. It is this—next to nature, which supplies it with the material that it converts into wealth. But it is even infinitely more than this. It is the prime basic condition for all human existence, and this to such an extent that, in a sense, we have to say that labour created man himself.

Many hundreds of thousands of years ago, during an epoch, not yet definitely determinable, of that period of the earth's history which geologists call the Tertiary period, most likely towards the end of it, a specially highly-developed race of anthropoid apes lived somewhere in the tropical zone—probably on a great continent that has now sunk to the bottom of the Indian

Ocean. Darwin has given us an approximate description of these ancestors of ours. They were completely covered with hair, they had beards and pointed ears, and they lived in bands in the trees.

Presumably as an immediate consequence of their mode of life, which in climbing assigns different functions to the hands than to the feet, these apes when walking on level ground began to disaccustom themselves to the aid of their hands and to adopt a more and more erect gait. This was *the decisive step in the transition from ape to man.*

*

For erect gait among our hairy ancestors to have become first the rule and in time a necessity presupposes that in the meantime diverse other functions increasingly devolved upon the hands. Even among the apes there already prevails a certain division in the employment of the hands and feet. As already mentioned, in climbing the hands are used differently from the feet. The former serve primarily for the collection and grasping of food, as already occurs in the use of the fore paws among lower mammals. Many monkeys use their hands to build nests for themselves in the trees or even, like the chimpanzee, to construct roofs between the branches for protection against the weather. With their hands they seize hold of clubs to defend themselves against enemies, or bombard the latter with fruits and stones. In captivity, they carry out with their hands a number of simple operations copied from human beings. But it is just here that one sees how great is the distance between the undeveloped hand of even the most anthropoid of apes and the human hand that has been highly perfected by the labour of hundreds of thousands of years. The number and general arrangement of the bones and muscles are the same in both; but the hand of the lowest savage can perform hundreds of operations that no monkey's hand can imitate. No simian hand has ever fashioned even the crudest of stone knives . . .

Thus the hand is not only the organ of labour, *it is also the product of labour.* Only by labour, by adaptation to ever new operations, by inheritance of the thus acquired special development of muscles, ligaments and, over longer periods of time, bones as well, and by the ever-renewed employment of this inherited finesse in new, more and more complicated operations, has the human hand attained the high degree of perfection that has enabled it to conjure into being the paintings of a Raphael, the statues of a Thorwaldsen, the music of a Paganini.

> FRIEDRICH ENGELS (1820–95), 'The Part Played by Labour in the Transition from Ape to Man', 1896

'An Evolutionary Fairy Tale'

'Pooh! pooh! pooh!' said the fairy. . . . 'Come here, and see what happens to people who do only what is pleasant.'

And she took out of one of her cupboards (she had all sorts of mysterious cupboards in the cracks of the rocks) the most wonderful waterproof book, full of such photographs as never were seen . . .

And on the title-page was written, 'The History of the great and famous nation of the Doasyoulikes, who came away from the country of Hardwork, because they wanted to play on the Jews'-harp all day long.'

In the first picture they saw these Doasyoulikes living in the land of Ready-made, at the foot of the Happy-golucky Mountains . . .

They lived very much such a life as those jolly old Greeks in Sicily, whom you may see painted on the ancient vases, and really there seemed to be great excuses for them, for they had no need to work.

Instead of houses, they lived in the beautiful caves of tufa, and bathed in the warm springs three times a day; and, as for clothes, it was so warm there that the gentlemen walked about in little beside a cocked hat and a pair of straps, or some light summer tackle of that kind; and the ladies all gathered gossamer in autumn (when they were not too lazy) to make their winter dresses.

They were very fond of music, but it was too much trouble to learn the piano or the violin; and, as for dancing, that would have been too great an exertion. So they sat on ant-hills all day long, and played on the Jews'-harp; and, if the ants bit them, why they just got up and went to the next ant-hill, till they were bitten there likewise.

And they sat under the flapdoodle-trees, and let the flapdoodle drop into their mouths; and under the vines, and squeezed the grape-juice down their throats; and, if any little pigs ran about ready roasted, crying, 'Come and eat me,' as was their fashion in that country, they waited till the pigs ran against their mouths, and then took a bite, and were content, just as so many oysters would have been.

They needed no weapons, for no enemies ever came near their land; and no tools, for everything was readymade to their hand; and the stern old fairy Necessity never came near them to hunt them up, and make them use their wits, or die.

And so on, and so on, and so on, till there were never such comfortable, easy-going, happy-go-lucky people in the world.

'Well, that is a jolly life,' said Tom.

'You think so?' said the fairy. 'Do you see that great peaked mountain there behind,' said the fairy, 'with smoke coming out of its top?'

'Yes.'

'And do you see all those ashes, and slag, and cinders, lying about?'

'Yes.'

'Then turn over the next five hundred years, and you will see what happens next.'

And behold the mountain had blown up like a barrel of gunpowder, and then boiled over like a kettle; whereby one-third of the Doasyoulikes were blown into the air, and another third were smothered in ashes; so that there was only one-third left.

'You see,' said the fairy, 'what comes of living on a burning mountain.'

'Oh, why did you not warn them?' said little Ellie.

'I did warn them all that I could. I let the smoke come out of the mountain; and wherever there is smoke there is fire. And I laid the ashes and cinders all about; and wherever there are cinders, cinders may be again. But they did not like to face facts, my dears, as very few people do; and so they invented a cock-and-bull story, which, I am sure, I never told them, that the smoke was the breath of a giant, whom some gods or other had buried under the mountain; and that the cinders were what the dwarfs roasted the little pigs whole with; and other nonsense of that kind. And, when folks are in that humour, I cannot teach them, save by the good old birch-rod.'

And then she turned over the next five hundred years: and there were the remnant of the Doasyoulikes, doing as they liked, as before. They were too lazy to move away from the mountain; so they said, If it has blown up once, that is all the more reason that it should not blow up again. And they were few in number: but they only said, The more the merrier, but the fewer the better fare. However, that was not quite true; for all the flapdoodle-trees were killed by the volcano, and they had eaten all the roast pigs, who, of course, could not be expected to have little ones. So they had to live very hard, on nuts and roots which they scratched out of the ground with sticks. Some of them talked of sowing corn, as their ancestors used to do, before they came into the land of Readymade; but they had forgotten how to make ploughs (they had forgotten even how to make Jews'-harps by this time), and had eaten all the seed-corn which they brought out of the land of Hardwork years since; and of course it was too much trouble to go away and find more. So they lived miserably on roots and nuts, and all the weakly little children had great stomachs, and then died.

'Why,' said Tom, 'they are growing no better than savages.'

'And look how ugly they are all getting,' said Ellie.

'Yes; when people live on poor vegetables instead of roast beef and plum-pudding, their jaws grow large, and their lips grow coarse, like the poor Paddies who eat potatoes.'

And she turned over the next five hundred years. And there they were all living up in trees, and making nests to keep off the rain. And underneath the trees lions were prowling about.

'Why,' said Ellie, 'the lions seem to have eaten a good many of them, for there are very few left now.'

'Yes,' said the fairy; 'you see it was only the strongest and most active ones who could climb the trees, and so escape.'

'But what great, hulking, broad-shouldered chaps they are,' said Tom; 'they are a rough lot as ever I saw.'

'Yes, they are getting very strong now; for the ladies will not marry any but the very strongest and fiercest gentlemen, who can help them up the trees out of the lions' way.'

And she turned over the next five hundred years. And in that they were fewer still, and stronger, and fiercer; but their feet had changed shape very oddly, for they laid hold of the branches with their great toes, as if they had been thumbs, just as a Hindoo tailor uses his toes to thread his needle.

The children were very much surprised, and asked the fairy whether that was her doing.

'Yes, and no,' she said, smiling. 'It was only those who could use their feet as well as their hands who could get a good living: or, indeed, get married; so that they got the best of everything, and starved out all the rest; and those who are left keep up a regular breed of toe-thumb-men, as a breed of shorthorns, or skye-terriers, or fancy pigeons is kept up.'

'But there is a hairy one among them,' said Ellie.

'Ah!' said the fairy, 'that will be a great man in his time, and chief of all the tribe.'

And, when she turned over the next five hundred years, it was true.

For this hairy chief had had hairy children, and they hairier children still; and every one wished to marry hairy husbands, and have hairy children too; for the climate was growing so damp that none but the hairy ones could live: all the rest coughed and sneezed, and had sore throats, and went into consumptions, before they could grow up to be men and women.

Then the fairy turned over the next five hundred years. And they were fewer still.

'Why, there is one on the ground picking up roots,' said Ellie, 'and he cannot walk upright.'

No more he could; for in the same way that the shape of their feet had altered, the shape of their backs had altered also.

'Why,' cried Tom, 'I declare they are all apes.'

'Something fearfully like it, poor foolish creatures,' said the fairy. 'They are grown so stupid now, that they can hardly think: for none of them have used their wits for many hundred years. They have almost forgotten, too, how to talk. For each stupid child forgot some of the words it heard from its stupid parents, and had not wits enough to make fresh words for itself. Beside, they are grown so fierce and suspicious and brutal that they keep out of each other's way, and mope and sulk in the dark forests, never hearing each other's voice, till they have forgotten almost what speech is like. I am afraid they will all be apes very soon, and all by doing only what they liked.'

And in the next five hundred years they were all dead and gone, by bad food and wild beasts and hunters; all except one tremendous old fellow with jaws like a jack, who stood full seven feet high; and M. Du Chaillu came up to him, and shot him, as he stood roaring and thumping his breast. And he remembered that his ancestors had once been men, and tried to say, 'Am I not a man and a brother?' but had forgotten how to use his tongue; and then he had tried to call for a doctor, but he had forgotten the word for one. So all he said was, 'Ubboboo!' and died.

And that was the end of the great and jolly nation of the Doasyoulikes. And, when Tom and Ellie came to the end of the book, they looked very sad and solemn; and they had good reason so to do, for they really fancied that the men were apes, and never thought, in their simplicity, of asking whether the creatures had hippopotamus majors in their brains or not; in which case, as you have been told already, they could not possibly have been apes, though they were more apish than the apes of all aperies.

'But could you not have saved them from becoming apes?' said little Ellie, at last.

'At first, my dear; if only they would have behaved like men, and set to work to do what they did not like. But the longer they waited, and behaved like the dumb beasts, who only do what they like, the stupider and clumsier they grew; till at last they were past all cure, for they had thrown their own wits away. It is such things as this that help to make me so ugly, that I know not when I shall grow fair.'

'And where are they all now?' asked Ellie.

'Exactly where they ought to be, my dear.'

CHARLES KINGSLEY (1819–75), The Water Babies, 1863

The creative and transforming power of human effort showed that work was something more than a tiresome necessity. From classical times onwards, moralists preached the virtues of labour. Work was an economic necessity; it was a divine command; and it benefited the whole community. Before the Fall of Man labour had been pleasurable rather than painful, but even in Eden there had been a duty to work.

But you, ever bearing my instruction in mind, must work, Perses, you who are of Zeus' stock, so that Hunger may shun you and august fair-crowned Demeter favour you and fill your granary with substance; for Hunger goes always with a workshy man. Gods and men disapprove of that man who lives without working, like in temper to the blunt-tailed drones who wear away the toil of the bees, eating it in idleness. You should embrace work-tasks in their due order, so that your granaries may be full of substance in its season. It is from work that men are rich in flocks and wealthy, and a working man is much dearer to the immortals. Work is no reproach, but not working is a reproach; and if you work, it will readily come about that a workshy man will envy you as you become wealthy. Wealth brings worth and prestige. But whatever your fortune, work is preferable, that is, if you turn your blight-witted heart from others' possessions towards work and show concern for livelihood as I tell you.

HESIOD (fl. c.700 BC), Works and Days, tr. M. L. West, 1988

Now, young master, there are these six disadvantages of idling. (The idler says) 'It's too cold,' and does no work: or 'It's too hot,' and does no work: or 'It's too early,' and does no work: or 'It's too late,' and does no work: or 'I'm too hungry,' and does no work: or 'I'm too full,' and does no work. So, as he lives with all these excuses about work, the wealth that has not yet come to him does not arise, and the wealth that has come goes to destruction.

> GAUTAMA SIDDHĀRTHA BUDDHA (*c.*563–483 BC), *Some Sayings of the Buddha According to the Pali Canon*, tr. F. L. Woodward, 1925

> The Sire of Gods and Men, with hard Decrees,
> Forbids our Plenty to be bought with Ease:
> And wills that Mortal Men, inur'd to toil,
> Shou'd exercise, with pains, the grudging Soil.
> Himself invented first the shining Share,
> And whetted humane Industry by Care:
> Himself did handy-crafts and Arts ordain;
> Nor suffer'd Sloath to rust his active Reign.

> VIRGIL (70–19 BC), *Georgics*, 36–29 BC, tr. John Dryden, 1697

And the Lord God formed man of the dust of the ground, and breathed into his nostrils the breath of life; and man became a living soul . . . And the Lord God took the man and put him into the garden of Eden to dress it and to keep it.

> Genesis 2: 7, 15

For this ye may understand that it is the will of God that every man and woman should labour busily. For if Adam and Eve had been occupied with labour, the serpent had not overcome them: for idleness is the devil's desire. Wherefore ye may know well it is the will of God that we should labour and put our body to penance for to flee sin. Thus did Adam and Eve, to example of all those that should come after them.

> ANON. PREACHER, '*Sermo de doctrina in Septuag*', 15th c.

> God would, that (void of painefull labor) he
> Should live in *Eden*, but not idlely,
> For idlenes pure innocence subverts,
> Defiles our bodie, and our soule perverts:

Yea sober'st men, it makes delicious,
To vertue dull, to vice ingenious.
But that first travell had no sympathy
With our since-travailes wretched cruelty,
Distilling sweat, and panting wanting wind,
Which was a scourge for *Adams* sinne assign'd.
　For *Edens* earth was then so fertile fat,
That he made only sweet assayes in that,
Of skilfull industry, and naked wrought
More for delight, then for the gaine he sought.
In briefe, it was a plesant exercise,
A labour like't, a paine much like the guise
Of cunning dancers, who although they skip,
Run, caper, vault, traverse, and turne, and trip,
From morne till even, at night againe full merry,
Renew their dance, of dancing never weary.
Or els of hunters, that with happy luck
Rousing betimes some often-breathed Buck,
Or goodly stag, their yelping hounds uncupple,
Wind lowd their horns, their whoops, and hallows dubble,
Spur-on and spare not, following their desire,
Themselves un-weary, though their Hacknies tyre.
But for in th'end of all their jolitie
Thear's found much stifnesse, sweat and vanity,
I rather match it to the pleasing paine
Of Angels pure, who ever sloath disdaine:
Or to the Sunnes calme course, who painles aye
About the welkin posteth night and day.

　　　Guillaume de Salluste, Sieur du Bartas (1544–90), *The Divine
　　　Weeks and Works*, 1578–84, tr. Joshua Sylvester, 1592–1608

Should man have wrought in Paradise?

　Yes: but not for need, and with trouble, as now: but with pleasure, to keep himself from idleness. Secondly, thereby to stir him up the more to contemplate heavenly things. And thirdly, to try the divers natures of grounds, and of those things that grow on the ground.

　　　Alexander Rosse (1591–1654), *The First Booke of Questions and
　　　Answers upon Genesis*, 1620

In the early Christian era, work was valued by monks and religious ascetics as a means of mortifying the flesh. But in the late medieval and early modern periods the positive value of work was increasingly stressed. Work was a religious duty and a means of protection against the sins that flowed from idleness. It was also a means of personal fulfilment. Human beings were born to labour and their work was a creative force.

For even when we were with you, this we commanded you, that if any would not work, neither should he eat.

For we hear that there are some which walk among you disorderly, working not at all, but are busybodies.

Now them that are such we command and exhort by our Lord Jesus Christ, that with quietness they work, and eat their own bread.

PAUL THE APOSTLE, First Epistle to the Thessalonians 3: 10

Idleness is the enemy of the soul. The brethren, therefore, must be occupied at stated hours in manual labour, and again at other hours in sacred reading. To this end we think that the times for each may be determined in the following manner. From Easter until September the 14th, the brethren shall start work in the morning and from the first hour until about the fourth do the tasks that have to be done. From the fourth hour until about the sixth let them apply themselves to reading. After the sixth hour, having left the table, let them rest on their beds in perfect silence, or if anyone wishes to read by himself, let him read so as not to disturb the others. Let Nones be said early, at the middle of the eighth hour; and let them again do what work has to be done until Vespers. But if the circumstances of the place or their poverty require them to gather the harvest themselves, let them not be discontented; for then are they truly monks when they live by the labour of their hands, like our fathers and the apostles. Yet let all things be done in moderation on account of the faint-hearted.

SAINT BENEDICT (c.480–c.547), *Rule for Monks*, c.530–40, tr. Justin McCann, 1970

The idle man grows dull in carnal desires, is cheerless in spiritual works, has no joy in the salvation of his soul, and does not become cheerful in helping his brother, but only craves and desires and performs everything in an idle fashion. *Acedia* corrupts the miserable mind which it inhabits with many misfortunes, which teach it many evil things. From it are born somnolence, laziness in good deeds, instability, roaming from place to place, lukewarmness in work, boredom, murmuring and vain talks. It is defeated by the soldier of Christ through reading, constancy in good deeds, the desire for the prize of future beatitude, confessing the temptation which is in the mind, stability of the place and of one's resolution, and the practice of some craft and work or prayer, and the perseverance in vigils. May the servant of God never be found idle! For the devil has greater difficulty in finding a spot for temptation in the man whom he finds employed in some good work, than in him whom he encounters idle and practising no good . . . Such then is the Christian who, when he arises in the morning from his bed of drunkenness, does not engage in any useful work, does not go to church to pray, does not hasten to hear the word of God, does not make an effort to give alms or to visit the sick or to help those who suffer injustice: but rather goes hunting abroad, or stirs quarrels and fights at home, or devotes himself to the dice or to useless stories and jokes while his food is being prepared by hardworking servants.

> RABANUS MAURUS, ABBOT OF FULDA (*c.*780–856), *De Ecclesiastica Disciplina*, 842–7, tr. Siegfried Wenzel, 1967

Should he be unable to work, either through infirmity or through his manner of praying or through some other employment of the mind or because God would have it so, then let him beg from folk, though always taking heed that he does not remain idle without praying. I say this because there are many whose teaching and practice is that there should be no working but always praying. As to this I say that unless a man has assurance from God in his soul that it is not his duty to work and tire his body, both to banish idleness and to procure necessities, then he should work and labour, honestly, in things that are honest and necessary to his neighbour, and useful to himself, according to the need.

> BLESSED SIMONE FIDATI (*c.*1290–1348), *The Christian Life*, 1333, tr. Walter Shewring, 1935

'Hear then,' said Hunger, 'and hold it in remembrance,
Let hounds-bread and horse-bread hold up the spirits
Of all bold beggars who should be bound to service.
Bring down their bellies with a bean diet,
And if they grumble and grutch, bid them go to labour.
He shall sup the sweeter who has so deserved it.'

*

'I would not grieve God,' said Piers, 'for all the goods about me.
Might I be sinless, and do as you say?' said Piers to Hunger.
'Yea, I assure you,' said Hunger, 'or else the Bible lies.
Go to the giant Genesis and the engendering of all things.
"In *sudore* and sorrow thou shalt earn thy meat,
And labour for thy livelihood," so our Lord commanded.
And Solomon says the same; I saw it in the Bible;
Piger prae frigore, shall not till his acre,
And so he shall bid and beg and none abet his hunger.

Matthew with the man's face maintains this teaching.
For *servus nequam* had a talent and would not trade with it,
And forfeited his lord's favour forever after.
The talent was taken from him, for he had not touched it,
And he took the talent who had ten to loan.
Then Holy Church heard the words of her master:
"He who hath shall have, and have help if need be,
And he who hath not shall not have; no man shall help him;
And what he thinks to have I will take from him."

Common Wit wills that each one labour,
In dyking or delving or travailing in prayers:
Contemplative life or active life are Christ's commandments.
The psalter says in the psalm *Beati omnes*
That he who feeds himself with his faithful labour
Is blessed by the Book in body and in spirit:
Labores manuum tuarum, etc.'

> WILLIAM LANGLAND (1330?–1386?), *The Vision of Piers Plowman*
> (*c.*1367–86), tr. Henry W. Wells, 1938

LUPSET: Master Pole, meseemeth you examine this matter somewhat too shortly, as though you would have all men to labour, to go to the plough, and exercise some craft: which is not necessary. For our mother the ground is so plenteous and bountiful, by the goodness of God and of nature given to her, that with little labour and tillage she will sufficiently nourish mankind none otherwise than she doth all beasts, fishes and fowls which are bred and brought up upon her, to whom we see she ministereth food with little labour or none, but of her own friendly benignity. Wherefore if a few of our people busy themself and labour therein, it is sufficient; the rest may live in triumph, at liberty and ease, free from all bodily labour and pain.

POLE: This is spoken, Master Lupset, even as though you judged man to be born for to live in idleness and pleasure, all thing referring and applying thereto. But, Sir, it is nothing so; but, contrary, he is born to labour and travail (after the opinion of the wise and ancient antiquity) none otherwise than a bird to fly, and not to live (as Homer saith some do) as an unprofitable weight and burden of the earth. For man is born to be as a governor, ruler and diligent tiller and inhabitant of this earth, as, some by labour of body to procure things necessary for the maintenance of man's life, some by wisdom and policy to keep the rest of the multitude in good order and civility. So that none be born to this idleness and vanity, to the which the most part of our people is much given and bent—but all to exercise themself in some fashion of life convenient to the dignity and nature of man.

> THOMAS STARKEY (1499?–1538), *A Dialogue between Reginald Pole and Thomas Lupset*, c.1533–6

In the reign of Henry VIII the bishops compiled a book of Christian doctrine called The Godly and Pious Institution of a Christian Man *(1537). One section in it read thus:*

And to them, to whom thou dost vouchsafe to give more than their own portion necessary for their vocation and degree, give thy grace, that they may be thy diligent and true dispensators and stewards, to distribute that they have over and above that is necessary, considering their estate and degree, to them that have need of it. For so, good Lord, thou dost provide for thy poor people that have nothing, by them which have of thy gift sufficient to relieve themselves and others.

When he saw the draft, the King ordered that it should be qualified by the insertion of the following:

But one thing herein is to be noted, that there be many folk which had lever live by the graffte of bekyng [begging] sloughfully than other work or labour for their living; truly, thcsc be none of them of whom before we spoke of; for we think it right necessary that such should be compelled by one means or other to serve the world with their bodily labour, thinking it small charity to bestow otherwise alms on them.

Our first father Adam toiled in the earth, according to God's commandment, and so gat his living. Cain was a ploughman. Abel was a shepherd. Jubal exercised music. Tubalcain was a smith, and a graver in metal. Noe was a planter of vineyards. Abraham, Lot, Isaac, and Jacob were ploughmen and shepherds. Joseph was a magistrate, and a public minister in the commonweal of Egypt, under king Pharao. Moses was a shepherd, and kept the sheep of Jethro his father-in-law, priest of Madian. The children of Israel got their living with hard and painful labour in Egypt, under king Pharao. David, before he was anointed king of Israel, was a shepherd. All the priests and Levites of the old law, every man according to his vocation, laboured by giving attendance in the temple, by killing of beasts, and offering sacrifices, by studying the scriptures of God, and teaching the same unto the people, &c. Amos the prophet was one of the shepherds at Therna. Abacuck the prophet travailed in husbandry. Christ himself was a carpenter. The apostles of Christ were fishers. Paul laboured with his own hands, and gat both his own living, and others' that were with him. St Luke was a physician, and (as some writeth) a painter also. Aquila was a maker of tents, of the which occupation St Paul was. Simon, St Peter's host, was a tanner. Dorcas, that virtuous woman, made garments with her own hands, and gave them to the poor. There was no good and godly man even from the beginning of the world, which hath not practised somewhat to get his living, and lived in some certain honest and godly vocation, wherein he might with a good conscience eat his bread.

THOMAS BECON (1512–67), *The Fortress of the Faithfull,* 1550

But we must labour and travail; as long as we be in this world we must be occupied.

> HUGH LATIMER (1492?–1555), 'The Third Sermon upon the Lord's Prayer', 1552

Passion.
    Sun, rise not yet then, let me rest a while,
For when thou risest, I must fall to toil;
The day, which gives to other men delight,
That is my mill to grind in till 'tis night.

    Sweet Sun, then being risen, speed thy motion
To cast thyself into the Western Ocean,
That when thy beams are vanished in the West,
The gentle night may call me home to rest.

    Long-look'd-for darkness, come then ease my sorrow,
Let me put off my yoke until tomorrow.
Refresh me with thy comforts while I stay,
I may have strength to labour when 'tis day.

*

    There, there [on Earth] I toil and labour like a brute,
I plough and sow, but others reap the fruit;
I dig for ore, but seldom touch the money,
I there am stung, but others suck the honey.

*

Discretion.
    But be content, 'tis not thy imperfection
In form, or substance, binds thee to subjection,
But only He that formed all doth say
Let some men rule, and other some obey

*

    Or why shouldst at thy working state repine?
When 'tis the state that God doth all enjoin:
When man would needs the fruit forbidden eat,
God tied him straight to labour for his meat.

    Then work, it is the will of thy Creator.
Besides, it makes thee eat, and sleep the better,
It preserves health, subdues the rebel sense,
And give much scope unto intelligence.

> EDWARD CALVER (*fl.* 1641–9), *Passion and Discretion in Youth, and Age,* 1641

The Country Parson hath not only taken a particular survey of the faults of his own parish, but a general also of the diseases of the time, that, so when his occasions carry him abroad, or bring strangers to him, he may be the better armed to encounter them. The great and national sin of this land he esteems to be idleness; great in itself, and great in consequence: for when men have nothing to do, then they fall to drink, to steal, to whore, to scoff, to revile, to all sorts of gamings. Come, say they, we have nothing to do, let's go to the tavern, or to the stews, or what not? Wherefore the parson strongly opposeth this sin, wheresoever he goes. And because idleness is twofold, the one in having no calling, the other in walking carelessly in our calling, he first represents to every body the necessity of a vocation. The reason of this assertion is taken from the nature of man, wherein God hath placed two great instruments, reason in the soul, and a hand in the body, as engagements of working; so that even in paradise man had a calling, and how much more out of paradise, when the evils which he is now subject unto, may be prevented, or diverted by reasonable employment. Besides, every gift or ability is a talent to be accounted for, and to be improved to our Master's advantage. Yet is it also a debt to our country to have a calling; and it concerns the commonwealth, that none should be idle, but all busied. Lastly, riches are the blessing of God, and the great instrument of doing admirable good; therefore all are to procure them honestly and seasonably when they are not better employed.

GEORGE HERBERT (1593–1633), *A Priest to the Temple*, 1652

My labour will sustain me.

JOHN MILTON (1608–74), *Paradise Lost*, 1667

Against Idleness and Mischief

I

How doth the little busy Bee
Improve each shining Hour,
And gather Honey all the day
From every opening Flower!

II

How skilfully she builds her Cell!
How neat she spreads the Wax!
And labours hard to store it well
With the sweet Food she makes.

III

In Works of Labour or of Skill
I would be busy too:
For *Satan* finds some Mischief still
For idle Hands to do.

IV

In Books, or Work, or healthful Play
Let my first Years be past,
That I may give for every Day
Some good Account at last.

Isaac Watts (1674–1748), 1715

I have a Boy but sixteen Years of Age, that thrashes me Wheat, Barley, Oats, Pease, Beans, or Thetches; and who, in October 1743, thrashed me out five Bushels of Hog-pease in one Day, and threw them out of the Chaff; and, tho' he is my Son, I favour him not, in Respect of Confinement and Labour; but, for his Encouragement, I give him small Wages: By this Means he is always in his Sphere, when he works hard. I have another Son, my Ploughman, that is so naturalised to Fatigue, by bringing him up in this Manner, that, if he is kept idle but one Day in the House, he protests it is more disagreeable to him, than Labouring all that Time.

William Ellis, farmer, of Little Gaddesden, Herts. (d. 1758), *The Modern Husbandman*, 1744

It is certain that any wild wish or vain imagination never takes such firm possession of the mind, as when it is found empty and unoccupied. The old peripatetic principle, that 'Nature abhors a Vacuum,' may be properly applied to the intellect, which will embrace any thing, however absurd or criminal, rather than be wholly without an object. Perhaps every man may date the predominance of those desires that disturb his life and contaminate his conscience from some unhappy hour when too much leisure exposed him to their incursions; for he has lived with little observation either on himself or others, who does not know that to be idle is to be vicious.

Samuel Johnson (1709–84), *The Rambler*, 8 Jan. 1751

No holidays were allowed, lest the habit of work should be broken, and a taste for idleness acquired.

John Stuart Mill (1806–73), on his childhood, *Autobiography*, 1873

Human society was envisaged as an association, each of whose members had a different role to perform. In the early Middle Ages it was said that there were three estates: the people, who cultivated the soil; the knights, who protected them; and the clergy, who prayed for their souls. This distinction was obsolete even when it was coined, for it took no account of the developing world of trade. As society grew increasingly complex, the number of occupations multiplied. By the eighteenth

*century, theorists had come to recognize that productivity rested upon an ever
expanding division of labour.*

Right so in the Church beeth needful these three offices: priesthood, knighthood [and] labourers. [To] priests [it falleth to] c[ut] away the void branches
of sins with the sword of their tongues. To knights it falleth to let wrongs and
thefts to be do[ne] and to maintain God's law and them that be teachers
thereof; and also to keep the land from enemies of other lands. And to
labourers it falleth to travail bodily and with their sore sweat getten out of the
earth [b]odily livelihood for them and for other parties. And these states
beeth also needful to the Church that none may well be without other. For if
priesthood lacked, the people for default for knowing of God's law should
wax wild on vices and die ghostly. And if knighthood lacked and men to rule
the people by law and hardness, thieves and enemies should so increase that
no man should live in peace. And if labourers were not, both priests and
knights must become acremen and herds, and else they should for default of
bodily sustenance die.

THOMAS WIMBLEDON (*fl.* 1386–9), '*Redde Racionem Villicacionis Tue*',
sermon preached in 1388

'This is a wild way without a leader
To follow each foot,' said the folk together.
But Perkin, the Plowman, answered, 'By Saint Peter,
I have half an acre to harrow by the highway!
Had I harrowed this half acre and sown it after,
I would go with you gladly and guide you thither.'

'That will be a long delay,' said a lady in a wimple;
'At what shall we women work in the meantime?'
'Some must sow the sack,' said Piers, 'to keep the seed from spilling.
And you lovely ladies with your long fingers,
Who have silk and sendal to sow when you are able,
Make chasubles for chaplains and for the church's honour.
Wives and widows, spin wool and linen;
Make cloth, I counsel you, and instruct your daughters.
Note how the needy and the naked are lying.
Get them some clothing, for truth commands it.
I shall lend them a livelihood unless the land fail us,
Both meat and bread for rich and poor folk,

let] prevent   *acremen*] cultivators

As long as I live, for the Lord's love in heaven.
And let all manner of men whom meat nourishes
Help those to work well who win your living!'

'By Christ,' quoth a knight, 'your command is honest!
But truly no one taught me how a team is driven;
But as I can,' quoth he, 'by Christ, I will do it!'
'By Saint Paul,' said Perkin, 'you proffer yourself so fairly,
That I shall serve and sweat and sow for us together,
And labour for your love as long as I am living,
In provision that you protect plowmen and churchmen
From wasters and the wicked by whom this world is ruined.
Go and hunt hardily for hares and foxes,
For boars and badgers that break down my hedges.
Find good falcons to fetch wild fowl,
For they come to my croft and crop my harvest.'

Then the knight commenced a courteous answer:
'To my power, Piers,' he said, 'I promise truly
To fulfil this offer though I should fight for you.
For as long as you live let me maintain you.'

    WILLIAM LANGLAND (1330?–86?), *The Vision of Piers Plowman,*
    *c.*1367–86, tr. Henry W. Wells, 1938

        Therefore doth heaven divide
The state of man in divers functions,
Setting endeavour in continual motion;
To which is fixed, as an aim or butt,
Obedience: for so work the honey-bees,
Creatures that by a rule in nature teach
The act of order to a peopled kingdom.
They have a king and officers of sorts;
Where some, like magistrates, correct at home,
Others, like merchants, venture trade abroad,
Others, like soldiers, armed in their stings,
Make boot upon the summer's velvet buds,
Which pillage they with merry march bring home
To the tent-royal of their emperor;
Who, busied in his majesty, surveys
The singing masons building roofs of gold,
The civil citizens kneading up the honey,
The poor mechanic porters crowding in
Their heavy burdens at his narrow gate,

The sad-eyed justice, with his surly hum
Delivering o'er to executors pale
The lazy yawning drone.

WILLIAM SHAKESPEARE (1564–1616), *King Henry V*, pr. 1600

It is evident, that, however urged by a sense of necessity, and a desire of convenience, or favoured by any advantages of situation and policy, a people can make no great progress in cultivating the arts of life, until they have separated, and committed to different persons, the several tasks, which require a peculiar skill and attention. The savage, or the barbarian, who must build and plant, and fabricate for himself, prefers, in the interval of great alarms and fatigues, the enjoyments of sloth to the improvement of his fortune: he is, perhaps, by the diversity of his wants, discouraged from industry; or, by his divided attention, prevented from acquiring skill in the management of any particular subject.

The enjoyment of peace, however, and the prospect of being able to exchange one commodity for another, turns, by degrees, the hunter and the warrior into a tradesman and a merchant. The accidents which distribute the means of subsistence unequally, inclination, and favourable opportunities, assign the different occupations of men; and a sense of utility leads them, without end, to subdivide their professions.

The artist finds, that the more he can confine his attention to a particular part of any work, his productions are the more perfect, and grow under his hands in the greater quantities. Every undertaker in manufacture finds, that the more he can subdivide the tasks of his workmen, and the more hands he can employ on separate articles, the more are his expences diminished, and his profits increased. The consumer too requires, in every kind of commodity, a workmanship more perfect than hands employed on a variety of subjects can produce; and the progress of commerce is but a continued subdivision of the mechanical arts.

Every craft may ingross the whole of a man's attention, and has a mystery which must be studied or learned by a regular apprenticeship. Nations of tradesmen come to consist of members who, beyond their own particular trade, are ignorant of all human affairs, and who may contribute to the preservation and enlargement of their commonwealth, without making its interest an object of their regard or attention. Every individual is distinguished by his calling, and has a place to which he is fitted. The savage, who knows no distinction but that of his merit, of his sex, or of his species, and to whom his community is the sovereign object of affection, is astonished to find, that in a scene of this nature, his being a man does not qualify him for any station whatever: he flies to the woods with amazement, distaste, and aversion.

> ADAM FERGUSON (1723–1816), *An Essay on the History of Civil Society*, 1767

For in so vast a City *Manufactures* will beget one another, and each *Manufacture* will be divided into as many parts as possible, whereby the Work of each *Artisan* will be simple and easie; As for Example. In the making of a *Watch*, If one Man shall make the *Wheels*, another the *Spring*, another shall Engrave the *Dial-plate*, and another shall make the *Cases*, then the *Watch* will be better and cheaper, than if the whole Work be put upon any one Man.

> SIR WILLIAM PETTY (1623–87), *Several Essays in Political Arithmetick*, 1699

The greatest improvement in the productive powers of labour, and the greater part of the skill, dexterity, and judgment with which it is any where directed, or applied, seem to have been the effects of the division of labour.

*

To take an example, therefore, from a very trifling manufacture; but one in which the division of labour has been very often taken notice of, the trade of the pin-maker; a workman not educated to this business (which the division of labour has rendered a distinct trade), nor acquainted with the use of the machinery employed in it (to the invention of which the same division of labour has probably given occasion), could scarce, perhaps, with his utmost industry, make one pin in a day, and certainly could not make twenty. But in the way in which this business is now carried on, not only the whole work is a peculiar trade, but it is divided into a number of branches, of which the greater part are likewise peculiar trades. One man draws out the wire, another straights it, a third cuts it, a fourth points it, a fifth grinds it at the top for receiving the head; to make the head requires two or three distinct operations; to put it on, is a peculiar business, to whiten the pins is another; it is even a trade by itself to put them into the paper; and the important business of making a pin is, in this manner, divided into about eighteen distinct operations, which, in some manufactories, are all performed by distinct hands, though in others the same man will sometimes perform two or three of them. I have seen a small manufactory of this kind where ten men only were employed, and where some of them consequently performed two or three distinct operations. But though they were very poor, and therefore but indifferently accommodated with the necessary machinery, they could, when they exerted themselves, make among them about twelve pounds of pins in a day. There are in a pound upwards of four thousand pins of a middling size. Those ten persons, therefore, could make among them upwards of forty-eight thousand pins in a day. Each person, therefore, making a tenth part of forty-eight thousand pins, might be considered as making four thousand eight hundred pins in a day. But if they had all wrought separately and independently, and without any of them having been educated to this peculiar business, they certainly could not each of them have made twenty, perhaps not one pin in a day; that is, certainly, not the two hundred and fortieth, perhaps not the four thousand eight hundredth part of what they are at present capable of performing, in consequence of a proper division and combination of their different operations

> ADAM SMITH (1723–90), *An Inquiry into the Nature and Causes of the Wealth of Nations*, 1776

When I look round upon those who are thus variously exerting their qualifications, I cannot but admire the secret concatenation of society, that links together the great and the mean, the illustrious and the obscure; and consider with benevolent satisfaction, that no man, unless his body or mind be totally disabled, has need to suffer the mortification of seeing himself useless or burdensome to the community: he that will diligently labour, in whatever occupation, will deserve the sustenance which he obtains, and the protection which he enjoys; and may lie down every night with the pleasing consciousness of having contributed something to the happiness of life.

> SAMUEL JOHNSON (1709–84), *The Adventurer*, 26 June 1753

As the range of possible employments multiplied, moralists insisted that the important thing was to have a calling of some kind. The nature of the work was less important, for all lawful occupations were meritorious.

Now if thou compare deed to deed, there is difference betwixt washing of dishes and preaching of the word of God; but as touching to please God, none at all.

> WILLIAM TYNDALE (c.1495–1536), *The Parable of the Wicked Mammon*, 1527

The Elixir

Teach me, my God and King,
In all things thee to see,
And what I do in any thing,
To do it as for thee:

Not rudely, as a beast,
  To runne into an action;
But still to make thee prepossest,
  And give it his perfection.

A man that looks on glasse,
  On it may stay his eye;
Or if he pleaseth, through it passe,
  And then the heav'n espie.

All may of thee partake:
  Nothing can be so mean,
Which with his tincture (for thy sake)
  Will not grow bright and clean.

A servant with this clause
  Makes drudgerie divine:
Who sweeps a room, as for thy laws,
  Makes that and th' action fine.

This is the famous stone
  That turneth all to gold:
For that which God doth touch and own
  Cannot for lesse be told.

GEORGE HERBERT (1593–1633), 1633

How shamed ladies'd be to have hands and arms like mine and how weak they'd be to do my work and how shocked to touch the dirty things even what i black my whole hands with every day—yet such things must be done and the lady's'd be the first to cry out if they was to find nobody to do it for 'em—so the lowest work i think is honourable in itself and the poor drudge is honourable too providing her mind isn't coarse and low as her work, both cause its useful and for be'en content with the station she is placed in.

HANNAH CULLWICK (1833–1909), *Diaries*, 1864

The Glory of the Garden

Our England is a garden that is full of stately views,
Of borders, beds and shrubberies and lawns and avenues,
With statues on the terraces and peacocks strutting by;
But the Glory of the Garden lies in more than meets the eye.

For where the old thick laurels grow, along the thin red wall,
You find the tool- and potting-sheds which are the heart of all;
The cold-frames and the hot-houses, the dungpits and the tanks,
The rollers, carts and drain-pipes, with the barrows and the planks.

And there you'll see the gardeners, the men and 'prentice boys
Told off to do as they are bid and do it without noise;
For, except when seeds are planted and we shout to scare the birds,
The Glory of the Garden it abideth not in words.

And some can pot begonias and some can bud a rose,
And some are hardly fit to trust with anything that grows;
But they can roll and trim the lawns and sift the sand and loam,
For the Glory of the Garden occupieth all who come.

Our England is a garden, and such gardens are not made
By singing:—'Oh, how beautiful!' and sitting in the shade,
While better men than we go out and start their working lives
At grubbing weeds from gravel-paths with broken dinner-knives.

There's not a pair of legs so thin, there's not a head so thick,
There's not a hand so weak and white, nor yet a heart so sick,
But it can find some needful job that's crying to be done,
For the Glory of the Garden glorifieth every one.

Then seek your job with thankfulness and work till further orders,
If it's only netting strawberries or killing slugs on borders;
And when your back stops aching and your hands begin to harden,
You will find yourself a partner in the Glory of the Garden.

Oh, Adam was a gardener, and God who made him sees
That half a proper gardener's work is done upon his knees,
So when your work is finished, you can wash your hands and pray
For the Glory of the Garden, that it may not pass away!
And the Glory of the Garden it shall never pass away!

Rudyard Kipling (1865–1936), 1911

In the nineteenth century the doctrine that work was a sacred duty incumbent upon everyone reached its apotheosis.

For there is a perennial nobleness, and even sacredness, in Work. Were he never so benighted, forgetful of his high calling, there is always hope in a man that actually and earnestly works: in Idleness alone is there perpetual despair. Work, never so Mammonish, mean, *is* in communication with Nature; the real desire to get Work done will itself lead one more and more to truth, to Nature's appointments and regulations which are truth.

The latest Gospel in this world is, Know thy work and do it. 'Know thyself': long enough has that poor 'self' of thine tormented thee; thou wilt never get to 'know' it, I believe! Think it not thy business, this of knowing thyself; thou art an unknowable individual: know what thou canst work at; and work at it, like a Hercules! That will be thy better plan.

It has been written, 'an endless significance lies in Work'; a man perfects himself by working. Foul jungles are cleared away, fair seed-fields rise instead, and stately cities; and withal the man himself first ceases to be a jungle and foul unwholesome desert thereby. Consider how, even in the meanest sorts of Labour, the whole soul of a man is composed into a kind of real harmony, the instant he sets himself to work! Doubt, Desire, Sorrow, Remorse, Indignation, Despair itself, all these like helldogs lie beleaguering the soul of the poor day-worker, as of every man: but he bends himself with free valour against his task, and all these are stilled, all these shrink murmuring far off into their caves. The man is now a man. The blessed glow of Labour in him, is it not as purifying fire, wherein all poison is burnt up, and of sour smoke itself there is made bright blessed flame! . . .

All true Work is sacred; in all true Work, were it but true hand-labour, there is something of divineness. Labour, wide as the Earth, has its summit in Heaven. Sweat of the brow; and up from that to sweat of the brain, sweat of the heart; which includes all Kepler calculations, Newton meditations, all Sciences, all spoken Epics, all acted Heroisms, Martyrdoms,—up to that 'Agony of bloody sweat,' which all men have called divine! O brother, if this is not 'worship,' then I say, the more pity for worship; for this is the noblest thing yet discovered under God's sky. Who art thou that complainest of thy life of toil? Complain not. Look up, my wearied brother; see thy fellow Workmen there, in God's Eternity; surviving there, they alone surviving: sacred Band of the Immortals, celestial Bodyguard of the Empire of Mankind. Even in the weak Human Memory they survive so long, as saints, as heroes, as gods; they alone surviving; peopling, they alone, the unmeasured solitudes of Time!

THOMAS CARLYLE (1795–1881), *Past and Present*, 1843

But do your work, and I shall know you. Do your work, and you shall reinforce yourself.

RALPH WALDO EMERSON (1803–82), 'Self-Reliance', 1841

'You're the waxwork child, are you not?' said Miss Monflathers.

'Yes, ma'am,' replied Nell, colouring deeply, for the young ladies had collected about her, and she was the centre on which all eyes were fixed.

'And don't you think you must be a very wicked little child,' said Miss Monflathers, who was of rather uncertain temper, and lost no opportunity of impressing moral truths upon the tender minds of the young ladies, 'to be a waxwork child at all?'

Poor Nell had never viewed her position in this light, and not knowing what to say, remained silent, blushing more deeply than before.

'Don't you know,' said Miss Monflathers, 'that it's very naughty and un-feminine, and a perversion of the properties wisely and benignantly trans-mitted to us, with expansive powers to be roused from their dormant state through the medium of cultivation?'

The two teachers murmured their respectful approval of this home-thrust, and looked at Nell as though they would have said that there indeed Miss Monflathers had hit her very hard. Then they smiled and glanced at Miss Monflathers, and then, their eyes meeting, they exchanged looks which plainly said that each considered herself smiler-in-ordinary to Miss Monflathers, and regarded the other as having no right to smile, and that her so doing was an act of presumption and impertinence.

'Don't you feel how naughty it is of you,' resumed Miss Monflathers, 'to be a waxwork child, when you might have the proud consciousness of assisting, to the extent of your infant powers, the manufactures of your country; of improving your mind by the constant contemplation of the steam-engine; and of earning a comfortable and independent subsistence of from two-and-ninepence to three shillings per week? Don't you know that the harder you are at work, the happier you are?'

' "How doth the little—" ' murmured one of the teachers, in quotation from Doctor Watts.

'Eh?' said Miss Monflathers, turning smartly round. 'Who said that?'

Of course the teacher who had not said it, indicated the rival who had, whom Miss Monflathers frowningly requested to hold her peace; by that means throwing the informing teacher into raptures of joy.

'The little busy bee,' said Miss Monflathers, drawing herself up, 'is applica-ble only to genteel children.

> "In books, or work, or healthful play"

is quite right as far as they are concerned; and the work means painting on velvet, fancy needlework, or embroidery. In such cases as these,' pointing to Nell, with her parasol, 'and in the case of all poor people's children, we should read it thus:

> "In work, work, work. In work alway
> Let my first years be past,
> That I may give for ev'ry day
> Some good account at last." '

A deep hum of applause rose not only from the two teachers, but from all the pupils, who were equally astonished to hear Miss Monflathers improvising after this brilliant style; for although she had been long known as a politician, she had never appeared before as an original poet. Just then somebody happened to discover that Nell was crying, and all eyes were again turned towards her.

CHARLES DICKENS (1812–70), *The Old Curiosity Shop*, 1841

Try and reconcile your mind thoroughly to the idea that this world, if we would be well and do well in it, is a world of work and not of idleness. This idea will, when heartily embraced, become like a part of yourself, and you will feel that you would on no account have it torn from you.

WILLIAM EWART GLADSTONE (1809–98), letter to his son Willy, 12 Mar. 1856

'But I like business,' said Pancks, getting on a little faster. 'What's a man made for?'

'For nothing else?' said Clennam.

Pancks put the counter question, 'What else?' It packed up, in the smallest compass, a weight that had rested on Clennam's life; and he made no answer.

'That's what I ask our weekly tenants,' said Pancks. 'Some of 'em will pull long faces to me, and say, Poor as you see us, master, we're always grinding, drudging, toiling, every minute we're awake. I say to them, What else are you made for? It shuts them up. They haven't a word to answer. What else are you made for? That clinches it.'

'Ah dear, dear, dear!' sighed Clennam.

'Here am I,' said Pancks, pursuing his argument with the weekly tenant. 'What else do you suppose I think I am made for? Nothing. Rattle me out of bed early, set me going, give me as short a time as you like to bolt my meals in, and keep me at it. Keep me always at it, and I'll keep you always at it, you keep somebody else always at it. There you are with the Whole Duty of Man in a commercial country.'

CHARLES DICKENS (1812–70), *Little Dorrit*, 1857

[The March girls experiment with a life of idleness.]

'May we, mother?' asked Meg, turning to Mrs March, who sat sewing, in what they called 'Marmee's corner.'

'You may try your experiment for a week, and see how you like it. I think by Saturday night you will find that all play and no work is as bad as all work and no play.'

'Oh, dear, no! it will be delicious, I'm sure,' said Meg complacently.

'I now propose a toast, as my "friend and pardner, Sairy Gamp," says. Fun for ever, and no grubbing!' cried Jo, rising, glass in hand, as the lemonade went round.

They all drank it merrily, and began the experiment by lounging for the rest of the day. Next morning, Meg did not appear till ten o'clock; her solitary breakfast did not taste nice, and the room seemed lonely and untidy; for Jo had not filled the vases, Beth had not dusted, and Amy's books lay scattered about. Nothing was neat and pleasant but 'Marmee's corner,' which looked as usual; and there Meg sat, to 'rest and read,' which meant yawn, and imagine what pretty summer dresses she would get with her salary. Jo spent the morning on the river, with Laurie, and the afternoon reading and crying over 'The Wide, Wide World,' up in the apple-tree. Beth began by rummaging everything out of the big closet, where her family resided; but, getting tired before half done, she left her establishment topsy-turvy, and went to her music, rejoicing that she had no dishes to wash. Amy arranged her bower, put on her best white frock, smoothed her curls, and sat down to draw, under the honey-suckles, hoping some one would see and inquire who the young artist was. As no one appeared but an inquisitive daddy-long-legs, who examined her work with interest, she went to walk, got caught in a shower, and came home dripping.

At tea-time they compared notes, and all agreed that it had been a delight-ful, though unusually long day. Meg, who went shopping in the afternoon, and got a 'sweet blue muslin,' had discovered, after she had cut the breadths off, that it wouldn't wash, which mishap made her slightly cross. Jo had burnt the skin off her nose boating, and got a raging headache by reading too long. Beth was worried by the confusion of her closet, and the difficulty of learning three or four songs at once; and Amy deeply regretted the damage done her frock, for Katy Brown's party was to be the next day; and now, like Flora McFlimsey, she had 'nothing to wear'. But these were mere trifles; and they assured their mother that the experiment was working finely. She smiled, said nothing, and, with Hannah's help, did their neglected work, keeping home pleasant, and the domestic machinery running smoothly. It was astonishing what a peculiar and uncomfortable state of things was produced by the 'rest-ing and revelling' process. The days kept getting longer and longer; the weather was unusually variable, and so were tempers; an unsettled feeling possessed every one, and Satan found plenty of mischief for the idle hands to do. As the height of luxury, Meg put out some of her sewing, and then found time hang so heavily that she fell to snipping and spoiling her clothes, in her attempts to furbish them up à la Moffat. Jo read till her eyes gave out, and she was sick of books; got so fidgety that even good-natured Laurie had a quarrel with her, and so reduced in spirits that she desperately wished she had gone with Aunt March. Beth got on pretty well, for she was constantly forgetting that it was to be *all play, and no work*, and fell back into her old ways now and then; but something in the air affected her, and, more than once, her tranquillity was much disturbed; so much so, that, on one occasion, she actually shook poor dear Joanna, and told her she was 'a fright.' Amy fared worst of all, for her resources were small; and, when her sisters left her to amuse and care for herself, she soon found that accomplished and important little self a great burden. She didn't like dolls, fairy-tales were childish, and one couldn't draw all the time; tea-parties didn't amount to much, neither did picnics, unless very well conducted. 'If one could have a fine house, full of nice girls, or go travelling, the summer would be delightful; but to stay at home with three selfish sisters and a grown-up boy was enough to try the patience of a Boaz,' complained Miss Malaprop, after several days devoted to pleasure, fretting, and *ennui*.

No one would own that they were tired of the experiment; but, by Friday night, each acknowledged to herself that she was glad the week was nearly done. Hoping to impress the lesson more deeply, Mrs March, who had a good deal of humour, resolved to finish off the trial in an appropriate manner; so she gave Hannah a holiday, and let the girls enjoy the full effect of the play system.

When they got up on Saturday morning, there was no fire in the kitchen, no breakfast in the dining-room, and no mother anywhere to be seen.

'Mercy on us! what *has* happened?' cried Jo, staring about her in dismay.

Meg ran upstairs, and soon came back again, looking relieved, but rather bewildered, and a little ashamed.

'Mother isn't sick, only very tired, and she says she is going to stay quietly in her room all day, and let us do the best we can. It's a very queer thing for her to do, she doesn't act a bit like herself; but she says it has been a hard week for her, so we mustn't grumble, but take care of ourselves.'

'That's easy enough, and I like the idea; I'm aching for something to do— that is, some new amusement, you know,' added Jo quickly.

In fact it *was* an immense relief to them all to have a little work, and they took hold with a will, but soon realised the truth of Hannah's saying, 'Housekeeping ain't no joke.' There was plenty of food in the larder, and, while Beth and Amy set the table, Meg and Jo got breakfast, wondering, as they did so, why servants ever talked about hard work.

'I shall take some up to mother, though she said we were not to think of her, for she'd take care of herself,' said Meg, who presided, and felt quite matronly behind the teapot.

So a tray was fitted out before any one began, and taken up, with the cook's compliments. The boiled tea was very bitter, the omelette scorched, and the biscuits speckled with saleratus; but Mrs March received her repast with thanks, and laughed heartily over it after Jo was gone.

'Poor little souls, they will have a hard time, I'm afraid; but they won't suffer, and it will do them good,' she said, producing the more palatable viands with which she had provided herself, and disposing of the bad breakfast, so that their feelings might not be hurt,—a motherly little deception, for which they were grateful.

[At the end of the day, which has been notable for the catastrophic failure of Jo's attempt at cooking for a dinner-party and the death, from neglect, of Pip the canary, the girls gather on the porch.]

'What a dreadful day this has been!' began Jo, usually the first to speak.

'It has seemed shorter than usual, but *so* uncomfortable,' said Meg.

'Not a bit like home,' added Amy.

'It can't seem so without Marmee and little Pip,' sighed Beth, glancing, with full eyes, at the empty cage above her head.

'Here's mother, dear, and you shall have another bird to-morrow, if you want it.'

As she spoke, Mrs March came and took her place among them, looking as if her holiday had not been much pleasanter than theirs.

'Are you satisfied with your experiment, girls, or do you want another week of it?' she asked, as Beth nestled up to her, and the rest turned toward her with brightening faces, as flowers turn toward the sun.

'I don't!' cried Jo decidedly.

'Nor I,' echoed the others.

'You think, then, that it is better to have a few duties, and live a little for others, do you?'

'Lounging and larking doesn't pay,' observed Jo, shaking her head. 'I'm tired of it, and mean to go to work at something right off.'

'Suppose you learn plain cooking; that's a useful accomplishment, which no woman should be without,' said Mrs March, laughing inaudibly at the recollection of Jo's dinner-party; for she had met Miss Crocker, and heard her account of it.

'Mother, did you go away and let everything be, just to see how we'd get on?' cried Meg, who had had suspicions all day.

'Yes; I wanted you to see how the comfort of all depends on each doing her share faithfully. While Hannah and I did your work, you got on pretty well, though I don't think you were very happy or amiable; so I thought, as a little lesson, I would show you what happens when every one thinks only of herself. Don't you feel that it is pleasanter to help one another, to have daily duties which make leisure sweet when it comes, and to bear and forbear, that home may be comfortable and lovely to us all?'

'We do, mother, we do!' cried the girls.

'Then let me advise you to take up your little burdens again; for though they seem heavy sometimes, they are good for us, and lighten as we learn to carry them. Work is wholesome, and there is plenty for every one; it keeps us from *ennui* and mischief, is good for health and spirits, and gives us a sense of power and independence better than money or fashion.'

'We'll work like bees, and love it too; see if we don't!' said Jo. 'I'll learn plain cooking for my holiday task; and the next dinner-party I have shall be a success.'

'I'll make the set of shirts for father, instead of letting you do it, Marmee. I can and I will, though I'm not fond of sewing; that will be better than fussing over my own things, which are plenty nice enough as they are,' said Meg.

'I'll do my lessons every day, and not spend so much time with my music and dolls. I am a stupid thing, and ought to be studying, not playing,' was Beth's resolution; while Amy followed their example, by heroically declaring, 'I shall learn to make buttonholes, and attend to my parts of speech.'

'Very good! then I am quite satisfied with the experiment, and fancy that we shall not have to repeat it; only don't go to the other extreme, and delve like slaves. Have regular hours for work and play; make each day both useful and pleasant, and prove that you understand the worth of time by employing it well. Then youth will be delightful, old age will bring few regrets, and life become a beautiful success, in spite of poverty.'

'We'll remember, mother!' and they did.

LOUISA MAY ALCOTT (1832–88), *Little Women*, 1867

The natural fruits of ability and hard work are careers distinguished above those of ordinary folk. Perhaps Jowett, as he grew older, tended to reckon each distinguished career as one more item in the statistical record of Balliol successes. Perhaps maintenance of the flow seemed to become an object in itself; the machine to be more important than the goods it delivered. I do not, myself, think that this was so; but that was how it looked to his detractors in other Oxford colleges, where the ever-mounting prestige of Balliol bred envy and not a little gall. As I see it, the heart of the matter lay in the living tradition of strenuous work which he succeeded in communicating to generations of Balliol undergraduates and supported by his own ceaseless example.

Many of these undergraduates, but for Jowett, would have idled through their critical three or four years at Oxford. How did he contrive to persuade them into doing what they had never intended to do? A clue is given by his advice to one rich young idler. 'You are a fool' he said to Walter Morrison. 'You must be sick of idling. It is too late for you to do much. But the class matters nothing. What does matter is the sense of power which comes from steady working.'

'The sense of *power*'?

What did he mean by that phrase, which hit Morrison so hard that it changed his whole life? Not mere power over the lives of others; money and position could provide that. Nor, even, power to stimulate the minds of other people. That was Jowett's own form of power; not communicable by teaching or example. What he meant, and what Morrison knew him to mean, was power over self: power in a man to control and direct his own life, instead of drifting on the currents of fortune and self-indulgence. It was a cunning lure, skilfully used.

GEOFFREY FABER (1889–1961), *Jowett*, 1957

Now I will conclude by, in my turn, offering you a faith, by beseeching you indeed to put your trust in work. Toil, young men, toil! I am quite conscious of the triteness of the advice. There is not a distribution of prizes at any school but it falls upon heedless, indifferent ears. None the less, I ask you to reflect upon it, and venture—I who have been nothing but a toiler—to tell you how great has been the benefit that I have derived from the long labour, the arduous accomplishment of which has occupied my whole life. My career began in hardship; I knew bitter misery and despair. Later on I lived a life of battle, I live it still; disparaged, scoffed at, covered with insults! Well, through all of this I have had but one faith, one fortifier—work. That which has sustained me has been the huge labour I imposed upon myself. Yonder, in front of me, I always beheld the goal towards which I was marching; and this it was—whenever the ills of life had laid me low—that sufficed to set me on my legs again and gave me the courage to march on and on, despite everything. The work I refer to is steady, settled work, the daily task, the self-imposed duty of making a forward step every day towards the accomplishment of one's allotted toil. How many times of a morning have I sat down at my table, with my head in confusion, lost, my mouth bitter, tortured by some great physical or moral anguish! And on each occasion, despite the rebellion of my sufferings, my task—after the first minutes of agony—brought me relief and comfort. I have invariably risen up from my daily toil with a feeling of consolation—my heart yet sore, perhaps, but nevertheless conscious that I was still erect, with strength enough to continue living until the morrow.

ÉMILE ZOLA (1840–1902), 'Life and Labour', address to Paris Students' Association, 1893

Quite apart from its productive value, work was valued by rulers and moralists as an indispensable form of social discipline. It kept the populace in check and prevented disorder.

... it is certain that employment and competencies do civilize all men and makes them tractable and obedient to superiors' commands, though otherwise ill-natured: none more intractable than idle beggars.

> PETER CHAMBERLEN (1601–83), *The Poore Mans Advocate,* 1649

It is commonly known and grown to be a proverb that women by nature are more talkative, so as greater care is to be had, and straight watch to be kept lest at any time, the locks and bars of wisdom and modesty being broken, the tongue, before being silent, do wander and stray abroad here and there. Whereunto it is a great help that a woman be constant and continuing in her labour; for even as the Apostle doth define idleness and slothfulness to be the seed of much talk in your widows, so continuance in labour is a singular remedy against rashness and forwardness of the tongue.

> JOHN DOD (1549?–1645) and WILLIAM HINDE (1569?–1629), *Bathshebas Instructions to Her Sonne Lemuel,* 1614

As a seething pot is cooled by stirring, so may lust be kept down by man's diligence in his calling. By this means the body of man is exercised, and his mind busied, and thus he [is] kept from idleness, which is a great cause of lust.

> WILLIAM GOUGE (1578–1653), *A Learned and Very Useful Commentary on the Whole Epistle to the Hebrewes,* 1655

Now as to the work of these supernumeraries [indigent people], let it be without expence of Foreign Commodities, and then 'tis no matter if it be employed to build a useless Pyramid upon Salisbury Plain, bring the Stones at Stonehenge to Tower-Hill, or the like; for at worst this would keep their mindes to discipline and obedience, and their bodies to a patience of more profitable labours when need shall require it.

> SIR WILLIAM PETTY (1623–87), *A Treatise of Taxes and Contributions,* 1662

Whether we consider the manual industry of the poor, or the intellectual exertions of the superior classes, we shall find that diligent occupation, if not criminally perverted from its purposes, is at once the instrument of virtue and the secret of happiness. Man cannot be safely trusted with a life of leisure.

HANNAH MORE (1745–1833), Christian Morals, 1813

In the glorification of 'work' and the never-ceasing talk about the 'blessing of labour', I see the same secret *arrière-pensée* as I do in the praise bestowed on impersonal acts of a general interest, viz. a fear of everything individual. For at the sight of work—that is to say, severe toil from morning till night—we have the feeling that it is the best police, viz. that it holds every one in check and effectively hinders the development of reason, of greed, and of desire for independence. For work uses up an extraordinary proportion of nervous force, withdrawing it from reflection, meditation, dreams, cares, love, and hatred; it dangles unimportant aims before the eyes of the worker and offers easy and regular gratification. Thus it happens that a society where work is continually being performed will enjoy greater security, and it is security which is now venerated as the supreme deity.

FRIEDRICH NIETZSCHE (1844–1900), The Dawn of Day, 1881, tr. J. M. Kennedy, 1911

There is no reason at all why people should wander about in a loafing and idle manner; if they are not earning their living they ought to be put under some control.

WINSTON CHURCHILL (1874–1965), as President of the Board of Trade, 18 Aug. 1909

Work was also thought to be indispensable for an individual's physical and psychic health.

Work: daily occupation to which man is condemned by his need and to which at the same time he owes his health, his subsistence, his peace of mind, his good sense and perhaps his virtue.

DENIS DIDEROT (1713–84) and JEAN LE ROND D'ALEMBERT (1717–83) eds., Encyclopédie, ou Dictionnaire raisonné des sciences, des arts et des métiers, 1751–80

For nothing in this life is worth so much for body and soul as well-ordered work. As to which Holy Scripture describes work in this manner: 'Work is the life of man and keeper of health. Work drives away occasion for sin, and makes man rest himself, is the relief of languor, a stay to illness, safety of the people, sharpener of all the senses, stepmother to idleness, duty to young people, and merit to old.' Hence he who would give up the joy of everlasting life takes care, says Scripture, that he does not work at all in this life.

NICOLE BOZON, 14th-century friar, tr. John Rose, 1913

A slothful man's imagination is apt to dress up labour in a horrible mask; but horrible as it is, idleness is more to be dreaded, and a life of poverty (its necessary consequence) is far more painful. It was the advice of Pythagoras, 'to choose the best kind of life', for that use would render it agreeable, reconciling men even to the roughest exercise. By practice, pains become at first easy, and in the progress pleasant; and this is so true, that whoever examines things will find, there can be no such thing as a happy life without labour, and that whoever doth not labour with his hands, must, in his own defence, labour with his brains.

GEORGE BERKELEY (1658–1753), *A Word to the Wise*, 1749

Providence has so ordered it, that a state of rest and inaction, however it may flatter our indolence, should be productive of many inconveniences; that it should generate such disorders, as may force us to have recourse to some labour, as a thing absolutely requisite to make us pass our lives with tolerable satisfaction; for the nature of rest is to suffer all the parts of our bodies to fall into a relaxation, that not only disables the members from performing their functions, but takes away the vigorous tone of fibre which is requisite for carrying on the natural and necessary secretions. At the same time, that in this languid inactive state, the nerves are more liable to the most horrid convulsions, than when they are sufficiently braced and strengthened. Melancholy, dejection, despair, and often self-murder, is the consequence of the gloomy view we take of things in this relaxed state of body. The best remedy for all these evils is exercise or *labour*; and labour is a surmounting of *difficulties*, an exertion of the contracting power of the muscles; and as such resembles pain, which consists in tension or contraction, in everything but degree. Labour is not only requisite to preserve the coarser organs in a state fit for their functions; but it is equally necessary to those finer and more delicate organs, on which, and by which, the imagination, and perhaps the other mental powers, act. Since it is probable, that not only the inferior parts of the soul, as the passions are called, but the understanding itself, makes use of some fine corporeal instruments in its operation; though what they are, and where they are, may be somewhat hard to settle: but that it does make use of such, appears from hence; that a long exercise of the mental powers induces a remarkable lassitude of the whole body; and, on the other hand, that great bodily labour, or pain, weakens, and sometimes actually destroys, the mental faculties. Now, as a due exercise is essential to the coarse muscular parts of the constitution, and that without this rousing they would become languid and diseased, the very same rule holds with regard to those finer parts we have mentioned; to have them in proper order, they must be shaken and worked to a proper degree.

EDMUND BURKE (1729–97), *A Philosophical Enquiry into the Origin of Our Ideas of the Sublime and Beautiful*, 1757

Writers, who themselves enjoyed sedentary lives, liked to emphasize the advantages of the regular exercise enjoyed by the labourer. They underrated the physical hardships and privations that went with manual toil. But how reassuring to think that the toiling swain was happier and healthier than the leisured classes who depended on his labours!

Usage of labour is a great thing; for it maketh, as saith Saint Bernard, the labourer to have strong arms and hard sinews; and Sloth maketh him feeble and tender.

GEOFFREY CHAUCER (*c*.1343–1400), 'The Parson's Tale', *The Canterbury Tales*, *c*.1387

The sleep of a labouring man is sweet, whether he eat little or much: but the abundance of the rich will not suffer him to sleep.

Ecclesiastes 5: 12

The board of industry,
By her own labour frugally supplied,
Gives to her food an admirable zest,
Unknown to indolence, which half asleep
With palateless indifference surveys
The smoking feast of plenty.

JAMES HURDIS (1763–1801), *The Village Curate*, 1788

For want of bodily labour, a multitude of the idle gentry, and rich people, and young people that are slothful, do heap up in the secret receptacles of the body a dunghill of unconcocted and excrementitious filth, and vitiate all the mass of humours which should be the fuel and oil of life, and die by thousands of untimely deaths (of fevers, palsies, convulsions, apoplexies, dropsies, consumptions, gout, etc.) more miserably than if thieves had murdered them by the highway, because it is their own doing and by their sloth they kill themselves.

RICHARD BAXTER (1615–91), *A Christian Directory*, 1673

O mortal man, who livest here by Toil,
Do not complain of this thy hard Estate;
That like an Emmet thou must ever moil,
Is a sad Sentence of an ancient Date:
And, certes, there is for it Reason great;
For, though sometimes it makes thee weep and wail,
And curse thy Stars, and early drudge and late,
Withouten That would come an heavier Bale,
Loose Life, unruly Passions, and Diseases pale.

JAMES THOMSON (1700–48), *The Castle of Indolence*, 1748

We ought to look on it as a mark of goodness in God that he has put us in this life under a necessity of labour, not only to keep mankind from the mischiefs that ill men at leisure are very apt to do. But it is a benefit even to the good and the virtuous, which are thereby preserved from the ills of idleness or the diseases that attend constant study in a sedentary life. Half the day employed in useful labour would supply the inhabitants of the earth with the necessities and conveniencies of life, in a full plenty, had not the luxury of Courts and, by their example, inferior Grandees found out idle and useless employment for themselves and others subservient to their pride and vanity, and so brought honest labour in useful and mechanical arts wholly into disgrace, whereby the studious and sedentary part of mankind as well as the rich and the noble have been deprived of that natural and true preservative against diseases. And 'tis to this that we may justly impute the Spleen and the gout and those other decays of health under which the lazily voluptuous, or busily studious part of men uselessly languish away a great part of their lives. How many shall we find amongst those who sit still either at their books or their pleasure, whom either the spleen or the gout does not rob of his thoughts or his limbs before he is got half his journey? And becomes a useless member of the commonwealth in that mature age which should make him most serviceable, whilst the sober and working artisan and the frugal laborious countryman performs his part well and cheerfully goes on in his business to a vigorous old age . . .

... those who at their first setting out eager in the pursuit of knowledge spare as little as they can of their time to the necessities of life to bestow it all upon their minds find it at last but an ill sort of husbandry, when they are fain to refund to the care of their decayed body a greater portion of their time than what they improvidently robbed them of. Six hours thus allotted to the mind, the other six might be employed in the provisions for the body and the preservation of health. Six hours' labour every day in some honest calling would at once provide necessities for the body and secure the health of it in the use of them. If this distribution of the twelve hours seem not fair nor sufficiently to keep up the distinction that ought to be in the ranks of men, let us change it a little. Let the Gentleman and scholar employ nine of the twelve on his mind in thought and reading and the other three in some honest labour. And the man of manual labour nine in work and three in knowledge. By which, all mankind might be supplied with what the real necessities and conveniency of life demand in greater plenty than they have now, and be delivered from that horrid ignorance and brutality to which the bulk of them is now everywhere given up.

JOHN LOCKE (1632–1704), 'Labour', 1693

As for bodily labour, it's a primitive institution of God, *It should earn its bread in the sweat of its brows*; labour being as proper for the body's health as eating is for its living; for what pains a man saves by ease, he will find in disease.

JOHN BELLERS (1654–1725), *Proposals for Raising a College of Industry*, 1696

I consider the Body as a System of Tubes and Glands, or to use a more Rustick Phrase, a Bundle of Pipes and Strainers, fitted to one another after so wonderful a manner as to make a proper Engine for the Soul to work with. This Description does not only comprehend the Bowels, Bones, Tendons, Veins, Nerves and Arteries, but every Muscle and every Ligature, which is a Composition of Fibres, that are so many imperceptible Tubes or Pipes interwoven on all sides with invisible Glands or Strainers.

This general Idea of a Human Body, without considering it in the Niceties of Anatomy, lets us see how absolutely necessary Labour is for the right Preservation of it. There must be frequent Motions and Agitations to mix, digest, and separate the Juices contained in it, as well as to clear and cleanse that Infinitude of Pipes and Strainers of which it is composed, and to give their solid Parts a more firm and lasting Tone. Labour or Exercise ferments the Humours, casts them into their proper Channels, throws off Redundancies, and helps Nature in those secret Distributions, without which the Body cannot subsist in its Vigour, nor the Soul act with Chearfulness.

I might here mention the Effects which this has upon all the Faculties of the Mind, by keeping the Understanding clear, the Imagination untroubled, and refining those Spirits that are necessary for the proper Exertion of our intellectual Faculties, during the present Laws of Union between Soul and Body. It is to a Neglect in this Particular that we must ascribe the Spleen, which is so frequent in Men of studious and sedentary Tempers, as well as the Vapours to which those of the other Sex are so often subject . . . and as for those who are not obliged to Labour, by the Condition in which they are born, they are more miserable than the rest of Mankind, unless they indulge themselves in that voluntary Labour which goes by the Name of Exercise.

JOSEPH ADDISON (1672–1719), *The Spectator*, 12 July 1711

In short, this whole country [Halifax], however mountainous, and that no sooner we were down one hill but we mounted another, is yet infinitely full of people; those people all full of business; not a beggar, not an idle person to be seen, except here and there an alms-house, where people antient, decrepid, and past labour, might perhaps be found; for it is observable, that the people here, however laborious, generally live to a great age, a certain testimony to the goodness and wholesomness of the country, which is, without doubt, as healthy as any part of England; nor is the health of the people lessen'd, but help'd and establish'd by their being constantly employ'd, and, as we call it, their working hard; so that they find a double advantage by their being always in business.

DANIEL DEFOE (1660–1731), *Tour through the Whole Island of Great Britain*, 1724–6

Better the toiling Swain, oh happier far!
Perhaps the happiest of the Sons of Men!
Who vigorous plies the Plough, the Team, or Car;
Who houghs the Field, or ditches in the Glen,
Delves in his Garden, or secures his Pen:
The Tooth of Avarice poisons not his Peace;
He tosses not in Sloth's abhorred Den;
From Vanity he has a full Release;
And, rich in Nature's Wealth, he thinks not of Increase.

Good Lord! how keen are his Sensations all!
His Bread is sweeter than the Glutton's Cates;
The Wines of France upon the Palate pall,

Compar'd with What his simple Soul elates,
The native Cup whose Flavour Thirst creates;
At one deep Draught of Sleep he takes the Night;
And for that Heart-felt Joy which Nothing mates,
Of the pure nuptial Bed the chaste Delight,
The Losel is to him a miserable Wight.

But what avail the largest Gifts of HEAVEN,
When sickening Health and Spirits go amiss?
How tasteless then Whatever can be given?
Health is the vital Principle of Bliss,
And Exercise of Health. In Proof of This,
Behold the Wretch, who slugs his Life away,
Soon swallow'd in Disease's sad Abyss;
While he whom Toil has brac'd, or manly Play,
Has light as Air each Limb, each Thought as clear as Day.

JAMES THOMSON (1700–48), *The Castle of Indolence*, 1748

A delightful feeling is experienced after a good sweating at work. Every nerve and tissue seems to be aglow with intensest life; the blood courses through the body and limbs freely and vigorously, and produces a sense of unspeakable physical pleasure. Sweating as the result of physical exercise has a powerful effect upon the mind, as well as upon the body; it clears the vision and invigorates the brain, and is a perfect medicine for many ailments, both mental and physical. If many of the languid and indolent, who never do any work or indulge in sturdy exercise, were suddenly to rouse themselves up and do sufficient physical labour, either for themselves or for someone else, to procure a good sweating at least twice a week, they would feel immeasurably better for it. Life would have a new meaning for them. They would eat better, rest better, and sleep better. They would feel fresher and stronger, altogether more active and vigorous, more sympathetic and satisfied. Though he is, as a rule, quite unaware of it, the workman derives considerably more physical pleasure from life than do those persons, mistakenly envied, who do nothing, for everything has a relish to him, while to the others all is flat and insipid. Truly work is the salt of life, and physical work at that, though there is a most passionate desire in many quarters to be well rid of it.

ALFRED WILLIAMS (1877–1930), *Life in a Railway Factory*, 1915

Losel] rake or profligate

Some maintained that hard physical work enhanced female beauty.

Oh, where are you going to, my pretty little dear,
With your red rosy cheeks and your coal-black hair?
I'm going a-milking, kind sir, she answered me:
And it's dabbling in the dew makes the milkmaids fair!

Suppose I were to clothe you, my pretty little dear,
In a green silken gown and the amethyst rare?
O no, sir, O no, sir, kind sir, she answered me,
For it's dabbling in the dew makes the milkmaids fair!

Suppose I were to carry you, my pretty little dear,
In a chariot with horses, a grey gallant pair?
O no, sir, O no, sir, kind sir, she answered me,
For it's dabbling in the dew makes the milkmaids fair!

Suppose I were to feast you, my pretty little dear,
With dainties on silver, the whole of the year?
O no, sir, O no, sir, kind sir, she answered me,
For it's dabbling in the dew makes the milkmaids fair!

O but London's a city, my pretty little dear,
And all men are gallant and brave that are there—
O no, sir, O no, sir, kind sir, she answered me,
For it's dabbling in the dew makes the milkmaids fair!

O fine clothes and dainties and carriages so rare
Bring grey to the cheeks and silver to the hair;
What's a ring on the finger if rings are round the eye?
But it's dabbling in the dew makes the milkmaids fair.

UNKNOWN (? Walter de la Mare) (1873–1956)

Occupation, then, bustling occupation—real down-right-work—either in the form of out-door exercise, or of attending to her household duties, a lady MUST take, if she wishes to have a good breast of milk;—if, in point of fact, she is desirous to have healthy offspring! For the ALMIGHTY is no respecter of persons! And HE has ordained that work shall be the lot of man and of woman too!—IT IS A BLESSED THING TO BE OBLIGED TO WORK.—If we do not work, we have all to pay a heavy penalty, in the form of loss of health and happiness!

PYE HENRY CHAVASSE (1810–79), *Advice to a Wife*, 1839

Pausing awhile, he proceeded anon, for none made answer.
Oh, if our high-born girls knew only the grace, the attraction,
Labour, and labour alone, can add to the beauty of women,
Truly the milliner's trade would quickly, I think, be at discount,
All the waste and loss in silk and satin be saved us,
Saved for purposes truly and widely productive——

                                                        That's right,
Take off your coat to it, Philip, cried Lindsay, outside in the garden,
Take off your coat to it, Philip.

                                        Well, then, said Hewson, resuming;
Laugh if you please at my novel economy; listen to this, though:
As for myself, and apart from economy wholly, believe me,
Never I properly felt the relation between men and women,
Though to the dancing-master I went perforce, for a quarter,
Where, in dismal quadrille, were good-looking girls in abundance,
Though, too, school-girl cousins were mine—a bevy of beauties—
Never (of course you will laugh, but of course all the same I shall say it),
Never, believe me, I knew of the feelings between men and women,
Till in some village fields in holidays now getting stupid,
One day sauntering 'long and listless,' as Tennyson has it,
Long and listless strolling, ungainly in hobbadehoyhood,
Chanced it my eye fell aside on a capless, bonnetless maiden,
Bending with three-pronged fork in a garden uprooting potatoes.
Was it the air? who can say? or herself, or the charm of the labour?
But a new thing was in me; and longing delicious possessed me,
Longing to take her and lift her, and put her away from her slaving.
Was it embracing or aiding was most in my mind? hard question!
But a new thing was in me, I, too, was a youth among maidens:
Was it the air? who can say? but in part 'twas the charm of the labour.

A. H. CLOUGH (1819–61), *The Bothie of Tober-na-Vuolich*, 1848

*No one had a greater appreciation of the contribution made by hard labour to
female beauty than the Victorian poet, barrister, and man about town, Arthur
Joseph Munby (1828–1910).*

Her handsome face, deep-bronzed by sun and wind;
Her strong, bare, sinewy arms and rugged hands,
Blacken'd with labour; and her peasant dress,
Rude, coarse in texture, yet most picturesque,
And suited to her situation and her ways;

All these, transfigured by that sentiment
Of lowly contrast to the man she served,
Grew dignified with beauty; and herself
A noble working woman, not ashamed
Of what her work had made her.

ARTHUR JOSEPH MUNBY (1828–1910), *Ann Morgan's Love*, 1896

Others admired the male body in action.

Blacksmiths with grimed and hairy chests environ the anvil,
Each has his main-sledge, they are all out, there is a great heat in the fire.

From the cinder-strew'd threshold I follow their movements,
The lithe sheer of their waists plays even with their massive arms,
Overhand the hammers swing, overhand so slow, overhand so sure,
They do not hasten, each man hits in his place.

WALT WHITMAN (1819–92), *Song of Myself*, 1881 edn.

Harry Ploughman

Hard as hurdle arms, with a broth of goldish flue
Breathed round; the rack of ribs; the scooped flank; lank
    { knee-nave;
Rope-over thigh; { kneebank; and barrelled shank—
    Héad and fóot, shoúldér and shánk—
By a grey eye's heed steered well, one crew, fall to;
      { barrowy brawn, his thew
Stånd at stress. Each limb's { barrowy-brawnèd thew
That onewhere curded, onewhere sucked or sank—
     Soáred ór sánk—,
Though as a beechbole firm, fínds his, as at a rollcall, rank
And features, ín flesh, whát deed he each must do—
    His sínew-sérvice whére dó.
He leans to it, Harry bends, look. Back, elbow, and liquid waist
In him, all quåil to the wallowing o' the plough. 'S cheek crímsons; curls
    { in a wínd liftéd, windláced—
Wag or crossbridle, { windloft or windlaced—
    { Wind-lilylocks-laced;
    { See his wínd-lílylócks-láced—;

Chŭrlsgrace too, chȋld of Amansstrength, how it hângs or hŭrls
{ Them
{ These—broȃd ín bluff híde his ftówning féet lashed! ráced
                               { cold fŭrls—
With, along them, cragiron under and { flame-fŭrls—
                         { With-a-fountain's shining-shot furls.
                         { With-a-wét-shéen-shót fúrls.

GERARD MANLEY HOPKINS (1844–89), 1887

Man Carrying Bale

The tough hand closes gently on the load;
    Out of the mind, a voice
Calls 'Lift!' and the arms, remembering well their work,
    Lengthen and pause for help.

Then a slow ripple flows along the body,
While all the muscles call to one another:
    'Lift!' and thc bulging bale
    Floats like a butterfly in June.

So moved the earliest carrier of bales,
    And the same watchful sun
Glowed through his body feeding it with light.
    So will the last one move,
And halt, and dip his head, and lay his load
Down, and the muscles will relax and tremble . . .
    Earth, you designed your man
    Beautiful both in labour, and repose.

HAROLD MONRO (1879–1932), 1917

Hedgers

Two labourers, young and stout limbed, brush the hedge
Left thick and wild for long years next Butler's Lane,
Where pools and ruts sink deep in early spring
And make rough way for loaded harvest wains.

With crotch and bill and busy hands they cut
To the quick those proud unruly bushes, pitch
The naked poles and faggots in due heap,
Burn the limp green and stubborn thorn in ditch.

Lit with the sunset rose and yellow flame,
Brown arm, worn corduroys and easy swing
Flash to their part in some heroic tale—
These men take on the livery of kings.

CLAUDE COLLEER ABBOTT (1889–1971), 1924

Work involved sociability, gossip, personal relationships, and indispensable human contact. Nowadays when people retire it is common for them to say that they will not miss the job, but that they will miss the people.

If you keep one servant, your work is done; if you keep two, it is half done; but if you keep three, you may do it yourself.

PROVERBIAL SAYING, often quoted by the miser John Elwes (1714–89)

Adam, well may we labour still to dress
This garden, still to tend plant, herb and flower,
Our pleasant task enjoined, but till more hands
Aid us, the work under our labour grows,
Luxurious by restraint; what we by day
Lop overgrown, or prune, or prop, or bind,
One night or two with wanton growth derides,
Tending to wild. Thou therefore now advise
Or hear what to my mind first thoughts present,
Let us divide our labours, you where choice
Leads you, or where most needs, whether to wind
The woodbine round this arbour, or direct
The clasping ivy where to climb, while I
In yonder spring of roses intermixt
With myrtle, find what to redress till noon:
For while so near each other thus all day
Our task we choose, what wonder if so near
Looks intervene and smiles, or object new
Casual discourse draw on, which intermits
Our day's work brought to little, though begun
Early, and the hour of supper comes unearn'd.

JOHN MILTON (1608–74), *Paradise Lost*, 1667

Laying stress upon importance of work has a greater effect than any other technique of living in the direction of binding the individual more closely to reality; in his work he is at least securely attached to a part of reality, the human community. Work is no less valuable for the opportunity it and the human relations connected with it provide for a very considerable discharge of libidinal component impulses, narcissistic, aggressive and even erotic, than because it is indispensable for subsistence and justifies existence in a society.

> SIGMUND FREUD (1856–1939), *Civilization and Its Discontents*, 1930, tr. Joan Riviere

He accompanied her up the hill, explaining to her the details of his forthcoming tenure of the other farm. They spoke very little of their mutual feelings; pretty phrases and warm expressions being probably unnecessary between such tried friends. Theirs was that substantial affection which arises (if any arises at all) when the two who are thrown together begin first by knowing the rougher sides of each other's character, and not the best till further on, the romance growing up in the interstices of a mass of hard prosaic reality. This good-fellowship—*camaraderie*—usually occurring through similarity of pursuits, is unfortunately seldom superadded to love between the sexes, because men and women associate, not in their labours, but in their pleasures merely. Where, however, happy circumstance permits its development, the compounded feeling proves itself to be the only love which is strong as death—that love which many waters cannot quench, nor the floods drown, beside which the passion usually called by the name is evanescent as steam.

> THOMAS HARDY (1840–1928), *Far from the Madding Crowd*, 1874

On completing his term of apprenticeship, and springing at once from a wage of eight or ten to one of thirty shillings or upwards per week, the new-fledged journeyman is generally as eager to pay his footing to those who are now his brother journeymen as they are to receive it; and a newly-married man is generally found to be liberally disposed towards his shopmates. Indeed it would be surprising if it were not so, for while a sovereign is the utmost expected from him, he receives, in the iron trade at least, an ovation from his shopmates, on his return to work after his marriage, that would be cheap at five times that amount. On the occasion of his marriage, a working man takes a few days' holiday, and on the day on which he returns to work does not come to the shop until after breakfast. Then he receives his ovation in the shape of what is technically called 'a ringing in.' Some of his intimates will know on what day he is to return, and at breakfast time on that day everything is got ready for welcoming him. Scouts are placed along the road he has to come, in

---

footing] fee payable by a workman upon entrance to a trade

order to signal his approach, and in the meantime the men and boys in the shop stand, hammer in hand, around boilers, plates of iron suspended from beams, or anything else that comes handy that will give out a good ringing sound when struck. The arrival of the subject of the demonstration is duly announced by the scouts; all stand to their posts, and, the instant he enters the shop, strike up, producing a thundering peal. In a large establishment, the Benedict of the occasion may have to pass through several shops before reaching the particular one in which he works. In that case the ringers in each shop, having rung him through their particular department, follow him as he passes out of it, until the whole body of them are assembled in his own shop, and then the peal reaches its grand climax. When it is considered that there are perhaps as many as five or six hundred men, all skilled in the use of the hammer, all hammering their best on high or sharp sounding material, the intensity of the peal may, and indeed *must*, be imagined, since it cannot be described. The ringing-in is continued for about five minutes, and then the proceedings are wound up with a hearty cheer. If such a demonstration as this is not cheap at a sovereign, then nothing in the shape of a demonstration can be cheap at any price.

> A JOURNEYMAN ENGINEER (Thomas Wright) (*fl.* 1867), *Some Habits and Customs of the Working Classes,* 1867

Soon as the rising Sun hath drank the Dew,
Another Scene is open'd to our View;
Our Master comes, and at his Heels a Throng
Of prattling Females, arm'd with Rake and Prong:
Prepar'd, whil'st he is here, to make his Hay;
Or, if he turns his Back, prepar'd to play.
But here, or gone, sure of this Comfort still,
Here's Company, so they may chat their fill:
And were their Hands as active as their Tongues,
How nimbly then would move their Rakes and Prongs.
The Grass again is spread upon the Ground,
Till not a vacant Place is to be found;
And while the piercing Sun-beams on it shine,
The Haymakers have time allow'd to dine:
That soon dispatch'd, they still sit on the Ground,
And the brisk Chat renew'd, a-fresh goes round:
All talk at once, but seeming all to fear,
That all they speak so well, the rest won't hear;
By quick degrees so high their Notes they strain,
That Standers-by can nought distinguish plain:
So loud their Speech, and so confus'd their Noise,

Scarce puzzled Echo can return a Voice;
Yet spite of this, they bravely all go on,
Each scorns to be, or seem to be, outdone:
Till (unobserv'd before) a low'ring Sky,
Fraught with black Clouds, proclaims a Shower nigh;
The tattling Croud can scarce their Garments gain,
Before descends the thick impetuous Rain:
Their noisy Prattle all at once is done,
And to the Hedge they all for Shelter run.

STEPHEN DUCK (1705–56), *The Thresher's Labour*, 1730

Forth goes the weeding dame, her daily task
To travel the green wheat-field, ancle-deep
In the fresh blade of harvest yet remote.
Now with exerted implement she checks
The growth of noisome weeds, to toil averse,
An animal gregarious, fond of talk.
Lo! where the gossipping banditti stand
Amid field idle all, and all alike
With shrill voice prating, fluent as the pye.
Far off let me the noisy group behold,
Nothing molested by their loud harangue,
And think it well to see the fertile field
By their red tunics peopled, and the frock
Of the white husbandman that ploughs hard by.

JAMES HURDIS (1763–1801), *The Favourite Village*, 1800

There was a man in the Stocks Department who had a desk close to mine and used to spend the whole of his lunch-time on the telephone. He would witter on. Some little time later, I noticed there was a woman at the back of the department who also spent her entire lunch-time on the telephone. It took me some further time to discover they were talking to one another and were conducting a love affair across this open-plan office.

DAVID VEREY (1950–), quoted in Cathy Courtney and Paul Thompson, *City Lives*, 1996

I ought to mention, though I may hardly illustrate, one faculty which is a great support to many of the men—I mean the masculine gift of 'humour.' Not playful-witted like the women, nor yet apt, like the women, to refresh their spirits in the indulgence of sentiment and emotion, but rather stolid and inclined to dim brooding thought, they are able to see the laughable side of their own misadventures and discomforts; and thanks to this they keep a sense of proportion, as though perceiving that if their labour accomplishes its end, it does not really matter that they get tired, or dirty, or wet through in doing it. This is a social gift, of small avail to the men working alone in their gardens; but it serves them well during the day's work with their mates, or when two or three of them together tackle some job of their own, such as cleaning out a well, or putting up a fowl-house. Then, if somebody gets splashed, or knocks his knuckles, and softly swears, his wrath turns to a grin as the little dry chuckle or the sly remark from the others reminds him that his feelings are understood.

GEORGE BOURNE (George Sturt) (1863–1927), *Change in the Village*, 1912

The lads of a large workshop devote the first day or two of the appearance of a new boy amongst them, to questioning him about himself and relatives, and more especially as to his designs about becoming the Stephenson or Watt of his day: in a word, to 'taking his measure.' Having ascertained his degree of gullibility, their next step will probably be to send him to the most ill-tempered man in the shop, with instructions to address him by some offensive nickname, and ask him for the loan of a half-round square, or some other non-existent and impossible tool: his reception by the man to whom he is sent on this fool's errand, and who is a stock victim of this particular pleas-antry, will be both astonishing and disagreeable. After this they will profess sorrow for the trick, and offer to make atonement by teaching him how to handle his hammer and chisel. When they have got him fairly to work, one of them will jerk the elbow of his hammer arm, and by that means cause him to hit his chisel hand. If he knocks a piece of skin off it, that is considered to add piquancy to the joke; and when he pulls a face and wrings his hand, he is told that it *couldn't have hurt him, as it wasn't on him a minute.*

A JOURNEYMAN ENGINEER (Thomas Wright) (*fl.* 1867), *Some Habits and Customs of the Working Classes*, 1867

When men are at work threshing wheat they are like they are when they train colts for the races. They make funny remarks. They work like the very deuce for a while and then lay off and maybe wrestle around.

Tar saw one young man, at work on the top of the stack of wheat, push another to the ground. Then he crawled back up and the two put down their forks and began to wrestle. There was a man on an elevated platform feeding the wheat into the separator, and he began to dance. He took a bundle of the wheat in his hands, shook it in the air, made a motion like a bird trying to fly that can't fly, and then began to dance again.

The two men on the stack wrestled as hard as they could, laughing all the time, and the old man by the fence near Tar growled at them, but you could tell he did not mean what he said.

The whole job of threshing came to a stop. All were intent on watching the struggle on the stack until one fellow had thrown the other to the ground.

Some women came along a lane bearing baskets and all the men went away from the machine to sit by the fence. It was in the middle of the afternoon but in the country when threshing is going on, people do like that. They eat and eat, just any time.

SHERWOOD ANDERSON (1876 1941), *Tar. A Mid-West Childhood*, 1926

They were all workers in this family. Everything was work to them. Uncle Tom was always sawing and hammering. He had made the chests of drawers and the tables in his house. Aunt Annie scrubbed and cooked. Cousin Gladys was always sewing and even when she came in from her factory, she had, as they said, 'something in her hands'—a brush, a broom, a cleaning cloth or scissors. Jim was a worker, too. He worked at the post office in the middle of the town. One day Uncle Tom took the boy on top of a tram and when they came near the post office, he said: 'Eh, look out this side and you'll see Gladys's Jim working. He's got a good job. Sometimes he's on nights. He's a night worker. Now, look out for him when the tram slows down.' The boy looked into the grey window of the post office as the tram passed by. Inside were dim rows of desks and people and presently he saw Jim in his shirt sleeves. He was carrying a large wastepaper basket.

'What's he doing?' said the boy.

'Sorting,' said Uncle Tom. 'Sorting the mail. His father put him into that job when he was fourteen.'

The boy saw Jim lift the wastepaper basket and then suddenly empty it over the head of another man who was sitting at a desk. He saw Jim laughing. He saw the man jump down and chase Jim across the office, laughing too.

'Larking about,' said Uncle Tom indignantly. 'That's government work.'

The boy stopped laughing. He was scared of Jim after this.

V. S. PRITCHETT (1900–97), 'The Night Worker', 1945

Gifts and Loans

They meet in the mornings over coffee,
their only bond, work, and being married
to other people. They begin with jokes
—the chairman, the weather, the awful journey—
delicately pacing out their common ground.

Later, they expand into description.
Families, who might not recognise themselves,
are called up in brisk bulletins,
edited for maximum entertainment.
(Gossip ignores their middle-aged laughter.)

She shows him a photo of her sons,
tanned and smiling over fishing-nets
one green June day when the light was perfect.
He talks about his daughters, both away
at college. They admire everything.

Through the months more curious, more honest,
they cultivate small permissions, remember
each other in the fading summer evenings,
and suddenly get up from their lives,
to hunt for a book, or pick some fruit.

No quarrels cloud the simple space between them.
They imagine how their adequate weekends
might shimmer with this other happiness
—and how, perhaps, they'd still end up with less
than haunts a gift of pears, a borrowed book.

CAROL RUMENS (1944–), 1981

Where the Sexes Meet

The metal shop whiffs of grease, old handrags.
We arrive here dressed as ourselves and button up
uniform blue overalls to hammer, weld, strip down,
bash out conveyors that line the factory floor.

Foremen are brown coats. Managers swank
in spotless white, fierce with creases, prowl
the yards, the cubby holes to catch you out.
Think they're up to all the dodges.

Women are wrapped and knotted in white aprons,
packed in rows across the factory, seated
at belts that never stop while their overseer
scans them from a platform made by us.

The air's chocolate over there, butter, jam.
That's where the sexes meet when machines break down,
where you chat each other between ovens,
across conveyors, when backs are turned.

GLYN WRIGHT (1949–), 1995

Office Friendships

Eve is madly in love with Hugh
And Hugh is keen on Jim.
Charles is in love with very few
And few are in love with him.

Myra sits typing notes of love
With romantic pianist's fingers.
Dick turns his eyes to the heavens above
Where Fran's divine perfume lingers.

Nicky is rolling eyes and tits
And flaunting her wiggly walk.
Everybody is thrilled to bits
By Clive's suggestive talk.

Sex suppressed will go berserk,
But it keeps us all alive.
It's a wonderful change from wives and work
And it ends at half past five.

GAVIN EWART (1916–95), 1966

Above all, work offered the pleasures of occupation: absorption in a task, release from other anxieties and pride in the constructive use of one's faculties.

Work is much more fun than fun.

NOËL COWARD (1899–1973), 1963

Seest thou a man diligent in his business? He shall stand before kings.

Proverbs 23: 29

Perfect freedom is reserved for the man who lives by his own work and in that work does what he wants to do.

R. G. COLLINGWOOD (1889–1943), *Speculum Mentis*, 1924

'The Signalwoman'

Of course I grumble at times. Who doesn't? How often have I cursed the job to all eternity on arriving at my cabin on a bitterly cold Monday morning to find everything frozen solid. Levers that seem to burn your hands when you touch them, they are so cold; points full of snow so that even an Amazon couldn't move the levers; signals pulled off on a Saturday night now frozen in that position, requiring a walk down the line and, after climbing up them, a good stiff clout with the coal hammer before they will drop to the 'on' position; water taps frozen, entailing a couple of hundred yards' walk to the next nearest tap, and a fire that refuses to burn in spite of the generous amount of paraffin you feed it. But when at last it does burn and the kettle is boiling and platelayers have arrived to salt the points, you settle down with a mug of tea and the morning paper, not really wishing to be anywhere else.

HOPE WISE (1924–), 1967, quoted in *Work*, ed. Ronald Fraser, 1968

The daily work of earning a livelihood affords particular satisfaction when it has been selected by free choice, *i.e.* when through sublimation it enables use to be made of existing inclinations, of instinctual impulses that have retained their strength, or are more intense than usual for constitutional reasons.

SIGMUND FREUD (1856–1939), *Civilization and Its Discontents*, 1930, tr. Joan Riviere

Milton produced *Paradise Lost* for the same reason that a silk worm produces silk. It was an activity of his nature.

KARL MARX (1818–93), *Theories of Surplus Value*, 1905–10, tr. G. A. Bonner and Emile Burns, 1951

I have written because it gave me pleasure, because it came natural to me, because it was like talking or breathing, besides the big fact that it was necessary for me to work for my children. That, however, was not the first motive, so that when I laugh inquiries off and say that it is my trade, I do it only by way of eluding the question which I have neither time nor wish to enter into.

*

When people comment upon the number of books I have written, and I say that I am so far from being proud of that fact that I should like at least half of them forgotten, they stare—and yet it is quite true; and even here I could no more go solemnly into them, and tell why I had done this or that, than I could fly. They are my work, which I like in the doing, which is my natural way of occupying myself, though they are never so good as I meant them to be. And when I have said that, I have said all that is in me to say.

MARGARET OLIPHANT (1828–97), *Autobiography*, 1899

You need not see what someone is doing
to know if it is his vocation,

you have only to watch his eyes:
a cook mixing a sauce, a surgeon

making a primary incision,
a clerk completing a bill of lading,

wear the same rapt expression,
forgetting themselves in a function.

How beautiful it is,
that eye-on-the-object look,

W. H. AUDEN (1907–73), *Horae Canonicae*, 1954

I scrape on again. Now I look to the other side, where Daddy is sitting; for him scraping potatoes is not just a little odd job, but a piece of precision work. When he reads, he has a deep wrinkle at the back of his head, but if he helps prepare potatoes, beans, or any other vegetables, then it seems as if nothing else penetrates. Then he has on his 'potato face', and he would never hand over an imperfectly scraped potato; it's out of the question when he makes that face.

ANNE FRANK (1929–45), *The Diary of a Young Girl*, 18 Aug. 1943, pub. 1947, tr. B. M. Mooyart-Doubleday, 1952

Pangur Bán

I and Pangur Bán, my cat,
'Tis a like task we are at;
Hunting mice is his delight,
Hunting words I sit all night.

Better far than praise of men
'Tis to sit with book and pen;
Pangur bears me no ill-will,
He too plies his simple skill.

'Tis a merry thing to see
At our tasks how glad are we,
When at home we sit and find
Entertainment to our mind.

Oftentimes a mouse will stray
In the hero Pangur's way;
Oftentimes my keen thought set
Takes a meaning in its net.

'Gainst the wall he sets his eye
Full and fierce and sharp and sly;
'Gainst the wall of knowledge I
All my little wisdom try.

When a mouse darts from its den,
O how glad is Pangur then!
O what gladness do I prove
When I solve the doubts I love!

So in peace our tasks we ply,
Pangur Bán, my cat, and I;
In our arts we find our bliss,
I have mine and he has his.

Practice every day has made
Pangur perfect in his trade;
I get wisdom day and night
Turning darkness into light.

Written in the 8th c. by an Irish monk. Tr. from the Gaelic by Robin
Flower, 1926

Sweet Content

Art thou poor, yet hast thou golden slumbers?
    O sweet content!
Art thou rich, yet is thy mind perplexed?
    O punishment!
Dost thou laugh to see how fools are vexed
To add to golden numbers, golden numbers?
O sweet content! O sweet, O sweet content!
    Work apace, apace, apace, apace;
    Honest labour bears a lovely face;
    Then hey nonny, nonny, hey nonny, nonny!

Canst drink the waters of the crisped spring?
    O sweet content!
Swim'st thou in wealth, yet sink'st in thine own tears?
    O punishment!
Then he that patiently want's burden bears
No burden bears, but is a king, a king!
O sweet content! O sweet, O sweet content!

Work apace, apace, apace, apace;
Honest labour bears a lovely face;
Then hey nonny, nonny, hey nonny, nonny!

THOMAS DEKKER (1570?–1632), HENRY CHETTLE (*c.*1560–1607?), and
WILLIAM HAUGHTON (*fl.* 1598), *The Pleasant Comodie of Patient Grissill,*
1603

I must add that the pleasingest way to pass one's time well is to employ it so.
For as when men are very attentively considering some object, a world of
others may pass by unregarded. So to those whose thoughts are very seriously
taken up with some business or other the hours steal by undiscernedly;
and such people you shall hear often complain that they want time, never
that it lies upon their hands.

ROBERT BOYLE (1627–91), 'Of Time and Idleness', wr. 1645–50

It may be proved, with much certainty, that God intends no man to live in this
world without working: but it seems to me no less evident that He intends
every man to be happy in his work. It is written, 'in the sweat of thy brow,' but
it was never written, 'in the breaking of thine heart,' thou shalt eat bread: and
I find that, as on the one hand, infinite misery is caused by idle people, who
both fail in doing what was appointed for them to do, and set in motion various springs of mischief in matters in which they should have no concern, so
on the other hand, no small misery is caused by over-worked and unhappy
people, in the dark views which they necessarily take up themselves, and force
upon others, of work itself. Were it not so, I believe the fact of their being
unhappy is in itself a violation of divine law, and a sign of some kind of folly
or sin in their way of life. Now in order that people may be happy in their
work, these three things are needed: They must be fit for it: They must not do
too much of it: and they must have a sense of success in it—not a doubtful
sense, such as needs some testimony of other people for its confirmation, but
a sure sense, or rather knowledge, that so much work has been done well, and
fruitfully done, whatever the world may say or think about it. So that in order
that a man may be happy, it is necessary that he should not only be capable of
his work, but a good judge of his work.

JOHN RUSKIN (1819–1900), *Pre-Raphaelitism,* 1851

If we except those miraculous and isolated moments fate can bestow on a
man, loving your work (unfortunately, the privilege of a few) represents the
best, most concrete approximation of happiness on earth. But this is a truth

not many know. This boundless region, the region of *le boulot*, the job, *il rusco*—of daily work, in other words—is less known than the Antarctic, and through a sad and mysterious phenomenon it happens that the people who talk most, and loudest, about it are the very ones who have never traveled through it. To exalt labor, in official ceremonies an insidious rhetoric is displayed, based on the consideration that a eulogy or a medal costs much less than a pay raise, and they are also more fruitful. There also exists a rhetoric on the opposite side, however, not cynical, but profoundly stupid, which tends to denigrate labor, to depict it as base, as if labor, our own or others', were something we could do without, not only in Utopia, but here, today; as if anyone who knows how to work were, by definition, a servant, and as if, on the contrary, someone who doesn't know how to work, or knows little, or doesn't want to, were for that very reason a free man. It is sadly true that many jobs are not lovable, but it is harmful to come on to the field charged with preconceived hatred. He who does this sentences himself, for life, to hating not only work, but also himself and the world. We can and must fight to see that the fruit of labor remains in the hands of those who work, and that work does not turn into punishment; but love or, conversely, hatred of work is an inner, original heritage, which depends greatly on the story of the individual and less than is believed on the productive structures within which the work is done.

PRIMO LEVI (1919–87), *The Wrench*, 1978, tr. William Weaver, 1986

Great is work, for every craftsman walks out with the implements of his calling, and is proud of them. Thus the weaver walks out with a shuttle in his ear. The dyer walks out with wool in his ear. The scribe walks out with his pen behind his ear. All are proud of their craft. God speaks of his work (Genesis 2: 3).

RABBI ELEAZAR BEN AZARIAH (*fl.* AD 80–120)

Sir, I am a true labourer: I earn that I eat, get that I wear, owe no man hate, envy no man's happiness, glad of other men's good, content with my harm, and the greatest of my pride is to see my ewes graze and my lambs suck.

WILLIAM SHAKESPEARE (1564–1616), *As You Like It*, 1599

The Noble-man's Generous Kindness

A Noble-man liv'd near a village of late,
Hard by a poor Thresher whose charge it was great:
He had seven children, and most of them small,
And none but his labour to keep them withal.

He never was given to idle and lurk;
For this Noble-man seeing [him] go daily to work
His flail with his bag, and his bottle of beer,
As cheerful as those that had hundreds a year.

Thus careful and constant each morning he went
To his daily labour, with joy and content;
So jocund and jolly, both whistle and sing,
As blithe and as brisk as a bird in the spring.

One morning this Noble-man, taking his walk,
He met with this Poor Man, and freely did talk;
He asked him many a question at large,
Familiarly talking concerning his charge.

'Thou hast many children I very well know,
Thy labour is hard, and thy wages is low,
And yet thou art cheerful: I pray tell me true,
How you do maintain them so well as you do.'

'I carefully carry home all that I earn,
Now daily experience by this I do learn;
That though it is possible we may live poor,
We still keep a ravenous wolf from the door.

'I reap and I mow, and I harrow and sow,
Sometimes I to hedging and ditching do go;
No work comes amiss, for I thresh and I plow;
Thus I eat my bread by the sweat of my brow.

'My wife she is willing to pull in the yoke,
We live like two lambs and we never provoke
Each other, but like to the labouring ant
We do our endeavour to keep us from want.

'And when I come home from my labour at night
To my wife and [my] children, in whom I delight,
To hear them come round me with tattling noise,—
Now these are the riches that Poor Man enjoys.

'Tho' I am as weary as weary may be,
The youngest I commonly dance on my knee;
I find that content is an absolute feast,
I never repin'd at my charge in the least.'

ANON., from a 17th-century ballad

Murat Halstead is dead. He was a most likable man. He lived to be not far short of eighty and he devoted about sixty years to diligent, hard slaving at editorial work. His life and mine make a curious contrast. From the time that my father died, March 24, 1847, when I was past eleven years old, until the end of 1856, or the first days of 1857, I worked—not diligently, not willingly, but fretfully, lazily, repiningly, complainingly, disgustedly, and always shirking the work when I was not watched. The statistics show that I was a worker during about ten years. I am approaching seventy-three and I believe I have never done any work since—unless I may call two or three years of lazy effort as reporter on the Pacific Coast by that large and honorable name—and so I think I am substantially right in saying that when I escaped from the printing office fifty or fifty-one years ago I ceased to be a worker and ceased permanently.

Piloting on the Mississippi River was not work to me; it was play—delightful play, vigorous play, adventurous play—and I loved it; silver mining in the Humboldt Mountains was play, only play, because I did not do any of the work; my pleasant comrades did it and I sat by and admired; my silver mining in Esmeralda was not work, for Higbie and Robert Howland did it and again I sat by and admired. I accepted a job of shoveling tailings in a quartz mill there, and that was really work and I had to do it myself, but I retired from that industry at the end of two weeks, and not only with my own approval but with the approval of the people who paid the wages. These mining experiences occupied ten months and came to an end toward the close of September, 1862.

I then became a reporter in Virginia City, Nevada, and later in San Francisco, and after something more than two years of this salaried indolence I retired from my position on the *Morning Call*, by solicitation. Solicitation of the proprietor. Then I acted as San Franciscan correspondent of the Virginia City *Enterprise* for two or three months; next I spent three months in pocket-mining at Jackass Gulch with the Gillis boys; then I went to the Sandwich Islands and corresponded thence for the Sacramento *Union* five or six months; in October, 1866, I broke out as a lecturer, and from that day to this I have always been able to gain my living without doing any work; for the writing of books and magazine matter was always play, not work. I enjoyed it; it was merely billiards to me.

I wonder why Murat Halstead was condemned to sixty years of editorial slavery and I let off with a lifetime of delightful idleness. There seems to be something most unfair about this—something not justifiable. But it seems to be a law of the human constitution that those that deserve shall not have and those that do not deserve shall get everything that is worth having. It is a sufficiently crazy arrangement, it seems to me.

MARK TWAIN (1835–1910), Autobiography, 7 July 1908, 1959 edn.

If men had the spirit of their calling in them, and a due measure of flame and heat in carrying it on, labour in it would be rather a pleasure than a trouble. In all other professions, those who follow them labour in them all the year long, and are hard at their business every day in the week. All men that are well suited in a profession that is agreeable to their genius and inclination are really the easier and the better pleased, the more they are employed in it. Indeed there is no trade nor course of life, except ours [that of the clergy], that does not take up the whole man.

GILBERT BURNET (1643–1715), *Discourse of the Pastoral Care*, 1692

This was not Samuel Johnson's view:

No, Sir; there is no profession to which a man gives a very great proportion of his time. It is wonderful when a calculation is made, how little the mind is actually employed in the discharge of any profession.

SAMUEL JOHNSON (1709–84), quoted in James Boswell, *The Life of Samuel Johnson*, 6 Apr. 1775, pub. 1791

Work

There is no point in work
   unless it absorbs you
   like an absorbing game.

If it doesn't absorb you
if it's never any fun,
   don't do it.

When a man goes out into his work
he is alive like a tree in spring,
he is living, not merely working.

When the Hindus weave thin wool into long, long
      lengths of stuff
With their thin dark hands and their wide dark eyes
      and their still souls absorbed
they are like slender trees putting forth leaves, a long
      white web of living leaf,
         the tissue they weave,
and they clothe themselves in white as a tree clothes
      itself in its own foliage.

As with cloth, so with houses, ships, shoes, wagons or
      cups or loaves.
Men might put them forth as a snail its shell, as a bird
      that leans
         its breast against its nest, to make it round,

> as the turnip models his round root, as the bush makes
> flowers or gooseberries,
> putting them forth, not manufacturing them,
> and cities might be as once they were, bowers grown out
> from the busy bodies of people.
> And so it will be again, men will smash the machines.
>
> At last, for the sake of clothing himself in his own leaf-
> like cloth
> tissued from his life,
> and dwelling in his own bowery house, like a beaver's
> nibbled mansion
> and drinking from cups that came off his fingers like
> flowers off their five-fold stem
> he will cancel the machines we have got.

D. H. LAWRENCE (1885–1930), 1929

The music of toiling men drew me down to the Volga. Even now it has an intoxicating effect and I remember very clearly that day when I first became aware of the heroic poetry of everyday life.

A great barge laden with goods from Persia ran aground on a rock below Kazan and smashed its bottom in. A gang of stevedores took me on to help unload the cargo. It was September, the wind was blowing upstream and made the waves angrily dance on the grey river as it savagely tore at their crests, whipping up a cold spray. The fifty men who made up the gang gloomily huddled under tarpaulins and old mats on the deck of an empty barge that a little tug had in tow, panting away as it scattered red sheaves of sparks into the driving rain.

Evening drew on. That leaden, watery sky sank low over the river and grew dark. The men swore and grumbled at the rain, at the wind, and at life as they lazily crawled round the deck trying to shelter from the cold and the wet. I thought that these men, who seemed to be half asleep, were incapable of any work and could never save that sinking cargo. Towards midnight we reached the shoals and moored our empty barge alongside the wreck. The foreman, a pock-faced, venomous, cunning old man with a filthy tongue and the eyes and nose of a kite, pulled his soaked cap off his bald head and shouted in the shrill voice of a woman: 'Time for prayers, lads!'

The stevedores bunched together into a black mass on the dark deck and growled like bears. The foreman finished his prayers first and screeched: 'Get some lamps! Come on, let's have some work out of you! Come on, lads, God help us!'

And those ponderous lazy men, drenched by the rain, began to show how they could work. Just as though they were going into battle they rushed onto the deck and down into the holds of the grounded barge, whooping, roaring and cracking jokes. Sacks of rice, boxes of raisins, hides, furs from Astrakhan, flew past me like feather cushions. Stocky figures tore by, urging each other on with their howling, whistling and violent swearing. It was hard to believe that these were the same morose, sluggish men who only a few minutes before had been gloomily complaining about life, rain and the cold—now they were working away gaily and quickly, and with great skill. The rain became heavier and colder, the wind rose and tugged at their shirts, blowing them up over their heads and baring their stomachs. In that damp murkiness, dark figures worked by the dim light of six lamps and their feet made a dull, thudding sound on the decks. They worked as though they had been starved of it and as though they had been waiting a long time for the sheer pleasure of throwing sacks weighing 160 pounds or more to each other, and tearing around with bales on their backs. And they worked as though they were playing a game, with all the gay enthusiasm of children, with that drunken joy of activity only surpassed in sweetness by a woman's embraces . . .

I joined in, grabbed some sacks, dragged them down and threw them to someone. Then I ran back for more and it seemed that I too was caught up with everything and whirling around in a mad dance. Those men could go on working furiously and gaily without getting tired, without sparing themselves, for months, for years, and they would have no trouble in seizing belfries and minarets in the town and taking them wherever they wanted to!

I spent that night in a state of ecstasy that I had never experienced before. My soul was brightened by the desire to spend my whole life in that half-insane rapture of work. Waves danced around the sides of the barges, rain lashed the decks, and the wind whistled over the river. In the greyish haze of the dawn half-wet naked figures ran swiftly and incessantly, shouting, laughing and revelling in their own strength and labour.

And suddenly the wind tore apart that heavy mass of clouds and a pinkish ray of sunlight gleamed in a clear blue patch of sky. Those gay animals greeted it with a friendly roar as they shook their wet hairy faces. I wanted to hug and kiss those two-legged beasts who worked so skilfully and deftly, so completely absorbed that they did not have a thought for themselves.

It seemed that nothing could withstand that joyful furious tempestuous surge of strength, that it was capable of working miracles on earth and of filling it overnight with beautiful palaces and cities, as it was told in prophetic fairy tales. After looking down on those toiling men for one or two minutes, the ray of sunlight failed to break through that dense bank of clouds and was drowned in it like a child in the sea. And now the rain turned into a heavy downpour.

'We can knock off now,' someone shouted, but he was angrily answered by the others: 'I'll knock *you* off!'

Right up to two o'clock, until the whole cargo had been loaded onto the other barge, those half-naked men worked without stopping in a torrential downpour and biting wind. All this made me understand with deep reverence what powerful forces enriched the world of men.

MAXIM GORKY (1868–1936), *My Universities*, 1923, tr. Ronald Wilks, 1979

The world of the ironworks is one in which there are constant suggestions of the ordinary operations of life raised to some strange, monstrous power, in which the land runs, not with water, but with fire, where the labourer leaning on his spade, is going to dig, not in fresh moist earth, but in a channel of molten flame; where, instead of stacking the crops, he stacks iron too hot for him to handle; where the tools laid out ready for his use are huge iron bars 10 feet long or more, taking several men to wield them. The onlooker, whose centre of activity lies among surroundings different from these, walks with wonder and misgiving through the lurid, reverberating works, seeing danger at every turn, and shudders at what seems to him the lot of the worker among such grim surroundings as these. But there is many a man employed in the works to whom these surroundings are even congenial, to whom the world coloured in black and flame-colour is a world he knows and understands, and that he misses when he is away from it. And there must be hundreds and thousands of people earning their livelihood in other ways, whose actual working hours are passed in a setting that will seem to many of us still less enviable: who, adding up figures or copying letters, see nothing but the walls of one small room round them for eight hours every day. For the actual nature of the occupation of the various branches of ironmaking may appear to some of us, given the requisite strength and the requisite health, to be preferable to many other of the callings which might presumably have been open to the people engaged in it, or, indeed, to those open to other classes of society who spend their lives in sedentary anxiety.

Many of the people who have to sit in a stuffy room and pore over pages in a bad light, would probably find their nerves, physical condition, digestion, and general outlook on life entirely different if they were, for instance, making trenches in the sand, taking out moulds, and throwing them to the next man to do the same. There is, no doubt, monotony in most occupations; but it is conceivable that the monotony of the work conducted in movement is not so penetrating as that which is conducted in immobility. It has not, at any rate, the deadly uniformity of being indoors, and even in England there are many days in the year when the weather is fine, and when the vapours from molten iron, ill-smelling though they be, cannot entirely sweep away the sweet breezes from the river. There are many of the men, no doubt, who look sullen at their work, many who look discontented; but so there are in all callings. In any Government office that you can name, I believe that there is as large a proportion of sullen and discontented faces as there is at the iron-works; indeed, there are probably more, because there have been more possibilities to choose from, and the area of disappointment is therefore greater. People differ in their conceptions and their definitions of happiness. A recent paraphrase of Aristotle has defined it thus: 'Happiness consists in living the best life that your powers command in the best way that your circumstances permit.' The man at the ironworks, who by his character and aptitude is safe to have regular employment, whose health is good, who has a sufficient wage to have a margin, and a wife that he cares about competent enough to administer it to the best advantage, who has a comfortable home and children of whom he is fond, seems to me to have as good a chance of happiness as most of his fellow creatures—and there is fortunately many a man at the works to whom this description can apply.

LADY (FLORENCE) BELL (1851–1930), *At the Works*, 1907

[Edwin Clayhanger, at the age of sixteen, discovers the pleasures of architectural draftsmanship.]

He no longer wanted to 'play' now. He despised play. His unique wish was to work. It struck him as curious and delightful that he really enjoyed work. Work indeed had become play. He could not do enough work to satisfy his appetite. And after the work of the day, scorning all silly notions about exercise and relaxation, he would spend the evening in his beautiful new attic, copying designs, which he would sometimes rise early to finish.

ARNOLD BENNETT (1867–1931), *Clayhanger*, 1910

But the quite happiest bit of manual work I ever did was for my mother in the old inn at Sixt, where she alleged the stone staircase to have become unpleasantly dirty, since last year. Nobody in the inn appearing to think it possible to wash it, I brought the necessary buckets of water from the yard myself, poured them into beautiful image of Versailles waterworks down the fifteen or twenty steps of the great staircase, and with the strongest broom I could find, cleaned every step into its corners. It was quite lovely work to dash the water and drive the mud, from each, with accumulating splash down to the next one.

JOHN RUSKIN (1819–1900), *Praeterita*, 1885–9

One day as we were discussing a matter of abiding interest to artists and writers, namely the tonic effect of work and the conduct of life, he [the painter Delacroix] said to me: 'Years ago, when I was young, I could settle down to work only when I had some pleasure in prospect for the evening. Some music, or dancing, or any other sort of entertainment. But nowadays I am no longer like a schoolboy; I can work without ceasing and without any hope of reward. Moreover,' he added, 'if only you knew how broad-minded and easy to please hard work makes one when it comes to pleasures! The man who has filled his working day to his own satisfaction will be quite happy in the company of the local street porter, playing cards with him!'

> CHARLES BAUDELAIRE (1821–67), *The Life and Work of Eugène Delacroix*, 1863, tr. P. E. Charvet, 1981

Work and boredom.—Looking for work in order to be paid: in civilized countries today almost all men are at one in doing that. For all of them work is a means and not an end in itself. Hence they are not very refined in their choice of work, if only it pays well. But there are, if only rarely, men who would rather perish than work without any *pleasure* in their work. They are choosy, hard to satisfy, and do not care for ample rewards, if the work itself is not the reward of rewards. Artists and contemplative men of all kinds belong to this rare breed, but so do even those men of leisure who spend their lives hunting, traveling, or in love affairs and adventures. All of these desire work and misery if only it is associated with pleasure, and the hardest, most difficult work if necessary. Otherwise, their idleness is resolute, even if it spells impoverishment, dishonor, and danger to life and limb. They do not fear boredom as much as work without pleasure; they actually require a lot of boredom if *their* work is to succeed. For thinkers and all sensitive spirits, boredom is that disagreeable 'windless calm' of the soul that precedes a happy voyage and cheerful winds. They have to bear it and must wait for its effect on them. Precisely this is what lesser natures cannot achieve by any means.

> FRIEDRICH NIETZSCHE (1844–1900), *The Gay Science* (1882; rev. 1887), tr. Walter Kaufmann, 1974

He often said: 'My programme is work. "Thou shalt gain thy bread in the sweat of thy brow" was written centuries ago. Immutable destiny, which none may change! What every one ought to do is to find progress in his profession, to try ever to do better, to be strong and clever in his trade, and be greater than his neighbor in talent and conscientiousness in his work. That for me is the only path. The rest is dream or calculation.'

> ALFRED SENSIER (1815–77), *Jean-François Millet: Peasant and Painter*, 1881, tr. Helena de Kay

He discovered at last a real adventure in the coal-mines. His father asked him to help in the firm. Gerald had been educated in the science of mining, and it had never interested him. Now, suddenly, with a sort of exultation, he laid hold of the world.

There was impressed photographically on his consciousness the great industry. Suddenly, it was real, he was part of it. Down the valley ran the colliery railway, linking mine with mine. Down the railway ran the trains, short trains of heavily-laden trucks, long trains of empty wagons, each one bearing in big white letters the initials: 'C. B. & Co.' These white letters on all the wagons he had seen since his first childhood, and it was as if he had never seen them, they were so familiar, and so ignored. Now at last he saw his own name written on the wall. Now he had a vision of power.

So many wagons, bearing his initial, running all over the country. He saw them as he entered London in the train, he saw them at Dover. So far his power ramified. He looked at Beldover, at Selby, at Whatmore, at Lethley Bank, the great colliery villages which depended entirely on his mines. They were hideous and sordid, during his childhood they had been sores in his consciousness. And now he saw them with pride. Four raw new towns, and many ugly industrial hamlets were crowded under his dependence. He saw the stream of miners flowing along the causeways from the mines at the end of the afternoon, thousands of blackened, slightly distorted human beings with red mouths, all moving subjugate to his will. He pushed slowly in his motorcar through the little market-top on Friday nights in Beldover, through a solid mass of human beings that were making their purchases and doing their weekly spending. They were all subordinate to him. They were ugly and uncouth, but they were his instruments. He was the God of the machine. They made way for his motor-car automatically, slowly.

He did not care whether they made way with alacrity, or grudgingly. He did not care what they thought of him. His vision had suddenly crystallised. Suddenly he had conceived the pure instrumentality of mankind. There had been so much humanitarianism, so much talk of sufferings and feelings. It was ridiculous. The sufferings and feelings of individuals did not matter in the least. They were mere conditions, like the weather. What mattered was the pure instrumentality of the individual. As a man as of a knife: does it cut well? Nothing else mattered.

Everything in the world has its function, and is good or not good in so far as it fulfils this function more or less perfectly. Was a miner a good miner? Then he was complete. Was a manager a good manager? That was enough. Gerald himself, who was responsible for all this industry, was he a good director? If he were, he had fulfilled his life. The rest was by-play.

The mines were there, they were old. They were giving out, it did not pay to work the seams. There was talk of closing down two of them. It was at this point that Gerald arrived on the scene.

He looked around. There lay the mines. They were old, obsolete. They were like old lions, no more good. He looked again. Pah! the mines were nothing but the clumsy efforts of impure minds. There they lay, abortions of a half-trained mind. Let the idea of them be swept away. He cleared his brain of them, and thought only of the coal in the under earth. How much was there?

There was plenty of coal. The old workings could not get at it, that was all. Then break the neck of the old workings. The coal lay there in its seams, even though the seams were thin. There it lay, inert matter, as it had always lain, since the beginning of time, subject to the will of man. The will of man was the determining factor. Man was the arch-god of earth. His mind was obedient to serve his will. Man's will was the absolute, the only absolute.

And it was his will to subjugate Matter to his own ends. The subjugation itself was the point, the fight was the be-all, the fruits of victory were mere results. It was not for the sake of money that Gerald took over the mines. He did not care about money, fundamentally. He was neither ostentatious nor luxurious, neither did he care about social position, not finally. What he wanted was the pure fulfilment of his own will in the struggle with the natural conditions. His will was now, to take the coal out of the earth, profitably. The profit was merely the condition of victory, but the victory itself lay in the feat achieved. He vibrated with zest before the challenge.

D. H. LAWRENCE (1885–1930), *Women in Love*, 1920

There's a good feeling when I'm out there on the road. There ain't nobody looking over your shoulder and watching what you're doing. When I worked in a warehouse, you'd be punching in and punching out, and bells ringing all the time. On those jobs, you're not thinking, you're just doing what they tell you. Sure, now I'm expected to bring her in on time, but a couple of hours one way or the other don't make no difference. And there ain't nobody but me to worry about how I get her there.

28-year-old trucker, quoted in Lillian B. Rubin, *Worlds of Pain*, 1972

Finally, it is evident that mental application or concentration or an intellectual accomplishment will result, especially in youthful persons, but in elder persons as well, in a simultaneous sexual excitement. This may be looked upon as the only justified basis for the otherwise so doubtful etiology of nervous disturbances from mental 'overwork'.

SIGMUND FREUD (1856–1939), 'Infantile Sexuality', *Three Contributions to the Theory of Sex*, 1905, tr. A. A. Brill, 1910

During a visit which I once paid to a manufactory of military clothing, I witnessed the following scene. In the midst of the uniform sound produced by some thirty sewing machines, I suddenly heard one of the machines working with much more velocity than the others. I looked at the person who was working it, a brunette of 18 or 20. While she was automatically occupied with the trousers she was making on the machine, her face became animated, her mouth opened slightly, her nostrils dilated, her feet moved the pedals with constantly increasing rapidity. Soon I saw a convulsive look in her eyes, her eyelids were lowered, her faced turned pale and was thrown backward; hands and legs stopped and became extended; a suffocated cry, followed by a long sigh, was lost in the noise of the workroom. The girl remained motionless a few seconds, drew out her handkerchief to wipe away the pearls of sweat from her forehead, and, after casting a timid and ashamed glance at her companions, resumed her work.

As I was leaving, I heard another machine at another part of the room in accelerated movement. The forewoman smiled at me, and remarked that that was so frequent that it attracted no notice.

> THÉSÉE POUILLET (b. 1849), *Essai médico-philosophique sur les formes, les causes, les signes, les conséquences et le traitement de l'onanisme chez la femme*, 1876, tr. Havelock Ellis, 1900

As the ex-slave, Frederick Douglass pointed out (above p. 19), singing at work is not necessarily a sign that pleasure is being taken in the task. But in early modern times it often was.

> Such servants are oftenest painfull and good,
>   that sing in their labour, as birdes in the wood.
>
> THOMAS TUSSER (1524?–80), *Five Hundred Points of Good Husbandrie*, 1557

> O fellow, come, the song we had last night.
> Mark it, Cesario, it is old and plain.
> The spinsters and the knitters in the sun,
> And the free maids that weave their thread with bones,
> Do use to chant it.
>
> WILLIAM SHAKESPEARE (1564–1616), *Twelfth Night*, wr. c.1600

> I heare the whistling Plough-man all day long,
> Sweetning his labour with a chearful song;
> His Bed's a Pad of *Straw*; his dyet, coarse;
> In both, he fares not better than his *Horse*;
> He seldom slakes his thirst, but from the *Pump*;

And yet his heart is blithe, his visage, plump;
His thoughts are ne'er acquainted with such things,
As Griefs or Fears; he only sweats and sings:

FRANCIS QUARLES (1592–1644), from 'On the Plough-man', 1632

I Hear America Singing

I hear America singing, the varied carols I hear,
Those of mechanics, each one singing his as it should be blithe and strong,
The carpenter singing his as he measures his plank or beam,
The mason singing his as he makes ready for work, or leaves off work,
The boatman singing what belongs to him in his boat, the deckhand singing
    on the steamboat deck,
The shoemaker singing as he sits on his bench, the hatter singing as he stands,
The wood-cutter's song, the ploughboy's on his way in the morning, or at
    noon intermission or at sundown,
The delicious singing of the mother, or of the young wife at work, or of the girl
    sewing or washing,
Each singing what belongs to him or her and to none else,
The day what belongs to the day—at night the party of young fellows, robust,
    friendly,
Singing with open mouths their strong melodious songs.

WALT WHITMAN (1819–92), 1881 edn.

Most of the men sang or whistled as they dug or hoed. There was a good deal of outdoor singing in those days. Workmen sang at their jobs; men with horses and carts sang on the road; the baker, the miller's man, and the fish-hawker sang as they went from door to door; even the doctor and parson on their rounds hummed a tune between their teeth. People were poorer and had not the comforts, amusements, or knowledge we have to-day; but they were happier. Which seems to suggest that happiness depends more upon the state of mind—and body, perhaps—than upon circumstances and events.

FLORA THOMPSON (1876–1947), *Lark Rise to Candleford*, 1945

What Happened to the Songs

Very seldom do they use the worksongs now. They don't use the worksongs in the fields chopping because they don't chop, they don't work the fields now like they used to work. They have tractors now to do the work we did with hoes. And the tractors plow up close and eliminate a lot of our work. The turnrows, they don't have to clean them no more because they got graders that grade off the turnrows.

Back then, you had to chop a row and back up, the squad would line up and clean off the turnrow, that called for a lot of chopping that high grass on the back of the turnrow. Probably clear across to the next ditch. Well, everybody would get together in union, in harmony. It made the work seem easy even when it's hard if you singing. Everybody chop together and pullin' together. It would be a lots easier now with the little choppin' they do if they did sing and work more closely together, 'cause now when they're not singing every man has probably got his lip stuck out 'cause he's got time to think. All you got to do is concentrate on your song and your rhythm and the time goes by.

But now everybody works individually in most cases. He won't even carry his part. When you working together in union in a line everybody carries his part. Now you liable to be in a line with nobody singing, maybe two or three squabbling about 'Move over, don't come hit me!' or 'Get your part!' That's all you hear all day. And it makes the work a little bit harder. Even though they're not working as hard as they did in the past.

Same thing applies in the woods. Now every now and then you get some of it. Some a the old convicts will get together, they'll work in the woods, mostly in that heavy timber. They'll call the old convicts to cut it down because the young ones can't handle it. They can't handle a axe like a old convict can. You take four or six around a tree and they'll sing it down, they'll sing it down in harmony, they'll sing and cut, and they'll have it down an hour quicker than those that's actually just runnin' their head and talkin' when they workin'. In union, when you workin' in union and singin' in union, it makes it a lot easier all around.

The oldtimers still sometimes sing. That is, if whoever is carrying the squad will let them. In some cases the boss won't let them sing.

Why?

You take in the system now, there's more educated men. Back in those days we was referrin' to when they did all the singing while they worked, the system couldn't hire educated men, they hired who they could, and they thought it was a big thing to let 'em sing. Which it was, it was helpin' the inmate. But now we have mostly college men, young college men, men that's finished college, still taking some classes in college, just carryin' squads, they never experienced that. And in most cases they don't know whether they can or whether they can't. They don't know whether they can permit 'em to sing or not and rather than step out of bounds and be wrong they say: 'Don't. Just knock off the singing and work.' Actually, we get more work done when there's singing then when we're silent. Because that leads into arguments and confusion if a man hasn't anything to occupy his mind. If his mind is occupied he's steady working in union.

The young mens don't get a chance to work with the older mens and they haven't experienced working with the older mens before. A lot of them have never been in the system before. And they crews they work with don't even know the songs, the worksongs that they work by. In most cases their world is so modernaire, they all daydreamin': they drivin' the Cadillacs and sleepin' on the silk sheets, you know. Living a fictitious life and daydreaming. But once they get to working with the older men, they learn the songs, and they try to carry them on when they can.

> ANONYMOUS TEXAS PRISONER, incarcerated *c.*1964–6, *Wake-up Dead Man: Afro-American Worksongs from Texas Prisons*, ed. Bruce Jackson, 1972

Work was commended as the most effective remedy for grief and unhappiness.

The labour we delight in physics pain.

> WILLIAM SHAKESPEARE (1564–1616), *Macbeth*, wr. 1606

Bodily labour keeps off Pain of Mind; and by doing so makes the Poor happy.

> FRANÇOIS, DUC DE LA ROCHEFOUCAULD (1613–80), *Moral Maxims and Reflections*, 1678, tr. George Stanhope, 1706

The safe and general antidote against sorrow is employment. It is commonly observed that among soldiers and seamen, though there is much kindness, there is little grief; they see their friend fall without any of that lamentation which is indulged in security and idleness, because they have no leisure to spare from the care of themselves; and whoever shall keep his thoughts equally busy, will find himself equally unaffected with irretrievable losses.

> SAMUEL JOHNSON (1709–84), *The Rambler*, 28 Aug. 1750

Up, and at the office all the morning; and so to it again after dinner and there busy late, choosing to imploy myself rather then go home to trouble with my wife.

> SAMUEL PEPYS (1633–1703), *Diary*, 7 Nov. 1668

During this conversation news had spread that two viziers of the bench and the mufti had been strangled in Constantinople, and several of their friends impaled. This catastrophe made a great stir everywhere for some hours. On their way back to the farm Pangloss, Candide, and Martin met a kindly old man who was taking the air at his door beneath an arbour of orange-trees. Pangloss, who was as curious as he was prone to philosophizing, asked him the name of the mufti who had just been strangled.

'I have no idea,' replied the fellow, 'and I never have known what any mufti or vizier was called. What you have just told me means absolutely nothing to me. I have no doubt that in general those who get involved in public affairs do sometimes come to a sad end and that they deserve it. But I never enquire what's going on in Constantinople. I am content to send my fruit for sale there from the garden I cultivate.'

Having said this, he invited the strangers into his house. His two daughters and two sons offered them several kinds of sorbet which they made themselves, some *kaïmak* sharpened with the zest of candied citron, some oranges, lemons, limes, pineapple, and pistachio nuts, and some Mocha coffee which had not been blended with that awful coffee from Batavia and the islands. After which the two daughters of this good Muslim perfumed the beards of Candide, Pangloss, and Martin.

'You must have a vast and magnificent property,' said Candide to the Turk.

'I have but twenty acres,' replied the Turk. 'I cultivate them with my children. Work keeps us from three great evils: boredom, vice, and need.'

Candide, on his way back to his farm, thought long and hard about what the Turk had said, and commented to Pangloss and Martin:

'That kind old man seems to me to have made a life for himself which is much preferable to that of those six Kings with whom we had the honour of having supper.'

'High rank can be very dangerous,' said Pangloss; 'all the philosophers say so. For the fact is, Eglon, King of the Moabites, was slain by Ehud; Absalom was hanged by the hair on his head and had three darts thrust through his heart; King Nadab, son of Jeroboam, was smitten by Baasha; King Elah by Zimri; Joram by Jehu; Athaliah by Jehoiada; and Kings Jehoiakim, Jehoiachin, and Zedekiah entered into captivity. You know what sort of deaths befell Croesus, Astyages, Darius, Dionysius of Syracuse, Pyrrhus, Perseus, Hannibal, Jugurtha, Ariovistus, Caesar, Pompey, Nero, Otho, Vitellius, Domitian, Richard II of England, Edward II, Henry VI, Richard III, Mary Stuart, Charles I, France's three Henris, and the Emperor Henri IV? You know . . .'

'I also know,' said Candide, 'that we must cultivate our garden.'

'You're right,' said Pangloss; 'for when man was placed in the garden of Eden, he was placed there *ut operaretur eum*—that he might work—which proves that man was not born to rest.'

'Let's get down to work and stop all this philosophizing,' said Martin. 'It's the only way to make life bearable.'

VOLTAIRE (1694–1778), Candide, 1759, tr. Roger Pearson, 1990

Without some fixed and steady occupation of labour—of business—of study—something which keeps in habitual exercise our physical or mental energies, and the better when it is both, it is impossible to make our existence glide smoothly—we must know moments, nay hours, of vexation and lassitude.

> FRANCES WRIGHT (1795–1852), letter to Julia Garnett, 4 Dec. 1825

Women, it is said, go mad much seldomer than men. I fancy if this be true it is in some degree owing to the little manual works in which they are constantly employed which regulate in some degree the current of ideas as the pendulum regulates the motion of the timepiece. I do not know if this is sense or nonsense but I am sensible that, if I was in solitary confinement without either the power of taking exercise or employing myself in study, six months would make me a madman or an idiot.

> SIR WALTER SCOTT (1771–1832), *Journal*, 29 Oct. 1826

There is nothing continually good but the habit of stubborn work. It releases an opium that numbs the soul.

> GUSTAVE FLAUBERT (1821–80), letter to Louise Colet, 26 July 1851, tr. Francis Steegmuller, 1980

'There's nothing but what's bearable as long as a man can work,' he said to himself: 'the natur o' things doesn't change, though it seems as if one's own life was nothing but change. The square o' four is sixteen, and you must lengthen your lever in proportion to your weight, is as true when a man's miserable as when he's happy; and the best o' working is, it gives you a grip hold o' things outside your own lot.'

As he dashed the cold water over his head and face, he felt completely himself again, and with his black eyes as keen as ever, and his thick black hair all glistening with the fresh moisture.

> GEORGE ELIOT (1819–90), *Adam Bede*, 1859

I am glad to hear of your farming. I like you to be so employed; still I should like you to do something besides. But one must judge one's friends according to *their* feelings, not one's own. We have always been very intimate, and very unlike. *Your* mind must be calm and tranquil before it can work. If I had enjoyed tranquillity and calm, I doubt whether I should ever have worked. It costs me so much, that if I were tolerably comfortable in inactivity, I should continue there. It has always been because my mind was uncomfortable at home that it sallied abroad to obtain, at any sacrifice, the relief of hard intellectual work. This is the case now.

I have no child to enjoy the little noise that my name may make. I do not believe that in such times as these the slightest influence can be obtained by such writings as mine, or even by any writings, except by the bad novels, which try to make us still more immoral and ill-conditioned than we are. Yet I rise at five, and sit for six hours before my paper, and often leave it still white. Sometimes I find what I am looking for, but find it painfully and imperfectly; sometimes I am in despair at not finding it at all. I leave work discontented with myself, and therefore with everything else. Why do I make these efforts? To escape from mental disquiet: while *you* cannot work unless you are already perfectly at ease.

ALEXIS DE TOCQUEVILLE (1805–59), letter to Gustave de Beaumont de
La Bonninière, 21 May 1858

It is well known, we are told, to physiologists, and the fact is not lost sight of in our treatment of the insane, that manual labour requiring a moderate amount of attention, such as the prosecution of a handicraft, has a remarkably composing tendency on the mind; but carpentering is perhaps the only male pursuit which combines the exact proportions of physical and mental exertion supposed to produce such beneficial results. Few men, however, are carpenters, whereas, speaking in general terms, all women can sew, and the very act of stitching we believe to be a complete and unfailing anodyne. The delicate fingers bend unconsciously to their task; the white hand flies to and fro as the dove flew round the Ark seeking the olive-branch on which it should find rest at last; the gentle head bends lower and lower, while thoughts, humbled by sorrow and chastened by resignation, wander further and further away. Presently the tears are dropping fast upon the pattern, be it the beads of a queen's embroidery or the hem of a peasant's smock; but like summer showers they do but clear the sky when they are over, and ere the hair is shook back, and the loving face looks up to thread the needle afresh, all is sunshine and peace once more.

G. J. WHYTE-MELVILLE (1821–78), *The Queen's Maries,* 1864

The cure for this ill is not to sit still,
Or frowst with a book by the fire;
But to take a large hoe and a shovel also,
And dig till you gently perspire.

RUDYARD KIPLING (1865–1936), from 'How the Camel Got His Hump',
1902

Such a hypnotic deadening of sensibility and susceptibility to pain, which presupposes somewhat rare powers, especially courage, contempt of opinion, intellectual stoicism, is less frequent than another and certainly easier *train-*

ing which is tried against states of depression. I mean *mechanical activity*. It is indisputable that a suffering existence can be thereby considerably alleviated. This fact is called to-day by the somewhat ignoble title of the 'Blessing of work.' The alleviation consists in the attention of the sufferer being absolutely diverted from suffering, in the incessant monopoly of the consciousness by action, so that consequently there is little room left for suffering—for *narrow* is it, this chamber of human consciousness!

> FRIEDRICH NIETZSCHE (1844–1900), *The Genealogy of Morals*, 1887, tr. Horace B. Samuel, 1910

You sound as if you keep busy—or are kept busy—and this keeps misery at bay to some extent. I tend to take to drink in such circumstances (incidentally, Patsy Strang, later Patsy Murphy, is now reputedly an alcoholic in Dublin. Another of my friends has been in hospital for the same thing. So I watch it). And of course *work*, paradoxically enough, *is* a comfort. One wakes up wanting to cut one's throat; one goes to work, & in 15 minutes one wants to cut someone else's—complete cure!

> PHILIP LARKIN (1922–85), letter to Winifred Bradshaw (née Arnott), 16 Nov. 1976

It is necessary to work, if not out of inclination, then at least out of desperation, since, all things considered, working causes less anxiety than does amusing oneself.

> CHARLES BAUDELAIRE (1821–67), *My Heart Laid Bare*, 1862–4

. . . working is a lot easier than living.

> JANE GARDAM (1928–), *The Queen of the Tambourine*, 1991

Work could also bring a sense of achievement and the satisfaction of a job well done.

Wherefore I perceive that there is nothing better, than that a man should rejoice in his own works.

> Ecclesiastes 3: 22

Honour the gardener! that patient man
Who from his schooldays follows up his calling,
Starting so modestly, a little boy

Red-nosed, red-fingered, doing what he's told,
Not knowing what he does or why he does it,
Having no concept of the larger plan.
But gradually, (if the love be there,
Irrational as any passion, strong,)
Enlarging vision slowly turns the key
And swings the door wide open on the long
Vistas of true significance. No more
Is toil a vacant drudgery, when purport
Attends each small and conscientious task,
—As the stone-mason setting yard by yard
Each stone in place, exalting not his gaze
To measure growth of structure or assess
That slow accomplishment, but in the end
Tops the last finial and, stepping back
To wipe the grit for the last time from eyes,
Sees that he built a temple,—so the true
Born gardener toils with love that is not toil
In detailed time of minutes, hours, and days,
Months, years, a life of doing each thing well;
The Life-line in his hand not rubbed away
As you might think, by constant scrape and rasp,
But deepened rather, as the line of Fate,
By earth imbedded in his wrinkled palm;
A golden ring worn thin upon his finger,
A signet ring, no ring of human marriage,
On that brown hand, dry as a crust of bread,
A ring that in its circle belts him close
To earthly seasons, and in its slow thinning
Wears out its life with his.

V. SACKVILLE-WEST (1892–1962), *The Garden*, 1946

The Old Workman

'Why are you so bent down before your time,
Old mason? Many have not left their prime
So far behind at your age, and can still
    Stand full upright at will.'

He pointed to the mansion-front hard by,
And to the stones of the quoin against the sky;
'Those upper blocks', he said, 'that there you see,
    It was that ruined me.'

There stood in the air up to the parapet
Crowning the corner height, the stones as set
By him—ashlar whereon the gales might drum
    For centuries to come.

'I carried them up', he said, 'by a ladder there;
The last was as big a load as I could bear;
But on I heaved; and something in my back
    Moved, as 'twere with a crack.

'So I got crookt. I never lost that sprain;
And those who live there, walled from wind and rain
By freestone that I lifted, do not know
    That my life's ache came so.

'They don't know me, or even know my name,
But good I think it, somehow, all the same
To have kept 'em safe from harm, and right and tight,
    Though it has broke me quite.

'Yes; that I fixed it firm up there I am proud,
Facing the hail and snow and sun and cloud,
And to stand storms for ages, beating round
    When I lie underground.'

THOMAS HARDY (1840–1928), 1922

'A Warning against Too Much Pride in One's Work'

If there be craftsmen in the monastery, let them practise their crafts with all humility, provided the abbot give permission. But if one of them be puffed up because of his skill in his craft, supposing that he is conferring a benefit on the monastery, let him be removed from his work and not return to it, unless he have humbled himself.

SAINT BENEDICT (*c.*480–*c.*547), *Rule for Monks*, *c.*530–40, tr. Justin McCann, 1970

There will never be a system invented which will do away with the necessity of work. Nature has seen to that. Idle hands and minds were never intended for any one of us. Work is our sanity, our self-respect, our salvation. So far from being a curse, work is the greatest blessing. Exact social justice flows only out of honest work. The man who contributes much should take away much. Therefore no element of charity is present in the paying of wages. The kind of workman who gives the business the best that is in him is the best kind of workman a business can have. And he cannot be expected to do this indefinitely without proper recognition of his contribution. The man who comes to the day's job feeling that no matter how much he may give, it will not yield him enough of a return to keep him beyond want, is not in shape to do his day's work. He is anxious and worried, and it all reacts to the detriment of his work.

But if a man feels that his day's work is not only supplying his basic need, but is also giving him a margin of comfort and enabling him to give his boys and girls their opportunity and his wife some pleasure in life, then his job looks good to him and he is free to give it of his best. This is a good thing for him and a good thing for the business. The man who does not get a certain satisfaction out of his day's work is losing the best part of his pay.

For the day's work is a great thing—a very great thing! It is at the very foundation of the world; it is the basis of our self-respect.

> HENRY FORD (1863–1947), in collaboration with Samuel Crowther, *My Life and Work*, 1922

I love all beauteous things,
 I seek and adore them;
God hath no better praise,
And man in his hasty days
 Is honoured for them.

I too will something make
 And joy in the making;
Altho' to-morrow it seem
Like the empty words of a dream
 Remembered on waking.

> ROBERT BRIDGES (1844–1930), 1890

Every one knows what it is to start a piece of work, either intellectual or muscular, feeling stale—or *oold*, as an Adirondack guide once put it to me. And everybody knows what it is to 'warm up' to his job. The process of warming up gets particularly striking in the phenomenon known as 'second wind.' On usual occasions we make a practice of stopping an occupation as soon as we meet the first effective layer (so to call it) of fatigue. We have then walked, played, or worked 'enough,' so we desist. That amount of fatigue is an efficacious obstruction on this side of which our usual life is cast. But if an unusual necessity forces us to press onward, a surprising thing occurs. The fatigue gets worse up to a certain critical point, when gradually or suddenly it passes away, and we are fresher than before. We have evidently tapped a level of new energy, masked until then by the fatigue-obstacle usually obeyed. There may be layer after layer of this experience. A third and a fourth 'wind' may supervene. Mental activity shows the phenomenon as well as physical, and in exceptional cases we may find, beyond the very extremity of fatigue-distress, amounts of ease and power that we never dreamed ourselves to own—sources of strength habitually not taxed at all, because habitually we never push through the obstruction, never pass those early critical points.

WILLIAM JAMES (1842–1910), 'The Energies of Men', 1907

I have this great comfort. It is only my present happiness in this world that can be damaged. My work, or at any rate a good lot of it, is done—nothing can undo it. The six published books, the novel, and the commonplace book—these are enough for one man. True, I should like to do a great deal more, and by no means despair of doing it, nevertheless, suppose I fail, I have still done not a little; and what I have done is square, genuine stuff.

SAMUEL BUTLER (1835–1902), *Note-Books*, wr. 1890–3, pub. 1934

Unfit for work: alone with poor dear father and his shadowlike mind and irresponsible character. Depressed, I take up a volume of Matthew Arnold's poems and read these words as the expression of the ideal life towards which I constantly strive:

> Of toil unsevered from tranquillity!
> Of labour, that in lasting fruit outgrows
> Far noisier schemes, accomplished in repose
> Too great for haste, too high for rivalry!

This state of toil unsevered from tranquillity I sometimes feel I have attained. Still, one is troubled (alas, too often troubled) with the foolish dreams of personal success and with a deep depression of personal failure. I love my work; that is my salvation; I delight in this slow stepping towards truth. Search after truth by the careful measurement of facts is the enthusiasm of my life. And of late this has been combined with a realization of the common aim of the great army of truth-seekers: the ennobling of human life. It has been enriched by the consciousness of the supreme unity of science, art, morality; the eternal trinity of the good, the beautiful and the true; knit together in the ideal towards which humanity is constantly striving, knowingly or unknowingly, with failure or success according to the ebb and flow of pure motive and honest purpose.

BEATRICE POTTER (later Webb) (1858–1943), diary, 17 Aug. 1889, *My Apprenticeship*, 1926

Some sorts of labor, though pursued systematically and continuously, seem never to become wearisome. This is the case with much intellectual labor, especially that of persons who are engaged in the pursuit of knowledge and in the satisfaction of man's insatiable curiosity about the things that surround him. Persons of artistic temperament—painters, musicians, poets—have often so strong an instinctive bent toward one kind of activity that nothing can hold them from it and nothing ever pall the pleasure of the exertion. And any occupation which satisfies the instinct of emulation has unceasing charm. He who can achieve things which few can achieve, and which many would like to achieve, rarely tires of his work. The actor, even though his occupation involves the monotonous and long-continued repetition of the most trifling details, never fails to get a thrill of pleasure from the breathless silence or stirring applause of his audience. Were he compelled to go through his part as often and as rigorously under the cold supervision of an indifferent supervisor, and under that only, how flat and stale it would become! For a similar reason, work of leadership and command almost always is continuously pleasurable. It satisfies the love of distinction and the desire for domination; and it has a real or apparent element of freedom. Hence the work of the employer commonly affords more satisfaction than that of the employee, and often is continued, from mere love of the doing as well as from habit, long after the reward or profit from the exertion has ceased to be valued.

F. W. Taussig (1859–1940), *Principles of Economics*, 1911

The differences in what labour means to different people could not be greater. For some, and probably a majority, it remains a stint to be performed. It may be preferable, especially in the context of social attitudes toward production, to doing nothing. Nevertheless it is fatiguing or monotonous or, at a minimum, a source of no particular pleasure. The reward rests not in the task but in the pay.

For others work, as it continues to be called, is an entirely different matter. It is taken for granted that it will be enjoyable. If it is not, this is a source of deep dissatisfaction or frustration. No one regards it as remarkable that the advertising man, tycoon, poet, or professor who suddenly finds his work unrewarding should seek the counsel of a psychiatrist. One insults the business executive or the scientist by suggesting that his principal motivation in life is the pay he receives. Pay is not unimportant. Among other things it is a prime index of prestige. Prestige—the respect, regard, and esteem of others—is in turn one of the more important sources of satisfaction associated with this kind of work. But, in general, those who do this kind of work expect to contribute their best regardless of compensation. They would be disturbed by any suggestion to the contrary.

John Kenneth Galbraith (1908–), *The Affluent Society*, 1958

For it is commonly said: completed labours are pleasant.

CICERO (106–43 BC), *De finibus bonorum et malorum,* 45 BC

[Edward Gibbon completes The History of the Decline and Fall of the Roman Empire.*]*

I have presumed to mark the moment of conception: I shall now commemorate the hour of my final deliverance. It was on the day, or rather night, of the 27th of June, 1787, between the hours of eleven and twelve, that I wrote the last lines of the last page, in a summer-house in my garden. After laying down my pen, I took several turns in a *berceau,* or covered walk of acacias, which commands a prospect of the country, the lake, and the mountains. The air was temperate, the sky was serene, the silver orb of the moon was reflected from the waters, and all nature was silent. I will not dissemble the first emotions of joy on the recovery of my freedom, and, perhaps, the establishment of my fame. But my pride was soon humbled, and a sober melancholy was spread over my mind, by the idea that I had taken an everlasting leave of an old and agreeable companion, and that whatsoever might be the future date of my History, the life of the historian must be short and precarious.

EDWARD GIBBON (1737–94), *Memoirs,* 1796

Labours once done be sweet . . . After painful labours and perils the remembrance of them is to him right pleasant.

RICHARD TAVERNER (1505?–75), *Proverbes or Adagies,* 1539

It was in 1885, after the completion of the Amiel translation, that I began 'Robert Elsmere.' . . . The book took me three years—nearly—to write. Again and again I found myself dreaming that the end was near, and publication only a month or two away; only to sink back on the dismal conviction that the second, or the first, or the third volume—or some portion of each— must be rewritten, if I was to satisfy myself at all. I actually wrote the last words of the last chapter in March 1887, and came out afterwards, from my tiny writing-room at the end of the drawing-room, shaken with tears, and wondering as I sat alone on the floor, by the fire, in the front room, what life would be like now that the book was done!

MRS HUMPHRY WARD (1851–1920), *A Writer's Recollections,* 1918

Work could thus become an obsessive addiction.

The truth is that in his last years, all the things we commonly call pleasure had disappeared from his life. One pleasure only, harsh, demanding, terrible, had replaced them all: work, which by then was no longer merely a passion but could well have been called a craving.

> CHARLES BAUDELAIRE (1821–67), *The Life and Work of Eugène Delacroix*, 1863, tr. P. E. Charvet, 1981

Work with some men is as besetting a sin as idleness with others.

> SAMUEL BUTLER (1835–1902), *Note-Books*, wr. 1890, pub. 1934

'Workaholism' is a word which I have invented. It is not in your dictionary. It means addiction to work, the compulsion or the uncontrollable need to work incessantly.

> W. E. OATES (1917–), *Confessions of a Workaholic*, 1971

You may wonder how such a busy man [Pliny the Elder] was able to complete so many volumes, many of them involving detailed study; and wonder still more when you learn that up to a certain age he practised at the bar, that he died at the age of fifty-five, and throughout the intervening years his time was much taken up with the important offices he held and his friendship with the Emperors. But he combined a penetrating intellect with amazing powers of concentration and the capacity to manage with the minimum of sleep.

From the feast of Vulcan onwards he began to work by lamplight, not with any idea of making a propitious start but to give himself more time for study, and would rise half-way through the night; in winter it would often be at midnight or an hour later, and two at the latest. Admittedly he fell asleep very easily, and would often doze and wake up again during his work. Before daybreak he would visit the Emperor Vespasian (who also made use of his nights) and then go to attend to his official duties. On returning home, he devoted any spare time to his work. After something to eat (his meals during the day were light and simple in the old-fashioned way), in summer when he was not too busy he would often lie in the sun, and a book was read aloud while he made notes and extracts. He made extracts of everything he read, and always said that there was no book so bad that some good could not be got out of it. After his rest in the sun he generally took a cold bath, and then ate something and had a short sleep; after which he worked till dinner time as if he had started on a new day. A book was read aloud during the meal and he took rapid notes. I remember that one of his friends told a reader to go back and repeat a word he had mispronounced. 'Couldn't you understand him?' said my uncle. His friend admitted that he could. 'Then why make him go back? Your interruption has lost us at least ten lines.' To such lengths did he carry his passion for saving time. In summer he rose from dinner while it was still light, in winter as soon as darkness fell, as if some law compelled him.

This was his routine in the midst of his public duties and the bustle of the city. In the country, the only time he took from his work was for his bath, and by bath I mean his actual immersion, for while he was being rubbed down and dried he had a book read to him or dictated notes. When travelling he felt free from other responsibilities to give every minute to work; he kept a secretary at his side with book and notebook, and in winter saw that his hands were protected by long sleeves, so that even bitter weather should not rob him of a working hour. For the same reason, too, he used to be carried about Rome in a chair. I can remember how he scolded me for walking; according to him I need not have wasted those hours, for he thought any time wasted which was not devoted to work. It was this application which enabled him to finish all those volumes, and to leave me 160 notebooks of selected passages, written in a minute hand on both sides of the page, so that their number is really doubled.

> PLINY THE YOUNGER (*c*.61–*c*.112), on his uncle, Pliny the Elder (23–79), tr. Betty Radice, 1969

Especially if they have beene formerly brought up to businesse, or to keepe much company, and upon a suddaine come to lead a sedentary life, it crucifies their soules, and seazeth on them in an instant, for whilst they are any waies imployed, in action, discourse, about any businesse, sport, or recreation, or in company to their liking, they are very well, but if alone, or idle, tormented instantly againe, one daies solitarinesse, one houres sometimes, doth them more harme, then a weekes physicke, labour and company can doe good. Melancholy seazeth on them forthwith being alone, and is such a torture, that as wise *Seneca* well saith, *malo mihi malè quam mollitèr esse,* I had rather be sicke then idle.

> ROBERT BURTON (1577–1640), *The Anatomy of Melancholy,* 1621

[His son describes the routine of the Puritan divine William Gouge (1578–1653).]

He did use to rise very early both winter and summer. In the winter he performed all the exercises of his private devotions before daylight; and in the summer time about four of the clock in the morning, by which means he had done half a day's work before others had begun their studies. If he heard any at their work before he had got to his study, he would say (as Demosthenes spoke concerning the smith) that he was much troubled that any should be at their calling before he was at his . . .

As for recreations, howsoever many pious persons do spend time therein, and that lawfully in warrantable recreations, yet he spent none therein . . . He hath been often heard to say that he took not any journey merely for pleasure in all his lifetime; study and pains having been always, both in youth and age, his chiefest pleasure and delight.

THOMAS GOUGE (1609–81), *A Narrative of the Life and Death of Doctor Gouge*, 1655

'A Puritan Divine's Resolution'

To be always doing, constant in studies, like Mr Calvin, who being asked why he was always at it, returned this answer: *Dominus cum venerit inveniet me laborantem*: when the Lord comes he shall find me working.

THOMAS CAWTON (1605–59), *The Life and Death of . . . Thomas Cawton*, 1662

[Sir John King (1638–77) was the top Chancery lawyer of his age. By the time of his death he was earning fees of £400 a day.]

His industry was so great that he never slept five hours together all those days that he designed to improve in his learning, and towards the latter end of his time not three hours together. Neither had he time to refresh nature by seasonable repasts and rest; his employment in his calling was so great, and overpressed by multitude of clients, which shortened his days.

A Memoir of the Life and Death of Sir John King by His Father, 1677

I may truly say
That they were as a proverb in the vale
For endless industry. When day was gone,
And from their occupations out of doors
The Son and Father were come home, even then,
Their labour did not cease; unless when all
Turned to the cleanly supper-board, and there,
Each with a mess of pottage and skimmed milk,
Sat round the basket piled with oaten cakes,
And their plain home-made cheese. Yet when the meal
Was ended, Luke (for so the Son was named)
And his old Father both betook themselves

To such convenient work as might employ
Their hands by the fire-side; perhaps to card
Wool for the Housewife's spindle, or repair
Some injury done to sickle, flail, or scythe,
Or other implement of house or field.

Down from the ceiling, by the chimney's edge,
That in our ancient uncouth country style
With huge and black projection overbrowed
Large space beneath, as duly as the light
Of day grew dim the Housewife hung a lamp;
An aged utensil, which had performed
Service beyond all others of its kind.
Early at evening did it burn—and late,
Surviving comrade of uncounted hours,
Which, going by from year to year, had found,
And left, the couple neither gay perhaps
Nor cheerful, yet with objects and with hopes,
Living a life of eager industry.

WILLIAM WORDSWORTH (1770–1850), from 'Michael', 1800

Happening to pass through Edinburgh in June, 1814, I dined one day with the gentleman in question (now the Honourable William Menzies, one of the Supreme Judges at the Cape of Good Hope), whose residence was then in George Street, situated very near to, and at right angles with, North Castle Street. It was a party of very young persons, most of them, like Menzies and myself, destined for the Bar of Scotland, all gay and thoughtless, enjoying the first flush of manhood, with little remembrance of the yesterday, or care for the morrow. When my companion's worthy father and uncle, after seeing two or three bottles go round, left the juveniles to themselves, the weather being hot, we adjourned to the library which had one large window looking northwards. After carousing there for an hour or more, I observed a shade had come over the aspect of my friend, who happened to be placed immediately opposite to myself, and said something that intimated a fear of his being unwell. 'No,' said he, 'I shall be well enough presently, if you will only let me sit where you are, and take my chair; for there is a confounded hand in sight of me here, which has often bothered me before, and now it won't let me fill my glass with a good will.' I rose to change places with him accordingly, and he pointed out to me this hand, which, like the writing on Belshazzar's wall, disturbed his hour of hilarity. 'Since we sat down,' he said, 'I have been watching it—it fascinates my eye—it never stops—page after page is finished and thrown on that heap of MS. and still it goes on unwearied—and so it will be till candles are brought in, and God knows how long after that. It is the same

every night—I can't stand a sight of it when I am not at my books.' 'Some
stupid, dogged, engrossing clerk, probably,' exclaimed myself, or some other
giddy youth in our society. 'No, boys,' said our host, 'I well know what hand
it is—'tis Walter Scott's.' This was the hand that, in the evenings of three
summer weeks, wrote the two last volumes of Waverley.

> J. G. LOCKHART (1794–1854), *Memoirs of the Life of Sir Walter Scott,*
> 1837–8

When Romney Leigh and I had parted thus,
I took a chamber up three flights of stairs
Not far from being as steep as some larks climb,
And there, in a certain house in Kensington,
Three years I lived and worked. Get leave to work
In this world—'tis the best you get at all;
For God, in cursing, gives us better gifts
Than men in benediction. God says, 'Sweat
For foreheads,' men say 'crowns,' and so we are crowned,
Ay, gashed by some tormenting circle of steel
Which snaps with a secret spring. Get work, get work;
Be sure 'tis better than what you work to get.

*

                         Day and night
I worked my rhythmic thought, and furrowed up
Both watch and slumber with long lines of life
Which did not suit their season. The rose fell
From either cheek, my eyes globed luminous
Through orbits of blue shadow, and my pulse
Would shudder along the purple-veinèd wrist
Like a shot bird. Youth's stern, set face to face
With youth's ideal: and when people came
And said, 'You work too much, you are looking ill,'
I smiled for pity of them who pitied me,
And thought I should be better soon perhaps
For those ill looks. Observe—'I' means in youth
Just *I*, the conscious and eternal soul
With all its ends, and not the outside life,
The parcel-man, the doublet of the flesh,
The so much liver, lung, integument,
Which make the sum of 'I' hereafter when
World-talkers talk of doing well or ill.
I prosper if I gain a step, although

A nail then pierced my foot: although my brain
Embracing any truth froze paralysed,
I prosper: I but change my instrument;
I break the spade off, digging deep for gold,
And catch the mattock up.
                              I worked on, on.
Through all the bristling fence of nights and days
Which hedges time in from the eternities,
I struggled—never stopped to note the stakes
Which hurt me in my course. The midnight oil
Would stink sometimes; there came some vulgar needs:
I had to live that therefore I might work,
And, being but poor, I was constrained, for life,
To work with one hand for the booksellers
While working with the other for myself
And art: you swim with feet as well as hands,
Or make small way. I apprehended this—
In England no one lives by verse that lives;
And, apprehending, I resolved by prose
To make a space to sphere my living verse.
I wrote for cyclopaedias, magazines,
And weekly papers, holding up my name
To keep it from the mud. I learnt the use
Of the editorial 'we' in a review
As courtly ladies the fine trick of trains,
And swept it grandly through the open doors
As if one could not pass through doors at all
Save so encumbered. I wrote tales beside,
Carved many an article on cherry-stones
To suit light readers—something in the lines
Revealing, it was said, the mallet-hand,
But that, I'll never vouch for: what you do
For bread, will taste of common grain, not grapes,
Although you have a vineyard in Champagne;
Much less in Nephelococcygia
As mine was, peradventure.
                              Having bread
For just so many days, just breathing-room
For body and verse, I stood up straight and worked
My veritable work. And as the soul
Which grows within a child makes the child grow—

Nephelococcygia] 'Cloud-cuckoo-land' in Aristophanes' *Birds*.

Or as the fiery sap, the touch from God,
Careering through a tree, dilates the bark
And roughs with scale and knob, before it strikes
The summer foliage out in a green flame—
So life, in deepening with me, deepened all
The course I took, the work I did. Indeed
The academic law convinced of sin;
The critics cried out on the falling off,
Regretting the first manner. But I felt
My heart's life throbbing in my verse to show
It lived, it also—certes incomplete,
Disordered with all Adam in the blood,
But even its very tumours, warts and wens
Still organised by and implying life.

ELIZABETH BARRETT BROWNING (1806–61), *Aurora Leigh*, 1857

'Take my own case,' he said. 'Maybe you envy me because I'm beginning to do good business, as the bourgeois say, publishing my books, making some money. Well, between you and me, it's getting me down. I've told you that already more than once, but you never believe me because for you, who find production so difficult and can make no headway with the public, happiness naturally means abundant production and being in the public eye, favourably or otherwise even . . . Get yourself accepted at the next Salon, go into the fray, paint more and more pictures, and then tell me whether you're as happy as you hoped to be! . . . The thing is, work has simply swamped my whole existence. Slowly but surely it's robbed me of my mother, my wife, and everything that meant anything to me. It's like a germ planted in the skull that devours the brain, spreads to the trunk and the limbs, and destroys the entire body in time. No sooner am I out of bed in the morning than work clamps down on me and pins me to my desk before I've even had a breath of fresh air. It follows me to lunch and I find myself chewing over sentences as I'm chewing my food. It goes with me when I go out, eats out of my plate at dinner and shares my pillow in bed at night. It's so completely merciless that once the process of creation is started, it's impossible for me to stop it, and it goes on growing and working even when I'm asleep . . . Outside that, nothing, nobody exists. I go up to see my mother, but I'm so absorbed that ten minutes afterwards I'm asking myself whether I've been up to her or not. As for my wife, she has no husband, poor thing; we're never really together any more, even when we're hand-in-hand! Sometimes I feel so acutely aware that I'm making them both unhappy that I'm overcome with remorse, for happiness in a home depends so much on kindness and frankness and gaiety. But do what I will, I can't escape entirely from the monster's clutches, and I'm soon back in the semi-conscious state that goes with creation and just as sullen and indifferent as I always am when I'm working. If the morning's writing's gone smoothly, all well and good; if it hasn't, all's *not* so good; and so the whole household laughs or cries to the whim of almighty Work! . . . That's the situation. I've nothing now I can call my own. In the bad old days I used to dream about foreign travel or restful holidays in the country. Now that I could have both, here I am hemmed in by work, with no hope of so much as a brisk walk in the morning, a free moment to visit an old friend, or a moment's self-indulgence! I haven't even a will of my own; it's become a habit now to lock my door on the world outside and throw my key out of the window . . . So there we are, cribbed and confined together, my work and me. And in the end it'll devour me, and that will be the end of that!'

ÉMILE ZOLA (1840–1902), *L'Œuvre*, 1886, tr. Thomas Walton, rev. Roger Pearson, 1993

[In 1855 Harriet Martineau wrote her autobiography in the belief that she had mortal heart disease and that her death was imminent. She lived for a further twenty-one years.]

In meditating on my course of life at that time, and gathering together the evidences of what I was learning and doing, I am less disposed than I used to be to be impatient with my friends for their incessant rebukes and remonstrances about over-work. From the age of fifteen to the moment in which I am writing, I have been scolded in one form or another, for working too hard; and I wonder my friends did not find out thirty years ago that there is no use in their fault-finding. I am heartily sick of it, I own; and there may be some little malice in the satisfaction with which I find myself dying, after all, of a disease which nobody can possibly attribute to over-work. Though knowing all along that my friends were mistaken as to what was moderate and what immoderate work, in other cases than their own (and I have always left *them* free to judge and act for themselves) I have never denied that less toil and more leisure would be wholesome and agreeable to me. My pleas have been that I have had no power of choice, and that my critics misjudged the particular case. Almost every one of them has proceeded on the supposition that the labour of authorship involved immense 'excitement;' and I, who am the quietest of quiet bodies, when let alone in my business, have been warned against 'excitement' till I am fairly sick of the word. One comfort has always been that those who were witnesses of my work-a-day life always came round to an agreement with me that literary labour is not necessarily more hurtfully exciting than any other serious occupation. My mother, alarmed at a distance, and always expecting to hear of a brain fever, used to say, amidst the whirl of our London spring days, 'My dear, I envy your calmness.' And a very intimate friend, one of the strongest remonstrants, told me spontaneously, when I had got through a vast pressure of work in her country house, that she should never trouble me more on that head, as she saw that my author-ship was the fulfilment of a natural function,—conducive to health of body and mind, instead of injurious to either. It would have saved me from much annoyance (kindly intended) if others had observed with the same good sense, and admitted conviction with equal candour. Authorship has never been with me a matter of choice. I have not done it for amusement, or for money, or for fame, or for any reason but because I could not help it. Things were pressing to be said; and there was more or less evidence that I was the person to say them. In such a case, it was always impossible to decline the duty for such reasons as that I should like more leisure, or more amusement, or more sleep, or more of any thing whatever. If my life *had* depended on more leisure and holiday, I could not have taken it. What wanted to be said must be said, for the sake of the many, whatever might be the consequences to the one worker concerned. Nor could the immediate task be put aside, from the remote consideration, for ever pressed upon me, of lengthening my life. The work called for to-day must not be refused for the possible sake of next month or next year. While feeling far less injured by toil than my friends took for granted I must be, I yet was always aware of the strong probability that my life would end as the lives of hard literary workers usually end,—in paralysis, with months or years of imbecil-ity. Every one must recoil from the prospect of being thus burdensome to friends and attendants; and it certainly was a matter of keen satisfaction to me, when my present fatal disease was ascertained, that I was released from that liability, and should die of something else, far less formidable to witnesses and nurses.

HARRIET MARTINEAU (1802–76), *Autobiography*, 1855

Extreme *busyness*, whether at school or college, kirk or market, is a symptom of deficient vitality; and a faculty for idleness implies a catholic appetite and a strong sense of personal identity. There is a sort of dead-alive, hackneyed people about, who are scarcely conscious of living except in the exercise of some conventional occupation. Bring these fellows into the country, or set them aboard ship, and you will see how they pine for their desk or their study. They have no curiosity; they cannot give themselves over to random provo-cations; they do not take pleasure in the exercise of their faculties for its own sake; and unless Necessity lays about them with a stick, they will even stand still. It is no good speaking to such folk: they *cannot* be idle, their nature is not generous enough: and they pass those hours in a sort of coma, which are not dedicated to furious moiling in the gold-mill. When they do not require to go to the office, when they are not hungry and have no mind to drink, the whole breathing world is a blank to them. If they have to wait an hour or so for a train, they fall into a stupid trance with their eyes open. To see them, you would suppose there was nothing to look at and no one to speak with; you would imagine they were paralysed or alienated: and yet very possibly they are hard workers in their own way, and have good eyesight for a flaw in a deed or a turn of the market. They have been to school and college, but all the time they had their eye on the medal; they have gone about in the world and mixed with clever people, but all the time they were thinking of their own affairs. As if a man's soul were not too small to begin with, they have dwarfed and narrowed theirs by a life of all work and no play; until here they are at forty, with a listless attention, a mind vacant of all material of amusement, and not one thought to rub against another, while they wait for the train. Before he was breeched, he might have clambered on the boxes; when he was twenty, he would have stared at the girls; but now the pipe is smoked out, the snuff-box empty, and my gentleman sits bolt upright upon a bench, with lamentable eyes. This does not appeal to me as being Success in Life.

ROBERT LOUIS STEVENSON (1850–94), 'An Apology for Idlers', 1881

[George Gissing celebrates his birthday.]

For me, it was a day of steady work, I am glad to say. Holidays of any kind I dread, for they only make resumption of work harder.

GEORGE GISSING (1857–1903), letter to Catherine Baseley, 23 Nov. 1886

Work of some sort or other was daily bread to Freud. He would have found a life of leisure unbearable. 'I could not contemplate with any sort of comfort a life without work. Creative imagination and work go together with me; I take no delight in anything else. That would be a prescription for happiness were it not for the terrible thought that one's productivity depends entirely on sensitive moods. What is one to do on a day when thoughts cease to flow and the proper words won't come? One cannot help trembling at this possibility. That is why, despite the acquiescence in fate that becomes an upright man, I secretly pray: no infirmity, no paralysis of one's powers through bodily distress. We'll die with harness on, as King Macbeth said.'

ERNEST JONES (1879–1958), *Sigmund Freud: Life and Work*, 1955

Leisure and idleness.—There is something of the American Indians, something of the ferocity peculiar to the Indian blood, in the American lust for gold; and the breathless haste with which they work—the distinctive vice of the new world—is already beginning to infect old Europe with its ferocity and is spreading a lack of spirituality like a blanket. Even now one is ashamed of resting, and prolonged reflection almost gives people a bad conscience. One thinks with a watch in one's hand, even as one eats one's midday meal while reading the latest news of the stock market; one lives as if one always 'might miss out on something.' 'Rather do anything than nothing': this principle, too, is merely a string to throttle all culture and good taste. Just as all forms are visibly perishing by the haste of the workers, the feeling for form itself, the ear and eye for the melody of movements are also perishing. The proof of this may be found in the universal demand for *gross obviousness* in all those situations in which human beings wish to be honest with one another for once—in their associations with friends, women, relatives, children, teachers, pupils, leaders, and princes: One no longer has time or energy for ceremonies, for being obliging in an indirect way, for *esprit* in conversation, and for any *otium* at all. Living in a constant chase after gain compels people to expend their spirit to the point of exhaustion in continual pretense and overreaching and anticipating others. Virtue has come to consist of doing something in less time than someone else. Hours in which honesty is *permitted* have become rare, and when they arrive one is tired and does not only want to 'let oneself go' but actually wishes to *stretch out* as long and wide and ungainly as one happens to be. This is how people now write *letters*, and the style and spirit of letters will always be the true 'sign of the times.'

If sociability and the arts still offer any delight, it is the kind of delight that slaves, weary of their work, devise for themselves. How frugal our educated—and uneducated—people have become regarding 'joy'! How they are becoming increasingly suspicious of all joy! More and more, *work* enlists all good conscience on its side; the desire for joy already calls itself a 'need to recuperate' and is beginning to be ashamed of itself. 'One owes it to one's health'—that is what people say when they are caught on an excursion into the country. Soon we may well reach the point where people can no longer give in to the desire for a *vita contemplativa* (that is, taking a walk with ideas and friends) without self-contempt and a bad conscience.

Well, formerly it was the other way around: it was work that was afflicted with the bad conscience. A person of good family used to conceal the fact that he was working if need compelled him to work. Slaves used to work, oppressed by the feeling that they were doing something contemptible: 'doing' itself was contemptible. 'Nobility and honor are attached solely to *otium* and *bellum*,' that was the ancient prejudice.

FRIEDRICH NIETZSCHE (1844–1900), *The Gay Science*, 1882, rev. 1887, tr. Walter Kaufmann, 1974

Doctor Baer was waiting in his inner office. With him was a colored man with a portable cardiograph like a huge suitcase. Stahr called it the lie detector. Stahr stripped to the waist, and the weekly examination began.

'How've you been feeling?'

'Oh—the usual,' said Stahr.

'Been hard at it? Getting any sleep?'

'No—about five hours. If I go to bed early, I just lie there.'

'Take the sleeping pills.'

'The yellow one gives me a hangover.'

'Take two red ones, then.'

'That's a nightmare.'

'Take one of each—the yellow first.'

'All right—I'll try. How've *you* been?'

'Say—I take care of myself, Monroe, I save myself.'

'The hell you do—you're up all night sometimes.'

'Then I sleep all next day.'

After ten minutes, Baer said:

'Seems OK. The blood pressure's up five points.'

'Good,' said Stahr. 'That's good, isn't it?'

'That's good. I'll develop the cardiographs tonight. When are you coming away with me?'

'Oh, some time,' said Stahr lightly. 'In about six weeks things'll ease up.'

Baer looked at him with a genuine liking that had grown over three years.

'You got better in thirty-three when you laid up,' he said. 'Even for three weeks.'

'I will again.'

No he wouldn't, Baer thought. With Minna's help he had enforced a few short rests years ago and lately he had hinted around, trying to find who Stahr considered his closest friends. Who could take him away and keep him away? It would almost surely be useless. He was due to die very soon now. Within six months one could say definitely. What was the use of developing the cardiograms? You couldn't persuade a man like Stahr to stop and lie down and look at the sky for six months. He would much rather die. He said differently, but what it added up to was the definite urge towards total exhaustion that he had run into before. Fatigue was a drug as well as a poison, and Stahr apparently derived some rare almost physical pleasure from working lightheaded with weariness. It was a perversion of the life force he had seen before, but he had almost stopped trying to interfere with it. He had cured a man or so—a hollow triumph of killing and preserving the shell.

F. Scott Fitzgerald (1896–1940), *The Last Tycoon*, 1941

There is, probably, no people on earth with whom business constitutes pleasure, and industry amusement, in an equal degree with the inhabitants of the United States of America. Active occupation is not only the principal source of their happiness, and the foundation of their national greatness, but they

are absolutely wretched without it, and instead of the *dolce far niente*, know
but the *horrors* of idleness: Business is the very soul of an American: he pur-
sues it, not as a means of procuring for himself and his family the necessary
comforts of life, but as the fountain of all human felicity.

From the earliest hour in the morning till late at night, the streets, offices,
and warehouses of the large cities are thronged by men of all trades and professions, each following his vocation like a *perpetuum mobile*, as if he never
dreamt of cessation from labor, or the possibility of becoming fatigued. If a
lounger should happen to be parading the street he would be sure to be jos-
tled off the side-walks, or to be pushed in every direction until he keeps time
with the rest. Should he meet a friend, he will only talk to him on *business*; and
if he retire to some house of entertainment he will again be entertained with
business. Wherever he goes the hum and bustle of *business* will follow him;
and when he finally sits down to his dinner, hoping there at least, to find an
hour of rest, he will discover to his sorrow that the Americans treat that as a
business too . . . it is as if all America were but one gigantic workshop, over the
entrance of which there is the blazing inscription, NO ADMISSION HERE,
EXCEPT ON BUSINESS.

> FRANCIS J. GRUND (1798–1863), *The Americans in Their Moral, Social
> and Political Relations*, 1837

The Mayor's hobby is work.

> MICHAEL PYE (1946–), quoting a colleague of Fiorello Henry La
> Guardia (1882–1947), Mayor of New York 1933–45, *Maximum City*, 1991

I believe that if a sociologist were to undertake a study of the work habits of
professional people, he would find that the habit of systematic overwork was
one of the most disagreeable late sequelae of the Second World War, when
nearly all non-combatants took the view that overwork was their contribution to the war effort. Nowadays it is still taken for granted that the senior
administrator takes home a case full of papers four days a week and should
feel guilty if he doesn't have to do so. As for holidays, it is taken as a matter of
course that the doctor, scientist, publisher, journalist, engineer and 'executive'
find their respective jobs so absorbing that they could perfectly well do without one. This is not because they are severally eaten up by ambition, avarice or
lust for self-advancement. It is above all because they have to run faster and
faster nowadays in order to remain in the same place (the Red Queen foresaw
it all). I suspect that if they were critically analysed, most job specifications
these days would turn out to be framed on the assumption of overwork, for a
good many responsible jobs are such that they simply cannot be done within
the compass of the ordinary working day.

> PETER MEDAWAR (1915–87), *Pluto's Republic*, 1982

Before they had gone three blocks the car got caught in a bad traffic jam and could barely crawl. Hopkins put his head back on the soft grey upholstery and closed his eyes. 'You've got to slow down!' the doctor had said. It seemed to Hopkins that people had been telling him that all his life.

It had started when he was a boy in public school. He had been editor of the school paper, and though he had been too small to excel at athletics, he had been manager of the football and basketball teams. He had stood at the top of his class scholastically, and whenever there had been a dance or a school play, he had always been chairman of the arrangements committee. 'You've got to slow down!' the teachers had told him. 'Take it easy, boy—you'll wear yourself out!'

At Princeton, where he had gone on a scholarship, it had been more of the same. He had headed the debating team, managed the football team, and engaged in a dozen other activities in addition to maintaining an almost straight A average in his studies. 'You've got to slow down!' his faculty adviser had told him. 'Take it easy!'

But he had not slowed down. Summers he had worked at all kinds of jobs, always astonishing his employers with his energy. After college had come a brief stint in the Army, a period during which his friends had kidded him about wanting to be a general. Upon being released from service in 1919, he had worked for a few years at a brokerage house before going to the United Broadcasting Corporation, which had just been started. A year later he had met Helen Perry, who had at the time been a fashionable beauty in New York. He had pursued her with all the zeal he always devoted to anything he wanted, and on June 3, 1921, he had married her. Up to that time, Hopkins had never had a failure in his life.

'You've got to slow down!' Helen had started saying, even before they were married, but unlike the teachers and faculty advisers, she had not let it go at that. As she discovered that it was Hopkins' habit to spend most of his evenings and week-ends at his office, she had become first annoyed, then indignant, and, finally, hurt and bewildered.

'Life isn't worth living like this,' she had said. 'I never see you! You've got to slow down!'

He had tried. Especially when their first child, Robert, had come, during the second year of their marriage, he had tried. He had come home every evening at six o'clock and conscientiously played with the baby and sat talking with his wife, and he had been genuinely appalled to find that the baby made him nervous, and that while he was talking to his wife, it was almost impossible for him to sit quietly. He had felt impelled to get up and pace up and down the room, jingling his change in his pockets and glancing at the clock. For the first time in his life he had started to drink heavily during those long evenings at home. Gradually he had started staying late at the office again—by that time he had already had a fairly important job at the United Broadcasting Corporation. Helen had remonstrated with him.

There had been recriminations, high-pitched arguments, and threats of divorce.

All right, it's a problem, he had said to himself after a particularly bitter scene—it's a problem that must be met head on, like all other problems. To Helen he had said, in a quiet voice, 'I don't want to have any more scenes— they wear us both out. I'm prepared to admit that whatever is wrong is entirely my fault. I am preoccupied with my work—I've been that way all my life, and it is nothing for which you should blame yourself.'

She had gone pale. 'Do you want a divorce?' she had asked.

'No,' he had said. 'Do you?'

'No.'

They had never talked about divorce again, but she had begun to refer to his preoccupation with work as a disease. 'You've got to do something about it,' she had said, and had suggested a psychiatrist.

For two years Hopkins had submitted to psychoanalysis. Five times a week he had lain on a couch in the psychoanalyst's apartment on Sixty-ninth Street and recalled his childhood. His father had been a cheerful, rather ineffectual man who, each afternoon upon returning from his job as assistant manager of a small paper mill in an upstate New York village, had spent most of his time rocking on the front porch of their shabby but comfortable house. His mother had been disappointed by the modesty of her husband's achievements and aspirations and had been bitterly condescending to him. Leaving her family to fend for itself most of the time, she had thrown all her energy into working for the local garden club and a bewildering variety of social and civic organizations. As she gained positions of leadership in these groups, her resentment at her serenely undistinguished husband had grown. Finally she had established herself in a separate room on the third floor of their house and, throughout most of Ralph's boyhood, had conducted herself like a great lady temporarily forced to live with poor relatives.

Hopkins was not an introspective man, but in recounting all this to the psychoanalyst, he had said, 'I always felt sorry for my father because my mother treated him so badly. She never gave me much time, either, except when I did something she thought was outstanding. Whenever I got a particularly good report card, or won anything, she'd take me up to her room to have tea alone with her. "We're two of a kind," she used to say. "We get things done." I suppose I got the impression from her that achievement means everything.'

Hopkins had felt quite proud of his efforts at self-diagnosis and had been surprised when the psychoanalyst had disregarded his suggestions in favour of much more bizarre 'explanations of neurosis.' He had said that Hopkins probably had a deep guilt complex, and that his constant work was simply an effort to punish and perhaps kill himself. The guilt complex was probably based on a fear of homosexuality, he had said. To Hopkins, who had never consciously worried about homosexuality, or guilt, this had seemed like so much rubbish, but he had tried to believe it, for the psychoanalyst had said it was necessary for him to believe to be cured, and Hopkins had wanted to be cured, in order to make his wife happy.

The trouble had been that every time he left the psychoanalyst's office the temptation to return to his own office and bury himself in work had been irresistible. At the end of two years he had become the youngest vice-president of United Broadcasting and had told his wife he simply wouldn't have time for psychoanalysis any longer.

SLOAN WILSON (1920–), The Man in the Grey Flannel Suit, 1956

Idleness, by contrast, brought boredom and frustration.

Fie upon this quiet life, I want work.

WILLIAM SHAKESPEARE (1564–1616), King Henry IV, Part I, pr. 1598

Work is good; it is truly a motive for life. Therefore unless you walk for the sake of walking, you do so for your work. *Where shall I turn, what shall I do?* are the voices of people grieving. Idleness is torture. In all times and places, nature abhors a vacuum.

THOMAS HOBBES (1588–1679), De Homine, 1658, tr. Charles T. Wood,
T. S. K. Scott-Craig, and Bernard Gert, 1972

> No pain's so painful are to those who know
> Their Soul's Authority, as lazy Rest:
> And on my foes, might I free Curses throw;
> My worst should be, what Drones esteem the best:
>   No Imprecations would I shoot, but this
>   And damn them to no Hell but Idleness.

JOSEPH BEAUMONT (1616–99), Psyche, or Love's Mystery, 1648

>   . . . with labour I must earn
> My bread; what harm? Idleness had been worse.

JOHN MILTON (1608–74), Paradise Lost, 1667

> Hard Labour's tedious everyone must own;
> But surely better such by far than none,
> The perfect Drone, the quite Impertinent,

Whose Life at nothing aims, but—to be spent;
Such Heaven visits for some mighty Ill;
'Tis sure the hardest Labour to sit still,
Hence that unhappy Tribe who Nought pursue;
Who sin for want of something else to do.

NATHANIEL AMES (1708–64), *An Astronomical Diary*, 1756

A mind always employed is always happy. This is the true secret, the grand recipe for felicity. The idle are the only wretched . . .

Be good and be industrious, and you will be what I shall most love in the world. Adieu my dear child. Yours affectionately,

THOMAS JEFFERSON (1743–1826), letter to his daughter Martha, 21 May 1787

But nature intended that we should be active, and we need some principle to incite us to action, when we happen not to be invited by any appetite or passion.

For this end, when strength and spirits are recruited by rest, nature has made total inaction as uneasy as excessive labour.

We may call this the principle of *activity*. It is most conspicuous in children, who cannot be supposed to know how useful and necessary it is for their improvement to be constantly employed. Their constant activity therefore appears not to proceed from their having some end constantly in view, but rather from this, that they desire to be always doing something, and feel uneasiness in total inaction.

Nor is this principle confined to childhood; it has great effects in advanced life.

When a man has neither hope, nor fear, nor desire, nor project, nor employment, of body or mind, one might be apt to think him the happiest mortal upon earth, having nothing to do but to enjoy himself; but we find him, in fact, the most unhappy.

He is more weary of inaction than ever he was of excessive labour. He is weary of the world, and of his own existence; and is more miserable than the sailor wrestling with a storm, or the soldier mounting a breach.

This dismal state is commonly the lot of the man who has neither exercise of body, nor employment of mind. For the mind, like water, corrupts and putrifies by stagnation, but by running purifies and refines.

THOMAS REID (1710–96), *Essays on the Active Powers of the Human Mind*, 1788

Every pupil was made to feel that there was work for him to do—that his happiness as well as his duty lay in doing that work well.

> BONAMY PRICE (1807–88), Mathematics Master at Rugby School
> 1832–50, on Thomas Arnold, Headmaster 1828–42

In the nineteenth century many middle-class women experienced the frustrations of a life of compulsory idleness.

'Caroline,' demanded Miss Keeldar, abruptly, 'don't you wish you had a profession—a trade?'

'I wish it fifty times a day. As it is, I often wonder what I came into the world for. I long to have something absorbing and compulsory to fill my head and hands, and to occupy my thoughts.'

'Can labour alone make a human being happy?'

'No; but it can give varieties of pain, and prevent us from breaking our hearts with a single tyrant master-torture. Besides, successful labour has its recompense; a vacant, weary, lonely, hopeless life has none.'

> CHARLOTTE BRONTË (1816–55), *Shirley*, 1849

Look at the poor lives we lead . . .

Mrs A. has the imagination, the poetry of a Murillo, and has sufficient power of execution to show that she might have had a great deal more. Why is she not a Murillo? From a material difficulty, not a mental one. If she has a knife and fork in her hands for three hours of the day, she cannot have a pencil or brush. Dinner is the great sacred ceremony of this day, the great sacrament. To be absent from dinner is equivalent to being ill. Nothing else will excuse us from it. Bodily incapacity is the only apology valid. If she has a pen and ink in her hands during other three hours, writing answers for the penny post, again, she cannot have her pencil, and so *ad infinitum* through life. People have no type before them in their lives, neither fathers nor mothers, nor the children themselves. They look at things in detail. They say, 'It is very desirable that A., my daughter, should go to such a party, should know such a lady, should sit by such a person.' It is true. But what standard have they before them of the nature and destination of man? The very words are rejected as pedantic. But might they not, at least, have a type in their minds that such an one might be a discoverer through her intellect, such another through her art, a third through her moral power?

Women often try one branch of intellect after another in their youth, *e.g.* mathematics. But that, least of all is compatible with the life of 'society.' It is impossible to follow up anything systematically. Women often long to enter some man's profession where they would find direction, competition (or rather opportunity of measuring the intellect with others) and, above all, time.

*

Now, why is it more ridiculous for a man than for a woman to do worsted work and drive out every day in the carriage? Why should we laugh if we were to see a parcel of men sitting round a drawing-room table in the morning, and think it all right if they were women?

Is man's time more valuable than woman's? or is the difference between man and woman this, that woman has confessedly nothing to do?

*

They have nothing to do.

Are they to be employed in sitting in the drawing-room saying words which may as well not be said, which could be said as well if *they* were not there?

Women often strive to live by intellect. The clear, brilliant, sharp radiance of intellect's moonlight rising upon such an expanse of snow is dreary, it is true, but some love its solemn desolation, its silence, its solitude—if they are but *allowed* to live in it; if they are not perpetually baulked or disappointed. But a woman cannot live in the light of intellect. Society forbids it. Those conventional frivolities, which are called her 'duties,' forbid it. Her 'domestic duties,' high-sounding words, which, for the most part, are bad habits (which she has not the courage to enfranchise herself from, the strength to break through) forbid it. What are these duties (or bad habits)?—Answering a multitude of letters which lead to nothing, from her so-called friends, keeping herself up to the level of the world that she may furnish her quota of amusement at the breakfast-table; driving out her company in the carriage. And all these things are exacted from her by her family which, if she is good and affectionate, will have more influence with her than the world.

What wonder, if, wearied out, sick at heart with hope deferred, the springs of will broken, not seeing clearly *where* her duty lies, she abandons intellect as a vocation and takes it only, as we use the moon, by glimpses through her tight-closed window shutters?

The family? It is too narrow a field for the development of an immortal spirit, be that spirit male or female. The chances are a thousand to one that, in that small sphere, the task for which that immortal spirit is destined by the qualities and the gifts which its Creator has placed within it, will not be found.

The family uses people, *not* for what they are, nor for what they are intended to be, but for what it wants them for—its own uses. It thinks of them not as what God has made them, but as the something which it has arranged that they shall be. If it wants someone to sit in the drawing-room, *that* someone is supplied by the family, though that member may be destined for science, or for education, or for active superintendence by God, *i.e.* by the gifts within.

This system dooms some minds to incurable infancy, others to silent misery . . .

They become incapable of consecutive or strenuous work.

What these suffer—even physically—from the want of such work no one can tell. The accumulation of nervous energy, which has had nothing to do during the day, makes them feel every night, when they go to bed, as if they were going mad; and they are obliged to lie long in bed in the morning to let it evaporate and keep it down. At last they suffer at once from disgust of the one and incapacity for the other—from loathing of conventional idleness and powerlessness to do work when they have it. 'Now go, you have seven hours,' say people, 'you have all the afternoon to yourself.' When they are all frittered away, they are to begin to work. When they are broken up into little bits, they are to hew away.

FLORENCE NIGHTINGALE (1820–1910), Cassandra, 1859

Here is the world around one mass of misery and evil! Not a paper do I take up but I see something about wretchedness and crime, and here I sit with health, strength, and knowledge, and able to do nothing, *nothing*—at the risk of breaking my mother's heart! I have pottered about cottages and taught at schools in the *dilettante* way of the young lady who thinks it her duty to be charitable; and I am told that it is my duty, and that I may be satisfied . . . Satisfied, when I know that every alley and lane of town or country reeks with vice and corruption, and that there is one cry for workers with brains and with purses! And here am I, able and willing, only longing to task myself to the uttermost, yet tethered down to the merest mockery of usefulness by conventionalities. I am a young lady forsooth!—I must not be out late; I must not put forth my views; I must not choose my acquaintance; I must be a mere helpless, useless being, growing old in a ridiculous fiction of prolonged childhood, affecting those graces of so-called sweet seventeen that I never had—because, because why? Is it for any better reason than because no mother can bear to believe her daughter no longer on the lists for matrimony?

CHARLOTTE M. YONGE (1823–1901), The Clever Woman of the Family, 1865

At all periods unemployment brought misery in its train.

Enforced leisure is an embarrassment which only those who have experienced it can possibly understand. It is an imposition, and should be treated as such. It represents a problem, the seriousness of which is tragic. Loss of skill and morale, physical and mental deterioration in the mass, cannot be viewed with equanimity. We do not realise how much we like work until we have none. The hopelessness and weariness of 'going after the job you know isn't there' imposes a stern self-discipline. The strain of keeping up appearances is not the best mental preparation for cultural occupation. The intrinsic value of leisure to the individual under these circumstances is almost negligible . . . Work is fundamental, there is no leisure without it.

> J. G. PATTERSON of the Industrial Welfare Society, *Industrial Welfare*, May 1934

She. Is there no work then to be got?
He. Not the least job—indeed there's not:
    The masters say their shops are full,
    And business either dead or dull;
    'They've goods enough' is all their cry,
    And yet no customers to buy;
    Their correspondents daily break—
    Their all's continually at stake;
    Scarce any money circulates,
    But paper due at distant dates;
    Their debts are large, and they must stay,
    For all are tardy now in pay:
    Respecting debts, both great and small,
    Happy to get them in at all;
    Many as desp'rate are confessed,
    And dubious e'en the very best.
She. Ah! I believe my heart will break.
He. You must these ills with patience take.
She. Preach the sea calm, when the winds rage;
    Can patience hungry mouths assuage?
    Will patience give your babes a meal,
    Who all the pangs of famine feel?
    For bread to me all day they cry,
    While I cannot their wants supply,
    Till through fatigue they fall asleep,
    Then wake again to call and weep.
    Will patience make your children still,
    Or their poor empty bellies fill?
    Our landlord, ask if he's content
    Your patience to receive for rent;
    The baker's bill will patience pay,
    Or send the butcher pleased away?
    While you are out in seeking work,

They join to use me like a Turk;
With threats and menaces pursue,
Of what they say they're bent to do;
In vain to them were patience thrown,
For frequently I lose my own.
He. Alas! what would you have me do?
She. Can't you some other trade pursue?
Perhaps you might some work obtain,
T' enable us to live again.
He. 'Tis all the same—all trades are dead;
Through town a gen'ral murmur's spread:
Besides, to take a trade in hand
I do not clearly understand—
Masters would call me stupid sot,
And say they've better workmen got;
'Think you,' they'd say, 'that we'll employ
A man our business to destroy?
Trade of itself is very lame;
You'd bring our shop at once to shame,
And hurt our credit and our name.
No, while good hands can be procured,
Bunglers ought not to be endured.'
Such, such would be the master's song,
While thus the men would use their tongue:
'Business is not already bad,
Though there's scarce any to be had,
But you an interloper come
Where all is full, and there's no room.
Too indolent you seem to be,
For such still love variety;
And like a lounging lazy drone,
You steal our trade and quit your own.'
Thus neither good success nor gains
Would recompense my honest pains.
She. What can we do?—Have you no friends
For fortune's frowns to make amends?
None that, in this our scene of woe,
A little succour would bestow?
He. I've tried them all a thousand ways;
All those who, in more prosp'rous days,
The firmest friendship to me swore,
And learned their bounty to implore;
But all in vain, their *words* were wind,
And, oh! their *deeds*—unkind, unkind.

It pains, it tortures me to speak
The cruelty I've met this week;
While I had money, I had friends,
Who meant to serve their private ends;
The friendship of these grov'ling men
Was to my circumstances then;
Now in the world no friendship reigns;
'Tis marred with interested stains;
And those who think this passion true,
An airy phantom but pursue;
Which when they vainly think they've caught,
Will 'scape them quick as nimble thought.
Of friendship judge by my success
In this our imminent distress:
The first whose heart I thought to touch
Was one who often promised much;
But he cried out with careless air,
'You're idle, that's the whole affair;
Do not on my good nature press;
I can't encourage idleness.'
Another, fond of hoarded pelf,
Replied, 'Indeed I'm poor myself.'
One said, 'You joke—you don't speak true,
I'm sure there's work enough to do;
Then learn to turn yourself about,
And seek some snug employment out;
Fortune will kindly for you carve:
While you have hands you cannot starve.'
Another cried, 'Why, go to sea,
You'll make yourself and family;
The sea you know will not refuse;
A better thing you cannot choose.'
This asks me if I thought him mad,
To lend where matters were so bad;
And that was quite amazed to find
That he should come across my mind.
Thus all in diff'rent ways denied,
And bid me for myself provide;
And tried to hide ingratitude,
Beneath advice or sayings shrewd.
She. Then at the last, what hope remains,
To end or mitigate our pains?
He. There's one dull light to cheer our gloom;
A workhouse is our certain doom.

Thither we all, alas! must go,
Where death will quickly end my woe.

ANON., 'Between an Unemployed Artist and His Wife', 1775

At all times it is a bewildering thing to the poor weaver to see his employer removing from house to house, each one grander than the last, till he ends in building one more magnificent than all, or withdraws his money from the concern, or sells his mill, to buy an estate in the country, while all the time the weaver, who thinks he and his fellows are the real makers of this wealth, is struggling on for bread for his children, through the vicissitudes of lowered wages, short hours, fewer hands employed, etc. And when he knows trade is bad, and could understand (at least partially) that there are not buyers enough in the market to purchase the goods already made, and consequently that there is no demand for more; when he would bear and endure much without complaining, could he also see that his employers were bearing their share; he is, I say, bewildered and (to use his own word) 'aggravated' to see that all goes on just as usual with the mill-owners. Large houses are still occupied, while spinners' and weavers' cottages stand empty, because the families that once filled them are obliged to live in rooms or cellars. Carriages still roll along the streets, concerts are still crowded by subscribers, the shops for expensive luxuries still find daily customers, while the workman loiters away his unemployed time in watching these things, and thinking of the pale, uncomplaining wife at home, and the wailing children asking in vain for enough of food,—of the sinking health, of the dying life of those near and dear to him. The contrast is too great. Why should he alone suffer from bad times?

ELIZABETH GASKELL (1810–65), *Mary Barton*, 1848

He who wishes to behold one of the most extraordinary and least-known scenes of this metropolis, should wend his way to the London Dock gates at half-past seven in the morning. There he will see congregated within the principal entrance masses of men of all grades, looks, and kinds; some in half-fashionable surtouts, burst at the elbows, with the dirty shirts showing through; others in greasy sporting jackets, with red pimpled faces; others in the rags of their half-slang gentility, with the velvet collars of their paletots worn through to the canvas; some in rusty black, with their waistcoats

Artist] artist or craftsman

fastened tight up to the throat; others, again, with the knowing thieves' curl on each side of the jaunty cap; whilst here and there you may see a big-whiskered Pole, with his hands in the pockets of his plaited French trousers. Some loll outside the gates, smoking the pipe which is forbidden within; but these are mostly Irish.

Presently you know, by the stream pouring through the gates, and the rush towards particular spots, that the 'calling foremen' have made their appearance. Then begins the scuffling and scrambling, and stretching forth of countless hands high in the air, to catch the eye of him whose voice may give them work. As the foreman calls from a book the names, some men jump upon the backs of the others, so as to lift themselves high above the rest, and attract the notice of him who hires them. All are shouting. Some cry aloud his surname, some his christian name; others call out their own names, to remind him that they are there. Now the appeal is made in Irish blarney, now in broken English. Indeed, it is a sight to sadden the most callous, to see *thousands* of men struggling for only one day's hire, the scuffle being made the fiercer by the knowledge that hundreds out of the number there assembled must be left to idle the day out in want. To look in the faces of that hungry crowd, is to see a sight that must be ever remembered. Some are smiling to the foreman to coax him into remembrance of them; others with their protruding eyes eager to snatch at the hoped-for pass. For weeks many have gone there, and gone through the same struggle, the same cries, and have gone away, after all, without the work they had screamed for.

From this it might be imagined that the work was of a peculiarly light and pleasant kind, and so, when I first saw the scene, I could not help imagining myself; but in reality the labour is of that heavy and continuous character that you would fancy only the best fed could withstand it. The work may be divided into three classes: wheel work, or that which is moved by the muscles of the legs and weight of the body; jigger or winch work, or that which is moved by the muscles of the arm—in each of these the labourer is stationary; but in the truck work, which forms the third class, the labourer has to travel over a space of ground greater or less in proportion to the distance which the goods have to be removed. The wheel work is performed somewhat on the system of the treadwheel, with this exception—that the force is applied inside, instead of outside the wheel. From six to eight men enter a wooden cylinder or drum, upon which are nailed battens, and the men, laying hold of ropes, commence treading the wheel round, occasionally singing the while, and stamping in time in a manner that is pleasant from its curiosity. The wheel is generally 16 feet in diameter and eight to nine feet broad, and the six or eight men treading within it will lift from 16 to 18 hundredweight, and often a ton, 40 times in an hour, an average of 27 feet high. Other men will get out a cargo of from 800 to 900 casks of wine, each cask averaging about 5 cwt, and being lifted about 18 feet, in a day-and-a-half. At trucking, each man is said to go, on an average, 30 miles a day, and two-thirds of that time he is moving $1\frac{1}{2}$ cwt at $6\frac{1}{2}$ miles per hour.

This labour, though requiring to be seen to be properly understood, must still appear so arduous, that one would imagine it was not of that tempting nature that 3,000 men could be found every day in London desperate enough to fight and battle for the privilege of getting 2s 6d by it; and even, if they fail in 'getting taken on' at the commencement of the day, that they should then retire to the appointed yard, there to remain hour after hour in the hope that the wind might blow them some stray ship, so that other 'gangs' might be wanted, and the calling foreman seek them there. It is a curious sight to see the men waiting in these yards to be hired at 4d per hour, for such are the terms given in the after-part of the day. There, seated on long benches ranged against the wall, they remain—some telling their miseries and some their crimes to one another, whilst others doze away their time. Rain or sunshine, there can always be found plenty ready to catch the stray shilling or eight pennyworth of work. By the size of the shed, you can tell how many men sometimes remain there in the pouring rain rather than run the chance of losing the stray hour's work. Some loiter on the bridges close by, and presently, as their practised eye or ear tells them that the calling foreman is in want of another gang, they rush forward in a stream towards the gate, though only six or eight at most can be hired out of the hundred or more that are waiting there. Again the same mad fight takes place as in the morning; there is the same jumping on benches, the same raising of hands, the same entreaties, and the same failure as before. It is strange to mark the change that takes place in the manner of the men when the foreman has left. Those that have been engaged go smiling to their labour. Indeed, I myself met on the quay just such a chuckling gang passing to their work. Those who are left behind give vent to their disappointment in abuse of him whom they had been supplicating and smiling at a few minutes before. Upon talking with some of the unsuccessful ones, they assured me that the men who had supplanted them had only gained their ends by bribing the foreman who had engaged them. This I made a point of inquiring into, and the deputy-warehousekeeper, of whom I sought the information, soon assured me, by the production of his book, that he himself was the gentleman who chose the men, the foreman merely executing his orders; and this, indeed, I find to be the custom throughout the dock.

HENRY MAYHEW (1812–87), *Morning Chronicle*, 26 Oct. 1849
[*see also* BEATRICE POTTER, pp. 59–60]

Out of Work

Alone at the shut of day was I,
With a star or two in a frost clear sky,
And the byre smell in the air.

I'd tramped the length and breadth o' the fen;
But never a farmer wanted men;
Naught doing anywhere.

A great calm moon rose back o' the mill,
And I told myself it was God's will
Who went hungry and who went fed.

I tried to whistle, I tried to be brave;
But the new ploughed fields smelt dank as the grave;
And I wished I were dead.

KENNETH H. ASHLEY, 1924

It was a procession.

In front marched a tall son of man, with white black-bearded face, long black hair, more like plumage than hair in its abundance and form, and he wore no hat. He walked straight as a soldier, but with long, slow steps, and his head hung so that his bare breast supported it, for he had no coat and his shirt was half open. He had knee-breeches, bare dark legs, and shoes on his feet. His hands were behind his back, as if he were handcuffed. Two men walked beside him in other men's black clothes and black hats worn grey—two unnoticeable human beings, snub-nosed, with small, rough beards, dull eyes, shuffling gait. Two others followed them close, each carrying one of the poles of a small white banner inscribed with the words: 'The Unemployed'. These also were unnoticeable, thin, grey, bent, but young, their clothes, their faces, their hair, their hats almost the same dry colour as the road. It was impossible to say what their features were, because their heads hung down and their hats were drawn well on to their heads, and their eyes were unseen. They could not keep step, nor walk side by side, and their banner was always shaky and always awry. Next, in no order, came three others of the same kind, shambling like the rest, of middle height, moderately ill-dressed, moderately thin, their hands in their pockets. In one of these I recognised the man who was born in Caermarthenshire. A cart came close behind, drawn by a fat grey donkey who needed no driving, for the one who rode in the cart had his back to the shafts, and, leaning forward on a tub into which money was expected to be thrown, he appeared to be talking to those who trailed at the back, for he waved an arm and wagged his yellow beard. He was fat, and dressed in a silk hat, frock-coat and striped trousers, almost too ancient to be ridiculous had they not kept company with a jaunty pair of yellow boots. He was midway between a seaside minstrel and a minister, had not one gesture destroyed the resemblance by showing that he wore no socks. Round about his coat also were the words: 'The Unemployed', repeated or crudely varied. Those whom he addressed were the fifteen or twenty who completed the procession but seemed not to

listen. They were all bent, young or middle-aged men, fair-haired, with unin-
tentional beards, road-coloured skins and slightly darker clothes. Many wore
overcoats, the collars turned up, and some had nothing under them except a
shirt, and one not that. All with hands in pockets, one carrying a pipe, all silent
and ashamed, struggled onward with bent knees. No two walked together;
there was no approach to a row or a column in their arrangement, nor was
there any pleasing irregularity as of plants grown from chance-scattered seed;
by no means could they have been made to express more feebleness, more
unbrotherliness, more lack of principle, purpose or control. Each had the
look of the meanest thief between his captors. Two blue, benevolent, impersonal policemen, large men, occasionally lifted their arms as if to help forwa￢d
the contemptible procession; sometimes, with a quick motion of the hand,
they caused the straggling rear to double their pace for a few yards by running
with knees yet more bent and coat-tails flapping and hands still deep in
pockets—only for a few yards, for their walking pace was their best, all having
the same strength, the same middle height, the same stride, though no two
could be seen keeping step.

The traffic thickened, and amidst the horses that nodded and trampled and
the motor-cars that fumed and fretted the procession was closed up into a
grey block behind the donkey-cart. On one side of the donkey was the black-
bearded man, his right arm now resting on the animal's neck; on the other
side the policemen; in front the standard-bearers hung down their heads and
held up their poles. Often the only remnant visible was the raven crest of the
leader.

The multitude on the pavement continued to press straight onward, or to
flit in and out of coloured shops. None looked at the standard, the dark man
and his cloudy followers, except a few of the smallest newspaper boys who had
a few spare minutes and rushed over to march with them in the hope of music
or a speech or a conflict. The straight flower-girl flashed her eyes as she stood
on the kerb, her left arm curving with divine grace round the shawl-hidden
child at her bosom, her left hand thrust out full of roses. The tender, well-
dressed women leaning on the arms of their men smiled faintly, a little pitiful,
but gladly conscious of their own security and pleasantness. Men with the
historic sense glanced and noted the fact that there was a procession. One
man, standing on the kerb, took a sovereign from his pocket, looked at it and
then at the unemployed, made a little gesture of utter bewilderment, and
dropping the coin down into the drain below, continued to watch. Comfortable clerks and others of the servile realised that here were the unemployed
about whom the newspapers had said this and that—('a pressing question'—
'a very complicated question not to be decided in a hurry'—'it is receiving the
attention of some of the best intellects of the time'—'our special reporter is
making a full investigation'—'who are the genuine and who are the impostors?'—'connected with Socialist intrigues')—and they repeated the word
'Socialism' and smiled at the bare legs of the son of man and the yellow boots

of the orator. Next day they would smile again with pride that they had seen the procession which ended in feeble, violent speeches against the Army and the Rich, in four arrests and an imprisonment. For they spoke in voices gentle with hunger. They were angry and uttered curses. One waved an arm against a palace, an arm that could scarcely hold out a revolver even were all the kings sitting in a row to tempt him. In the crowd and disturbance the leader fell and fainted. They propped him in their arms and cleared a space about him. 'Death of Nelson', suggested an onlooker, laughing, as he observed the attitude and the knee-breeches. 'If he had only a crown of thorns . . .' said another, pleased by the group. 'Wants a bit of skilly and real hard work,' said a third.

> Edward Thomas (1878–1917), *The South Country*, 1909

It is a weird experience, this, of wandering through England in search of a job. You keep your heart up so long as you have something in your stomach, but when hunger steals upon you, then you despair. Footsore and listless at the same time, you simply lose all interest in the future . . .

Nothing wearies one more than walking about hunting for employment which is not to be had. It is far harder than real work. The uncertainty, the despair, when you reach a place only to discover that your journey is fruitless, are frightful. I've known a man say, 'Which way shall I go today?' Having no earthly idea which way to take, he tosses up a button. If the button comes down on one side he treks east; if on the other, he treks west.

You can imagine the feeling when, after walking your boots off, a man says to you, as he jingles sovereigns in his pocket, 'Why don't you work?' That is what happened to me as I scoured the country between London and Liverpool, asking all the way for any kind of work to help me along.

> Will Crooks (1852–1921), quoted in George Haw, *From Workhouse to Westminster: The Life Story of Will Crooks MP*, 1907

Closed Works

There was a steel rail up from the clay-pit.
The truck, hauled up by a winch on a wire hawser,
Went through the doors at the top of a high tower,
Reaching there, was levelled, was seized by the two grinning men
(Grinning and waving to one looking up to them, admiring them)
Who, pressing a lever, tilted the truck so that the clay
Tumbled and rumbled down into the tower.
                              Uprighted with a toss,

The empty truck, on a slack windlass, down clattered the slope
Jangling bang clattering. O lovely the speed, the clanging and ringing and
So to have driven one dancing or ruddy-faced wild with excitement
At the sight of the truck under the bridge where I stood, whether
(Whether smell of the nettles, the tar, white hawthorn in summer;
Or reek of bonfires; allotment smells, men on allotments in autumn);
Prying between the planks of the bridge at the booming and the
   and the slow upward long creep or
Glimpsing the jangling quick clattering
   a downward sweet swoop
Of the truck to the bottom: the bottom where it bumped and it rumped
On a beamy, wood-soddy dumbness of buffers, where it waited
For the tipping of clay-mud, the clay from the hoppers
(Which men pedal like scooters round rims of the clay-pit
Rims round the clay-pit are railed; men loading the hoppers on rails—
Then one foot on the plate, the other is scooting till, grabbing up speed,
They lifted both feet on the plate of the hoppers, so running till thump
At the funnel or chute) and how they would pour
The chugg-cloddy lovely, the downy grey mass into the chute
Dumping, and thumping in the underneath truck, and then once again
The slow, the upward long creep, wire-hawser warblingly tight,
So grumpling under the bridge, and you peer through the planks
Of the bridge, and you see it—passing below you—the lovely,
The lovely, the loaded, the wire-pulled-up-through
Up-going, big-loaded, steady, thick-loaded
Truck
Up to the tower, where it levelled and stopped, was tipped
(By two waiting men, dirty their faces, but waving and grinning and fine)
Stumbling and mumbling its clay. Then righted
Clanging
   rang down truck
To the boof of buffers.
O, those Brick Works!

Today I took my young son to show this vast excitement and glory.
But I find the brick-works to be now closed.
I attempt to translate a marvellously remembered text
But by necessity find failure.
There is an exhausted hole where the clay was used.
The rails around the rim are uprooted.
There are no hoppers; there is no truck;
(The bridge is insecure and the slope is rotting),
There are no two smiling men;
The tower is empty.
No noise.

Yet: All that was dug down for was built up with?
Or (more simply): Works Closed?

FRANCIS BERRY (1915–), 1961

In Bombay

Time passes even when unemployed.

After summer the incessant monologue of rain.
There is a professional touch to it all.
I have been employed as many times
as unemployed.
And now I am unemployed.
Repetition does not make it easier.

In the beginning one leaves the house
in the morning as usual.
Pretences increase, imaginary interviews
outnumber unimaginary ones.
Waiting to be interviewed is a
test by itself.

Unemployed, one makes friends who
are unemployed.
Picked up at the employment bureau
where silence is articulate.
The unemployed dare not lose their temper.

The afternoons are reserved for exhibitions,
libraries, bookstalls.
Movies. Today it was *Wait until Dark*
for the second time.
I am an outsider in an auditorium of
college students.

The boys are quick with gilded wit, the
girls gay dolls
with 'Choosy Cherry' lips and expensive eyes.
My white-washed presence marred the
illustration.

Of course, when unemployed, the need to spend,
to do everything in excess, increases.

Cursing comes easily, when a hundred-rupee
note is lost or stolen
it is God who is a so and so.

Unemployed people try to sleep at any
time of the day.

TARA PATEL (1949–), 1992

So, though some continued to regard work as a tedious and wearisome feature of the human condition, others concluded that it was a psychological necessity.

In the sweat of thy brow shalt thou labour! was Jehovah's curse on Adam. And this is labour for [Adam] Smith, a curse. 'Tranquillity' appears as the adequate state, as identical with 'freedom' and 'happiness'. It seems quite far from Smith's mind that the individual, 'in his normal state of health, strength, activity, skill, facility', also needs a normal portion of work, and of the suspension of tranquillity. Certainly, labour obtains its measure from the outside, through the aim to be attained and the obstacles to be overcome in attaining it. But Smith has no inkling whatever that this overcoming of obstacles is in itself a liberating activity—and that, further, the external aims become stripped of the semblance of merely external natural urgencies, and become posited as aims which the individual himself posits—hence as self-realization, objectification of the subject, hence real freedom, whose action is, precisely, labour. He is right, of course, that, in its historic forms as slave-labour, serf-labour, and wage-labour, labour always appears as repulsive, always as *external forced labour,* and not-labour, by contrast, as 'freedom, and happiness'.

*

A. Smith, by the way, has only the slaves of capital in mind. For example, even the semi-artistic worker of the Middle Ages does not fit into his definition.

KARL MARX (1818–83), *Grundrisse,* 1953, tr. Martin Nicolaus, 1973

There is no craving or demand of the human mind more constant and insatiable than that for exercise and employment; and this desire seems the foundation of most of our passions and pursuits.

DAVID HUME (1711–76), 'Of Interest', 1741–2

Some few months ago I read in a paper the report of a speech made to the assembled work-people of a famous firm of manufacturers (as they are called). The speech was a very humane and thoughtful one, spoken by one of the leaders of modern thought: the firm to whose people it was addressed was and is famous not only for successful commerce, but also for the consideration and goodwill with which it treats its work-people, men and women. No wonder, therefore, that the speech was pleasant reading; for the tone of it was that of a man speaking to his friends who could well understand him and from whom he need hide nothing; but towards the end of it I came across a sentence, which set me a-thinking so hard, that I forgot all that had gone before. It was to this effect, and I think nearly in these very words, 'Since no man would work if it were not that he hoped by working to earn leisure:' and the context showed that this was assumed as a self-evident truth.

Well, for many years I have had my mind fixed on what I in my turn regarded as an axiom which may be worded thus: No work which cannot be done without pleasure in the doing is worth doing; so you may think I was much disturbed at a grave and learned man taking such a completely different view of it with such calmness of certainty. What a little way, I thought, has all Ruskin's fire and eloquence made in driving into people so great a truth, a truth so fertile of consequences!

Then I turned the intrusive sentence over again in my mind: 'No man would work unless he hoped by working to earn leisure:' and I saw that this was another way of putting it: first, all the work of the world is done against the grain: second, what a man does in his 'leisure' is not work.

A poor bribe the hope of such leisure to supplement the other inducement to toil, which I take to be the fear of death by starvation: a poor bribe; for the most of men, like those Yorkshire weavers and spinners (and the more part far worse than they), work for such a very small share of leisure that, one must needs say that if all their hope be in that, they are pretty much beguiled of their hope!

So I thought, and this next, that if it were indeed true and beyond remedy, that no man would work unless he hoped by working to earn leisure, the hell of theologians was but little needed; for a thickly populated civilised country, where, you know, after all people must work at something, would serve their turn well enough. Yet again I knew that this theory of the general and necessary hatefulness of work was indeed the common one, and that all sorts of people held it, who without being monsters of insensibility grew fat and jolly nevertheless . . .

For I tried to think what would happen to me if I were forbidden my ordinary daily work; and I knew that I should die of despair and weariness, unless I could straightway take to something else which I could make my daily work: and it was clear to me that I worked not in the least in the world for the sake of earning leisure by it, but partly driven by the fear of starvation or disgrace, and partly, and even a very great deal, because I love the work itself: and as for my leisure: well I had to confess that part of it I do indeed spend as a dog does—in contemplation, let us say; and like it well enough: but part of it also I spend in work: which work gives me just as much pleasure as my bread-earning work—neither more nor less; and therefore could be no bribe or hope for my work-a-day hours.

Then next I turned my thought to my friends: mere artists, and therefore, you know, lazy people by prescriptive right: I found that the one thing they enjoyed was their work, and that their only idea of happy leisure was other work, just as valuable to the world as their work-a-day work: they only differed from me in liking the dog-like leisure less and the man-like labour more than I do.

I got no further when I turned from mere artists, to important men—public men: I could see no signs of their working merely to earn leisure: they all worked for the work and the deeds' sake. Do rich gentlemen sit up all night in the House of Commons for the sake of earning leisure? if so, 'tis a sad waste of labour. Or Mr Gladstone? he doesn't seem to have succeeded in winning much leisure by tolerably strenuous work; what he does get he might have got on much easier terms, I am sure.

> WILLIAM MORRIS (1834–96), 'The Prospects of Architecture in Civilization', 1880

No, I don't like work. I had rather laze about and think of all the fine things that can be done. I don't like work—no man does—but I like what is in the work,—the chance to find yourself. Your own reality—for yourself, not for others—what no other man can ever know. They can only see the mere show, and never can tell what it really means.

> JOSEPH CONRAD (1857–1924), *Heart of Darkness*, 1899

The truth seems to be that as human nature is constituted, man rapidly degenerates unless he has some hard work to do, some difficulties to overcome; and that some strenuous exertion is necessary for physical and moral health. The fulness of life lies in the development and activity of as many and as high faculties as possible. There is intense pleasure in the ardent pursuit of any aim, whether it be success in business, the advancement of art and science, or the improvement of the condition of one's fellow-beings. The highest constructive work of all kinds must often alternate between periods of over-strain and periods of lassitude and stagnation; but for ordinary people, for those who have no strong ambitions, whether of a lower or a higher kind, a moderate income earned by moderate and fairly steady work offers the best opportunity for the growth of those habits of body, mind, and spirit in which alone there is true happiness.

> ALFRED MARSHALL (1842–1924), *Principles of Economics*, 1890

Now, Katherine, what do you mean by health? And what do you want it for?

Answer: By health I mean the power to live a full, adult, living, breathing life in close contact with what I love—the earth and the wonders thereof—the sea—the sun. All that we mean when we speak of the external world. I want to enter into it, to be part of it, to live in it, to learn from it, to lose all that is superficial and acquired in me and to become a conscious direct human being. I want, by understanding myself, to understand others. I want to be all that I am capable of becoming so that I may be (and here I have stopped and waited and waited and it's no good—there's only one phrase that will do) *a child of the sun*. About helping others, about carrying a light and so on, it seems false to say a single word. Let it be at that. *A child of the sun.*

Then I want to *work*. At what? I want so to live that I work with my hands and my feeling and my brain. I want a garden, a small house, grass, animals, books, pictures, music. And out of this, the expression of this, I want to be writing. (Though I may write about cabmen. That's no matter.)

But warm, eager, living life—to be rooted in life—to learn, to desire to know, to feel, to think, to act. That is what I want. And nothing less. That is what I must try for.

> KATHERINE MANSFIELD (1888–1923), *Journal*, 10 Oct. 1922. (This was the last entry. She died on 9 Jan. 1923.)

Toads Revisited

Walking around in the park
Should feel better than work:
The lake, the sunshine,
The grass to lie on,

Blurred playground noises
Beyond black-stockinged nurses—
Not a bad place to be.
Yet it doesn't suit me,

Being one of the men
You meet of an afternoon:
Palsied old step-takers,
Hare-eyed clerks with the jitters,

Waxed-fleshed out-patients
Still vague from accidents,
And characters in long coats
Deep in the litter-baskets—

All dodging the toad work
By being stupid or weak.
Think of being them!
Hearing the hours chime,

Watching the bread delivered,
The sun by clouds covered,
The children going home;
Think of being them,

Turning over their failures
By some bed of lobelias,
Nowhere to go but indoors,
No friends but empty chairs—

No, give me my in-tray,
My loaf-haired secretary,
My shall-I-keep-the-call-in-Sir:
What else can I answer,

When the lights come on at four
At the end of another year?
Give me your arm, old toad;
Help me down Cemetery Road.

PHILIP LARKIN (1922–85), 1964

III. ALL IN A DAY'S WORK

In modern times work gives society its collective rhythms and shapes the day for individuals. Typically, work starts in the morning, is punctuated by breaks and ends in the late afternoon. Those who work night shifts or stay late in the office are highly conscious of being outside the normal routine. Most people work a five-day week, followed by a two-day weekend break. During the year there will be several periods of seasonal holiday, and at some point the individual will take some weeks of annual holiday. This regular and predictable cycle of work and non-work breaks up the time and gives structure to our lives.

It was not always like this. The regular working week is a relatively modern invention and so is the annual period of holiday. In earlier and simpler societies work was more likely to be oriented by task than by time. Milkmaids worked in the morning and the evening, but had the middle of the day off. Between sowing and harvest peasants had intervals of relative leisure. Shepherds were busy during lambing and sheep-shearing, but otherwise had a great deal of spare time. Even industry was highly seasonal at first.

In the early modern period craftsmen and labourers were expected to work during all the hours of daylight, which meant that they had a longer day in the summer than in the winter. They put in more hours than their modern equivalents, though very probably they worked less intensively during them. Holidays were irregular, coinciding with the festivals of the church year. Sundays were supposed to be days off from work, but only during the nineteenth century did it become usual for employees in Britain to be given an additional day or half-day off each week, along with several weeks' paid holiday each year and the annual Bank holidays prescribed by Act of Parliament in 1871.

In modern times the distinction between work and leisure has been further enhanced by the separation between the home and the workplace. When people lived on their agricultural holdings and when the craftsman's house was his workshop, work and leisure were intermingled. Holidays were not private occasions, but were celebrated at home by the whole working community. Children and old people were not separated from the world of work, but participated in it to the best of their ability. The segregation of children in schools was as unusual as compulsory retirement for the elderly.

Today, however, work and home are normally quite separate. Going to work usually involves getting up at a different time, putting on different clothes and making a journey of ever increasing length. The division between the public world of work and business and the private life of family and domesticity is sometimes so great that individuals display totally different personalities in the two contexts. Dickens's description of Wemmick in his 'castle' at Walworth (pp. 264–7 below) brilliantly foreshadows this process. The separateness of the two spheres is strictly enforced, and when it is breached, as in the telephone call from the office to the home, we feel the need to apologize.

Beginning work nowadays thus involves a decisive movement out of the domestic circle into the public arena. Instead of being a barely visible process of gradual initiation, as it used to be, it has become a distinct rite of initiation. A job has to be found; and the young person's first day at work can be a traumatic ordeal.

LOOKING FOR A JOB

Becker's Law. It is much harder to find a job than to keep one.

JULES BECKER of Becker & Co., San Francisco

In the Northern part of Oxfordshire, about Banbury and Bloxham, it has always been the custom at set times of year, for young people to meet to be hired as servants; which meeting, at Banbury they call the Mop; at Bloxham the Statute, where they all sort themselves, and carry their badges according as they are qualified; the carters standing in one place with their whips, and the Shepherds in another with their crooks; but the maids, as far as I could observe, stood promiscuously: which custom I had scarce I think noted, but that it seems to be as old as our Saviour, and to illustrate his Parable in St Matthew's Gospel, where the laborers are said to stand in the mercat to be hired.

ROBERT PLOT (1640–96), *The Natural History of Oxfordshire*, 1677

In hiring of a servant you are first to make sure that he be set at liberty, after that to inquire of him where he was born, in what service he hath been, with what labour he hath been most exercised, and whether he can do such and such things; and after that to go to his master, or some neighbour of his that you are acquainted with, and tell them that you are about to hire such a servant and so know of them whether he be true and trusty, if he be a gentle and quiet fellow, whether he be addicted to company-keeping or no, and lastly to know what wages he had the year before. But if he have any of the forenamed ill properties, your best way will be to forbear hiring of him.

In hiring of maid-servants you are to make choice of such as are good milkers, and to have a care of such as are of a sluggish and sleepy disposition, for danger of fire; and never to hire such as are too near their friends, for occasion is said to make a thief, and being hired you are not to commit over much to their trust, but to see into all things yourself and to keep as much as you can under lock and key.

When you are about to hire a servant, you are to call them aside and to talk privately with them concerning their wage. If the servants stand in a church-yard, they usually call them aside and walk to the back side of the church, and there treat of their wage. And so soon as you have hired them, you are to call to them for their tickets, and thereby shall you be secured from all future danger. Their tickets cost them 2d a piece, and some masters will give them that 2d again, but that is in the master's choice, unless they condition so before the servant be hired.

HENRY BEST, Yorkshire farmer (c.1592–1647), *Farming Book*, 1642

The examination at the Internal Navigation was certainly not to be so much dreaded as that at the Weights and Measures; but still there was an examination; and Charley, who had not been the most diligent of schoolboys, approached it with great dread after a preparatory evening passed with the assistance of his cousin and Mr Norman.

Exactly at ten in the morning he walked into the lobby of his future work-shop, and found no one yet there but two aged seedy messengers. He was shown into a waiting-room, and there he remained for a couple of hours, during which every clerk in the establishment came to have a look at him. At last he was ushered into the Secretary's room.

'Ah!' said the Secretary, 'your name is Tudor, isn't it?'

Charley confessed to the fact.

'Yes,' said the Secretary, 'I have heard about you from Sir Gilbert de Salop.' Now Sir Gilbert de Salop was the great family friend of this branch of the Tudors. But Charley, finding that no remark suggested itself to him at this moment concerning Sir Gilbert, merely said, 'Yes, sir.'

'And you wish to serve the Queen?' said the Secretary.

Charley, not quite knowing whether this was a joke or not, said that he did.

'Quite right—it is a very fair ambition,' continued the great official func-tionary—'quite right—but, mind you, Mr Tudor, if you come to us you must come to work. I hope you like hard work; you should do so, if you intend to remain with us.'

Charley said that he thought he did rather like hard work. Hereupon a senior clerk standing by, though a man not given to much laughter, smiled slightly, probably in pity at the unceasing labour to which the youth was about to devote himself.

'The Internal Navigation requires great steadiness, good natural abilities, considerable education, and—and—and no end of appli-cation. Come, Mr Tudor, let us see what you can do.' And so saying, Mr

Oldeschole, the Secretary, motioned him to sit down at an office table opposite to himself.

Charley did as he was bid, and took from the hands of his future master
an old, much-worn quill pen, with which the great man had been signing
minutes.

'Now,' said the great man, 'just copy the few first sentences of that leading
article—either one will do,' and he pushed over to him a huge newspaper.

To tell the truth, Charley did not know what a leading article was, and so he
sat abashed, staring at the paper.

'Why don't you write?' asked the Secretary.

'Where shall I begin, sir?' stammered poor Charley, looking piteously into
the examiner's face.

'God bless my soul! there; either of those leading articles,' and leaning over
the table, the Secretary pointed to a particular spot.

Hereupon Charley began his task in a large, ugly, round hand, neither that
of a man nor of a boy, and set himself to copy the contents of the paper. 'The
name of Pacifico stinks in the nostril of the British public. It is well known
to all the world how sincerely we admire the vers*i*tility of Lord Palmerston's
genius; how cordially we s*i*mpathize with his patriotic energies. But the admiration which even a Palmerston inspires must have a bound, and our s*i*mpa-
thy may be called on too far. When we find ourselves asked to pay———'. By this
time Charley had half covered the half-sheet of foolscap which had been put
before him, and here at the word 'pay' he unfortunately suffered a large blot of
ink to fall on the paper.

'That won't do, Mr Tudor, that won't do—come, let us look,' and stretching
over again, the Secretary took up the copy.

'Oh dear! oh dear! this is very bad; versatility with an "i!"—sympathy with
an "i!" sympathize with an "i!" Why, Mr Tudor, you must be very fond of "i's"
down in Shropshire.'

Charley looked sheepish, but of course said nothing.

'And I never saw a viler hand in my life. Oh dear, oh dear, I must send you
back to Sir Gilbert. Look here, Snape, this will never do—never do for the
Internal Navigation, will it?'

Snape, the attendant senior clerk, said, as indeed he could not help saying,
that the writing was very bad.

'I never saw worse in my life,' said the Secretary. 'And now, Mr Tudor, what
do you know of arithmetic?'

Charley said that he thought he knew arithmetic pretty well;—'at least
some of it,' he modestly added.

'Some of it!' said the Secretary, slightly laughing. 'Well, I'll tell you what—
this won't do at all;' and he took the unfortunate manuscript between his
thumb and forefinger. 'You had better go home and endeavour to write something a little better than this. Mind, if it is not very much better it won't do.
And look here; take care that you do it yourself. If you bring me the writing of

any one else, I shall be sure to detect you. I have not any more time now; as to arithmetic, we'll examine you in "some of it" to-morrow.'

So Charley, with a faint heart, went back to his cousin's lodgings and waited till the two friends had arrived from the Weights and Measures. The men there made a point of staying up to five o'clock, as is the case with all model officials, and it was therefore late before he could get himself properly set to work. But when they did arrive, preparations for calligraphy were made on a great scale; a volume of Gibbon was taken down, new quill pens, large and small, and steel pens by various makers were procured; cream-laid paper was provided, and ruled lines were put beneath it. And when this was done, Charley was especially cautioned to copy the spelling as well as the wording.

He worked thus for an hour before dinner, and then for three hours in the evening, and produced a very legible copy of half a chapter of the 'Decline and Fall.'

'I didn't think they examined at all at the Navigation,' said Norman.

'Well, I believe it's quite a new thing,' said Alaric Tudor. 'The schoolmaster must be abroad with a vengeance, if he has got as far as that.'

And then they carefully examined Charley's work, crossed his t's, dotted his i's, saw that his spelling was right, and went to bed.

Again, punctually at ten o'clock, Charley presented himself at the Internal Navigation; and again saw the two seedy old messengers warming themselves at the lobby fire. On this occasion he was kept three hours in the waiting-room, and some of the younger clerks ventured to come and speak to him. At length Mr Snape appeared, and desired the acolyte to follow him. Charley, supposing that he was again going to the awful Secretary, did so with a palpitating heart. But he was led in another direction into a large room, carrying his manuscript neatly rolled in his hand. Here Mr Snape introduced him to five other occupants of the chamber; he, Mr Snape himself, having a separate desk there, being, in official parlance, the head of the room. Charley was told to take a seat at a desk, and did so, still thinking that the dread hour of his examination was soon to come. His examination, however, was begun and over. No one ever asked for his calligraphic manuscript, and as to his arithmetic, it may be presumed that his assurance that he knew 'some of it,' was deemed to be adequate evidence of sufficient capacity. And in this manner, Charley Tudor became one of the Infernal Navvies.

ANTHONY TROLLOPE (1815–82), *The Three Clerks*, 1857

'A Sinister Employer'

'I have been a governess for five years,' said she, 'in the family of Colonel Spence Munro, but two months ago the Colonel received an appointment at Halifax, in Nova Scotia, and took his children over to America with him, so that I found myself without a situation. I advertised and I answered advertisements, but without success. At last the little money which I had saved began to run short, and I was at my wits' end as to what I should do.

'There is a well-known agency for governesses in the West End called West-away's, and there I used to call about once a week in order to see whether anything had turned up which might suit me. Westaway was the name of the founder of the business, but it is really managed by Miss Stoper. She sits in her own little office, and the ladies who are seeking employment wait in an ante-room, and are then shown in one by one, when she consults her ledgers, and sees whether she has anything which would suit them.

'Well, when I called last week I was shown into the little office as usual, but I found that Miss Stoper was not alone. A prodigiously stout man with a very smiling face, and a great heavy chin which rolled down in fold upon fold over his throat, sat at her elbow with a pair of glasses on his nose, looking very earnestly at the ladies who entered. As I came in he gave quite a jump in his chair, and turned quickly to Miss Stoper:

' "That will do," said he; "I could not ask for anything better. Capital! capital!" He seemed quite enthusiastic, and rubbed his hands together in the most genial fashion. He was such a comfortable-looking man that it was quite a pleasure to look at him.

' "You are looking for a situation, miss?" he asked.

' "Yes, sir."

' "As governess?"

' "Yes, sir."

' "And what salary do you ask?"

' "I had four pounds a month in my last place with Colonel Spence Munro."

' "Oh, tut, tut! sweating—rank sweating!" he cried, throwing his fat hands out into the air like a man who is in a boiling passion. "How could anyone offer so pitiful a sum to a lady with such attractions and accomplishments?"

' "My accomplishments, sir, may be less than you imagine," said I. "A little French, a little German, music and drawing—"

' "Tut, tut!" he cried. "This is all quite beside the question. The point is, have you or have you not the bearing and deportment of a lady? There it is in a nutshell. If you have not, you are not fitted for the rearing of a child who may some day play a considerable part in the history of the country. But if you have, why, then how could any gentleman ask you to condescend to accept anything under the three figures? Your salary with me, madam, would commence at a hundred pounds a year."

'You may imagine, Mr Holmes, that to me, destitute as I was, such an offer seemed almost too good to be true. The gentleman, however, seeing perhaps the look of incredulity upon my face, opened a pocket-book and took out a note.

' "It is also my custom," said he, smiling in the most pleasant fashion until his eyes were just two shining slits, amid the white creases of his face, "to advance to my young ladies half their salary beforehand, so that they may meet any little expenses of their journey and their wardrobe."

'It seemed to me that I had never met so fascinating and so thoughtful a man. As I was already in debt to my tradesmen, the advance was a great convenience, and yet there was something unnatural about the whole transaction which made me wish to know a little more before I quite committed myself.

' "May I ask where you live, sir?" said I.

' "Hampshire. Charming rural place. The Copper Beeches, five miles on the far side of Winchester. It is the most lovely country, my dear young lady, and the dearest old country house."

' "And my duties, sir? I should be glad to know what they would be."

' "One child—one dear little romper just six years old. Oh, if you could see him killing cockroaches with a slipper! Smack! smack! smack! Three gone before you could wink!" He leaned back in his chair and laughed his eyes into his head again.'

> ARTHUR CONAN DOYLE (1859–1930), 'The Copper Beeches', *The Adventures of Sherlock Holmes,* 1892

Once Boris suggested that I should go to Les Halles and try for a job as a porter. I arrived at half-past four in the morning, when the work was getting into its swing. Seeing a short fat man in a bowler hat directing some porters, I went up to him and asked for work. Before answering he seized my right hand and felt the palm.

'You are strong, eh?' he said.

'Very strong,' I said untruly.

'*Bien.* Let me see you lift that crate.'

It was a huge wicker basket full of potatoes. I took hold of it, and found that, so far from lifting it, I could not even move it. The man in the bowler hat watched me, then shrugged his shoulders and turned away. I made off. When I had gone some distance I looked back and saw *four* men lifting the basket onto a cart. It weighed three hundredweight, possibly. The man had seen that I was no use, and taken this way of getting rid of me.

> GEORGE ORWELL (1903–50), *Down and Out in Paris and London,* 1933

Will Consider Situation

These here are words of radical advice for a young man looking for a job;
Young man, be a snob.
Yes, if you are in search of arguments against starting at the bottom,
Why I've gottom.
Let the personnel managers differ;
It's obvious that you will get on faster at the top than at the bottom because
there are more people at the bottom than at the top so naturally the
competition at the bottom is stiffer.

If you need any further proof that my theory works,
Well, nobody can deny that presidents get paid more than vice-presidents and
    vice-presidents get paid more than clerks.
Stop looking at me quizzically;
I want to add that you will never achieve fortune in a job that makes you
    uncomfortable physically.
When anybody tells you that hard jobs are better for you than soft jobs be sure
    to repeat this text to them,
Postmen tramp around all day through rain and snow just to deliver people's
    in cozy air-conditioned offices checks to them.
You don't need to interpret tea leaves stuck in a cup
To understand that people who work sitting down get paid more than people
    who work standing up.
Another thing about having a comfortable job is you not only accumulate
    more treasure;
You get more leisure.
So that when you find you have worked so comfortably that your waistline is
    a menace,
You correct it with golf or tennis.
Whereas if in an uncomfortable job like piano-moving or stevedoring you
    indulge,
You have no time to exercise, you just continue to bulge.
To sum it up, young man, there is every reason to refuse a job that will make
    heavy demands on you corporally or manually,
And the only intelligent way to start your career is to accept a sitting position
    paying at least twenty-five thousand dollars annually.

                                           Ogden Nash (1902–71), 1941

'Ask her to come up,' he said.

Lady Julia Fish was a handsome middle-aged woman of the large blonde type, of a personality both breezy and commanding. She came into the room a few moments later like a galleon under sail, her resolute chin and her china-blue eyes proclaiming a supreme confidence in her ability to get anything she wanted out of anyone. And Lord Tilbury, having bowed stiffly, stood regarding her with a pop-eyed hostility. Even setting aside her loathsome family connexions, there was a patronizing good humour about her manner which he resented. And certainly, if Lady Julia Fish's manner had a fault, it was that it resembled a little too closely that of the great lady of a village amusedly trying to make friends with the backward child of one of her tenants.

'Well, well, well,' she said, not actually patting Lord Tilbury on the head but conveying the impression that she might see fit to do so at any moment, 'you're looking very bonny. Biarritz did you good.'

Lord Tilbury, with the geniality of a trapped wolf, admitted to being in robust health.

'So this is where you get out all those jolly little papers of yours, is it? I must say I'm impressed. Quite awe-inspiring, all that ritual on the threshold. Admirals in the Swiss Navy making you fill up forms with your name and business, and small boys in buttons eyeing you as if anything you said might be used in evidence against you.'

'What *is* your business?' asked Lord Tilbury.

'The practical note!' said Lady Julia, with indulgent approval. 'How stimulating that is. Time is money, and all that. Quite. Well, cutting the preamble, I want a job for Ronnie.'

Lord Tilbury looked like a trapped wolf who had thought as much.

'Ronnie?' he said coldly.

'My son. Didn't you meet him at Biarritz? He was there. Small and pink.'

Lord Tilbury drew in breath for the delivery of the nasty blow.

'I regret . . .'

'I know what you're going to say. You're very crowded here. Fearful congestion, and so on. Well, Ronnie won't take up much room. And I shouldn't think he could do any actual harm to a solidly established concern like this. Surely you could let him mess about at *something*? Why, Sir Gregory Parsloe, our neighbour down in Shropshire, told me that you were employing his nephew, Monty. And while I would be the last woman to claim Ronnie is a mental giant, at least he's brighter than young Monty Bodkin.'

A quiver ran through Lord Tilbury's stocky form. This woman had unbared his secret shame. A man who prided himself on never letting himself be worked for jobs, he had had a few weeks before a brief moment of madness when, under the softening influence of a particularly good public dinner, he had yielded to the request of the banqueter on his left that he should find a place at Tilbury House for his nephew.

He had regretted the lapse next morning. He had regretted it more on seeing the nephew. And he had not ceased to regret it now.

'That,' he said tensely, 'has nothing to do with the case.'

'I don't see why. Swallowing camels and straining at gnats is what I should call it.'

'Nothing,' repeated Lord Tilbury, 'to do with the case.'

He was beginning to feel that this interview was not working out as he had anticipated. He had meant to be strong, brusque, decisive—the man of iron. And here this woman had got him arguing and explaining—almost in a position of defending himself. Like so many people who came into contact with her, he began to feel that there was something disagreeably hypnotic about Lady Julia Fish.

'But what do you want your son to work here *for*?' he asked, realizing as he spoke that a man of iron ought to have scorned to put such a question.

Lady Julia considered.

'Oh, a pittance. Whatever the dole is you give your slaves.'

Lord Tilbury made himself clearer.

'I mean, why? Has he shown any aptitude for journalism?' This seemed to amuse Lady Julia.

'My dear man,' she said, tickled by the quaint conceit, 'no member of my family has ever shown any aptitude for anything except eating and sleeping.'

'Then why do you want him to join my staff?'

'Well, primarily, to distract his mind.'

'What!'

'To distract his . . . well, yes, I suppose in a loose way you could call it a mind.'

'I don't understand you.'

'Well, it's like this. The poor half-wit is trying to marry a chorus-girl, and it seemed to me that if he were safe at Tilbury House, inking his nose and getting bustled about by editors and people, it might take his mind off the tender passion.'

Lord Tilbury drew a long, deep, rasping breath. The weakness had passed. He could be strong now. This outrageous insult to the business he loved had shattered the spell which those china-blue eyes and that confident manner had been weaving about him. He spoke curtly, placing his thumbs in the armholes of his waistcoat to lend emphasis to his remarks.

'I fear you have mistaken the functions of Tilbury House, Lady Julia.'

'I beg your pardon?'

'We publish newspapers, magazines, weekly journals. We are not a Home for the Lovelorn.'

P. G. WODEHOUSE (1881–1975), *Heavy Weather*, 1933

It has been said that the modern English do not like work. It cannot be said that they do not look for it and ask for it. The day after this advertisement appeared, the postal heavens opened and a hurricane of letters fell upon Twigg and Dersingham. Into Angel Pavement all that day there poured a bewildering stream of replies. It seemed as if street after street, whole suburbs, had been waiting for this particular opening. There were, it appeared, dozens of men with vast connections in the furnishing trade and the most thorough, the most intimate knowledge of veneers and inlays, and most of these men, though they had apparently refused scores of offers recently, were only too willing to assist Messrs Twigg and Dersingham. Then there were men who had not perhaps exactly a connection but had been for years, so to speak, on the fringe of the furnishing trade, men who had sold pianos, who had given removing estimates, who had done a little valuing, who knew something about upholstering. Then there were older men, ex-officers many of them, who knew about all kinds of things and were ready to enclose the most astonishing testimonials, who admitted that the furnishing trade and veneers and inlays were all new to them but who felt that they could soon learn all there was to know, and in the meantime were anxious to show how they could command men and to display their unusual ability to organise. And, last of all, there were the public school men, fellows who knew nothing about veneers and inlays and did not even pretend to care about them, but pointed out that they could drive cars, manage an estate, organise anything or anybody, and were willing to go out East, being evidently under the impression that Twigg and Dersingham had probably a couple of tea plantations as well as a business in veneers and inlays. These correspondents expressed themselves in every imaginable sort of handwriting and on every conceivable kind of notepaper, from superior parchment to dirty little pink bits that had been saved up in a box on the mantelpiece, but in one particular they were all alike: they were all keen, all energetic.

'This tells you something about the old country, doesn't it?' said Mr Golspie, who always talked as if he came from some newer one. He and Mr Dersingham and Mr Smeeth had been going through the pile.

'It's only the slump,' said Mr Dersingham.

J. B. PRIESTLEY (1894–1984), *Angel Pavement*, 1930

Walker's outer office was impressive. As soon as Tom saw it, he knew he was being seriously considered for a job, and maybe a pretty good one. Walker had two secretaries, one chosen for looks, apparently, and one for utility. A pale-yellow carpet lay on the floor, and there was a yellow leather armchair for callers. Walker himself was closeted in an inner office which was separated from the rest of the room by a partition of opaque glass brick.

The utilitarian secretary told Tom to wait. It was extremely quiet. Neither of the two girls was typing, and although each had two telephones on her desk and an interoffice communication box, there was no ringing or buzzing. Both the secretaries sat reading typewritten sheets in black notebooks. After Tom had waited about half an hour, the pretty secretary, with no audible or visible cue, suddenly looked up brightly and said, 'Mr Walker will see you now. Just open the door and go in.'

Tom opened the door and saw a fat pale man sitting in a high-backed upholstered chair behind a kidney-shaped desk with nothing on it but a blotter and pen. He was in his shirt sleeves, and he weighed about two hundred and fifty pounds. His face was as white as a marshmallow. He didn't stand up when Tom came in, but he smiled. It was a surprisingly warm, spontaneous smile, as though he had unexpectedly recognized an old friend. 'Thomas Rath?' he said. 'Sit down! Make yourself comfortable! Take off your coat!'

Tom thanked him and, although it wasn't particularly warm, took off his coat. There wasn't any place to put it, so, sitting down in the comfortable chair in front of Walker's desk, he laid the coat awkwardly across his lap.

'I've read the application forms you filled out, and it seems to me you might be qualified for a new position we may have opening up here,' Walker said. 'There are just a few questions I want to ask you.' He was still smiling. Suddenly he touched a button on the arm of his chair and the back of the chair dropped, allowing him to recline, as though he were in an airplane seat. Tom could see only his face across the top of the desk.

'You will excuse me,' Walker said, still smiling. 'The doctor says I must get plenty of rest, and this is the way I do it.'

Tom couldn't think of anything more appropriate to say than 'It looks comfortable . . .'

'Why do you want to work for the United Broadcasting Corporation?' Walker asked abruptly.

'It's a good company . . .' Tom began hesitantly, and was suddenly impatient at the need for hypocrisy. The sole reason he wanted to work for United Broadcasting was that he thought he might be able to make a lot of money there fast, but he felt he couldn't say that. It was sometimes considered fashionable for the employees of foundations to say that they were in it for the money, but people were supposed to work at advertising agencies and broadcasting companies for spiritual reasons.

'I believe,' Tom said, 'that television is developing into the greatest medium for mass education and entertainment. It has always fascinated me, and I would like to work with it . . .'

'What kind of salary do you have in mind?' Walker asked. Tom hadn't expected the question that soon. Walker was still smiling.

'The salary isn't the primary consideration with me,' Tom said, trying desperately to come up with stock answers to stock questions. 'I'm mainly interested in finding something useful and worth while to do. I have personal responsibilities, however, and I would hope that something could be worked out to enable me to meet them . . .'

'Of course,' Walker said, beaming more cheerily than ever. 'I understand you applied for a position in the public-relations department. Why did you choose that?'

Because I heard there was an opening, Tom wanted to say, but quickly thought better of it and substituted a halting avowal of lifelong interest in public relations. 'I think my experience in working with *people* at the Schanenhauser Foundation would be helpful,' he concluded lamely.

'I see,' Walker said kindly. There was a short silence before he added, 'Can you write?'

'I do most of the writing at the Schanenhauser Foundation,' Tom said. 'The annual report to the trustees is my job, and so are most of the reports on individual projects. I used to be editor of my college paper.'

'That sounds fine,' Walker said casually. 'I have a little favour I want to ask of you. I want you to write me your autobiography.'

'What?' Tom asked in astonishment.

'Nothing very long,' Walker said. 'Just as much as you can manage to type out in an hour. One of my girls will give you a room with a typewriter.'

'Is there anything in particular you want me to tell you about?'

'Yourself,' Walker said, looking hugely pleased. 'Explain yourself to me. Tell me what kind of person you are. Explain why we should hire you.'

'I'll try,' Tom said weakly.

'You'll have precisely an hour,' Walker said. 'You see, this is a device I use in employing people—I find it most helpful. For this particular job, I have twenty or thirty applicants. It's hard to tell from a brief interview whom to choose, so I ask them all to write about themselves for an hour. You'd be surprised how revealing the results are . . .'

He paused, still smiling, Tom said nothing.

'Just a few hints,' Walker continued. 'Write anything you want, but at the end of your last page, I'd like you to finish this sentence: "The most significant fact about me is . . ."'

'The most significant fact about me is . . .' Tom repeated idiotically.

'The results, of course, will be entirely confidential.' Walker lifted a bulky arm and inspected his wrist watch. 'It's now five minutes to twelve,' he concluded. 'I'll expect your paper on my desk at precisely one o'clock.'

SLOAN WILSON (1920–), *The Man in the Grey Flannel Suit*, 1955

You will be Hearing from us Shortly

You feel adequate to the demands of this position?
What qualities do you feel you
Personally have to offer?

                                        Ah

Let us consider your application form.
Your qualifications, though impressive, are
Not, we must admit, precisely what
We had in mind. Would you care
To defend their relevance?

                                        Indeed

Now your age. Perhaps you feel able
To make your own comment about that,
Too? We are conscious ourselves
Of the need for a candidate with precisely
The right degree of immaturity.

                                        So glad we agree

And now a delicate matter: your looks.
You do appreciate this work involves
Contact with the actual public? Might they,
Perhaps, find your appearance
Disturbing?

                                       Quite so

And your accent. That is the way
You have always spoken, is it? What
Of your education? Were
You educated? We mean, of course,
Where were you educated?
                   And how
Much of a handicap is that to you,
Would you say?

               Married, children,
We see. The usual dubious
Desire to perpetuate what had better
Not have happened at all. We do not
Ask what domestic disasters shimmer
Behind that vaguely unsuitable address.

And you were born—?
                                    Yes. Pity.

So glad we agree.
                           U. A. Fanthorpe (1929–), 1982

BEGINNERS

Caleb's shepherding began in childhood; at all events he had his first experience of it at that time. Many an old shepherd, whose father was shepherd before him, has told me that he began to go with the flock very early in life, when he was no more than ten to twelve years of age. Caleb remembered being put in charge of his father's flock at the tender age of six. It was a new and wonderful experience, and made so vivid and lasting an impression on his mind that now, when he is past eighty, he speaks of it very feelingly as of something which happened yesterday.

It was harvesting time, and Isaac, who was a good reaper, was wanted in the field, but he could find no one, not even a boy, to take charge of his flock in the meantime, and so to be able to reap and keep an eye on the flock at the same time he brought his sheep down to the part of the down adjoining the field. It was on his 'liberty,' or that part of the down where he was entitled to have his flock. He then took his very small boy, Caleb, and placing him with the sheep told him they were now in his charge; that he was not to lose sight of them, and at the same time not to run about among the furze-bushes for fear of treading on an adder. By and by the sheep began straying off among the furze-bushes, and no sooner would they disappear from sight than he imagined they were lost for ever, or would be unless he quickly found them, and to find them he had to run about among the bushes with the terror of adders in his mind, and the two troubles together kept him crying with misery all the time. Then, at intervals, Isaac would leave his reaping and come to see how he was getting on, and the tears would vanish from his eyes, and he would feel very brave again, and to his father's question he would reply that he was getting on very well.

Finally his father came and took him to the field, to his great relief; but he did not carry him in his arms; he strode along at his usual pace and let the little fellow run after him, stumbling and falling and picking himself up again and running on. And by and by one of the women in the field cried out, 'Be you not ashamed, Isaac, to go that pace and not bide for the little child! I do b'lieve he's no more'n seven year—poor mite!'

'No more'n six,' answered Isaac proudly, with a laugh.

W. H. HUDSON (1841–1922), *A Shepherd's Life*, 1910

'A Childhood in the Fens about 1850 to 1860'

In the very short schooling that I obtained, I learnt neither grammar nor writing. On the day that I was eight years of age, I left school, and began to work fourteen hours a day in the fields, with from forty to fifty other children of whom, even at that early age, I was the eldest. We were followed all day long by an old man carrying a long whip in his hand which he did not forget to use. A great many of the children were only five years of age. You will think that I am exaggerating, but I am *not*; it is as true as the Gospel. Thirty-five years ago is the time I speak of, and the place, Croyland in Lincolnshire, nine miles from Peterborough. I could even now name several of the children who began at the age of five to work in the gangs, and also the name of the ganger.

We always left the town, summer and winter, the moment the old Abbey clock struck six. Anyone who has read *Hereward the Wake*, by Charles Kingsley, will have read a good description of this Abbey. We had to walk a very long way to our work, never much less than two miles each way, and very often five miles each way. The large farms all lay a good distance from the town, and it was on those farms that we worked. In the winter, by the time we reached our work, it was light enough to begin, and of course we worked until it was dark and then had our long walk home. I never remember to have reached home sooner than six and more often seven, even in winter. In the summer, we did not leave the fields in the evening until the clock had struck six, and then of course we must walk home, and this walk was no easy task for us children who had worked hard all day on the ploughed fields.

In all the four years I worked in the fields, I never worked one hour under cover of a barn, and only once did we have a meal in a house. And I shall never forget that one meal or the woman who gave us it. It was a most terrible day. The cold east wind (I suppose it was an east wind, for surely no wind ever blew colder), the sleet and snow which came every now and then in showers seemed almost to cut us to pieces. We were working upon a large farm that lay half-way between Croyland and Peterborough. Had the snow and sleet come continuously we should have been allowed to come home, but because it only came at intervals, of course we had to stay. I have been out in all sorts of weather but never remember a colder day. Well, the morning passed along somehow. The ganger did his best for us by letting us have a run in our turns, but that did not help us very much because we were too numbed with the cold to be able to run much. Dinner-time came, and we were preparing to sit down under a hedge and eat our cold dinner and drink our cold tea, when we saw the shepherd's wife coming towards us, and she said to our ganger, 'Bring these children into my house and let them eat their dinner there.' We went into that very small two-roomed cottage, and when we got into the largest room there was not standing room for us all, but this woman's heart was large, even if her house was small, and so she put her few chairs and table out into the garden, and then we all sat down in a ring upon the floor. She then placed in our midst a very large saucepan of hot boiled potatoes, and bade us help ourselves. Truly, although I have attended scores of grand parties and banquets since that time, not one of them has seemed half as good to me as that meal did. I well remember that woman. She was one of the plainest women I ever knew; in fact she was what the world would call quite ugly, and yet I can't think of her even now without thinking of that verse in one of our hymns, where it says,

> No, Earth has angels though their forms are moulded
> But of such clay as fashions all below,
> Though harps are wanting, and bright pinions folded,
> We know them by the love-light on their brow.

MRS BURROWS (*d. ante* 1931), quoted in *Life as We Have Known It* by Co-operative Working Women, ed. Margaret Llewelyn Davies, 1931

Mother Wept

> Mother wept, and father sighed;
>   With delight a-glow
> Cried the lad, 'To-morrow,' cried,
>   'To the pit I go.'

Up and down the place he sped,
    Greeted old and young,
Far and wide the tidings spread,
    Clapt his hands and sung.

Came his cronies; some to gaze
    Wrapt in wonder; some
Free with counsel; some with praise;
    Some with envy dumb.

'May he,' many a gossip cried,
    'Be from peril kept;'
Father hid his face and sighed,
    Mother turned and wept.

JOSEPH SKIPSEY (1832–1903), 1886

When we reached the carré, a large square hall between the dwelling-house and the pensionnat, she paused, dropped my hand, faced, and scrutinized me. I was flushed, and tremulous from head to foot; tell it not in Gath, I believe I was crying. In fact, the difficulties before me were far from being wholly imaginary; some of them were real enough; and not the least substantial lay in my want of mastery over the medium through which I should be obliged to teach. I had, indeed, studied French closely since my arrival in Villette; learning its practice by day, and its theory in every leisure moment at night, to as late an hour as the rule of the house would allow candle-light, but I was far from yet being able to trust my powers of correct oral expression.

'Dites donc,' said madame sternly, 'vous sentez-vous réellement trop faible?'

I might have said 'Yes,' and gone back to nursery obscurity, and there, perhaps, mouldered for the rest of my life; but, looking up at madame, I saw in her countenance a something that made me think twice ere I decided. At that instant, she did not wear a woman's aspect, but rather a man's. Power of a particular kind strongly limned itself in all her traits, and that power was not *my* kind of power: neither sympathy, nor congeniality, nor submission, were the emotions it awakened. I stood—not soothed, nor won, nor overwhelmed. It seemed as if a challenge of strength between opposing gifts was given, and I suddenly felt all the dishonour of my diffidence—all the pusillanimity of my slackness to aspire.

'Will you,' said she, 'go backward or forward?' indicating with her hand, first, the small door of communication with the dwelling-house, and then the great double portals of the classes or school-rooms.

pensionnat] boarding school   '*Dites donc,*' . . . *trop faible?*'] 'Tell me, then, do you really
feel too weak?'

'En avant,' I said.

'But,' pursued she, cooling as I warmed, and continuing the hard look, from very antipathy to which I drew strength and determination, 'can you face the classes, or are you over-excited?'

She sneered slightly in saying this—nervous excitability was not much to madame's taste.

'I am no more excited than this stone,' I said, tapping the flag with my toe: 'or than you,' I added, returning her look.

'Bon! But let me tell you these are not quiet, decorous English girls you are going to encounter. Ce sont des Labassecouriennes, rondes, franches, brusques, et tant soit peu rebelles.'

I said: 'I know; and I know, too, that though I have studied French hard since I came here, yet I still speak it with far too much hesitation—too little accuracy to be able to command their respect: I shall make blunders that will lay me open to the scorn of the most ignorant. Still I mean to give the lesson.'

'They always throw over timid teachers,' said she.

'I know that, too, madame; I have heard how they rebelled against and persecuted Miss Turner'—a poor, friendless English teacher, whom madame had employed, and lightly discarded; and to whose piteous history I was no stranger.

'C'est vrai,' said she, coolly. 'Miss Turner had no more command over them than a servant from the kitchen would have had. She was weak and wavering; she had neither tact nor intelligence, decision nor dignity. Miss Turner would not do for these girls at all.'

I made no reply, but advanced to the closed school-room door.

'You will not expect aid from me, or from any one,' said madame. 'That would at once set you down as incompetent for your office.'

I opened the door, let her pass with courtesy, and followed her. There were three school-rooms, all large. That dedicated to the second division, where I was to figure, was considerably the largest, and accommodated an assemblage more numerous, more turbulent, and infinitely more unmanageable than the other two. In after days, when I knew the ground better, I used to think sometimes (if such a comparison may be permitted), that the quiet, polished, tame first division, was to the robust, riotous, demonstrative second division, what the English House of Lords is to the House of Commons.

The first glance informed me that many of the pupils were more than girls—quite young women; I knew that some of them were of noble family (as nobility goes in Labassecour), and I was well convinced that not one amongst them was ignorant of my position in madame's household. As I mounted the

'En avant,'] 'Forward.'   *'Ce sont . . . peu rebelles.'*] 'They are Belgian girls, frank, outspoken, offhand, and ever so slightly rebellious.'   *'C'est vrai.'*] 'That's true.' *Labassecour*] Belgium (the 'farmyard')

estrade (a low platform, raised a step above the flooring), where stood the teacher's chair and desk, I beheld opposite to me a row of eyes and brows that threatened stormy weather—eyes full of an insolent light, and brows hard and unblushing as marble. The continental 'female' is quite a different being to the insular 'female' of the same age and class: I never saw such eyes and brows in England. Madame Beck introduced me in one cool phrase, sailed from the room, and left me alone in my glory.

I shall never forget that first lesson, nor all the undercurrent of life and character it opened up to me. Then first did I begin rightly to see the wide difference that lies between the novelist's and poet's ideal 'jeune fille,' and the said 'jeune fille' as she really is.

It seemed that three titled belles in the first row had sat down predetermined that a *bonne d'enfants* should not give them lessons in English. They knew they had succeeded in expelling obnoxious teachers before now; they knew that madame would at any time throw overboard a professeur or maîtresse who became unpopular with the school—that she never assisted a weak official to retain his place—that if he had not strength to fight, or tact to win his way—down he went: looking at 'Miss Snowe' they promised themselves an easy victory.

Mesdemoiselles Blanche, Virginie, and Angélique opened the campaign by a series of titterings and whisperings; these soon swelled into murmurs and short laughs, which the remoter benches caught up and echoed more loudly. This growing revolt of sixty against one, soon became oppressive enough; my command of French being so limited, and exercised under such cruel constraint.

Could I but have spoken in my own tongue, I felt as if I might have gained a hearing; for, in the first place, though I knew I looked a poor creature, and in many respects actually was so, yet nature had given me a voice that could make itself heard, if lifted in excitement or deepened by emotion. In the second place, while I had no flow, only a hesitating trickle of language, in ordinary circumstances, yet—under stimulus such as was now rife through the mutinous mass—I could, in English, have rolled out readily phrases stigmatizing their proceedings as such proceedings deserved to be stigmatized; and then with some sarcasm, flavoured with contemptuous bitterness, for the ringleaders, and relieved with easy banter for the weaker, but less knavish followers, it seemed to me that one might possibly get command over this wild herd and bring them into training, at last. All I could now do was to walk up to Blanche—Mademoiselle de Melcy, a young baronne—the eldest, tallest, handsomest, and most vicious—stand before her desk, take from under her hand her exercise-book, remount the estrade, deliberately read the composition, which I found very stupid, and as deliberately, and in the face of the whole school, tear the blotted page in two.

bonne d'enfants] nursery governess

This action availed to draw attention and check noise. One girl alone, quite in the background, persevered in the riot with undiminished energy. I looked at her attentively. She had a pale face, hair like night, broad strong eyebrows, decided features, and a dark, mutinous, sinister eye: I noted that she sat close by a little door, which door, I was well aware, opened into a small closet where books were kept. She was standing up for the purpose of conducting her clamour with freer energies. I measured her stature and calculated her strength. She seemed both tall and wiry; but, so the conflict were brief and the attack unexpected, I thought I might manage her.

Advancing up the room, looking as cool and careless as I possibly could, in short, *ayant l'air de rien*; I slightly pushed the door and found it was ajar. In an instant, and with sharpness, I had turned on her. In another instant she occupied the closet, the door was shut, and the key in my pocket.

It so happened that this girl, Dolores by name and a Catalonian by race, was the sort of character at once dreaded and hated by all her associates; the act of summary justice above noted, proved popular: there was not one present but, in her heart, liked to see it done. They were stilled for a moment; then a smile—not a laugh—passed from desk to desk: then—when I had gravely and tranquilly returned to the estrade, courteously requested silence, and commenced a dictation as if nothing at all had happened—the pens travelled peacefully over the pages, and the remainder of the lesson passed in order and industry.

'C'est bien,' said Madame Beck, when I came out of class, hot and a little exhausted. 'Ça ira.'

She had been listening and peeping through a spy-hole the whole time.

From that day I ceased to be nursery-governess, and became English teacher. Madame raised my salary; but she got thrice the work out of me she had extracted from Mr Wilson, at half the expense.

Charlotte Brontë (1816–55), Villette, 1853

I stumbled after Mr Jones up a dark, narrow, iron staircase till we emerged through a trap-door into a garret at the top of the house. I recoiled with disgust at the scene before me; and here I was to work—perhaps through life! A low lean-to room, stifling me with the combined odours of human breath and perspiration, stale beer, the sweet sickly smell of gin, and the sour and hardly less disgusting one of new cloth. On the floor, thick with dust and dirt, scraps of stuff and ends of thread, sat some dozen haggard, untidy, shoeless men, with a mingled look of care and recklessness that made me shudder. The windows were tight closed to keep out the cold winter air; and the condensed breath ran in streams down the panes, chequering the dreary outlook

ayant l'air de rien] looking as if I had nothing on my mind

of chimney tops and smoke. The conductor handed me over to one of the men.

'Here, Crossthwaite, take this younker and make a tailor of him. Keep him next you, and prick him up with your needle if he shirks.'

He disappeared down the trap-door, and mechanically, as if in a dream, I sat down by the man and listened to his instructions, kindly enough bestowed. But I did not remain in peace two minutes. A burst of chatter rose as the foreman vanished, and a tall, bloated, sharp-nosed young man next me bawled in my ear,——

'I say, young'un, fork out the tin and pay your footing at Conscrumption Hospital?'

'What do you mean?'

'Aint he just green?—Down with the stumpy—a tizzy for a pot of half-and-half.'

'I never drink beer.'

'Then never do,' whispered the man at my side; 'as sure as hell's hell, it's your only chance.'

There was a fierce, deep earnestness in the tone which made me look up at the speaker, but the other instantly chimed in,——

'Oh, yer don't, don't yer, my young Father Mathy? then yer'll soon learn it here if yer want to keep yer victuals down.'

'And I have promised to take my wages home to my mother.'

'O criminy! hark to that, my coves! here's a chap as is going to take the blunt home to his mammy.'

'T'aint much of it the old'un 'll see,' said another. 'Ven yer pockets it at the Cock and Bottle, my kiddy, yer won't find much of it left o' Sunday mornings.'

'Don't his mother know he's out?' asked another; 'and won't she know it——

> Ven he's sitting in his glory
> Half-price at the Victory.

Oh! no, ve never mentions her—her name is never heard. Certainly not, by no means. Why should it?'

'Well, if yer won't stand a pot,' quoth the tall man, 'I will, that's all, and blow temperance. "A short life and a merry one," says the tailor——

> The ministers talk a great deal about port,
>   And they makes Cape wine very dear,
> But blow their hi's if ever they tries
>   To deprive a poor cove of his beer.

Here, Sam, run to the Cock and Bottle for a pot of half-and-half to my score.'

A thin, pale lad jumped up and vanished, while my tormentor turned to me:

'I say, young'un, do you know why we're nearer heaven here than our neighbours?'

'I shouldn't have thought so,' answered I with a *naïveté* which raised a laugh, and dashed the tall man for a moment.

'Yer don't? then I'll tell yer. A cause we're a top of the house in the first place, and next place yer'll die here six months sooner nor if yer worked in the room below. Aint that logic and science, Orator?' appealing to Crossthwaite.

'Why?' asked I.

'A cause you get all the other floors' stinks up here as well as your own. Concentrated essence of man's flesh, is this here as you're a-breathing. Cellar work-room we calls Rheumatic Ward, because of the damp. Ground-floor's Fever Ward—them as don't get typhus gets dysentery, and them as don't get dysentery gets typhus—your nose'd tell yer why if you opened the back windy. First floor's Ashmy Ward—don't you hear 'um now through the cracks in the boards, a-puffing away like a nest of young locomotives? And this here most august and upper-crust cockloft is the Conscrumptive Hospital. First you begins to cough, then you proceeds to expectorate—spittoons, as you see, perwided free gracious for nothing—fined a kivarten if you spits on the floor—

> Then your cheeks they grows red, and your nose it grows thin,
> And your bones they stick out, till they comes through your skin:

and then, when you've sufficiently covered the poor dear shivering bare backs of the hairystocracy——

> Die, die, die,
> Away you fly,
> Your soul is in the sky!

as the hinspired Shakespeare wittily remarks.'

And the ribald lay down on his back, stretched himself out, and pretended to die in a fit of coughing, which last was, alas! no counterfeit, while poor I, shocked and bewildered, let my tears fall fast upon my knees.

CHARLES KINGSLEY (1819–75), Alton Locke, 1850

And such as would take advantage of a greenhorn's inexperience and credulity in playing him tricks. Such as when Billy Higgs, one of the senior apprentices whose behests it was Harry's duty to obey, sent him to the stores for the 'long stand'. Harry went, unsuspectingly, made his request, wondering on the shape and use of the instrument. The storekeeper answered, solemnly:

'Long stand? Oh, aye, just stand there,' and went on with his work. Minutes elapsed: Harry watched the traffic of boys coming with brass checks and going with tools. Jack Lindsay, a thickset boy with a ready grin and a fondness of striking pugilistic attitudes for no reason at all, came up whistling: ''Allo, 'Arry,' he said, 'What y' standin' there for?' Harry told him. Jack shook his head and said, sympathetically: 'They mek y' wait for that summat awful.' He went off chuckling. Soon Harry began to blush and to wonder why all the apprentices who now came up looked at him as though he was some odd animal: they grinned or laughed, nudged each other and winked. Bill Simmons, blue-eyed, over-grown, with an unruly mop of hair and a chronic habit of prefixing almost every noun he used with the idiomatic term for copulation, laughed and said to his companion, Sam Hardie, an undersized, bow-legged, low browed boy with long, strong, ape-like arms: 'Did y' ever, Sam. They ain't gev him the—stand yet!'

With a sickly grin Harry asked him the meaning of the joke. Sam, grinning, advised him to ask the storekeeper. Blushing, Harry turned to the busy man who had forgotten all about him: 'Hey,' he protested, mildly indignant: 'Hey, what about that there long stand?'

The man looked up: 'What! Ain't you gone *yet*?' he asked, raising his brows.

'I come here for long stand an' you told me . . .'

'Well, y' bin standin' there hafe an hour . . . Ain't that long enough?'

Truth dawned; red in the face Harry licked his lips, turned on his heel and slunk away. 'You might ha' told me,' he said, reproachfully, to Bill Simmons and the others. Bill sniggered: 'Wait till *you* see some gawp doin' the same. See whether you tell him.'

WALTER GREENWOOD (1903–74), Love on the Dole, 1933

It was with but weak knees and a slight catch in her breathing that she came up to the great shoe company at Adams and Fifth Avenue and entered the elevator. When she stepped out on the fourth floor there was no one at hand, only great aisles of boxes piled to the ceiling. She stood, very much frightened, awaiting some one, when a young man with some order slips in his hand got off the elevator.

'Who is it you want?' he asked her.

'Mr Brown.'

'Oh,' he said.

Presently Mr Brown came up. He did not seem to recognize her.

'What is it you want?' he questioned.

Carrie's heart sank.

'You said I should come this morning to see about work—'

'Oh,' he interrupted. 'Um—yes. What is your name?'

'Carrie Meeber.'

'Yes,' said he. 'You come with me.'

He led the way through dark, box-lined aisles which had the smell of new shoes until they came to an iron door which opened into the factory proper. There was a large low-ceiled room with clacking, rattling machines at which men in white shirt sleeves and blue gingham aprons were working. She followed him diffidently through the clattering automatons, keeping her eyes straight before her and flushing slightly. They crossed to a far corner and took an elevator to the sixth floor. Out of the array of machines and benches Mr Brown signaled a foreman.

'This is the girl,' he said, and turning to Carrie, 'you go with him.' He then returned and Carrie followed her new superior to a little desk in a corner, which he used as a kind of official center.

'You've never worked at anything like this before, have you?' he questioned rather sternly.

'No sir,' she answered.

He seemed rather annoyed at having to bother with such help, but put down her name and then led her across to where a line of girls were sitting on a line of stools in front of a line of clacking machines. On the shoulder of one of the girls who was punching eye holes in one piece of the upper, by the aid of the machine, he put his hand.

'You,' he said, 'show this girl how to do what you're doing. When you get through, come to me.'

The girl so addressed rose promptly and gave Carrie her place.

'It isn't hard to do,' she said, bending over. 'You just take this so, fasten it with this clamp and start the machine.'

She suited action to word, fastened the piece of leather (which was eventually to form the right half of the upper of a man's shoe) by little adjustable clamps, and pushed a small steel rod at the side of the machine. The latter jumped to the task of punching, with sharp, snapping clicks, cutting circular bits of leather out of the side of the upper, leaving the holes which eventually were to hold the laces. After observing a few times, the girl let her work at it alone. Seeing that it was being fairly well done, she went away.

The pieces of leather came from the girl at the machine to her right, and were passed on to the girl at her left. Carrie saw at once that an average speed was necessary or the work would pile up on her and all those below would be delayed. She had no time to look about, and bent anxiously to her task, managing to do fairly well. The girls at her left and right realized her predicament and feelings, and, in a way, tried to aid her as much as they dared by working slower.

*

As the morning wore on the room became hotter. She felt the need of a breath of fresh air and a drink of water but did not venture to stir. The stool she sat on was without a back or footrest and she began to feel uncomfortable. She found after a time that her back was beginning to ache. She twisted and turned from one position to another slightly different, but it did not ease her for long. She was beginning to weary.

'Stand up, why don't you,' said the girl at her right, without any form of introduction. 'They won't care.'

Carrie looked at her gratefully. 'I guess I will,' she said.

She stood up from her stool and worked that way for awhile, but it was a more difficult position. Her neck and shoulders ached in bending over.

The spirit of the place was one which impressed itself on her in a rough way. She did not venture to look around any, but above the clack of the machines she could hear an occasional remark. She could also note a thing or two out of the side of her eye.

'Did you see Harry last night?' said the girl at her left, addressing her neighbor.

'No.'

'You ought to have seen the tie he had on. Gee, but he was a mark.'

'S-s-t,' said the other girl, bending over her work. The first silenced instantly, assuming a solemn face. The foreman passed slowly along, eyeing each worker distinctly. The moment he was gone, the conversation was resumed again.

'Say,' began the girl at her left, 'what jeh think he said?'

'I don't know.'

'He said he saw us with Eddie Harris at Martin's that night.'

'No!' They both giggled.

A youth with tan-colored hair that needed clipping very badly came shuffling along between the machines, bearing a basket of leather findings under his left arm, and pressed against his stomach. When near Carrie he stretched out his right hand and gripped one girl under the arm.

'Aw, let go,' she exclaimed angrily—'Duffer.'

He only grinned broadly in return.

'Rubber,' he called back as she looked after him. There was nothing of the gallant in him.

Carrie got so at last that she could scarcely sit still. Her legs began to tire and she felt as if she would give anything to get up and stretch. Would noon never come? It seemed as if she had worked an entire day already. She was not hungry at all, but weak, and her eyes were tired straining at the one point where the eye-punch came down and clipped the small piece out of the leather. The girl at the right noticed her squirmings and felt sorry for her. She was concentrating herself too thoroughly—what she did really required less mental and physical strain. There was nothing to be done, however. The halves of the uppers came piling steadily down. Her hands began to ache at the wrists and then in the fingers, and toward the last she seemed one mass of dull complaining muscles, fixed in an eternal position and performing a single mechanical movement which became more and more distasteful until at last it was absolutely nauseating. When she was most wondering whether the strain would ever cease, a dull-sounding bell clanged somewhere down an elevator shaft and the end came. In an instant there was a buzz of action and conversation. All the girls instantly left their stools and hurried away into an adjoining room; men passed through, coming from some department which opened on the right. The whirring wheels began to sing in a steadily modifying key until at last they died away in a low buzz. There was an audible stillness in which the common voice sounded strange.

Carrie gladly got up and sought her lunch box. She was stiff, a little dizzy and very thirsty. On the way to the small space portioned off by wood, where all the wraps and lunches were kept, she encountered the foreman, who stared at her hard.

'Well,' he said, 'did you get along all right?'

'I think so,' she replied, very respectfully.

THEODORE DREISER (1871–1945), *Sister Carrie*, 1900

He sniffed the clean and eager smell
Of crushed wild garlic as he thrust
Beneath the sallows; and a spell
He stood there munching a thick crust—
The fresh tang giving keener zest
To bread and cheese, and watched a pair
Of wagtails preening wing and breast,
Then running, flirting tails in air
And pied plumes sleeked to silky sheen,
Chasing each other in and out
The wet wild garlic's white and green.

And then, remembering, with a shout
And rattle whirring, he ran back
Again into the Fair Maid's Mead
To scare the rascal thieves and black
That flocked from far and near to feed
Upon the sprouting grain. As one
They rose with clapping rustling wings—
Rooks, starlings, pigeons, in the sun
Circling about him in wide rings,
And plovers hovering over him
In mazy interweaving flight
Until it made his young wits swim
To see them up against the light,
A dazzling dance of black and white
Against the clear blue April sky—

Wings on wings in flashing flight
Swooping low and soaring high,
Swooping, soaring, fluttering, flapping,
Tossing, tumbling, swerving, dipping.
Chattering, cawing, creaking, clapping,
Till he felt his senses slipping,
And gripped his corncrake rattle tight
And flourished it above his head
Till every bird was out of sight,
And laughed when all had flown and fled
To think that he, and all alone,
Could put so many thieves to rout.

Then, sitting down upon a stone,
He wondered if the school were out—
The school where only yesterday
He'd sat at work among his mates,
At work that now seemed children's play
With pens and pencils, books and slates . . .

He'd liked that room, he'd liked it all—
The window steaming when it rained,
The sunlight dancing on the wall
Among the glossy charts and maps,
The blotchy stain beside the clock
That only he of all the chaps
Knew for a chart of Dead Man's Rock
That lies in Tiger Island Bay—
The reef on which the schooners split
And founder, that would bear away
The treasure chest of Cut-Throat-Kit
That's buried under Black Bill's bones
Beneath the purple pepper tree . . .
A trail of clean-sucked cherry-stones
Which you must follow carefully
Across the dunes of yellow sand
Leads winding upward from the beach
Till, with a pistol in each hand
And cutlass 'twixt your teeth, you reach . . .

Plumping their fat crops peacefully
Were plovers, pigeons, starlings, rooks,
Feeding on every side while he
Was in the land of story-books.
He raised his rattle with a shout

And scattered them with yell and crake . . .
A man must mind what he's about
. And keep his silly wits awake,
Not go woolgathering, if he'd earn
His wage. And soon, no schoolboy now,
He'd take on a man's job and learn
To build a rick and drive a plough
Like father.

                              Up against the sky,
Beyond the spinney and the stream,
With easy stride and steady eye
He saw his father drive his team,
Turning the red marl gleaming wet
Into long furrows clean and true:
And, dreaming there, he longed to set
His young hand to the ploughshare too.

                    WILFRID GIBSON (1878–1962), from 'The Plough,' 1917

Meantime Teta Elzbieta had taken Stanislovas to the priest, and gotten a
certificate to the effect that he was two years older than he was; and with it the
little boy now sallied forth to make his fortune in the world. It chanced that
Durham had just put in a wonderful new lard machine, and when the special
policeman in front of the time station saw Stanislovas and his document, he
smiled to himself, and told him to go—'*Czia! Czia!*' pointing. And so
Stanislovas went down a long stone corridor and up a flight of stairs, which
took him into a room lighted by electricity, with the new machines for filling
lard cans at work in it. The lard was finished on the floor above, and it came in
little jets, like beautiful, wriggling, snow-white snakes of unpleasant odor.
There were several kinds and sizes of jets, and after a certain precise quantity
had come out, each stopped automatically, and the wonderful machine made
a turn, and took the can under another jet, and so on, until it was filled neatly
to the brim, and pressed tightly and smoothed off. To attend to all this and fill
several hundred cans of lard per hour there were necessary two human creatures, one of whom knew how to place an empty lard can on a certain spot
every few seconds, and the other of whom knew how to take a full lard can off
a certain spot every few seconds and set it upon a tray.

And so, after little Stanislovas had stood gazing timidly about him for a few
minutes, a man approached him, and asked what he wanted, to which
Stanislovas said, 'Job.' Then the man said, 'How old?' and Stanislovas
answered, 'Sixtin.' Once or twice every year a State inspector would come
wandering through the packing plants, asking a child here and there how old

he was; and so the packers were very careful to comply with the law, which cost them as much trouble as was now involved in the boss's taking the document from the little boy, and glancing at it, and then sending it to the office to be filed away. Then he set someone else at a different job, and showed the lad how to place a lard can every time the empty arm of the remorseless machine came to him; and so was decided the place in the universe of little Stanislovas, and his destiny till the end of his days. Hour after hour, day after day, year after year, it was fated that he should stand upon a certain square foot of floor from seven in the morning until noon, and again from half past twelve till half past five, making never a motion and thinking never a thought, save for the setting of lard cans. In summer the stench of the warm lard would be nauseating, and in winter the cans would all but freeze to his naked little fingers in the unheated cellar. Half the year it would be dark as night when he went in to work, and dark as night again when he came out, and so he would never know what the sun looked like on weekdays. And for this, at the end of the week, he would carry home three dollars to his family, being his pay at the rate of five cents per hour—just about his proper share of the total earnings of the million and three-quarters of children who are now engaged in earning their livings in the United States.

Upton Sinclair (1878–1968), The Jungle, 1906

On the Monday morning the boy got up at six to start work . . . His mother packed his dinner in a small, shut-up basket, and he set off at a quarter to seven to catch the 7.15 train. Mrs Morel came to the entry-end to see him off.

It was a perfect morning. From the ash-tree the slender green fruits that the children call 'pigeons' were twinkling gaily down on a little breeze, into the front gardens of the houses. The valley was full of a lustrous dark haze, through which the ripe corn shimmered, and in which the steam from Minton pit melted swiftly. Puffs of wind came. Paul looked over the high woods of Aldersley, where the country gleamed, and home had never pulled at him so powerfully.

'Good morning, mother,' he said, smiling, but feeling very unhappy.

'Good morning,' she replied cheerfully and tenderly . . .

At eight o'clock he climbed the dismal stairs of Jordan's Surgical Appliance Factory, and stood helplessly against the first great parcel-rack, waiting for somebody to pick him up. The place was still not awake. Over the counters were great dust sheets. Two men only had arrived, and were heard talking in a corner, as they took off their coats and rolled up their shirt-sleeves. It was ten past eight. Evidently there was no rush of punctuality. Paul listened to the voices of the two clerks. Then he heard someone cough, and saw in the office at the end of the room an old, decaying clerk, in a round smoking-cap of black velvet embroidered with red and green, opening letters. He waited and waited. One of the junior clerks went to the old man, greeted him cheerily and loudly. Evidently the old 'chief' was deaf. Then the young fellow came striding importantly down to his counter. He spied Paul.

'Hello!' he said. 'You the new lad?'

'Yes,' said Paul.

'H'm! What's your name?'

'Paul Morel.'

'Paul Morel? All right, you come on round here.' . . .

Paul was led round to a very dark corner.

'This is the "Spiral" corner,' said the clerk. 'You're Spiral, with Pappleworth. He's your boss, but he's not come yet. He doesn't get here till half-past eight. So you can fetch the letters, if you like, from Mr Melling down there.'

The young man pointed to the old clerk in the office.

'All right,' said Paul.

'Here's a peg to hang your cap on. Here are your entry ledgers. Mr Pappleworth won't be long.'

And the thin young man stalked away with long, busy strides over the hollow wooden floor.

After a minute or two Paul went down and stood in the door of the glass office. The old clerk in the smoking-cap looked down over the rim of his spectacles.

'Good morning,' he said, kindly and impressively. 'You want the letters for the Spiral department, Thomas?'

Paul resented being called 'Thomas'. But he took the letters and returned to his dark place, where the counter made an angle, where the great parcel-rack came to an end, and where there were three doors in the corner. He sat on a high stool and read the letters—those whose handwriting was not too difficult. They ran as follows:

'Will you please send me at once a pair of lady's silk spiral thigh-hose, without feet, such as I had from you last year; length, thigh to knee, etc.' Or 'Major Chamberlain wishes to repeat his previous order for a silk non-elastic suspensory bandage.'

Many of the letters, some of them in French or Norwegian, were a great puzzle to the boy. He sat on his stool nervously awaiting the arrival of his 'boss'. He suffered tortures of shyness when, at half-past eight, the factory girls for upstairs trooped past him.

Mr Pappleworth arrived, chewing a chlorodyne gum, at about twenty to nine, when all the other men were at work. He was a thin, sallow man with a red nose, quick, staccato, and smartly but stiffly dressed. He was about thirty-six years old. There was something rather 'doggy', rather smart, rather 'cute and shrewd, and something warm, and something slightly contemptible about him.

'You my new lad?' he said.

Paul stood up and said he was.

'Fetched the letters?'

Mr Pappleworth gave a chew to his gum.

'Yes.'

'Copied 'em?'

'No.'

'Well, come on then, let's look slippy. Changed your coat?'

'No.'

'You want to bring an old coat and leave it here.' He pronounced the last words with the chlorodyne gum between his side teeth. He vanished into darkness behind the great parcel-rack, reappeared coatless, turning up a smart striped shirt-cuff over a thin and hairy arm. Then he slipped into his coat. Paul noticed how thin he was, and that his trousers were in folds behind. He seized a stool, dragged it beside the boy's, and sat down.

'Sit down,' he said.

Paul took a seat.

Mr Pappleworth was very close to him. The man seized the letters, snatched a long entry-book out of a rack in front of him, flung it open, seized a pen, and said:

'Now look here. You want to copy these letters in here.' He sniffed twice, gave a quick chew at his gum, stared fixedly at a letter, then went very still and absorbed, and wrote the entry rapidly, in a beautiful flourishing hand. He glanced quickly at Paul.

'See that?'

'Yes.'

'Think you can do it all right?'

'Yes.'

'All right then, let's see you.'

He sprang off his stool. Paul took a pen. Mr Pappleworth disappeared. Paul rather liked copying the letters, but he wrote slowly, laboriously, and exceedingly badly . . .

The day was very long. All morning the work-people were coming to speak to Mr Pappleworth. Paul was writing or learning to make up parcels, ready for the midday post. At one o'clock, or, rather, at a quarter to one, Mr Pappleworth disappeared to catch his train: he lived in the suburbs. At one o'clock, Paul, feeling very lost, took his dinner-basket down into the stockroom in the basement, that had the long table on trestles, and ate his meal hurriedly, alone in that cellar of gloom and desolation. Then he went out of doors. The brightness and the freedom of the streets made him feel adventurous and happy. But at two o'clock he was back in the corner of the big room. Soon the work-girls went trooping past, making remarks. It was the commoner girls who worked upstairs at the heavy tasks of truss-making and the finishing of artificial limbs. He waited for Mr Pappleworth, not knowing what to do, sitting scribbling on the yellow order-paper. Mr Pappleworth came at twenty minutes to three. Then he sat and gossiped with Paul, treating the boy entirely as an equal, even in age.

In the afternoon there was never very much to do, unless it were near the week-end, and the accounts had to be made up. At five o'clock all the men went down into the dungeon with the table on trestles, and there they had tea, eating bread-and-butter on the bare, dirty boards, talking with the same kind of ugly haste and slovenliness with which they ate their meal. And yet upstairs the atmosphere among them was always jolly and clear. The cellar and the trestles affected them.

After tea, when all the gases were lighted, *work* went more briskly. There was the big evening post to get off. The hose came up warm and newly pressed from the workrooms. Paul had made out the invoices. Now he had the packing up and addressing to do, then he had to weigh his stock of parcels on the scales. Everywhere voices were calling weights, there was the chink of metal, the rapid snapping of string, the hurrying to old Mr Melling for stamps. And at last the postman came with his sack, laughing and jolly. Then everything slacked off, and Paul took his dinner-basket and ran to the station to catch the eight-twenty train. The day in the factory was just twelve hours long.

D. H. LAWRENCE (1885–1930), *Sons and Lovers*, 1913

THE DAILY GRIND

Man goeth forth unto his work and to his labour until the evening.

Psalms 104: 23

London's Summer Morning

Who has not wakcd to list the busy sounds
Of summer's morning, in the sultry smoke
Of noisy London? On the pavement hot
The sooty chimney-boy, with dingy face
And tatter'd covering, shrilly bawls his trade,
Rousing the sleepy housemaid. At the door
The milk-pail rattles, and the tinkling bell
Proclaims the dustman's office; while the street
Is lost in clouds impervious. Now begins
The din of hackney-coaches, waggons, carts;
While tinmen's shops, and noisy trunk-makers,
Knife-grinders, coopers, squeaking cork-cutters,

Fruit barrows, and the hunger-giving cries
Of vegetable venders, fill the air.
Now every shop displays its varied trade,
And the fresh-sprinkled pavement cools the feet
Of early walkers. At the private door
The ruddy housemaid twirls the busy mop,
Annoying the smart 'prentice, or neat girl,
Tripping with band-box lightly. Now the sun
Darts burning splendour on the glittering pane,
Save where the canvas awning throws a shade
On the gay merchandize. Now, spruce and trim,
In shops (where beauty smiles with industry),
Sits the smart damsel; while the passenger
Peeps through the window, watching every charm.
Now pastry dainties catch the eye minute
Of humming insects, while the limy snare
Waits to enthral them. Now the lamp-lighter
Mounts the tall ladder, nimbly venturous,
To trim the half-fill'd lamp; while at his feet
The pot-boy yells discordant! All along
The sultry pavement, the old-clothes man cries
In tone monotonous, and side-long views
The area for his traffic: now the bag
Is slily open'd, and the half-worn suit
(Sometimes the pilfer'd treasure of the base
Domestic spoiler), for one half its worth,
Sinks in the green abyss. The porter now
Bears his huge load along the burning way;
And the poor poet wakes from busy dreams,
To paint the summer morning.

MARY ROBINSON (1758–1800), 1806

Get Up

'Get up!' the caller calls, 'Get up!'
    And in the dead of night,
To win the bairns their bite and sup,
    I rise a weary wight.

My flannel dudden donn'd, thrice o'er
    My birds are kiss'd, and then
I with a whistle shut the door,
    I may not ope again.

JOSEPH SKIPSEY (1837–1903), 1886

London Bridge! It is the climax, the apotheosis, as it were, of all thus far seen. So crowded is the canvas, so full of movement, it dazes one. Life sweeps over the bridge like the rush of the sea by the sides of a ship—always Citywards. In thousands they advance, leaning forward, with long, quick strides, eager to be there! Swiftly they flash past, and still they come and come, like the silent, shadowy legions of a dream. Somehow they suggest the dogged march of an army in retreat, with its rallying point far ahead, and the enemy's cavalry pressing on its rear. Looking down upon the swarming masses, with the dark sullen river for a background, they fuse into one monstrous organism, their progress merges in the rhythmic swaying of one mammoth breathing thing. Stand in the midst of the mighty current of men! A wearied, languorous feeling creeps over you, as face follows face, and eyes in thousands swim by. It is the hypnotic influence of the measureless, the unfathomable, the you-know-not-what of mystery and elusiveness in life, stealing your senses away.

During an hour these multitudes in drab march past to the relentless City, to barter what they have of value for their daily bread. The monotony of the endless parade is overpowering, numbing; and minute by minute the railway station, not a stone's throw away, yields up fresh battalions for this sublime muster of citizens. Within the station itself is being enacted a scene which is an impressive combination of order and disorder. A train rushes alongside a platform. In a twinkling its passengers are thronging to the exits. A few seconds more and the place is clear. The empty train disappears to make way for another, whose impatient whistle is already heard. Again a crowd of passengers melts, and another springs up in its place. The train is again shunted, and the metals it vacates are speedily covered. And so proceeds like clockwork the arrangement—so simple and so intricate—for the mobilisation of the army of business men who pour in one wonderful phalanx across the noble bridge.

For a full hour it continues. Then, as the clock points to ten, there are gaps in the ranks. The tide of life suddenly slackens. The reinforcements grow weaker. Traffic once more moves freely in opposite directions; for the invasion of the morning is consummated. Business has begun.

P. F. WILLIAM RYAN (1873–1939), 'Going to Business in London', 1902

> Unreal City,
> Under the brown fog of a winter dawn,
> A crowd flowed over London Bridge, so many,
> I had not thought death had undone so many.
> Sighs, short and infrequent, were exhaled,
> And each man fixed his eyes before his feet.
> Flowed up the hill and down King William Street,

To where Saint Mary Woolnoth kept the hours
With a dead sound on the final stroke of nine.

T. S. ELIOT (1888–1965), *The Waste Land*, 1922

Any one who three or four years ago chose to spend an hour from 9.45 to 10.45 a.m. in strolling about Whitehall and its neighbourhood on the morning of any week-day during the Parliamentary Session might see the gradations of the official hierarchy exhibited in a curious combination of persons and times. For the first quarter of an hour or twenty minutes the streets are crowded with men and women, mostly young, on the whole healthy and intelligent in appearance, neatly but not as a rule smartly dressed—a picked sample of the great class loosely known as the 'lower middle class', solid, decent, kindly, trustworthy. As the hour of ten approaches, the pace quickens; for most of them belong to grades that are liable to mild reprimand if they are not in their place of work by the hour, or a minute or two later. They represent almost entirely the lower ranks of the Civil Service—typists, junior executive and clerical officers, assistant accountants, junior technicians, and so forth. There are a few of higher rank—Private Secretaries who need a little time before their chiefs arrive, Assistant Secretaries, Legal Advisers, and even Heads of Departments who make a habit of early arrival, or who, not being greatly addicted to such a habit, on this particular morning have some particular worm to catch: but these will be lost (to the eye of the human observer) in the masses of subordinates. By five minutes past ten this crowd will have disappeared through the great doors, and for the following ten minutes or so there will be visible a much smaller, less hurried, and predominantly masculine procession moving towards the same doors. These are the NCOs and junior commissioned officers of the civilian army—higher clerical and executive officers, Assistant Principals and Principals, and men holding fairly responsible technical appointments. The half-hour from 10.15 to 10.45 a.m. is the time when the potentates of the Service may usually be seen walking briskly, but without undignified haste, to their places of power. They are practically all men of mature age, from forty to sixty or sixty-five, of good and sometimes fine physique (far better on the whole than the 10 o'clock crowd, allowance being made for the difference in age), well-dressed in a quiet style. To an eye used to distinguish the grades of English society most of them will appear at once what they are—able cultivated men of the upper middle class. A few have the aspect of pillars of state:

deep on his front engraven
Deliberation sits and public care.

But even in the Civil Service solemnity may be the mask of an uneasy weakness: and conversely the permanent Head of a great Department, steadily carrying a heavy load of work, power, and responsibility, is sometimes a lively rollicking person who manifestly enjoys life and its good things.

By 10.45 a.m. or thereabouts the Higher Civil Service has vanished from the streets except for one or two men who have some special reason for late arrival or retain unyielding the habits of the age before the Flood, when in many of the great Offices even the First Division juniors did not profess to begin work till 11 a.m.

H. E. DALE (1875–1954), *The Higher Civil Service of Great Britain*, 1941

REST DURING WORK

But sweet Vicissitudes of Rest and Toyl
Make easy Labour, and renew the Soil.
VIRGIL (70–19 BC), *Georgics*, 36–29 BC, tr. John Dryden, 1697

Haymaking

After night's thunder far away had rolled
The fiery day had a kernel sweet of cold,
And in the perfect blue the clouds uncurled,
Like the first gods before they made the world
And misery, swimming the stormless sea
In beauty and in divine gaiety.
The smooth white empty road was lightly strewn
With leaves—the holly's Autumn falls in June—
And fir cones standing up stiff in the heat.
The mill-foot water tumbled white and lit
With tossing crystals, happier than any crowd
Of children pouring out of school aloud.
And in the little thickets where a sleeper
For ever might lie lost, the nettle creeper
And garden-warbler sang unceasingly;
While over them shrill shrieked in his fierce glee
The swift with wings and tail as sharp and narrow

As if the bow had flown off with the arrow.
Only the scent of woodbine and hay new mown
Travelled the road. In the field sloping down,
Park-like, to where its willows showed the brook,
Haymakers rested. The tosser lay forsook
Out in the sun; and the long waggon stood
Without its team: it seemed it never would
Move from the shadow of that single yew.
The team, as still, until their task was due,
Beside the labourers enjoyed the shade
That three squat oaks mid-field together made
Upon a circle of grass and weed uncut,
And on the hollow, once a chalk pit, but
Now brimmed with nut and elder-flower so clean.
The men leaned on their rakes, about to begin,
But still. And all were silent. All was old,
This morning time, with a great age untold,
Older than Clare and Cobbett, Morland and Crome,
Than, at the field's far edge, the farmer's home,
A white house crouched at the foot of a great tree.
Under the heavens that know not what years be
The men, the beasts, the trees, the implements
Uttered even what they will in times far hence—
All of us gone out of the reach of change—
Immortal in a picture of an old grange.

EDWARD THOMAS (1878–1917), 1915

The Corn Harvest

Summer!
the painting is organized
about a young

reaper enjoying his
noonday rest
completely

relaxed
from his morning labors
sprawled

in fact sleeping
unbuttoned
on his back

the women
have brought him his lunch
perhaps

a spot of wine
they gather gossiping
under a tree

whose shade
carelessly
he does not share the

resting
center of
their workaday world

WILLIAM CARLOS WILLIAMS (1883–1963), *Pictures from Brueghel,* 1962

[In 1586 hundreds of labourers, carts, and oxen were recruited from neighbouring towns to assist in the rebuilding of Dover Harbour.]

In all this time, and among all these people, there was never any tumult, fray, nor falling out to the disquieting or disturbing of the works, which by that means were the better applied, and with less interruption. For they never ceased working the whole day, save that at eleven of the clock before noon, as also at six of the clock in the evening, there was a flag usually held up by the sergeant of the town, in the top of a tower, except the tide or extraordinary business forced the officers to prevent the hour, or to make some small delay and stay there. And presently upon the sign given, there was a general shout made by all the workers; and wherever any cart was at that instant either empty or laden, there was it left, till one of the clock after noon or six of the clock in the morning, when they returned to their business. But by the space of half an hour before the flag of liberty was hanged out, all the cart-drivers entered into a song, where, although the ditty was barbarous, and the note rustical, the matter of no moment, and all but a jest, yet it is not unworthy of some brief note of remembrance; because the tune, or rather the noise thereof was extraordinary, and (being delivered with the continual voice of such a multitude) was very strange. In this and some other respect, I will set down their ditty, the words of which were these:

O Harry hold up thy hat, it's eleven a clock,
   and a little, little, little, little past:
My bow is broken, I would unyoke,
   my foot is sore, I can work no more.

RAPHAEL HOLINSHED (d. 1580?), JOHN HOOKER (alias Vowell)
(1526–1601), *et al., Chronicles of England, Scotlande, and Irelande*,
1586–7

Consisting more often than not of sandwiches eaten at the desk or a sausage
and beer in a crammed and raucous pub, followed by a walk or some shopping or a glance at a museum, the lunch hour is, for most of us, the high point
of the working day, the watershed that divides the brightness and the bustle of
the morning from the somnolent melancholy of the afternoon. (Given the
prevalence of afternoon slumber, enlightened office managers should bow to
the inevitable and provide let-down canvas beds, so enabling their employees
to give of their best later on.) The traditional office lunch—bibulous, protracted and indiscreet—looms large in the mythology of office life, though
Perrier culture, Yuppiedom and recession have done grave damage to its age-
old rituals.

The prospect of a long, congenial lunch, in which any business that needs
to be aired will be crammed in at the coffee stage after gossip, children and
holidays have held the floor, gives the prospective luncher something to look
forward to—particularly if the other party is paying, so removing all worries
about whether and how such a meal can be justified on expenses. It's advisable
to clear one's desk before stepping sharply out in the direction of the edibles:
though this in itself is unlikely to protect the late luncher, sneaking in by the
back exit at 4.30, his breath hot with alcoholic fumes and his hair in disarray,
from a flurry of angry or anxious notes to say that the Boss has been looking
for him all afternoon, and is highly unamused. Pausing briefly to straighten
his clothing and rinse out his mouth, the late luncher hurries nervously down
to the Inner Sanctum, only to discover that the Boss has quite forgotten why
it was he needed to see him so badly. As is so often the case in office life, one's
presence is what matters, rather than the work itself.

JEREMY LEWIS (1942–), *The Chatto Book of Office Life*, 1992

RECREATION AND WEEKENDS

Each day men sell little pieces of themselves in order to try to buy them back
each night and weekend with the coin of 'fun'.

C. WRIGHT MILLS (1919–62), *White Collar*, 1951

All work and no play makes Jack a dull boy.

> JAMES HOWELL (1593–1666), *Proverbs*, 1659, in *Lexicon Tetraglotton*, 1660

The town [Kirtling, Cambridgeshire] was then my grandfather's, consisting of tillage farms, and small dairies, so that business was usually done by noon, and it was always the custom for the youth of the town, who were men or maid servants, and children, to assemble, after horses baited, either upon the green or (after haysel) in a close accustomed to be so used, and there all to play till milking time, and supper at night. The men to football, and the maids, with whom we children commonly mixed, being not proof for the turbulence of the other party, to stoolball, and such running games as they knew. And all this without mixing men and women, as in dancing with fiddle, but apart. No idle or lascivious frolics between them, and at last all parting to their stations. I mention this because it seems to me to have been a better condition of country living than I ever observed anywhere else, and being at those years free from all cares, made a happier state than all honour and wealth can boast of.

> ROGER NORTH (1651?–1734), *Autobiography*, 1887

For it is not to be doubted, but as God has given man things profitable, so hath he allowed him honest comfort, delight and recreation in all the works of his hands. No, all his labours under the sun without this are troubles and vexation of mind. For what is greedy gain without delight, but moiling and turmoiling in slavery? But comfortable delight, with content, is the good of everything, and the pattern of Heaven. A morsel of bread with comfort, is better by far than a fat ox with unquietness. And who can deny but that the principal end of an orchard is the honest delight of one wearied with the work of his lawful calling? The very works of, and in, an orchard and garden, are better than the ease and rest of and from other labours. When God has made a man after his own image, in a perfect state, and would have him to represent himself in authority, tranquillity, and pleasure upon the earth, he placed him in Paradise. What was Paradise, but a garden and orchard of trees and herbs, full of pleasure and nothing there but delights? The gods of the earth, resembling the great God of Heaven in authority, majesty, and abundance of all things, wherein is there most delight and whither do they withdraw themselves from the troublesome affairs of their estate, being tired with the hearing and judging of litigious controversies, choked (as it were) with the close airs of their sumptuous buildings, their stomachs cloyed with variety of banquets, their

haysel] the hay season

ears filled and overburdened with tedious discoursings? Whither, but into their Orchards, made and prepared, dressed and destined for that purpose, to renew and refresh their senses, and to call home their over-wearied spirits. No, it is (no doubt) a comfort to them to set open their casements into a most delicate garden and orchard, whereby they may not only see that wherein they so much delighted, but also to give fresh, sweet and pleasant air to their galleries and chambers.

WILLIAM LAWSON (*fl.* 1618), *A New Orchard and Garden*, 1618

> To every Cot the Lord's indulgent mind,
> Has a small space for Garden-ground assign'd;
> Here—till return of morn dismiss'd the farm—
> The careful Peasant plies the sinewy arm,
> Warm'd as he works and casts his look around
> On every foot of that improving ground;
> It is his own he sees; his Master's eye,
> Peers not about, some secret fault to spy;
> Nor voice severe is there, nor censure known;—
> Hope, profit, pleasure,—they are all his own.
> Here grow the humble C[h]*ives* and hard by them,
> The *Leek* with crown globose and reedy stem;
> High climb his Pulse in many an even row,
> Deep strike the ponderous roots in soil below,
> And herbs of potent smell and pungent taste,
> Give a warm relish to the Night's repast.
> Apples and Cherries grafted by his hand,
> And cluster'd Nuts for neighbouring market stand.
> Nor thus concludes his labour; near the Cot,
> The Reed-fence rises round some favourite spot;
> Where rich Carnations, Pinks with purple eyes,
> Proud Hyacinths, the least some Florist's prize,
> Tulips tall-stemm'd and pounc'd Auricula's rise.

GEORGE CRABBE (1754–1832), *The Parish Register*, 1807

Long-striding and ungainly, they walk home; between six o'clock and seven you may be sure of seeing some of them coming up the hill from the town, alone or by twos and threes. They speak but little; they look tired and stern; very often there is nothing but a twinkle in their eyes to prove to you that they are not morose. But in fact they are still taking life seriously; their thoughts, and hopes too, are bent on the further work they mean to do when they shall have had their tea. For the more old-fashioned men allow themselves but little rest, and in many a cottage garden of an evening you may see the father of the family soberly at work, and liking it too. If his wife is able to come and look on and chatter to him, or if he can hear her laughing with a friend in the next garden, so much the better; but he does not stop work. Impelled, as I shall show later, by other reasons besides those of economy, many of the men make prodigiously long days of it, at least during the summer months. I have known them to leave home at five or even four in the morning, walk five or six miles, do a day's work, walk back in the evening so as to reach home at six or seven o'clock, and then, after a meal, go on again in their gardens until eight or nine. They seem to be under some spiritual need to keep going; their conscience enslaves them. So they grow thin and gaunt in body, grave and very quiet in their spirits. But sullen they very rarely are. With rheumatism and 'the 'ump' combined a man will sometimes grow exasperated and be heard to speak irritably, but usually it is a very amiable 'Good-evening' that greets you from across the hedge where one of these men is silently digging or hoeing.

The nature of their work, shall I say, tends to bring them to quietness of soul? I hesitate to say it, because, though work upon the ground with spade or hoe has such a soothing influence upon the amateur, there is a difference between doing it for pleasure during a spare hour and doing it as a duty after a twelve hours' day, and without any prospect of holiday as long as one lives. Nevertheless it is plain to be seen that, albeit their long days too often reduce them to a state of apathy, these quiet and patient men experience no less often a compensating delight in the friendly feeling of the tool responding to their skill, and in the fine freshness of the soil as they work it, and in the solace, so varied and so unfailingly fresh, of the open air. Thus much at least I have seen in their looks, and have heard in their speech. On a certain June evening when it had set in wet, five large-limbed men, just off their work on the railway, came striding past me up the hill. They had sacks over their shoulders; their clothes and boots, from working in gravel all day, were of the same yellowish-brown colour as the sacks; they were getting decidedly wet; but they looked enviably easy-going and unconcerned. As they went by me one after another, one sleepy-eyed man, comfortably smoking his pipe, vouchsafed no word or glance. But the others, with friendly sidelong glance at me, all spoke; and their placid voices were full of rich contentment. 'Good-night'; 'Nice *rain*'; 'G'd-evenin''; and, last of all, '*This*'ll make the young taters grow!' The man who said this looked all alert, as if the blood were dancing in him with enjoyment of the rain; his eyes were beaming with pleasure. So the five passed up the hill homewards, to have some supper, and then, perhaps, watch and listen to the rain on their gardens until it was time to go to bed.

GEORGE BOURNE (George Sturt) (1863–1927), *Change in the Village*, 1912

There is a class of men in Manchester, unknown even to many of the inhabitants, and whose existence will probably be doubted by many, who yet may claim kindred with all the noble names that science recognises. I said in 'Manchester,' but they are scattered all over the manufacturing districts of Lancashire. In the neighbourhood of Oldham there are weavers, common handloom weavers, who throw the shuttle with unceasing sound, though Newton's 'Principia' lies open on the loom, to be snatched at in work hours, but revelled over in meal times, or at night. Mathematical problems are received with interest, and studied with absorbing attention by many a broad-spoken, common-looking factory-hand. It is perhaps less astonishing that the more popularly interesting branches of natural history have their warm and devoted followers among this class. There are botanists among them, equally familiar with either the Linnaean or the Natural system, who know the name and habitat of every plant within a day's walk from their dwellings; who steal the holiday of a day or two when any particular plant should be in flower, and tying up their simple food in their pocket-hand-kerchiefs, set off with single purpose to fetch home the humble-looking weed. There are entomologists, who may be seen with a rude-looking net, ready to catch any winged insect, or a kind of dredge, with which they rake the green and slimy pools; practical, shrewd, hard-working men, who pore over every new specimen with real scientific delight. Nor is it the common and more obvious divisions of Entomology and Botany that alone attract these earnest seekers after knowledge. Perhaps it may be owing to the great annual town-holiday of Whitsun-week so often falling in May or June, that the two great beautiful families of Ephemeridæ and Phryganidæ have been so much and so closely studied by Manchester workmen, while they have in a great measure escaped general observation. If you will refer to the preface to Sir J. E. Smith's Life (I have it not by me, or I would copy you the exact passage), you will find that he names a little circumstance corroborative of what I have said. Being on a visit to Roscoe, of Liverpool, he made some inquiries from him as to the habitat of a very rare plant, said to be found in certain places in Lancashire. Mr Roscoe knew nothing of the plant; but stated, that if any one could give him the desired information, it would be a hand-loom weaver in Manchester, whom he named. Sir J. E. Smith proceeded by boat to Manchester, and on arriving at that town, he inquired of the porter who was carrying his luggage if he could direct him to So and So.

'Oh, yes,' replied the man. 'He does a bit in my way;' and, on further investigation, it turned out, that both the porter, and his friend the weaver, were skilful botanists; and able to give Sir J. E. Smith the very information which he wanted.

Such are the tastes and pursuits of some of the thoughtful, little understood, working men of Manchester.

ELIZABETH GASKELL (1810–65), *Mary Barton*, 1848

All day he shoves the pasteboard in
The slick machine that turns out boxes,
A box a minute; and its din

Is all his music, as he stands
And feeds it; while his jaded brain
Moves only out and in again
With the slick motion of his hands,
Monotonously making boxes,
A box a minute—all his thoughts
A slick succession of empty boxes.

But, when night comes, and he is free
To play his fiddle, with the music
His whole soul moves to melody;
No more recalling day's dumb round,
His reckless spirit sweeps and whirls
On surging waves and dizzy swirls
And eddies of enchanted sound;
And in a flame-winged flight of music
Above the roofs and chimneys soars
To ride the starry tides of music.

WILFRID GIBSON (1878–1962), from 'The Release', 1928

And on the seventh day God ended his work which he had made; and he rested on the seventh day from all his work which he had made.

And God blessed the seventh day, and sanctified it; because that in it he had rested from all his work which God had created and made.

Genesis 2: 3–4

Industrious races find it very troublesome to endure leisure: it was a master-piece of *English* instinct to make the Sabbath so holy and so boring that the English begin unconsciously to lust again for their work- and week-day. It is a kind of cleverly invented, cleverly inserted *fast*, the like of which is also encountered frequently in the ancient world (although, in fairness to south-ern peoples, not exactly in regard to work).

FRIEDRICH NIETZSCHE (1844–1900), *Beyond Good and Evil*, 1886, tr. Walter Kaufmann, 1966

Apart from its religious aspect or the question of its divine origin, Sunday is to the great majority of civilized mankind a most blessed day. To all classes of society its calm and quiet, and comparative relaxation from the bustle and labour of the business of life—the clamour and weariness of which pen-etrates beyond the immediate circle of the toilers and spinners—must bring something of joy and contentment. It is a day on which many of the wicked cease from troubling, and the weary are at rest—a day which brings happiness alike to the truly religious, who regard it as a day more specially devoted to the service of their Master; to the dressily religious, who look upon it as a day, and the church or chapel as the most fitting place, for the triumphal inauguration of new bonnets or new dresses; and the church-courtshiply-religious, who, in church or on the way to or from it, manage to exchange at least glances and signals with the beloved beings from whom an unkind fate, in the shape of a limited income or a stern parent, or something of that kind, wholly divides them on other days; but to none does it bring greater happiness than to working men, and by none is it more eagerly looked forward to, or keenly appreciated. To them it is literally a day of rest—a day but for the existence of which the portion of the primal curse that decreed that man should earn his bread by the sweat of his brow would to them be a curse indeed! It is the greatest of all boons to labouring humanity, the brightest of the flowers that has been left them since the Fall, and is regarded by them as an inestimable treasure, even though the trail of the serpent is over it, inasmuch as the joys of the day are somewhat dimmed by the sad reflection that Sunday comes but once a week, and that in this uncertain climate of ours, those disastrous events, wet Sundays, are of frequent occurrence. But, taken with all its imperfections, the day is still itself alone, and stands out in joyous pre-eminence from the other six commonplace days of the week.

> A JOURNEYMAN ENGINEER (Thomas Wright) (*fl.* 1867), *Some Habits and Customs of the Working Classes,* 1867

Very soon the City itself would be standing over until Monday: the crowds of brokers and cashiers and clerks and typists and hawkers would have vanished from its pavements, the bars would be forlorn, the teashops nearly empty or closed; its trams and buses, no longer clamouring for a few more yards of space, would come gliding easily through misty blue vacancies like ships going down London River; and the whole place, populated only by caretakers and policemen among the living, would sink slowly into quietness; the very bank-rate would be forgotten; and it would be left to drown itself in reverie, with a drift of smoke and light fog across its old stones like the return of an army of ghosts. Until—with a clatter, a clang, a sudden raw awakening—Monday.

Papers were swept into drawers, letters were stamped in rows, blotters were shut, turned over, put away, ledgers and petty cash boxes were locked up, typewriters were covered, noses were powdered, cigarettes and pipes were lit, doors were banged, and stairs were noisy with hasty feet. The week was done. Out they came in their thousands into Angel Pavement, London Wall, Moorgate Street, Cornhill and Cheapside. They were so thick along Finsbury Pavement that the Moorgate Tube Station seemed like a monster sucking them down into its hot rank inside.

J. B. PRIESTLEY (1894–1984), *Angel Pavement*, 1930

But mark—not the whole week do we pass thus,—
No, nor whole day. Heaven, for ease' sake, forbid!
Half of the day (and half of that might serve,
Were all the world active and just as we)
Is mixed with the great throng, playing its part
Of toil and pain; we could not relish else
Our absolute comfort; nay, should almost fear
Heaven counted us not worthy to partake
The common load with its great hopes for all,
But held us flimsy triflers—gnats i' the sun—
Made but for play, and so to die, unheavened.
Oh, hard we work, and carefully we think,
And much we suffer! but the line being drawn
'Twixt work and our earth's heav'n, well do we draw it,
Sudden, and sharp, and sweet; and in an instant
Are borne away, like knights to fairy isles,
And close our gates behind us on the world.

LEIGH HUNT (1784–1859), from 'Our Cottage', 1836

Week-end

I

The train! The twelve o'clock for paradise.
    Hurry, or it will try to creep away.
Out in the country everyone is wise:
    We can be only wise on Saturday.
There you are waiting, little friendly house:
    Those are your chimney-stacks with you between,
Surrounded by old trees and strolling cows,
    Staring through all your windows at the green.
Your homely floor is creaking for our tread;
    The smiling teapot with contented spout
Thinks of the boiling water, and the bread
    Longs for the butter. All their hands are out
        To greet us, and the gentle blankets seem
        Purring and crooning: 'Lie in us, and dream.'

II

The key will stammer, and the door reply,
　　The hall wake, yawn, and smile; the torpid stair
Will grumble at our feet, the table cry:
　　'Fetch my belongings for me; I am bare.'
A clatter! Something in the attic falls.
　　A ghost has lifted up his robes and fled.
The loitering shadows move along the walls;
　　Then silence very slowly lifts his head.
The starling with impatient screech has flown
　　The chimney, and is watching from the tree.
They thought us gone for ever: mouse alone
　　Stops in the middle of the floor to see.
　　　　　Now all you idle things, resume your toil.
　　　　　Hearth, put your flames on. Sulky kettle, boil.

III

Contented evening; comfortable joys;
　　The snoozing fire, and all the fields are still:
Tranquil delight, no purpose, and no noise—
　　Unless the slow wind flowing round the hill.
'Murry' (the kettle) dozes; little mouse
　　Is rambling prudently about the floor.
There's lovely conversation in this house:
　　Words become princes that were slaves before.
What a sweet atmosphere for you and me
　　The people that have been here left behind . . .
Oh, but I fear it may turn out to be
　　Built of a dream, erected in the mind:
　　　　　So if we speak too loud, we may awaken
　　　　　To find it vanished, and ourselves mistaken.

*

VI

Morning! Wake up! Awaken! All the boughs
　　Are rippling on the air across the green.
The youngest birds are singing to the house.
　　Blood of the world!—and is the country clean?
Disturb the precinct. Cool it with a shout.
　　Sing as you trundle down to light the fire.
Turn the encumbering shadows tumbling out,
　　And fill the chambers with a new desire.
Life is no good, unless the morning brings
　　White happiness and quick delight of day.

These half-inanimate domestic things
  Must all be useful, or must go away.
    Coffee, be fragrant. Porridge in my plate,
    Increase the vigour to fulfil my fate.

VII

The fresh air moves like water round a boat.
  The white clouds wander. Let us wander too.
The whining wavering plover flap and float.
  That crow is flying after that cuckoo.
Look! Look! . . . They're gone. What are the great trees calling?
  Just come a little farther, by that edge
Of green, to where the stormy ploughland, falling
  Wave upon wave, is lapping to the hedge.
Oh, what a lovely bank! Give me your hand.
  Lie down and press your heart against the ground.
Let us both listen till we understand,
  Each through the other, every natural sound . . .
    I can't hear anything to-day, can you,
    But, far and near: 'Cuckoo! Cuckoo! Cuckoo!'?

VIII

The everlasting grass—how bright, how cool!
  The day has gone too suddenly, too soon.
There's something white and shiny in that pool—
  Throw in a stone, and you will hit the moon.
Listen, the church-bell ringing! Do not say
  We must go back to-morrow to our work.
We'll tell them we are dead: we died to-day.
  We're lazy. We're too happy. We will shirk.
We're cows. We're kettles. We'll be anything
  Except the manikins of time and fear.
We'll start away to-morrow wandering,
  And nobody will notice in a year . . .
    Now the great sun is slipping under ground.
    Grip firmly!—How the earth is whirling round.

IX

Be staid; be careful; and be not too free.
Temptation to enjoy your liberty
May rise against you, break into a crime,
And smash the habit of employing Time.
It serves no purpose that the careful clock
  Mark the appointment, the officious train
Hurry to keep it, if the minutes mock

Loud in your ear: 'Late. Late. Late. Late again.'
Week-end is very well on Saturday:
On Monday it's a different affair—
A little episode, a trivial stay
In some oblivious spot somehow, somewhere.
On Sunday night we hardly laugh or speak:
Week-end begins to merge itself in Week.

X

Pack up the house, and close the creaking door.
The fields are dull this morning in the rain.
It's difficult to leave that homely floor.
Wave a light hand; we will return again.
(What was that bird?) Good-bye, ecstatic tree,
Floating, bursting, and breathing on the air.
The lonely farm is wondering that we
Can leave. How every window seems to stare!
That bag is heavy. Share it for a bit.
You like that gentle swashing of the ground
As we tread? . . .
It is over. Now we sit
Reading the morning paper in the sound
Of the debilitating heavy train.
London again, again. London again.

HAROLD MONRO (1879–1932), 1917

But the most noticeable holiday, the most thoroughly self-made and characteristic of them all, is that greatest of small holidays—Saint Monday.

Which portion of the great unwashed first instituted the worship of this Saint is a disputed point; but to the tailors, who are amongst its most ardent devotees, the honour is usually ascribed. The institution is a comparatively recent one, and its origin is not very difficult to trace. The general introduction of steam as a motive power, and the rapid invention of machinery applicable to all kinds of manufacturing work, gave rise to a numerous body of highly skilled and highly paid workmen, who soon found themselves in a position to successfully oppose the employers of labour on some of the debatable grounds between capital, and labour, their most notable victories being the definite establishment of ten hours as the standard of a day's work, and the securing of an extra rate of payment for all hours worked above that number; and also the laying the foundation of the Saturday half-holiday movement, by obtaining the privilege—never afterwards abrogated—of leaving work at four o'clock on Saturdays. These workmen would at the end of the week put off their working clothes with a sense of relief, and, thinking far more of how they should enjoy themselves to the most advantage during the Saturday evening and Sunday, than of what would become of the working clothes in the meantime, the consequence was that on the Monday morning, when they had once more to appear 'with harness on their back,' and awoke at the usual time for donning it, the harness was not always forthcoming, especially in the case of those men who were only lodgers. The clean jacket and trousers or overalls that were supposed to be on the chair at the bedside would, after an exasperating search, be discovered at the bottom of the clothes-basket, unaired, and minus some important button, in consequence of which latter circumstance, the unfortunate wearer would have to run to work holding himself together as it were. The coat, which is substituted for the shop jacket in going to and from the workshop, and which is an indispensable appendage of the mechanical dignity, would not be found on its usual nail, for the reason that the landlady had stuffed it under the sofa with other objectionable art-icles that were considered too vulgar or too suggestive of work, to be allowed to meet the sight of the guests who on the previous day had attended her gen-teel Sunday tea-party; and when the coat was disinterred from its hiding-place, the cap, which was supposed to be in the pocket of it, would be missing. Having, however, by this time not a moment to spare, the unhappy victim to mislaid clothing would dash off, keeping a sharp look-out to avoid tripping himself with the flying laces of his unlaced shoes. By running, the half-dressed and breathless martyr to Monday morning circumstances would just manage to rush through the workshop gates as they were closing, but only, alas! to find that he had forgotten—had left in the pockets of the clothes turned off on the Saturday—the ticket, the giving in of which would alone enable him to start work. In consequence of this he would be compelled to return home, cursing his fate at having had his early rising and hard run for nothing, and oppressed with the distressing consciousness of having lost a quarter (of a day) without having the compensatory pleasure of spending it in bed. Driven by their sufferings in this respect to take some bold measure for their own relief, a large number of the operative engineers adopted the practice of regularly losing the morning quarter on Mondays, a proceeding which no other body of workmen would have dared at that time, when steam power and machine work were making engineering *the* trade of the day, to have carried out! and which there can be no reasonable doubt originated the holiday of Saint Monday. The sufferers from mislaid clothing and forgotten tickets having established this custom for their own benefit, others soon began to avail themselves of its advantages. Did a man feel more than usually inclined for a 'lie-in' after his Sunday-evening ramble, he would remember him that it was Monday morning, and indulge himself in the luxury of 'a little more sleep and a little more slumber;' or did a 'lushington' get a drop too much at the suburban inn to which *his* Sunday-evening ramble had led him, he would remember, when he came to 'think of his head in the morning,' that it was Monday, and have another turn round in the sheets, instead of turning out, as he would had to have done on any other working morning. Then if a man had any business to transact, he would ask for Monday as being a broken day at any rate; and sometimes, when going to work after breakfast, two or three thirsty souls who had been losing the first quarter, would turn into a public-house for a morning dram, and perhaps end in 'making a day of it.' And so the thing went on, extending in course of time to other trades, until it culminated in the canonization and setting apart of Monday as the avowed and self-constituted holiday of the pleasure-loving portion of 'the million.'

A JOURNEYMAN ENGINEER (Thomas Wright) (*fl.* 1867), *Some Habits and Customs of the Working Classes*, 1867

HOLIDAYS

I've waited longing for today:
Spindle, bobbin, and spool, away!
In joy and bliss I'm off to play
   Upon this high holiday.

Spindle, bobbin, and spool, away,
For joy that it's a holiday!

The dirt upon the floor's unswept,
The fireplace isn't cleaned and kept,
I haven't cut the rushes yet
   Upon this high holiday.

Spindle, bobbin, etc.

The cooking herbs I must fetch in,
And fix my kerchief under my chin.
Darling Jack, lend me a pin
   To fix me well this holiday!

Spindle, bobbin, etc.

Now midday has almost come,
And all my chores are still not done:
I'll clean my shoes till they become
   Bright for a high holiday.

Spindle, bobbin, etc.

In pails the milk has got to go;
I ought to spread this bowl of dough—
It clogs my nails and fingers so
    As I knead this holiday!

    Spindle, bobbin, etc.

Jack will take me on my way,
And with me he will want to play:
I needn't fear my lady's nay
    On such a high holiday!

    Spindle, bobbin, etc.

And when we stop beside the track
At the inn this Sunday, Jack
Will wet my whistle and pay my whack
    As on every holiday.

    Spindle, bobbin, etc.

Then he'll take me by the hand
And lay me down upon the land
And make my buttocks feel like sand
    Upon this high holiday.

    Spindle, bobbin, etc.

In he'll push and out he'll go,
With me beneath him lying low:
'By God's death, you do me woe
    Upon this high holiday!'

    Spindle, bobbin, etc.

Soon my belly began to swell
As round and great as any bell;
And to my dame I dared not tell
    What happened to me that holiday.

    Spindle, bobbin, and spool, away,
    For joy that it's a holiday!

                    ANON., 15th c., tr. Brian Stone, 1964

But besides Sundays I had a day at Easter, and a day at Christmas, with a full
week in the summer to go and air myself in my native fields of Hertfordshire.
This last was a great indulgence; and the prospect of its recurrence, I believe,

alone kept me up through the year, and made my durance tolerable. But when the week came round, did the glittering phantom of the distance keep touch with me? or rather was it not a series of seven uneasy days, spent in restless pursuit of pleasure, and a wearisome anxiety to find out how to make the most of them? Where was the quiet, where the promised rest? Before I had a taste of it, it was vanished. I was at the desk again, counting upon the fifty-one tedious weeks that must intervene before such another snatch would come. Still the prospect of its coming threw something of an illumination upon the darker side of my captivity. Without it, as I have said, I could scarcely have sustained my thraldom.

CHARLES LAMB (1775–1834), 'The Superannuated Man', 1825

It is the long vacation in the regions of Chancery Lane. The good ships Law and Equity, those teak-built, copper-bottomed, iron-fastened, brazen-faced, and not by any means fast-sailing Clippers, are laid up in ordinary. The Flying Dutchman, with a crew of ghostly clients imploring all whom they may encounter to peruse their papers, has drifted, for the time being, Heaven knows where. The Courts are all shut up; the public offices lie in a hot sleep; Westminster Hall itself is a shady solitude where nightingales might sing, and a tenderer class of suitors than is usually found there, walk.

The Temple, Chancery Lane, Serjeants' Inn, and Lincoln's Inn even unto the Fields, are like tidal harbours at low water; where stranded proceedings, offices at anchor, idle clerks lounging on lop-sided stools that will not recover their perpendicular until the current of Term sets in, lie high and dry upon the ooze of the long vacation. Outer doors of chambers are shut up by the score, messages and parcels are to be left at the Porter's Lodge by the bushel. A crop of grass would grow in the chinks of the stone pavement outside Lincoln's Inn Hall, but that the ticket-porters, who have nothing to do beyond sitting in the shade there, with their white aprons over their heads to keep the flies off, grub it up and eat it thoughtfully.

There is only one Judge in town. Even he only comes twice a week to sit in chambers. If the country folks of those assize towns on his circuit could see him now! No full-bottomed wig, no red petticoats, no fur, no javelin-men, no white wands. Merely a close-shaved gentleman in white trousers and a white hat, with sea-bronze on the judicial countenance, and a strip of bark peeled by the solar rays from the judicial nose, who calls in at the shell-fish shop as he comes along, and drinks iced ginger-beer!

The bar of England is scattered over the face of the earth. How England can get on through four long summer months without its bar—which is its acknowledged refuge in adversity, and its only legitimate triumph in prosperity—is beside the question; assuredly that shield and buckler of Britannia are not in present wear. The learned gentleman who is always so tremendously indignant at the unprecedented outrage committed on the feelings of his client by the opposite party, that he never seems likely to recover it, is doing infinitely better than might be expected, in Switzerland. The learned gentleman who does the withering business, and who blights all opponents with his gloomy sarcasm, is as merry as a grig at a French watering-place. The learned gentleman who weeps by the pint on the smallest provocation, has not shed a tear these six weeks. The very learned gentleman who has cooled the natural heat of his gingery complexion in pools and fountains of law, until he has become great in knotty arguments for term-time, when he poses the drowsy Bench with legal 'chaff,' inexplicable to the uninitiated and to most of the initiated too, is roaming, with a characteristic delight in aridity and dust, about Constantinople. Other dispersed fragments of the same great Palladium are to be found on the canals of Venice, at the second cataract of the Nile, in the baths of Germany, and sprinkled on the sea-sand all over the English coast. Scarcely one is to be encountered in the deserted region of Chancery Lane. If such a lonely member of the bar do flit across the waste, and come upon a prowling suitor who is unable to leave off haunting the scenes of his anxiety, they frighten one another, and retreat into opposite shades.

It is the hottest long vacation known for many years. All the young clerks are madly in love, and, according to their various degrees, pine for bliss with the beloved object, at Margate, Ramsgate, or Gravesend. All the middle-aged clerks think their families too large. All the unowned dogs who stray into the Inns of Court, and pant about staircases and other dry places, seeking water, give short howls of aggravation. All the blind men's dogs in the streets draw their masters against pumps, or trip them over buckets. A shop with a sun-blind, and a watered pavement, and a bowl of gold and silver fish in the window, is a sanctuary. Temple Bar gets so hot, that it is, to the adjacent Strand and Fleet Street, what a heater is in an urn, and keeps them simmering all night.

CHARLES DICKENS (1812–70), Bleak House, 1853

Peace

a study

He stood, a worn-out City clerk—
    Who'd toiled, and seen no holiday,
For forty years from dawn to dark—
    Alone beside Caermarthen Bay.

He felt the salt spray on his lips;
    Heard children's voices on the sands;
Up the sun's path he saw the ships
    Sail on and on to other lands;

And laughed aloud. Each sight and sound
    To him was joy too deep for tears;
He sat him on the beach, and bound
    A blue bandana round his ears:

And thought how, posted near his door,
    His own green door on Camden Hill,
Two bands at least, most likely more,
    Were mingling at their own sweet will

Verdi with Vance. And at the thought
    He laughed again, and softly drew
That Morning Herald that he'd bought
    Forth from his breast, and read it through.

CHARLES STUART CALVERLEY (1831–84), 1866

It is Bank Holiday today, and the streets are overcrowded with swarms of people. Never is so clearly to be seen the vulgarity of the people as at these holiday times. Their notion of a holiday is to rush in crowds to some sweltering place, such as the Crystal Palace, and there sit and drink and quarrel themselves into stupidity. Miserable children are lugged about, yelling at the top of their voices, and are beaten because they yell. Troops of hideous creatures drive wildly about the town in gigs, donkey-carts, cabbage-carts, dirt-carts, and think it enjoyment. The pleasure of peace and quietness, of rest for body and mind, is not understood. Thousands are tempted by cheap trips to go off for the day to the seaside, and succeed in wearying themselves to death, for the sake of eating a greasy meal in a Margate Coffee-shop, and getting five minutes' glimpse of the sea through eyes blinded with dirt and perspiration. Places like Hampstead Heath and the various parks and commons are packed with screeching drunkards, one general mass of dust and heat and rage and exhaustion. Yet this is the best kind of holiday the people are capable of.

It is utterly absurd, this idea of setting aside single days for great public holidays. It will never do anything but harm. What we want is a general shortening of working hours all the year round, so that, for instance, all labour would be over at 4 o'clock in the afternoon. Then the idea of hours of leisure would become familiar to the people and they would learn to make some sensible use of them. Of course this is impossible so long as we work for working's sake. All the world's work—all that is really necessary for the health and comfort and even luxury of mankind—could be performed in three or four hours each day. There is so much labour just because there is so much money-grubbing. Every man has to fight for a living with his neighbour, and the grocer who keeps his shop open till half an hour after midnight has an advantage over him who closes at twelve. Work in itself is *not an end; only a means;*

but we nowadays make it an end, and three-fourths of the world cannot understand anything else.

> GEORGE GISSING (1857–1903), letter to his sister Margaret, 29 May 1892

THE DAY'S WORK COMPLETED

Rest is the end of all motion, and the last perfection of all things that labour. Labours in us are journeys, and even in them which feel no weariness by any work, yet they are but ways whereby to come unto that which bringeth not happiness till it do bring rest. For as long as anything we desire is unattained we rest not.

Let us not here take rest for idleness. They are idle whom the painfulness of action causeth to avoid those labours, whereunto both God and nature bindeth them: they rest which either cease from their work when they have brought it unto perfection, or else give over a meaner labour because a worthier and better is to be undertaken.

> RICHARD HOOKER (1554–1600), *Of the Laws of Ecclesiastical Polity*, 1593–7

After Apple-Picking

My long two-pointed ladder's sticking through a tree
Toward heaven still,
And there's a barrel that I didn't fill
Beside it, and there may be two or three
Apples I didn't pick upon some bough.
But I am done with apple-picking now.
Essence of winter sleep is on the night,
The scent of apples: I am drowsing off.
I cannot rub the strangeness from my sight
I got from looking through a pane of glass
I skimmed this morning from the drinking trough
And held against the world of hoary grass.
It melted, and I let it fall and break.
But I was well
Upon my way to sleep before it fell,
And I could tell
What form my dreaming was about to take.
Magnified apples appear and disappear,
Stem end and blossom end,
And every fleck of russet showing clear.

My instep arch not only keeps the ache,
It keeps the pressure of a ladder-round.
I feel the ladder sway as the boughs bend.
And I keep hearing from the cellar bin
The rumbling sound
Of load on load of apples coming in.
For I have had too much
Of apple-picking: I am overtired
Of the great harvest I myself desired.
There were ten thousand thousand fruit to touch,
Cherish in hand, lift down, and not let fall.
For all
That struck the earth,
No matter if not bruised or spiked with stubble,
Went sure to the cider-apple heap
As of no worth.
One can see what will trouble
This sleep of mine, whatever sleep it is.
Were he not gone,
The woodchuck could say whether it's like his
Long sleep, as I describe its coming on,
Or just some human sleep.

ROBERT FROST (1874–1963), 1914

Evenen in the Village

Now the light o' the west is a-turn'd to gloom,
    An' the men be at hwome vrom ground;
An' the bells be a-zendèn all down the Coombe
    From tower, their mwoansome sound.
        An' the wind is still,
        An' the house-dogs do bark,
An' the rooks be a-vled to the elems high an' dark,
    An' the water do roar at mill.

An' the flickerèn light drough the window-peäne
    Vrom the candle's dull fleäme do shoot,
An' young Jemmy the smith is a-gone down leäne,
    A-playèn his shrill-vaïced flute.
        An' the miller's man
        Do zit down at his ease
On the seat that is under the cluster o' trees,
    Wi' his pipe an' his cider can.

WILLIAM BARNES (1801–86), 1844

So spends many a farmer of the old stamp his day, and at night he takes his seat on the settle, under the old wide chimney—his wife has her little work-table set near—the 'wenches' darning their stockings, or making up a cap for Sunday, and the men sitting on the other side of the hearth with their shoes off. He now enjoys of all things to talk over his labours and plans with the men—they canvass the best method of doing this and that—lay out the course of to-morrow—what land is to be broke up, or laid down; where barley, wheat, oats, etc., shall be sown, or if they be growing, when they shall be cut. In harvest-time, lambing-time, in potato setting and gathering time, in fact, almost all summer long, there is no sitting on the hearth—it is out of bed with the sun, and after the long hard day—supper, and to bed again.

WILLIAM HOWITT (1792–1879), *The Rural Life of England*, 1838

All hands worked on in silence for some minutes, until the church clock began to strike six. Before the first stroke had died away, Sandy Jim had loosed his plane and was reaching his jacket; Wiry Ben had left a screw half driven in, and thrown his screw-driver into his tool-basket; Mum Taft, who, true to his name, had kept silence throughout the previous conversation, had flung down his hammer as he was in the act of lifting it; and Seth, too, had straightened his back, and was putting out his hand towards his paper cap. Adam alone had gone on with his work as if nothing had happened. But observing the cessation of the tools, he looked up, and said, in a tone of indignation,—

'Look there, now! I can't abide to see men throw away their tools i' that way, the minute the clock begins to strike, as if they took no pleasure i' their work, and was afraid o' doing a stroke too much.'

Seth looked a little conscious, and began to be slower in his preparations for going; but Mum Taft broke silence, and said,—

'Ay, ay, Adam lad, ye talk like a young un. When y' are six-an'-forty like me, istid o' six-an'-twenty, ye wonna be so flush o' workin' for nought.'

'Nonsense,' said Adam, still wrathful. 'What's age got to do with it, I wonder? Ye arena getting stiff yet, I reckon. I hate to see a man's arms drop down as if he was shot, before the clock's fairly struck, just as if he'd never a bit o' pride and delight in 's work. The very grindstone 'ull go on turning a bit after you loose it.'

'Bodderation, Adam!' exclaimed Wiry Ben; 'lave a chap aloon, will 'ee? Ye war a-finding faut wi' preachers a while agoo—y' are fond enough o' preachin' yoursen. Ye may like work better nor play, but I like play better nor work; that'll 'commodate ye—it laves ye th' more to do.'

With this exit speech, which he considered effective, Wiry Ben shouldered his basket and left the workshop, quickly followed by Mum Taft and Sandy Jim.

GEORGE ELIOT (1819–80), *Adam Bede*, 1859

It was the hour of the unyoking of men. In the highways and byways of Clerkenwell there was a thronging of released toilers, of young and old, of male and female. Forth they streamed from factories and workrooms, anxious to make the most of the few hours during which they might live for themselves. Great numbers were still bent over their labour, and would be for hours to come, but the majority had leave to wend stablewards. Along the main thoroughfares the wheel-track was clangorous; every omnibus that clattered by was heavily laden with passengers; tarpaulins gleamed over the knees of those who sat outside. This way and that the lights were blurred into a misty radiance; overhead was mere blackness, whence descended the lashing rain. There was a ceaseless scattering of mud; there were blocks in the traffic, attended with rough jest or angry curse; there was jostling on the crowded pavement. Public-houses began to brighten up, to bestir themselves for the evening's business. Streets that had been hives of activity since early morning were being abandoned to silence and darkness and the sweeping wind.

GEORGE GISSING (1857–1903), *The Nether World*, 1889

At first with such discourse, and afterwards with conversation of a more general nature, did Mr Wemmick and I beguile the time and the road, until he gave me to understand that we had arrived in the district of Walworth.

It appeared to be a collection of back lanes, ditches, and little gardens, and to present the aspect of a rather dull retirement. Wemmick's house was a little wooden cottage in the midst of plots of garden, and the top of it was cut out and painted like a battery mounted with guns.

'My own doing,' said Wemmick. 'Looks pretty; don't it?'

I highly commended it. I think it was the smallest house I ever saw; with the queerest gothic windows (by far the greater part of them sham), and a gothic door, almost too small to get in at.

'That's a real flagstaff, you see,' said Wemmick, 'and on Sundays I run up a real flag. Then look here. After I have crossed this bridge, I hoist it up—so—and cut off the communication.'

The bridge was a plank, and it crossed a chasm about four feet wide and two deep. But it was very pleasant to see the pride with which he hoisted it up and made it fast; smiling as he did so, with a relish and not merely mechanically.

'At nine o'clock every night, Greenwich time,' said Wemmick, 'the gun fires. There he is, you see! And when you hear him go, I think you'll say he's a Stinger.'

The piece of ordnance referred to, was mounted in a separate fortress, constructed of lattice-work. It was protected from the weather by an ingenious little tarpaulin contrivance in the nature of an umbrella.

'Then, at the back,' said Wemmick, 'out of sight, so as not to impede the idea of fortifications—for it's a principle with me, if you have an idea, carry it out and keep it up—I don't know whether that's your opinion——'

I said, decidedly.

'At the back, there's a pig, and there are fowls and rabbits; then, I knock together my own little frame, you see, and grow cucumbers; and you'll judge at supper what sort of a salad I can raise. So, sir,' said Wemmick, smiling again, but seriously too, as he shook his head, 'if you can suppose the little place besieged, it would hold out a devil of a time in point of provisions.'

Then, he conducted me to a bower about a dozen yards off, but which was approached by such ingenious twists of path that it took quite a long time to get at; and in this retreat our glasses were already set forth. Our punch was cooling in an ornamental lake, on whose margin the bower was raised. This piece of water (with an island in the middle which might have been the salad for supper) was of a circular form, and he had constructed a fountain in it, which, when you set a little mill going and took a cork out of a pipe, played to that powerful extent that it made the back of your hand quite wet.

'I am my own engineer, and my own carpenter, and my own plumber, and my own gardener, and my own Jack of all Trades,' said Wemmick, in acknowledging my compliments. 'Well; it's a good thing, you know. It brushes the Newgate cobwebs away, and pleases the Aged. You wouldn't mind being at once introduced to the Aged, would you? It wouldn't put you out?'

I expressed the readiness I felt, and we went into the Castle. There, we found, sitting by a fire, a very old man in a flannel coat: clean, cheerful, comfortable, and well cared for, but intensely deaf.

'Well aged parent,' said Wemmick, shaking hands with him in a cordial and jocose way, 'how am you?'

'All right, John; all right!' replied the old man.

'Here's Mr Pip, aged parent,' said Wemmick, 'and I wish you could hear his name. Nod away at him, Mr Pip; that's what he likes. Nod away at him, if you please, like winking!'

'This is a fine place of my son's, sir,' cried the old man, while I nodded as hard as I possibly could. 'This is a pretty pleasure-ground, sir. This spot and these beautiful works upon it ought to be kept together by the Nation, after my son's time, for the people's enjoyment.'

'You're as proud of it as Punch; ain't you, Aged?' said Wemmick, contemplating the old man, with his hard face really softened; '*there's* a nod for you;' giving him a tremendous one; '*there's* another for you;' giving him a still more tremendous one; 'you like that, don't you? If you're not tired, Mr Pip—though I know it's tiring to strangers—will you tip him one more? You can't think how it pleases him.'

I tipped him several more, and he was in great spirits. We left him bestirring himself to feed the fowls, and we sat down to our punch in the arbour; where Wemmick told me as he smoked a pipe that it had taken him a good many years to bring the property up to its present pitch of perfection.

'Is it your own, Mr Wemmick?'

'Oh yes,' said Wemmick, 'I have got hold of it, a bit at a time. It's a freehold, by George!'

'Is it, indeed? I hope Mr Jaggers admires it?'

'Never seen it,' said Wemmick. 'Never heard of it. Never seen the Aged. Never heard of him. No; the office is one thing, and private life is another. When I go into the office, I leave the Castle behind me, and when I come into the Castle, I leave the office behind me. If it's not in any way disagreeable to you, you'll oblige me by doing the same. I don't wish it professionally spoken about.'

Of course I felt my good faith involved in the observance of his request. The punch being very nice, we sat there drinking it and talking, until it was almost nine o'clock. 'Getting near gunfire,' said Wemmick then, as he laid down his pipe; 'it's the Aged's treat.'

Proceeding into the Castle again, we found the Aged heating the poker, with expectant eyes, as a preliminary to the performance of this great nightly ceremony. Wemmick stood with his watch in his hand, until the moment was come for him to take the red-hot poker from the Aged, and repair to the battery. He took it, and went out, and presently the Stinger went off with a Bang that shook the crazy little box of a cottage as if it must fall to pieces, and made every glass and teacup in it ring. Upon this, the Aged—who I believe would have been blown out of his armchair but for holding on by the elbows—cried out exultingly, 'He's fired! I heerd him!' and I nodded at the old gentleman until it is no figure of speech to declare that I absolutely could not see him.

The interval between that time and supper, Wemmick devoted to showing me his collection of curiosities. They were mostly of a felonious character; comprising the pen with which a celebrated forgery had been committed, a distinguished razor or two, some locks of hair, and several manuscript confessions written under condemnation—upon which Mr Wemmick set particular value as being, to use his own words, 'every one of 'em Lies, sir.' These were agreeably dispersed among small specimens of china and glass, various neat trifles made by the proprietor of the museum, and some tobacco-stoppers carved by the Aged. They were all displayed in that chamber of the Castle into which I had been first inducted, and which served, not only as the general sitting-room but as the kitchen too, if I might judge from a saucepan on the hob, and a brazen bijou over the fireplace designed for the suspension of a roasting-jack.

There was a neat little girl in attendance, who looked after the Aged in the day. When she had laid the supper-cloth, the bridge was lowered to give her means of egress, and she withdrew for the night. The supper was excellent; and though the Castle was rather subject to dry-rot insomuch that it tasted like a bad nut, and though the pig might have been farther off, I was heartily pleased with my whole entertainment. Nor was there any drawback on my little turret bedroom, beyond there being such a very thin ceiling between me and the flagstaff, that when I lay down on my back in bed, it seemed as if I had to balance that pole on my forehead all night.

Wemmick was up early in the morning, and I am afraid I heard him cleaning my boots. After that, he fell to gardening, and I saw him from my gothic window pretending to employ the Aged, and nodding at him in a most devoted manner. Our breakfast was as good as the supper, and at half-past eight precisely we started for Little Britain. By degrees, Wemmick got dryer and harder as we went along, and his mouth tightened into a post-office again. At last, when we got to his place of business and he pulled out his key from his coat-collar, he looked as unconscious of his Walworth property as if the Castle and the drawbridge and the arbour and the lake and the fountain and the Aged, had all been blown into space together by the last discharge of the Stinger.

CHARLES DICKENS (1812–70), *Great Expectations*, 1861

'Evening in Buffalo, New York'

The day fell, its weight gathered like mud on the shoes, as the laboring crowd teemed out of namesake yards and works, embarked on another delivery, lugging the carcass home to a tenement. The fume of soap was replaced on the sidewalks and in the trolleys by that of sweat and industrial leavings, by worn wools and flannels. One worked to rest. One worked to drink. Dark came, doors closed. Windows, incredibly small given the universal scale of night, spilled light onto streets darkened further by the redundant shade of elms. The smallness of the windows against the blackness would have amazed a pedestrian out emptying the dog. They were patches cut from the fabric of privacy. Behind them, within them, gravity bent bodies into grace. For the first time since early morning, flesh (not just hands) met purposefully. Laps came into use again, and loins. The workday was just a means of keeping bodies apart.

VERLYN KLINKENBORG (1953–   ), *The Last Fine Time*, 1991

When the laborious Plow-man hath by day
Worri'd himself, and Earth, and water'd it
With his own sweat; cool night his head doth lay
Safe on his bed, and teach him to forget
   His toilesome work; whilst soft and gentle sleep
   Yeilds him a crop of pleasant dreams to reap.

JOSEPH BEAUMONT (1616–99), *Psyche, or Love's Mysterie*, 1648

When Adam thus to Eve: Fair consort, the hour
Of night, and all things now retired to rest
Mind us of like repose, since God hath set
Labour and rest, as day and night to men
Successive, and the timely dew of sleep
Now falling with soft slumbrous weight inclines
Our eyelids; other creatures all day long
Rove idle unemployed, and less need rest;
Man hath his daily work of body or mind
Appointed, which declares his dignity,
And the regard of heaven on all his ways;
While other animals unactive range,
And of their doings God takes no account.
To morrow ere fresh morning streak the east
With first approach of light, we must be risen,
And at our pleasant labour, to reform
Yon flowery arbours, yonder alleys green,
Our walk at noon, with branches overgrown,
That mock our scant manuring, and require
More hands than ours to lop their wanton growth:
These blossoms also, and those dropping gums,
That lie bestrewn unsightly and unsmooth,
Ask riddance, if we mean to tread with ease;
Meanwhile, as nature wills, night bids us rest.

JOHN MILTON (1608–74), *Paradise Lost*, 1667

The sleep of a labouring man is sweet.

Ecclesiasticus 5: 10

There is a poignancy in preparing for the night shift, the feeling is really one of tragedy. This is where the unnaturalness begins. Everyone but you is going home to rest, to revel in the sweet society of wife and children, or parents, to enjoy the greatest pleasure of the workers' day—the evening meal, the happy fireside, a few short hours of simple pleasure or recreation and, afterwards, the honey-dew of slumber. As you walk along the lane or street towards the factory you meet the toilers in single file, or two abreast, or marching like an army, in compact squads and groups, or straggling here and there. The boys and youths move smartly and quickly, laughing and talking; the men proceed more soberly, some upright with firm step and cheerful countenance, others bent and stooping, dragging their weary limbs along in silence like tired warriors retreating after the hard-fought battle.

There is also the inward sense and knowledge of evening, for, however much you may deceive your external self, you cannot deceive Nature. Forget yourself as much as you please, she always remembers the hour and the minute; she is far more painstaking and punctual than we are. The time of day fills you with a sweet sadness. The summer sun entering into the broad, gold-flooded west, the soft, autumn twilight, or the gathering shades of the winter evening, all tell the same story. It is drawing towards night; night that was made for man, when very nature reposes; night for pleasure and rest, for peace, joy, and compensations, while you—here are you off to sweat and slave for twelve dreary hours in a modern inferno, in the Cyclops' den, with the everlasting wheels, the smoke and steam, the flaring furnace and piles of blazing hot metal all around you.

ALFRED WILLIAMS (1877–1930), *Life in a Railway Factory*, 1915

Part Two
Kinds of Work

IV. WOMEN'S WORK AND CHILD LABOUR

WOMEN'S WORK

In the Western world today there are virtually no forms of work that women do not perform. They can be soldiers, judges, priests, university vice-chancellors, even prime ministers. But before the twentieth century most societies confined certain occupations to members of one sex. Typically, this sexual division of labour involved men in venturing out of the household to engage in public activities, while women stayed behind to take care of the house, to prepare food and clothing, and to bring up the children. In the days before factories and supermarkets this meant that women did a great deal more than mere 'house-work': the sixteenth-century housewife described by Thomas Tusser was a hard-working manager and producer whose activities were economically as important as those of her husband. Widows of well-to-do merchants or tradesmen often carried on with their husbands' businesses. But for the most part women who worked outside the household were confined to work of low status and low remuneration.

Woman of Africa
Sweeper
Smearing floors and walls
With cow dung and black soil
Cook, *ayah*, the baby tied on your back
Vomiting,
Washer of dishes.
Planting, weeding, harvesting
Storekeeper, builder
Runner of errands.
Cart, lorry,
Donkey . . .

Woman of Africa
What are you not?

O<small>KOT</small> P'B<small>ITEK</small> (1931–82), Song of Ocol, 1967

Who can find a virtuous woman? for her price is far above rubies.

The heart of her husband doth safely trust in her, so that he shall have no need of spoil.

She will do him good and not evil all the days of her life.

She seeketh wool, and flax, and worketh willingly with her hands.

She is like the merchants' ships; she bringeth her food from afar.

She riseth also while it is yet night, and giveth meat to her household, and a portion to her maidens.

She considereth a field, and buyeth it: with the fruit of her hands she planteth a vineyard.

She girdeth her loins with strength, and strengtheneth her arms.

She perceiveth that her merchandise is good: her candle goeth not out by night.

She layeth her hands to the spindle, and her hands hold the distaff.

She stretcheth out her hand to the poor; yea, she reacheth forth her hands to the needy.

She is not afraid of the snow for her household: for all her household are clothed with scarlet.

She maketh herself coverings of tapestry; her clothing is silk and purple.

Her husband is known in the gates, when he sitteth among the elders of the land.

She maketh fine linen, and selleth it; and delivereth girdles unto the merchant.

Strength and honour are her clothing; and she shall rejoice in time to come.

She openeth her mouth with wisdom; and in her tongue is the law of kindness.

She looketh well to the ways of her household, and eateth not the bread of idleness.

Proverbs 31: 10–27

Then if this be a society, and consisteth only of freemen, the least part thereof must be of two. The naturalest and first conjunction of two toward the making of a further society of continuance is of the husband and wife after a diverse sort each having care of the family: the man to get, to travail abroad, to defend: the wife, to save that which is gotten, to tarry at home to distribute that which cometh from the husband's labour for nurture of the children and family of them both, and to keep all at home neat and clean.

Sir Thomas Smith (1513–77), *De Republica Anglorum*, 1583

Wherever individuals join their actions for a common end that is not absolutely simple, some division of labour spontaneously arises. We see this even in such a transitory incident as a picnic. Immediately a spot for the repast has been decided on, some begin to unpack the hampers, others to collect fern for sitting upon and presently, while the ladies lay the cloth and arrange the knives and forks, one of the gentlemen fetches water from a spring and another takes down the wine to be cooled in the neighbouring stream.

HERBERT SPENCER (1820–1903), *The Principles of Sociology,* 1877–96

What Works a Wife Should Do in General

When thou art up and ready, then first sweep thy house, dress up thy dish-board, and set all things in good order within thy house. Milk thy cows, suckle thy calves, strain up thy milk, take up thy children and array them, and provide for thy husband's breakfast, dinner, supper, and for thy children and servants, and take thy part with them. And to order corn and malt to the mill, to bake and brew withal when need is. And meet it to the mill, and from the mill, and see that thou have thy measure again beside the toll, or else the miller dealeth not truly with thee, or else thy corn is not dry as it should be.

Thou must make butter, and cheese when thou mayest, serve thy swine both morning and evening, and give thy poultry meat in the morning; and when time of the year cometh, thou must take heed how thy hens, ducks, and geese do lay, and to gather up their eggs, and when they wax broody, to set them there as no beasts, swine, nor other vermin hurt them. And thou must know that all whole-footed fowls will sit a month, and all cloven-footed fowls will sit but three weeks, except a peahen and great fowls, as cranes, bustards, and such other. And when they have brought forth their birds, to see that they be well kept from the kites, crows, polecats and other vermin.

And in the beginning of March, or a little before, is time for a wife to make her garden, and to get as many good seeds and herbs as she can, and especially such as be good for the pot, and to eat: and as often as need shall require, it must be weeded, for else the weeds will overgrow the herbs. And also in March is time to sow flax and hemp: . . . and thereof may they make sheets, table-cloths, towels, shirts, smocks, and such other necessaries, and therefore let thy distaff be always ready for a pastime, that thou be not idle. And undoubtedly a woman cannot get her living honestly with spinning on the distaff, but it stops a gap, and must needs be had . . .

It is convenient for a husband to have sheep of his own, for many causes, and then maybe his wife have part of the wool, to make her husband and her-self some clothes. And at the least way, she may have the locks of the sheep, either to make clothes or blankets and coverlets, or both. And if she have no wool of her own, she may take wool to spin off cloth-makers, and by that means she may have a convenient living, and much time to do other work. It is a wife's occupation, to winnow all manner of corn, to make malt, to wash and wring, to make hay, shear corn, and in time of need to help her husband to fill the muck-wain or dung-cart, drive the plough, to load hay, corn, and such other. And to go or ride to the market, to sell butter, cheese, milk, eggs, chickens, capons, hens, pigs, geese, and all manner of corn. And also to buy all manner of necessary things belonging to the household, and to make a true reckoning and account to her husband, what she hath paid.

JOHN FITZHERBERT (d. 1531), *The Book of Husbandry*, 1534

A woman's work is never done.

Title of a ballad, 1629

'The Tudor Housewife's Day'

Morning Workes

Get up in the morning as soone as thou wilt,
with overlong slugging good servant is spilt.

Some slovens from sleeping no sooner get up,
but hand is in aumbrie, and nose in the cup.

Some worke in the morning may trimly be donne,
that all the day after can hardly be wonne.

Good husband without it is needfull there be,
good huswife within as needfull as he.

Sluts corners avoided shall further thy health,
much time about trifles shall hinder thy wealth.

Set some to peele hempe or else rishes to twine,
to spin and to card, or to seething of brine.

Set some about cattle, some pasture to vewe,
some mault to be grinding against ye do brewe.

*

Breakefast Doings

Call servants to breakefast by day starre appere,
a snatch and to worke, fellowes tarrie not here.

Let huswife be carver, let pottage be heate,
a messe to eche one, with a morsell of meate.

*

aumbrie] pantry   *rishes*] rushes

Cookerie

Good cooke to dresse dinner, to bake and to brewe,
deserves a rewarde, being honest and trewe.

Good diligent turnebroch and trustie withall,
is sometime as needfull as some in the hall.

Dairie

Good huswife in dairie, that needes not be tolde,
deserveth hir fee to be paid hir in golde.

Ill servant neglecting what huswiferie saies,
deserveth hir fee to be paid hir with baies.

Good droie to serve hog, to helpe wash, and to milke,
more needfull is truelie than some in their silke.

Though homelie be milker, let cleanlie be cooke,
for a slut and a sloven be knowne by their looke.

Though cat (a good mouser) doth dwell in a house,
yet ever in dairie have trap for a mouse.

Take heede how thou laiest the bane for the rats,
for poisoning servant, thy selfe and thy brats.

Scouring

Though scouring be needfull, yet scouring too mutch,
is pride without profit, and robbeth thine hutch.

Keepe kettles from knocks, set tubs out of Sun,
for mending is costlie, and crackt is soone dun.

Washing

Maids, wash well and wring well, but beat ye wot how,
if any lack beating, I feare it be yow.

In washing by hand, have an eie to thy boll,
for launders and millers, be quick of their toll.

Go wash well, saith Sommer, with sunne I shall drie,
go wring well, saith Winter, with winde so shall I.

*

turnebroch] boy who turns the spit   *baies*] chidings   *droie*] drudge

Evening Workes

When hennes go to roost go in hand to dresse meate,
serve hogs and to milking and some to serve neate.

Where twaine be ynow, be not served with three,
more knaves in a companie worser they bee.

For everie trifle leave ianting thy nag,
but rather make lackey of Jack boie thy wag.

Make servant at night lug in wood or a log,
let none come in emptie but slut and thy dog.

Where pullen use nightly to pearch in the yard,
there two legged foxes keepe watches and ward.

See cattle well served, without and within,
and all thing at quiet ere supper begin.

No clothes in garden, no trinkets without,
no doore leave unbolted, for feare of a dout.

Thou woman whom pitie becommeth the best,
graunt all that hath laboured time to take rest.

*

Declare after Supper, take heede thereunto,
what worke in the morning ech servant shall do.

After Supper Matters

Remember those children whose parents be poore,
which hunger, yet dare not crave at thy doore.

Thy Bandog that serveth for diverse mishaps,
forget not to give him thy bones and thy scraps.

*

Such keies lay up safe, ere ye take ye to rest,
of dairie, of buttrie, of cubboord and chest.

*

The day willeth done whatsoever ye bid,
the night is a theefe, if ye take not good hid.

Wash dishes, lay leavens, save fire and away,
locke doores and to bed, a good huswife will say.

THOMAS TUSSER (1524?–80), *Five Hundred Pointes of Good Husbandrie*,
1557

ianting] driving   *Bandog*] fierce dog, kept tied up   *keies*] keys   *leavens*] put
barm and meal together, to ferment

I told him I had perhaps differing notions of matrimony from what the received custom had given us of it; that I thought a woman was a free agent as well as a man, and was born free, and, could she manage herself suitably, might enjoy that liberty to as much purpose as the men do; that the laws of matrimony were indeed otherwise, and mankind at this time acted quite upon other principles; and those such, that a woman gave herself entirely away from herself in marriage, and capitulated only to be at best but an upper servant, and from the time she took the man she was no better or worse than the servant among the Israelites who had his ears bored, that is, nailed to the door-post, who by that act gave himself up to be a servant during life.

That the very nature of the marriage contract was, in short, nothing but giving up liberty, estate, authority, and everything to the man, and the woman was indeed a mere woman ever after, that is to say, a slave.

He replied that though in some respects it was as I had said, yet I ought to consider that as an equivalent to this the man had all the care of things devolved upon him; that the weight of business lay upon his shoulders, and as he had the trust, so he had the toil of life upon him, his was the labour, his the anxiety of living; that the woman had nothing to do but to eat the fat and drink the sweet, to sit still and look round her, be waited on and made much of, be served and loved and made easy, especially if the husband acted as became him; and that, in general, the labour of the man was appointed to make the woman live quiet and unconcerned in the world; that they had the name of subjection without the thing, and if in inferior families they had the drudgery of the house and care of the provisions upon them, yet they had indeed much the easier part. For, in general, the women had only the care of managing, that is, spending what their husbands get; and that a woman had the name of subjection indeed, but that they generally commanded not the men only, but all they had, managed all for themselves, and where the man did his duty the woman's life was all ease and tranquillity, and that she had nothing to do but to be easy and to make all that were about her both easy and merry.

DANIEL DEFOE (1661–1731), Roxana, 1724

Curly Locks

Curly locks, Curly locks,
  Wilt thou be mine?
Thou shalt not wash dishes
  Nor yet feed the swine,
But sit on a cushion
  And sew a fine seam,
And feed upon strawberries,
  Sugar and cream.

Traditional

Then, for my meaning as to women's work, what *should* I mean, but scrubbing furniture, dusting walls, sweeping floors, making the beds, washing up the crockery, ditto the children, and whipping them when they want it,—mending their clothes, cooking their dinners,—and when there are cooks more than enough, helping with the farm work, or the garden, or the dairy? Is *that* plain speaking enough? Have I not fifty times over, in season and out of season, dictated and insisted and asseverated and—what stronger word else there may be—that the essentially right life for all womankind is that of the Swiss Paysanne?

JOHN RUSKIN (1819–1900), *Fors Clavigera*, 1883

It always seems to me that a hard-worked woman is better and happier for her work. It is in the nature of women to be fond of carrying weights; you may see them in omnibuses and carriages, always preferring to hold their baskets or their babies on their knees, to setting them down on the seats by their sides. A woman, whose modern dress includes I know not how many cubic feet of space, has hardly ever pockets of a sufficient size to carry small articles; for she prefers to load her hands with a bag or other weighty object. A nursery-maid, who is on the move all day, seems the happiest specimen of her sex; and, after her, a maid-of-all-work who is treated fairly by her mistress.

FRANCIS GALTON (1822–1911), *Art of Travel*, 1872

Millet wrote to Thoré concerning three of his own pictures, then exhibited at Martinet's, and which were very much admired:

In the 'Woman Going to Draw Water,' I tried to show that she was not a water-carrier, or even a servant, but a woman going to draw water for the house, for soup, for her husband and children; that she should not seem to be carrying any greater or less weight than the buckets full; that under the sort of grimace which the weight on her shoulders causes, and the closing of the eyes at the sunlight, one should see a kind of homely goodness. I have avoided (as I always do with horror) anything that can verge on the sentimental. I wanted her to do her work good-naturedly and simply, without thinking anything about it,—as if it were a part of her daily labor, the habit of her life. I wanted to show the coolness of the well, and meant that its antique form should suggest that many before her had come there to draw water.

ALFRED SENSIER (1815–77), *Jean-François Millet: Peasant and Painter*, 1881, tr. Helena de Kay

The Cossack spends most of his time in the cordon, in action, or in hunting and fishing. He hardly ever works at home. When he stays in the village it is an exception to the general rule and then he is holiday-making. All Cossacks make their own wine, and drunkenness is not so much a general tendency as a rite, the non-fulfilment of which would be considered apostasy. The Cossack looks upon a woman as an instrument for his welfare; only the unmarried girls are allowed to amuse themselves. A married woman has to work for her husband from youth to very old age: his demands on her are the Oriental ones of submission and labour. In consequence of this outlook women are strongly developed both physically and mentally, and though they are—as everywhere in the East—nominally in subjection, they possess far greater influence and importance in family-life than Western women. Their exclusion from public life and inurement to heavy male labour give the women all the more power and importance in the household. A Cossack, who before strangers considers it improper to speak affectionately or needlessly to his wife, when alone with her is involuntarily conscious of her superiority. His house and all his property, in fact the entire homestead, has been acquired and is kept together solely by her labour and care. Though firmly convinced that labour is degrading to a Cossack and is only proper for a Nogáy labourer or a woman, he is vaguely aware of the fact that all he makes use of and calls his own is the result of that toil, and that it is in the power of the woman (his mother or his wife) whom he considers his slave, to deprive him of all he possesses. Besides, the continuous performance of man's heavy work and the responsibilities entrusted to her have endowed the Grebénsk women with a peculiarly independent masculine character and have remarkably developed their physical powers, common sense, resolution, and stability. The women are in most cases stronger, more intelligent, more developed, and handsomer than the men.

> Lev Nikolaevich Tolstoy (1828–1910), 'The Cossacks', 1862, tr. Louise and Aylmer Maude, 1935

The Labouring Woman

You married men and women too, give ear unto my song,
I'll tell you of a circumstance that will not keep you long,
I heard a man the other day and he was as savage as a Turk,
He was grumbling at his wife, saying, 'She never did any work.'

So men don't grumble at your wives. For I'm sure there's none of you
Can tell the daily labour that a woman has to do.

Says he, you lazy hussy, now I really must confess
I'm weary and tired of keeping you all in your idleness,
'Indeed,' the wife made answer. 'I work as hard as you.
So I will just run through the list what a woman has to do.

At six o'clock each morning when to work you do go,
I have to rise and light the fire and the bellows for to blow,
I have to set the breakfast things and get the kettle boiled.
Besides you know I have to wash and dress the youngest child.

When breakfast it is over you know I make a rule,
To get the children ready and send them off to school.
I have to shake and make the beds and sweep the room also,
And then clean the window and empty the chamber po.

Four times a day I have to cook your wants to supply,
Breakfast, dinner, tea and supper I have to stew and fry,
I hardly get a moment's rest I have to run here and there.
Then I have to scrub the tables down likewise the stooles & chair.

I have to wash the sheets and blankets, the pinafores and frocks,
Gowns, petticoats and pillow slips, shirts, handkerchiefs & smocks,
I have to nurse the infant and wash the napkins too.
There's no man can imagine what a woman has to do.

A woman's work is never done, let her do her best and try.
From morning until bed time I'm sure you can't deny;
So men if you would happy be don't rail at women so,
But think of your mother how she put up with you.

Some men will curse their wives, and kick them it is true,
But a man without a woman whatever would he do;
So men if you would happy be don't treat your wives with shame,
For when a woman does her best she cannot be to blame.

So men don't grumble at your wife, for I'm sure there's none of you
Can tell the daily labour that a woman has to do.'

> Irish street ballad, 19th c.

Then she took home her husband to her and kept him years after as long as he
lived and had full much labour with him, for in his last days he turned childish again and lacked reason, [so] that he could not do his own easement to go
to a stool or else he would not, but as a child voided his natural digestion in his
linen clothes where he sat, by the fire or at the table, which it were, he would
spare no place. And therefore was her labour much that more in washing and
wringing.

> MARGERY KEMPE (*c*.1373–*c*.1439), *The Book of Margery Kempe, c*.1436

Lineage

My grandmothers were strong.
They followed plows and bent to toil.
They moved through fields sowing seed.
They touched earth and grain grew.
They were full of sturdiness and singing.
My grandmothers were strong.

My grandmothers are full of memories
Smelling of soap and onions and wet clay
With veins rolling roughly over quick hands
They have many clean words to say.
My grandmothers were strong.
Why am I not as they?

MARGARET WALKER (1915–), 1942

The ritual enactment of housekeeping typically links its performer back in time to the company of female ancestors . . . Just as family stories or memorabilia may be handed down within families, so may traditional ways of doing certain tasks . . . To do a task precisely as you observed or were taught by your mother or grandmother is to experience a portion of what they each once did . . . The ritual enactment of housework thus helps provide continuity from one generation of women to another. Consequently, although housework as it is generally practiced is a solitary occupation, some sense of community is provided by the method of doing, when that method reflects the performance of earlier women.

KATHRYN ALLEN RABUZZI (1938–), *The Sacred and the Feminine: Toward a Theology of Housework,* 1982

With merry lark this maiden rose,
And straight about the house she goes,
With swapping besom in her hand;
And at her girdle in a band,
A jolly bunch of keys she wore
Her petticoat fine laced before,
Her tail tucked up in trimmest guise
A napkin hanging o'er her eyes,
To keep off dust and dross of walls
That often from the windows falls.
Though she was smug, she took small ease,
For thrifty girls are glad to please;
She won the love of all the house,
And pranked it like a pretty mouse,
And sure at every word she spake,
A goodly curtsy could she make;
A stirring housewife every where,
That bent both back and bones to bear.
She never slepèd much by night,

But rose sometimes by candle-light
To card and spin, or sew her smock;
There could no sooner crow a cock,
But she was up, to sleek her clothes,
And would be sweet as any rose.
Full cleanly still the girl would go
And handsome in a house also,
As ever saw I country wench.
She sweepèd under every bench,
And shaked the cushions in their kind;
When out of order she did find
A rush, a straw or little stick
She could it mend, she was so quick
About her business every hour.
This maid was called her mistress' flower.

THOMAS CHURCHYARD (1520?–1604), from 'A Fayned Fancye', 1575

'Janet, listen to me.' 'What am I to listen to? Haven't I anything else to do?' 'And what hast thou to do that takes so long?' 'I am making the beds, setting straight the cushions on the forms, chairs, benches, tuffets and stools, and I am cleaning the solar [parlour], the chamber, the house and the kitchen.' 'Thou'rt a good girl and I praise thee.' 'Well, ma'am, I do your will not my own.' 'Tell Jehan that he is slow.' 'Where is he, ma'am?' 'How do I know? I expect he is by thy side.' 'Why do you say that, ma'am?' 'Because he is ready enough to follow thee round about the beds, when thou'rt alone.' 'Saint Mary, ma'am, what are you talking about? Upon my oath, he hates nothing so much as me.' Here follows a somewhat *inconvenant* anecdote of the rout of Jehan, whose intentions are not at all honourable, by Janet, which causes her mistress to exclaim 'O Dieu! Janet, art thou as innocent as thou makest out? Come down and bring towels and linen and coal, and take the bellows and blow up the fire, take the tongs and mend it so that it burns, boil the pots, fry some fat, lay the table and bring the long cloth, put water in the hand-basin.' 'Ma'am, where are the copper, the cauldron and our pans?' 'Art thou blind? dost thou not see them all beside the cupboard?' 'You're right, ma'am.' 'Thou hast still to wash and scour the pewter bottles, the quart and pint pots, platters, bowls and saucers, and put all this iron gear in its proper place, the roasting-iron, the flesh-hook, the trivet, the covers of the pots, and the spits, and then go for wine.' 'Where shall I go?' 'Go where you see most people and I will tell you what wine to get.'

14th-century Franco-Flemish vocabulary, as rendered by Eileen Power, *The Goodman of Paris*, 1928

When icicles hang by the wall,
  And Dick the shepherd blows his nail,
And Tom bears logs into the hall,
  And milk comes frozen home in pail,
When blood is nipp'd and ways be foul,
Then nightly sings the staring owl,
    To-whit!
To-who!—a merry note,
While greasy Joan doth keel the pot.

When all aloud the wind doth blow,
  And coughing drowns the parson's saw,
And birds sit brooding in the snow,
  And Marian's nose looks red and raw,
When roasted crabs hiss in the bowl,
Then nightly sings the staring owl,
    To-whit!
To-who!—a merry note,
While greasy Joan doth keel the pot.

WILLIAM SHAKESPEARE (1564–1616), *Love's Labour's Lost*, pr. 1598

May it please your Lordships, &c. According to an order from your Lordships bearing date the sixth of December 1633. we went into the storehouses where the new Soape is kept at Lambeth, Saint Katherines and the Strand, and from thence we tooke indifferently Sixteene small vessels out of a multitude marked by the assay Master, wee caused those Sixteene small vessels to bee brought to the Guild-Hall, and tooke one halfe firkin out of those sixteene, and sent for one other firkin of the sequestred Old Soape, commonly called Crowne Soape, and so marked; and weighing out an equall proportion or quantitie of each sort of Soape, We caused two Laundresses indifferently chosen to wash therewith, and wee did plainely perceive, that the new white Soape did with a very small difference lather much better then the Old Crowne Soape did, and that the Clothes washed with the said new Soape, (being dryed) were as white and sweeter then the Clothes washed with the Old Crowne Soape. And forasmuch as a generall complaint was made, that the new white Soape did fret the skin from their hands that washed therewith, and that it did spoile and burne the Clothes; Wee have according to your Lordships further Order received Certificates from above fourescore persons, of which number there are foure Countesses, and five Viscountesses, and divers other Ladies and Gentlewomen of great credite and quality, besides common Laundresses and others, who have a long time used the same White Soape; who generally certifie, that the new white Soape washeth whiter and sweeter then the Old Soap, and many of them certifie that they finde it goeth further, and that it neither fretteth their maids hands, nor spoileth their Linnen that hath beene washed therewith, as hath beene reported. All which Certificates wee have returned to your Lordships, according to your Order. Wee further returne to your Lordships divers Petitions complaining of the new Soape, with some two or three hundred names set thereunto, which upon examination wee finde to bee clamorous, and either to bee set to without the knowledge of the parties there named, or procured by persons who had no experience of the said Soape, and indeavoring to discover the parties there named, wee did finde out but very few of them, and those of meane condition, whereof the first was Bedrid, the second lay in Childbed, and the husbands of both disavowed the complaints, one other alleaged the complaints of her Laundresse, whose name she knew not, and disavowed her owne name in the Petition; neither did wee finde any other whose names were used, that did speake materially to the complaint, onely one Mistris Sweeting affirmed, that she found that the new Soape did wash fine Cloathes reasonable well, but of coarse clothes not so well.

A Proclamation Concerning Soape and Soape-makers, 23 Jan. 1634

Sonnet

On Mistress Nicely, a Pattern for Housekeepers

*Written after seeing Mrs Davenport in her
Character at Covent Garden*

She was a woman peerless in her station,
   With household virtues wedded to her name;
   Spotless in linen, grass-bleached in her fame,
And pure and clear-starched in her reputation;—
Thence in my Castle of Imagination
She dwells for evermore, the dainty dame,
To keep all airy draperies from shame,
And all dream-furniture in preservation;
There walketh she with keys quite silver-bright,
In perfect hose, and shoes of seemly black,
   Apron and stomacher of lily-white,
And decent order follows in her track:
   The burnished plate grows lustrous in her sight,
And polished floors and tables shine her back.

THOMAS HOOD (1797–1845), *The Plea of the Midsummer Fairies*, 1827

Mrs Davenport] In *The School of Reform, or, How to Rule a Husband* by Thomas Morton

'The Sin of Taking Too Much Pleasure in Housework'

As for matters of Huswifery, when God puts them upon you it would bee sin either to refuse them or to perform them negligently, and therefore the ignorance of them is a great shame and Danger for women that intend Marriage. But to seek these kinds of Businesses for pleasure, and to make them your delights, and to pride yourselves for your care and curiositie in them, is a great vanitie and Folly at the best, and to neglect better things and more necessarie by pretence of being imployed in these things is surely, though a common Practize, yet a peice of sinfull Hypocrisie. Doe them therefore, when God puts them upon you, and doe them carefully and well, and God shall reward you, however the things themselves bee but meane, accepting them at your hands as if they were greater matters, when they are done and undergone out of Obedience to his Command. But let your Delight bee onely in the better part.

Mary Farrar (Ferrar) (1550–1634), letter to her daughters, 1632

When bright Orion glitters in the skies
In winter nights, then early we must rise;
The weather ne'er so bad, wind, rain or snow,
Our work appointed, we must rise and go,
While you on easy beds may lie and sleep,
Till light does through your chamber-windows peep.
When to the house we come where we should go,
How to get in, alas! we do not know:
The maid quite tired with work the day before,
O'ercome with sleep; we standing at the door,
Oppressed with cold, and often call in vain,
Ere to our work we can admittance gain.
But when from wind and weather we get in,
Briskly with courage we our work begin;
Heaps of fine linen we before us view,
Whereon to lay our strength and patience too;
Cambrics and muslins, which our ladies wear,
Laces and edgings, costly, fine and rare,
Which must be washed with utmost skill and care;
With holland shirts, ruffles and fringes too,
Fashions which our forefathers never knew.
For several hours here we work and slave,
Before we can one glimpse of daylight have;
We labour hard before the morning's past,
Because we fear the time runs on too fast.
   At length bright Sol illuminates the skies,

And summons drowsy mortals to arise;
Then comes our mistress to us without fail,
And in her hand, perhaps, a mug of ale
To cheer our hearts, and also to inform
Herself what work is done that very morn;
Lays her commands upon us, that we mind
Her linen well, nor leave the dirt behind.
Not this alone, but also to take care
We don't her cambrics nor her ruffles tear;
And these most strictly does of us require,
To save her soap and sparing be of fire;
Tells us her charge is great, nay furthermore,
Her clothes are fewer than the time before.
Now we drive on, resolved our strength to try,
And what we can we do most willingly;
Until with heat and work, 'tis often known,
Not only sweat but blood runs trickling down
Our wrists and fingers: still our work demands
The constant action of our lab'ring hands.
     Now night comes on, from whence you have relief,
But that, alas! does but increase our grief.
With heavy hearts we often view the sun,
Fearing he'll set before our work is done;
For, either in the morning or at night,
We piece the summer's day with candlelight.
Though we all day with care our work attend,
Such is our fate, we know not when 'twill end.
When evening's come, you homeward take your way;
We, till our work is done, are forced to stay,
And, after all our toil and labour past,
Sixpence or eightpence pays us off at last;
For all our pains, no prospect can we see
Attend us, but old age and poverty.

MARY COLLIER (1690?–*c*.1762), *The Woman's Labour*, 1739

'Twas on a Monday morning
When I beheld my darling,
She looked so neat and charming
     In every high degree;
She looked so neat and charming O,
A-washing of her linen, O;
     Dashing away with the smoothing iron,
     She stole my heart away.

'Twas on a Tuesday morning
When I beheld my darling
A-starching of her linen, O.

'Twas on a Wednesday morning
When I beheld my darling
A-hanging out her linen, O.

'Twas on a Thursday morning
When I beheld my darling
A-ironing of her linen, O.

'Twas on a Friday morning
When I beheld my darling
A-folding of her linen, O.

'Twas on a Saturday morning
When I beheld my darling
A-airing of her linen, O.

'Twas on a Sunday morning
When I beheld my darling,

She looked so neat and charming
    In every high degree;
She looked so neat and charming O,
A-wearing of her linen, O;
    Dashing away with the smoothing iron,
    She stole my heart away.

                                        Traditional song

Washing-Day

Come, Muse, and sing the dreaded Washing-Day.
Ye who beneath the yoke of wedlock bend,
With bowed soul, full well ye ken the day
Which week, smooth sliding after week brings on
Too soon;—for to that day nor peace belongs
Nor comfort;—ere the first gray streak of dawn,
The red-armed washers come and chase repose.
Nor pleasant smile, nor quaint device of mirth,
E'er visited that day: the very cat,
From the wet kitchen scared and reeking hearth,
Visits the parlour,—an unwonted guest.
The silent breakfast-meal is soon dispatched;
Uninterrupted, save by anxious looks

Cast at the lowering sky, if sky should lower.
From that last evil, O preserve us heavens!
For should the skies pour down, adieu to all
Remains of quiet: then expect to hear
Of sad disasters,—dirt and gravel stains
Hard to efface, and loaded lines at once
Snapped short,—and linen-horse by dog thrown down,
And all the petty miseries of life.
Saints have been calm while stretched upon the rack,
And Guatimozin smiled on burning coals;
But never yet did housewife notable
Greet with a smile a rainy washing-day.
—But grant the welkin fair, require not thou
Who call'st thyself perchance the master there,
Or study swept, or nicely dusted coat,
Or usual 'tendance;—ask not, indiscreet,
Thy stockings mended, though the yawning rents
Gape wide as Erebus; nor hope to find
Some snug recess impervious; shouldst thou try
The 'customed garden walks, thine eye shall rue
The budding fragrance of thy tender shrubs,
Myrtle or rose, all crushed beneath the weight
Of coarse checked apron,—with impatient hand
Twitched off when showers impend: or crossing lines
Shall mar thy musing, as the wet cold sheet
Flaps in thy face abrupt. Woe to the friend
Whose evil stars have urged him forth to claim
On such a day the hospitable rites!
Looks, blank at best, and stinted courtesy,
Shall he receive. Vainly he feeds his hopes
With dinner of roast chicken, savoury pie,
Or tart or pudding:—pudding he nor tart
That day shall eat; nor, though the husband try,
Mending what can't be helped, to kindle mirth
From cheer deficient, shall his consort's brow
Clear up propitious:—the unlucky guest
In silence dines, and early slinks away.
I well remember, when a child, the awe
This day struck into me; for then the maids,
I scarce knew why, looked cross, and drove me from them:
Nor soft caress could I obtain, nor hope

Guatimozin] the last Aztec emperor, tortured by the Spaniards

Usual indulgencies, jelly or creams,
Relic of costly suppers, and set by
For me their petted one; or buttered toast,
When butter was forbid; or thrilling tale
Of ghost, or witch, or murder—so I went
And sheltered me beside the parlour fire:
There my dear grandmother, eldest of forms,
Tended the little ones, and watched from harm,
Anxiously fond, though oft her spectacles
With elfin cunning hid, and oft the pins
Drawn from her ravelled stocking, might have soured
One less indulgent.—
At intervals my mother's voice was heard,
Urging dispatch: briskly the work went on,
All hands employed to wash, to rinse, to wring,
To fold, and starch, and clap, and iron, and plait.
Then would I sit me down, and ponder much
Why washings were. Sometimes through hollow bowl
Of pipe amused we blew, and sent aloft
The floating bubbles; little dreaming then
To see, Mongolfier, thy silken ball
Ride buoyant through the clouds—so near approach
The sports of children and the toils of men.
Earth, air, and sky, and ocean, hath its bubbles,
And verse is one of them—this most of all.

ANNA LAETITIA BARBAULD (1743–1824), 1797

Grandma always kept her white hair in curlers until a late hour in the afternoon, when she changed into one of her spotted blue dresses. The only day on which she looked less than neat was Monday. On this terrible day she pinned a man's cloth cap to her hair, kirtled a rough skirt above her knees, put on a pair of wooden clogs and went out to the scullery to start the great weekly wash of sheets, pillow-cases, towels, table-cloths and clothes. They were first boiled in a copper, then she moved out to a wash-tub by the pump in the cobbled yard and she turned the linen round and round with the three-legged wooden 'dolly'—as tall as myself—every so often remarking for her neighbours to hear that her linen was of better quality, better washed, whiter and cleaner than the linen of any other woman in the town; that the sight of her washing hanging on the line—where my grandfather had to peg and prop it—would shame the rest of the world and the final ironing be a blow to all rivals. The house smelled of suds and ironing. Her clogs clattered in the yard. But, sharp at five o'clock she changed as usual and sat down to read the *British Weekly*.

On Tuesday, she made her first baking of the week. This consisted of different kinds of bread and I watched it rise in its pans to its full beauty before the fire; on Thursday, she made her second baking, concentrating less on bread than on pies, her Madeira cake, her seed-cake, her Eccles cakes, her puffs, her lemon-curd or jam tarts and tarts of egg 'custard', operations that lasted from seven in the morning until five in the afternoon once more. The 'bake' included, of course, the scouring of pans and saucepans which a rough village girl would help her with. At the end, the little creature showed no sign of being tired, but would 'lay' there was no better cook in the town than herself and pitied the cooking of her sisters.

On Wednesdays she turned out the house. This cleaning was ferocious. The carpets were all taken up and hung on a line, my grandfather got out a heavy stick to beat them while she stood beside him saying things like 'Eeh Willyum, I can't abide dirt.'

*

After the carpets, the linoleum was taken up and Grandma was down on her knees scrubbing the floor boards. Then came hours of dusting and polishing.

'Woman,' Granda often said on Wednesdays, standing very still and thundery and glaring at her, 'lay not up your treasure on earth where moth and dust doth corrupt.'

'Eeh Willyum,' she would reply, 'wipe your boots outside. Ah can't abide a dirty doormat. Mrs So-and-so hasn't whitened her step since Monday.'

And once more she would settle down as pretty as a picture to an evening, making another rag rug or perhaps crocheting more and more lace for her dresses, her table-centres and her doilies. By the time she was eighty years old she had stored away several thousand of these doilies, chests full of them; and of course they were superior to the work of any other woman in the country. In old age, she sent boxes of them to her younger son who had emigrated to Canada, thinking he might be 'in want'.

V. S. PRITCHETT (1900–97), *A Cab at the Door*, 1968

[In 1860 Hannah Cullwick was a general servant to Mr Jackson, an upholsterer living at 22 Carlton Villas, Kilburn, London. She kept a diary at the request of the well-to-do admirer of working women, Arthur Joseph Munby, whom she married in 1873 after a secret eighteen-year-long courtship.]

Opened the shutters & Lighted the kitchen fire. Shook my sooty things in the dusthole & emptied the soot there. Swept & dusted the rooms & the hall. Laid the hearth & got breakfast up. Clean'd 2 pairs of boots. Made the beds & emptied the slops. Clean'd & wash'd the breakfast things up. Clean'd the plate; clean'd the knives & got dinner up. Clean'd away. Clean'd the kitchen up; unpack'd a hamper. Took two chickens to Mrs Brewer's & brought the mes-

sage back. Made a tart & pick'd & gutted two ducks & roasted them. Clean'd
the steps & flags on my knees. Blackleaded the scraper in front of the house;
clean'd the street flags too on my knees. Wash'd up in the scullery. Clean'd the
pantry on my knees & scour'd the tables. Scrubbed the flags around the house
& clean'd the window sills. Got tea at 9 for the master & Mrs Warwick in my
dirt, but Ann carried it up. Clean'd the privy & passage & scullery floor on my
knees. Wash'd the dog & clean'd the sinks down. Put the supper ready for Ann
to take up, for I was too dirty & tired to go upstairs. Wash'd in a bath & to bed
without feeling any the worse for yesterday.

HANNAH CULLWICK (1833–1909), Diaries, 14 July 1860

Every year I myself make 1,825 beds (5 × 365), cook, serve and wash up after
24 × 365 meals, walk approximately 3,000 miles in the performance of my
household duties, and sweep up several tons of dirt, but I don't feel very Distinguished on that account; only unutterably bored and fed-up; and I think it
very likely that if I were a Russian woman, and able to (or maybe made to?)
swap all that in order to make a million rivets a week or turn out a distinguished, not to say honourable, number of screw nuts and bolts every day, I
should be just as bored and fed-up.

MARGARET WHEELER (1908–), letter to George Bernard Shaw, 29 Mar. 1950

I don't much like cleaning windows. Ladders wobble.
You can get mugged by buckets. Upper windows
gleam when I'm twelve feet up but look worse
than before they were washed when I've clambered down.
You can see both sides at once—the liberal dilemma—
so it's often hard to decide what's splashed the glass—
soup or a passing bird. I feel watched by
opponents of aerosol cans, by consciousness-raisers,
by looming aproned figures from childhood,
by all those sparkling television girls
who show the smiling easy way to clean.
I can be brisk, keeping my mind on the job,
or switch my hand to on and watch the sky.

any the worse] What Hannah wasn't 'any the worse for' seems to have been going up inside the
chimney, sometimes naked and sometimes in her shift, in order to sweep down soot; for at the
beginning of the day's entry she says 'shook my sooty things'. She did so to please Munby,
although at her own initial suggestion.

I can brood on reading the signs, on whether
it's healthier to reflect or concentrate.
In any case the smears show up at night
and there in the darkened glass that shape again,
that anti-heroine, that dismal clown with the
oh-so-predictable foot in a bucket of suds,
the yell from the teetering ladder, the comical angst.

MARGARET SCOTT (1934–), Housework, 1988

Many of the women get into a frame of mind in which they simply accept, in a sort of inertia, what life brings them, as though they had given up the idea, if they ever had it, of the possibility of making anything better of it.

Mrs N., for instance, a woman who had been bright and cheerful in her girlhood, with a temperament not very buoyant, perhaps, but not the reverse, became gradually swamped and crushed by the necessary and inevitable work that fell to her lot. She had had six children in rapid succession, in itself enough to affect any woman's health, especially one whose condition does not admit of her being careful after the children have been born. Two children had died, which meant that she had had the additional strain of anxiety, grief, nervous shock. Her life, she said, seemed to be one ceaseless, relentless round, in which—no doubt from her incapacity to arrange it, but that, after all, was part of her misfortune—there was absolutely no time for leisure. She got up early in the morning, soon after her husband had started for his work, did some cleaning, lighted the fire, cooked the breakfast, got the children up, washed them, fed them, sent them off to school, did the house, tidied, cooked the dinner—either for the husband to have at home or to send to him—mended and washed, got the tea ready, and no sooner had she 'got cleared away and washed up' than bedtime for the children began. Then the husband's supper and food had to be put ready for him to take that night, if he was working on the 10 p.m. shift, or next morning, if on the 6 a.m. shift. Then to bed. And the next morning the round began again, with never one moment, so she said, to rest or sit down; no change of thought, no relief. The outlook of every day to this woman and others like her may truly present itself as discouraging to one who has not a cheerful, courageous disposition to begin with.

LADY (FLORENCE) BELL (1851–1930), At the Works, 1907

Thoughts after Ruskin

Women reminded him of lilies and roses.
Me they remind rather of blood and soap,
Armed with a warm rag, assaulting noses,
Ears, neck, mouth and all the secret places.

Armed with a sharp knife, cutting up liver,
Holding hearts to bleed under a running tap,
Gutting and stuffing, pickling and preserving,
Scalding, blanching, broiling, pulverizing,
—All the terrible chemistry of their kitchens.

Their distant husbands lean across mahogany
And delicately manipulate the market,
While safe at home, the tender and the gentle
Are killing tiny mice, dead snap by the neck,
Asphyxiating flies, evicting spiders,
Scrubbing, scouring aloud, disturbing cupboards,
Committing things to dustbins, twisting, wringing,
Wrists red and knuckles white and fingers puckered,
Pulpy, tepid. Steering screaming cleaners
Around the nags of furniture, they straighten
And haul out sheets from under the incontinent
And heavy old, stoop to importunate young,
Tugging, folding, tucking, zipping, buttoning,
Spooning in food, encouraging excretion,
Mopping up vomit, stabbing cloth with needles,
Contorting wool around their knitting needles,
Creating snug and comfy on their needles.

Their huge hands! their everywhere eyes! their voices
Raised to convey across the hullabaloo,
Their massive thighs and breasts dispensing comfort,
Their bloody passages and hairy crannies,
Their wombs that pocket a man upside down!

And when all's over, off with overalls,
Quickly consulting clocks, they go upstairs,
Sit and sigh a little, brushing hair,
And somehow find, in mirrors, colours, odours,
Their essences of lilies and of roses.

ELMA MITCHELL (1919–), 1976

In domestic work, with or without the aid of servants, woman makes her home her own, finds social justification, and provides herself with an occupation, an activity, that deals usefully and satisfyingly with material objects—shining stoves, fresh, clean clothes, bright copper, polished furniture—but provides no escape from immanence and little affirmation of individuality. Such work has a negative basis: cleaning is getting rid of dirt, tidying up is eliminating disorder. And under impoverished conditions no satisfaction is possible; the hovel remains a hovel in spite of woman's sweat and tears: 'nothing in the world can make it pretty'. Legions of women have only this endless struggle without victory over the dirt. And for even the most privileged the victory is never final.

Few tasks are more like the torture of Sisyphus than housework, with its endless repetition: the clean becomes soiled, the soiled is made clean, over and over, day after day. The housewife wears herself out marking time: she makes nothing, simply perpetuates the present. She never senses conquest of a positive Good, but rather indefinite struggle against negative Evil. A young pupil writes in her essay: 'I shall never have house-cleaning day'; she thinks of the future as constant progress towards some unknown summit; but one day, as her mother washes the dishes, it comes over her that both of them will be bound to such rites until death. Eating, sleeping, cleaning—the years no longer rise up towards heaven, they lie spread out ahead, grey and identical. The battle against dust and dirt is never won . . .

But it is a sad fate to be required without respite to repel an enemy instead of working towards positive ends, and very often the housekeeper submits to it in a kind of madness that may verge on perversion, a kind of sado-masochism. The maniac housekeeper wages her furious war against dirt, blaming life itself for the rubbish all living growth entails. When any living being enters her house, her eye gleams with a wicked light: 'Wipe your feet, don't tear the place apart, leave that alone!' She wishes those of her household would hardly breathe; everything means more thankless work for her. Severe, preoccupied, always on the watch, she loses *joie de vivre*, she becomes overprudent and avaricious. She shuts out the sunlight, for along with that come insects, germs and dust, and besides, the sun ruins silk hangings and fades upholstery; she scatters naphthalene, which scents the air. She becomes bitter and disagreeable and hostile to all that lives; the end is sometimes murder.

> SIMONE DE BEAUVOIR (1908–86), *The Second Sex*, 1949, tr. H. M. Parshley, 1953

I often feel at the end of the day that all my efforts have been of no avail. I remember all the polishing and cleaning, washing and ironing, that will have to be done all over again, and like many other housewives I wish that my life could be a bit more exciting sometimes. But when the evening fire glows, when the house becomes a home, then it seems to me that this is perhaps the path to true happiness.

> ANON. HOUSEWIFE in Woodford, London, c.1957–9, quoted in Peter Willmott and Michael Young, *Family and Class in a London Suburb*, 1965

Washing-up

(for Hilda Cotterill)

Our mother, hater of parties and occasions,
Made much of the washing-up after. It became an exorcising,
A celebration. Outsiders gone, the kitchen choked
With leftovers, disordered courses, mucky fiddly forks,
The alarming best glasses. She worked a system,
A competition. First we stacked the mess
In regular order: glasses, cutlery, plates
(Each in their kind); saucepans and base things last.

Then we began. She washed, I wiped; to the first to finish,
The prize of *putting-away.* A wiper-up
Should finish first. I never did, for mother
Slaved in a bacchic frenzy, scattering Vim
And purity, splashing new libations
Of suds and scalding water, piling with exquisite fingers
(Unringed for the occasion) the china in ranks,
Knives all together. I was made slow by her passion.

And as we worked she sang. My doughty mother—
Who lived through wars and took life seriously,
Never read fiction, seldom laughed at jokes—
My sorcerer-mother sang grand opera,
Parodied makeshift words and proper music.
Softly awoke her heart, without too much bathos,
But *Samso-o-o-n* got her going, and she never
Took *Trovatore* seriously: *Ah, I have sighed to rest me*
Deep in the quiet grave she'd serenade
The carving-knife, from that a short step
To saucepans and the Jewel Song: *Marguerita, this is not I.*
High-born maiden I must be, high-born maiden . . .
Her mezzo skidding along coloratura country,
My laughter rattling the stacks. The men
Came down to hear. And as she nipped
Between cupboards (having won), she added the footwork
Of humbler songs: *Home James, and don't spare*
The horses. This night has been ruin for me. Home James,
And don't spare the horses. I'm ruined as ruined can be
With a pert little mime. She liked these ruined maids,
Or about to be. *No! No! A thousand times no!*
You cannot buy my caress. No! No! A thousand times no!
I'd rather die than say yes. But her feet denied it.

Lastly, when all was done, her party-piece
True to the self she seldom let us see:
I feel so silly when the moon comes out . . .
Then, everything purged and placed, we'd go to bed.

O I remember my magical mother dancing
And singing after the party, under the airer
With the used tea towels hanging up to dry.

U. A. FANTHORPE (1929–   ), 1987

I can't walk from one end of my kitchen to the other without querying my motives or comparing myself unfavourably with two warring tribes of ideal types. If I leave the house without clearing up the breakfast dishes, I'm a bad housekeeper. If I do clear them, I'm a pushover, because really I ought to have asked Frank. If he clears them without my asking, then I'm luckier, at least according to the latest statistics, than 97 per cent of women in this country. If I forget to thank him, I'm a shrew. If I do thank him, I'm setting up the expectation that household chores, if he does them, are favours, and not duties, and so I become my own worst enemy.

MAUREEN FREELY (1952–   ), *What about Us? An Open Letter to the Mothers Feminism Forgot*, 1995

HOUSEWORK BY MEN

So long as household tasks were regarded as women's business, the sight of men attempting to make themselves useful in the home seemed irresistibly comic.

For Men in Aprons

Of the disappointingly few letters I have received in response to my offer, made a month ago in this paper, to help you with your household problems, perhaps the most interesting is one which deals with the vexed question of getting cold porridge out of the crevices of saucepans. But before I answer this point in detail, may I permit myself the luxury of a general reflection on saucepans?

In the old pre-war days, it will be remembered, when in some sudden emergency we offered our assistance at the sink, it was always clearly understood that we men did not concern ourselves with saucepans—nor indeed with any cooking utensil likely to have dried foodstuffs adhering tenaciously to its sides and bottom. We did the plates and cutlery and we held the glasses momentarily under the tap. But the rest was women's work; somebody would do it in the morning. Those spacious days are over. Nothing, literally nothing, is nowadays considered too revolting for a man to touch. When I say that men have been known to tackle those brown earthenware jars used for Lancashire hot-pot, from the rims of which (for this is not the place to speak of their unimaginable interiors) the jagged ridges of caked and blackened gravy must be chipped off with a chisel, when I mention this simple fact returning husbands will, I think, gain some notion of the pass to which we have come.

Very well, then. Now to my correspondent, whose name I decipher as Brandsop or (more improbably) Brushoff. He writes:

'I can get most of the porridge out all right with the scratcher, but it won't do the corners or the part where the handle joins the top of the saucepan. Poking about with a skewer is fatiguing work and makes me late with the fireplaces, nor does it really do the job properly. I am at my wits' end and would give up porridge altogether, if we could get any eggs, bacon, kidneys or fish.'

Well, this is a problem that has puzzled most of us in our time. Nor is it to be solved by any such drastic expedient as dropping porridge off the menu, because (apart from any other considerations) exactly the same difficulty crops up with boiled milk. So let's face it boldly, shall we?

When Mr Brandsop speaks of the 'scratcher' he is referring undoubtedly to that bundle of twisted wire which is usually kept in a soap-dish on the draining-board or under the plate-rack, and he is absolutely right to use it for the main interior surfaces of the pan. Used fearlessly, with a brisk rotatory movement, the scratcher will clear up the most stubborn situation in no time. But it is not designed to penetrate nooks and crannies. For such pockets of resistance as the corners of a saucepan and (as Mr Brandsop well says) the junction of the handle with the main framework, a special instrument has been devised and is to be found in any well-appointed scullery. If Mr Brandsop will look round he may find a piece of apparatus resembling a bundle of twigs bound about the middle with a metal clasp. It is often balanced behind the kitchen taps, where these are close enough together to afford a lodgment, and may have escaped his observation. The correct name for this thing is not known to me; it is referred to in this house as the 'scritcher,' and the name, which conveys with some fidelity the greater precision and delicacy with which it scratches, will serve as well as another. Now, having possessed yourself of scratcher *and* scritcher, here is the way to go to work. First scour out with the scratcher, rinse and pour away. Most of the porridge will now be embedded in the scratcher, but that need not concern you. Bad as things are, the time has not yet come when we men are expected to clean the scratcher. Next take the scritcher and scritch lightly but firmly in all the crevices. Rinse again. Finish by whisking round the rim of the saucepan in such a way that half the bristles of the scritcher are inside and half out. Give it a final rinse, mop out and hang up or hurl under the dresser according to local custom . . .

I have spent so long over this very important problem of saucepans that I have only time now to deal very briefly with a point raised by Mr Joseph Twill, of Mole's End, Gloucestershire. He wants to know whether it is possible to stop milk boiling over, and suggests that a really deep saucepan might conceivably be a solution.

I propose to answer Mr Twill's question by enunciating a number of rules for milk-boilers. They are based on common sense and a wide experience of mopping up milk both on gas and electric stoves.

1. *Never* boil milk. Heat it till turgid and remove.

2. It is impossible to combine the heating of milk with any other pursuit whatsoever. (The same rule applies to the toasting of bread under a grill. Thus to attempt to heat milk and toast bread at the same time—a very common fault—is the height of insanity. The only thing to be said for it is that the milk in boiling over puts the toast out.)

3. An unwatched pot boils *immediately*.

4. Half a pint of milk brought to a temperature of 100° Centigrade rises to a height greater than the walls of the saucepan, *irrespective of the dimensions of the saucepan*. To take an extreme case, if a jug of milk were poured into the crater of Vesuvius, Pompeii would inevitably be engulfed a second time.

5. The speed at which boiling milk rises from the bottom of the pan to any point beyond the top is greater than the speed at which the human brain and hand can combine to snatch the confounded thing off.

Follow these rules, Mr Twill, and you will be all right. But keep a dish-cloth handy.

H. F. ELLIS (1907–   ), *Punch*, 13 Feb. 1946

You never saw such a commotion up and down a house, in all your life, as when my Uncle Podger undertook to do a job. A picture would have come home from the frame-maker's, and be standing in the dining-room, waiting to be put up; and Aunt Podger would ask what was to be done with it, and Uncle Podger would say:

'Oh, you leave that to *me*. Don't you, any of you, worry yourselves about that. *I'll* do all that.'

And then he would take off his coat, and begin.

He would send the girl out for sixpen'orth of nails, and then one of the boys after her to tell her what size to get; and, from that, he would gradually work down, and start the whole house.

'Now you go and get me my hammer, Will,' he would shout; 'and you bring me the rule, Tom; and I shall want the step-ladder, and I had better have a kitchen-chair, too; and, Jim! you run round to Mr. Goggles, and tell him, "Pa's kind regards, and hopes his leg's better; and will he lend him his spirit-level?" And don't you go, Maria, because I shall want somebody to hold me the light; and when the girl comes back, she must go out again for a bit of picture-cord; and Tom!—where's Tom?—Tom, you come here; I shall want you to hand me up the picture.'

And then he would lift up the picture, and drop it, and it would come out of the frame, and he would try to save the glass, and cut himself; and then he would spring round the room, looking for his handkerchief. He could not find his handkerchief, because it was in the pocket of the coat he had taken off, and he did not know where he had put the coat, and all the house had to leave off looking for his tools, and start looking for his coat; while he would dance round and hinder them.

'Doesn't anybody in the whole house know where my coat is? I never came across such a set in all my life—upon my word I didn't. Six of you!—and you can't find a coat that I put down not five minutes ago! Well, of all the——'

Then he'd get up, and find that he had been sitting on it, and would call out:

'Oh, you can give it up! I've found it myself now. Might just as well ask the cat to find anything as expect you people to find it.'

And, when half an hour had been spent in tying up his finger, and a new glass had been got, and the tools, and the ladder, and the chair, and the candle had been brought, he would have another go, the whole family, including the girl and the charwoman, standing round in a semi-circle, ready to help. Two people would have to hold the chair, and a third would help him up on it, and hold him there, and a fourth would hand him a nail, and a fifth would pass him up the hammer, and he would take hold of the nail, and drop it.

'There!' he would say, in an injured tone, 'now the nail's gone.'

And we would all have to go down on our knees and grovel for it, while he would stand on the chair, and grunt, and want to know if he was to be kept there all the evening.

The nail would be found at last, but by that time he would have lost the hammer.

'Where's the hammer? What did I do with the hammer? Great heavens! Seven of you, gaping round there, and you don't know what I did with the hammer?'

We would find the hammer for him, and then he would have lost sight of the mark he had made on the wall, where the nail was to go in, and each of us had to get up on the chair, beside him, and see if we could find it; and we would each discover it in a different place, and he would call us all fools, one after another, and tell us to get down. And he would take the rule, and re-measure, and find that he wanted half thirty-one and three-eighths inches from the corner, and would try to do it in his head, and go mad.

And we would all try to do it in our heads, and all arrive at different results, and sneer at one another. And in the general row, the original number would be forgotten, and Uncle Podger would have to measure it again.

He would use a bit of string this time, and at the critical moment, when the old fool was leaning over the chair at an angle of forty-five, and trying to reach a point three inches beyond what was possible for him to reach, the string would slip, and down he would slide on to the piano, a really fine musical effect being produced by the suddenness with which his head and body struck all the notes at the same time.

And Aunt Maria would say that she would not allow the children to stand round and hear such language.

At last, Uncle Podger would get the spot fixed again, and put the point of the nail on it with his left hand, and take the hammer in his right hand. And, with the first blow, he would smash his thumb, and drop the hammer, with a yell, on somebody's toes.

Aunt Maria would mildly observe that, next time Uncle Podger was going to hammer a nail into the wall, she hoped he'd let her know in time, so that she could make arrangements to go and spend a week with her mother while it was being done.

'Oh! you women, you make such a fuss over everything,' Uncle Podger would reply, picking himself up. 'Why, I *like* doing a little job of this sort.'

And then he would have another try, and, at the second blow, the nail would go clean through the plaster, and half the hammer after it, and Uncle Podger be precipitated against the wall with force nearly sufficient to flatten his nose.

Then we had to find the rule and the string again, and a new hole was made; and, about midnight, the picture would be up—very crooked and insecure, the wall for yards round looking as if it had been smoothed down with a rake, and everybody dead beat and wretched—except Uncle Podger.

'There you are,' he would say, stepping heavily off the chair on to the charwoman's corns, and surveying the mess he had made with evident pride. 'Why, some people would have had a man in to do a little thing like that!'

JEROME K. JEROME (1859–1927), *Three Men in a Boat*, 1889

CHILD WORKERS

Only in modern times has it become normal to segregate children from the world of work by keeping them in school until their late teens or in college until their twenties. Before the late nineteenth century most children in Britain began work as soon as they were physically capable of doing so. Only a minority of parents could afford full-time education for their offspring. Work was thus a normal experience for most children. In many parts of the world it still is.

So homewards and took up a boy that had a lanthorn, that was picking up of rags, and got him to light me home. And had great discourse with him how he could get sometimes three or four bushels of rags in a day, and gat 3d a bushel for them. And many other discourses, what and how many ways there are for poor children to get their livings honestly.

SAMUEL PEPYS (1633–1703), *Diary*, 25 Mar. 1661

I have sufficiently shew'd already, why going to School was Idleness if compar'd to Working, and exploded this sort of Education in the Children of the Poor, because it Incapacitates them ever after for downright Labour, which is their proper Province, and in every Civil Society a Portion they ought not to repine or grumble at, if exacted from them with Discretion and Humanity.

BERNARD DE MANDEVILLE (1670–1733), *The Fable of the Bees*, 1714–23

. . . as I pass'd this part of the country in the year 1723, the manufacturers assured me, that there was not in all the eastern and middle part of Norfolk, any hand, unemploy'd, if they would work; and that the very children after four or five years of age, could every one earn their own bread.

DANIEL DEFOE (1660–1731), *Tour through the Whole Island of Great Britain*, 1724–6

The Chimney-Sweeper's Complaint

A chimney-sweeper's boy am I;
    Pity my wretched fate!
Ah, turn your eyes; 'twould draw a tear,
    Knew you my helpless state.

Far from my home, no parents I
    Am ever doomed to see;
My master, should I sue to him,
    He'd flog the skin from me.

Ah, dearest madam, dearest sir,
    Have pity on my youth;
Though black, and covered o'er with rags,
    I tell you naught but truth.

My feeble limbs, benumbed with cold,
    Totter beneath the sack,
Which ere the morning dawn appears
    Is loaded on my back.

My legs you see are burnt and bruised,
    My feet are galled by stones,
My flesh for lack of food is gone,
    I'm little else but bones.

Yet still my master makes me work,
    Nor spares me day or night;
His 'prentice boy he says I am,
    And he will have his right.

'Up to the highest top,' he cries,
    "There call out *chimney-sweep!*'
With panting heart and weeping eyes,
    Trembling I upwards creep.

But stop! no more—I see him come;
    Kind sir, remember me!
Oh, could I hide me under ground,
    How thankful should I be!

MARY ALCOCK (née Cumberland) (*c.*1742–98), 1799

The Emperour of Russia has made an attempt to improve the condition of the serfs throughout his vast dominions but the proposal has been met with such ill will by his barbarous nobility that he will hardly be able yet to carry out his benevolent plans.

    We need hardly waste our sensibility on the bondage of these soil tillers nor on the Slave miseries so feelingly depicted so long when this last report of the parliamentary commissioners on the subject of juvenile labour in our own vaunted country be reflected on. In the collieries of the North of England and East of Scotland and in Wales children from three years old are employed naked nearly to drag or push trucks of coal through passages in which they cannot stand half filled with mire, totally dark, where they labour till exhausted day after day, year after year, without instruction or change, badly fed and harshly treated—the details are actually horrible and have haunted me painfully this whole day. Parents carry their infants into these places of torture partly from the brutality resulting from their own cheerless lives, partly from the hope of gain, as their wages are encreased according to the number of victims they can supply for this unholy traffick. My God, what a race of pigmys both in person and intellect must be the result of such a child-hood, such a youth, deformed limbs, stunted size, an idiot vacant stare har-rowed the feelings of the Commissioners; reading this and recollecting the happy slaves in the Mauritius, lightly tasked, well fed, well dressed and singing merrily without a thought of care, I cannot but feel that people are often deceived by sounds—the name of slavery—the name of liberty—have ideas annexed to them very very different from the reality. One can't advocate the system of one human being daring to appropriate to himself absolutely the possession of another, his equal in the eye of God. Yet the slave owner is seldom as depraved in the management of his gangs of purchased workmen as are the owners of our British Collieries in the case of their free labourers; nor did we ever hear of the lash of the slave driver being more cruelly applied than by the overseers of these bands of wretched children. It has turned me quite sick, it is dreadful.

ELIZABETH GRANT OF ROTHIEMURCHUS (1797–1885), *The Highland Lady in Ireland: Journals 1840–50*, 11 May 1842, 1991 edn.

The Foddering Boy

The foddering boy along the crumping snows
With straw band belted legs & folded arm
Hastens & on the blast that keenly blows
Oft turns for breath & beats his fingers warm
& shakes the lodging snows from off his cloaths
Buttoning his doublet closer from the storm
& slouching his brown beaver oer his nose
Then faces it agen—& seeks the stack
Within its circling fence—were hungry lows
Expecting cattle making many a track
About the snows—impatient for the sound
When in hugh fork fulls trailing at his back
He litters the sweet hay about the ground
& brawls to call the staring cattle round

JOHN CLARE (1793–1864), 1821–2

Nineteen miles to the Isle of Wight,
Shall I get there by candle light?
Yes, if your fingers go lissom and light,
You'll get there by candle light.

*

Nineteen long lines hanging over my door,
The faster I work it'll shorten my score,
But if I do play, it'll stick to a stay,

So ho! little fingers, and twink it away.
for after tomorrow comes my wedding day.

Verses sung by child workers in early-19th-century Buckinghamshire
and Northamptonshire

*[Written during the parliamentary debates on the author's Bill for the regulation
of child labour in mills and factories, 1832.]*

The Factory Girl's Last Day

'Twas on a winter's morning,
   The weather wet and wild,
Three hours before the dawning
   The father roused his child;
Her daily morsel bringing,
   The darksome room he paced,
And cried, 'The bell is ringing,
   My hapless darling, haste!'

'Father, I'm up, but weary,
   I scarce can reach the door,
And long the way and dreary,—
   O carry me once more!
To help us we've no mother;
   And you have no employ;
They killed my little brother,—
   Like him I'll work and die!'

Her wasted form seemed nothing,—
   The load was at his heart;
The sufferer he kept soothing
   Till at the mill they part.

The overlooker met her,
   As to her frame she crept,
And with his thong he beat her,
   And cursed her as she wept.

Alas! what hours of horror
   Made up her latest day;
In toil, and pain, and sorrow,
   They slowly passed away:
It seemed, as she grew weaker,
   The threads the oftener broke,

The rapid wheels ran quicker,
    And heavier fell the stroke.

The sun had long descended,
    But night brought no repose;
Her day began and ended
    As cruel tyrants chose.
At length a little neighbour
    Her halfpenny she paid
To take her last hour's labour,
    While by her frame she laid.

At last, the engine ceasing,
    The captives homeward rushed;
She thought her strength increasing—
    'Twas hope her spirits flushed:
She left but often tarried,
    She fell and rose no more,
Till, by her comrades carried,
    She reached her father's door.

All night, with tortured feeling,
    He watched his speechless child;
While, close beside her kneeling,
    She knew him not, nor smiled.
Again the factory's ringing
    Her last perceptions tried;
When, from her straw-bed springing,
    ''Tis time!' she shrieked, and died!

That night a chariot passed her,
    While on the ground she lay;
The daughters of her master
    An evening visit pay:
Their tender hearts were sighing
    As negro wrongs were told,—
While the white slave lay dying,
    Who earned their father's gold!

                    MICHAEL THOMAS SADLER (1780–1835)

V. WORKING THE LAND AND SEA

For the bulk of human history most work has been agricultural work. Only during the last century or so has it been possible in the advanced economies of the West to leave the business of food production to a small minority of the population.

FARM LABOURERS

The Labourer

There he goes, tacking against the fields'
Uneasy tides. What have the centuries done
To change him? The same garments, frayed with light
Or seamed with rain, cling to the wind-scoured bones
And shame him in the eyes of the spruce birds.
Once it was ignorance, then need, but now
Habit that drapes him on a bush of cloud
For life to mock at, while the noisy surf
Of people dins far off at the world's rim.
He has been here since life began, a vague
Movement among the roots of the young grass.
Bend down and peer beneath the twigs of hair,
And look into the hard eyes, flecked with care;
What do you see? Notice the twitching hands,
Veined like a leaf, and tough bark of the limbs,
Wrinkled and gnarled, and tell me what you think.
A wild tree still, whose seasons are not yours,
The slow heart beating to the hidden pulse
Of the strong sap, the feet firm in the soil?
No, no, a man like you, but blind with tears
Of sweat to the bright star that draws you on.

R. S. THOMAS (1913–), 1955

We meet with certain wild animals, male and female, spread over the country. They are black and tann'd, united to the earth, which they are always digging and turning up and down with an unweary'd resolution. They have something like an articulate voice; when they stand on their feet they discover a manlike face, and indeed are men; at night they retire into their burries, where they live on black bread, water and raisins. They spare other men the trouble of sowing, labouring, and reaping for their maintenance, and deserve, one would think, that they should not want the bread they themselves sow.

JEAN DE LA BRUYÈRE (1645–96), *The Characters,* 1688, 'made English by several hands', 1699

Four in the Morning

At four this day of June I rise:
The dawn-light strengthens steadily;
Earth is a cerule mystery,
As if not far from Paradise
     At four o'clock,

Or else near the Great Nebula,
Or where the Pleiads blink and smile:
(For though we see with eyes of guile
the grisly grin of things by day,
     At four o'clock

They show their best.) . . . In this vale's space
I am up the first, I think. Yet, no,
A whistling? and the to-and-fro
Wheezed whettings of a scythe apace
     At four o'clock? . . .

—Though pleasure spurred, I rose with irk:
Here is one at compulsion's whip
Taking his life's stern stewardship
With blithe uncare, and hard at work
     At four o'clock!

THOMAS HARDY (1840–1928), 1925

'I did oftens go out to work at four in the mornin', as a boy,' Luke Hulle remarked one day, when haymaking had begun and he was busy mowing, 'and plenty o' times did not leave stable till seven o' evenings. But we was happy, and didn't mind nothin'. There wasn't the pride in them days as is now; and us meant workin'. There was a sight more o' friendliness then as well—folks did seem more all alike, and not one above another; and us was content. But what be it now? Why now 'tis—if one o' the youngsters hasn't got three or four suits and three or four pairs o' boots, they bain't satisfied. And what's a-goin' to satisfy such as they?

'I tell yer as they looks upon comin' on the land as a punishment; and what's more, there be many o' the fathers o' the youngest on 'em do look on it in the same fashion. Why, here's my neighbour, Harry Clegg, a-talking of his varmint of a son, says to me this way: "Well, if he don't turn over a new leaf soon, he'll go straight on the farm, that's what he'll do—straight on the farm!" "For why not?" says I; "'tain't no disgrace in it, be ther'?" Oi look again at such sayin' as this. There's Bill Brooks a-talkin' of his son 'listin', and says: "None of our family hasn't come to that *yet*, and they bain't a-goin' to now—the very idea!" I lets him have it a bit, arter that, and Harry Clegg the same; and now they knows my leanings.

'But, lor' bless yer, some o' the mothers ain't no better, and aids and abets such foolishness in 'em, if, for the matter of that, they ain't afear'd on 'em. You knows as well as me as a 'ooman can lead a man a'most where she do like. Can't a-been about the world a lot wi'out havin' seen summut o' that. Ay; seen scores led away and brought to ruin wi' it, I have. Wull, it be the same here. The lads about knows as no girl 'll look at 'em while they bides on a farm: don't lead to nothin', they says: do lead, 'wever, to nothin' but hard work, in a cottage stuck away alone, and no variety.

'And there's plenty comes along and tells 'em the same, and talks o' the callin' o' the land as the lowest o' the low. So the young folks forgets the old as you might say, and all as was in 'em; dresses theirselves up, gets off to the towns, and comes back wi' town manners and town gait; but the main of it be all sham, just as it be all pride at bottom.'

Ernest Gambier-Parry (1853–1936), *The Spirit of the Old Folk*, 1913

The Waggoner

The old waggon drudges through the miry lane
    By the skulking pond where the pollards frown,
Notched, dumb, surly images of pain;
    On a dulled earth the night droops down.

Wincing to slow and wistful airs
    The leaves on the shrubbed oaks know their hour,
And the unknown wandering spoiler bares
    The thorned black hedge of a mournful shower.

Small bodies fluster in the dead brown wrack
　　As the stumbling shaft-horse jingles past,
And the waggoner flicks his whip a crack:
　　The odd light flares on shadows vast

Over the lodges and oasts and byres
　　Of the darkened farm; the moment hangs wan
As though nature flagged and all desires.
　　But in the dim court the ghost is gone

From the hug-secret yew to the penthouse wall,
　　And stooping there seems to listen to
The waggoner leading the gray to stall,
　　As centuries past itself would do.

EDMUND BLUNDEN (1896–1974), 1920

Every autumn, if possible, or in the earliest spring, there was one journeying at least to river-sides for rushes, in anticipation of the spring task of 'hop-tying.' The rushes were brought home (I remember stumbling through them with wonder the first time I entered Bettesworth's cottage), and strewn on the floor, that they might be trodden into lissomness; and there they remained for weeks, as it were promising May. For in May, when the hops are 'poled' and the young growth is beginning its swift ascension, women must to the plantations with their rushes, and carefully tie the new hop shoots each to its pole. It is a weary, cramping task, followed day after day, and ill-paid on piece-work terms, yet not without compensations fluttering down upon the women with the spring sunshine or shower.

The hops once tied, there would be no further room for Mrs Bettesworth in the gardens until September, when the picking commenced; but meanwhile other field-work would be plentiful enough. With June comes in the airy upland hay-making; that of the deep water-meadows follows it close, and before the hay is well got in there is the corn harvest beginning, in which women's work was not yet superfluous when Lucy Bettesworth was younger. And then autumn brought its own less thrilling tasks, that left the fields desolate and naked to the oncoming of winter, beginning with the potato harvest in weather still sun-softened, ending with the swede-trimming on bleak and frozen hillsides amongst the folded sheep. It would be erroneous to suppose that Mrs Bettesworth's life at all these varied toils could have been enviable— it was a life of crushing fatigue, of stinging hardship; but to think it only hardship and fatigue would be almost equally wrong. For it is not credible that she could live thirty years in the sunlight without caring for it or without appetite for the tonic of air. Be that as it may, for nearly that length of time, not counting what preceded her marriage, she was wholly of the fields. 'Twenty-seven year', says Bettesworth, 'she went with me down into Sussex. The farmer used to ask after her. "'Ave ye brought the little dark woman?" he used to say.' That she could undertake this annual pilgrimage is evidence of her detachment from things domestic. She had no family, and therefore nothing to keep her at home. Through those dim twenty-seven years at least, her history, whatever it may have been, must have unfolded chiefly in the open air.

As a worker 'the little dark woman' maintained an efficiency still remembered with respect by her husband—a competent judge. Throughout middle-life, he boasts, she was 'as strong as a little donkcy. See her out with the shcep-fold, liftin' they great hurdles, and then go out and cut up a bushel o' swedes, and out with it for 'em. Strong as any *man*! That was out here on So-and-So's farm. No mistake, she 'ave worked 'ard.' She has also endured bravely. 'I've knowed my wife', remarked her husband once, 'since we bin married, come 'ome with daglets of ice's big 's yer thumb hangin' from her skirts. Yes, daglets of ice.' (*Can't you hear?* is implied in the old man's impatient repetition.) 'That was trimmin' swedes, with men goin' in front of her to sweep the snow away from 'em. Well, *some* body got to do it; if they didn't, th' sheep 'd starve. So there she bin, with the men sweepin' and she follerin' of 'em, purpose for to keep the sheep goin'. That was in these fields up here'; and Bettesworth points now to Mr What's-his-name's farm. For the whole neighbourhood has been the scene of old Lucy's labours.

GEORGE BOURNE (George Sturt) (1863–1927), *Lucy Bettesworth*, 1913

A few women still did field work, not with the men, or even in the same field as a rule, but at their own special tasks, weeding and hoeing, picking up stones, and topping and tailing turnips and mangel; or, in wet weather, mending sacks in a barn. Formerly, it was said, there had been a large gang of field women, lawless, slatternly creatures, some of whom had thought nothing of having four or five children out of wedlock. Their day was over; but the reputation they had left behind them had given most country-women a distaste for 'goin' afield'. In the 'eighties about half a dozen of the hamlet women did field work, most of them being respectable middle-aged women who, having got their families off hand, had spare time, a liking for an open-air life, and a longing for a few shillings a week they could call their own.

Their hours, arranged that they might do their housework before they left home in the morning and cook their husband's meal after they returned, were from ten to four, with an hour off for dinner. Their wage was four shillings a week. They worked in sunbonnets, hobnailed boots and men's coats, with coarse aprons of sacking enveloping the lower part of their bodies. One, a Mrs Spicer, was a pioneer in the wearing of trousers; she sported a pair of her husband's corduroys. The others compromised with ends of old trouser legs worn as gaiters. Strong, healthy, weather-beaten, hard as nails, they worked

through all but the very worst weathers and declared they would go 'stark,
staring mad' if they had to be shut up in a house all day.

FLORA THOMPSON (1876–1947), *Lark Rise to Candleford*, 1945

SHEPHERDS AND MILKMAIDS

Dorastus, repaying her curtesie with a smiling countenance, began to parlie
with her on this manner.

Faire maide (quoth he) either your want is great, or a shepheards life very
sweete, that your delight is in such country labors. I can not conceive what
pleasure you should take, unlesse you meane to imitate the nymphes, being
yourself so like a Nymph. To put me out of this doubt, shew me what is to be
commended in a shepherdes life, and what pleasures you have to countervaile
these drudging laboures. *Fawnia* with blushing face made him this ready
aunswere.

Sir, what richer state then content, or what sweeter life then quiet? we shepheards are not borne to honor, nor bcholding unto beautie: the lesse care we
have to fcare fame or fortune: we count our attire brave inough if warme
inough, and our foode dainty, if to suffice nature: our greatest enemie is the
wolfe: our onely care in safe keeping our flock: in stead of courtlie ditties we
spend the daies with cuntry songs: our amorous conceites are homely
thoughtes: delighting as much to talke of Pan and his cuntrey prankes, as
Ladies to tell of *Venus* and her wanton toyes. Our toyle is in shifting the
fouldes, and looking to the Lambes, easie laboures: oft singing and telling tales,
homely pleasures: our greatest welth not to covet, our honor not to climbe,
our quiet not to care. Enuie looketh not so lowe as shepheards: Shepheards
gaze not so high as ambition: we are rich in that we are poore with content,
and proud onely in this, that we have no cause to be proud.

ROBERT GREENE (1558–92), *Pandosto: The Triumph of Time*, 1588

O God! methinks it were a happy life,
To be no better than a homely swain;
To sit upon a hill, as I do now,
To carve out dials quaintly, point by point,
Thereby to see the minutes how they run,
How many make the hour full complete;
How many hours bring about the day;

How many days will finish up the year;
How many years a mortal man may live.
When this is known, then to divide the times:
So many hours must I tend my flock;
So many hours must I take my rest;
So many hours must I contemplate;
So many hours must I sport myself;
So many days my ewes have been with young;
So many weeks ere the poor fools will ean;
So many years ere I shall shear the fleece:

So minutes, hours, days, months and years,
Pass'd over to the end they were created,
Would bring white hairs unto a quiet grave.
Ah, what a life were this! how sweet! how lovely!
Gives not the hawthorn-bush a sweeter shade
To shepherds looking on their silly sheep,
Than doth a rich embroider'd canopy
To kings that fear their subjects' treachery?

WILLIAM SHAKESPEARE (1564–1616), *King Henry VI, Part 3*, pr. 1594

'Washing Sheep'

Or rushing thence, in one diffusive Band,
They drive the troubled Flocks, by many a Dog
Compell'd, to where the mazy-running Brook
Forms a deep Pool: This Bank abrupt and high,
And That fair-spreading in a pebbled Shore.
Urg'd to the giddy Brink, much is the Toil,
The Clamour much of Men, and Boys, and Dogs,
Ere the soft fearful People to the Flood
Commit their woolly Sides. And oft the Swain,
On some impatient seizing, hurls them in:
Embolden'd then, nor hesitating more,
Fast, fast, they plunge amid the flashing Wave,
And panting labour to the farther Shore.
Repeated This, till deep the well-wash'd Fleece
Has drunk the Flood, and from his lively Haunt
The Trout is banish'd by the sordid Stream;

ean] lamb

Heavy, and dripping, to the breezy Brow
Slow-move the harmless Race: where, as they spread
Their swelling Treasures to the sunny Ray,
Inly disturb'd, and wondering what this wild
Outrageous Tumult means, their loud Complaints
The Country fill; and, toss'd from Rock to Rock,
Incessant Bleatings run around the Hills.

JAMES THOMSON (1700–48), 'Summer', *The Seasons*, 1726–30

To sing of shepherds is an easy task;
The happy youth assumes the common strain,
A nymph his mistress and himself a swain;
With no sad scenes he clouds his tuneful prayer,
But all, to look like her, is painted fair.
I grant indeed that fields and flocks have charms,
For him that gazes or for him that farms;
But when amid such pleasing scenes I trace
The poor laborious natives of the place,
And see the mid-day sun, with fervid ray,
On their bare heads and dewy temples play;
While some, with feebler hands and fainter hearts,
Deplore their fortune, yet sustain their parts,
Then shall I dare these real ills to hide,
In tinsel trappings of poetic pride?

GEORGE CRABBE (1754–1832), *The Village*, 1788

... about sixe or seven a Clock, I walke out into a Common that lyes hard by the house where a great many young wenches keep Sheep and Cow's and sitt in the shade singing of Ballads; I goe to them and compare theire voyces and Beauty's to some Ancient Shepherdesses that I have read of and finde a vaste difference there, but trust mee I think these are as innocent as those could bee. I talke to them, and finde they want nothing to make them the happiest People in the world, but the knoledge that they are soe. most comonly when wee are in the middest of our discourse one looks aboute her and spyes her Cow's goeing into the Corne and then away they all run, as if they had wing's at theire heels. I that am not soe nimble stay behinde, & when I see them driveing home theire Cattle I think tis time for mee to retyre too.

DOROTHY OSBORNE (1627–95), letter to her future husband, William Temple, 2–4 June 1653

The Milkmaid o' the Farm

O Poll's the milk-maïd o' the farm!
  An' Poll's so happy out in groun',
Wi' her white païl below her eärm
  As if she wore a goolden crown.

An' Pool don't zit up half the night,
  Nor lie vor half the day a-bed;
An' zoo her eyes bc sparklèn bright,
  An' zoo her cheäks be bloomèn red.

In zummer mornens, when the lark
  Do rouse the litty lad an' lass
To work, then she's the vu'st to mark
  Her steps along the dewy grass.

An' in the evenen, when the zun
  Do sheen ageän the western brows
O' hills, where bubblèn brooks do run,
  There she do zing bezide her cows.

An' ev'ry cow of hers do stand,
  An' never overzet her païl;
Nor try to kick her nimble hand,
  Nor switch her wi' her heavy taïl.

Noo leädy, wi' her muff an' vaïl,
  Do walk wi' sich a steätely tread
As she do, wi' her milkèn païl
  A-balanc'd on her comely head.

An' she, at mornen an' at night,
  Do skim the yollow cream, an' mwold
An' wring her cheeses red an' white,
  An' zee the butter vetch'd an' roll'd.

An' in the barken or the ground,
  The chaps do always do their best
To milk the vu'st their own cows round,
  An' then help her to milk the rest.

Zoo Poll's the milk-maïd o' the farm!
  An' Poll's so happy out in groun',
Wi' her white païl below her eärm,
  As if she wore a goolden crown.

WILLIAM BARNES (1801–86), 1862

The Farmer's Boy

Forth comes the Maid, and like the morning smiles;
The Mistress too, and follow'd close by Giles.
A friendly tripod forms their humble seat,
With pails bright scour'd, and delicately sweet.
Where shadowing elms obstruct the morning ray,
Begins the work, begins the simple lay;
The full-charg'd udder yields its willing streams,
While Mary sings some lover's amorous dreams;
And crouching Giles beneath a neighbouring tree
Tugs o'er his pail, and chants with equal glee;
Whose hat with tatter'd brim, of nap so bare,
From the cow's side purloins a coat of hair,
A mottled ensign of his harmless trade,
An unambitious, peaceable cockade.
As unambitious too that cheerful aid
The Mistress yields beside her rosy Maid;
With joy she views her plenteous reeking store,
And bears a brimmer to the dairy-door;
Her cows dismiss'd, the luscious mead to roam,
Till eve again recall them loaded home.
And now the Dairy claims her choicest care,
And half her household find employment there:
Slow rolls the churn, its load of clogging cream
At once foregoes its quality and name:
From knotty particles first floating wide
Congealing butter's dash'd from side to side;
Streams of new milk through flowing coolers stray,
And snow-white curd abounds, and wholesome whey.
Due north th' unglazed windows, cold and clear,
For warming sunbeams are unwelcome here.
Brisk goes the work beneath each busy hand,
And Giles must trudge, whoever gives command;
A Gibeonite, that serves them all by turns:
He drains the pump, from him the faggot burns;
From him the noisy Hogs demand their food;
While at his heels run many a chirping brood,
Or down his path in expectation stand,
With equal claims upon his strewing hand.
Thus wastes the morn, till each with pleasure sees
The bustle o'er, and press'd the new-made cheese.

ROBERT BLOOMFIELD (1766–1823), The Farmer's Boy, 1800

RURAL CRAFTS

In the room from which this cheerful blaze proceeded he beheld a girl seated on a willow chair, and busily working by the light of the fire, which was ample, and of wood. With a bill-hook in one hand, and a leather glove much too large for her on the other, she was making spars—such as are used by thatchers—with great rapidity. She wore a leather apron for this purpose, which was also much too large for her figure. On her left hand lay a bundle of the straight smooth hazel rods called spar-gads—the raw material of her manufacture: on her right a heap of chips and ends—the refuse—with which the fire was maintained: in front a pile of the finished articles. To produce them she took up each gad, looked critically at it from end to end, cut it to length, split it into four, and sharpened each of the quarters with dexterous blows which brought it to a triangular point precisely resembling that of a bayonet . . .

The young woman laid down the bill-hook for a moment, and examined the palm of her right hand, which unlike the other was ungloved, and showed little hardness or roughness about it. The palm was red and blistering, as if her present occupation were as yet too recent to have subdued it to what it worked in. As with so many right hands born to manual labour, there was nothing in its fundamental shape to bear out the physiological conventionalism that gradations of birth show themselves primarily in the form of this member. Nothing but a cast of the die of Destiny had decided that the girl should handle the tool; and the fingers which clasped the heavy ash haft might have skilfully guided the pencil or swept the string, had they only been set to do it in good time.

THOMAS HARDY (1840–1928), *The Woodlanders*, 1887

I never saw it, but I judge it must have been a noble sight—the loading of a timber-carriage in the woods. For the trees had been criss-cross, anyhow, as they fell; yet when they were brought home they lay evenly on the carriage—butt-end foremost always; and it must have involved no end of patient skill in the carters, and of well-applied strength in the straining horses, to get them there. Often clay covering the wheels betokened difficult forest ways; often there had been a six or seven mile journey after the loading was finished; but I don't remember timber ever being brought to my yard too late to be unloaded before dark, though sometimes of a winter evening the dusk would be deepening before all had gone and the yard was quiet again.

And anyhow the unloading—what a display of sense and skill and patience and good-temper it was! The carters laid their skids from wheel to ground or to trees previously thrown down there—laid them and chained them to the wheels; and then one by one the trees were rolled or slid down the skids to the stack until the carriage was cleared. Levers were needed for all this—an old waggon-shaft or so—and one or two wheelwrights came out from the shop, or may be a blacksmith from the smithy, to lend a hand. Truly it was worth while to get away from bench or forge. The wheelwrights had a sort of connoisseurs' interest in the timber; besides, some ingenuity was often called for in the unloading: the horses stood about, to be spoken to or patted; and always it was good to be with the carters. These men, old acquaintances from a near village, had rustic talk and anecdotes, rustic manners. I never saw them other than quietly wise. To watch them at work, unhurried, understanding one another and seeing with keen-glancing eyes what to do, was to watch (unawares, and that is best) the traditional behaviour of a whole country-side of strong and good-tempered Englishmen. With the timber and the horses they seemed to bring the lonely woodlands, the far-off roads, into the little town.

GEORGE STURT (1863–1927), *The Wheelwright's Shop*, 1923

Hedger

To me the A Major Concerto has been dearer
Than ever before, because I saw one weave
Wonderful patterns of bright green, never clearer
Of April; whose hand nothing at all did deceive
Of laying right
The stakes of bright
Green lopped-off spear-shaped, and stuck notched, crooked-up;
Wonder was quickened at workman's craftsmanship
But clumsy were the efforts of my stiff body
To help him in the laying of bramble, ready
Of mind, but clumsy of muscle in helping; rip
Of clothes unheeded, torn hands. And his quick moving
Was never broken by any danger, his loving
Use of the bill or scythe was most deft, and clear—
Had my piano-playing or counterpoint
Been so without fear
Then indeed fame had been mine of most bright outshining;
But never have I known singer or piano-player
So quick and sure in movement as this hedge-layer
This gap-mender, of quiet courage unhastening.

IVOR GURNEY (1890–1937), *c.*1922–5

Diggers of long standing from time immemorial who have worked at digging from generation to generation have reached the highest degree of perfection in farm work. One should see how a digger cuts the land, cutting out, for example, a pond—how much dirt he puts in a wheelbarrow, how he hauls the wheelbarrow! One should see how he handles pieces of sod with a shovel! To what perfection, to what elegance the work is taken! A digger seems to work slowly: he carefully looks over the layout of the job, as if to orient himself better. He carefully selects the type of shovel he needs, digs the earth slowly, accurately so that there will not be a single crumb left, not a single crumb falls from the spade, he knows that this will all be wasted work, that all of these crumbs will have to be lifted again to the same height from which they fell. It is impossible not to admire diggers' work all the more since you do not see that the digger has made any special effort, that he has suffered over the work, that he has exerted his muscles in any special way. There is none of this. He works as if he were playing, as if it were very easy: he digs out the sod, the blocks of dirt of a pud's weight each and takes it out to the wheelbarrow just as if he were cutting slices of cheese. This is all done so easily that it seems as if you could do it yourself . . .

The diggers' skill at farm work stands out even more clearly if you look at the same work as it is done by ordinary peasants who are not diggers. I have only to look at the spot from which they have taken the dirt to determine unerringly who did the work: diggers or ordinary peasants. Where it was not diggers who took the dirt it is immediately obvious that people did an enormous amount of unproductive labor, that they wasted their strength uselessly. Peasants, however, almost never take on real digging work now and if a ditch or pond needs to be dug in the village, they hire diggers.

ALEKSANDR NIKOLAEVICH ENGELGARDT (1832–93), *Letters from the Country 1872–87*, 1879, tr. Cathy A. Frierson, 1993

Mole Catcher

With coat like any mole's, as soft and black,
And hazel bows bundled beneath his arm,
With long-helved spade and rush bag on his back,
The trapper plods alone about the farm:
And spies new mounds in the ripe pasture-land,
And where the lob-worms writhe up in alarm
And easy sinks the spade, he takes his stand
Knowing the moles' dark highroad runs below:
Then sharp and square he chops the turf, and day
Gloats on the opened turnpike through the clay.

Out from his wallet hurry pin and prong,
And trap, and noose to tie it to the bow;
And then his grand arcanum, oily and strong,
Found out by his forefather years ago

To scent the peg and witch the moles along.
The bow is earthed and arched ready to shoot
And snatch the death-knot fast round the first mole
Who comes and snuffs well pleased and tries to root
Past the sly nose peg; back again is put
The mould, and death left smirking in the hole.
The old man goes and tallies all his snares
And finds the prisoners there and takes his toll.

And moles to him are only moles; but hares
See him afield and scarcely cease to nip
Their dinners, for he harms not them; he spares
The drowning fly that of his ale would sip
And throws the ant the crumbs of comradeship.
And every time he comes into his yard
Grey linnet knows he brings the groundsel sheaf,
And clatters round the cage to be unbarred,
And on his finger whistles twice as hard.—
What his old vicar says, is his belief,
In the side pew he sits and hears the truth;
And never misses once to ring his bell
On Sundays night and morn, nor once since youth
Has heard the chimes afield, but has heard tell
There's not a peal in England sounds so well.

EDMUND BLUNDEN (1896–1974), 1920

MOWERS AND HAYMAKERS

'Mowing'

The Birds salute us as to Work we go,
And a new Life seems in our Breasts to glow.
A-cross one's Shoulder hangs a Scythe well steel'd,
The Weapon destin'd to unclothe the Field:
T'other supports the Whetstone, Scrip, and Beer;
That for our Scythes, and These our selves to chear.
And now the Field design'd our Strength to try
Appears, and meets at last our longing Eye;
The Grass and Ground each chearfully surveys,
Willing to see which way th' Advantage lays.
As the best Man, each claims the foremost Place,

And our first Work seems but a sportive Race:
With rapid Force our well-whet Blades we drive,
Strain every Nerve, and Blow for Blow we give:
Tho' but this Eminence the Foremost gains,
Only t' excel the rest in Toil and Pains.
But when the scorching Sun is mounted high,
And no kind Barns with friendly Shades are nigh,
Our weary Scythes entangle in the Grass,
And Streams of Sweat run trickling down a-pace;
Our sportive Labour we too late lament,
And wish that Strength again, we vainly spent.
Thus in the Morn a Courser I have seen,
With headlong Fury scour the level Green,
Or mount the Hills, if Hills are in his way,
As if no Labour could his Fire allay,
Till the meridian Sun with sultry Heat,
And piercing Beams hath bath'd his Sides in Sweat;
The lengthen'd Chace scarce able to sustain,
He measures back the Hills and Dales with pain.
With Heat and Labour tir'd, our Scythes we quit,
Search out a shady Tree, and down we sit;
From Scrip and Bottle hope new Strength to gain;
But Scrip and Bottle too are try'd in vain.
Down our parch'd Throats we scarce the Bread can get,
And quite o'er-spent with Toil, but faintly eat;
Nor can the Bottle only answer all,
Alas! the Bottle and the Beer's too small.
Our Time slides on, we move from off the Grass,
And each again betakes him to his Place.
Not eager now, as late, our Strength to prove,
But all contented regular to move:
Often we whet, as often view the Sun,
To see how near his tedious Race is run;
At length he vails his radiant Face from sight,
And bids the weary Traveller good-night:
Homewards we move, but so much spent with Toil,
We walk but slow, and rest at every Stile.
Our good expecting Wives, who think we stay.
Got to the Door, soon eye us in the way;
Then from the Pot the Dumpling's catch'd in haste,
And homely by its side the Bacon's plac'd.
Supper and Sleep by Morn new Strength supply,
And out we set again our Works to try . . .

STEPHEN DUCK (1705–56), *The Thresher's Labour*, 1730

The personal matter that occupied Levin while he was talking with his brother was this. The year before, when visiting a field that was being mown, he had lost his temper with his steward, and to calm himself had used a remedy of his own—he took a scythe from one of the peasants and himself began mowing.

He liked this work so much that he went mowing several times: he mowed all the meadow in front of his house, and when spring came he planned to devote several whole days to mowing with the peasants. Since his brother's arrival, however, he was in doubt whether to go mowing or not. He did not feel comfortable at the thought of leaving his brother alone all day long, and he also feared that Koznyshev might laugh at him. But while walking over the meadow he recalled the impression mowing had made on him, and almost made up his mind to do it. After his irritating conversation with his brother he again remembered his intention.

'I need physical exercise; without it my character gets quite spoilt,' thought he, and determined to go and mow, however uncomfortable his brother and the peasants might make him feel . . .

Next morning Constantine got up earlier than usual, but giving instructions about the farming delayed him, and when he came to the meadow each man was already mowing his second swath.

From the hill, as he came to his first swath, he could see, in the shade at his feet, a part of the meadow that was already mown, with the green heaps of grass and dark piles of coats thrown down by the mowers.

As he drew nearer, the peasants—following each other in a long straggling line, some with coats on, some in their shirts, each swinging his scythe in his own manner—gradually came into sight. He counted forty-two of them.

They moved slowly along the uneven bottom of the meadow, where a weir had once been. Levin recognized some of his own men. Old Ermil, wearing a very long white shirt, was swinging his scythe, with his back bent; young Vaska, who had been in Levin's service as coachman, and who at each swing of his scythe cut the grass the whole width of his swath; and Titus, Levin's mowing master, a thin little peasant, who went along without stopping, mowing his wide swath as if in play.

Levin dismounted and, tethering his horse by the roadside, went up to Titus, who fetched another scythe from behind a bush and gave it to Levin.

'It's ready, master! Like a razor, it will mow of itself,' said Titus, taking off his cap and smiling as he handed the scythe.

Levin took it and began to put himself in position. The peasants, perspiring and merry, who had finished their swaths came out on to the road one after another, and laughingly exchanged greetings with their master. They all looked at him, but no one made any remark until a tall old man with a shrivelled, beardless face, wearing a sheep-skin jacket, stepped out on to the road and addressed him:

'Mind, master! Having put your hand to the plough, don't look back!'

And Levin heard the sound of repressed laughter among the mowers.

'I will try not to lag behind,' he said, taking his place behind Titus and wait-ing his turn to fall in.

'Mind!' repeated the old man.

Titus made room for Levin, and Levin followed him. By the roadside the grass was short and tough, and Levin, who had not done any mowing for a long time and was confused by so many eyes upon him mowed badly for the first ten minutes, though he swung his scythe with much vigour. He heard voices behind him:

'It's not properly adjusted, the grip is not right. See how he has to stoop!' said one.

'Hold the heel lower,' said another.

'Never mind! It's all right: he'll get into it,' said the old man. 'There he goes . . .'

'You are taking too wide a swath, you'll get knocked up.' . . . 'He's the mas-ter, he must work; he's working for himself!' . . . 'But look how uneven!' . . . 'That's what the likes of us used to get a thump on the back for.'

They came to softer grass, and Levin, who was listening without replying, followed Titus and tried to mow as well as possible. When they had gone some hundred steps Titus was still going on without pausing, showing no signs of fatigue, while Levin was already beginning to fear he would not be able to keep up, he felt so tired.

He swung his scythe, feeling almost at the last gasp, and made up his mind to ask Titus to stop. But just at that moment Titus stopped of his own accord, stooped, took up some grass and wiped his scythe with it. Levin straightened himself, sighed, and looked back. The peasant behind him was still mowing but was obviously tired too, for he stopped without coming even with Levin and began whetting his scythe. Titus whetted his own and Levin's, and they began mowing again.

The same thing happened at Levin's second attempt. Titus swung his scythe, swing after swing, without stopping and without getting tired. Levin followed, trying not to lag behind, but it became harder and harder until at last the moment came when he felt he had no strength left, and then Titus again stopped and began whetting his scythe. In this way they finished the swaths. They were long, and to Levin seemed particularly difficult; but when it was done and Titus with his scythe over his shoulder turned about and slowly retraced his steps, placing his feet on the marks left on the mown sur-face by the heels of his boots, and Levin went down his own swath in the same way, then—in spite of the perspiration that ran down his face in streams and dripped from his nose, and though his back was as wet as if the shirt had been soaked in water—he felt very light-hearted. What gave him most pleasure was the knowledge that he would be able to keep up with the peasants.

The only thing marring his joy was the fact that his swath was not well mown. 'I must swing the scythe less with my arms and more with the whole of my body,' he thought, comparing Titus's swath, cut straight as if by measure, with his own, on which the grass lay scattered and uneven.

As Levin was aware, Titus had been mowing this swath with special rapidity, probably to put his master to the test, and it chanced to be a very long one. The next swaths were easier, but still Levin had to work with all his might to keep even with the peasants. He thought of nothing and desired nothing, except not to lag behind and to do his work as well as possible. He heard only the swishing of the scythes and saw only the receding figure of Titus, the convex half-circle of the mown piece before him, and the grasses and heads of flowers falling in waves about the blade of his scythe, and in the background the end of the swath where he would rest.

Suddenly he was conscious of a pleasant coolness on his hot perspiring shoulders, without knowing what it was or whence it came. He glanced up at the sky whilst whetting his scythe. A dark cloud was hanging low overhead, and large drops of rain were falling. Some of the peasants went to put on their coats; others as well as Levin felt pleasure in the refreshing rain and merely moved their shoulders up and down.

They came to the end of another swath. They went on mowing for some time and had really no idea whether it was late or early. His work was undergoing a change which gave him intense pleasure. While working he sometimes forgot for some minutes what he was about, and felt quite at ease; then his mowing was nearly as even as that of Titus. But as soon as he began thinking about it and trying to work better, he at once felt how hard the task was and mowed badly . . .

After breakfast Levin got placed between a humorous old man who invited him to be his neighbour and a young peasant who had only got married last autumn and was now out for his first summer's mowing.

The old man went along holding himself erect, moving with regular, long steps, turning out his toes, and with a precise and even motion that seemed to cost him no more effort than swinging his arms when walking, he laid the grass in a level high ridge, as if in play or as if the sharp scythe of its own accord whizzed through the juicy grass.

Young Mishka went behind Levin. His pleasant young face, with a wisp of grass tied round the forehead over his hair, worked all over with the effort; but whenever anyone glanced at him he smiled. Evidently he would have died rather than confess that the work was trying.

Between these two went Levin. Now, in the hottest part of the day, the work did not seem so hard to him. The perspiration in which he was bathed was cooling, and the sun which burnt his back, his head and his arm— bare to the elbow—added to his strength and perseverance in his task, and those unconscious intervals when it became possible not to think of what he was doing recurred more and more often. The scythe seemed to mow of itself. Those were happy moments. Yet more joyous were the moments when, reaching the river at the lower end of the swaths, the old man would wipe his scythe with the wet grass, rinse its blade in the clear water, and dipping his whetstone-box in the stream, would offer it to Levin.

'A little of my kvas? It's good!' said he, with a wink.

And really Levin thought he had never tasted any nicer drink than this lukewarm water with green stuff floating in it and a flavour of the rusty tin box. And then came the ecstasy of a slow walk, one hand resting on the scythe, when there was leisure to wipe away the streams of perspiration, to breathe deep, to watch the line of mowers, and to see what was going on around in forest and field.

The longer Levin went on mowing, the oftener he experienced those moments of oblivion when his arms no longer seemed to swing the scythe, but the scythe itself his whole body, so conscious and full of life; and as if by magic, regularly and definitely without a thought being given to it, the work accomplished itself of its own accord. These were blessed moments.

> LEV NIKOLAEVICH TOLSTOY (1828–1910), *Anna Karenina*, 1875–7, tr. Louise and Aylmer Maude, 1918

Next morning, before it was yet broad day, I awoke, and thought of the mowing. The birds were already chattering in the trees beside my window, all except the nightingale, which had left and flown away to the Weald, where he sings all summer by day as well as by night in the oaks and the hazel spinneys, and especially along the little river Adur, one of the rivers of the Weald. The birds and the thought of the mowing had awakened me, and I went down the stairs and along the stone floors to where I could find a scythe; and when I took it from its nail, I remembered how, fourteen years ago, I had last gone out with my scythe, just so, into the fields at morning. In between that day and this were many things, cities and armies, and a confusion of books, mountains and the desert, and horrible great breadths of sea.

When I got out into the long grass the sun was not yet risen, but there were already many colours in the eastern sky, and I made haste to sharpen my scythe, so that I might get to the cutting before the dew should dry. Some say that it is best to wait till all the dew has risen, so as to get the grass quite dry from the very first. But, though it is an advantage to get the grass quite dry, yet it is not worth while to wait till the dew has risen. For, in the first place, you lose many hours of work (and those the coolest), and next—which is more important—you lose that great ease and thickness in cutting which comes of the dew. So I at once began to sharpen my scythe.

There is an art also in the sharpening of a scythe, and it is worth describing carefully. Your blade must be dry, and that is why you will see men rubbing the scythe-blade with grass before they whet it. Then also your rubber must be quite dry, and on this account it is a good thing to lay it on your coat and keep it there during all your day's mowing. The scythe you stand upright, with the blade pointing away from you, and you put your left hand firmly on the back of the blade, grasping it: then you pass the rubber first down one side of the blade-edge and then down the other, beginning near the handle and going on to the point and working quickly and hard. When you first do this you will, perhaps, cut your hand; but it is only at first that such an accident will happen to you.

To tell when the scythe is sharp enough this is the rule. First the stone clangs and grinds against the iron harshly; then it rings musically to one note; then, at last, it purrs as though the iron and stone were exactly suited. When you hear this, your scythe is sharp enough; and I, when I heard it that June dawn, with everything quite silent except the birds, let down the scythe and bent myself to mow.

When one does anything anew, after so many years, one fears very much for one's trick or habit. But all things once learnt are easily recoverable, and I very soon recovered the swing and power of the mower. Mowing well and mowing badly—or rather not mowing at all—are separated by very little; as is also true of writing verse, of playing the fiddle, and of dozens of other things, but of nothing more than of believing. For the bad or young or untaught mower without tradition, the mower Promethean, the mower original and contemptuous of the past, does all these things: He leaves great crescents of grass uncut. He digs the point of the scythe hard into the ground with a jerk. He loosens the handles and even the fastening of the blade. He twists the blade with his blunders, he blunts the blade, he chips it, dulls it, or breaks it clean off at the tip. If any one is standing by he cuts him in the ankle. He sweeps up into the air wildly, with nothing to resist his stroke. He drags up earth with the grass, which is like making the meadow bleed. But the good mower who does things just as they should be done and have been for a hundred thousand years, falls into none of these fooleries. He goes forward very steadily, his scythe-blade just barely missing the ground, every grass falling; the swish and rhythm of his mowing are always the same.

So great an art can only be learnt by continual practice; but this much is worth writing down, that, as in all good work, to know the thing with which you work is the core of the affair. Good verse is best written on good paper with an easy pen, not with a lump of coal on a whitewashed wall. The pen thinks for you; and so does the scythe mow for you if you treat it honourably and in a manner that makes it recognize its service. The manner is this. You must regard the scythe as a pendulum that swings, not as a knife that cuts. A good mower puts no more strength into his stroke than into his lifting. Again, stand up to your work. The bad mower, eager and full of pain, leans forward and tries to force the scythe through the grass. The good mower, serene and able, stands as nearly straight as the shape of the scythe will let him, and follows up every stroke closely, moving his left foot forward. Then also let every stroke get well away. Mowing is a thing of ample gestures, like drawing a cartoon. Then, again, get yourself into a mechanical and repetitive mood: be thinking of anything at all but your mowing, and be anxious only when there seems some interruption to the monotony of the sound. In this mowing should be like one's prayers—all of a sort and always the same, and so made that you can establish a monotony and work them, as it were, with half your mind: that happier half, the half that does not bother.

HILAIRE BELLOC (1870–1953), from 'The Mowing of a Field', 1906

The Mower

The rooks travelled home,
The milch cows went lowing,
And down in the meadow,
An old man was mowing.

His shirt rank with sweat,
His neck stained with grime;
But he moved like the cadence
And sweetness of rhyme.

He moved like the heavy-winged
Rooks, the slow cows,
He moved like the vane
On the roof of the house.

The foam of the daisies
Was spread like a sea,
The spikes of red sorrel
Came up past his knee.

The sorrel, the clover,
The buttercups gold—
A man that was dirty
And twisted and old—

But again and again
Like an eddy he was,
He moved like the wind
In his own tasselled grass.

SYLVIA LYND (1888–1952), 1916

Hay-Meäken

'Tis merry ov a zummer's day,
Where vo'k be out a-meäkèn haÿ;
Where men an' women in a string
Do ted or turn the grass, an' zing,
Wi' cheemèn vaïces, merry zongs,

A-tossèn o' their sheenèn prongs
Wi' eärms a-zwangèn left an' right,
In colour'd gowns an' shirt sleeves white;
Or, wider spread, a reäkèn round
The rwosy hedges o' the ground,
Where Sam do zee the speckled sneäke,
An' try to kill en wi' his reäke;
An' Poll do jump about an' squall,
To zee the twistèn slooworm crawl.

'Tis merry where a gaÿ-tongued lot
Ov haÿ-meäkers be all a-squot,
On lightly-russlèn haÿ a-spread
Below an elem's lofty head,
To rest their weary limbs an' munch
Their bit o' dinner, or their nunch;
Where teethy reäkes do lie all round
By picks a-stuck up into ground.
An' wi' their vittles in their laps,
An' in their tinnèn cups their draps
O' cider sweet, or frothy eäle,
Their tongues do run wi' joke an' teäle.

An' when the zun, so low an' red,
Do sheen above the leafy head
O' zome broad tree, a-rizèn high
Avore the vi'ry western sky,
'Tis merry where all han's do goo
Athirt the groun', by two an' two,
A-reäkèn, over humps an' hollors,
The russlèn grass up into rollers.
An' woone do row it into line,
An' woone do clwose it up behine;
An' a'ter them the little bwoys
Do stride an' fling their eärms all woys,
Wi' busy picks an' proud young looks
A-meäkèn up their tiny pooks.
An' zoo 'tis merry out among
The vo'k in haÿ-vield all day long.

WILLIAM BARNES (1801–86), 1844

The notion that peasants are joyous, that the typical moment to represent a man in a smock-frock is when he is cracking a joke and showing a row of sound teeth, that cottage matrons are usually buxom, and village children necessarily rosy and merry, are prejudices difficult to dislodge from the artistic mind, which looks for its subjects into literature instead of life. The painter is still under the influence of idyllic literature, which has always expressed the imagination of the cultivated and town-bred, rather than the truth of rustic life. Idyllic ploughmen are jocund when they drive their team afield; idyllic shepherds make bashful love under hawthorn bushes; idyllic villagers dance in the chequered shade and refresh themselves, not immoderately, with spicy nutbrown ale. But no one who has seen much of actual ploughmen thinks them jocund; no one who is well acquainted with the English peasantry can pronounce them merry. The slow gaze, in which no sense of beauty beams, no humour twinkles,—the slow utterance, and the heavy slouching walk, remind one rather of that melancholy animal the camel, than of the sturdy countryman, with striped stockings, red waistcoat, and hat aside, who represents the traditional English peasant. Observe a company of haymakers. When you see them at a distance, tossing up the forkfuls of hay in the golden light, while the wagon creeps slowly with its increasing burthen over the meadow, and the bright green space which tells of work done gets larger and larger, you pronounce the scene 'smiling,' and you think these companions in labour must be as bright and cheerful as the picture to which they give animation. Approach nearer, and you will certainly find that haymaking time is a time for joking, especially if there are women among the labourers; but the coarse laugh that bursts out every now and then, and expresses the triumphant taunt, is as far as possible from your conception of idyllic merriment. That delicious effervescence of the mind which we call fun, has no equivalent for the northern peasant, except tipsy revelry; the only realm of fancy and imagination for the English clown exists at the bottom of the third quart pot.

GEORGE ELIOT (1819–80), 'The Natural History of German Life', 1856

Hay for the Horses

He had driven half the night
From far down San Joaquin
Through Mariposa, up the
Dangerous mountain roads,
And pulled in at eight a.m.
With his big truckload of hay
          behind the barn.
With winch and ropes and hooks
We stacked the bales up clean
To splintery redwood rafters
High in the dark, flecks of alfalfa
Whirling through shingle-cracks of light,
Itch of haydust in the
          sweaty shirt and shoes.

At lunchtime under Black oak
Out in the hot corral,
—The old mare nosing lunchpails
Grasshoppers crackling in the weeds—
'I'm sixty-eight,' he said,
'I first bucked hay when I was seventeen.
I thought, that day I started,
I sure would hate to do this all my life.
And dammit, that's just what
I've gone and done.'

GARY SNYDER (1930–), 1962

TILLERS OF THE SOIL

Nor is the Profit small, the Peasant makes;
Who smooths with Harrows, or who pounds with Rakes
The crumbling Clods: Nor *Ceres* from on high
Regards his Labours with a grudging Eye;
Nor his, who plows across the furrow'd Grounds,
And on the Back of Earth inflicts new Wounds:
For he with frequent Exercise Commands
Th' unwilling Soil, and tames the stubborn Lands.

VIRGIL (70–19 BC), *Georgics*, 36–29 BC, tr. John Dryden, 1697

The toils of husbandmen are great, and their ways and manner of life scant, narrow and full of hardship, which makes the poorer sort of people, born and bred to misery, take to that, as the calling which is most suitable to their mean birth, breeding and spirits.

EDWARD WATERHOUSE (1619–70), *Fortescutus Illustratus*, 1663

'The Aborigines of Wiltshire'

In North Wiltshire, and like the vale of Gloucestershire (a dirty clayey country) the Indigenæ, or Aborigines, speake drawling; they are phlegmatique, skins pale and livid, slow and dull, heavy of spirit: hereabout is but little tillage or hard labour, they only milk the cowes and make cheese; they feed chiefly on milke meates, which cooles their braines too much, and hurts their inventions. These circumstances make them melancholy, contemplative, and malicious; by consequence whereof come more law suites out of North Wilts, at least double to the Southern parts. And by the same reason they are generally more apt to be fanatiques . . .

*

On the downes, sc. the south part, where 'tis all upon tillage, and where the shepherds labour hard, their flesh is hard, their bodies strong: being weary after hard labour, they have not leisure to read and contemplate of religion, but goe to bed to their rest, to rise betime the next morning to their labour.

JOHN AUBREY (1626–97), *The Natural History of Wiltshire, c.*1656

The Yeoman

He tills the soil to-day,
Surly and grave, his difficult wage to earn.
Cities of discontent, the sickened nerve,
Are still a fashion that he will not learn.
His way is still the obstinate old way,
Even though his horses stare above the hedge,
And whinny, while the tractor drives its wedge
Where they were wont to serve,
And iron robs them of their privilege.
Still is his heart not given
To such encroachments on a natural creed;
Not wholly given, though he bows to need
By urgency and competition driven,
And vanity, to follow with the tide.
Still with a secret triumph he will say,
'Tractor for sand, maybe, but horse for clay,'
And in his calling takes a stubborn pride
That nature still defeats
The frowsty science of the cloistered men,
Their theory, their conceits;
The faith within him still derides the pen,
Experience his text-book. What have they,
The bookish townsmen in their dry retreats,
Known of December dawns, before the sun
Reddened the east, and fields were wet and grey?
When have they gone, another day begun,
By tracks into a quagmire trodden,

With sacks about their shoulders and the damp
Soaking until their very souls were sodden,
To help a sick beast, by a flickering lamp,
With rough words and kind hands?
Or felt their boots so heavy and so swere
With trudging over cledgy lands,
Held fast by earth, being to earth so near?

Book-learning they have known.
They meet together, talk, and grow most wise,
But they have lost, in losing solitude,
Something—an inward grace, the seeing eyes,
The power of being alone;
The power of being alone with earth and skies,
Of going about a task with quietude,
Aware once of earth's surrounding mood
And of an insect crawling on a stone.

V. SACKVILLE-WEST (1892–1962), *The Land*, 1926

Of Drivers of Ploughs

The skill of the drivers lies in knowing how to drive a team of oxen level, without beating, goading or ill-treating them. They should not be mournful men or wrathful, but cheerful, singing and joyous, so that by their tunes and songs the oxen may in some measure be heartened.

Fleta, 13th c., tr. H. G. Richardson and G. O. Sayles, 1955

As I went on my way, weeping for sorrow,
I saw a poor man beside me bending over the plough.
His coat was of a coarse cloth called 'cary'.
His hood was full of holes, so that his hair showed through.
From his knobbly, thickly-patched shoes,
His toes peeped out as he plodded over the land.
His stockings hung over round his heels,
Bedaubed in mud as he followed the plough.
From a pair of mean mittens made of rags
His fingers stuck out, covered in dirt.
This man wallowed in mud almost to his ankles.
Four enfeebled heifers went ahead of him,
So wretched were they, you could tell every rib.
His wife walked beside him with a long stick,

In a short gown, cut very high.
She was wrapped in a winnowing sheet to keep her from the weather,
Walking barefoot on the icy ground, she left a trail of blood behind her.
And at the side of the field lay a small bread-crock.
And in it was a little child, tightly wrapped.
And two more of two years old on the other side.
And they all sang one song that was pitiful to hear.
They all cried one cry, a song full of sorrow.
The poor man sighed sorely, and said, 'Children, be quiet!'

ANON., Pierce the Ploughman's Creed, c.1394

I do not remember when I have been more satisfied and pleased with my lot; even to-day the memory of that job gives me great pleasure. In thinking about it now it has come upon me with rather an unpleasant shock, that as far as I can see, I have ploughed my last furrow, as my present farm in England is now all grass, and I do not possess any ploughs. This thought saddens me, for ploughing is the king of jobs. In itself it is all-sufficing and soul-satisfying. You English townsfolk, who sneer at Hodge plodding at the plough tail, do not realize that he pities you, in that you cannot plough and have never known the joy of ploughing.

'But how monotonous and boring it must be,' you will say, and in the saying you will display your ignorance, for ploughing is the most charming disguise that work can wear. The plough is a perfect implement. The coulter cuts the side of the furrow slice: the share cuts the under side; and the turn-furrow or mouldboard inverts the whole. Therefore, if you are a competent ploughman, you are performing a perfect operation, and since when has perfection been monotonous?

When once you have acquired the knack of it, it goes with the effortless urge of a sailing boat. The plough, which looks so clumsy and uncouth, changes its character. In conjunction with your team of horses, it becomes a glorious galleon, which you steer proudly over the rolling fields like some mariner of old. It is no longer an ugly, awkward, inanimate thing, but a delicately flexible instrument, which responds to your lightest touch.

As you become intimate with it, you find that you have ceased to be the operator of a mere farm implement. You and the plough have become one, a common intelligence with but one idea only, to plough—on and on and on. Your mind stands calmly aloof, rejoicing in a thing in which it has no conscious part, noting with a detached satisfaction the perfect furrow which falls away on your right in an infinite ribbon.

A. G. STREET (1892–1966), Farmer's Glory, 1932

Cynddylan on a Tractor

Ah, you should see Cynddylan on a tractor.
Gone the old look that yoked him to the soil;
He's a new man now, part of the machine,
His nerves of metal and his blood oil.
The clutch curses, but the gears obey
His least bidding, and lo, he's away
Out of the farmyard, scattering hens.
Riding to work now as a great man should,
He is the knight at arms breaking the fields'
Mirror of silence, emptying the wood
Of foxes and squirrels and bright jays.
The sun comes over the tall trees
Kindling all the hedges, but not for him
Who runs his engine on a different fuel.
And all the birds are singing, bills wide in vain,
As Cynddylan passes proudly up the lane.

R. S. THOMAS (1913–), 1952

HARVESTERS

Another field rose high with waving grain;
With bended sickles stand the reaper train:
Here stretch'd in ranks the levell'd swarths are found,
Sheaves heap'd on sheaves here thicken up the ground.
With sweeping stroke the mowers strow the lands;
The gatherers follow, and collect in bands;
And last the children, in whose arms are borne
(Too short to gripe them) the brown sheaves of corn.
The rustic monarch of the field descries,
With silent glee, the heaps around him rise.
A ready banquet on the turf is laid,
Beneath an ample oak's expanded shade.
The victim ox the sturdy youth prepare;
The reaper's due repast, the woman's care.

HOMER, *The Iliad*, c.750 BC, tr. Alexander Pope, 1715–20

The Morning past, we sweat beneath the Sun;
And but uneasily our Work goes on.
Before us we perplexing Thistles find,

And Corn blown adverse with the ruffling Wind:
Behind our Backs the Female Gleaners wait,
Who sometimes stoop, and sometimes hold a Chat.
Each Morn we early rise, go late to Bed,
And lab'ring hard, a painful Life we lead:
For Toils, scarce ever ceasing, press us now,
Rest never does, but on the Sabbath show,
And barely that, our Master will allow.
Nor, when asleep, are we secure from Pain,
We then perform our Labours o'er again:
Our mimic Fancy always restless seems,
And what we act awake, she acts in Dreams.
Hard Fate! Our Labours ev'n in Sleep don't cease,
Scarce *Hercules* e'er felt such Toils as these.
At length in Rows stands up the well-dry'd Corn,
A grateful Scene, and ready for the Barn.
Our well-pleas'd Master views the Sight with joy,
And we for carrying all our Force employ.
Confusion soon o'er all the Field appears,
And stunning Clamours fill the Workmens Ears;
The Bells, and clashing Whips, alternate sound,
And rattling Waggons thunder o'er the Ground.
The Wheat got in, the Pease, and other Grain,
Share the same Fate, and soon leave bare the Plain:
In noisy Triumph the last Load moves on,
And loud Huzza's proclaim the Harvest done.
Our Master joyful at the welcome Sight,
Invites us all to feast with him at Night.
A Table plentifully spread we find,
And Jugs of humming Beer to cheer the Mind;
Which he, too generous, pushes on so fast,
We think no Toils to come, nor mind the past.
But the next Morning soon reveals the Cheat,
When the same Toils we must again repeat:
To the same Barns again must back return,
To labour there for room for next Year's Corn.

STEPHEN DUCK (1705–56), *The Thresher's Labour*, 1730

The Twilight now came on, and our Road lay thro Hop Grounds, where every creature (even at that hour) was employ'd in Picking Hops, with their whole Families; For the little Children in their Cradles (a pleasant and novel sight) were strew'd, dispersedly amidst The Hop Gardens:—The Twinkling Lights aided the Imagination and made me fancy it like a scene in a Pantomime Dance.

JOHN BYNG (1742–1813), *A Tour into Kent,* 1790

What a scene was that cornfield under the hot August sky! Fiery red glowed the faces of the harvestmen, against the golden background, a sea of waving wheat, the famed ruddy-hued wheat of Talavera. Not a cloud obscured the burning blue heavens, whilst beyond the standing corn showed here and there a bit of foliage, lofty hedge starred with wild roses or low pollard oaks of deep rich green.

As the afternoon drew on, the sultriness increased, and such brilliant contrasts of colour grew more intense. Southern warmth and gorgeousness seemed to invest the Suffolk harvest field. But the bucolic mood of the reapers had passed. Whilst the sickles moved automatically backwards and forwards, not a word passed their lips, a regiment of deaf-mutes were hardly quieter. From time to time, at a signal of the leader, each stood up, wiped his brow, shook himself, took a draught of beer, interchanged a word with his fellow, then resumed work vigorously as before.

The sun sank behind the pollard oaks and twilight succeeded, hardly bringing coolness. A little later, although no breeze sprang up, pleasant freshness lightened their labours; another and yet another drink from the master's can lent new strength; long after moon-rising, that mechanical swing of forty arms, that gleam of twenty sickles went on. Deep, almost solemn silence reigned over the cornfield. Only the rustle of footsteps and wheat falling on the stover broke the stillness, a stillness and monotony emblematic of these noiseless, unheroic lives, the tide of human existence that perpetually ebbs and flows, leaving no memory behind.

MATILDA BETHAM-EDWARDS (1836–1919), *The Lord of the Harvest,* 1899

Toil on heroes! harvest the products!
Not alone on those warlike fields the Mother of All,
With dilated form and lambent eyes watch'd you.

Toil on heroes! toil well! handle the weapons well!
The Mother of All, yet here as ever she watches you.

Well-pleased America thou beholdest,
Over the fields of the West those crawling monsters,
The human-divine inventions, the labor-saving implements;
Beholdest moving in every direction imbued as with life the revolving
    hay-rakes,

stover] stubble

The steam-power reaping-machines and the horse-power machines,
The engines, thrashers of grain and cleaners of grain, well separating the
        straw, the nimble work of the patent pitchfork,
Beholdest the newer saw-mill, the southern cotton-gin, and the rice-cleanser.
Beneath thy look O Maternal,
With these and else and with their own strong hands the heroes harvest.

All gather and all harvest,
Yet but for thee O Powerful, not a scythe might swing as now in security,
Not a maize-stalk dangle as now its silken tassels in peace.

Under thee only they harvest, even but a wisp of hay under thy great face only,
Harvest the wheat of Ohio, Illinois, Wisconsin, every barbed spear under
        thee,
Harvest the maize of Missouri, Kentucky, Tennessee, each ear in its light-
        green sheath,
Gather the hay to its myriad mows in the odorous tranquil barns,
Oats to their bins, the white potato, the buckwheat of Michigan, to theirs;
Gather the cotton in Mississippi or Alabama, dig and hoard the golden the
        sweet potato of Georgia and the Carolinas,
Clip the wool of California or Pennsylvania,
Cut the flax in the Middle States, or hemp or tobacco in the Borders,
Pick the pea and the bean, or pull apples from the trees or bunches of grapes
        from the vines,
Or aught that ripens in all these States or North or South,
Under the beaming sun and under thee.

                    WALT WHITMAN (1819–92), from 'The Return of the Heroes', 1881 edn.

No one knew the day—the last day of doom of the golden race; every one
knew it was nigh. One evening there was a small square piece cut at one side,
a little notch, and two shocks stood there in the twilight. Next day the village
sent forth its army with their crooked weapons to cut and slay. It used to be an
era, let me tell you, when a great farmer gave the signal to his reapers; not a
man, woman, or child that did not talk of that. Well-to-do people stopped
their vehicles and walked out into the new stubble. Ladies came, farmers, men
of low degree, everybody—all to exchange a word or two with the workers.
These were so terribly in earnest at the start they could scarcely acknowledge
the presence even of the squire. They felt themselves so important, and were
so full, and so intense and one-minded in their labour, that the great of the
earth might come and go as sparrows for aught they cared. More men and
more men were put on day by day, and women to bind the sheaves, till the vast
field held the village, yet they seemed but a handful buried in the tunnels of
the golden mine: they were lost in it like the hares, for as the wheat fell, the
shocks rose behind them, low tents of corn. Your skin or mine could not have

stood the scratching of the straw, which is stiff and sharp, and the burning of the sun, which blisters like red-hot iron. No one could stand the harvest-field as a reaper except he had been born and cradled in a cottage, and passed his childhood bareheaded in July heats and January snows. I was always fond of being out of doors, yet I used to wonder how these men and women could stand it, for the summer day is long, and they were there hours before I was up. The edge of the reap-hook had to be driven by force through the stout stalks like a sword, blow after blow, minute after minute, hour after hour; the back stooping, and the broad sun throwing his fiery rays from a full disc on the head and neck. I think some of them used to put handkerchiefs doubled up in their hats as pads, as in the East they wind the long roll of the turban about the head, and perhaps they would have done better if they had adopted the custom of the South and wound a long scarf about the middle of the body, for they were very liable to be struck down with such internal complaints as come from great heat. Their necks grew black, much like black oak in old houses. Their open chests were always bare, and flat, and stark, and never rising with rounded bust-like muscle as the Greek statues of athletes.

The breast-bone was burned black, and their arms, tough as ash, seemed cased in leather. They grew visibly thinner in the harvest-field, and shrunk together—all flesh disappearing, and nothing but sinew and muscle remaining. Never was such work. The wages were low in those days, and it is not long ago, either—I mean the all-year-round wages; the reaping was piece-work at so much per acre—like solid gold to men and women who had lived on dry bones, as it were, through the winter. So they worked and slaved, and tore at the wheat as if they were seized with a frenzy; the heat, the aches, the illness, the sunstroke, always impending in the air—the stomach hungry again before the meal was over, it was nothing. No song, no laugh, no stay—on from morn till night, possessed with a maddened desire to labour, for the more they could cut the larger the sum they would receive; and what is man's heart and brain to money? So hard, you see, is the pressure of human life that these miserables would have prayed on their knees for permission to tear their arms from the socket, and to scorch and shrivel themselves to charred human brands in the furnace of the sun.

Does it not seem bitter that it should be so? Here was the wheat, the beauty of which I strive in vain to tell you, in the midst of the flowery summer, scourging them with the knot of necessity; that which should give life pulling the life out of them, rendering their existence below that of the cattle, so far as the pleasure of living goes. Without doubt many a low mound in the church-yard—once visible, now level—was the sooner raised over the nameless dead because of that terrible strain in the few weeks of the gold fever. This is human life, real human life—no rest, no calm enjoyment of the scene, no generous gift of food and wine lavishly offered by the gods—the hard fist of necessity for ever battering man to a shapeless and hopeless fall.

RICHARD JEFFERIES (1848–87), *Field and Hedgerow*, 1889

'Harvesting Wheat in California'

The sprocket adjusted, the engineer called up the gang, and the men took their places. The fireman stoked vigorously, the two sack-sewers resumed their posts on the sacking platform, putting on the goggles that kept the chaff from their eyes. The separator-man and header-man gripped their levers.

The harvester, shooting a column of thick smoke straight upward, vibrating to the top of the stack hissed, clanked, and lurched forward. Instantly motion sprang to life in all its component parts: the header knives, cutting a thirty-six foot swath, gnashed like teeth; beltings slid and moved like smooth-flowing streams; the separator whirred, the agitator jarred and crashed; cylinders, augers, fans, seeders and elevators, drapers and chaff-carriers clattered, rumbled, buzzed, and clanged. The steam hissed and rasped, the ground reverberated a hollow note, and the thousands upon thousands of wheat stalks, sliced and slashed in the clashing shears of the header, rattled like dry rushes in a hurricane as they fell inward, and were caught up by an endless belt, to disappear into the bowels of the vast brute that devoured them.

It was that and no less. It was the feeding of some prodigious monster, insatiable, with iron teeth, gnashing and threshing into the fields of standing wheat; devouring always, never glutted, never satiated, swallowing an entire harvest, snarling and slobbering in a welter of warm vapour, acrid smoke, and blinding, pungent clouds of chaff. It moved belly-deep in the standing grain—a hippopotamus, half mired in river ooze, gorging rushes, snorting, sweating; a dinosaur wallowing through thick, hot grasses, floundering there, crouching, grovelling there as its vast jaws crushed and tore and its enormous gullet swallowed, incessant, ravenous, and inordinate.

S. Behrman, very much amused, changed places with one of the sack-sewers, allowing him to hold his horse while he mounted the sacking platform and took his place. The trepidation and jostling of the machine shook him till his teeth chattered in his head. His ears were shocked and assaulted by a myriad-tongued clamor, clashing steel, straining belts, jarring woodwork; while the impalpable chaff powder from the separators settled like dust in his hair, his ears, eyes, and mouth.

Directly in front of where he sat on the platform was the chute from the cleaner, and from this into the mouth of a half-full sack spouted an unending gush of grain, winnowed, cleaned, threshed, ready for the mill.

The pour from the chute of the cleaner had for S. Behrman an immense satisfaction. Without an instant's pause a thick rivulet of wheat rolled and dashed tumultuous into the sack. In half a minute—sometimes in twenty seconds—the sack was full, was passed over to the second sewer, the mouth reeved up, and the sack dumped out upon the ground, to be picked up by the wagons and hauled to the railroad.

S. Behrman, hypnotized, sat watching that river of grain. All that shrieking, bellowing machinery, all that gigantic organism, all the months of labour, the ploughing, the planting, the prayers for rain, the years of preparation, the heartaches, the anxiety, the foresight, all the whole business of the ranch, the work of horses, of steam, of men and boys, looked to this spot—the grain chute from the harvester into the sacks. Its volume was the index of failure or success, of riches or poverty. And at this point the labour of the rancher ended. Here, at the lip of the chute, he parted company with his grain, and from here the wheat streamed forth to feed the world. The yawning mouths of the sacks might well stand for the unnumbered mouths of the People, all agape for food; and here, into these sacks, at first so lean, so flaccid, attenuated like starved stomachs, rushed the living stream of food, insistent, interminable, filling the empty, fattening the shrivelled, making it sleek and heavy and solid.

FRANK NORRIS (1870–1902), *The Octopus*, 1901

Cotton Pickers Wanted—placards on the road, handbills out, orange-colored handbills—Cotton Pickers Wanted.

Here, up this road, it says.

The dark green plants stringy now, and the heavy bolls clutched in the pod. White cotton spilling out like popcorn.

Like to get our hands on the bolls. Tenderly, with the fingertips.

I'm a good picker.

Here's the man, right here.

I aim to pick some cotton.

Got a bag?

Well, no, I ain't.

Cost ya a dollar, the bag. Take it out o' your first hunderd and fifty. Eighty cents a hunderd first time over the field. Ninety cents second time over. Get your bag there. One dollar. 'F you ain't got the buck, we'll take it out of your first hunderd and fifty. That's fair, and you know it.

Sure it's fair. Good cotton bag, last all season. An' when she's wore out, draggin', turn 'er aroun', use the other end. Sew up the open end. Open up the wore end. And when both ends is gone, why, that's nice cloth! Makes a nice pair of summer drawers. Makes nightshirts. And well, hell—a cotton bag's a nice thing.

Hang it around your waist. Straddle it, drag it between your legs. She drags light at first. And your finger-tips pick out the fluff, and the hands go twisting into the sack between your legs. Kids come along behind; got no bags for the kids—use a gunny sack or put it in your ol' man's bag. She hangs heavy, some, now. Lean forward, hoist 'er along. I'm a good hand with cotton. Finger-wide, boll-wise. Jes' move along talkin', an' maybe singin' till the bag gets heavy. Fingers go right to it. Fingers know. Eyes see the work—and don't see it.

Talkin' across the rows—

They was a lady back home—won't mention no names—had a nigger kid all of a sudden. Nobody knowed before. Never did hunt out the nigger. Couldn' never hold up her head no more. But I started to tell—she was a good picker.

Now the bag is heavy, boost it along. Set your hips and tow it along, like a work horse. And the kids pickin' into the old man's sack. Good crop here. Gets thin in the low places, thin and stringy. Never seen no cotton like this here California cotton. Long fiber, bes' damn cotton I ever seen. Spoil the lan' pretty soon. Like a fella wants to buy some cotton lan'—Don' buy her, rent her. Then when she's cottoned on down, move someplace new.

Lines of people moving across the fields. Finger-wise. Inquisitive fingers snick in and out and find the bolls. Hardly have to look.

Bet I could pick cotton if I was blind. Got a feelin' for a cotton boll. Pick clean, clean as a whistle.

Sack's full now. Take her to the scales. Argue. Scale man says you got rocks to make weight. How 'bout him? His scales is fixed. Sometimes he's right, you got rocks in the sack. Sometimes you're right, the scales is crooked. Sometimes both; rocks an' crooked scales. Always argue, always fight. Keeps your head up. An' his head up. What's a few rocks? Jus' one, maybe. Quarter pound? Always argue.

Back with the empty sack. Got our own book. Mark in the weight. Got to. If they know you're markin', then they don't cheat. But God he'p ya if ya don' keep your own weight.

This is good work. Kids runnin' aroun'. Heard 'bout the cotton-pickin' machine?

Yeah, I heard.

Think it'll ever come?

Well, if it comes—fella says it'll put han'-pickin' out.

Come night. All tired. Good pickin', though. Got three dollars, me an' the ol' woman an' the kids.

The cars move to the cotton-fields. The cotton camps set up. The screened high trucks and trailers are piled high with white fluff. Cotton clings to the fence wires, and cotton rolls in little balls along the road when the wind blows. And clean white cotton, going to the gin. And the big, lumpy bales standing, going to the compress. And cotton clinging to your clothes and stuck to your whiskers. Blow your nose, there's cotton in your nose.

Hunch along now, fill up the bag 'fore dark. Wise fingers seeking in the bolls. Hips hunching along, dragging the bag. Kids are tired, now in the evening. They trip over their feet in the cultivated earth. And the sun is going down.

Wisht it would last. It ain't much money, God knows, but I wisht it would last.

JOHN STEINBECK (1902–68), *The Grapes of Wrath*, 1939

The Hock-Cart, or, Harvest Home

To the Right Honourable, Mildmay, Earle of Westmorland

Come Sons of Summer, by whose toile,
We are the Lords of Wine and Oile:
By whose tough labours, and rough hands,
We rip up first, then reap our lands.
Crown'd with the eares of corne, now come,
And, to the Pipe, sing Harvest home.
Come forth, my Lord, and see the Cart
Drest up with all the Country Art.
See, here a *Maukin*, there a sheet,
As spotlesse pure, as it is sweet:
The Horses, Mares, and frisking Fillies,
(Clad, all, in Linnen, white as Lillies.)
The Harvest Swaines, and Wenches bound
For joy, to see the *Hock-cart* crown'd.
About the Cart, heare, how the Rout
Of Rurall Younglings raise the shout;
Pressing before, some coming after,
Those with a shout, and these with laughter.
Some blesse the Cart; some kisse the sheaves;
Some prank them up with Oaken leaves:
Some crosse the Fill-horse; some with great
Devotion, stroak the home-borne wheat:
While other Rusticks, lesse attent
To Prayers, then to Merryment,
Run after with their breeches rent.
Well, on, brave boyes, to your Lords Hearth,
Glitt'ring with fire; where, for your mirth,
Ye shall see first the large and cheefe
Foundation of your Feast, Fat Beefe:
With Upper Stories, Mutton, Veale
And Bacon, (which makes full the meale)
With sev'rall dishes standing by,
As here a Custard, there a Pie,
And here all tempting Frumentie.
And for to make the merry cheere,
If smirking Wine be wanting here,
There's that, which drowns all care, stout Beere;
Which freely drink to your Lords health,
Then to the Plough, (the Common-wealth)

Maukin] mop   *crosse the Fill-horse*] bestride the shaft-horse

Next to your Flailes, your Fanes, your Fatts;
Then to the Maids with Wheaten Hats:
To the rough Sickle, and crookt Sythe,
Drink frollick boyes, till all be blythe.
Feed, and grow fat; and as ye eat,
Be mindfull, that the lab'ring Neat
(As you) may have their fill of meat.
And know, besides, ye must revoke
The patient Oxe unto the Yoke,
And all goe back unto the Plough
And Harrow, (though they'r hang'd up now.)
And, you must know, your Lords word's true,
Feed him ye must, whose food fils you.
And that this pleasure is like raine,
Not sent ye for to drowne your paine,
But for to make it spring againe.

ROBERT HERRICK (1591–1674), *Hesperides*, 1648

On the morning of the harvest home dinner everybody prepared themselves for a tremendous feast, some to the extent of going without breakfast, that the appetite might not be impaired. And what a feast it was! Such a bustling in the farm-house kitchen for days beforehand; such boiling of hams and roasting of sirloins; such a stacking of plum puddings, made by the Christmas recipe; such a tapping of eighteen-gallon casks and baking of plum loaves would astonish those accustomed to the appetites of to-day. By noon the whole parish had assembled, the workers and their wives and children to feast and the sprinkling of the better-to-do to help with the serving. The only ones absent were the aged bedridden and their attendants, and to them, the next day, portions, carefully graded in daintiness according to their social standing, were carried by the children from the remnants of the feast. A plum pudding was considered a delicate compliment to an equal of the farmer; slices of beef or ham went to the 'better-most poor'; and a ham-bone with plenty of meat left upon it or part of a pudding or a can of soup to the commonalty.

Long tables were laid out of doors in the shade of a barn, and soon after twelve o'clock the cottagers sat down to the good cheer, with the farmer carving at the principal table, his wife with her tea urn at another, the daughters of the house and their friends circling the tables with vegetable dishes and beer jugs, and the grandchildren, in their stiff, white, embroidered frocks, dashing hither and thither to see that everybody had what they required. As a background there was the rick-yard with its new yellow stacks and, over all, the mellow sunshine of late summer.

Fanes] fans   *Fatts*] casks

Passers-by on the road stopped their gigs and high dog-carts to wave greetings and shout congratulations on the weather. If a tramp looked wistfully in, he was beckoned to a seat on the straw beneath a rick and a full plate was placed on his knees. It was a picture of plenty and goodwill.

It did not do to look beneath the surface. Laura's father, who did not come into the picture, being a 'tradesman' and so not invited, used to say that the farmer paid his men starvation wages all the year and thought he made it up to them by giving that one good meal. The farmer did not think so, because he did not think at all, and the men did not think either on that day; they were too busy enjoying the food and the fun.

After the dinner there were sports and games, then dancing in the home paddock until twilight, and when, at the end of the day, the farmer, carving indoors for the family supper, paused with knife poised to listen to the last distant 'Hooray!' and exclaimed, 'A lot of good chaps! A lot of good chaps, God bless 'em!' both he and the cheering men were sincere, however mistaken.

FLORA THOMPSON (1876–1947), Lark Rise to Candleford, 1945

Harvest—End

At Dagenhams, long after sun was set,
While light still tarried, waggons rumbled back
Their swaying loads toward the half built stack

Where, from afar, the labourers stood clear,
Dark figures twirling heavy sheaves to feed
The man who shook and settled them to his need.

Like mummers in an old morality
They moved across the sky's deep summer dusk,
Miming their simple parts with heave and thrust

In a play that is the oldest of them all,
The strife where might of man and earth are matched
Till the house of corn be built four-square and thatched.

CLAUDE COLLEER ABBOTT (1889–1971), 1924

THRESHERS

The Grove receives us next;
Between the upright shafts of whose tall elms
We may discern the thresher at his task.

Thump after thump resounds the constant flail,
That seems to swing uncertain, and yet falls
Full on the destined ear. Wide flies the chaff;
The rustling straw sends up a frequent mist
Of atoms, sparkling in the noonday beam.
Come hither, ye that press your beds of down
And sleep not; see him sweating o'er his bread
Before he eats it—'Tis the primal curse,
But softened into mercy; made the pledge
Of cheerful days, and nights without a groan.

WILLIAM COWPER (1731–1800), *The Task*, 1785

Or to the Farm, where, high on trampled stacks,
The labourers stir themselves amain
To feed with hasty sheaves of grain
The deaf'ning engine's boisterous maw,
And snatch again,
From to-and-fro tormenting racks,
The toss'd and hustled straw;
Whilst others tend the shedded wheat
That fills yon row of shuddering sacks,
Or shift them quick, and bind them neat,
And dogs and boys with sticks
Wait, murderous, for the rats that leave the ruin'd ricks;
And, all the bags being fill'd and rank'd fivefold, they pour
The treasure on the barn's clean floor.
And take them back for more,
Until the whole bared harvest beauteous lies
Under our pleased and prosperous eyes.

COVENTRY PATMORE (1823–96), *Amelia*, 1878

FISHING FOLK

'On the Lancashire Coast, 1636'

Heere through the wasshie sholes
We spye an owld man wading for the soles
And flukes and rayes, which the last morning tide

flukes] flounders

Had stayd in nets, or did att anchor ride
Uppon his hooks; him we fetch up, and then
To our goodmorrowe, 'Welcomme gentlemen,'
He sayd, and more, 'you gentlemen at ease,
Whoe money have, and goe where ere you please,
Are never quiett; wearye of the daye,
You now comme hether to drive time away:
Must time be driven? longest day with us
Shutts in to soone, as never tedious
Unto our buisnesse; making, mending nett,
Preparing hooks and baits, wherewith to gett
Cod, whiting, place, uppon the sandie shelvs,
Where with to feede the markett and our selvs.'
Happie ould blade, whoe in his youth had binne
Roving at sea when Essex Cales did winne,
So now he lives.

RICHARD JAMES (1592–1638), *Iter Lancastrense*, WR. 1636

The Fisher's Life

What joy attends the fisher's life!
    Blow, winds, blow!
The fisher and his faithful wife!
    Row, boys, row!
He drives no plough on stubborn land,
His fields are ready to his hand;
No nipping frosts his orchards fear,
He has his autumn all the year!

The husbandman has rent to pay,
    Blow, winds, blow!
And seed to purchase every day,
    Row, boys, row!
But he who farms the rolling deeps
Though never sowing, always reaps;
The ocean's fields are fair and free,
There are no rent days on the sea!

ANON., 1861

Cales] Cadiz in 1596

Wick harbour is surrounded on the land side by hundreds of erections, look-ing like abortive attempts at building wood houses, some twenty feet square, for the walls are only about three feet high. These are the gutting troughs. Round them stood rows of what close inspection led you to conclude were women, though at first sight you might be excused for having some doubts respecting their sex. They all wore strange-shaped canvas garments, so bespattered with blood and the entrails and scales of fish as to cause them to resemble animals of the ichthyological kingdom, recently divested of their skin, undergoing perhaps one of those transitions set forth in Mr Darwin's speculative book 'On the Origin of Species.' And if a man may become a monkey, or has been a whale, why should not a Caithness damsel become a herring?

Badinage apart, the women do cast their skins. Work over, they don gay dresses, and, flaunting in colours, you would not know the girls that you meet in the evening to be those whom you saw in the morning coated with blood and viscera.

Sixty-five women, side by side, and all silent! A wonder this, you will think; but if you saw the movement of hands and arms you would admit that to keep these going at the rapid rate which they do, is quite sufficient muscular exercise.

Let us watch the operations. First, the herrings are carried as fast as pos-sible in baskets from the boats to the gutting-troughs until the boats are emp-tied of their scaly treasures. Then, the women, familiarly called gutters, pounce upon the herrings like a bird of prey, seize their victims, and, with a rapidity of motion which baffles your eye, deprive the fish of their viscera. The operation, which a damsel not quite so repulsive as her companions obligingly performed for me at slow time, is thus effected. The herring is seized in the left hand, and by two dexterous cuts made with a sharp short knife in the neck an opening is effected sufficiently large to enable the viscera and liver to be extracted. These with the gills are thrown into a barrel, the gutted fish being cast among his eviscerated companions. Try your hand, as I did, at this apparently simple process, and ten to one but your first cut will decapitate the herring. If this does not happen, you will mangle the fish so seriously in your attempts to eviscerate it that you will render it entirely unworthy of the honour of being packed with its skilfully gutted companions. And even if you succeed in disembowelling a herring artistically, you will probably spend many minutes in the operation, whereas the Wick gutters—I timed them—gut on an average twenty-six herrings per minute.

At this rapid rate you no longer wonder at the silence that prevails while the bloody work is going on, nor at the incarnadined condition of the women. How habit deadens feeling!

CHARLES WELD (1813–69), *Two Months in the Highlands, Orcadia and Skye*, 1860

In the morning when the sardine fleet has made a catch, the purse-seiners waddle heavily into the bay blowing their whistles. The deep-laden boats pull in against the coast where the canneries dip their tails into the bay. The figure is advisedly chosen, for if the canneries dipped their mouths into the bay the canned sardines which merged from the other end would be, metaphorically at least, even more horrifying. Then cannery whistles scream and all over the town men and women scramble into their clothes and come running down to the Row to go to work. Then shining cars bring the upper classes down: superintendents, accountants, owners, who disappear into offices. Then from the town pour Wops and Chinamen and Polaks, men and women in trousers and rubber coats and oilcloth aprons. They come running to clean and cut and pack and cook and can the fish. The whole street rumbles and groans and screams and rattles while the silver rivers of fish pour in out of the boats and the boats rise higher and higher in the water until they are empty. The canneries rumble and rattle and squeak until the last fish is cleaned and cut and cooked and canned, and then the whistles scream again and the dripping, smelly, tired Wops and Chinamen and Polaks, men and women, struggle out and droop their ways up the hill into the town and Cannery Row becomes itself again—quiet and magical.

JOHN STEINBECK (1902–68), *Cannery Row*, 1945

VI. ALL MANNER OF OCCUPATIONS

The more complex the society, the more elaborate the range of occupations that go on within it. In the modern world the division of labour has proceeded so far that a mere list of all the occupations that now exist, if one could compile it, would more than fill this book.* So only a selection can be represented here.

TEXTILE WORKERS

Bessy and Her Spinning Wheel

O leeze me on my spinnin-wheel,
And leeze me on my rock and reel;
Frae tap to tae that cleeds me bien,
And haps me fiel and warm at e'en!
I'll set me down and sing and spin,
While laigh descends the simmer sun,
Blest wi' content, and milk and meal,
O leeze me on my spinnin-wheel.—

On ilka hand the burnies trot,
And meet below my theekit cot;
The scented birk and hawthorn white
Across the pool their arms unite,
Alike to screen the birdie's nest,
And little fishes' callor rest:
The sun blinks kindly in the biel'
Where, blythe I turn my spinnin wheel.—

---

* A *Classification of Occupations*, published by the British Office of Population Censuses and Surveys in 1980, lists over 23,000.

leeze me on] lief is me, I am delighted by   *rock*] distaff   *tae*] toe   *cleeds*] clothes   *bien*] comfortably   *haps*] covers   *fiel*] cosily   *laigh*] low   *simmer*] summer   *ilka*] each   *burnies*] streams   *trot*] bustle   *theekit*] thatched   *birk*] birch tree   *callor*] cool   *blinks*] gleams   *biel'*] shelter

On lofty aiks the cushats wail,
And Echo cons the doolfu' tale;
The lintwhites in the hazel braes,
Delighted, rival ithers lays:
The craik amang the claver hay,
The pairtrick whirrin o'er the ley,
The swallow jinkin round my shiel,
Amuse me at my spinnin wheel.—

Wi' sma' to sell, and less to buy,
Aboon distress, below envy,
O wha wad leave this humble state,
For a' the pride of a' the Great?
Amid their flairing, idle toys,
Amid their cumbrous, dinsome joys,
Can they the peace and pleasure feel
Of Bessy at her spinnin wheel!

ROBERT BURNS (1759–96), 1792

Within one roome being large and long,
There stood two hundred Loomes full strong:
Two hundred men the truth is so,
Wrought in these Loomes all in a row.
By every one a pretty boy,
Sate making quils with mickle ioy;
And in another place hard by,
An hundred women merily,
Were carding hard with ioyfull cheere,
Who singing sate with voices cleere.
And in a chamber close beside,
Two hundred maidens did abide,
In petticoates of Stammell red,
And milke-white kerchers on their head:
Their smocke-sleeves like to winter snow,
That on the Westerne mountaines flow,
And each sleeve with a silken band,
Was featly tied at the hand.
These pretty maids did never lin,

aiks] oaks   cushats] wood pigeons   lintwhite] linnet   braes] river banks
ithers] others'   craik] corncrake   claver] clover   jinkin] darting
shiel] hut   flairing] gaudy   dinsome] noisy   Stammell] coarse cloth
lin] cease

But in that place all day did spin:
And spinning so with voices meet,
Like Nightingals they sung full sweet.
Then to another roome came they,
Where children were in poore aray:
And every one sate picking wool,
The finest from the course to cull:
The number was seven score and ten,
The children of poore silly men:
And these their labours to requite,
Had every one a penny at night,
Beside their meat and drinke all day,
Which was to them a wondrous stay.
Within another place likewise,
Full fifty proper men he spies,
And these were Shearemen every one,
Whose skill and cunning there was showne:
And hard by them there did remaine,
Full fourscore Rowers taking paine.
A Dye-house likewise had he then,
Wherein he kept full forty men:
And likewise in his fulling Mill,
Full twenty persons kept he still.

THOMAS DELONEY (1560?–1600), *The Pleasant Historie of John Winchcomb, in His Younguer Yeares Called Jack of Newbery*, wr. *c*.1597

By gentle steps
Up-raised, from room to room we slowly walk,
And view with wonder and with silent joy
The sprightly scene, where many a busy hand,
Where spoles, cards, wheels, and looms, with motion quick,
And ever-murmuring sound, the unwonted sense
Wrap in surprise. To see them all employed,
All blithe, it gives the spreading heart delight,
As neither meats, nor drinks, nor aught of joy
Corporeal, can bestow. Nor less they gain
Virtue than wealth, while, on their useful works
From day to day intent, in their full minds
Evil no place can find. With equal scale

Rowers] workers who put a nap on the cloth

Some deal abroad the well-assorted fleece;
These card the short, those comb the longer flake;
Others the harsh and clotted lock receive,
Yet sever and refine with patient toil,
And bring to proper use. Flax too, and hemp,
Excite their diligence. The younger hands
Ply at the easy work of winding yarn
On swiftly-circling engines, and their notes
Warble together, as a choir of larks.

JOHN DYER (1699–1757), *The Fleece*, 1757

The Song of the Shirt

With fingers weary and worn,
    With eyelids heavy and red,
A Woman sat, in unwomanly rags,
    Plying her needle and thread—
Stitch! stitch! stitch!
    In poverty, hunger, and dirt,
And still with a voice of dolorous pitch
    She sang the 'Song of the Shirt!'

'Work! work! work!
    While the cock is crowing aloof!
And work—work—work,
    Till the stars shine through the roof!
It's O! to be a slave
    Along with the barbarous Turk,
Where woman has never a soul to save,
    If this is Christian work!

'Work—work—work
    Till the brain begins to swim,
Work—work—work
    Till the eyes are heavy and dim!
Seam, and gusset, and band,
    Band, and gusset, and seam,
Till over the buttons I fall asleep
    And sew them on in a dream!

'O, Men with Sisters dear!
    O Men! with Mothers and Wives!
It is not linen you're wearing out,
    But human creatures' lives!

Stitch—stitch—stitch,
    In poverty, hunger, and dirt,
Sewing at once, with a double thread,
    A Shroud as well as a Shirt.

'But why do I talk of Death?
    That Phantom of grisly bone,
I hardly fear this terrible shape,
    It seems so like my own—
It seems so like my own
    Because of the fasts I keep;
O God! that bread should be so dear,
    And flesh and blood so cheap!

'Work—work—work!
    My labour never flags;
And what are its wages? A bed of straw,
    A crust of bread—and rags.
 That shatter'd roof—and this naked floor—
    A table—a broken chair—
And a wall so blank, my shadow I thank
    For sometimes falling there!

'Work—work—work!
    From weary chime to chime,
Work—work—work—
    As prisoners work for crime!
Band, and gusset, and seam,
    Seam, and gusset, and band,
Till the heart is sick, and the brain benumb'd,
    As well as the weary hand.

'Work—work—work,
    In the dull December light,
And work—work—work,
    When the weather is warm and bright—
While underneath the eaves
    The brooding swallows cling,
As if to show me their sunny backs
    And twit me with the spring.

'O, but to breathe the breath
    Of the cowslip and primrose sweet!—
With the sky above my head,
    And the grass beneath my feet;

For only one short hour
   To feel as I used to feel,
Before I knew the woes of want
   And the walk that costs a meal!

'O but for one short hour!
   A respite however brief!
No blessed leisure for Love or Hope,
   But only time for Grief!
A little weeping would ease my heart,
   But in their briny bed
My tears must stop, for every drop
   Hinders needle and thread.

'Seam, and gusset, and band,
   Band, and gusset, and seam,
Work, work, work,
   Like the Engine that works by Steam!
A mere machine of iron and wood
   That toils for Mammon's sake—
Without a brain to ponder and craze,
   Or a heart to feel—and break!'

—With fingers weary and worn,
   With eyelids heavy and red,
A Woman sat, in unwomanly rags,
   Plying her needle and thread—
Stitch! stitch! stitch!
   In poverty, hunger, and dirt,
And still with a voice of dolorous pitch,—
Would that its tone could reach the Rich!—
   She sang this 'Song of the Shirt!'

THOMAS HOOD (1799–1845), 1843

It is a curious fact that the production of precisely those articles which serve
the personal adornment of the ladies of the bourgeoisie involves the saddest
consequences for the health of the workers. We have already seen this in the
case of the lace-makers, and come now to the dress-making establishments of
London for further proof. They employ a mass of young girls—there are said
to be 15,000 of them in all—who sleep and eat on the premises, come usually
from the country, and are therefore absolutely the slaves of their employers.
During the fashionable season, which lasts some four months, working
hours, even in the best establishments, are fifteen, and, in very pressing cases,
eighteen a day; but in most shops work goes on at these times without any set

regulation, so that the girls never have more than six, often not more than three or four, sometimes, indeed, not more than two hours in the twenty-four, for rest and sleep, working nineteen to twenty hours, if not the whole night through, as frequently happens! The only limit set to their work is the absolute physical inability to hold the needle another minute. Cases have occurred in which these helpless creatures did not undress during nine consecutive days and nights, and could only rest a moment or two here and there upon a mattress, where food was served them ready cut up in order to require the least possible time for swallowing. In short, these unfortunate girls are kept by means of the moral whip of the modern slave-driver, the threat of discharge, to such long and unbroken toil as no strong man, much less a delicate girl of 14 to 20 years, can endure. In addition to this, the foul air of the workroom and sleeping places, the bent posture, the often bad and indigestible food, all these causes, but above all the long hours of work combined with almost total exclusion from fresh air, entail the saddest consequences for the health of the girls. Enervation, exhaustion, debility, loss of appetite, pains in the shoulders, back, and hips, but especially headache, begin very soon; then follow curvatures of the spine, high, deformed shoulders, leanness, swelled, weeping, and smarting eyes, which soon become short-sighted; coughs, narrow chests, shortness of breath, and all manner of disorders in the development of the female organism.

In many cases the eyes suffer so severely that incurable blindness follows; but if the sight remains strong enough to make continued work possible, consumption usually soon ends the sad life of these milliners and dressmakers. Even those who leave this work at an early age retain permanently injured health, a broken constitution; and, when married, bring feeble and sickly children into the world. All the medical men interrogated by the commissioner agreed that no method of life could be invented better calculated to destroy health and induce early death.

> FRIEDRICH ENGELS (1820–95), *The Condition of the Working Class in England*, 1845, tr. Florence Kelley-Wischnewetsky, 1887

The Fur-Pullers of South London

The inquirer who turns aside out of that historic street from which one April day there started long ago a famous and jocund company of pilgrims—where today a sadder stream of humanity ceaselessly ebbs and flows—and who plunges under one of the narrow archways on its western side, will find himself at once face to face with the lowest depths to which the toil of women can be dragged. Here, in an endless network of pestilential courts and alleys, into which can penetrate no pure, purging breath of heaven, where the plants languish and die in the heavy air, and the very flies seem to lose the power of flight and creep and crawl in sickly, loathsome adhesion to mouldering walls and ceilings—here, without one glimpse of the beauty of God's fair world, or of the worth and dignity of that human nature made after the image of the Divine, we find the miserable poverty-stricken rooms of the fur-pullers.

To apply the word 'homes' to dens such as these is cruel mockery. There are no 'kindred points' between them and heaven.

Of all these home-workers the fur-pullers are the hardest to find. Whether it is from some strange sense of the degradation of their work, some faint glimmer of the divine spark of self-respect, which makes them seek to hide from prying eyes; or whether it is merely from a vague terror lest discovery by the mysterious higher powers should deprive them of their last means of buying a crust of bread, the fact remains that they hide themselves away with a curious persistence. If you want to find them, the surest and quickest method is to inquire of the swarms of neglected, unwashed children who are always to be found playing on the greasy pavements 'where the lady lives who does fur-pulling'. A dozen names will be instantly shouted out, with graphic descriptions of the owners and their abodes. Changes of residence are too much an affair of every day for either parents or children in these parts to burden themselves with remembering the numbers even of the houses in which they themselves are lodged for the time being.

It is the business of the fur-puller, broadly speaking, to remove the long coarse hairs from rabbit skins; the skins and the collected hairs having each their further uses. Accordingly, as we approach the first of those tenement dwellings to which the inquiry is directed, the countless miscellaneous odours of the alley are absorbed in one which overpowers the rest—the sickly, unmistakable smell of uncleaned skins. On entering the house the air becomes thick with the millions of almost impalpable hairs which float in it. They force their way through every chink and crevice, clinging to everything they touch, and lying piled in layers of horrible dust on the dilapidated and dirty staircase.

Groping your way upwards, avoiding as carefully as possible all contact with the walls and low ceilings, and guided by the ever-increasing density of the 'fluff', you enter a back attic in which two of the fur-pullers are at work.

The room is barely eight feet square, even less, because of its accumulation of dirt; and it has to serve for day and night alike. Pushed into one corner is the bed, a dirty pallet tied together with string, upon which is piled a black heap of bedclothes. On one half of the table are the remains of breakfast—a crust of bread, a piece of butter, and a cracked cup, all thickly coated with the all-pervading hairs. The other half is covered with pulled skins, waiting to be taken into 'shop'. The window is tightly closed, because such air as can find its way in from the stifling court below would force the hairs into the noses and eyes and lungs of the workers, and make life more intolerable for them than it already is. To the visitor, indeed, the choking sensation caused by the passage of the hairs into the throat, and the nausea from the smell of the skins, is at first almost too overpowering for speech.

The two prematurely aged women—whose unkempt, matted hair is almost hidden under a thick covering of fluff, and whose clothing is of the scantiest, seeming to consist of bits of sacking fashioned into some semblance of garments—are sitting on low stools before a roughly made deal trough, into which they throw the long upper hairs of the skin, reducing them to the fine, silky down growing next to the skin itself, which is afterwards manufactured into felt hats. The heaps of skins by their side are dried, but uncleaned, and still covered with congealed blood.

EDITH F. HOGG, in *The Nineteenth Century*, Nov. 1897

Skirt Machinist

I am making great big skirts
For great big women—
Amazons who've fed and slept
Themselves inhuman.

Such long skirts, not less than two
And forty inches.
Thirty round the waist for fear
The webbing pinches.

There must be tremendous tucks
On those round bellies.
Underneath the limbs will shake
Like wine-soft jellies.

I am making such big skirts
And all so heavy,
I can see the wearers at
A lord-mayor's levee.

I, who am so small and weak
I have hardly grown,
Wish the skirts I'm making less
Unlike my own.

LESBIA HARFORD (1889–1927), pub. 1991

'Look at those spangles, Miss Bart—every one of 'em sewed on crooked.'

The tall forewoman, a pinched perpendicular figure, dropped the condemned structure of wire and net on the table at Lily's side, and passed on to the next figure in the line.

There were twenty of them in the work-room, their fagged profiles, under exaggerated hair, bowed in the harsh north light above the utensils of their art; for it was something more than an industry, surely, this creation of ever-varied settings for the face of fortunate womanhood. Their own faces were sallow with the unwholesomeness of hot air and sedentary toil, rather than with any actual signs of want: they were employed in a fashionable millinery establishment, and were fairly well clothed and well paid; but the youngest among them was as dull and colourless as the middle-aged. In the whole work-room there was only one skin beneath which the blood still visibly played; and that now burned with vexation as Miss Bart, under the lash of the forewoman's comment, began to strip the hat-frame of its over-lapping spangles.

*

Lily had taken up her work early in January: it was now two months later, and she was still being rebuked for her inability to sew spangles on a hat-frame. As she returned to her work she heard a titter pass down the tables. She knew she was an object of criticism and amusement to the other work-women. They were, of course, aware of her history—the exact situation of every girl in the room was known and freely discussed by all the others—but the knowledge did not produce in them any awkward sense of class distinction: it merely explained why her untutored fingers were still blundering over the rudiments of the trade. Lily had no desire that they should recognize any social difference in her; but she had hoped to be received as their equal, and perhaps before long to show herself their superior by a special deftness of touch, and it was humiliating to find that, after two months of drudgery, she still betrayed her lack of early training. Remote was the day when she might aspire to exercise the talents she felt confident of possessing; only experienced workers were entrusted with the delicate art of shaping and trimming the hat, and the forewoman still held her inexorably to the routine of preparatory work.

She began to rip the spangles from the frame, listening absently to the buzz of talk which rose and fell with the coming and going of Miss Haines's active figure. The air was closer than usual, because Miss Haines, who had a cold, had not allowed a window to be opened even during the noon recess; and Lily's head was so heavy with the weight of a sleepless night that the chatter of her companions had the incoherence of a dream.

'I *told* her he'd never look at her again; and he didn't. I wouldn't have, either—I think she acted real mean to him. He took her to the Arion Ball, and had a hack for her both ways . . . She's taken ten bottles, and her headaches don't seem no better—but she's written a testimonial to say the first bottle cured her, and she got five dollars and her picture in the paper . . . Mrs Trenor's hat? The one with the green Paradise? Here, Miss Haines—it'll be ready right off . . . That was one of the Trenor girls here yesterday with Mrs George Dorset. How'd I know? Why, Madam sent for me to alter the flower in that Virot hat—the blue tulle: she's tall and slight, with her hair fuzzed out—a good deal like Mamie Leach, on'y thinner . . .'

On and on it flowed, a current of meaningless sound, on which, startlingly enough, a familiar name now and then floated to the surface. It was the strangest part of Lily's strange experience, the hearing of these names, the seeing the fragmentary and distorted image of the world she had lived in reflected in the mirror of the working-girls' minds. She had never before suspected the mixture of insatiable curiosity and contemptuous freedom with which she and her kind were discussed in this underworld of toilers who lived on their vanity and self-indulgence. Every girl in Mme Regina's workroom knew to whom the headgear in her hands was destined, and had her opinion of its future wearer, and a definite knowledge of the latter's place in the social system. That Lily was a star fallen from that sky did not, after the first stir of curiosity had subsided, materially add to their interest in her. She had fallen, she had 'gone under,' and true to the ideal of their race, they were awed only by success—by the gross tangible image of material achievement. The consciousness of her different point of view merely kept them at a little distance from her, as though she were a foreigner with whom it was an effort to talk.

'Miss Bart, if you can't sew those spangles on more regular I guess you'd better give the hat to Miss Kilroy.'

Lily looked down ruefully at her handiwork. The forewoman was right: the sewing on of the spangles was inexcusably bad. What made her so much more clumsy than usual? Was it a growing distaste for her task, or actual physical disability? She felt tired and confused: it was an effort to put her thoughts together. She rose and handed the hat to Miss Kilroy, who took it with a suppressed smile.

'I'm sorry; I'm afraid I am not well,' she said to the forewoman.

Miss Haines offered no comment. From the first she had augured ill of Mme Regina's consenting to include a fashionable apprentice among her workers. In that temple of art no raw beginners were wanted, and Miss Haines would have been more than human had she not taken a certain pleasure in seeing her forebodings confirmed.

'You'd better go back to binding edges,' she said drily.

EDITH WHARTON (1862–1937), *The House of Mirth*, 1905

SAILORS

A sea-captain, whose home was in the west,
Was there—a Dartmouth man, for all I know.
He rode a cob as well as he knew how,

And was dressed in a knee-length woollen gown.
From a lanyard round his neck, a dagger hung
Under his arm. Summer had tanned him brown.
As rough a diamond as you'd hope to find,
He'd tapped and lifted many a stoup of wine
From Bordeaux, when the merchant wasn't looking.
He hadn't time for scruples or fine feeling,
For if he fought, and got the upper hand,
He'd send his captives home by sea, not land.
But as for seamanship, and calculation
Of moon, tides, currents, all hazards at sea,
For harbour-lore, and skill in navigation,
From Hull to Carthage there was none to touch him.
He was shrewd adventurer, tough and hardy.
By many a tempest had his beard been shaken.
And he knew all the harbours that there were
Between the Baltic and Cape Finisterre,
And each inlet of Britanny and Spain.
The ship he sailed was called 'The Magdalen'.

GEOFFREY CHAUCER (*c*.1343–1400), 'General Prologue', *The Canterbury Tales*, *c*.1387, tr. David Wright, 1985

Nothing is more common than to hear people say, 'Are not sailors very idle at sea? What can they find to do?' This is a natural mistake, and, being frequently made, is one which every sailor feels interested in having corrected. In the first place, then, the discipline of the ship requires every man to be at work upon *something* when he is on deck, except at night and on Sundays. At all other times you will never see a man, on board a well-ordered vessel, standing idle on deck, sitting down, or leaning over the side. It is the officers' duty to keep everyone at work, even if there is nothing to be done but to scrape the rust from the chain cables. In no state prison are the convicts more regularly set to work, and more closely watched. No conversation is allowed among the crew at their duty, and though they frequently do talk when aloft, or when near one another, yet they stop when an officer is nigh.

With regard to the work upon which the men are put, it is a matter which probably would not be understood by one who has not been at sea. When I first left port, and found that we were kept regularly employed for a week or two, I supposed that we were getting the vessel into sea trim, and that it would soon be over, and we should have nothing to do but to sail the ship; but I found that it continued so for two years, and at the end of the two years there was as much to be done as ever. As has often been said, a ship is like a lady's watch, always out of repair. When first leaving port, studding-sail gear is to be rove, all the running rigging to be examined, that which is unfit for use to be got down, and new rigging rove in its place; then the standing rigging is to be overhauled, replaced, and repaired in a thousand different ways; and wherever any of the numberless ropes or the yards are chafing or wearing upon it, their 'chafing-gear,' as it is called, must be put on. This chafing-gear consists of worming, parcelling, roundings, battens, and service of all kinds—rope-yarns, spun-yarn, marline, and seizing-stuffs. Taking off, putting on, and mending the chafing-gear alone, upon a vessel, would find constant employment for a man or two men, during working hours, for a whole voyage.

The next point to be considered is, that all the 'small stuffs' which are used on board a ship—such as spun-yarn, marline, seizing-stuff, etc., etc.—are made on board. The owners of a vessel buy up incredible quantities of 'old junk,' which the sailors unlay, and, after drawing out the yarns, knot them together, and roll them up in balls. These 'rope-yarns' are constantly used for various purposes, but the greater part is manufactured into spun-yarn. For this purpose, every vessel is furnished with a 'spun-yarn winch,' which is very simple, consisting of a wheel and spindle. This may be heard constantly going on deck in pleasant weather; and we had employment, during a great part of the time, for three hands, in drawing and knotting yarns, and making spun-yarn.

Another method of employing the crew is 'setting up' rigging. Whenever any of the standing rigging becomes slack (which is continually happening) the seizings and coverings must be taken off, tackles got up, and, after the rigging is bowsed well taut, the seizings and coverings replaced, which is a very nice piece of work. There is also such a connection between different parts of a vessel, that one rope can seldom be touched without altering the place of another. You cannot stay a mast aft by the back-stays without slacking up the head-stays, etc., etc. If we add to this all the tarring, greasing, oiling, varnishing, painting, scraping, and scrubbing which is required in the course of a long voyage, and also remember this is all to be done in *addition to* watching at night, steering, reefing, furling, bracing, making and setting sail, and pulling, hauling, and climbing in every direction, one will hardly ask, 'What can a sailor find to do at sea?'

If, after all this labour—after exposing their lives and limbs in storms, wet and cold—

> Wherein the cub-drawn bear would couch,
> The lion and the belly-pinched wolf
> Keep their furs dry,—

the merchants and captains think that their men have not earned their twelve dollars a month (out of which they clothe themselves), and their salt beef and hard bread, they keep them picking oakum—*ad infinitum*. This is the usual resource upon a rainy day, for then it will not do to work upon rigging; and when it is pouring down in floods, instead of letting the sailors stand about in sheltered places, and talk, and keep themselves comfortable, they are separated to different parts of the ship, and kept at work picking oakum. I have seen oakum stuff placed about in different parts of the ship, so that the sailors might not be idle in the snatches between the frequent squalls upon crossing the equator. Some officers have been so driven to find work for the crew in a ship ready for sea, that they have set them to pounding the anchors (often done) and scraping the chain cables. The 'Philadelphia Catechism' is—

> Six days shalt thou labour and do all thou art able,
> And on the seventh—holystone the decks and scrape the cable.

This kind of work, of course, is not kept up off Cape Horn, Cape of Good Hope, and in extreme north and south latitudes; but I have seen the decks washed down and scrubbed when the water would have frozen if it had been fresh, and all hands kept at work upon the rigging, when we had on our pea-jackets, and our hands so numb that we could hardly hold our marline-spikes.

RICHARD HENRY DANA (1815–82), *Two Years Before the Mast*, 1840

A thorough sailor must understand much of other avocations. He must be a bit of an embroiderer, to work fanciful collars of hempen lace about the shrouds; he must be something of a weaver, to weave mats of rope-yarns for lashings to the boats; he must have a touch of millinery, so as to tie graceful bows and knots, such as *Matthew Walker's roses*, and *Turk's heads*; he must be a bit of a musician, in order to sing out at the halyards; he must be a sort of jeweller, to set dead-eyes in the standing rigging; he must be a carpenter, to enable him to make a jury-mast out of a yard in case of emergency; he must be a sempstress, to darn and mend the sails; a ropemaker, to twist *marline* and *Spanish foxes*; a blacksmith, to make hooks and thimbles for the blocks: in short, he must be a sort of Jack of all trades, in order to master his own. And this, perhaps, in a greater or less degree, is pretty much the case with all things else; for you know nothing till you know all; which is the reason we never know any thing.

A sailor, also, in working at the rigging, uses special tools peculiar to his calling—*fids, serving-mallets, toggles, prickers, marlingspikes, palms, heavers*, and many more. The smaller sort he generally carries with him from ship to ship in a sort of canvas reticule.

The estimation in which a ship's crew hold the knowledge of such accomplishments as these, is expressed in the phrase they apply to one who is a clever practitioner. To distinguish such a mariner from those who merely '*hand, reef, and steer*,' that is, run aloft, furl sails, haul ropes, and stand at the wheel, they

say he is '*a sailor-man*;' which means that he not only knows how to reef a
topsail, but is an artist in the rigging.

HERMAN MELVILLE (1819–91), *Redburn*, 1849

Round and Round

The lighthouse keeper's world is round,
Belongings skipping in a ring—
All that a man may want, therein,
A wife, a wireless, bread, jam, soap,
Yet day by night his straining hope
Shoots out to live upon the sound
The spinning waves make while they break
For their own endeavor's sake—
The lighthouse keeper's world is round.

He wonders, winding up the stair
To work the lamp which lights the ships,
Why each secured possession skips
With face towards the center turned,
From table-loads of books has learned
Shore-worlds are round as well, not square,
But there things dance with faces out-
ward turned: faces of fear and doubt?
He wonders, winding up the stair.

When it is calm, the rocks are safe
To take a little exercise
But all he does is fix his eyes
On that huge totem he has left
Where thoughts dance round what will not shift—
His secret inarticulate grief.
Waves have no sun, but are beam-caught
Running below his feet, wry salt,
When, in a calm, the rocks are safe.

THOM GUNN (1929–), 1954

CRAFTSMEN

So every carpenter and workmaster, that laboureth night and day: and they
that cut and grave seals, and are diligent to make great variety, and give themselves to counterfeit imagery, and watch to finish a work:

The smith also sitting by the anvil, and considering the iron work, the vapour of the fire wasteth his flesh, and he fighteth with the heat of the furnace: the noise of the hammer and the anvil is ever in his ears, and his eyes look still upon the pattern of the thing that he maketh; he setteth his mind to finish his work, and watcheth to polish it perfectly.

So doth the potter sitting at his work, and turning the wheel about with his feet, who is alway carefully set at his work, and maketh all his work by number;

He fashioneth the clay with his arm, and boweth down his strength before his feet; he applieth himself to lead it over; and he is diligent to make clean the furnace:

All these trust to their hands: and every one is wise in his work.

Without these cannot a city be inhabited: and they shall not dwell where they will, nor go up and down:

They shall not be sought for in publick counsel, nor sit high in the congregation: they shall not sit on the judges' seat, nor understand the sentence of judgment: they cannot declare justice and judgment: and they shall not be found where parables are spoken.

But they will maintain the state of the world, and [all] their desire is in the work of their craft.

Ecclesiasticus 38: 24–34

Castes, principally decided by birth, are organized hierarchically by occupation and by ritual. The various occupations are ranked in terms of the ritualistic significance of the kind of work. Hence, among the artisans and others the ranking of institutions is thus:

1 The goldsmith, because gold is the noblest of metals
2 The carpenter, because he builds the temples
3 The blacksmith, because iron is inferior to wood, being used for killing
4 The coppersmith, because copper is inferior to iron, being used by women for cooking
5 The sculptor, because stone is inferior to copper
6 The potter, because clay is inferior to stone
7 The barber, because he performs a task in which there is a risk of pollution
8 The washerman, because he handles dirty things
9 The leatherworker, because leather defiles.

K. ISHWARAN (1922–   ), *Shivapur: A South Indian Village*, 1968

Métier.   This name is given to all professions which require the use of the arms, and which are limited to a certain number of mechanical operations that the worker repeats incessantly. I do not know why a vile idea is attached to this word; it is trades that bring us all the things necessary for life. Anyone who will take the trouble to walk through the workshops, will see there utility joined to the greatest proofs of sagacity . . . I leave it to those who have some principle of equity, to judge whether it is reason or prejudice that makes us look at such essential men with such a disdainful eye. The poet, the philosopher, the orator, the statesman, the warrior, the hero would be entirely nude, and would lack bread, without this artisan, the object of their cruel scorn.

> DENIS DIDEROT (1713–84) and JEAN LE ROND D'ALEMBERT (1717–83) eds., *Encyclopédie, ou Dictionnaire raisonné des sciences, des arts et des métiers*, 1751–80, tr. William H. Sewell Jr, 1980

A great axe first she gave, that two ways cut,
In which a fair well-polish'd helm was put,
That from an olive bough receiv'd his frame.
A plainer then. Then led she, till they came
To lofty woods that did the isle confine.
The fir-tree, poplar, and heav'n-scaling pine,
Had there their offspring. Of which, those that were
Of driest matter, and grew longest there,
He choos'd for lighter sail. This place thus shown,
The Nymph turn'd home. He fell to felling down,
And twenty trees he stoop'd in little space,
Plain'd, used his plumb, did all with artful grace.
In mean time did Calypso wimbles bring.
He bor'd, clos'd, nail'd, and order'd ev'ry thing,
And look how much a ship-wright will allow
A ship of burden (one that best doth know
What fits his art) so large a keel he cast,
Wrought up her decks, and hatches, side-boards, mast,
With willow watlings arm'd her to resist
The billows' outrage, added all she miss'd,
Sail-yards, and stern for guide. The Nymph then brought
Linen for sails, which with dispatch he wrought,
Gables, and halsters, tacklings. All the frame
In four days' space to full perfection came.

> HOMER, *The Odyssey*, c.725 BC, tr. George Chapman, 1616

wimbles] gimlets   *halsters*] cables and hawsers

Bell Ringer

Carswell, George, is the name,
Rang the bells here, Wells Cathedral,
Seventy-six deafening years, this brass
On the south wall says so;
The silent memorandum of my fame.
Pulled hard at every festival,
Saw from my loft the seasons pass.
Rang in fog, blossom and harvest time, snow;
Mainly tenor, began in 1810,
When in my cocky 'teens,
Learning from the older men,
What every ringer has to know,
The sequence of the rounds and queens.
Was ready with bob majors at Waterloo,
Parties then in all the hotels,
Bonfires, dancing, and hullabaloo;
A peal of muffled bells
Mourned the mad old king,
But merry grandsire triples for the little Victoria;
We fired the bells for her son's christening,
Making one continuous Gloria.
How many times have I bowed my back
Beneath the broad beams of the tower,
Held the swaying ropes, taut and slack,
At weddings of the county families,
Pale daughters, trembling at the knees,
Puffy knights in velvet and lace,
Dowagers with poodles and pedigrees,
Ringing the sharp changes, hour after hour,
Sprinkling a proud shower of wealth
Over moated swans and market place.
Yet, I do not know what they all came to see,
Those crowds of gawking spectators,
The early closing day they buried me,
Or what they thought the fuss was all about;
The lads up in the tower they drank my health
And, bless them, saw me grandly out
To a long and lively set of Steadman Caters.

LEONARD CLARK (1905–), 1968

The Line-Gang

Here come the line-gang pioneering by.
They throw a forest down less cut than broken.
They plant dead trees for living, and the dead
They string together with a living thread.
They string an instrument against the sky
Wherein words, whether beaten out or spoken,
Will run as hushed as when they were a thought.
But in no hush they string it: they go past
With shouts afar to pull the cable taut,
To hold it hard until they make it fast.
To ease away—they have it. With a laugh
And oath of towns that set the wild at naught,
They bring the telephone and telegraph.

ROBERT FROST (1874–1963), 1916

The Carpenter

With a jack plane in his hands
My father the carpenter
Massaged the wafering wood,
Making it white and true.

He was skilful with his saws,
Handsaw, bowsaw, hacksaw,
And ripsaw with fishes' teeth
That chewed a plank in a second.

He was fond of silver bits,
The twist and countersink—
And the auger in its pit
Chucking shavings over its shoulder.

I remember my father's hands,
For they were supple and strong
With fingers that were lovers—
Sensuous strokers of wood:

He fondled the oak, the strong-man
Who holds above his head
A record-breaking lift
Of thick commingled boughs;

And he touched with his finger tips
Dark boards of elm and alder,
Spruce, and cherry for lathes
That turned all days to spring.

My father's hands were tender
Upon my tender head,
But they were massive on massive
Beam for building a house,

And delicate on the box wood
Leaning against the wall
As though placed there in a corner
For a moment and then forgotten,

And expert as they decoded
Archives unlocked by the axe—
The pretty medullary rays
Once jammed with a traffic of food

To a watched and desired tree
That he marked and felled in the winter,
The tracks of tractors smashing
The ground where violets grew,

Then bound in chains and dragged
To the slaughtering circular saw:
A railway dulcimer
Rang the passing bell

Of my father's loved ones,
Though there was no grief in him
Caressing the slim wood, hearing
A robin's piccolo song.

CLIFFORD DYMENT (1914–71), 1955

1st Removal Man. What was Ceylon like?
Dave. Beautiful island. Being a carpenter I used to watch the local carpenters at work. They used to make their own tools and sometimes they'd
show me. They'd sit out on the beach fashioning the boats or outside their
houses planing and chiselling away at their timber, and they let me sit with
them once they knew I was also building boats. And you know, one day, as I
watched, I made a discovery—the kind of discovery you discover two or three
times in a lifetime. I discovered an old truth: that a man is made to work and
that when he works he's giving away something of himself, something very
precious—

ARNOLD WESKER (1932–), *I'm Talking about Jerusalem*, 1960

Your soul was lifted by the wings to-day
Hearing the master of the violin:
You praised him, praised the great Sebastian too
Who made that fine Chaconne; but did you think
Of old Antonio Stradivari?—him
Who a good century and half ago
Put his true work in that brown instrument
And by the nice adjustment of its frame
Gave it responsive life, continuous
With the master's finger-tips and perfected
Like them by delicate rectitude of use.
Not Bach alone, helped by fine precedent
Of genius gone before, nor Joachim
Who holds the strain afresh incorporate
By inward hearing and notation strict
Of nerve and muscle, made our joy to-day:
Another soul was living in the air
And swaying it to true deliverance
Of high invention and responsive skill:—
That plain white-aproned man who stood at work
Patient and accurate full fourscore years,
Cherished his sight and touch by temperance,
And since keen sense is love of perfectness
Made perfect violins, the needed paths
For inspiration and high mastery.

No simpler man than he: he never cried,
'Why was I born to this monotonous task
Of making violins?' or flung them down
To suit with hurling act a well-hurled curse
At labour on such perishable stuff.
Hence neighbours in Cremona held him dull,
Called him a slave, a mill-horse, a machine,
Begged him to tell his motives or to lend
A few gold pieces to a loftier mind.
Yet he had pithy words full fed by fact;
For Fact, well-trusted, reasons and persuades,
Is gnomic, cutting, or ironical,
Draws tears, or is a tocsin to arouse—
Can hold all figures of the orator
In one plain sentence; has her pauses too—
Eloquent silence at the chasm abrupt
Where knowledge ceases. Thus Antonio
Made answers as Fact willed, and made them strong.

GEORGE ELIOT (1819–80), from 'Stradivarius', 1873

Elegy for Alfred Hubbard

Hubbard is dead, the old plumber;
who will mend our burst pipes now,
the tap that has dripped all the summer,
testing the sink's overflow?

No other like him. Young men with knowledge
of new techniques, theories from books,
may better his work straight from college,
but who will challenge his squint-eyed looks

in kitchen, bathroom, under floorboards,
rules of thumb which were often wrong;
seek as erringly stopcocks in cupboards,
or make a job last half as long?

He was a man who knew the ginnels,
alleyways, streets—the whole district,
family secrets, minor annals,
time-honoured fictions fused to fact.

Seventy years of gossip muttered
under his cap, his tufty thatch,
so that his talk was slow and clotted,
hard to follow, and too much.

As though nothing fell, none vanished,
and time were the maze of Cheetham Hill,
in which the dead—with jobs unfinished—
waited to hear him ring the bell.

For much he never got round to doing,
but meant to, when weather bucked up,
or worsened, or when his pipe was drawing,
or when he'd finished this cup.

I thought time, he forgot so often,
had forgotten him, but here's Death's pomp
over his house, and by the coffin
the son who will inherit his blowlamp,

tools, workshop, cart, and cornet
(pride of Cheetham Prize Brass Band),
and there's his mourning widow, Janet,
stood at the gate he'd promised to mend.

Soon he will make his final journey;
shaved and silent, strangely trim,
with never a pause to talk to anybody: how arrow-like, for him!

In St Mark's Church, whose dismal tower
he pointed and painted when a lad,
they will sing his praises amidst flowers
while, somewhere, a cellar starts to flood,

and the housewife banging his front-door knocker
is not surprised to find him gone,
and runs for Thwaite, who's a better worker,
and sticks at a job until it's done.

TONY CONNOR (1930–), 1962

I was introduced to old George, a Cotswold mason. He is in his seventies but
still at it. When I met him he was engaged in the almost lost art of dry-walling,
pulling down some ramshackle old walls and converting their materials into
smooth solid ramparts. He was a little man, with a dusty puckered face and an
immense upper lip so that he looked like a wise old monkey; and he had spent
all his long life among stones. There were bits of stone all over him. He handled the stones about him, some of which he showed to us, at once easily and
lovingly, as women handle their babies. He was like a being that had been created out of stone, a quarry gnome. He was a pious man, this old George, and
when he was not talking about stone and walls, he talked in a very quiet
though evangelical strain about his religious beliefs, which were old and simple. Being a real craftsman, knowing that he could do something better than
you or I could do it, he obviously enjoyed his work, which was not so much
toil exchanged for so many shillings but the full expression of himself, his sign
that he was Old George the mason and still at it. Bad walls, not of his building,
were coming down, and good walls were going up. The stones in them fitted
squarely and smoothly and were a delight to the eye and a great contentment
to the mind, so weary of shoddy and rubbish. I have never done anything in
my life so thoroughly and truly as that old mason did his building. If I could
write this book, or any other book, as well as he can build walls, honest dry
walls, I should be the proudest and happiest man alive. Old George has always
been a mason, and his father and grandfather were masons before him; they
were all masons, these Georges; they built the whole Cotswolds: men of their
hands, men with a trade, craftsmen. I do not know for what pittances they
worked, or how narrow and frugal their lives must have been, but I do know
that they were not unhappy men; they knew what they could do and they were
allowed to do it; they were not taught algebra and chemistry and then flung

into a world that did not even want their casual labour: they were not robbed of all the dignity and sweetness of real work; they did not find themselves lost and hopeless in a world that neither they nor anyone else could understand; they did not feel themselves to be tiny cogs in a vast machine that was running down; they had a good trade in their fingers, solid work to do, and when it was done—and there it was, with no mistake about it, ready to outlast whole dynasties—they could take their wages and go home and be content. I am glad I met old George and saw him at work. And if ever we do build Jerusalem in this green and pleasant land, I hope he will be there, doing the dry-walling.

J. B. PRIESTLEY (1894–1984), *English Journey*, 1934

He asked for the foreman, and looked round among the new traceries, mullions, transoms, shafts, pinnacles, and battlements standing on the bankers half worked, or waiting to be removed. They were marked by precision, mathematical straightness, smoothness, exactitude: there in the old walls were the broken lines of the original idea; jagged curves, disdain of precision, irregularity, disarray.

For a moment there fell on Jude a true illumination; that here in the stone yard was a centre of effort as worthy as that dignified by the name of scholarly study within the noblest of the colleges.

THOMAS HARDY (1840–1928), *Jude the Obscure*, 1895

A Truthful Song

I

THE BRICKLAYER:
I tell this tale, which is strictly true,
Just by way of convincing you
How very little, since things were made,
Things have altered in the building trade.

A year ago, come the middle of March,
We was building flats near the Marble Arch,
When a thin young man with coal-black hair
Came up to watch us working there.

Now there wasn't a trick in brick or stone
Which this young man hadn't seen or known;
Nor there wasn't a tool from trowel to maul
But this young man could use 'em all!

Then up and spoke the plumbyers bold,
Which was laying the pipes for the hot and cold:
'Since you with us have made so free,
Will you kindly say what your name might be?'

The young man kindly answered them:
'It might be Lot or Methusalem,
Or it might be Moses (a man I hate),
Whereas it is Pharaoh surnamed the Great.

'Your glazing is new and your plumbing's strange,
But otherwise I perceive no change;
And in less than a month if you do as I bid
I'd learn you to build me a Pyramid!'

II

THE SAILOR:
I tell this tale, which is stricter true,
Just by way of convincing you
How very little, since things was made,
Things have altered in the shipwright's trade.

In Blackwall Basin yesterday
A China barque re-fitting lay,
When a fat old man with snow-white hair
Came up to watch us working there.

Now there wasn't a knot which the riggers knew
But the old man made it—and better too;
Nor there wasn't a sheet, or a lift, or a brace,
But the old man knew its lead and place.

Then up and spoke the caulkyers bold,
Which was packing the pump in the afterhold:
'Since you with us have made so free,
Will you kindly tell what your name might be?'

The old man kindly answered them:
'It might be Japheth, it might be Shem,
Or it might be Ham (though his skin was dark),
Whereas it is Noah, commanding the Ark.

'Your wheel is new and your pumps are strange,
But otherwise I perceive no change;
And in less than a week, if she did not ground,
I'd sail this hooker the wide world round!'

BOTH:
We tell these tales, which are strictest true,
Just by way of convincing you
How very little, since things was made,
Anything alters in any one's trade!

RUDYARD KIPLING (1865–1936), 1910

Bricklaying is one of the oldest of our trades. For hundreds of years there has been little or no improvement made in the implements and materials used in this trade, nor in fact in the method of laying bricks. In spite of the millions of men who have practised this trade, no great improvement has been evolved for many generations. Here, then, at least, one would expect to find but little gain possible through scientific analysis and study. Mr Frank B. Gilbreth, a member of our Society, who had himself studied bricklaying in his youth, became interested in the principles of scientific management, and decided to apply them to the art of bricklaying. He made an intensely interesting analysis and study of each movement of the bricklayer, and one after another eliminated all unnecessary movements and substituted fast for slow motions. He experimented with every minute element which in any way affects the speed and the tiring of the bricklayer.

He developed the exact position which each of the feet of the bricklayer should occupy with relation to the wall, the mortar box, and the pile of bricks, and so made it unnecessary for him to take a step or two toward the pile of bricks and back again each time a brick is laid.

He studied the best height for the mortar box and brick pile, and then designed a scaffold, with a table on it, upon which all of the materials are placed, so as to keep the bricks, the mortar, the man, and the wall in their proper relative positions. These scaffolds are adjusted, as the wall grows in height, for all of the bricklayers by a laborer especially detailed for this purpose, and by this means the bricklayer is saved the exertion of stooping down to the level of his feet for each brick and each trowelful of mortar and then straightening up again. Think of the waste of effort that has gone on through all these years, with each bricklayer lowering his body, weighing, say, 150 pounds, down two feet and raising it up again every time a brick (weighing about 5 pounds) is laid in the wall! And this each bricklayer did about one thousand times a day.

As a result of further study, after the bricks are unloaded from the cars, and before bringing them to the bricklayer, they are carefully sorted by a laborer, and placed with their best edge up on a simple wooden frame, constructed so as to enable him to take hold of each brick in the quickest time and in the most advantageous position. In this way the bricklayer avoids either having to turn the brick over or end for end to examine it before laying it, and he saves, also, the time taken in deciding which is the best edge and end to place on the outside of the wall. In most cases, also, he saves the time taken in disentangling the brick from a disorderly pile on the scaffold. This 'pack' of bricks (as Mr Gilbreth calls his loaded wooden frames) is placed by the helper in its proper position on the adjustable scaffold close to the mortar box.

We have all been used to seeing bricklayers tap each brick after it is placed on its bed of mortar several times with the end of the handle of the trowel so as to secure the right thickness for the joint. Mr Gilbreth found that by tempering the mortar just right, the bricks could be readily bedded to the proper depth by a downward pressure of the hand with which they are laid. He insisted that his mortar mixers should give special attention to tempering the mortar, and so save the time consumed in tapping the brick.

Through all of this minute study of the motions to be made by the bricklayer in laying bricks under standard conditions, Mr Gilbreth has reduced his movements from eighteen motions per brick to five, and even in one case to as low as two motions per brick. He has given all of the details of this analysis to the profession in the chapter headed 'Motion Study,' of his book entitled 'Bricklaying System,' published by Myron C. Clerk Publishing Company, New York and Chicago; E. F. N. Spon, of London.

> FREDERICK WINSLOW TAYLOR (1856–1915), *The Principles of Scientific Management*, 1911

The Builders

Staggering slowly, and swaying
Heavily at each slow foot's lift and drag,
With tense eyes careless of the roar and throng,
That under jut and jag
Of half-built wall and scaffold streams along,
Six bowed men straining strong
Bear, hardly lifted, a huge lintel stone.
This ignorant thing and prone,
Mere dumbness, blindly weighing,
A brute piece of blank death, a bone
Of the stark mountain, helpless and inert,
Yet draws each sinew till the hot veins swell
And sweat-drops upon hand and forehead start,
Till with short pants the suffering heart
Throbs to the throat, where fiercely hurt
Crushed shoulders cannot heave; till thought and sense
Are nerved and narrowed to one aim intense,
One effort scarce to be supported longer!
What tyrant will in man or God were stronger

To summon, thrall and seize
The exaction of life's uttermost resource
That from the down-weighed breast and aching knees
To arms lifted in pain
And hands that grapple and strain
Upsurges, thrusting desperate to repel
The pressure and the force
Of this, which neither feels, nor hears, nor sees?

LAURENCE BINYON (1869–1943), 1908

Visitors to Oxford and indeed many members of the University who are sometimes puzzled or annoyed by the unexpected appearance of scaffolding and the lengthy periods during which college and university buildings are surrounded and concealed by scaffolding may not be aware that what may appear to be a random process is governed by a traditional and carefully worked out procedure. Its principles were negotiated some years ago by the intercollegiate committee of college Bursars and representatives of the T. G. W. and Building and Allied Trades Unions. Full details of the procedures are confidential but it can be said that in straightforward cases involving no special technical complexities the current operating rules involve twelve stages. They are as follows:

Stage one: Scaffolding is erected without prior warning, so as not to provoke needless feelings of apprehension, alarm, or annoyance on the part of those inhabitants of college or university buildings whose premises are scaffolded.

Stage two: A period of at least one week elapses between erection of the scaffolding and the beginning of any operation.

Stage three: More scaffolding is erected than is needed for whatever the scaffolding is erected for.

Stage four: When the scaffolding is erected no more than two persons work on it simultaneously whatever the size of the scaffolding.

Stage five: When the operations for which the scaffolding is erected are completed the scaffolding is not disturbed or dismantled for a minimum period of 10 days (or if in Lent 21 days).

Stage six: The scaffolders are asked when the scaffolding will be dismantled and they say that it will be dismantled 'almost immediately'.

Stage seven: The scaffolding is not dismantled almost immediately.

Stage eight: The scaffolders are asked why the scaffolding has not been dismantled almost immediately and they say that the dismantlers are busy but dismantling will begin soon (or within 10 days, allowing for Bank Holidays).

Stage nine: The scaffolding is not dismantled soon or within 10 days, even allowing for Bank Holidays.

Stage ten: After a further period, whose duration has not been exactly specified, dismantlers (to a number of not more than two) begin to dismantle the scaffolding, if possible by dropping items of scaffolding from the top of the scaffolding to the ground without warning.

Stage eleven: Scaffolding lorries arrive and are parked (if possible double parked) outside the college or university building in question and scaffolding poles are piled at all convenient points of egress.

Stage twelve: Inspection of damage caused by the dismantlers requires the erection of further scaffolding, in accordance with the above operating procedures.

It must be conceded that, however meticulously operated, these working rules have on occasion caused disgruntlement. Several College Governing Bodies are said to be considering proposals to provide for the erection of some form of permanent college scaffolding. This would avoid the alarm and annoyance caused by the unexpected appearance of temporary scaffolding and make for a significant improvement in the tranquillity of academic life.

GEOFFREY MARSHALL (1929–), *Oxford Magazine*, 1987

'Building a Roman Road'

First comes the task of preparing the ditches,
Marking the borders, and deeply as needed,
Delving into the earth's interior;
Then with other stuff filling the furrows,
Making a base for the crown of the roadway,
Lest the soil sink, or deceptive foundations
Furnish the flagstones with treacherous bedding;
Then to secure the roadway with cobbles
Close-packed, and also ubiquitous wedges.
How many hands are working together!
Some fell the forest while some denude mountains,
Some smooth boulders and baulks with iron;
Others with sand that is heated, and earthy
Tufa, assemble the stones of the structure.
Some with labour drain pools ever thirsty;
Some lead the rivulets far to the distance.

STATIUS (AD 45/early 50s–96), *Silvae*, *c.*95, tr. K. D. White, 1984

'The Seventeenth-century Barber'

TERMS OF ART USED IN BARBING AND SHAVING

Take the chair, is for the person to be trimmed, to sit down.

Clear the neck, is to unbutton and turn down the collar of the man's neck.

Clothe him, is to put a trimming cloth before him, and to fasten it about his neck.

Comb round the hair, is to ready the hair with a wide tooth comb.

Powder the hair, is to puff sweet powder into it.

Rub the hair with a napkin, is to dry it from its sweatiness and filth in the head.

Comb out the hair, and *power it*, is to comb the hair straight with a wide tooth horn comb.

Comb it smooth and *even* with a box comb.

Comb it against the grain, is to comb it round the head upwards to the crown.

Walk your combs, is to use two combs, in each hand one, and to comb the hair with one after the other.

Quiver the combs, is to use them as if they were scratching on each side the temples.

Quiver the head round, is to scratch it with the combs all over.

Divide the hair, is to lay it straight, or part it on the top of the head, even with the nose.

Cut it up in heights, that is to cut as each person will have it, for there is variety of ways in cutting of hair, as

> *Cutting it all off the top*, and so they use it that wear periwigs.
>
> *Cutting it close*, so that the remainder stands upright; this is called *round cutting*, and *prick-eared cutting*, because the hair is so short that it scarce covers the ears.
>
> *Cutting in falls*, when the hair is cut to fall down each side the head, and extends itself to the shoulders. This is termed *parting of the hair*.

Jessamine the hair, is to put jessamy [jasmine perfume] on the palms of your hands and rub it on the hair, and in the hair, by putting the locks between your hands, and rubbing the hands together.

Powder the hair.

Clap on the cap, and divide the hair alike on each side.

Curl up the hair, is to roll it about a pair of curling or beard irons, and thrust it under the cap.

Handle the basin, and *Ball*, pour in the water.

Lather the face, is to wash the beard with the suds which the ball maketh by chafing it in the warm water.

Hand the razor, set it in a right order between the thumb and fingers.

Shave the beard, is to take off superfluous hairs.

Wash the face, with a ball and water, or a sweet ball.

Clear the face from the ball, is to wash it over with clean water to take off the soapiness.

Dry the face, is airing of a napkin (if cold weather) and drying off the wet.

Trim the beard, take away straggling hairs, and cut it thinner.

Take off the cap, and fall the hair.

Comb out the hair.

Hold him the glass, to see his new-made face, and to give the barber instructions where it is amiss.

Take off the linens.

Brush his clothes.

Present him with his hat, and, according to his hire, he makes a bow, with 'your humble servant, sir'.

RANDLE HOLME (1627–99), *The Academy of Armory*, 1688

Alex at the Barber's

He is having his hair cut. Towels are tucked
About his chin, his mop scalped jokingly.
The face in the mirror is his own face.

The barber moves and chats among the green
And methylated violet, snipper-snips,
Puts scissors down, puts in a plaited flex,

And like a surgeon with his perfumed hands
Presses the waiting skull and shapes the base.
He likes having his hair cut, and the man

Likes cutting it. The radio drones on.
The eyes in the mirror are his own eyes.
While the next chair receives the Demon Blade,

A dog-leg razor nicks a sideburn here;
As from a sofa there a sheet is whisked
And silver pocketed. The doorbell pings.

The barber, frowning, grips the ragged fringe
And slowly cuts. Upon the speckled sheet
The bits fall down and now his hair is cut.

The neighing trams outside splash through the rain.
The barber tests the spray for heat and rubs
Lemon shampoo into his spiky hair.

Bent with his head above the running bowl,
Eyes squeezed shut, he does not see the water
Gurgle and sway like twisted sweetpaper

Above the waste, but, for a moment, tows
A sleigh of polished silver parrots through
Acres of snow, exclaiming soundlessly.

Then towel round head. Head swung gently up.
Eyes padded. As the barber briskly rubs,
The smile in the mirror is his own smile.

JOHN FULLER (1937–), 1961

MINERS

The miner thus through perils digs his way,
Equal to theirs, and deeper than the sea!
Drawing, in pestilential steams, his breath,
Resolv'd to conquer, though he combats Death.
Night's gloomy realms his pointed steel invades,
The courts of Pluto, and infernal shades:
He cuts through mountains, subterraneous lakes,
Plying his work, each nervous stroke he takes
Loosens the earth, and the whole cavern shakes.
Thus, with his brawny arms, the Cyclops stands,
To form Jove's lightning, with uplifted hands,
The ponderous hammer with a force descends,
Loud as the thunder which his art intends;
And as he strikes, with each resistless blow
The anvil yields, and Etna groans below.

THOMAS YALDEN (1670–1736), from 'To Sir Humphry Mackworth: On the Mines, Late of Sir Carbery Price', 1701

I suppose that there are in Great Britain upwards of an hundred thousand people employed in lead, tin, iron, copper, and coal mines; these unhappy wretches scarce ever see the light of the sun; they are buried in the bowels of the earth; there they work at a severe and dismal task, without the least prospect of being delivered from it; they subsist upon the coarsest and worst sort of fare; they have their health miserably impaired, and their lives cut short, by being perpetually confined in the close vapour of these malignant minerals. An hundred thousand more at least are tortured without remission by the suffocating smoke, intense fires, and constant drudgery necessary in refining and managing the products of those mines.

EDMUND BURKE (1727–97), A Vindication of Natural Society, 1753

The Miner's Catechism

Q. Rehearse the articles of thy belief.

A. I believe that my master, who is a Coal Owner, sinks his capital in a coal pit in expectation of making a princely fortune in a short time, and that his Viewers are hard task-masters, and that it is them who make such hard laws as these: Thou shalt not send any foul coal, splint, or stone to bank among the good coals, or if thou dost thou shalt pay threepence a quart for it; and if thou sends a tub to bank not containing the quantity specified in the bond, thou shalt not have any pay for the same . . .

Q. What dost thou chiefly learn in the articles of thy belief?

A. First, I learn to believe that the Coal Owner wants his work done as cheap as possible. Secondly, That the Viewer gets as much money as possible from the workmen so that he may accumulate as large a fortune as possible. Thirdly, That the Overman will do anything the Owner or Viewer tells him to do.

Q. You said that your godfathers and godmothers did promise for you, that you should keep your master's commandments, tell me how many there be.

A. Ten.

Q. Which be they?

A. The same that the Master spake on the day that he read the bond, saying, I am thy Master who hath bound thee to the Coal Pits, and for twelve months thou shalt remain in bondage to me.

I. Thou shalt have no other Master but me.

II. Thou shalt work for no other Master, neither shalt thou give thy services to any otherman, for I thy Master am a jealous man, and I will visit thee with heavy fines and punishments if thou break any of my commandments.

III. Thou shalt say no manner of evil of me, but shalt say I am a good master although I act as a tyrant towards thee; for I will not hold thee guiltless if thou say any manner of evil of my name.

IV. Remember thou work six days in the week, and be very thankful that I allow thee the seventh day to recruit thy exhausted strength, for I, thy Master, want as much work out of thee as possible, and if it suits me to give thee only two, three, or more days in the week, be very thankful that I give thee any work at all, for I only look at my interest, not thine.

V. Honour me thy Master, honour my Viewers, my Overman, and my Agents, so that thy days may be long in my service.

VI. Thou shalt work thyself to death and commit self-murder.

VII. Thou shalt exhaust thyself with work to hinder thee from committing adultery.

VIII. Thou shalt not steal anything from thy Master altho' I give thee no money for working for me.

IX. Thou shalt not bear witness against me or any of my agents for any misdemeanor we may commit.

X. Thou shalt not covet thy Master's house, thou shalt not covet thy Master's wife, nor his servants, nor his lands, nor his carriage, nor his horses nor any thing that is his.

Q. What dost thou chiefly learn from these commandments?

A. I learn two things, my duty towards my master, and my duty towards myself.

Q. What is thy duty towards thy master?

A. My duty towards my master is to work honestly for him and not to waste his substance, while I remain his servant.

Q. What is thy duty towards thyself?

A. My duty towards myself is to work a fair day's work for a fair day's wage, and to hinder my master from being a tyrant over me.

> Published in 1844 during the coal miners' strike in North-Eastern England

The four hewers had just spread themselves out, each lying at a different height, so as to cover the whole expanse of the coal-face. They were separated by boards, hung on hooks, which caught the coal as they hewed it away; they each worked over about four metres of the seam at a time; and the seam was so thin, hardly more than half a metre thick at that point, that they were more or less flattened between the roof and the wall, dragging themselves around on their knees and elbows, unable to turn round without bruising their shoulders. In order to get at the coal, they had to stay stretched out on one side, with their necks twisted, so that they could swing their arms far enough back to wield their short-handled picks at an angle.

First of all there was Zacharie, at the bottom; Levaque and Chaval were on the next two shelves up; and then right at the top came Maheu. Each one hewed away at the shale bedrock, hollowing it out with his pick; then he made two vertical cuts in the seam, and levered the block out by forcing an iron wedge into the top. The coal was soft, so the blocks broke up into little pieces which rolled down their stomachs and thighs. As these pieces were caught by the boards and piled up beneath the hewers, the latter gradually disappeared from view, and became walled into their narrow crevices.

It was Maheu who suffered most from this. At the top the temperature reached thirty-five degrees, and there was no air, so in time you could die of suffocation. In order to see what he was doing, he had had to fix his lamp on to a nail over his head, which in the end made his blood run hot. But his torment was aggravated by the wetness. The rock above him was only a few centimetres away from his face and large drops of water streamed from it rapidly and relentlessly, falling with an apparently obstinate rhythm, always hitting the same spot. However much he twisted and turned his neck backwards and sideways, the drops kept splashing his face, spattering and slapping him remorselessly. After a quarter of an hour, he was soaked, covered in his own sweat as well, giving off a stream of dirty, warm vapour. That morning a persistent dripping in one of his eyes made him swear. He didn't want to stop cutting, and hacked away so furiously that he shook with the vibrations, wedged between his two levels of rock, like a greenfly caught between the pages of a book which threatened to slam suddenly shut.

Not a word was exchanged. They were all hacking away, their irregular blows setting up a dull, distant-sounding, but pervasive barrage of noise. The sound had a harsh timbre in the thick air, which stifled any echo at birth. And the darkness seemed to be coloured an unnatural black, with swirling waves of coal-dust, and vapours which hung heavy on the eyelids. The wicks of the lamps, beneath their gauze chimneys, failed to penetrate the gloom with their small red glow. Hardly anything could be seen at the coal-face, whose wide mouth led diagonally upwards like a wide but shallow chimney, where the soot had been gathering for a decade of winters to form an impenetrable blackness. Ghostly figures could be seen gesticulating, as a stray gleam revealed at random an arched hip, a muscular arm, or a grim face, camouflaged as if for some crime. Sometimes, as a block of coal was dislodged, its surface or corners would suddenly sparkle like crystal. Then everything would be plunged into darkness again, the picks battering away with their heavy, dull blows, and nothing was audible but chesty breathing, and tired or painful grunts and groans, muffled by the heavy air and the sound of running water.

ÉMILE ZOLA (1840–1902), *Germinal*, 1885, tr. Peter Collier, 1993

In the metabolism of the Western world the coal-miner is second in importance only to the man who ploughs the soil. He is a sort of grimy caryatid upon whose shoulders nearly everything that is *not* grimy is supported. For this reason the actual process by which coal is extracted is well worth watching, if you get the chance and are willing to take the trouble.

When you go down a coal-mine it is important to try and get to the coal face when the 'fillers' are at work. This is not easy, because when the mine is working visitors are a nuisance and are not encouraged, but if you go at any other time, it is possible to come away with a totally wrong impression. On a Sunday, for instance, a mine seems almost peaceful. The time to go there is when the machines are roaring and the air is black with coal dust, and when you can actually see what the miners have to do. At those times the place is like hell, or at any rate like my own mental picture of hell. Most of the things one imagines in hell are there—heat, noise, confusion, darkness, foul air, and, above all, unbearably cramped space. Everything except the fire, for there is no fire down there except the feeble beams of Davy lamps and electric torches which scarcely penetrate the clouds of coal dust.

When you have finally got there—and getting there is a job in itself: I will explain that in a moment—you crawl through the last line of pit props and see opposite you a shiny black wall three or four feet high. This is the coal face. Overhead is the smooth ceiling made by the rock from which the coal has been cut; underneath is the rock again, so that the gallery you are in is only as high as the ledge of coal itself, probably not much more than a yard. The first impression of all, overmastering everything else for a while, is the frightful, deafening din from the conveyor belt which carries the coal away. You cannot see very far, because the fog of coal dust throws back the beam of your lamp, but you can see on either side of you the line of half-naked kneeling men, one to every four or five yards, driving their shovels under the fallen coal and flinging it swiftly over their left shoulders. They are feeding it on to the conveyor belt, a moving rubber belt a couple of feet wide which runs a yard or two behind them. Down this belt a glittering river of coal races constantly. In a big mine it is carrying away several tons of coal every minute. It bears it off to some place in the main roads where it is shot into tubs holding half a ton, and thence dragged to the cages and hoisted to the outer air.

It is impossible to watch the 'fillers' at work without feeling a pang of envy for their toughness. It is a dreadful job that they do, an almost superhuman job by the standards of an ordinary person. For they are not only shifting monstrous quantities of coal, they are also doing it in a position that doubles or trebles the work. They have got to remain kneeling all the while—they could hardly rise from their knees without hitting the ceiling—and you can easily see by trying it what a tremendous effort this means. Shovelling is comparatively easy when you are standing up, because you can use your knee and thigh to drive the shovel along; kneeling down, the whole of the strain is thrown upon your arm and belly muscles. And the other conditions do not exactly make things easier. There is the heat—it varies, but in some mines it is suffocating—and the coal dust that stuffs up your throat and nostrils and collects along your eyelids, and the unending rattle of the conveyor belt, which in that confined space is rather like the rattle of a machine-gun. But the fillers look and work as though they were made of iron. They really do look like iron—hammered iron statues under the smooth coat of coal dust which clings to them from head to foot. It is only when you see miners down the mine and naked that you realize what splendid men they are. Most of them are small (big men are at a disadvantage in that job) but nearly all of them have the most noble bodies; wide shoulders tapering to slender supple waists, and small pronounced buttocks and sinewy thighs, with not an ounce of waste flesh anywhere. In the hotter mines they wear only a pair of thin drawers, clogs, and knee-pads; in the hottest mines of all, only the clogs and knee-pads. You can hardly tell by the look of them whether they are young or old. They may be any age up to sixty or even sixty-five, but when they are black and naked they all look alike. No one could do their work who had not a young man's body, and a figure fit for a guardsman at that; just a few pounds of extra flesh on the waistline, and the constant bending would be impossible. You can never forget that spectacle once you have seen it—the line of bowed, kneeling figures, sooty black all over, driving their huge shovels under the coal with stupendous force and speed. They are on the job for seven and a half hours, theoretically without a break, for there is no time 'off'. Actually they snatch a quarter of an hour or so at some time during the shift to eat the food they have brought with them, usually a hunk of bread and dripping and a bottle of cold tea. The first time I was watching the 'fillers' at work I put my hand upon some dreadful slimy thing among the coal dust. It was a chewed quid of tobacco. Nearly all the miners chew tobacco, which is said to be good against thirst . . .

It is not long since conditions in the mines were worse than they are now. There are still living a few very old women who in their youth have worked underground, with a harness round their waists and a chain that passed between their legs, crawling on all fours and dragging tubs of coal. They used to go on doing this even when they were pregnant. And even now, if coal could not be produced without pregnant women dragging it to and fro, I fancy we should let them do it rather than deprive ourselves of coal. But most of the time, of course, we should prefer to forget that they were doing it. It is so with all types of manual work; it keeps us alive, and we are oblivious of its existence. More than anyone else, perhaps, the miner can stand as the type of the manual worker, not only because his work is so exaggeratedly awful, but also because it is so vitally necessary and yet so remote from our experience, so invisible, as it were, that we are capable of forgetting it as we forget the blood in our veins. In a way it is even humiliating to watch coal-miners working. It raises in you a momentary doubt about your own status as an 'intellectual' and a superior person generally. For it is brought home to you, at least while you are watching, that it is only because miners sweat their guts out that superior persons can remain superior. You and I and the editor of the *Times Lit. Supp.*, and the Nancy poets and the Archbishop of Canterbury and Comrade X, author of *Marxism for Infants*—all of us *really* owe the comparative decency of our lives to poor drudges underground, blackened to the eyes, with their throats full of coal dust, driving their shovels forward with arms and belly muscles of steel.

GEORGE ORWELL (1903–50), *The Road to Wigan Pier*, 1937

SMITHS AND METALWORKERS

Swarte-smeked smethes, smatered with smoke,
Drive me to deth with den of here dintes:
Swich nois on nightes ne herd men never,

What knavene cry and clatering of knockes!
The cammede kongons cryen after 'Col! col!'
And blowen here bellewes that all here brain brestes.
'Huf, puf,' seith that on, 'Haf, paf,' that other.
They spitten and sprawlen and spellen many spelles,
They gnawen and gnacchen, they grones togidere,
And holden hem hote with here hard hamers.
Of a bole hide ben here barm-felles,
Here shankes ben shakeled for the fere-flunderes.
Hevy hameres they han that hard ben handled,
Stark strokes they striken on a steled stocke.
'Lus, bus, las, das,' rowten by rowe.
Swiche dolful a dreme the Devil it todrive!
The maister longeth a litil and lasheth a lesse,
Twineth hem twein and toucheth a treble.
'Tik, tak, hic, hac, tiket, taket, tik, tak,
Lus, bus, lus, das'. Swich lif they leden,
Alle clothemeres, Christ hem give sorwe!
May no man for brenwateres on night han his rest.

ANON., *c.*1425–50

R. T. Davies translated the above as:

Smoke-blackened smiths, begrimed with smoke, drive me to death with the din of their blows: such noise by night no man ever heard, what crying of workmen and clattering of blows! The snub-nosed (crooked?) changelings cry out for, 'Coal! coal!' and blow their bellows fit to burst their brains. 'Huf, puf', says that one, and 'Haf, paf', the other. They spit and sprawl and tell many tales, they gnaw and gnash, they groan together, and keep themselves hot with their hard hammers. Of a bull's hide are their leather aprons, their legs are protected against the fiery sparks. Heavy hammers they have that are handled hard, strong blows they strike on an anvil of steel. 'Lus, bus, las, das', they crash in turn. May the Devil put an end to so miserable a racket. The master-smith lengthens a little piece of iron, hammers a smaller piece, twists the two together and strikes a treble note (?) Such a life they lead, all smiths who clothe horses in iron armour, may Heaven punish them! For smiths who burn water (when they cool hot iron in it) no man can sleep at night.

1963

See, pale and hollow-eyed, in his blue shirt,
Before the scorching furnace, reeking stands
The weary smith. A thund'ring water-wheel

Alternately uplifts his cumbrous pair
Of roaring bellows. He torments the coal,
And stirs the melting ore, till all resolv'd;
Then with vast forceps seizes the bright mass,
And drags it glowing to the anvil. Eye
Can scarce attend it, so intense the heat.
He bears it all, and with one arm lets free
Th'impatient stream. The heavy wheel uplifts
Slowly, and suddenly lets fall, the loud
And awful hammer, that confounds the ear,
And makes the firm earth tremble. He the block
Shapes, to the blow obsequious; cooler grown,
He stays his floodgate, once again provokes
The dying cinder, and his half-done work
Buries in fire. Again he plucks it forth,
And once more lifts it to the sturdy anvil.
There beaten long, and often turn'd, at length
'Tis done. He bears it hissing to the light,
An iron bar. Behold it well. What is't,
But a just emblem of the lot of virtue?
For in this naughty world she cannot live,
Nor rust contract, nor mingle with alloy.
So the great Judge, to make her worthy heav'n,
Submits her to the furnace and the anvil;
Till molten, bruis'd, and batter'd, she becomes
Spotless and pure, and leaves her dross behind.
    Who can repine and think his lot severe,
Who well considers this? The slaving smith,
That wipes his flowing brow so fast, his bread
Earns at the bitter cost, expense of health.
In summer's hottest day he feeds his forge,
And stands expos'd to the distressful fire,
That almost broils him dead. Yet what complaint
Makes he at fortune? He is well content
To toil at his infernal work, and breathe
A torrid atmosphere, to earn at best
Scanty subsistence in this pinching world.
Ye idle rich, consider this, nor aim
At places, pensions, titles, coronets.
Ye lazy clerks, consider this, nor sue
For benefices, canonries, and mitres.
All might inherit ease, would they not long
To fill a braver office, and at times
Look down, and see how hard the drudging poor

Toils for a bare subsistence. Be content,
And happiness shall turn and follow you.

> JAMES HURDIS (1763–1801), *The Village Curate*, 1788

The Village Blacksmith

Under a spreading chestnut-tree
    The village smithy stands;
The smith, a mighty man is he,
    With large and sinewy hands;
And the muscles of his brawny arms
    Are strong as iron bands.

His hair is crisp, and black, and long,
    His face is like the tan;
His brow is wet with honest sweat,
    He earns whate'er he can,
And looks the whole world in the face,
    For he owes not any man.

Week in, week out, from morn till night,
    You can hear his bellows blow;
You can hear him swing his heavy sledge,
    With measured beat and slow,
Like a sexton ringing the village bell,
    When the evening sun is low.

And children coming home from school
    Look in at the open door;
They love to see the flaming forge,
    And hear the bellows roar,
And catch the burning sparks that fly
    Like chaff from a threshing-floor.

He goes on Sunday to the church,
    And sits among his boys;
He hears the parson pray and preach,
    He hears his daughter's voice,
Singing in the village choir,
    And it makes his heart rejoice.

It sounds to him like her mother's voice,
    Singing in Paradise!
He needs must think of her once more,
    How in the grave she lies;
And with his hard, rough hand he wipes
    A tear out of his eyes.

Toiling—rejoicing—sorrowing,
     Onward through life he goes;
Each morning sees some task begin,
     Each evening sees it close;
Something attempted, something done,
     Has earned a night's repose.

Thanks, thanks to thee, my worthy friend,
     For the lesson thou hast taught!
Thus at the flaming forge of life
     Our fortunes must be wrought;
Thus on its sounding anvil shaped
     Each burning deed and thought.

HENRY WADSWORTH LONGFELLOW (1807–82), 1841

The blacksmith never left his fire alone. Staring into it, in constant watch for 'the heat'—that moment of moments when the iron could be properly hammered—staring, watching, he was for ever fidgeting about with it. Now, it seemed to be flaring too freely, and he sprinkled water on it with the little stubby heath broom kept in the trough at his right hand. Now he worried at the coal with his small sharp-pointed poker, bright of handle. Sometimes he would (with frown of great annoyance) poke out from the very heart of the fire a blazing mass of what looked to me like coal, and push it scornfully away over the further edge of the hearth, to fall on to the growing heap of clinkers there: for in fact this was but molten 'dirt', not good coal. If such a piece of clinker found its way between the two ends of iron to be welded together, Will grew almost frantic until he had poked it out, lest it should spoil the 'shut'. This sort of thing went on amidst Will's talk of his parsnips or potatoes— how, digging some 'taters' after a drought, he had got nothing bigger than 'nuts and warnuts'; or of the grapevine over his father's cottage in Frensham village; or of a blacksmith neighbour working in another shop; or of—any other country chatter that came uppermost.

Then, in the midst of it, he would signal to his helper—the smith at another forge or perhaps one of the wheelwrights—and the said helper promptly got into position with the sledge.

For the moment was come. Old Will had got his heat. Indeed, flaming sparks were whirling up the chimney; a pinch of sand had been thrown into the fire to keep the iron from 'burning'; unaccustomed eyes like mine could not look into the intolerable brightness; the iron was melting. One more push down then of the bellows lever, and I too had to hasten out, to help lift the tyre on the anvil and to help hold it there while able men 'shut' one side of it. I was not quite an able man myself—too feeble of arm and too fumbling. Moreover, as employer, I could not afford to be too obviously a laughing-stock. Besides, a third man—or boy—was really often needed, with heavy tyres. I was that man—or boy. So I saw the tyre-shutting, and was of some slight use too.

The second half of the shut required another heat. Accordingly the tyre, turned over, was lifted back into the fire, the bellows were blown again, the whole process was gone over a second time. But, after the 'striker', panting a little it may be, at last put down his sledge (a chinking of the hand-hammer on the anvil was the signal to him to leave off, as a lighter chinking had kept time for him all along) old Will still continued, hammering out the bruises or 'squats' left by the sledge. So he worked up the edges of the new tyre until it matched the rest of the bar.

GEORGE STURT (1883–1927), The Wheelwright's Shop, 1923

Where the city's ceaseless crowd moves on the livelong day,
Withdrawn I join a group of children watching, I pause aside with them.

By the curb toward the edge of the flagging,
A knife-grinder works at his wheel sharpening a great knife,
Bending over he carefully holds it to the stone, by foot and knee,
With measured tread he turns rapidly, as he presses with light but firm hand,
Forth issue then in copious golden jets,
Sparkles from the wheel.

WALT WHITMAN (1819–92), from 'Sparkles from the Wheel', 1871

In a large and lofty building, supported by pillars of iron, with great black apertures in the upper walls, open to the external air; echoing to the roof with the beating of hammers and roar of furnaces, mingled with the hissing of red-hot metal plunged in water, and a hundred strange unearthly noises never heard elsewhere; in this gloomy place, moving like demons among the flame and smoke, dimly and fitfully seen, flushed and tormented by the burning fires, and wielding great weapons, a faulty blow from any one of which must have crushed some workman's skull, a number of men laboured like giants. Others, reposing upon heaps of coals or ashes, with their faces turned to the black vault above, slept or rested from their toil. Others again, opening the white-hot furnace-doors, cast fuel on the flames, which came rushing and roaring forth to meet it, and licked it up like oil. Others drew forth, with clashing noise, upon the ground, great sheets of glowing steel, emitting an insupportable heat, and a dull deep light like that which reddens in the eyes of savage beasts.

CHARLES DICKENS (1812–70), The Old Curiosity Shop, 1841

Not many even of the inhabitants of a manufacturing town know the vast machinery of system by which the bodies of workmen are governed, that goes on unceasingly from year to year. The hands of each mill are divided into watches that relieve each other as regularly as the sentinels of an army. By night and day the work goes on, the unsleeping engines groan and shriek, the fiery pools of metal boil and surge. Only for a day in the week, in half-courtesy to public censure, the fires are partially veiled; but as soon as the clock strikes midnight, the great furnaces break forth with renewed fury, the clamor begins with fresh, breathless vigor, the engines sob and shriek like 'gods in pain.'

As Deborah hurried down through the heavy rain, the noise of these thousand engines sounded through the sleep and shadow of the city like far-off thunder. The mill to which she was going lay on the river, a mile below the city-limits. It was far, and she was weak, aching from standing twelve hours at the spools. Yet it was her almost nightly walk to take this man his supper, though at every square she sat down to rest, and she knew she should receive small word of thanks.

Perhaps, if she had possessed an artist's eye, the picturesque oddity of the scene might have made her step stagger less, and the path seem shorter; but to her the mills were only 'summat deilish to look at by night.'

The road leading to the mills had been quarried from the solid rock, which rose abrupt and bare on one side of the cinder-covered road, while the river, sluggish and black, crept past on the other. The mills for rolling iron are simply immense tent-like roofs, covering acres of ground, open on every side. Beneath these roofs Deborah looked in on a city of fires, that burned hot and fiercely in the night. Fire in every horrible form: pits of flame waving in the wind; liquid metal-flames writhing in tortuous streams through the sand; wide caldrons filled with boiling fire, over which bent ghastly wretches stirring the strange brewing; and through all, crowds of half-clad men, looking like revengeful ghosts in the red light, hurried, throwing masses of glittering fire. It was like a street in Hell. Even Deborah muttered, as she crept through, ''T looks like t' Devil's place!' It did—in more ways than one.

> REBECCA HARDING DAVIS (1831–1910), on Wheeling, Virginia (now West Virginia), *Life in the Iron Mills*, 1861

To the outsider, indeed, part of the absorbing interest of watching the manufacture of iron is that in this country, at any rate, it is all done by human hands, and not by machinery. From the moment when the ironstone is lifted off the trucks, then dropped into the kilns, afterwards taken to the furnace, and then drawn out of it, it has not been handled by any other means than the arms of powerful men, whose strength and vigilance are constantly strained almost to breaking-point. It cannot be too often repeated what the risk is of dealing with a thing which you encounter only in terms of liquid fire. The path of the ironworker is literally strewn with danger, for as he walks along, the innocent-looking fragment, no longer glowing, may be a piece of hot iron of which the touch, if he stepped upon it, is enough to cripple him; one splash of the molten stream may blind him; if he were to stumble as he walks along the edge of that sandy platform where the iron is bubbling and rushing into the moulds he would never get up again. The men move about among these sur-roundings with the reckless—often too reckless—unconcern of long habit. You may see as you pass a man standing engaged in thickening the end of a bar of iron by leisurely twirling it round and round in a vessel full of red-hot slag, of which he will then allow a portion to cool on it, and doing it as calmly as though he were stirring round a pan of water.

When the moment comes to open the furnace for the next casting, the requisite time having elapsed since the last, a hole is drilled through the bot-tom of the 'hearth' in the solid piece of clay with which the furnace was closed the last time it was tapped. This is done by a great iron bar, held by three men, being thrust again and again against the clay, clearing away the loose rubbish and beginning to make the hole, against which it is then held in position by two men, while two others deal alternate blows on it with big hammers. It is done as quickly and regularly as though by machinery, the top of the crowbar hit fair and square with a clang at every blow, and the men who are striking are surrounded by a group of others waiting. These last are slaggers, mine-fillers, and others, come away from their special job to help in this one. They all stand intently concentrated on the moment when the clay shall finally yield. When that moment has come, the bar, with a mighty effort, is withdrawn, and the blazing stream rushes out in foaming and leaping red-hot waves through the opening into the deep main channel prepared for it. The heat to those stand-ing on the bank of that molten river is almost unbearable, the glare hardly to be endured. The onlooker is half blinded, half choked, as the flood rushes fiercely past him.

LADY (FLORENCE) BELL (1851–1930), *At the Works,* 1907

'If you think this is rough, wait till you see the foundry,' said Wilcox, with a grim smile, and set off again at his brisk terrier's trot. Even this warning did not prepare Robyn for the shock of the foundry. They crossed another yard, where hulks of obsolete machinery crouched, bleeding rust into their blankets of snow, and entered a large building with a high vaulted roof hidden in gloom. This space rang with the most barbaric noise Robyn had ever experienced. Her first instinct was to cover her ears, but she soon realised that it was not going to get any quieter, and let her hands fall to her sides. The floor was covered with a black substance that looked like soot, but grated under the soles of her boots like sand. The air reeked with a sulphurous, resinous smell, and a fine drizzle of black dust fell on their heads from the roof. Here and there the open doors of furnaces glowed a dangerous red, and in the far corner of the building what looked like a stream of molten lava trickled down a curved channel from roof to floor. The roof itself was holed in places, and melting snow dripped to the floor and spread in muddy puddles. It was a place of extreme temperatures: one moment you were shivering in an icy draught from some gap in the outside wall, the next you felt the frightening heat of a furnace's breath on your face. Everywhere there was indescribable mess, dirt, disorder. Discarded castings, broken tools, empty canisters, old bits of iron and wood, lay scattered around. Everything had an improvised, random air about it, as if people had erected new machines just where they happened to be standing at the time, next to the debris of the old. It was impossible to believe that anything clean and new and mechanically efficient could come out of this place. To Robyn's eye it resembled nothing so much as a medieval painting of hell—though it was hard to say whether the workers looked more like devils or the damned. Most of them, she observed, were Asian or Caribbean, in contrast to the machine shop where the majority had been white.

Wilcox led her up a twisted and worn steel staircase to a prefabricated office perched on stilts in the middle of the building, and introduced her to the general manager, Tom Rigby, who looked her up and down once and then ignored her. Rigby's young assistant regarded her with more interest, but was soon drawn into a discussion about production schedules. Robyn looked around the office. She had never seen a room that had such a forlorn, unloved look. The furniture was dirty, damaged and mismatched. The lino on the floor was scuffed and torn, the windows nearly opaque with grime, and the walls looked as if they had never been repainted since the place was constructed. Fluorescent strip lighting relentlessly illuminated every sordid detail. The only splash of colour in the drab decor was the inevitable pin-up, on the wall above the desk of Rigby's young assistant: last year's calendar, turned to the page for December, depicting a grinning topless model tricked out in fur boots and ermine-trimmed bikini pants. Apart from her, the only item in the room that didn't look old and obsolete was the computer over which the three men were crouched, talking earnestly.

Bored, she stepped outside, onto a steel gallery overlooking the factory floor. She surveyed the scene, feeling more than ever like Dante in the Inferno. All was noise, smoke, fumes and flames. Overalled figures, wearing goggles, facemasks, helmets or turbans, moved slowly through the sulphurous gloom or crouched over their inscrutable tasks beside furnaces and machines.

'Here—Tom said you'd better put this on.'

Wilcox had appeared at her side. He thrust into her hands a blue plastic safety helmet with a transparent visor.

'What about you?' she asked, as she put it on. He shrugged and shook his head. He hadn't even got a coat or overall to cover his business suit. Some kind of macho pride, presumably. The boss must appear invulnerable.

'Visitors have to,' said Tom Rigby. 'We're responsible, like.'

A very loud hooter started bleating frantically, and made Robyn jump.

Rigby grinned: 'That's the KW, they've got it going again.'

'What was the matter with it?' said Wilcox.

'Just a valve, I think. You should show her.' He jerked his head in Robyn's direction. 'Something worth seeing, the KW, when she's on song.'

'What's a KW?' Robyn asked.

'Kunkel Wagner Automatic Moulding Line,' said Wilcox.

'The boss's pride and joy,' said Rigby. 'Only installed a few weeks back. You should show her,' he said again to Wilcox.

'All in due course,' said Wilcox. 'The pattern shop first.'

The pattern shop was a haven of relative peace and quiet, reminiscent of cottage industry, a place where carpenters fashioned the wooden shapes that contributed the first stage of the moulding process. After that she saw men making sand moulds, first by hand, and then with machines that looked like giant waffle-irons. It was there that she saw women working alongside the men, lifting the heavy-looking mouldings, reeking of hot resin, from the machines, and stacking them on trolleys. She listened uncomprehendingly to Wilcox's technical explanations about the drag and the cope, core boxes and coffin moulds. 'Now we'll have a dekko at the cupola,' he shouted. 'Watch your step.'

The cupola turned out to be a kind of gigantic cauldron erected high in one corner of the building where she had earlier noticed what looked like volcanic lava trickling downwards. 'They fill it up continuously with layers of coke and iron—scrap-iron and pig-iron—and limestone, and fire it with oxygenated air. The iron melts, picking up the correct amount of carbon from the coke, and runs out of the tap-hole at the bottom.' He led her up another tortuous steel staircase, its steps worn and buckled, across improvised bridges and rickety gangways, up higher and higher, until they were crouching next to the very source of the molten metal. The white-hot stream flowed down a crudely-fashioned open conduit, passing only a couple of feet from Robyn's toecaps. It was like a small pinnacle in Pandemonium, dark and hot, and the two squatting Sikhs who rolled their white eyeballs and flashed their teeth in her direction, poking with steel rods at the molten metal for no discernible purpose, looked just like demons on an old fresco.

The situation was so bizarre, so totally unlike her usual environment, that there was a kind of exhilaration to be found in it, in its very discomfort and danger, such as explorers must feel, she supposed, in a remote and barbarous country. She thought of what her colleagues and students might be doing this Wednesday morning—earnestly discussing the poetry of John Donne or the novels of Jane Austen or the nature of modernism, in centrally heated, carpeted rooms. She thought of Charles at the University of Suffolk, giving a lecture, perhaps, on Romantic landscape poetry, illustrated with slides. Penny Black would be feeding more statistics on wife-beating in the West Midlands into her data-base, and Robyn's mother would be giving a coffee morning for some charitable cause in her Liberty-curtained lounge with a view of the sea. What would they all think if they could see her now?

DAVID LODGE (1935–), *Nice Work*, 1988

FACTORY WORKERS

It may even be doubted, whether the measure of national capacity increases with the advancement of arts. Many mechanical arts, indeed, require no capacity; they succeed best under a total suppression of sentiment and reason; and ignorance is the mother of industry as well as of superstition. Reflection and fancy are subject to err; but a habit of moving the hand, or the foot, is independent of either. Manufactures, accordingly, prosper most, where the mind is least consulted, and where the workshop may, without any great effort of imagination, be considered as an engine, the parts of which are men.

ADAM FERGUSON (1723–1816), *An Essay on the History of Civil Society*, 1767

We enter at once on a new scene—the interior of a pin manufactory . . . It does, indeed, look more like an outhouse in a state of dilapidation than a place where artizans assemble to pursue a thriving trade; but the interior will prove that the latter is its real purpose. We proceed through several departments of busy employment: in one there are children winding slender wire, which, being passed through a machine by steam-power, is drawn out by men. Here, the boys work, generally, under their fathers; and whatever we may think of their close, protracted confinement, the labour itself is not severe. In the next room we find many little fellows, more fatiguingly employed, being perpetually on foot, walking to and fro, assisting their seniors by the operation of straightening the coiled wire furnished by the drawers, which the men cut into lengths and point. Next we find a third part of boys, mixed with about an equal number of men: they spin, by a very exact, monotonous process, some wire into a spiral shape, which is subsequently cut into rings, forming heads for the pins. Hither to, we have found no girls, nor very little children; but enter the next department, and the scene will change.

Here is a room, if we can call it by that name, eight yards in length, by six in breadth, and about nine feet high. A row of small, dingy windows, along each side, admit such light as there is; and here, seated before machines unlike any that we have yet surveyed, are about fifty children, of whom the eldest may be thirteen; but the general age is less, much less—they are mere babes. Near each of them is placed a quantity of the prepared heads, from which they pick out one with the pointed head of the wires, also supplied to them, and passing it up the shank, they fix it at the blunt end; and holding the pin obliquely under a small hammer, turn it round until, with four or five smart strokes, it is properly secured in its place. Such is the general aspect of the apartment, such the employment of its inmates, and just as we now behold them they have been engaged since eight o'clock in the morning, with the certainty of carrying it on till eight in the evening: how much longer they may, on any pretext, be detained, no one can tell.

Stunted in their growth, bony, pallid, and most wretchedly unhealthy in their looks; filthy beyond expression in their persons, with scarcely rags enough to hold decently together, these miserable little beings appear conscious of but two objects capable of attracting their notice beyond the work about which their poor dirty little hands are incessantly moving. One of these is the very small fireplace, where an exceedingly scanty portion of fuel is just emitting smoke enough to prove that fire smoulders beneath. Towards this, many a longing look is cast, while the blue lips quiver, and the teeth chatter, and the fingers are well-nigh disabled from moving by the benumbing influence of cold. One might suppose that the crowding of so many living creatures within that confined space, would ensure heat enough; but oppressive as the air feels, it evidently brings no warmth to them. Empty stomachs, and curdling blood, never set in motion by exercise or play, will produce a chill not to be overcome by these damp exhalations, even if the frequent entrance of a draught of colder though not purer air from neighbouring workshops did not increase it: and as to the fire, it may serve to speak of, to think about, to look towards, but for any purpose of warmth, such as these poor infants require, the grate might just as well be empty.

But another object divides their attention: a woman on whose hard features many violent passions have conspired to plough indelible lines, whose inflated nostril, compressed lip, and restless eye, bespeak alike a cruel disposition, and watchfulness for means to gratify it, stalks to and fro, with a supple cane in her hand, intent to catch at a case of delinquency—a false movement, a momentary flagging of energy, a slight indication of the drowsiness peculiarly inevitable in children, when limb and spirit are fatigued, the mind unoccupied, and natural playfulness wholly restrained—sufficient to warrant the application of the well-known weapon to their poor little heads or shoulders. Occasionally she disappears, as if to invite a feeling of momentary security; and then, perhaps, some of the small hammers will tap less vigorously on the heads of the pins; some cramped fingers are stretched, and some half-frozen ones are held in the mouth for the comfortable refreshment of a warm breath: some little bare feet are briskly rubbed together, or perhaps some kind-hearted brother might take his baby-sister on his knee, and chafe her arms and ancles, numbed with the bitter cold of such unnatural stagnation: but, noiselessly, yet rapidly, the watcher re-enters, the cane is uplifted, and in the sudden acceleration of machinery something is gained by the traffickers in infant life; while only a few among the delinquents get any blows worth speaking of; and perhaps a lock or two of flaxen hair may be twitched out by her left, while her right hand administers the passing switch to some culprit, flurried by the sudden surprise into a blundering movement!

*

It is fatiguing to prolong the observation of these wretched little automata, with their small hammers, so monotonously sounding on the dirty-looking manufacture before them. The pins are not yet whitened or polished, and nothing here looks neat, nothing feels comfortable. You might be tempted to stroke the head of some pretty, engaging child, and to try whether a smile would not call up some answering expression of gladness in its heavy countenance, but your hand shrinks from the contact of that uncleanly hair, and you *cannot* smile with such an aggregate of infant misery before you.

> CHARLOTTE ELIZABETH TONNA (formerly Phelan) (1790–1846), *The Wrongs of Woman*, 1843

The supervision of machinery, the joining of broken threads, is no activity which claims the operative's thinking powers, yet it is of a sort which prevents him from occupying his mind with other things. We have seen, too, that this work affords the muscles no opportunity for physical activity. Thus it is, properly speaking, not work, but tedium, the most deadening, wearing process conceivable. The operative is condemned to let his physical and mental powers decay in this utter monotony, it is his mission to be bored every day and all day long from his eighth year.

> FRIEDRICH ENGELS (1820–95), *The Condition of the Working Class in England*, 1845, tr. Florence Kelley-Wischnewetsky, 1887

The first thing, then, which strikes the observer as an essential and fundamental part of the factory system, is the comparative lightness of the actual labour—the comparatively small amount of physical strength required in any of the processes. In truth, the engine is the worker. The operative is the superintendent of the engine's labours . . . Watchfulness, intelligent attention, and manual quickness to repair and supply accidental defects are what he requires.

The question then comes to be, whether or no this species of labour necessarily invades and consumes the frame by its irksomeness and continuity more than ruder kinds of work—by the absolute exhaustion which they produce. The affirmative of this proposition was the ground taken by Mr Sadler's Factory Committee in their report and is the ground taken still by the keener opponents of the factory system. I cannot yet venture to speak positively, but I can venture to state my belief that that ground will be found untenable. What species of labour is not irksome? Find that out and nine-tenths of the human race will willingly bind themselves apprentice to acquire it. Daily toil of a uniform and an unchanging character—as in the nature of things all toil to be steadily valuable must be—does necessarily involve a certain degree of irksomeness. The ploughman over his furrow, the blacksmith over his anvil, the sailor upon his watch—so long as human nature continues to be human nature—long for the conclusion of his task. So also do the spinners and weavers who work by hand; and so, doubtless, often must the spinners and weavers who work hand-in-hand with steam. Irksomeness in a greater or less degree is inseparable from labour. He who divides the one from the other eludes the primeval curse . . .

We have been told that labour carried on in great *ateliers,* by great bodies of operatives disciplined to work in steady conjunction with the uniform movements of machinery, is in itself something anomalous and unnatural. That it is something novel in the world's history, all may admit; that it is an organisation of human and mechanical power, requiring to be strictly watched and judiciously checked, is what few will deny; that it possesses so far as the consumer is concerned, palpable and immense advantages, is unquestioned on all hands; and that it may be so conducted as to benefit the producer, as well and as much as the consumer, is an assertion which I believe to be capable of clear and unquestioned demonstration.

ANGUS BETHUNE REACH (1821–56), Morning Chronicle, 22 Oct. 1849

I have not been able to discover that repetitive labour injures a man in any way. I have been told by parlour experts that repetitive labour is soul- as well as body-destroying, but that has not been the result of our investigations. There was one case of a man who all day long did little but step on a treadle release. He thought that the motion was making him one-sided; the medical examination did not show that he had been affected but, of course, he was changed to another job that used a different set of muscles. In a few weeks he asked for his old job again. It would seem reasonable to imagine that going through the same set of motions daily for eight hours would produce an abnormal body, but we have never had a case of it. We shift men whenever they ask to be shifted and we should like regularly to change them—that would be entirely feasible if only the men would have it that way. They do not like changes which they do not themselves suggest. Some of the operations are undoubtedly monotonous—so monotonous that it seems scarcely possible that any man would care to continue long at the same job. Probably the most monotonous task in the whole factory is one in which a man picks up a gear with a steel hook, shakes it in a vat of oil, then turns it into a basket. The motion never varies. The gears come to him always in exactly the same place, he gives each one the same number of shakes, and he drops it into a basket which is always in the same place. No muscular energy is required, no intelligence is required. He does little more than wave his hands gently to and fro— the steel rod is so light. Yet the man on that job has been doing it for eight solid years. He has saved and invested his money until now he has about forty thousand dollars—and he stubbornly resists every attempt to force him into a better job!

The most thorough research has not brought out a single case of a man's mind being twisted or deadened by the work. The kind of mind that does not like repetitive work does not have to stay in it. The work in each department is classified according to its desirability and skill into Classes 'A,' 'B,' and 'C,' each class having anywhere from ten to thirty different operations. A man comes directly from the employment office to 'Class C.' As he gets better he goes into 'Class B,' and so on into 'Class A,' and out of 'Class A' into tool making or some supervisory capacity. It is up to him to place himself. If he stays in production it is because he likes it.

> HENRY FORD (1863–1947), in collaboration with Samuel Crowther, *My Life and Work*, 1922

Anyone who has worked at all in a factory knows how deathly conveyor belt work is. At first it is difficult to keep up, and when you're tired it is quite merciless. After a while, when you have become fairly used to it, the fact that you can't work faster is also infuriating. Sometimes, when things are going well, you feel that you could go fast for a while, and maybe slow up later when you were tired. But no, you must work at exactly the prescribed speed, making exactly the same movements, being careful to be as economical with energy as possible, learning not to put your back into it but to use only your arms, learning how to use the wrists the same way every day so the muscles are strengthened and don't go on aching. It looks so easy, and it is, but it's important to make it as easy as possible. One false move repeated three thousand times is a painful mistake.

I had often wondered what people thought about, working on assembly lines all day. The answer is nothing. The work needs just enough concentration to keep the mind occupied. I had thought it would be a time when I could sit and think for hours on end. But my mind was blank. The monotony permeates every corner of the brain. The rhythm deadens every thought. I found myself repeating tables endlessly just for the sake of doing something. One afternoon I got up to 500 times 500. From the miserable and expressionless faces of the other girls, I doubt whether they were thinking much either. Just cakes and more cakes and more cakes.

POLLY TOYNBEE (1946–), *A Working Life*, 1971

'It went quick this morning, didn't it?'

'Yes, it went lovely and quick between eleven and twelve, but it dragged after that, I thought.'

'Yes, just after the twelve o'clock buzzer. It started to drag then.'

'Funny, wasn't it? It usually goes so quick after the twelve o'clock buzzer.'

'I hope it will go as quick this afternoon.'

'Hope so. You can always tell, can't you? If it goes quick up to half-past two, then it's going to go quick all the afternoon.'

'It's funny, that.'

MASS-OBSERVATION, *War Factory: A Report*, 1943

My first workday. Up at 5:00 a.m. It's still dark when I go out. The eastern mountains are glowing faintly, but I can still see the stars shining brightly in the sky. The street is lit by a few scattered lamps. It's a forty-minute walk to the factory. Unfortunately, the plant I have to work in is at the farthest corner of the factory compound. I can't find the canteen and miss breakfast.

I have really been fooled by the seeming slowness of the conveyor belt. No one can understand how it works without experiencing it. Almost as soon as I begin, I am dripping with sweat. Somehow, I learn the order of the work motions, but I'm totally unable to keep up with the speed of the line. My work gloves make it difficult to grab as many tiny bolts as I need, and how many precious seconds do I waste doing just that? I do my best, but I can barely finish one gear box out of three within the fixed length of time. If a different-model transmission comes along, it's simply beyond my capacity. Some skill is needed, and a new hand like me can't do it alone. I'm thirsty as hell, but workers can neither smoke nor drink water. Going to the toilet is out of the question. Who could have invented a system like this? It's designed to make workers do nothing *but* work and to prevent any kind of rest. Yet the man beside me the other day deftly handled his hammer, put the bolts into their grooves with both hands, and fastened them with a nut runner (a power screwdriver that can tighten six bolts simultaneously), seemingly with no difficulty.

The conveyor starts at 6:00 a.m. and doesn't stop until 11:00 a.m. One box of transmissions arrives on the conveyor belt every minute and twenty seconds with unerring precision. When the line stops at eleven o'clock, we tear off our gloves and leave our positions as quickly as we can. We wash our greasy hands and run to the toilet, then rush to the canteen about a hundred yards away where we wait in another line to get our food. After standing five hours, my legs are numb and stiff. My new safety shoes are so heavy that I feel I can barely move. I put my ticket into a box, take an aluminum tray, a pair of chopsticks, a plate of food, a tea cup, and a bowl of rice. I'm still unfamiliar with the routine and have a hard time finding a seat at one of the long tables. Finally, just as I'm settling down to eat, I have the sensation that the trays on the table are moving slowly sideways as if they're on a conveyor belt! At 11:45, the line starts again. There's not much time to rest since ten minutes before work starts we have to begin preparing a large enough supply of parts for the afternoon assemblage . . .

The first shift ends at 2:15 p.m. Already, the man on the next shift is standing beside me, waiting for me to finish. As soon as I put my hammer down on the belt, he picks it up and begins precisely where I left off. A baton pass, and neatly done, too.

Still, it turns out I'm not finished! I have to spend thirty more minutes replenishing the supply parts for the afternoon shift. I also have to pick up the parts I've scattered on the floor. Damn! My legs ache the entire forty-minute walk back to the dorm. I'm bone tired. Is this the life for a worker in a great enterprise, a famous auto company, proud of being tops in Japan and the third in the world?

> SATOSHI KAMATA (1938–), *Japan in the Passing Lane: An Insider's Account of Life in a Japanese Auto Factory*, 1980, tr. Tatsuru Akimoto, 1982

SHOPKEEPERS AND SALESMEN

The Grocer

'the kingdom of God cometh not with observation'
—James Joyce to Lady Gregory

The grocer's hair is parted like a feather
by two swift brushes and a dab of brilliantine.

His cheesewire is a sun-dial selling by the hour.
He brings it down at four and five o'clock,

the wooden T gripped like a corkscrew.
Greaseproof squares curl in diamonds on a hook.

He takes, and orientates the chock of cheese,
swoops his hand away, leaves it on the choppy scales.

Tortoise-necked, he reads the price aloud
and fingers do their automatic origami.

He shakes the air into a paper bag and,
eggs pickpocketed inside, trapezes it.

Coins are raked with trident hand,
trickled into the till—palm out,

with thumb crooked over the stigma,
he smiles like a modest quattrocento Christ.

CRAIG RAINE (1944–   ), 1978

It seems now at this time, when all goods are packeted, and self-service is the order of the day, almost incredible the amount of work involved in serving just one customer under the old conditions. We sold some goods for which there was no room in the shop, such things as potatoes, corn for chickens, barley meal, bran and other animal feeding-stuffs which had to be measured in pint, quart or gallon measures and packed in paper bags. Another article was common salt, which came to the shop in long thick bars, from which we had to cut a thick slice to be sold for $1\frac{1}{2}$ d. Yet another commodity was a long bar of household soap which might be bought whole or in halves or quarters and, for a change from solids, there was draught vinegar, to be drawn off into a measure and transferred to customer's own bottle or jug. All these goods and others too were stored in rooms behind the shop and had to be fetched and weighed or measured as needed. The shop assistant's job was not a light one in those days, neither was it a clean one. So many things to weigh and so much to fetch and carry played havoc with our hands and with our overalls. We had a little retreat where we could wash our hands, in cold water, but too many trips to 'Scarborough', as it came to be called, were apt to be frowned upon. So we just wiped our hands on our overalls—and that was that!

WINIFRED GRIFFITHS (b. 1895), a shop assistant during the First World War, *Autobiography* (unpub.), in John Burnett, *Useful Toil*, 1974

The milkman never argues; he works alone and no one speaks to him; the
city is asleep when he is on the job; he puts a bottle on six hundred
porches and calls it a day's work; he climbs two hundred wooden
stairways; two horses are company for him; he never argues.

CARL SANDBURG (1878–1967), from 'Psalm of those who go forth before daylight', 1918

The indentures that bound Kipps to Mr Shalford were antique and complex; they insisted on the latter gentleman's parental privileges, they forbade Kipps to dice and game, they made him over, body and soul, to Mr Shalford for seven long years, the crucial years of his life. In return there were vague stipulations about teaching the whole art and mystery of the trade to him, but as there was no penalty attached to negligence, Mr Shalford, being a sound, practical, business man, considered this a mere rhetorical flourish, and set himself assiduously to get as much out of Kipps and to put as little into him as he could in the seven years of their intercourse.

What he put into Kipps was chiefly bread and margarine, infusions of chicory and tea-dust, colonial meat by contract at threepence a pound, potatoes by the sack, and watered beer. If, however, Kipps chose to buy any supplementary material for growth, Mr Shalford had the generosity to place his kitchen resources at his disposal free—if the fire chanced to be going. He was also allowed to share a bedroom with eight other young men, and to sleep in a bed which, except in very severe weather, could be made, with the help of his overcoat and private underlinen, not to mention newspapers, quite sufficiently warm for any reasonable soul. In addition, Kipps was taught the list of fines, and how to tie up parcels, to know where goods were kept in Mr Shalford's systematised shop, to hold his hands extended upon the counter, and to repeat such phrases as 'What can I have the pleasure——?' 'No trouble, I 'ssure you,' and the like; to block, fold, and measure materials of all sorts, to lift his hat from his head when he passed Mr Shalford abroad, and to practise a servile obedience to a large number of people. But he was not, of course, taught the 'cost' mark of the goods he sold, nor anything of the method of buying such goods. Nor was his attention directed to the unfamiliar social habits and fashions to which his trade ministered. The use of half the goods he saw sold and was presently to assist in selling he did not understand; materials for hangings, cretonnes, chintzes, and the like; serviettes, and all the bright, hard whitewear of a well-ordered house; pleasant dress materials, linings, stiffenings; they were to him from first to last no more than things, heavy and difficult to handle in bulk, that one folded up, unfolded, cut into lengths, and saw dwindle and pass away out into that mysterious, happy world in which the Customer dwells. Kipps hurried from piling linen table-cloths, that were, collectively, as heavy as lead, to eat off oilcloth in a gas-lit dining-room underground, and he dreamt of combing endless blankets beneath his overcoat, spare undershirt, and three newspapers. So he had at least the chance of learning the beginnings of philosophy.

In return for these benefits he worked so that he commonly went to bed exhausted and footsore. His round began at half-past six in the morning, when he would descend, unwashed and shirtless, in old clothes and a scarf, and dust boxes and yawn, and take down wrappers and clean the windows until eight. Then in half an hour he would complete his toilet, and take an austere breakfast of bread and margarine and what only an Imperial Englishman would admit to be coffee, after which refreshment he ascended to the shop for the labours of the day.

H. G. WELLS (1866–1946), Kipps, 1905

No Buyers

A Street Scene

A load of brushes and baskets and cradles and chairs
    Labours along the street in the rain:
With it a man, a woman, a pony with whiteybrown hairs.—
    The man foots in front of the horse with a shambling sway
      At a slower tread than a funeral train,
    While to a dirge-like tune he chants his wares,
Swinging a Turk's-head brush (in a drum-major's way
      When the bandsmen march and play).

A yard from the back of the man is the whiteybrown pony's nose:
He mirrors his master in every item of pace and pose:
      He stops when the man stops, without being told,
    And seems to be eased by a pause; too plainly he's old,
        Indeed, not strength enough shows
      To steer the disjointed waggon straight,
    Which wriggles left and right in a rambling line,
    Deflected thus by its own warp and weight,
And pushing the pony with it in each incline.

      The woman walks on the pavement verge,
        Parallel to the man:
    She wears an apron white and wide in span,
And carries a like Turk's-head, but more in nursing-wise:
      Now and then she joins in his dirge,
      But as if her thoughts were on distant things.
      The rain clams her apron till it clings.—
So, step by step, they move with their merchandize,
      And nobody buys.

THOMAS HARDY (1840–1928), 1925

I deal with farmers, things like dips and feed.
Every third month I book myself in at
The ------ Hotel in ----ton for three days.
The boots carries my lean old leather case
Up to a single, where I hang my hat.
One beer, and then 'the dinner', at which I read
The ----*shire Times* from soup to stewed pears.
Births, deaths. For sale. Police court. Motor spares.

Afterwards, whisky in the Smoke Room: Clough,
Margetts, the Captain, Dr Watterson;
Who makes ends meet, who's taking the knock,
Government tariffs, wages, price of stock.
Smoke hangs under the light. The pictures on
The walls are comic—hunting, the trenches, stuff
Nobody minds or notices. A sound
Of dominoes from the Bar. I stand a round.

Later, the square is empty: a big sky
Drains down the estuary like the bed
Of a gold river, and the Customs House
Still has its office lit. I drowse
Between ex-Army sheets, wondering why
I think it's worth while coming. Father's dead:
He used to, but the business now is mine.
It's time for change, in nineteen twenty-nine.

PHILIP LARKIN (1922–85), from 'Livings', 1971

When white-collar people get jobs, they sell not only their time and energy but their personalities as well. They sell by the week or month their smiles and their kindly gestures and they must practice the prompt repression of resentment and aggression. For these intimate traits are of commercial relevance and required for the more efficient and profitable distribution of goods and services.

C. WRIGHT MILLS (1916–62), *White Collar*, 1953

Executive

I am a young executive. No cuffs than mine are cleaner;
I have a Slimline brief-case and I use the firm's Cortina.
In every roadside hostelry from here to Burgess Hill
The *maîtres d'hôtel* all know me well and let me sign the bill.

You ask me what it is I do. Well actually, you know,
I'm partly a liaison man and partly PRO.
Essentially I integrate the current export drive
And basically I'm viable from ten o'clock till five.

For vital off-the-record work—that's talking transport-wise—
I've a scarlet Aston-Martin—and does she go? She flies!
Pedestrians and dogs and cats—we mark them down for slaughter.
I also own a speed-boat which has never touched the water.

She's built of fibre-glass, of course. I call her 'Mandy Jane'
After a bird I used to know—No soda, please, just plain—
And how did I acquire her? Well to tell you about that
And to put you in the picture I must wear my other hat.

I do some mild developing. The sort of place I need
Is a quiet country market town that's rather run to seed.
A luncheon and a drink or two, a little *savoir faire*—
I fix the Planning Officer, the Town Clerk and the Mayor.

And if some preservationist attempts to interfere
A 'dangerous structure' notice from the Borough Engineer
Will settle any buildings that are standing in our way—
The modern style, sir, with respect, has really come to stay.

JOHN BETJEMAN (1906–84), 1974

SOLDIERS

Come, let me tell you the woes of the soldier, and how many are his superiors: the general, the troop-commander, the officer who leads, the standard-bearer, the lieutenant, the scribe, the commander of fifty, and the garrison-captain. They go in and out in the halls of the palace, saying: 'Get labourers!' He is awakened at any hour. One is after him as after a donkey. He toils until the Aten (the sun-disc) sets in his darkness of night. He is hungry, his belly hurts; he is dead while yet alive. When he receives a grain-ration, having been released from duty, it is no good for grinding.

He is called up for Syria. He may not rest. There are no clothes, no sandals. The weapons of war are assembled at the fortress of Sile [starting-point for the campaigns into the Levant]. His march is uphill through mountains. He drinks water every third day; it is smelly and tastes of salt. His body is ravaged by illness. The enemy comes, surrounds him with missiles, and life recedes from him. He is told: 'Quick, forward, valiant soldier! Win for yourself a good name!' He does not know what he is about. His body is weak, his legs fail him. When victory is won, the captives are handed over to his majesty, to be taken to Egypt. The foreign woman faints on the march; she hangs herself on the soldier's neck. His knapsack drops, another grabs it while he is burdened with the woman. His wife and children are in the village; he dies and does not reach it. If he comes out alive, he is worn out from marching. Be he at large, be he detained, the soldier suffers. If he leaps and joins the deserters, all his people are imprisoned. He dies on the edge of the desert, and there is none to perpetuate his name. He suffers in death as in life. A big sack is brought for him; he does not know his resting place.

From an Ancient Egyptian schoolbook (Papyrus Lansing), c.1195–1080
BC, tr. by Miriam Lichtheim, 1976

Today my strength has been cropped away by my too plentiful tribulations: but perhaps from the look of the stubble you can guess what my ripeness was. Ares and Athene granted me a courage which carried me through the press of battle. When once I had determined my tactics against an enemy, no inkling of death would visit my high heart. I would post a chosen party in ambush and then thrust far beyond its leaders to bring down with my spear any opponent less nimble than myself upon his feet. That was the fighting me: but labour I never could abide, nor the husbandry which breeds healthy children. My fancies were set upon galleys and wars, pikes and burnished javelins, the deadly toys that bring shivers to men of ordinary mould. I think such tastes came to me from heaven. Each man sports the activity he enjoys.

HOMER, *The Odyssey*, c.725 BC, tr. T. E. Shaw (Lawrence of Arabia), 1932

'The Roman Soldier's Hardships'

Then the toil, the great toil of the march; the load of more than half a month's provisions, the load of any requisite needed, the load of the stake for intrenchment; for shield, sword, helmet are reckoned a burden by our soldiers as little as their shoulders, arms and hands; for weapons they say are the soldiers' limbs, and these they carry handy so that, should need arise, they fling aside their burdens and have their weapons as free for use as their limbs. Look at the training of the legions, the double, the attack, the battle-cry, what an amount of toil it means! Hence comes the courage in battle that makes them ready to face wounds. Bring up a force of untrained soldiers of equal courage: they will seem like women. Why is there such a difference between raw and veteran soldiers as we have lately had experience of? Recruits have usually the advantage in age, but it is habit which teaches men to endure toil and despise wounds.

CICERO (103–43 BC), *Tusculan Disputations*, 45 BC, tr. J. E. King, 1927

I had a very short time of being a soldier, which hath not lasted above six weeks, and I like it as a commendable way of breeding for a young gentleman, if they consort themselves with such as are civil, and their quarrel lawful. For as idleness is the nurse of all evil, enfeebling the parts both of mind and body, this employment of a soldier's is contrary unto it. For it greatly improves them, by enabling his body to labour, his mind to watchfulness, and so, by a contempt of all things but the employment he is in, he shall not much care how hard he lies, nor how meanly he fares. Whereas the independence of a private life makes one insolent, and not easily brought under subjection. This business of a soldier will learn him to be dutiful and obedient to his commanders without reply, how equal and just it is. It makes one not over fond of this life, but willing to resign it.

SIR HENRY SLINGSBY (1602–58), *Diary*, 1639

. . . we walked on through several out-courts, till we came into a place my friend told me was Scotland Yard, where gentlemen soldiers lie basking in the sun, like so many lazy swine upon a warm dunghill. I stood a little while ruminating on the great unhappiness of such a life, and could not restrain my thoughts from giving a character of that unfortunate wretch, who in time of war, hazards his life for sixpence a day, and that perhaps ne'er paid him, and in time of peace has nothing to do but to mount the guard and loiter.

A foot soldier is commonly a man who for the sake of wearing a sword, and the honour of being termed a gentleman, is coaxed from a handicraft trade, whereby he might live comfortably, to bear arms for his King and Country, whereby he has the hopes of nothing but to live starvingly. His lodging is as near Heaven as his quarters can raise him, and his soul generally as near Hell as a profligate life can sink him, for to speak without swearing he thinks a scandal to his post. He makes many a meal upon tobacco which keeps the inside of his carcase as nasty as his shirt. He's a champion for the Church, because he fights for religion, though he never hears prayers except they be read upon a drumhead. He can never pass by a brandy shop with twopence in his pocket, for he naturally loves strong waters, as a Turk loves coffee.

No man humbles himself more upon the committing of a fault, for he bows his head to his heels, and lies bound by the hour to his good behaviour. He is a man of undaunted courage; dreading no enemy so much as he does the wooden horse, which makes him hate to be mounted, and rather chooses to be a foot soldier. He makes a terrible figure in a country town, and makes the old women watch their poultry more than a gang of gipsies.

When once he has been in a battle, it's a hard matter to get him out of it, for wherever he comes he's always talking of the action, in which he was posted in the greatest danger, and seems to know more of the matter than the General. He's one that loves fighting no more than other men, though perhaps, a dozen of drink and an affront, will make him draw his sword, yet a pint and a good word, will make him put it up again. The best end he can expect to make, is to

wooden horse] instrument of punishment

die in the bed of honour, and the greatest living marks of his bravery, to recommend him at once to the world's praise and pity, are crippled limbs, with
which I shall leave him to beg a better livelihood.

> To a cobbler's awl, or butcher's knife,
>   Or a porter's knot commend me,
> But from a soldier's lazy life,
>   Good Heaven, I pray, defend me.

NED WARD (1667–1731), The London Spy, 1703

'The Royal Welch Fusiliers in the First World War'

Dunn went on. 'These Welshmen are peculiar. They won't stand being
shouted at. They'll do anything if you explain the reason for it. They will do
and die, but they have to know their reason why. The best way to make them
behave is not to give them too much time to think. Work them off their feet.
They are good workmen. Officers must work too, not only direct the work.
Our time-table is like this. Breakfast at eight o'clock in the morning, clean
trenches and inspect rifles, work all morning; lunch at twelve, work again
from one till about six, when the men feed again. 'Stand-to' at dusk for about
an hour, work all night, 'stand-to' for an hour before dawn. That's the general
programme. Then there's sentry duty. The men do two-hour sentry spells,
then work two hours, then sleep two hours. At night sentries are doubled, so
our working parties are smaller. We officers are on duty all day and divide up
the night in three-hourly watches.'

ROBERT GRAVES (1895–1985), Goodbye to All That, 1929

Work and Freedom

> Even small events that others might not notice,
> I found hard to forget. In Auschwitz truly
> I had no reason to complain of boredom.
> If an incident affected me too deeply
> I could not go straight home to my wife and children.
> I would ride my horse till the terrible picture faded.
> Often at night I would wander through the stables
> And seek relief among my beloved horses.
> At home my thoughts, often and with no warning,
> Turned to such things. When I saw my children playing
> Or observed my wife's delight over our youngest,
> I would walk out and stand beside the transports,

The firepits, crematoriums, or gas-chambers.
My wife ascribed my gloom to some annoyance
Connected with my work but I was thinking,
'How long will our happiness last?' I was not happy
Once the mass exterminations had started.

My work, such unease aside, was never-ending,
My colleagues untrustworthy, those above me
Reluctant to understand or even to listen—
Yet everyone thought the commandant's life was heaven.
My wife and children, true, were well looked after.
Her garden was a paradise of flowers.
The prisoners, trying no doubt to attract attention,
Never once failed in little acts of kindness.
Not one of them, in our house, was badly treated:
My wife would have loved to give the prisoners presents—
And as for the children, they begged for cigarettes for them,
Especially for those who worked in the garden and brought them
Tortoises, martens, lizards, cats. Each Sunday
We'd walk to the stables, never omitting the kennels
Where the dogs were kept. My children loved all creatures
But most of all our foal and our two horses.
In summer they splashed in the wading pool, but their greatest
Joy was to bathe together with Daddy—who had
Limited hours, alas, for these childish pleasures.
My wife said, 'Think of us, not only the service.'
How could she know what lay so heavily on me?
(It made life hard, this excessive sense of duty.)

When Auschwitz was divided, Pohl in a kindly
And quite exceptional gesture gave me the option
—Perhaps as recompense for this last assignment—
To head DK or to run Sachsenhausen.
I had one day to decide. At first the thought of
Uprooting myself from Auschwitz made me unhappy,
So involved had I grown in its tasks and troubles.
But in the end I was glad to gain my freedom.

VIKRAM SETH (1952–), 1990

There was no such thing as 'free' time in Basic Training. The evenings and
weekends were fully occupied, mainly by cleaning and polishing equipment,
or in army jargon 'bull'. Someone had obviously given considerable thought

to this part of our training. First of all we were issued with brasses that were green and deeply corroded, and therefore had to be rubbed for hours with emery paper before the application of 'Brasso' produced any effect. Our boots had a dull, orange-peel surface, which is of course a characteristic feature of good waterproof foot-wear, but we had to eradicate the dimples and produce a patent-leather shine. The approved method was to heat a spoon handle over a candle and to rub the boots with it, squeezing out the oil and smoothing out the surface. This process naturally ruined the boots *qua* boots, but such functional considerations were irrelevant within the mystique of 'bull'. Some of the lads used more drastic methods, such as rubbing a hot iron over the boots, or even covering them with polish and setting fire to them. In addition to brasses and boots, there was webbing to be blancoed and clothing to be pressed. When we were first issued with webbing Baker ordered us to scrub off the existing, deeply ingrained khaki blanco. 'I want them white,' he said. Four hours' scrubbing with cold water produced a dirty grey. The next day we were instructed to blanco the webbing again in exactly the same colour as that in which it had been issued . . .

Pressing was somewhat difficult for me at first, because I had never pressed a single garment in my life before I was called up. The usual pressing technique was to use the iron over a sheet of brown paper which had been wetted with a shaving brush. The hiss of steam and the pungent odour of scorched brown paper are still inextricably connected with the Army in my mind, like the whine of shells and the smell of cordite in the memories of war-veterans. I minimized the pressing by using my own pyjamas and underpants. I pressed the Army's issue once, according to the regulation measurements, and kept them undisturbed for kit layouts throughout my service, carrying them carefully from place to place in polythene bags.

The amount of equipment that was required to be laid out for inspection in the mornings was subtly increased during the period of Basic Training, starting with a few items and culminating in a series of full kit-layouts which kept us working late into the night. An additional vexation was the occasional 'Fire Picquet', a quaintly-named duty which consisted in parading with the guard in steel helmets and peeling potatoes for two hours in a small annexe to the cookhouse, awash with freezing water and potato peel. One had heard of this sort of thing of course,—peeling potatoes was more or less a cartoonist's cliché for depicting the Army—but it came as a shock, to me at least, to find myself doing it. I had supposed that it was some kind of punishment, and probably obsolete, like flogging. I felt the same, only more strongly, about cookhouse fatigues.

DAVID LODGE (1935–), *Ginger, You're Barmy*, 1962

SWEEPERS, CLEANERS, AND SHOVELLERS

And as I have mentioned the word labour, I cannot help saying that a great deal of nonsense is being written and talked nowadays about the dignity of manual labour. There is nothing necessarily dignified about manual labour at all, and most of it is absolutely degrading. It is mentally and morally injurious to man to do anything in which he does not find pleasure, and many forms of labour are quite pleasureless activities, and should be regarded as such. To sweep a slushy crossing for eight hours on a day when the east wind is blowing is a disgusting occupation. To sweep it with mental, moral, or physical dignity seems to me to be impossible. To sweep it with joy would be appalling. Man is made for something better than disturbing dirt. All work of that kind should be done by a machine.

OSCAR WILDE (1854–1900), 'The Soul of Man under Socialism', 1891

Of the 'Pure'-Finders

Dogs'-dung is called 'Pure,' from its cleansing and purifying properties.

The name of 'Pure-finders,' however, has been applied to the men engaged in collecting dogs'-dung from the public streets only, within the last 20 or 30 years. Previous to this period there appears to have been no men engaged in the business, old women alone gathered the substance, and they were known by the name of 'bunters,' which signifies properly gatherers of rags; and thus plainly intimates that the rag-gatherers originally added the collecting of 'Pure' to their original and proper vocation. Hence it appears that the bone-grubbers, rag-gatherers, and pure-finders, constituted formerly but one class of people, and even now they have, as I have stated, kindred characteristics.

The pure-finders meet with a ready market for all the dogs'-dung they are able to collect, at the numerous tanyards in Bermondsey, where they sell it by the stable-bucket full, and get from 8d to 10d per bucket, and sometimes 1s and 1s 2d for it, according to its quality. The 'dry limy-looking sort' fetches the highest price at some yards, as it is found to possess more of the alkaline, or purifying properties; but others are found to prefer the dark moist quality. Strange as it may appear, the preference for a particular kind has suggested to the finders of Pure the idea of adulterating it to a very considerable extent; this is effected by means of mortar broken away from old walls, and mixed up with the whole mass, which it closely resembles; in some cases, however, the mortar is rolled into small balls similar to those found. Hence it would appear, that there is no business or trade, however insignificant or contemptible, without its own peculiar and appropriate tricks . . .

The pure-finder may at once be distinguished from the bone-grubber and rag-gatherer; the latter, as I have before mentioned, carries a bag, and usually a stick armed with a spike, while he is most frequently to be met with in back streets, narrow lanes, yards and other places, where dust and rubbish are likely to be thrown out from the adjacent houses. The pure-finder, on the contrary, is often found in the open streets, as dogs wander where they like. The pure-finders always carry a handle basket, generally with a cover, to hide the contents, and have their right hand covered with a black leather glove; many of them, however, dispense with the glove, as they say it is much easier to wash their hands than to keep the glove fit for use. The women generally have a large pocket for the reception of such rags as they may chance to fall in with, but they pick up those only of the very best quality, and will not go out of their way to search even for them. Thus equipped they may be seen pursuing their avocation in almost every street in and about London, excepting such streets as are now cleansed by the 'street orderlies,' of whom the pure-finders grievously complain, as being an unwarrantable interference with the privileges of their class.

The pure collected is used by leather-dressers and tanners, and more especially by those engaged in the manufacture of morocco and kid leather from the skins of old and young goats, of which skins great numbers are imported, and of the roans and lambskins which are the sham morocco and kids of the 'slop' leather trade, and are used by the better class of shoemakers, bookbinders, and glovers, for the inferior requirements of their business. Pure is also used by tanners, as is pigeon's dung, for the tanning of the thinner kinds of leather, such as calf-skins, for which purpose it is placed in pits with an admixture of lime and bark.

HENRY MAYHEW (1812–87), *London Labour and the London Poor*, 1861–2

I took the place of another man who had been sent to do some job or other in the opposite end of the mill. My partner in shovelling was again a smallish man, competent with a shovel but not a very energetic worker, so that my lack of experience did not show up a great deal. I had never been used to a shovel, and like all others who have not earned their livings with one I imagined there was nothing in it. It looked so easy to thrust into the pile and lift up a heap of stuff, step backwards with one foot and throw the load neatly over the left shoulder as you straightened up. I kept a surreptitious eye on my partner and did exactly as he did, but after three fillings of the skip I was pouring with perspiration in trying to keep pace with his easy, rhythmical movements. We were not on piecework, but the big hopper up in the roof was running dangerously low and the foreman wanted it full. Three skips running in turn could fill it faster than the mills could eat it up, but the defection of one supply-line made all the difference and meant that we had to go all out to keep the mills going. By teatime I was feeling it badly; my back was cracking with the constant bending up and down and my hands were fearfully sore. I sat down on the plank resting on a few bricks which comprised the messroom, and leaned back gratefully against the cool whitewashed wall to eat and drink. There was an open brazier on the floor upon which we could warm our tea-jacks, and for twenty minutes we luxuriated before getting stiffly to our feet again.

Four more hours to go. They were four of the longest hours I had ever known. I shovelled mechanically, piling up the skip and pushing it along the rails to the hoist, tipping it and running it back empty under its own momentum while we followed wearily after. Then down to it again, bending and lifting, settling the load on the big number seven square-faced shovels and heaving it into the skip at our backs. It was a warm evening, and we pulled off our shirts and worked stripped to the waist to keep cool. The dust settled on our skins and worked its way into the open pores as we perspired, and when the end of the shift came we looked pretty sights. There was no thought of washing, and we just shook some of the dust out of our clothes and thankfully went home.

The next morning found me in such a state that I really did not think I could do another shift. When I had arrived home the previous night I had been actually unable to turn the door-handle because of the agonising blisters on my hands, and I had had to kick the door gently for the landlady to come and open it. I tried to wash, but the dust was engrained in the skin and refused to come off unless a nailbrush were used, and you can't use a nailbrush on soft blisters. The backs of my hands where they had rubbed against my knees in shovelling were deprived of skin, and from head to foot I was one throbbing ache. I thought hard as to what I should do, looking doubtfully at my hands as I tried to open and shut them. If I jibbed at any more punishment, I should be out of a job again; maybe the pain would wear off in a few days. But my hands worried me. I could not hold a knife or fork firmly, let alone a shovel; and to close my fists was agony. I deferred a decision until after dinner, as I would not be leaving for work until about half-past one.

I was still undecided at one o'clock, but I had dressed in my dusty working clothes, buckled on my belt, and left my boots unlaced because I could not do them up. I tried my hands again, opening and shutting them, and they felt a little better. I got up, picked up my food-box, and set off to work.

The long walk down to the works eased the stiffness from my legs, and altogether I had nearly recovered my spirits by the time I got into the mill. There was the skip again, and the two shovels lying on the floor where the morning shift had left them, and my mate of yesterday cleaning loose bits from under his feet ready for a start. Neither of us had shaved. I took off my coat, rolled up my sleeves, and caught hold of the shovel. There was only one way to go about it, and that was to grip loosely with my fingertips until such time as my hands should warm up and fold properly round the thick handle with its steel

strappings, and with many wincings as my sore body protested against movement I bent down and drove into the heap.

Four hours afterwards I was all right. I was glad I had stuck it. My hands
were burning, but not too painfully, and I had worked off the excruciating
pain in the small of my back. By dint of careful imitation of the methods of my
partner I got into the rhythm of the throw, and made up for my still obvious
lack of skill by lifting much more than he did with the shovel. I had a lot to
learn about this business, but towards the end of the shift I was conceited
enough to think that I had mastered the job. How far I was from being anywhere near mastery I was yet to discover, because the technique of the shovel,
if one is to be a real artist with it, demands long practice. A navvy, using his
shield-shaped excavating shovel in a trench with a bad bottom, does wonders,
but in a long time; he would be a useless partner in a ten-ton wagon, and the
corporation employee, lifting little bits in the street, would have died of fright
had he seen our shovels.

IFAN EDWARDS (b. 1898), *No Gold on My Shovel,* 1947

It was to this building that Jurgis came daily, as if dragged by an unseen hand.
The month of May was an exceptionally cool one, and his secret prayers were
granted; but early in June there came a record-breaking hot spell, and after
that there were men wanted in the fertilizer mill.

The boss of the grinding room had come to know Jurgis by this time, and
had marked him for a likely man; and so when he came to the door about two
o'clock this breathless hot day, he felt a sudden spasm of pain shoot through
him—the boss beckoned to him! In ten minutes more Jurgis had pulled off
his coat and overshirt, and set his teeth together and gone to work. Here was
one more difficulty for him to meet and conquer!

His labor took him about one minute to learn. Before him was one of the
vents of the mill in which the fertilizer was being ground—rushing forth in a
great brown river, with a spray of the finest dust flung forth in clouds. Jurgis
was given a shovel, and along with half a dozen others it was his task to shovel
this fertilizer into carts. That others were at work he knew by the sound, and
by the fact that he sometimes collided with them; otherwise they might as well
not have been there, for in the blinding dust-storm a man could not see six
feet in front of his face. When he had filled one cart he had to grope around
him until another came, and if there was none on hand he continued to grope
till one arrived. In five minutes he was, of course, a mass of fertilizer from
head to feet; they gave him a sponge to tie over his mouth, so that he could
breathe, but the sponge did not prevent his lips and eyelids from caking up
with it and his ears from filling solid. He looked like a brown ghost at twilight—from hair to shoes he became the color of the building and of everything in it, and, for that matter, a hundred yards outside it. The building had
to be left open, and when the wind blew Durham and Company lost a great
deal of fertilizer.

Working in his shirt-sleeves, and with the thermometer at over a hundred, the phosphates soaked in through every pore of Jurgis's skin, and in five minutes he had a headache, and in fifteen was almost dazed. The blood was pounding in his brain like an engine's throbbing; there was a frightful pain in the top of his skull, and he could hardly control his hands. Still, with the memory of his four months' siege behind him, he fought on, in a frenzy of determination; and half an hour later he began to vomit—he vomited until it seemed as if his inwards must be torn into shreds. A man could get used to the fertilizer mill, the boss had said, if he would only make up his mind to it; but Jurgis now began to see that it was a question of making up his stomach.

At the end of that day of horror he could scarcely stand. He had to catch himself now and then, and lean against a building and get his bearings. Most of the men, when they came out, made straight for a saloon—they seemed to place fertilizer and rattlesnake poison in one class. But Jurgis was too ill to think of drinking—he could only make his way to the street and stagger on to a car. He had a sense of humor, and later on, when he became an old hand, he used to think it fun to board a streetcar and see what happened. Now, however, he was too ill to notice it—how the people in the car began to gasp and sputter, to put handkerchiefs to their noses, and transfix him with furious glances. Jurgis only knew that a man in front of him immediately got up and gave him a seat; and that half a minute later the two people on each side of him got up; and that in a full minute the crowded car was nearly empty—those passengers who could not get room on the platform having gotten out to walk.

Of course Jurgis had made his home a miniature fertilizer mill a minute after entering. The stuff was half an inch deep in his skin—his whole system was full of it, and it would have taken a week not merely of scrubbing, but of vigorous exercise, to get it out of him. As it was, he could be compared with nothing known to men, save that newest discovery of the savants, a substance which emits energy for an unlimited time, without being itself in the least diminished in power. He smelt so that he made all the food at the table taste, and set the whole family to vomiting; for himself it was three days before he could keep anything upon his stomach—he might wash his hands, and use a knife and fork, but were not his mouth and throat filled with the poison?

UPTON SINCLAIR (1878–1968), *The Jungle*, 1906

SERVANTS

Scene V—Verona.   A Hall in CAPULET's *house.*

MUSICIANS *waiting.   Enter* SERVINGMEN.

First Serv.   Where's Potpan, that he helps not to take away? he shift a trencher! he scrape a trencher!

Sec. Serv.   When good manners shall lie all in one or two men's hands, and they unwashed too, 'tis a foul thing.

First Serv.   Away with the joint-stools, remove the court-cupboard, look to the plate. Good thou, save me a piece of marchpane; and, as thou lovest me, let the porter let in Susan Grindstone and Nell. Antony! and Potpan!

Sec. Serv.   Ay, boy; ready.

First Serv.   You are looked for and called for, asked for and sought for in the great chamber.

Third Serv.   We cannot be here and there too.

Sec. Serv.   Cheerly, boys; be brisk awhile, and the longer liver take all.

[*They retire behind.*]

WILLIAM SHAKESPEARE (1564–1616), *Romeo and Juliet*, wr. *c*.1595

It is required that such as we commonly call serving-men should have, beside the office of waiting, some other particular calling, unless they tend on men of great place and state. For only to wait and give attendance is not a sufficient calling, as common experience telleth. For waiting-servants, by reason they spend most of their time in eating and drinking, sleeping and gaming after dinner and after supper, do prove the most unprofitable members both in Church and Commonwealth. For when either their good masters die, or they be turned out of their office for some misdemeanour, they are fit for no calling, being unable to labour; and thus they give themselves either to beg or steal.

WILLIAM PERKINS (1558–1602), *A Treatise of the Vocations, or Callings of Men*, 1603

I knew one bredd a servant, and by accident grew rich. His caracter was industrious and servile, and from a walking surveyor of the excise was taken into a revenew-farme, and so by others' braines got his estate. He built an house in Norfolk, and adorned it with a park, gardens, and planting without, and curiosity (as he thought) of finishing and furniture within. But in truth nothing was well done, but what related to servants. The capitall part of his house was paltry, but kitchen, daiery, brewhouse, &c., for a duke, supposing he delighted often to visit them; but his rooms of enterteinement, as also the face and profile of the whole house abroad, such as a citisen would contrive at Hackney. A framed lanthorne upon the roof, shass windoes, and an elegant court yard, and within some right wainscote, which from the native plainness was the best, and frequent carving, but that mean; much of painting, and pretended guilding, but in truth laker, which in time grew pale, and despicable; and the painting for most part of various affected colours, which please the ignorant, but nauseate the knowing; windoe plans and chimnys all marble. But the rooms low, windoes broad, which increast that defect; no back stairs to the cheif apartments; in the gardens, much fountaine work, but spoiled by a monster of a wooden tower in sight, which raised the water; and that water conveyed not onely to the offices, but most rooms in the house to moisten and mould every thing. Nor was his way of living various, being all vain and ostentatious, without judgment, and extended principally in things which servants rather than masters admire: that is, profusion in dyet and wine, such as he used to comend, hoping to partake, and whereby he sought that which in his course of life and fortune went for great and glorious. One pasage was diverting when I saw the house, the servant took out a pannell of wainscot and said there my master hangs his old hatts, then lifted up a board of the floor, here my master sets his old shoos. And yet this man had spent 20,000 in his building, and thought of nothing, but the out-doing a neighbour nobleman who had built, and, being a court favorite, lived in splendor. In short, in spight of all this pretension, the servant stared you in the face; and had he bin but the bailif, and his wife cook laundry and dairey woman, his house had not bin amiss. It was hard to suggest any thing for ease and saving of servants which was not there done; and if it had bin told him, an engin was contrived to make brooms sweep of themselves, he had endeavoured to procure it.

ROGER NORTH (1651?–1734), *Of Building*, wr. 1698

Scene.   An old-fashioned house.

[*Enter* HARDCASTLE, *followed by three or four awkward* SERVANTS.]

Hardcastle.   Well, I hope you're perfect in the table exercise I have been teaching you these three days. You all know your posts and your places, and can shew that you have been used to good company, without ever stirring from home.

Omnes.   Ay, ay.

Hardcastle.   When company comes, you are not to pop out and stare, and then run in again, like frighted rabbits in a warren.

Omnes.   No, no.

Hardcastle.   You, Diggory, whom I have taken from the barn, are to make a shew at the side-table; and you, Roger, whom I have advanced from the plough, are to place yourself behind *my* chair. But you're not to stand so, with your hands in your pockets. Take your hands from your pockets, Roger; and from your head, you blockhead you. See how Diggory carries his hands. They're a little too stiff, indeed, but that's no great matter.

Diggory.   Ay, mind how I hold them. I learned to hold my hands this way, when I was upon drill for the militia. And so being upon drill——

Hardcastle.   You must not be so talkative, Diggory. You must be all atten-tion to the guests. You must hear us talk, and not think of talking; you must see us drink, and not think of drinking; you must see us eat, and not think of eating.

Diggory.   By the laws, your worship, that's parfectly unpossible. Whenever Diggory sees yeating going forward, ecod he's always wishing for a mouthful himself.

Hardcastle.   Blockhead! Is not a belly-full in the kitchen as good as a belly-full in the parlour? Stay your stomach with that reflection.

Diggory.   Ecod I thank your worship, I'll make a shift to stay my stomach with a slice of cold beef in the pantry.

Hardcastle.   Diggory, you are too talkative. Then if I happen to say a good thing, or tell a good story at table, you must not all burst out a laughing, as if you made part of the company.

Diggory.   Then ecod your worship must not tell the story of Ould Grouse in the gun-room: I can't help laughing at that—he! he! he!—for the soul of me. We have laughed at that these twenty years—ha! ha! ha!

Hardcastle.   Ha! ha! ha! The story is a good one. Well, honest Diggory, you may laugh at that—but still remember to be attentive. Suppose one of the company should call for a glass of wine, how will you behave? A glass of wine, Sir, if you please (*to* Diggory)—Eh, why don't you move?

Diggory.   Ecod, your worship, I never have courage till I see the eatables and drinkables brought upo' the table, and then I'm as bauld as a lion.

Hardcastle.   What, will no body move?

First Serv.   I'm not to leave this pleace.

Sec. Serv.   I'm sure it's no pleace of mine.

Third Serv.   Nor mine, for sartain.

Diggory.   Wauns, and I'm sure it canna be mine.

Hardcastle.   You numbskulls! and so while, like your betters, you are quarrelling for places, the guests must be starved. O you dunces! I find I must begin all over again.—But don't I hear a coach drive into the yard? To your posts you blockheads. I'll go in the mean time and give my old friend's son a hearty reception at the gate.   [*Exit* HARDCASTLE]

Diggory.   By the elevens, my pleace is gone quite out of my head.

Roger.   I know that my pleace is to be every where.

First Serv.   Where the devil is mine?

Sec. Serv.   My pleace is to be no where at all; and so Ize go about my business.   [*Exeunt* SERVANTS, *running about as if frighted, different ways.*]

OLIVER GOLDSMITH (1730?–74), *She Stoops to Conquer*, 1773

The Rival Josephs

Would you see a man that's slow,
Come and see our footman Joe,
Most unlike the bounding roe,
Or an arrow from a bow,
Or the flight direct of crow,
Is the pace of footman Joe.
Snails, contemptuous as they go,
In their motions outrun Joe,
Crabs that hobble to and fro,
Look behind and laugh at Joe,
An acre many a man could mow,
Ere across it creepeth Joe.
Danube, Severn, Trent, and Po,
Backward to their source might flow,
Ere dispatch be made by Joe.
Letters to a Plenipo,
Send not by our footman Joe.
Would you Job's full merit know,
Ring the bell, and wait for Joe.
Is your purse or credit low,
Let your debts be paid by Joe;
Legal process none can show,
If your lawyers move like Joe.

Epitaph

Death, at last, our common foe,
Must trip up the heels of Joe,
And a stone shall tell below
How, scarce changed, sleepeth Joe:
For when the final trump shall blow,
The last that comes will still be Joe.

R. H. BARHAM (1788–1845), 1881

Martha was blunt and plain-spoken to a fault; otherwise she was a brisk, well-meaning, but very ignorant girl. She had not been with us a week before Miss Matilda and I were astounded one morning by the receipt of a letter from a cousin of hers, who had been twenty or thirty years in India, and who had lately, as we had seen by the 'Army List,' returned to England, bringing with him an invalid wife, who had never been introduced to her English relations. Major Jenkyns wrote to propose that he and his wife should spend a night at

Cranford, on his way to Scotland—at the inn, if it did not suit Miss Matilda to receive them into her house; in which case they should hope to be with her as much as possible during the day. Of course, it *must* suit her, as she said; for all Cranford knew that she had her sister's bedroom at liberty; but I am sure she wished the Major had stopped in India and forgotten his cousins out and out.

'Oh! how must I manage?' asked she, helplessly. 'If Deborah had been alive, she would have known what to do with a gentleman-visitor. Must I put razors in his dressing-room? Dear! dear! and I've got none. Deborah would have had them. And slippers, and coat-brushes?' I suggested that probably he would bring all these things with him. 'And after dinner, how am I to know when to get up, and leave him to his wine? Deborah would have done it so well; she would have been quite in her element. Will he want coffee, do you think?' I undertook the management of the coffee, and told her I would instruct Martha in the art of waiting, in which it must be owned she was terribly deficient; and that I had no doubt Major and Mrs Jenkyns would understand the quiet mode in which a lady lived by herself in a country town. But she was sadly fluttered. I made her empty her decanters, and bring up two fresh bottles of wine. I wished I could have prevented her being present at my instructions to Martha; for she frequently cut in with some fresh direction, muddling the poor girl's mind, as she stood open-mouthed, listening to us both.

'Hand the vegetables round,' said I (foolishly, I see now—for it was aiming at more than we could accomplish with quietness and simplicity): and then, seeing her look bewildered, I added, 'Take the vegetables round to people, and let them help themselves.'

'And mind you go first to the ladies,' put in Miss Matilda. 'Always go to the ladies before gentlemen, when you are waiting.'

'I'll do it as you tell me, ma'am,' said Martha; 'but I like lads best.'

ELIZABETH GASKELL (1810–65), Cranford, 1853

Without and Within

My coachman, in the moonlight there,
  Looks through the side-light of the door;
I hear him with his brethren swear,
  As I could do,—but only more.

Flattening his nose against the pane,
  He envies me my brilliant lot,
Breathes on his aching fist in vain,
  And dooms me to a place more hot.

He sees me into supper go,
  A silken wonder by my side,
Bare arms, bare shoulders, and a row
  Of flounces, for the door too wide.

He thinks how happy is my arm,
  'Neath its white-gloved and jewelled load;
And wishes me some dreadful harm,
  Hearing the merry corks explode.

Meanwhile I inly curse the bore
  Of hunting still the same old coon,
And envy him, outside the door,
  The golden quiet of the moon.

The winter wind is not so cold
  As the bright smile he sees me win,
Nor the host's oldest wine so old
  As our poor gabble, sour and thin.

I envy him the rugged prance
  By which his freezing feet he warms,
And drag my lady's chains, and dance,
  The galley-slave of dreary forms.

Oh could he have my share of din,
  And I his quiet!—past a doubt
'Twould still be one man bored within,
  And just another bored without.

J. RUSSELL LOWELL (1819–91), 1869

WAITRESSES AND WAITERS

I would recommend any grumbling discontented person to pay a visit to Liverpool, merely for the purpose of witnessing a specimen of the art of living well and cheap, as regards the very important affair of dinner. There, chance led me on one particular occasion to Keels's Hotel, which is, I think, in the large street leading from the Mansion House to St George's Dock; however, at all events, it is what is called highly respectable, both as to its position and elevation. Having mistaken the hour of departure of one of the boats, I was directed hither by the policeman, who, to his recommendation, added in an awful cadence, that '*the magistrates themselves very often dined there.*'

When I entered the coffee-room, near a score of people were seated at different tables, some with their hats on, but all busily eating their dinner, and a chair and a table were provided for myself by a good-looking and very smartly dressed young woman, who officiated as waiter. Constant communication was held with the bar at the head of the room, at which three or four other females presided. Upon inquiring what I could have for dinner, the young lady produced the *carte*, whence it appeared that there really was everything that an Englishman could possibly desire, in the matter of roasted and boiled meats, meat pies, and pastry. Neither was the adage '*bis dat qui citò dat*,'—(He gives doubly who gives quickly,)—within these walls forgotten, for here a hungry man has no sooner made his selection, than in half a minute the smoke of the dish is curling under his nose. I think I never partook of a more glorious round of beef than that of which a plateful was placed before me, together with a delicate lily-white heart of a young cabbage. Next came a delightful apple dumpling well sugared, the fruit transparent, and the crust excellent. The garniture of the table was homely but clean, the dishes and covers of queen's metal, as highly polished as silver. And after having eaten a sufficient quantity to satisfy any reasonable appetite, the charge for the whole was only *one shilling*. To conclude—I asked a gentleman sitting at an adjoining table how much it was customary to give the waiter, to which he replied, with a look of surprise—nothing. Had I not come to the conclusion long before, I certainly should have arrived at it now, namely, that so long as an individual can procure so very good a dinner for a shilling, and be waited upon by a tidy young woman into the bargain, England cannot be, in spite of a vast deal of modern philosophy, so very bad a country to live in.

The young person referred to was really the pink of her profession, her movements being quiet, quick, dexterous, and I may add, graceful in a great degree. With no one to assist her, she waited upon a score of people, who were no sooner satisfied than they went away, and were replaced by others; so that the whole set were nearly changed twice over during the half hour that I remained in the room. Her eyes were in every corner at the same moment; every guest found his wants attended to, as soon almost as he was aware of them himself. At all events she was never for a moment still, dropping a fork to one, a piece of bread to another, craving pardon of a third, as she reached across the table for a huge mug, and somewhat in the attitude of a flying Mercury, exposed precisely as much as was decent and proper of a well turned leg, and then away she would go to another quarter, wriggling about, in a way of her own, though somewhat in the French style, as if her feet were tied together, or like a figure on wheels wound up by clock-work. Such an active being surely never could be still,—even in her sleep.

The more the business on her hands, the more rapid the succession of her smiles, which she dispersed gratuitously all around. Every man in the room was sure to obtain one, and if he happened to be young, certainly two, yet the '*hoc age*,' *mind what you're at*, was always uppermost in her mind; and though she simpered and flirted, and even now and then put on a languishing air, as if suffering either by Cupid or the hot weather, no item, meanwhile, of things furnished on any body's account was forgotten in the bill, and thus she went on from morning to night, attending to the interests of her employer, serving the customers, and in perpetual motion between the coffee-room and the bar, so that no ant was ever seen at his work more lively and busy.

Notwithstanding this incessant occupation, she found time for her toilette. Her dress was in the style of a smart lady's maid. That is to say, she wore a figured muslin gown with full sleeves, and a small black silk apron. Her stays were tightly laced, her clothes well put on, and her feet neat to perfection. Her cap was adorned with blue ribands, and covered a profusion of ringlets.

Twelve months had rolled away, when on paying to this hotel a second and last visit, I saw the same young woman, on the same spot, performing the duties of the same office, in precisely the same manner, and in the same good humour with herself and all the rest of the world; and there still, I have no doubt, any other body who chooses to make the experiment, in twelve months more, provided she change not her condition, may also find her.

> Sir George Head (1782–1855), *A Home Tour through the Manufacturing Districts of England in the Summer of 1835*, 1836

Waitress

At one they hurry in to eat.
Loosed from the office job they sit
But somehow emptied out by it
And eager to fill up with meat.
　Salisbury Steak with Garden Peas.

The boss who orders them about
Lunches elsewhere and they are free
To take a turn at ordering me.
I watch them hot and heavy shout:
　Waitress I want the Special please.

My little breasts, my face, my hips,
My legs they study while they feed
Are not found on the list they read
While wiping gravy off their lips.
　Here Honey gimme one more scoop.

I dream that while they belch and munch
And talk of Pussy, Ass, and Tits,
And sweat into their double knits,
I serve them up their Special Lunch:
　Bone Hash, Grease Pie, and Leather Soup.

> Thom Gunn (1929–), 1982

The Wail of the Waiter

All day long, at Scott's or Menzies', I await the gorging crowd,
Panting, penned within a pantry, with the blowflies humming loud.
There at seven in the morning do I count my daily cash,
While the home-returning reveller calls for 'soda and a dash'.
And the weary hansom-cabbies set the blinking squatters down,
Who, all night, in savage freedom, have been 'knocking round the town'.
Soon the breakfast gong resounding bids the festive meal begin,
And, with appetites like demons, come the gentle public in.
'Toast and butter!' 'Eggs and coffee!' 'Waiter, mutton chops for four!'
'Flatheads!' 'Ham!' 'Beef!' 'Where's the mustard?' 'Steak and onions!' 'Shut
    the door!'
Here sits Bandicoot, the broker, eating in a desperate hurry,
Scowling at his left-hand neighbour, Cornstalk from the Upper Murray,
Who with brandy-nose empurpled, and with blue lips cracked and dry,
In incipient delirium shoves the eggspoon in his eye.
'Bloater paste!' 'Some *tender* steak, sir?' 'Here, *confound* you, where's my
    chop?'
'Waiter!' 'Yessir!' '*Waiter*!' 'Yessir!!'—running till I'm fit to drop.
Then at lunch time—fearful crisis! In by shoals the gorgers pour,
Gobbling, crunching, swilling, munching—ten times hungrier than
    before.
'Glass of porter!' '*Ale* for me, John!' 'Where's my stick?' 'And where's my
    hat!'
'Oxtail soup!' '*I* asked for curry!' 'Cold boiled beef, and cut it fat!'
'Irish stew!' 'Some pickled cabbage!' 'What, no *beans*?' 'Bring *me* some
    pork!'
'Soup, sir?' 'Yes. You grinning idiot, can I eat it with a FORK?'
'Take care, waiter!' 'Beg your pardon.' 'Curse you, have you two left legs?'
'I asked for *bread* an hour ago, sir!' 'Now then, have you *laid* those eggs?'
'Sherry!' 'No, I called for *beer*—of all the fools I ever saw!'
'Waiter!' 'Yessir!' 'WAITER!!' 'Here, sir!' 'Damme, sir, this steak is RAW!'

Thus amid this hideous Babel do I live the livelong day,
While my memory is going, and my hair is turning grey.
All my soul is slowly melting, all my brain is softening fast,
And I know that I'll be taken to the Yarra Bend at last.
For at night from fitful slumbers I awaken with a start,
Murmuring of steak and onions, babbling of apple-tart.
While to me the Poet's cloudland a gigantic kitchen seems,
And those mislaid table-napkins haunt me even in my dreams
Is this right?—Ye sages tell me!—Does a man live but to eat?
Is there nothing worth enjoying but one's miserable meat?

Is the mightiest task of Genius but to swallow buttered beans,
And has Man but been created to demolish pork and greens?
Is there no *unfed* Hereafter, where the round of chewing stops?
Is the atmosphere of heaven clammy with perpetual chops?
Do the friends of Mr Naylor sup on spirit-reared cow-heel?
Can the great Alexis Soyer really say 'Soyez tranquille?'
Or must I bring spirit beefsteak grilled in spirit regions hotter
For the spirit delectation of some spiritual squatter?
Shall I in a spirit kitchen hear the spirit blowflies humming,
Calming spiritual stomachs with a spiritual 'Coming!'?
Shall—but this is idle chatter, I have got my work to do.
'WAITER!!' 'Yessir.' 'Wake up, stupid! Biled calves' feet for Number Two!'

MARCUS CLARKE (1846–81), 1870

It was amusing to look round the filthy little scullery and think that only a double door was between us and the dining-room. There sat the customers in all their splendour—spotless table-cloths, bowls of flowers, mirrors and gilt cornices and painted cherubim; and here, just a few feet away, we in our disgusting filth. For it really was disgusting filth. There was no time to sweep the floor till evening, and we slithered about in a compound of soapy water, lettuce-leaves, torn paper and trampled food. A dozen waiters with their coats off, showing their sweaty armpits, sat at the table mixing salads and sticking their thumbs into the cream pots. The room had a dirty mixed smell of food and sweat. Everywhere in the cupboards, behind the piles of crockery, were squalid stores of food that the waiters had stolen. There were only two sinks, and no washing basin, and it was nothing unusual for a waiter to wash his face in the water in which clean crockery was rinsing. But the customers saw nothing of this. There were a coco-nut mat and a mirror outside the dining-room door, and the waiters used to preen themselves up and go in looking the picture of cleanliness.

It is an instructive sight to see a waiter going into a hotel dining-room. As he passes the door a sudden change comes over him. The set of his shoulders alters; all the dirt and hurry and irritation have dropped off in an instant. He glides over the carpet, with a solemn priest-like air. I remember our assistant *maître d'hôtel*, a fiery Italian, pausing at the dining-room door to address an apprentice who had broken a bottle of wine. Shaking his fist above his head he yelled (luckily the door was more or less soundproof):

'*Tu me fais chier.* Do you call yourself a waiter, you young bastard? You a waiter! You're not fit to scrub floors in the brothel your mother came from. *Maquereau!*'

Words failing him, he turned to the door; and as he opened it he farted loudly, a favourite Italian insult.

Then he entered the dining-room and sailed across it dish in hand, grace-ful as a swan. Ten seconds later he was bowing reverently to a customer. And you could not help thinking, as you saw him bow and smile, with that benign smile of the trained waiter, that the customer was put to shame by having such an aristocrat to serve him.

> GEORGE ORWELL (1903–50), *Down and Out in Paris and London*, 1933

SHADIER TRADES

In the [19]80s *sex work* was coined by activists in the prostitutes' movement to describe a range of commercial sex. Porn stars, erotic dancers, peep show per-formers, sex writers, and others in the trade made it obvious that the prosti-tutes' movement should broaden its language. Thus the inclusive *sex worker*. But *sex work* is also code. In two words, 'selling sex is just another occupation.' *Sex work* sidesteps any pejorative meanings associated with *to prostitute* (the verb) and *prostitute* (the person).

As an activist hooker, I have helped to promote the fashionable status of the term *sex work* (and, apparently, of actual sex workers). Sometimes I have my regrets. *Sex work* doesn't sound immoral, but it doesn't sound like fun, either.

> TRACY QUAN, New York prostitute, letter to the *New York Review of Books*, 5 Nov. 1992

Editor Whedon

To be able to see every side of every question;
To be on every side, to be everything, to be nothing long;
To pervert truth, to ride it for a purpose,
To use great feelings and passions of the human family
For base designs, for cunning ends,
To wear a mask like the Greek actors—
Your eight-page paper—behind which you huddle,
Bawling through the megaphone of big type:
'This is I, the giant.'
Thereby also living the life of a sneak-thief,
Poisoned with the anonymous words
Of your clandestine soul.
To scratch dirt over scandal for money,
And exhume it to the winds for revenge,

Or to sell papers,
Crushing reputations, or bodies, if need be,
To win at any cost, save your own life.
To glory in demoniac power, ditching civilization,
As a paranoiac boy puts a log on the track
And derails the express train.
To be an editor, as I was.
Then to lie here close by the river over the place
Where the sewage flows from the village,
And the empty cans and garbage are dumped,
And abortions are hidden.

EDGAR LEE MASTERS (1868–1950), 1915

In order to the better describing of the Tricks of the Bawds and Procurers about Town, I shall conclude our NIGHT RAMBLER FOR OCTOBER with exhibiting the following account, given by a young woman who was taken in the Streets a picking up men, carried before a Justice of Peace, and sent to Bridewell, where a friend of hers, pittying her Condition, thought himself obliged in Charity to Visit, Examine, and Exhort her to a Reformation of Life.

The account she gave was thus. Being about 16 years of Age, said she, and reputed handsome, I lived with an Ordinary Tradesman in town, but neither his Wages nor way of living suited with my haughty Mind, for I did very much admire finery in others, and was impatient to be as fine as they. A Bawd happening to observe me, she implored one of her Emissaries to come and tell me that if I would be a Chambermaid, she could help me to a very good place, where I should have six pound a year and fine Cloaths. This pleas'd me to the Life, and the Old Bawd who was one of those that pretends to help Servant-Maids to Places, told me that the Gentlewoman would come to her House such a day to see me, and praid me not to fail being there by that time. Mistrusting nothing, thither I went, where I found a Gentlewoman richly Clad, and thought my self very happy in meeting with such a Mistress; she gave her self out to be a Merchants Widdow, that her Husband had left her a plentiful Estate, and if I pleased her I should want for nothing, so that the Bargain being maid, I went to her in a little time after. I had not been long with her, till she told me that she was to go a visiting, and that I must dress my self to go with her, and alledging that my own Cloaths would disgrace her, she put me on a fine Suit, which she said belong'd to a Niece of hers in the Country——out we went, and after passing through many turnings and windings, we came to an House where she told me she was to visit a certain Lady, who I afterwards understood by sad experience to be one of her own imployment. There we staid Dinner, and my Mistress pretending I was a friend of hers, who served her both as a Companion and a Maid, they would needs have me sit at Dinner with them. The Table was very well covered, and our fare was Luscious and Dainty, and just as we had begun to eat comes in a young Spark whom the pretended Lady called her Kindsman, and invited him to sit down, having din'd plentifully and drunk largely of Rich Wine, my Mistress ordered me to withdraw into the next room till she called me, which accordingly I did, I was scarcely well sat down till I heard a Clinking of Money, which I understood since was the Price of my Chastity; and a little after that the Gallant comes into the room where I was, and one of them lockt the door behind him, I shrecht and made a noise finding my self betrayed, but to no purpose, for there was no body near that would relieve me, so that after many presents offered, and struggling so long as I was able, I was at last overcome. The Gallant did not stir out of the room that night and next morning comes in the pretended Lady with Cordials, Wines, and Bisket, and told me impudently that she hopt I was pleas'd with my Treatment. I rail'd at her, and flew at her face crying out for help, but all was in vain, so that the Spark tumbled me down upon the Bed till she got out and lockt the door behind her. Then he flattered me with all imaginable Craft, told me I should neither want for Money, Fine Cloaths, nor the best of Entertainment if I would be patient and comply with his desires: And when I was a sleep, through weariness and Grief, he stole out of the Room, and did not return again till night.

In the mean time the Old Beldam with a couple of other young Women, whom she had debaucht came in to me with a dish of Fruit curiously drest and Wine, and Sweet-meats in plenty, and the young Women told me straight that they themselves had been served in the same manner, and tho' they were as much enrag'd at first as I was, yet truly now they likt it very well, they eat, and wore, and sleept as well as any Ladies; and when they had a mind to have Money from their Sparks it was but to be a little Coy, and then they lay'd it by to maintain them in Age and Sickness; and when one Gallant was weary of em they found means to get another, which said they, is a much better life surely then to be a druge in any Trades man's House; and at last they told me in plain Terms, that out of the room I should not come till I were brought to their bow, and that I should rather die then they would either hazard a Carts-Arse or the Pillory for me. This I took to be a Sentance of death past against me if I did not comply with their humour, and therefore was forced to dissemble my doing so, and having plaid two or three hours at Cards with me, and shewed the fine presents they had received from their Gallants, night approacht when they made up the bed, brought me all sorts of Linnen for my use, and bid me prepare to receive my Spark with more kindness. Upon his return, he presented me with a Ring, and Gloves, and my own Corruption complying with the Circumstances and Tentations I was quickly enurd to, and enamour'd on that course of Life, but a month being over my Spark grew cool in his Amours, and sparing of his presents; and at last he abandoned me quite. Then I was reduced to the necessity either of Complying with the further direction of the Old Bawd, or of being stript of all I had, and either murdered or turned out of doors naked in the night time, and at best be exposed to shame and disgrace . . .

> Attr. to JOHN DUNTON (1659–1733), *The Night-Walker, or, Evening Rambles in Search after Lewd Women,* 1696

INTERVIEWER: You don't think, then, that there's anything wrong in not working for your living?
ROBERT ALLERTON (a professional criminal): But I do work for my living. Most crime—unless it's the senseless, petty-thieving sort—is quite hard work, you know. Planning a job, working out all the details of the best way to do it, and then carrying it out, under a lot of nervous strain and tension—and having to run round afterwards, if it's goods, fencing the stuff, getting a good price for it, delivering it to the fence, and so on—all this needs a lot of thinking and concentration.

> Quoted in TONY PARKER (1923–) and ROBERT ALLERTON (*c.*1929–), *The Courage of His Convictions,* 1962

Young Jerry, walking with the stool under his arm at his father's side along sunny and crowded Fleet Street, was a very different Young Jerry from him of the previous night, running home through darkness and solitude from his grim pursuer. His cunning was fresh with the day, and his qualms were gone with the night—in which particulars it is not improbable that he had compeers in Fleet Street and the City of London, that fine morning.

'Father,' said Young Jerry, as they walked along: taking care to keep at arm's length and to have the stool well between them: 'what's a Resurrection-Man?'

Mr Cruncher came to a stop on the pavement before he answered, 'How should I know?'

'I thought you knowed everything, father,' said the artless boy.

'Hem! Well,' returned Mr Cruncher, going on again, and lifting off his hat to give his spikes free play, 'he's a tradesman.'

What's his goods, father?' asked the brisk Young Jerry.

'His goods,' said Mr Cruncher, after turning it over in his mind, 'is a branch of Scientific goods.'

'Persons' bodies, ain't it, father?' asked the lively boy.

'I believe it is something of that sort,' said Mr Cruncher.

'Oh, father, I should so like to be a Resurrection-Man when I'm quite growed up!'

Mr Cruncher was soothed, but shook his head in a dubious and moral way. 'It depends upon how you dewelop your talents. Be careful to dewelop your talents, and never to say no more than you can help to nobody, and there's no telling at the present time what you may not come to be fit for.' As Young Jerry, thus encouraged, went on a few yards in advance, to plant the stool in the shadow of the Bar, Mr Cruncher added to himself: 'Jerry, you honest trades-man, there's hopes wot that boy will yet be a blessing to you, and a recompense to you for his mother!'

CHARLES DICKENS (1812–70), *A Tale of Two Cities*, 1859

Somerset, glass in hand, contemplated the strange fanatic before him, and listened to his heated rhapsody with indescribable bewilderment. He looked him in the face with curious particularity; saw there the marks of education; and wondered the more profoundly.

'Sir,' he said—'for I know not whether I should still address you as Mr Jones—'

'Jones, Brietman, Higginbotham, Pumpernickel, Daviot, Henderland, by all or any of these you may address me,' said the plotter; 'for all I have at some time borne. Yet that which I most prize, that which is most feared, hated, and obeyed, is not a name to be found in your directories; it is not a name current in post-offices or banks; and indeed, like the celebrated clan M'Gregor, I may justly describe myself as being nameless by day. But,' he continued, rising to his feet, 'by night, and among my desperate followers, I am the redoubted Zero.'

Somerset was unacquainted with the name; but he politely expressed surprise and gratification. 'I am to understand,' he continued, 'that, under this alias, you follow the profession of a dynamiter?'

The plotter had resumed his seat and now replenished the glasses.

'I do,' he said. 'In this dark period of time, a star—the star of dynamite—has risen for the oppressed; and among those who practise its use, so thick beset with dangers and attended by such incredible difficulties and disappointments, few have been more assiduous, and not many—' He paused, and a shade of embarrassment appeared upon his face—'not many have been more successful than myself.'

'I can imagine,' observed Somerset, 'that, from the sweeping consequences looked for, the career is not devoid of interest. You have, besides, some of the entertainment of the game of hide-and-seek. But it would still seem to me—I speak as a layman—that nothing could be simpler or safer than to deposit an infernal machine and retire to an adjacent county to await the painful consequences.'

'You speak, indeed,' returned the plotter, with some evidence of warmth, 'you speak, indeed, most ignorantly. Do you make nothing, then, of such a peril as we share this moment? Do you think it nothing to occupy a house like this one, mined, menaced, and, in a word, literally tottering to its fall?'

'Good God!' ejaculated Somerset.

'And when you speak of ease,' pursued Zero, 'in this age of scientific studies, you fill me with surprise. Are you not aware that chemicals are proverbially as fickle as woman, and clockwork as capricious as the very devil? Do you see upon my brow these furrows of anxiety? do you observe the silver threads that mingle with my hair? Clockwork, clockwork has stamped them on my brow—chemicals have sprinkled them upon my locks! No, Mr Somerset,' he resumed, after a moment's pause, his voice still quivering with sensibility, 'you must not suppose the dynamiter's life to be all gold. On the contrary: you cannot picture to yourself the bloodshot vigils and the staggering disappointments of a life like mine. I have toiled (let us say) for months, up early and down late; my bag is ready, my clock set; a daring agent has hurried with white face to deposit the instrument of ruin; we await the fall of England, the massacre of thousands, the yell of fear and execration; and lo! a snap like that of a child's pistol, an offensive smell, and the entire loss of so much time and plant! If,' he continued musingly, 'we had been merely able to recover the lost bags, I believe, with but a touch or two, I could have remedied the peccant engine. But what with the loss of plant and the almost insuperable scientific difficulties of the task, our friends in France are almost ready to desert the chosen medium. They propose, instead, to break up the drainage system of cities and sweep off whole populations with the devastating typhoid pestilence: a tempting and scientific project: a process, indiscriminate indeed, but of idyllical simplicity. I recognize its elegance; but, sir, I have something of the poet in my nature; something, possibly, of the tribune. And, for my small part, I shall remain devoted to that more emphatic, more striking, and (if you please) more popular method of the explosive bomb. Yes,' he cried, with unshaken hope, 'I will still continue, and I feel it in my bosom I shall yet succeed.'

ROBERT LOUIS STEVENSON (1850–94), The Dynamiter, 1885

Every year I bury a couple hundred of my townspeople. Another two or three dozen I take to the crematory to be burned. I sell caskets, burial vaults, and urns for the ashes. I have a sideline in headstones and monuments. I do flowers on commission.

Apart from the tangibles, I sell the use of my building: eleven thousand square feet, furnished and fixtured with an abundance of pastel and chair rail and crown moldings. The whole lash-up is mortgaged and remortgaged well into the next century. My rolling stock includes a hearse, two Fleetwoods, and a mini-van with darkened windows our price list calls a service vehicle and everyone in town calls the Dead Wagon.

I used to use the *unit pricing method*—the old package deal. It meant that you had only one number to look at. It was a large number. Now everything is itemized. It's the law. So now there is a long list of items and numbers and italicized disclaimers, something like a menu or the Sears Roebuck Wish Book, and sometimes the federally mandated options begin to look like cruise control or rear-window defrost. I wear black most of the time, to keep folks in mind of the fact we're not talking Buicks here. At the bottom of the list there is still a large number.

In a good year the gross is close to a million, 5 per cent of which we hope to call profit. I am the only undertaker in this town. I have a corner on the market.

THOMAS LYNCH (1948–), *The Undertaking*, 1997

VII. HEAD WORK

But when it is said, all men should labour, it is not so straitly meant that all men should use handy labour: but, as there be divers sorts of labour, some of the mind, and some of the body, and some of both, so every one, (except by reason of age, debility of body, or want of health he be unapt to labour at all,) ought, both for the getting of his own living honestly and for to profit others, in some kind of labour to exercise himself, according as the vocation where-unto God hath called him shall require. So that whosoever doeth good to the common weal and society of men with his industry and labour, whether it be by governing the common weal publicly, or by bearing public office or min-istry, or by doing any common necessary affairs of his country, or by giving counsel, or by teaching and instructing others, or by what other means soever he be occupied, so that a profit and benefit redound thereof unto others, the same person is not to be accounted idle, though he work no bodily labour, nor is to be denied his living, (if he attend his vocation,) though he work not with his hands. Bodily labour is not required of them which by reason of their vocation and office are occupied in the labour of the mind to the profit and help of others.

ANON., perhaps John Jewel (1522–71), *An Homily against Idleness*, 1563

I value highly the work done by a great master even though he may have spent little time over it.

Works are not to be judged by the amount of useless labour spent on them but by the worth of the skill and mastery of their author. Were it not so, one would not pay a larger sum to a lawyer for giving an hour's attention to an important case than to a weaver for all the cloth he weaves during a lifetime or to a peasant who toils all day at his digging.

Attr. to MICHELANGELO BUONAROTTI (1475–1564)

These seven sciences [grammar, logic, rhetoric, arithmetic, geometry, music and astronomy] be called liberal sciences ... because they be most meet and expedient to be learned of gentlemen and of free men, for it is illiberal and servile to get the living with hand and sweat of the body.

WILLIAM ALLEY (1510?–70), *The Poore Mans Library*, 1571

The more a man labours with his mind, which is mental labour, and the less with his hands, which is bodily labour, the higher he is in the scale of labourers: all must agree to that whether they will or no. This is a real distinction in nature, and can no more be got rid of by laws, constitutions, and form of government, than the complexion of the face, or colour of the eyes . . . It is upon this ground, that there ever have been, and ever will be, high and low, rich and poor, masters and servants.

THEODORE SEDGWICK (1780–1839), *Public and Private Economy*, 1836

'Trades and professions'—these are themes the Muse,
Left to her freedom, would forbear to choose;

GEORGE CRABBE (1754–1832), *The Borough*, 1810

The Managers

In the bad old days it was not so bad:
    The top of the ladder
Was an amusing place to sit; success
    Meant quite a lot—leisure
And huge meals, more palaces filled with more
    Objects, books, girls, horses
Than one would ever get round to, and to be
    Carried uphill while seeing
Others walk. To rule was a pleasure when
    One wrote a death-sentence
On the back of the Ace of Spades and played on
    With a new deck. Honours
Are not so physical or jolly now,
    For the species of Powers
We are used to are not like that. Could one of them
    Be said to resemble
The Tragic Hero, the Platonic Saint,
    Or would any painter
Portray one rising triumphant from a lake
    On a dolphin, naked,
Protected by an umbrella of cherubs? Can
    They so much as manage
To behave like genuine Caesars when alone
    Or drinking with cronies,
To let their hair down and be frank about
    The world? It is doubtful.
The last word on how we may live or die
    Rests today with such quiet

Men, working too hard in rooms that are too big,
   Reducing to figures
What is the matter, what is to be done.
   A neat little luncheon
Of sandwiches is brought to each on a tray,
   Nourishment they are able
To take with one hand without looking up
   From papers a couple
Of secretaries are needed to file,
   From problems no smiling
Can dismiss. The typewriters never stop
   But whirr like grasshoppers
In the silent siesta heat as, frivolous
   Across their discussions,
From woods unaltered by our wars and our vows
   There drift the scents of flowers
And the songs of birds who will never vote
   Or bother to notice
Those distinguishing marks a lover sees
   By instinct and policemen
Can be trained to observe. Far into the night
   Their windows burn brightly
And, behind their backs bent over some report,
   On every quarter,
For ever like a god or a disease
   There on the earth the reason
In all its aspects why they are tired, the weak,
   The inattentive, seeking
Someone to blame. If, to recuperate
   They go a-playing, their greatness
Encounters the bow of the chef or the glance
   Of the ballet-dancer
Who cannot be ruined by any master's fall.
   To rule must be a calling,
It seems, like surgery or sculpture; the fun
   Neither love nor money
But taking necessary risks, the test
   Of one's skill, the question,
If difficult, their own reward. But then
   Perhaps one should mention
Also what must be a comfort as they guess
   In times like the present
When guesses can prove so fatally wrong,
   The fact of belonging

To the very select indeed, to those
    For whom, just supposing
They do, there will be places on the last
    Plane out of disaster.
No; no one is really sorry for their
    Heavy gait and careworn
Look, nor would they thank you if you said you were.

                  W. H. AUDEN (1907–73), 1948

FINANCE

The first of all English games is making money. That is an all-absorbing game; and we knock each other down oftener in playing at that, than at football, or any other roughest sport: and it is absolutely without purpose; no one who engages heartily in that game ever knows why. Ask a great money-maker what he wants to do with his money,—he never knows. He doesn't make it to do anything with it. He gets it only that he *may* get it. 'What will you make of what you have got?' you ask. 'Well, I'll get more,' he says. Just as, at cricket, you get more runs. There's no use in the runs, but to get more of them than other people is the game. And there's no use in the money, but to have more of it than other people is the game. So all that great foul city of London there,—rattling, growling, smoking, stinking,—a ghastly heap of fermenting brick-work, pouring out poison at every pore,—you fancy it is a city of work? Not a street of it! It is a great city of play; very nasty play, and very hard play, but still play. It is only Lord's cricket-ground without the turf:—a huge billiard-table without the cloth, and with pockets as deep as the bottomless pit; but mainly a billiard-table, after all.

        JOHN RUSKIN (1819–1900), *The Crown of Wild Olive*, 1866

Her father employed her as an agent and accountant; an employment in which she showed marvellous acuteness and patience; it not only gave her habits of business and accuracy, but let her into a familiarity with the modes of thought and terms of expression among the people which she could in no other way have acquired. The exactness of arithmetical calculations far from disgusting her by its dryness, was agreeable to the honesty of her mind, and the apparently monotonous business of adding up columns of accounts was a pleasure to her, so much did she like to make her totals agree and complete her admirably-kept account books.

        FRANCES ANNE EDGEWORTH (1769–1865), *A Memoir of Maria Edgeworth* (1768–1849), 1867

The mature young lady is a lady of property. The mature young gentleman is a gentleman of property. He invests his property. He goes, in a condescending amateurish way, into the City, attends meetings of Directors, and has to do with traffic in Shares. As is well known to the wise in their generation, traffic in Shares is the one thing to have to do with in this world. Have no antecedents, no established character, no cultivation, no ideas, no manners; have Shares. Have Shares enough to be on Boards of Direction in capital letters, oscillate on mysterious business between London and Paris, and be great. Where does he come from? Shares. Where is he going to? Shares. What are his tastes? Shares. Has he any principles? Shares. What squeezes him into Parliament? Shares. Perhaps he never of himself achieved success in anything, never originated anything, never produced anything! Sufficient answer to all; Shares. O mighty Shares! To set those blaring images so high, and to cause us smaller vermin, as under the influence of henbane or opium, to cry out night and day, 'Relieve us of our money, scatter it for us, buy us and sell us, ruin us, only we beseech ye take rank among the powers of the earth, and fatten on us!'

CHARLES DICKENS (1812–70), Our Mutual Friend, 1865

Every muzhik, given the chance, is a kulak; he is an exploiter, but as long as he is a landed peasant, as long as he labors, works, works the land himself, this is still not a true kulak: he does not think to take everything for himself, he does not think how good it would be if everyone were poor, in need, he does not act in this spirit. Of course, he makes use of another man's need, he makes him work for him, but he does not build his well-being on the need of others, but builds on his own labor. From such a peasant of the land you will hear, 'I love the land, I love work, if I go to sleep and my arms and legs don't hurt from work, I am ashamed; it seems like I didn't finish something, like I lived all day for nothing.' Such a peasant of the land also has his favorite horse that is not for sale, such a muzhik takes pleasure in his buildings, his livestock, his hemp field, his grain. And not at all just because these provide him with so many rubles. He expands his farm not with the goal of profit alone; he works to the point of exhaustion, he does not get full, he does not eat his fill. Such a peasant of the land never has a big gut the way a real kulak does.

Only in the village of B, is there a real kulak in the entire 'Happy Little Corner.' This one does not love the land, or farming, or labor; this one loves only money. This one will not say that he is ashamed when his arms and legs don't hurt when he goes to sleep; this one, on the contrary, says, 'work loves fools,' 'a fool works, but a smart man, having put his hands in his pockets, strolls, and runs things with his brains.' This one prides himself on his fat gut, he prides himself on the fact that he himself does little work, 'People who owe me do all my mowing, threshing and put it in the barn.' This kulak works with the land in an offhand way, he does not expand his farm, he does not increase the number of livestock, horses, he does not plough up fields. With this one, everything is built not on the land, not on farming, not on labor, but on capital, in which he deals, which he gives out on loans with interest. His idol is money, and he thinks only about its increase. He inherited his capital, which was acquired in some unknown, but somehow unclean manner, long ago, during serfdom still, it lay hidden, and made its appearance only after the Emancipation. He lends this capital for interest and this is called 'running things with his brains.'

> Aleksandr Nikolaevich Englegardt (1832–93), *Letters from the Country 1872–87*, 1882, tr. Cathy A. Frierson, 1993

[Curtis Jadwin is a Chicago speculator who has set out to corner the market in wheat.]

But all this took not only his every minute of time, but his every thought, his every consideration. He who had only so short a while before considered the amount of five million bushels burdensome, demanding careful attention, was now called upon to watch, govern, and control the tremendous forces latent in a line of forty million. At times he remembered the Curtis Jadwin of the spring before his marriage, the Curtis Jadwin who had sold a pitiful million on the strength of the news of the French import duty, and had considered the deal 'big.' Well, he was a different man since that time. Then he had been suspicious of speculation, had feared it even. Now he had discovered that there were in him powers, capabilities, and a breadth of grasp hitherto unsuspected. He could control the Chicago wheat market; and the man who could do that might well call himself 'great,' without presumption. He knew that he overtopped them all—Gretry, the Crookes gang, the arrogant, sneering Bears, all the men of the world of the Board of Trade. He was stronger, bigger, shrewder than them all. A few days now would show, when they would all wake to the fact that wheat, which they had promised to deliver before they had it in hand, was not to be got except from him, and at whatever price he chose to impose. He could exact from them a hundred dollars a bushel if he chose, and they must pay him the price or become bankrupts.

By now his mind was upon this one great fact—May Wheat—continually. It was with him the instant he woke in the morning. It kept him company during his hasty breakfast; in the rhythm of his horses' hoofs, as the team carried him down town he heard, 'Wheat—wheat—wheat, wheat—wheat—wheat.' No sooner did he enter La Salle Street than the roar of traffic came to his ears as the roar of the torrent of wheat which drove through Chicago from the Western farms to the mills and bakeshops of Europe. There at the foot of the street the torrent swirled once upon itself, forty million strong, in the eddy which he told himself he mastered. The afternoon waned; night came on. The day's business was to be gone over; the morrow's campaign was to be planned;

little, unexpected side-issues, a score of them, a hundred of them, cropped out from hour to hour; new decisions had to be taken each minute. At dinner-time he left the office, and his horses carried him home again, while again their hoofs upon the asphalt beat out unceasingly the monotone of the one refrain, 'Wheat—wheat—wheat, wheat—wheat—wheat.' At dinner-table he could not eat. Between each course he found himself going over the day's work, testing it, questioning himself—'Was this rightly done?' 'Was that particular decision sound?' 'Is there a loop-hole here?' 'Just what was the meaning of that despatch?' After the meal the papers, contracts, statistics, and reports which he had brought with him in his Gladstone bag were to be studied. As often as not Gretry called, and the two, shut in the library, talked, discussed, and planned till long after midnight.

Then at last, when he had shut the front door upon his lieutenant and turned to face the empty, silent house, came the moment's reaction. The tired brain flagged and drooped; exhaustion, like a weight of lead, hung upon his heels. But somewhere a hall clock struck, a single, booming note, like a gong—like the signal that would unchain the tempest in the Pit to-morrow morning. Wheat—wheat—wheat, wheat—wheat—wheat! Instantly the jaded senses braced again, instantly the wearied mind sprang to its post. He turned out the lights, he locked the front door. Long since the great house was asleep. In the cold, dim silence of the earliest dawn Curtis Jadwin went to bed, only to lie awake, staring up into the darkness, planning, devising new measures, reviewing the day's doings, while the faint tides of blood behind the eardrums murmured ceaselessly to the overdriven brain, 'Wheat—wheat—wheat, wheat—wheat—wheat. Forty million bushels, forty million, forty million.'

FRANK NORRIS (1870–1902), The Pit, 1903

An interview with Lord Rothschild had to be amazingly rapid . . . He came in, placed a watch on his desk, and intimated that the interview would last five minutes, or three, or even less. In that space of time he absorbed in his right ear—on the other he was deaf—an extraordinary grasp of what was said to him, made one or two shrewd comments, and then dismissed you to stalk off to some other room to listen to another proposal in the same manner. In this way he got through an extraordinary amount of work.

Manchester Guardian, 1 Apr. 1915

The business of an issuing house comes, on the whole, into the creative category. The 'vetting' of a concern, in which part of our business I was mostly engaged, involves enlivening human contacts as well as the checking of figures. There was plenty of variety in our days; the one great drawback was the

spasmodic character of the business. It is not every day in the week that business concerns, or cities, or foreign countries, want to raise large sums of
money, or if they do, that their agents pass the doors of Rothschild's, of
Baring's, of Morgan Grenfell's, of Lazard's, and of Higginson's in order to turn
in at 41 Threadneedle Street. Not every day of the week nor, in years of slump
and unemployment, in every month of the year. We had idle months as well
as idle weeks and idle days; and these I found dispiriting. I felt like the young
men one sees drooping in those very smart shops in Bond Street, where all the
wares are so precious, and every price so high, that only once or twice in a day
does a customer drop in. At such times I used to envy civil servants and dons,
and all whose work is regular and unaffected by 'cycles' and 'depressions.' And
I dare say such dons and civil servants as I was acquainted with envied me, and
would gladly have exchanged the regularity of their underpaid jobs for the
fitfulness of my overpaid one. I call it overpaid, because in good times my
rewards had no relation to my skill, abilities, or character. Financiers—and
under this name I include stockbrokers and jobbers and bankers and discount
and acceptance houses—are not, like other professional men such as lawyers,
doctors, or architects, paid by the job and in proportion to their skill and
expertness in doing the job. They are paid by a commission on the volume of
business they handle, and while they may quite properly put it to the credit of
their own expertise and integrity that business is brought to themselves and
not to others, the volume of that business depends upon conditions over
which they have no control whatsoever. Their skill and cleverness remain
constant in good times or bad; but their earnings depend upon trade cycles,
industrial conditions, and all the ups and downs of getting and spending in all
parts of the busy world. If you live on rake-offs, as we did, it is the size of the
heap, not your skill with the rake, that counts. I was fortunate in belonging to
an excellent firm whose name stood high, and have a lively sense of what I
owed to the energy and capacity of my senior partners, who could nose out
and capture business for which there was much competition. But there would
have been a satisfaction I have never known in standing upon my own feet,
and in earning, by my own efforts, a living conformable to my deserts. What I
have lost, however, in self-approbation, my family has gained in comfort and
security. How right Clough was to sing:

> How pleasant it is to have money, heigh ho!
> How pleasant it is to have money.

L. E. JONES (Sir Lawrence Jones) (1885–1969), *Georgian Afternoon*, 1958

Louis Franc was a Belgian who became a partner in Samuel Montagu. He had
one of the quickest minds as an arbitrageur that I've ever come across. He
built up an enormous business at Montagu and an enormous private fortune.
He made a remark which left a lasting impression on me. He was looking at

the portfolio of his investments and he said, 'Henry, I'm living on the income of the income of the income.' That was a considerable achievement.

LORD BENSON (1909–95), quoted in Cathy Courtney and Paul Thompson, *City Lives*, 1996

The investment-banking firm of Pierce & Pierce occupied the fiftieth, fifty-first, fifty-second, fifty-third, and fifty-fourth floors of a glass tower that rose up sixty stories from out of the gloomy groin of Wall Street. The bond trading room, where Sherman worked, was on the fiftieth. Every day he stepped out of an aluminium-walled elevator into what looked like the reception area of one of those new London hotels catering to the Yanks. Near the elevator door was a fake fireplace and an antique mahogany mantelpiece with great bunches of fruit carved on each corner. Out in front of the fake fireplace was a brass fence or fender, as they called it in country homes in the west of England. In the appropriate months a fake fire glowed within, casting flickering lights upon a prodigious pair of brass andirons. The wall surrounding it was covered in more mahogany, rich and reddish, done in linen-fold panels carved so deep, you could *feel* the expense in the tips of your fingers by just looking at them.

All of this reflected the passion of Pierce & Pierce's chief executive officer, Eugene Lopwitz, for things British. Things British—library ladders, bow-front consoles, Sheraton legs, Chippendale backs, cigar cutters, tufted club chairs, Wilton-weave carpet—were multiplying on the fiftieth floor at Pierce & Pierce day by day. Alas, there wasn't much Eugene Lopwitz could do about the ceiling, which was barely eight feet above the floor. The floor had been raised one foot. Beneath it ran enough cables and wires to electrify Guatemala. The wires provided the power for the computer terminals and telephones of the bond trading room. The ceiling had been lowered one foot, to make room for light housings and air-conditioning ducts and a few more miles of wire. The floor had risen; the ceiling had descended; it was as if you were in an English mansion that had been squashed.

No sooner did you pass the fake fireplace than you heard an ungodly roar, like the roar of a mob. It came from somewhere around the corner. You couldn't miss it. Sherman McCoy headed straight for it, with relish. On this particular morning, as on every morning, it resonated with his very gizzard.

He turned the corner, and there it was: the bond trading room of Pierce & Pierce. It was a vast space, perhaps sixty by eighty feet, but with the same eight-foot ceiling bearing down on your head. It was an oppressive space with a ferocious glare, writhing silhouettes, and the roar. The glare came from a wall of plate glass that faced south, looking out over New York Harbor, the

Statue of Liberty, Staten Island, and the Brooklyn and New Jersey shores. The writhing silhouettes were the arms and torsos of young men, few of them older than forty. They had their suit jackets off. They were moving about in an agitated manner and sweating early in the morning and shouting, which created the roar. It was the sound of well-educated young white men baying for money on the bond market.

'Pick up the fucking phone, please!' a chubby, pink-faced member of the Harvard Class of 1976 screamed at someone two rows of desks away. The room was like a newspaper city room in that there were no partitions and no signs of visible rank. Everyone sat at light gray metal desks in front of veal-colored computer terminals with black screens. Rows of green-diode letters and numbers came skidding across.

'I said please pick up the fucking phone! I mean holy shit!' There were dark half-moons in the armpits of his shirt, and the day had just begun.

A member of the Yale Class of 1973 with a neck that seemed to protrude twelve inches out of his shirt stared at a screen and screamed over the telephone at a broker in Paris: 'If you can't see the fucking screen . . . Oh, for Christ's sake, Jean-Pierre, that's the *buyer*'s five million! The *buyer*'s! Nothing further's coming in!'

Then he covered the telephone with his hand and looked straight up at the ceiling and said out loud to no one, except Mammon, 'The frogs! The fucking frogs!'

Four desks away, a member of the Stanford Class of 1979 was sitting down, staring at a sheet of paper on his desk and holding a telephone to his ear. His right foot was up on the stirrup of a portable shoeshine stand, and a black man named Felix, who was about fifty—or was he about sixty?—was humped over his foot, stropping his shoe with a high-shine rag. All day long Felix moved from desk to desk, shining the shoes of young bond traders and salesmen as they worked, at three dollars per, counting the tip. Seldom was a word exchanged; Felix scarcely registered on their maculae. Just then Stanford '79 rose from his chair, his eyes still fastened on the sheet of paper, the telephone still at his ear—and his right foot still on the shoeshine stirrup—and he shouted: 'Well then, why do you think everybody's stripping the fucking twenty-years?'

Never took his foot off the shoeshine stand! What powerful legs he must have! thought Sherman. Sherman sat down before his own telephone and computer terminals. The shouts, the imprecations, the gesticulations, the fucking fear and greed, enveloped him, and he loved it. He was the number one bond salesman, 'the biggest producer,' as the phrase went, in the bond trading room of Pierce & Pierce on the fiftieth floor, and he loved the very roar of the storm.

'This Goldman order really fucked things up good!'

'—step up to the fucking plate and—'

'—bid 8¹/₂—'
'I'm away by two thirty-seconds!'
'Somebody's painting you a fucking picture! Can't you see that?'
'I'll take an order and buy 'em at 6-plus!'
'Hit the five-year!'
'Sell five!'
'You couldn't do ten?'
'You think this thing continues up?'
'Strip fever in the twenty-year! That's all these jerks keep talking about!'
'—a hundred million July-nineties at the buck
'—naked short—'
'Jesus Christ, what's going on?'
'I don't fucking believe this!'
'Holy fucking shit?' shouted the Yale men and the Harvard men and the Stanford men. 'Ho-lee fuc-king shit.'

How these sons of the great universities, these legatees of Jefferson, Emerson, Thoreau, William James, Frederick Jackson Turner, William Lyons Phelps, Samuel Flagg Bemis, and the other three-name giants of American scholarship—how these inheritors of the *lux* and the *veritas* now flocked to Wall Street and to the bond trading room of Pierce & Pierce! How the stories circulated on every campus! If you weren't making $250,000 a year within five years, then you were either grossly stupid or grossly lazy. That was the word. By age thirty, $500,000—and that sum had the taint of the mediocre. By age forty you were either making a million a year or you were timid and incompetent. *Make it now!* That motto burned in every heart, like myocarditis.

Tom Wolfe (1931–), *Bonfire of the Vanities*, 1987

The Old Books

They were beautiful, the old books, beautiful I tell you.
You've no idea, you young ones with all those machines;
There's no point in telling you; you wouldn't understand.
You wouldn't know what the word beautiful means.
I remember Mr Archibald—the old man, not his son—
He said to me right out: 'You've got a beautiful hand,
Your books are a pleasure to look at, real works of art.'
You youngsters with your ball-points wouldn't understand.
You should have seen them, my day book, and sales ledger:
The unused lines were always cancelled in red ink.
You wouldn't find better kept books in the City;
But it's no good talking: I know what you all think:

'He's old. He's had it. He's living in the past,
The poor old sod.' Well, I don't want your pity,
My forty-seventh Christmas with the firm. Too much to drink.
You're staring at me, pitying. I can tell by your looks.
You'll never know what it was like, what you've missed.
You'll never know. My God, they were beautiful, the old books.

VERNON SCANNELL (1922–), 1965

OFFICE WORKERS

The Man in the Bowler Hat

I am the unnoticed, the unnoticeable man:
The man who sat on your right in the morning train:
The man you looked through like a windowpane:
The man who was the colour of the carriage, the colour of the mounting
Morning pipe smoke.

I am the man too busy with a living to live,
Too hurried and worried to see and smell and touch:
The man who is patient too long and obeys too much
And wishes too softly and seldom.

I am the man they call the nation's backbone,
Who am boneless—playable catgut, pliable clay:
The Man they label Little lest one day
I dare to grow.

I am the rails on which the moment passes,
The megaphone for many words and voices:
I am graph, diagram,
Composite face.

I am the led, the easily-fed,
The tool, the not-quite-fool,
The would-be-safe-and-sound,
The uncomplaining bound,
The dust fine-ground,
Stone-for-a-statue waveworn pebble-round.

A. S. J. TESSIMOND (1902–62), *Voices in a Giant City*, 1947

[In the Counting House, 1903]

Occupying a corner of the long desk was dear old Buddimore, sweetly Irish to the backbone. He wore a frayed top hat and a frayed top coat (the only one in the Firm to do so, and the poorest paid). Buddimore was a pleasant looking man, with a striking black moustache. He was for ever working on his ledger—never uttering a sound—never wasting a moment. But somehow he could never manage to arrive at work on time; he was always two or three minutes after nine—a heinous offence, for nobody else failed to be at his desk punctually in this too well-ordered Victorian office.

At one o'clock sharp, Buddimore would carefully lay down his pen, blow his nose violently, take from his desk the *Daily Telegraph*, adjourn with it to the lavatory, come back and open a newspaper packet containing a hunk of bread and a piece of cheese. These he ate while reading. Just on the stroke of two, he would clean the desk, blow his nose violently for the second time, wipe his moustache carefully and be ready with his pen just as ever-punctual boss Almond arrived with heavy, quick tread.

SYDNEY MOSELEY (1888–1961), *The Private Diaries*, 1960

April 10

It is disgraceful how late some of the young clerks are at arriving. I told three of them that if Mr Perkupp, the principal, heard of it, they might be discharged.

Pitt, a monkey of seventeen, who has only been with us six weeks, told me 'to keep my hair on!' I informed him I had had the honour of being in the firm twenty years, to which he insolently replied that I 'looked it.' I gave him an indignant look, and said: 'I demand from you some respect, sir.' He replied: 'All right, go on demanding.' I would not argue with him any further. You cannot argue with people like that.

April 11

I was half-an-hour late at the office, a thing that has never happened to me before. There has recently been much irregularity in the attendance of the clerks, and Mr Perkupp, our principal, unfortunately chose this very morning to pounce down upon us early. Someone had given the tip to the others. The result was that I was the only one late of the lot. Buckling, one of the senior clerks, was a brick, and I was saved by his intervention. As I passed by Pitt's desk, I heard him remark to his neighbour; 'How disgracefully late some of the head clerks arrive!' This was, of course, meant for me. I treated the observation with silence, simply giving him a look, which unfortunately had the effect of making both of the clerks laugh. Thought afterwards it would have been more dignified if I had pretended not to have heard him at all.

April 28

At the office, the new and very young clerk Pitt, who was very impudent to me a week or so ago, was late again. I told him it would be my duty to inform Mr Perkupp, the principal. To my surprise, Pitt apologized most humbly and in a most gentlemanly fashion. I was unfeignedly pleased to notice this improvement in his manner towards me, and told him I would look over his unpunctuality. Passing down the room an hour later, I received a hard smack in the face from a rolled-up ball of hard foolscap. I turned round sharply, but all the clerks were apparently riveted to their work. I am not a rich man, but I would give half-a-sovereign to know whether that was thrown by accident or design.

GEORGE (1847–1912) and WEEDON (1852–1919) GROSSMITH, *The Diary of a Nobody*, 1892

[In the Post Office]

Working hours in such small post offices as that where Laura was employed were then from the arrival of the seven o'clock morning mail till the office was closed at night, with no weekly half-day off and Sunday not entirely free, for there was a Sunday morning delivery of letters and an outward mail to be made up in the evening. Slave's hours, she was told by those employed directly by Government in the larger post offices, where they worked an eight-hour-day. And so they would have been had life moved at its present-day pace. At that time life moved in a more leisurely manner; the amount of business transacted in such village post offices was smaller and its nature more simple, there were no complicated forms with instructions for filling in to be dealt out to the public, no Government allowances to be paid, and the only pensions were the quarterly ones to ex-Service men, of whom there would not be more than three or four in such a place. During the day there were long, quiet intervals in which meals could be taken in comparative peace, or reading or knitting were possible, while where two were engaged in the business, as at Candleford Green, there were opportunities of getting out into the fresh air.

Most important of all, there was leisure for human contacts. Instead of rushing in a crowd to post at the last moment, villagers would stroll over the green in the afternoon to post their letters and stay for a chat, often bringing an apple or a pear or a nosegay from their gardens for Laura. There was always at least one pot of cut flowers in the office, pink moss-roses, sweet williams and lad's love in summer, and in autumn the old-fashioned yellow-and-bronze button chrysanthemums which filled cottage gardens at that time.

In time Laura came to know these regular customers well. Some letter or telegram they had received or were sending opened the way to confidences and often, afterwards, she was treated as an old friend and would ask if the daughter in Birmingham had made a good recovery from her confinement, or if the son in Australia was having better luck, or how the wife's asthma was, or if the husband had succeeded in getting the job he was trying for. And they would ask Laura if her people at home were well, or compliment her upon a new cotton frock she was wearing, or ask her if she liked such-and-such a flower, because they had some at home they could bring her.

FLORA THOMPSON (1876–1947), *Lark Rise to Candleford,* 1945

His appearance was deceptive. He looked what he ought to have been, in the opinion of a few thousand hasty and foolish observers of this life, and what he was not—a grey drudge. They could easily see him as a drab ageing fellow for ever toiling away at figures of no importance, as a creature of the little foggy City street, of crusted ink-pots and dusty ledgers and day books, as a typical troglodyte of this dingy and absurd civilisation. Angel Pavement and its kind, too hot and airless in summer, too raw in winter, too wet in spring, and too smoky and foggy in autumn, assisted by long hours of artificial light, by hasty breakfasts and illusory lunches, by walks in boots made of sodden cardboard and rides in germ-haunted buses, by fuss all day and worry at night, had blanched the whole man, had thinned his hair and turned it grey, wrinkled his forehead and the space at each side of his short grey moustache, put eyeglasses at one end of his nose and slightly sharpened and reddened the other end, and given him a prominent Adam's apple, drooping shoulders and a narrow chest, pains in his joints, a perpetual slight cough, and a hay-fevered look at least one week out of every ten. Nevertheless, he was not a grey drudge. He did not toil on hopelessly. On the contrary, his days at the office were filled with important and exciting events, all the more important and exciting because they were there in the light, for just beyond them, all round them, was the darkness in which lurked the one great fear, the fear that he might take part no longer in these events, that he might lose his job. Once he stopped being Twigg and Dersingham's cashier, what was he? He avoided the question by day, but sometimes at night, when he could not sleep, it came to him with all its force and dreadfully illuminated the darkness with little pictures of shabby and broken men, trudging round from office to office, haunting the Labour Exchanges and the newspaper rooms of Free Libraries, and gradually sinking into the workhouse and the gutter.

J. B. PRIESTLEY (1894–1984), *Angel Pavement,* 1930

Among the clerks there was the weedy lewd and sarcastic Mr Drake, a sandy-haired man who invented the day's dirty jokes and backed horses. At a desk under the long iron-barred windows, sat a respectable puffing middle-aged man with a dirty collar, the shipping clerk, his desk a confusion of bills of lading, delivery orders, weight slips. An inaccurate and over-worked man, he was always losing important documents and was often blown up by one of the angry partners, the sons of Mr Kenneth. There was Mr Clark, a dark, drawling defiant figure who looked like a boxer. He was the invoice clerk. He would stand warming himself by the fire, unmoving, even if the head cashier arrived, until the clock struck nine. If the cashier glared at him, Mr Clark stood his ground and said: 'Nine o'clock is my time.'

The arrival of the head cashier set the office in motion and something like a chapel service began. He was a tall, grizzled, melancholy man who stood at his desk calling over figures to an assistant, like a preacher at a burial. He was famous for his sigh. It was a dull noise coming from low down in his body. 'Um ha ha,' he said. And sometimes he would call to an idling clerk:

'Press on, Mr Drake.'

'Press on what?' Mr Drake would mutter.

'Your old woman,' from Mr Clark.

'I did that last night,' sniggered Mr Drake. 'The air raid upset her.'

'Sit on her head,' called Mr Clark.

Conversations that were carried across the office in penetrating mutters. The head cashier's stomach noise pleased everyone. If he left the office for a moment, it was ten to one that Mr Haylett would mimic it and bang his desk lid up and down, like a schoolboy.

About nine arrived the only two women employed in the main office—there were five sacred typists upstairs. These two women were quarrelling sisters. Women were in the post-corset, pre-brassiere period and it was the joy of the office to exclaim at the jumpings, bobbings and swingings of a pair of breasts. One lady combined a heavy white blouseful with an air of swan-like disdain.

'Things are swinging free this morning, do you not observe, Mr Clark?' Drake would say.

'Do you fancy fish for lunch?' Mr Clark would reply, nodding to the prettier sister.

The elder girl raised her nose, the pretty one shrugged her shoulders and pouted.

Hour after hour, the cashier and the swan carried on their duet.

'Feb. 2 By Goods. Cash £872 11. 4.'

And the swan answered:

'£872 11. 4.'

'Comm. and dis. £96 16. 2,' intoned the cashier. 'Um, ha, ha.' The mournful sing-song enchanted us.

At 9.30 the 'lady secretaries' arrived. They were the secretaries of the partners, their little breasts jumping too and their high heels clattering. These girls were always late.

'The troops stay so late,' sniggered Mr Drake. 'How can a working girl get to work?'

V. S. PRITCHETT (1900–97), *A Cab at the Door*, 1968

The office politics bred caste. Caste at Pemberton's was as clearly defined as ranks in an army.

At the top were the big chiefs, the officers of the company, and the heads of departments—Mr Pemberton and his sons, the treasurer, the general manager, the purchasing-agent, the superintendents of the soda-fountain-syrup factory, of the soap-works, of the drug-laboratories, of the toilet-accessories shops, the sales-manager, and Mr S. Herbert Ross. The Olympian council were they; divinities to whom the lesser clerks had never dared to speak. When there were rumors of 'a change,' of 'a cut-down in the force,' every person on the office floor watched the chiefs as they assembled to go out to lunch together—big, florid, shaven, large-chinned men, talking easily, healthy from motoring and golf, able in a moment's conference at lunch to 'shift the policy' and to bring instant poverty to the families of forty clerks or four hundred workmen in the shops. When they jovially entered the elevator together, some high-strung stenographer would rush over to one of the older women to weep and be comforted . . . An hour from now her tiny job might be gone.

Even the chiefs' outside associates were tremendous, buyers and diplomatic representatives; big-chested men with watch-chains across their beautiful tight waistcoats. And like envoys-extraordinary were the efficiency experts whom Mr Pemberton occasionally had in to speed up the work a bit more beyond the point of human endurance . . . One of these experts, a smiling and pale-haired young man who talked to Mr Ross about the new poetry, arranged to have office-boys go about with trays of water-glasses at ten, twelve, two, and four. Thitherto, the stenographers had wasted a great deal of time in trotting to the battery of water-coolers, in actually being human and relaxed and gossipy for ten minutes a day. After the visitation of the expert the girls were so efficient that they never for a second stopped their work— except when one of them would explode in hysteria and be hurried off to the rest-room. But no expert was able to keep them from jumping at the chance to marry anyone who would condescend to take them out of this efficient atmosphere.

Just beneath the chiefs was the caste of bright young men who would some day have the chance to be beatified into chiefs. They believed enormously in the virtue of spreading the blessings of Pemberton's patent medicines; they worshipped the house policy. Once a month they met at what they called 'punch lunches,' and listened to electrifying addresses by Mr S. Herbert Ross or some other inspirer, and turned fresh, excited eyes on one another, and vowed to adhere to the true faith of Pemberton's, and not waste their evenings in making love, or reading fiction, or hearing music, but to read diligently about soap and syrups and window displays, and to keep firmly before them the vision of fifteen thousand dollars a year. They had quite the best time of anyone at Pemberton's, the bright young men. They sat, in silk shirts and new ties, at shiny, flat-topped desks in rows; they answered the telephone with an air; they talked about tennis and business conditions, and were never, never bored.

Intermingled with this caste were the petty chiefs, the office-managers and book-keepers, who were velvety to those placed in power over them, but twangily nagging to the girls and young men under them. Failures themselves, they eyed sourly the stenographers who desired two dollars more a week, and assured them that while *personally* they would be *very* glad to obtain the advance for them, it would be 'unfair to the other girls.' They were very strong on the subject of not being unfair to the other girls, and their own salaries were based on 'keeping down overhead.' Oldish men they were, wearing last-year hats and smoking Virginia cigarettes at lunch; always gossiping about the big chiefs, and at night disappearing to homes and families in New Jersey or Harlem. Awe-encircled as the very chiefs they appeared when they lectured stenographers, but they cowered when the chiefs spoke to them, and tremblingly fingered their frayed cuffs.

SINCLAIR LEWIS (1885–1951), *The Job*, 1916

The Railway Clerk

It isn't my fault.
I do what I'm told
but still I am blamed.
This year, my leave application
was twice refused.
Every day there is so much work
and I don't get overtime.
My wife is always asking for more money.
Money, money, where to get money?
My job is such, no one is giving bribe,
while other clerks are in fortunate position,
and no promotion even because I am not graduate.

I wish I was bird.

I am never neglecting my responsibility,
I am discharging it properly,
I am doing my duty,
but who is appreciating?
Nobody, I am telling you.

My desk is too small,
the fan is not repaired for two months,
three months.
I am living far off in Borivli,
my children are neglecting studies,
how long this can go on?

Once a week, I see film
and then I am happy, but not otherwise.
Also, I have good friends,
that is only consolation.
Sometimes we are meeting here or there
and having long chat.
We are discussing country's problems.
Some are thinking of foreign
but due to circumstances, I cannot think.
My wife's mother is confined to bed
and I am only support.

NISSIM EZEKIEL (1924–), 1976

Office Party

This holy night in open forum
   Miss McIntosh, who handles Files,
Has lost one shoe and her decorum.
   Stately, the frozen chairman smiles

On Media, desperately vocal.
   Credit, though they have lost their hopes
Of edging toward an early Local,
   Finger their bonus envelopes.

The glassy boys, the bursting girls
   Of Copy, start a Conga clatter
To a swung carol. Limply curls
   The final sandwich on the platter

Till hark! a herald Messenger
   (Room 414) lifts loudly up
His quavering tenor. Salesmen stir
   Libation for his Lily cup.

'Noel,' he pipes, 'Noel, Noel.'
   Some wag beats tempo with a ruler.
And the plump blonde from Personnel
   Is sick behind the water cooler.

PHYLLIS MCGINLEY (1905–78), 1932

Hard at Work, Off and On

My first job was in a British merchant bank in Hamburg. I typed bills of lading in German: sometimes to this day my fingers take on a life of their own and flicker out at lightning speed the words *& Cie GmbH* or *Aktiengesellschaft* in the middle of a harmless article. Meanwhile I find my back straightening and my feet clicking together under the table, as if I were once more under the eye of Frau Seier and Frau Haas.

They ran a tight ship, those ladies: it was understood that one arrived at five to nine—not nine o'clock; one went out for lunch sharp at one, whether one felt like it or not; wiping the Sauerkraut from one's lips one returned at 1.55 and remained static until five. One did not go swanning off to lean on the photocopier, nor spend more than three minutes in the Ladies: one worked. If there were no bills of lading one sat demurely waiting for more, or took instruction in the German language from Frau Seier. She liked to give me a proverb a day to memorise: *Ohne fleiss, kein preis* (without labour is no reward) was a favourite. So was *Morgen, morgen, nur nicht heute sagen alle faulen Leute*, which translates as, 'Tomorrow, tomorrow, not today, is what the lazy people say!'

You will understand my awed nostalgia for these days when I tell you that Frau S. was only 20, two years older than me. And this was in 1968, when the London office scene meant feckless dollybirds with hangovers: when I stayed with a schoolfriend who was temping off Piccadilly, I nearly fainted with shock at the reckless informality of her office. Since then I have never made the mistake of thinking that the Germans got rich by accident.

But the great thing about that office was that when five o'clock came, it emptied. All the men who had removed their jackets to reveal a dismal vista of string vests worn under transparent white nylon shirts, put them back on and vamoosed. We girls switched out the desk-lamps and followed, exchanging the odd proverb ('All that glisters is not gold, Fräulein Purves! *Gute nacht!*' '*Schön' dank, Frau Seier!* Without labour is no reward!'). Idyllic, really.

Because at least one knew where one stood. One had served one's hours. Since then my destiny has lain in more unstructured workplaces. People drift in between nine and whenever, eat sandwiches while on the phone one day and vanish to John Lewis for three hours the next; they are still riffling through filing-cabinets when the cleaners turn up at six. Some have keys, and go out to the pub for two hours before returning to 'clear up a few little jobs' at their desks and spill a can of diet soda into the word-processor.

The next morning someone else will beat the rush-hour by turning up at 7.30, and absent-mindedly swig the flat dregs of the Diet Coke before discovering there is a fag-end in it. Someone else is working from home, or engaged in some baroque jobshare which involves either both parties turning up and getting in one another's way, or else vanishing in a joint flurry of faxes. Increasingly, one rings people in their offices to be told, 'I'm not sure whether she's due in this morning.' Frau Seier wouldn't like it. *GmbH. Aktiengesellschaft.* Sorry.

I actually rather approve of flexible hours, being a disciple of the business guru Charles Handy, who says that it is degrading to buy people's time rather than their achievement. But human nature tends towards one-upmanship, and flexible working is a perfect lever for making one's fellow-man uncomfortable. Plant a bugged briefcase in any workplace and before long you will hear the words, 'Off home early, then?' followed by a mumbled, 'Yah—well—I've put in a lot of office lunches and Saturdays lately.'

You may imagine the scornful curl of the lip with which the saintly figure at the desk greets this. Even though it might be perfectly true, and even though the assailant may be on fixed hours and be the kind of paranoid clock-watcher who won't pick up a phone at 1.59 if his lunchbreak lasts till two. Despite all this, the barb sticks.

In offices which open every day—such as newspapers—some men who wish to signal that they are working outside their allocated hours go to the desperate lengths of appearing in the office in a fluffy pullover instead of a jacket at the weekend. They might as well have someone knit the words 'My day off' on to the chest and have done with it.

But if some flexible workers do suffer from the 'Off home early then?' form of harassment, possibly they should examine their consciences. Have they never done the opposite? Floated past a preoccupied colleague at 5.30 and said, 'You work too hard. There are other things in life, you know'? This—with its subtext implying that one has no friends or invitations, and ends the day watching *Blind Date* in a lonely little flat—is possibly the world's most annoying remark. Especially when what you are finishing is, come to think of it, supposed to be their job

By the time you whirl your chair round to say so, however, the swine will have vanished, leaving only a whiff of Eau Sauvage. I suppose you could always stick your head out of the window and shout 'OFF HOME EARLY, THEN?' But he might not hear.

LIBBY PURVES (1950–), The Times, 9 Mar. 1992

CLERGY, DOCTORS, AND LAWYERS

[Verses spoken extempore by Dean Swift on his curate's complaint of hard duty.]

> I March'd three miles thro' scorching sand,
> With zeal in heart, and notes in hand;
> I rode four more to great St *Mary*,
> Using four legs when two were weary.
> To three fair virgins I did tie men
> In the close bands of pleasing hymen.
> I dipp'd two babes in holy-water,
> And purify'd their mothers after.

Within an hour, and eke a half,
I preached three congregations deaf,
Which, thundring out with lungs long-winded,
I chopp'd so fast, that few there minded.
My Emblem, the labourious sun,
Saw all these mighty labours done,
Before one race of his was run;
All this perform'd by *Robert Hewit*,
What mortal else cou'd e'er go through it!

JONATHAN SWIFT (1667–1745), 1734

It follows of course, that setting up one species of religion, in preference to others, or nationalizing it, by countenancing, protecting, and supporting in idleness and luxury such drones as MUFTIS, POPES, TA-HO-CHANGS, GREAT LAMAS, PARSONS, ARCHBISHOPS, DEACONESSES, RECTORS, HIGH-PRIESTS, ELDERS, FAKIRS, BISHOPS, DEACONS, MUSTAPHIS, ARCHDEACONS, DRUIDS, PRIESTESES, LEVITES, PRIORS, CANNONS, DEANS, PRIESTS, DOCTORS OF DIVINITY, HO-CHANGS, NUNS, RABBIS, MUNKS, ABBES, CARMELITES, JESUITS, CARTHUSIANS, DOMINICANS, FRANCISCANS, LADY ABBESSES, MASORITES, LAMAS, CARDINALS, EMIRS, VICARS, PROPHETS, PREBENDS, TALAPOINS, BONZES, BRAMINS, APOSTLES, SEERS, PRIMON-TRES, BENEDICTINES, JACOBINES, FEUILLANS, BERNARDINES, FRERES DE L'ORDRE DE LA MERCY, CORDELIERS, CAPUCHINS, RECOLLECTS, FRERES DE LA CHARITE, MINIMES, ORATORIANS, CHARTREUX, PREDICATEURS, PICPUCES, CARMES, AUGUSTINS, URSULINES, CALVERIANS, CLERINES, SOEURS DE LA CROIX, BARNABITES, SOEURS DE LA CHARITE, ANNONCIATS, SOEURS DE ST THOMAS, CARMES DE CHAUSSEE, PETIT PERES, DAMES DE ST CLAIRE, LAZARISTS, ORDRE DE ST BENOIT, DAMES DE LA VISITATION, CELESTINES, CHAPITRE NOBLE DES FEMMES, CHANOINS, TRAPISTES, INCAS, FRIARS, CURATES, CLERGYMEN, CHAPLAINS, and other such useless beings, or *as they emphatically style each other* IMPUDENT IMPOSTORS, who being too proud and lazy to work, have availed themselves of man's credulity, and the corruption of the executive power, to get laws enacted, enabling them to steal with impunity from the laborious and industrious citizens; and who not content with thus cheating mankind, have contrived to defraud each other in the division of the spoil, by giving to one, because he wears a cap of a particular form, and of his own invention, TEN OR TWELVE THOUSAND POUNDS A YEAR, whilst the poor devils who read all their tenets to the infat-uated multitude are allowed by these *meek, moderate, temperate, sober, honest, chaste, virtuous, modest, dignified*, and *superior* interpreters of what, *as they say of each other*, each impiously chooses to call God's holy word, perhaps FIFTEEN OR TWENTY POUNDS A YEAR; but then their motto is *patience, and perhaps I may be a cardinal, bishop, pope, mufti, Ta-ho-chang, Great Lama, or high-priest;* it follows, I say, that these establishments, which produce such caterpillars, who pretend that an all just God has sent them to devour the good things of this world, without contributing to the labour of producing them, can be attended with no other consequence than that unhappy one of exciting the most rancorous animosities and implacable resentments betwixt those whose immediate interest consists in preserving the utmost cordiality, harmony, and fraternity, with each other, because they are at every instant endeavouring to gain superiority the one over the other, by engendering the most vicious hatred in their followers against all who happen to dissent from their particular doctrine; I therefore propose, as religion is a subject merely of opinion, and consequently ought to be free as the circumambient air, not to suffer the building, at other than private expence, any CATHEDRAL, MOSQUE, SYNAGOGUE, CONVENT, PAGOD, CHURCH, MONASTERY, TABERNACLE, CONVENTICLE, ABBEY, MEETING-HOUSE, NUNNERY, PANTHEON, CHAPEL, TEMPLE, ALTAR, or other edifice, to be appropriated to the purpose of what is called NATIONAL RELIGIOUS WORSHIP; or the endowment of any MONASTRY or NUNNERY; or the existence of any tythes, or other provision for what are called the REGULAR and NATIONAL CLERGY.

WILLIAM HODGSON (1745–1851), *The Commonwealth of Reason,* 1795

'Of course I have always intended to go into a profession. I have never looked at it in the same light as you do. I have always intended to make my own way, and have no doubt that I shall do so. I have quite made up my mind about it now.'

'About what, George?'

'I shall go into orders, and take a college living.'

'Orders!' said Sir Lionel; and he expressed more surprise and almost more disgust at this idea than at that other one respecting the attorney scheme.

'Yes; I have been long doubting; but I think I have made up my mind.'

'Do you mean that you wish to be a parson, and that after taking a double-first?'

'I don't see what the double-first has to do with it, sir. The only objection I have is the system of the establishment. I do not like the established church.'

'Then why go into it?' said Sir Lionel, not at all understanding the nature of his son's objection.

'I love our liturgy, and I like the ritual; but what we want is the voluntary principle. I do not like to put myself in a position which I can, in fact, hold whether I do the duties of it or no. Nor do I wish—'

'Well; I understand very little about all that; but, George, I had hoped something better for you. Now, the army is a beggarly profession unless a man has a private fortune; but, upon my word, I look on the church as the worst of the two. A man *may* be a bishop of course; but I take it he has to eat a deal of dirt first.'

'I don't mean to eat any dirt,' said the son.

'Nor to be a bishop, perhaps,' replied the father.

They were quite unable to understand each other on this subject. In Sir Lionel's view of the matter, a profession was—a profession. The word was understood well enough throughout the known world. It signified a calling by which a gentleman, not born to the inheritance of a gentleman's allowance of good things, might ingeniously obtain the same by some exercise of his abilities. The more of these good things that might be obtained, the better the profession; the easier the labour also, the better the profession; the less restriction that might be laid on a man in his pleasurable enjoyment of the world, the better the profession. This was Sir Lionel's view of a profession, and it must be acknowledged that, though his view was commonplace, it was also common sense; that he looked at the matter as a great many people look at it; and that his ideas were at any rate sufficiently intelligible. But George Bertram's view was different, and much less easy of explanation. He had an idea that in choosing a profession he should consider, not so much how he should get the means of spending his life, but how he should in fact spend it. He would have, in making this choice, to select the pursuit to which he would devote that amount of power and that amount of life which God should allot to him. Fathers and mothers, uncles and aunts, guardians and grandfathers, was not this a singular view for a young man to take in looking at such a subject?

Anthony Trollope (1815–82), *The Bertrams*, 1859

'What time do you get up?'

'Oh!—ah!—sometimes half-past six; not often, though;' for I remembered only twice that I had done so during the past summer.

She turned her head, and looked at me.

'Father is up at three; and so was mother till she was ill. I should like to be up at four.'

'Your father up at three! Why, what has he to do at that hour?'

'What has he not to do? He has his private exercise in his own room; he always rings the great bell which calls the men to milking; he rouses up Betty, our maid; as often as not, he gives the horses their feed before the man is up—for Jem, who takes care of the horses, is an old man; and father is always loth to disturb him; he looks at the calves, and the shoulders, heels, traces, chaff, and corn, before the horses go a-field; he has often to whip-cord the plough-whips; he sees the hogs fed; he looks into the swill-tubs, and writes his orders for what is wanted for food for man and beast; yes, and for fuel, too. And then, if he has a bit of time to spare, he comes in and reads with me—but only

English; we keep Latin for the evenings, that we may have time to enjoy it; and then he calls in the man to breakfast, and cuts the boys' bread and cheese, and sees their wooden bottles filled, and sends them off to their work;—and by this time it is half-past six, and we have our breakfast. There is father!' she exclaimed, pointing out to me a man in his shirt-sleeves, taller by the head than the other two with whom he was working. We only saw him through the leaves of the ash-trees growing in the hedge, and I thought I must be confusing the figures, or mistaken: that man still looked like a very powerful labourer, and had none of the precise demureness of appearance which I had always imagined was the characteristic of a minister. It was the Reverend Ebenezer Holman, however. He gave us a nod as we entered the stubble-field; and I think he would have come to meet us, but that he was in the middle of giving some directions to his men. I could see that Phillis was built more after his type than her mother's. He, like his daughter, was largely made, and of a fair, ruddy complexion, whereas hers was brilliant and delicate. His hair had been yellow or sandy, but now was grizzled. Yet his grey hairs betokened no failure in strength. I never saw a more powerful man—deep chest, lean flanks, well-planted head. By this time we were nearly up to him; and he interrupted himself and stepped forwards, holding out his hand to me, but addressing Phillis.

'Well, my lass, this is cousin Manning, I suppose. Wait a minute, young man, and I'll put on my coat, and give you a decorous and formal welcome But—— Ned Hall, there ought to be a water-furrow across this land: it's a nasty, stiff, clayey, dauby bit of ground, and thou and I must fall to, come next Monday—I beg your pardon, cousin Manning—and there's old Jem's cottage wants a bit of thatch; you can do that job to-morrow, while I am busy.' Then, suddenly changing the tone of his deep bass voice to an odd suggestion of chapels and preachers, he added, 'Now I will give out the psalm: "Come all harmonious tongues," to be sung to "Mount Ephraim" tune.'

He lifted his spade in his hand, and began to beat time with it; the two labourers seemed to know both words and music, though I did not; and so did Phillis: her rich voice followed her father's, as he set the tune; and the men came in with more uncertainty, but still harmoniously. Phillis looked at me once or twice, with a little surprise at my silence; but I did not know the words. There we five stood, bareheaded, excepting Phillis, in the tawny stubble-field, from which all the shocks of corn had not yet been carried—a dark wood on one side, where the wood-pigeons were cooing; blue distance, seen through the ash-trees, on the other. Somehow, I think that, if I had known the words, and could have sung, my throat would have been choked up by the feeling of the unaccustomed scene.

ELIZABETH GASKELL (1810–65), *Cousin Phillis*, 1864

An East-End Curate

A small blind street off East Commercial Road;
      Window, door; window, door;
      Every house like the one before,
Is where the curate, Mr Dowle, has found a pinched abode.
Spectacled, pale, moustache straw-coloured, and with a long thin face,
Day or dark his lodgings' narrow doorstep does he pace.

A bleached pianoforte, with its drawn silk plaitings faded,
Stands in his room, its keys much yellowed, cyphering, and abraded,
'Novello's Anthems' lie at hand, and also a few glees,
And 'Laws of Heaven for Earth' in a frame upon the wall one sees.

He goes through his neighbours' houses as his own, and none regards,
And opens their back-doors off-hand, to look for them in their yards:
A man is threatening his wife on the other side of the wall,
But the curate lets it pass as knowing the history of it all.

Freely within his hearing the children skip and laugh and say:
      'There's Mister Dow-well! There's Mister Dow-well!'
          in their play;
      And the long, pallid, devoted face notes not,
But stoops along abstractedly, for good, or in vain, God wot!

                             THOMAS HARDY (1840–1928), 1924

A Correct Compassion

To Mr Philip Allison, after watching him perform a Mitral Stenosis
Valvulotomy in the General Infirmary at Leeds

Cleanly, sir, you went to the core of the matter.
Using the purest kind of wit, a balance of belief and art,
You with a curious nervous elegance laid bare
The root of life, and put your finger on its beating heart.

The glistening theatre swarms with eyes, and hands, and eyes.
On green-clothed tables, ranks of instruments transmit a sterile gleam.
The masks are on, and no unnecessary smile betrays
A certain tension, true concomitant of calm.

Here we communicate by looks, though words,
Too, are used, as in continuous historic present
You describe our observations and your deeds.
All gesture is reduced to its result, an instrument.

She who does not know she is a patient lies
Within a tent of green, and sleeps without a sound
Beneath the lamps, and the reflectors that devise
Illuminations probing the profoundest wound.

A calligraphic master, improvising, you invent
The first incision, and no poet's hesitation
Before his snow-blank page mars your intent:
The flowing stroke is drawn like an uncalculated inspiration.

A garland of flowers unfurls across the painted flesh.
With quick precision the arterial forceps click.
Yellow threads are knotted with a simple flourish.
Transfused, the blood preserves its rose, though it is sick.

Meters record the blood, measure heart-beats, control the breath.
Hieratic gesture: scalpel bares a creamy rib; with pincer knives
The bone quietly is clipped, and lifted out. Beneath,
The pink, black-mottled lung like a revolted creature heaves,

Collapses; as if by extra fingers is neatly held aside
By two ordinary egg-beaters, kitchen tools that curve
Like extraordinary hands. Heart, laid bare, silently beats. It can hide
No longer yet is not revealed.—'A local anaesthetic in the cardiac nerve.'

Now, in firm hands that quiver with a careful strength,
Your knife feels through the heart's transparent skin; at first,
Inside the pericardium, slit down half its length,
The heart, black-veined, swells like a fruit about to burst,

But goes on beating, love's poignant image bleeding at the dart
Of a more grievous passion, as a bird, dreaming of flight, sleeps on
Within its leafy cage.—'It generally upsets the heart
A bit, though not unduly, when I make the first injection.'

Still, still the patient sleeps, and still the speaking heart is dumb.
The watchers breathe an air far sweeter, rarer than the room's.
The cold walls listen. Each in his own blood hears the drum
She hears, tented in green, unfathomable calms.

'I make a purse-string suture here, with a reserve
Suture, which I must make first, and deeper,
As a safeguard, should the other burst. In the cardiac nerve
I inject again a local anaesthetic. Could we have fresh towels to cover

All these adventitious ones. Now can you all see.
When I put my finger inside the valve, there may be a lot
Of blood, and it may come with quite a bang. But I let it flow,
In case there are any clots, to give the heart a good clean-out.

Now can you give me every bit of light you've got.'
We stand on the benches, peering over his shoulder.
The lamp's intensest rays are concentrated on an inmost heart.
Someone coughs.—'If you have to cough, you will do it outside this
    theatre.'—'Yes, sir.'

'How's she breathing, Doug? Do you feel quite happy?'—'Yes, fairly
Happy.'—'Now. I am putting my finger in the opening of the valve.
I can only get the tip of my finger in.—It's gradually
Giving way.—I'm inside.—No clots.—I can feel the valve

Breathing freely now around my finger, and the heart working.
Not too much blood. It opened very nicely.
I should say that anatomically speaking
This is a perfect case.—Anatomically.

For, of course, anatomy is not physiology.'
We find we breathe again, and hear the surgeon hum.
Outside, in the street, a car starts up. The heart regularly
Thunders.—'I do not stitch up the pericardium.

It is not necessary.'—For this is imagination's other place,
Where only necessary things are done, with the supreme and grave
Dexterity that ignores technique; with proper grace
Informing a correct compassion, that performs its love, and makes it live.

JAMES KIRKUP (1918–), 1952

The operating table was in the centre of the bare, tiled room, directly under the wide lamp that hung like a huge inverted saucer from the ceiling. It was completely invisible, as about twenty figures in white gowns were packed round it like tube passengers in the rush-hour. These were mostly students. The operating team was made up of Sir Lancelot himself, who was a head higher than anyone else in the room; his theatre Sister, masked and with all her hair carefully tucked into a sterile white turban, standing on a little plat-form beside him; his senior houseman, Mr Stubbins, and his registrar, Mr Crate, assisting him from the opposite side; and his anæsthetist, sitting on a small metal piano stool beside a chromium-plated barrow of apparatus at the head of the table, reading the *Daily Telegraph*. On the outskirts of this scrum two nurses in sterile clothes dashed round anxiously, dishing out hot sterilized instruments from small metal bowls like waiters serving spaghetti. A theatre porter, also gowned and masked, leant reflectively on a sort of towel rail used for counting the swabs, and another strode in with a fresh cylinder of oxygen on his shoulder. The only indication that there was a patient present at all was a pair of feet in thick, coarse-knitted bed-socks that stuck pathetically from one end of the audience.

As soon as Sir Lancelot spoke the group round the table opened, as if he were Aladdin at the mouth of his cave. I walked unhappily into the centre. My companions closed tightly behind me, and I found myself wedged against the table opposite Sir Lancelot with a man who played in the second row of the hospital forwards immediately behind me. Escape was therefore out of the question, on physical as well as moral grounds.

The operation was on the point of starting. The patient was still invisible, as the body was covered with sterile towels except for a clean-shaved strip of lower abdomen on the right-hand side of which the operating light was focussed diagnostically. I couldn't even see if it was a young man or a woman.

Having forced me into a ringside seat, Sir Lancelot then appeared to dismiss me from his mind. He paused to adjust the cuff of the rubber glove that stretched over his bony hand. Stubbins and Crate were waiting with gauze dabs, and the theatre sister was threading needles with catgut as unconcernedly as if she was going to darn her stockings.

'Stubbins,' said Sir Lancelot chattily, making a three-inch incision over the appendix, 'remind me to look into Fortnum's on my way home, there's a good lad. My missus'll give me hell if I forget her dried ginger again. I suppose it was all right for me to start?' he asked the anæsthetist.

The *Daily Telegraph* rustled slightly in assent.

I was surprised. Dried ginger in an operating theatre? Shopping lists disturbing the sanctity of surgery? And the *Daily Telegraph*?

'I've got a damn funny story to tell you lads,' went on Sir Lancelot affably, deepening his incision. 'Make you all laugh. Happened to me last week. An old lady turned up in my rooms in Harley Street . . . Sister!' he exclaimed in a tone of sudden annoyance. 'Do you expect me to operate with a jam-spreader? This knife's a disgrace.'

He threw it on the floor. Without looking at him she handed him another.

'That's better,' Sir Lancelot growled. Then, in his previous tone, as though he were two people making conversation, he went on: 'Where was I? Oh yes, the old lady. Well, she said she'd come to see me on the advice of Lord—Lord Someoneorother, I can't remember these damn titles—whom I'd operated on last year. She said she was convinced she'd got gallstones.

'Now look here, Stubbins, can't you and Crate keep out of each other's way? Your job is to use that gauze swab sensibly, not wave it around like a Salvation Army banner. How the devil do you think I can operate properly if everything's wallowing in blood? Why am I always cursed with assistants who have a couple of left hands? And I want a clip, Sister. Hurry up, woman, I can't wait all night!'

Sir Lancelot had cut through the abdominal wall while he was talking, like a child impatient to see inside a Christmas parcel.

'Well,' he went on, all affability again, seemingly conducting the operation with the concentration of a gossipy woman knitting a pair of socks, 'I said to this old lady "Gallstones, eh? Now, my dear, what makes you think you've got gallstones?" And I've never seen anyone look so embarrassed in my life!'

He returned to the operation.

'What's this structure, gentlemen?'

A reply came from under a student's mask on the edge of the crowd.

'Quite correct, whoever you are,' said Sir Lancelot, but without any congratulation in his voice. 'Glad to see you fellers remember a little fundamental anatomy from your two years in the rooms . . . so I wondered what was up. After all, patients don't get embarrassed over gallstones. It's only piles and things like that, and even then it's never the old ladies who are coy but the tough young men. Remember that bit of advice, gentlemen . . . Come on, Stubbins, wake up! You're as useless as an udder on a bull.'

He produced the appendix from the wound like a bird pulling a worm from the ground, and laid it and the attached intestine on a little square of gauze.

'Then the old lady said to me, "As a matter of fact, Sir Lancelot, I've been passing them all month . . ." Don't lean on the patient, Stubbins! If I'm not tired you shouldn't be, and I can give you forty or fifty years, my lad.'

'So now we come to the interesting part of the story. She showed me a little box, like those things you send out pieces of wedding cake in . . . Sister! What in the name of God are you threading your needles with? This isn't catgut, it's rope. What's that, woman?' He leant the red ear that stuck out below his cap towards her. 'Speak up, don't mutter to yourself. I'm not being rude, damn you! I'm never rude in the theatre. All right, tell your Matron, but give us a decent ligature. That's more like it. Swab, man, swab. Stubbins, did I ever tell you about the Matron when she was a junior theatre nurse? She had a terrible crush on a fellow house-surgeon of mine—chap called Bungo Ross, used to drink like a fish and a devil for the women. Became a respected GP in Bognor or somewhere. Died last year. I wrote a damn good obituary for him in the *British Medical Journal.* I'm tying off the appendicular artery gentlemen. See? What's that, Stubbins? Oh, the old lady. Cherry stones.'

He tossed the appendix into a small enamel bowl held for him by Stubbins.

'Looks a bit blue this end, George,' he said in the direction of the anæsthetist. 'All right, I suppose?' The anæsthetist was at the time in the corner of the theatre talking earnestly to one of the nurses who had been serving out the instruments. Theatre kit is unfair to nurses; it makes them look like white bundles. But one could tell from the rough shape of this one, from the little black-stockinged ankles below her gown and the two wide eyes above her mask, that the parcel would be worth the unwrapping. The anæsthetist jumped back to his trolley and began to twiddle the knobs on it. Sister, who was already in a wild temper, injected the nurse with a glance like a syringeful of strychnine.

'Forceps, Sister!' bellowed Sir Lancelot. She handed him a pair which he looked at closely, snapping them together in front of his mask. For some reason they displeased him, so he threw them over the heads of the crowd at the opposite wall. This caused no surprise to anyone, and seemed to be one of his usual habits. She calmly handed him another pair.

'Swabs correct, Sister, before I close? Good. Terribly important that, gentlemen. Once you've left a swab inside a patient you're finished for life. Courts, damages, newspapers, and all that sort of thing. It's the only disaster in surgery the blasted public thinks it knows anything about. Cut their throats when they're under the anæsthetic, yes, but leave anything inside and you're in the *News of the World* in no time. Shove in the skin stitches, Stubbins. What's the next case? Tea? Excellent. Operating always makes me thirsty.'

RICHARD GORDON (1921–), *Doctor in the House*, 1952

It's the humdrum, day-in, day-out, everyday work that is the real satisfaction of the practice of medicine; the million and a half patients a man has seen on his daily visits over a forty-year period of weekdays and Sundays that make up his life. I have never had a money practice; it would have been impossible for me. But the actual calling on people, at all times and under all conditions, the coming to grips with the intimate conditions of their lives, when they were being born, when they were dying, watching them die, watching them get well when they were ill, has always absorbed me.

I lost myself in the very properties of their minds; for the moment at least I actually became *them*, whoever they should be, so that when I detached myself from them at the end of a half hour of intense concentration over some illness which was affecting them, it was as though I were reawakening from a sleep. For the moment I myself did not exist, nothing of myself affected me. As a consequence I came back to myself, as from any other sleep, rested.

WILLIAM CARLOS WILLIAMS (1883–1963), *Autobiography*, 1951

The Oedipus Complex

'Good morning, Mr P,' said Mr Pollfax, rinsing and drying his hands after the last patient. 'How's Mr P.?' I was always Mr P. until I sat in the chair and he switched the lamp on and had my mouth open. Then I got a peerage.

'That's fine, my lord,' said Mr Pollfax having a look inside.

Dogged, with its slight suggestion of doggish, was the word for Mr Pollfax. He was a short man, jaunty, hair going thin with jaunty buttocks and a sway to his walk. He had two lines, from habitual grinning, cut deep from the nostrils, and scores of lesser lines like the fine hair of a bird's nest round his egg-blue eyes. There was something innocent, heroic and determined about Mr Pollfax, something of the English Tommy in tin hat and full pack going up the line. He suggested in a quiet way—war.

He was the best dentist I ever had. He got you into the chair, turned on the light, tapped around a bit with a thing like a spoon and then, dropping his white-coated arm to his side, told you a story. Several more stories followed in his flat Somerset voice, when he had your mouth jacked up. And then removing the towel and with a final 'Rinse that lot out', he finished with the strangest story of all and let you go. A month or so later the bill came in. Mr Pollfax presents his compliments and across the bottom of it, in his hand, 'Be good'. I have never known a dentist like Mr Pollfax.

'Open, my lord,' said Mr Pollfax. 'Let's see what sort of life his lordship has been leading. Still smoking that filthy pipe, I see. I shall have to do some cleaning up.'

He tapped around and then dropped his arm. A look of anxiety came on his face. 'Did I tell you that one about the girl who went to the Punch and Judy show? No? Nor the one about the engine-driver who was put on sentry duty in Syria? You're sure? When did I see you last? What was the last one I told you? That sounds like last April? Lord, you *have* been letting things go. Well,' said Mr Pollfax, tipping back my head and squirting something on to a tooth, 'we'll have a go at that root at the back. It's not doing you any good. It was like this. There was a girl sitting on the beach at Barmouth with her young man watching a Punch and Judy show . . .' (Closer and closer came Mr Pollfax's head, lower and lower went his voice.)

He took an instrument and began chipping his way through the tooth and the tale.

'Not bad, eh?' he said, stepping back with a sudden shout of laughter.

'Ah,' I mouthed.

'All right, my lord,' said Mr Pollfax, withdrawing the instrument and relapsing into his dead professional manner. 'Spit that lot out.'

He began again.

There was just that root, Mr Pollfax was saying. It was no good there. There was nothing else wrong; he'd have it out in a couple of shakes.

'Though, my lord,' he said, 'you did grow it about as far back in your throat as you could, didn't you, trying to make it as difficult as you could for Mr Pollfax? What we'll do first of all is to give it a dose of something.'

He swivelled the dish of instruments towards me and gave a tilt to the lamp. I remembered that lamp because once the bulb had exploded, sending glass all over the room. It was fortunate, Mr Pollfax said at the time, that it had blown the other way and none of it had hit me, for someone might have brought a case for damages against someone—which reminded him of the story of the honeymoon couple who went to a small hotel in Aberdeen . . .

'Now,' said Mr Pollfax, dipping things in little pots and coming to me with an injection needle; 'open wide, keep dead still. I was reading Freud the other day. There's a man. Oedipus complex? Ever read about that? Don't move, don't breathe, you'll feel a prick, but for God's sake don't jump. I don't want it to break in your gum. I've never had one break yet, touch wood, but they're thin, and if it broke off you'd be in a nursing home three weeks and Mr Pollfax would be down your throat looking for it. The trouble about these little bits of wire is they move a bit farther into the system every time you swallow.'

'There now,' said Mr Pollfax.

'Feel anything? Feel it prick?' he said. 'Fine.'

He went to a cupboard and picked out the instrument of extraction and then stood, working it up and down like a gardener's secateurs in his hand. He studied my face. He was a clean-shaven man and looked like a priest in his white coat.

'Some of the stories you hear!' exclaimed Mr Pollfax. 'And some of the songs. I mean where I come from. "The Lot that Lily Lost in the Lottery"— know that one? Is your skin beginning to tingle, do you feel it on the tip of your tongue yet? That's fine, my lord. I'll sing it to you.'

Mr Pollfax began to sing. He'd give it another minute, he said, when he'd done with Lily; he'd just give me the chorus of 'The Night Uncle's Waistcoat Caught Fire.'

'Tra la la,' sang Mr Pollfax.

'I bet,' said Mr Pollfax sadistically, 'one side of his lordship's face has gone dead and his tongue feels like a pin cushion.'

'Blah,' I said.

'I think,' he said, 'we'll begin.'

So Mr Pollfax moved round to the side of me, got a grip on my shoulders and began to press on the instrument in my mouth. Pressing and drawing firmly he worked upon the root. Then he paused and increased the pressure. He seemed to be hanging from a crowbar fixed to my jaw. Nothing happened. He withdrew.

'The Great Flood begins,' said Mr Pollfax putting a tube in my mouth and taking another weapon from the tray.

The operation began again. Mr Pollfax now seemed to hang and swing on the crowbar. It was not successful.

'Dug himself in, has he?' muttered Mr Pollfax. He had a look at his instruments. 'You can spit, my lord,' he said.

Mr Pollfax now seized me with great determination, hung, swung, pressed and tugged with increased energy.

'It's no good you thinking you're going to stay in,' said Mr Pollfax in mid-air, muttering to the root. But the instrument slipped and a piece of tooth broke off as he spoke.

'So that's the game is it?' said Mr Pollfax withdrawing. 'Good rinse, my lord, while Mr Pollfax considers the position.'

He was breathing hard.

Oh well, he said, there were more ways than one of killing a cat. He'd get the drill on it. There were two Jews standing outside Buckingham Palace when a policeman came by, he said, coming at me with the drill which made a whistling noise like a fishing line as he drew it through. The tube gurgled in my mouth. I was looking, as I always did at Mr Pollfax's, at the cowls busily twirling on the chimneys opposite. Wind or no wind these cowls always seemed to be twirling round. Two metal cowls on two yellow chimneys. I always remember them.

'Spit, my lord,' said Mr Pollfax, changing to a coarser drill. 'Sorry old man, if it slipped, but Mr Pollfax is not to be beaten.'

The drill whirred again, skidding and whining; the cowls twirled on the chimneys, Mr Pollfax's knuckles were on my nose. What he was trying to do, he said, was to get a purchase.

Mr Pollfax's movements got quicker. He hung up the drill, he tapped impatiently on the tray, looking for something. He came at me with something like a button-hook. He got it in. He levered like a signal man changing points.

'I'm just digging,' he said. Another piece of tooth broke off.

Mr Pollfax started when he heard it go and drew back.

'Mr Pollfax in a dilemma,' he said.

Well, he'd try the other side. Down came the drill again. There were beads of sweat on his brow. His breath was shorter.

'You see,' exclaimed Mr Pollfax suddenly and loudly, looking angrily up at his clock. 'I'm fighting against time. Keep that head this way, hold the mouth. That's right. Sorry, my lord, I've got to bash you about, but time's against me.'

'Why, damn this root,' said Mr Pollfax hanging up again. 'It's wearing out my drill. We'll have to saw. Mr Pollfax *is* up against it.'

His face was red now, he was gasping and his eyes were glittering. A troubled and emotional look came over Mr Pollfax's face.

'I've been up against it in my time,' exclaimed Mr Pollfax forcefully between his teeth. 'You heard me mention the Oedipus complex to you?'

'Blah,' I managed.

'I started well by ruining my father. I took every penny he had. That's a good start, isn't it?' he said, speaking very rapidly. 'Then I got married. Perfectly happy marriage, but I went and bust it up. I went off with a French girl and her husband shot at us out in the car one day. I was with that girl eighteen months and she broke her back in a railway accident and I sat with her six months watching her die. Six ruddy months. I've been through it. Then my mother died and my father was going to marry again, a girl young enough to be his daughter. I went up and took that girl off him, ran off to Hungary with her, married her and we've got seven children. Perfect happiness at last. I've been through the mill,' said Mr Pollfax, relaxing his chin and shining a torch down my mouth, 'but I've come out in the end.'

'A good rinse, my noble lord,' said Mr Pollfax.

'The oldest's fourteen,' he said, getting the saw. 'Clever girl. Very clever with her hands.'

He seized me again. Did I feel anything? Well, thank God for that, said Mr Pollfax. Here we'd been forty minutes with this damned root.

'And I bet you're thinking why didn't Lord Pollfax let sleeping dogs lie, like the telephone operator said. Did I tell you that one about the telephone operator? That gum of yours is going to be sore.'

He was standing legs apart, chin trembling, eyes blinking, hacking with the button-hook, like a wrestler putting on a headlock.

'Mr Pollfax with his back against the wall,' he said, between his teeth.

'Mr Pollfax making a last-minute stand,' he hissed.

'On the burning deck!' he gasped.

'Whence,' he added, 'all but he had fled.'

'Spit,' he said. 'And now let's have another look.' He wiped his brow. 'Don't say anything. Keep dead still. For God's sake don't let it hear you. My lords, ladies and gentlemen, pray silence for Mr Pollfax. It's coming, it isn't. No, it isn't. It is. It is. There,' he cried, holding a fragment in his fingers.

He stood gravely to attention.

> 'And his chief beside,
> Smiling the boy fell dead.'

said Mr Pollfax. 'A good and final spit, my lord and prince.'

V. S. PRITCHETT (1900–97), 1945

Mrs Gamp curtseyed all round, and signified her wish to be conducted to the scene of her official duties. The chambermaid led her, through a variety of intricate passages, to the top of the house; and pointing at length to a solitary door at the end of a gallery, informed her that yonder was the chamber where the patient lay. That done, she hurried off with all the speed she could make.

Mrs Gamp traversed the gallery in a great heat from having carried her large bundle up so many stairs, and tapped at the door, which was immediately opened by Mrs Prig, bonneted and shawled and all impatience to be gone. Mrs Prig was of the Gamp build, but not so fat; and her voice was deeper and more like a man's. She had also a beard.

'I began to think you warn't a coming!' Mrs Prig observed, in some displeasure.

'It shall be made good to-morrow night,' said Mrs Gamp, 'honorable. I had to go and fetch my things.' She had begun to make signs of enquiry in reference to the position of the patient and his overhearing them—for there was a screen before the door—when Mrs Prig settled that point easily.

'Oh!' she said aloud, 'he's quiet, but his wits is gone. It an't no matter wot you say.'

'Anythin to tell afore you goes, my dear?' asked Mrs Gamp, setting her bundle down inside the door, and looking affectionately at her partner.

'The pickled salmon,' Mrs Prig replied, 'is quite delicious. I can partick'ler recommend it. Don't have nothink to say to the cold meat, for it tastes of the stable. The drinks is all good.'

Mrs Gamp expressed herself much gratified.

'The physic and them things is on the drawers and manklesbelf,' said Mrs Prig, cursorily. 'He took his last slime draught at seven. The easy chair an't soft enough. You'll want his piller.'

Mrs Gamp thanked her for these hints, and giving her a friendly good night, held the door open until she had disappeared at the other end of the gallery. Having thus performed the hospitable duty of seeing her safely off, she shut it, locked it on the inside, took up her bundle, walked round the screen, and entered on her occupation of the sick chamber.

'A little dull, but not so bad as might be,' Mrs Gamp remarked. 'I'm glad to see a parapidge, in case of fire, and lots of roofs and chimley-pots to walk upon.'

It will be seen from these remarks that Mrs Gamp was looking out of window. When she had exhausted the prospect, she tried the easy chair, which she indignantly declared was 'harder than a brickbadge.' Next she pursued her researches among the physic-bottles, glasses, jugs, and teacups; and when she had entirely satisfied her curiosity on all these subjects of investigation, she untied her bonnet-strings and strolled up to the bedside to take a look at the patient.

A young man—dark and not ill-looking—with long black hair, that seemed the blacker for the whiteness of the bed-clothes. His eyes were partly open, and he never ceased to roll his head from side to side upon the pillow, keeping his body almost quiet. He did not utter words; but every now and then gave vent to an expression of impatience or fatigue, sometimes of surprise; and still his restless head—oh, weary, weary hour!—went to and fro without a moment's intermission.

Mrs Gamp solaced herself with a pinch of snuff, and stood looking at him with her head inclined a little sideways, as a connoisseur might gaze upon a doubtful work of art. By degrees, a horrible remembrance of one branch of her calling took possession of the woman; and stooping down, she pinned his wandering arms against his sides, to see how he would look if laid out as a dead man. Hideous as it may appear, her fingers itched to compose his limbs in that last marble attitude.

'Ah!' said Mrs Gamp, walking away from the bed, 'he'd make a lovely corpse!'

She now proceeded to unpack her bundle; lighted a candle with the aid of a fire-box on the drawers; filled a small kettle, as a preliminary to refreshing herself with a cup of tea in the course of the night; laid what she called 'a little bit of fire,' for the same philanthropic purpose; and also set forth a small tea-board, that nothing might be wanting for her comfortable enjoyment. These preparations occupied so long, that when they were brought to a conclusion it was high time to think about supper; so she rang the bell and ordered it.

'I think, young woman,' said Mrs Gamp to the assistant chambermaid, in a tone expressive of weakness, 'that I could pick a little bit of pickled salmon, with a nice little sprig of fennel, and a sprinkling of white pepper. I takes new bread, my dear, with jest a little pat of fresh butter, and a mossel of cheese. In case there should be sech a thing as a cowcumber in the ouse, will you be so kind as bring it, for I'm rather partial to 'em, and they does a world of good in a sick room. If they draws the Brighton Tipper here, I takes *that* ale at night, my love; it bein considered wakeful by the doctors. And whatever you do, young woman, don't bring more than a shillingsworth of gin-and-water warm when I rings the bell a second time: for that is always my allowance, and I never takes a drop beyond!'

Having preferred these moderate requests, Mrs Gamp observed that she would stand at the door until the order was executed, to the end that the patient might not be disturbed by her opening it a second time; and therefore she would thank the young woman to 'look sharp.'

A tray was brought with everything upon it, even to the cucumber; and Mrs Gamp accordingly sat down to eat and drink in high good humour. The extent to which she availed herself of the vinegar, and supped up that refreshing fluid with the blade of her knife, can scarcely be expressed in narrative.

'Ah!' sighed Mrs Gamp, as she meditated over the warm shillings-worth, 'what a blessed thing it is—living in a wale—to be contented! What a blessed thing it is to make sick people happy in their beds, and never mind one's self as long as one can do a service! I don't believe a finer cowcumber was ever grow'd. I'm sure I never see one!'

She moralised in the same vein until her glass was empty, and then administered the patient's medicine, by the simple process of clutching his windpipe to make him gasp, and immediately pouring it down his throat.

'I a'most forgot the piller, I declare!' said Mrs Gamp, drawing it away. 'There! Now he's as comfortable as he can be, I'm sure! I must try to make myself as much so as I can.'

With this view, she went about the construction of an extemporaneous bed in the easy chair, with the addition of the next easy one for her feet. Having formed the best couch that the circumstances admitted of, she took out of her bundle a yellow nightcap, of prodigious size, in shape resembling a cabbage; which article of dress she fixed and tied on with the utmost care, previously divesting herself of a row of bald old curls that could scarcely be called false, they were so very innocent of anything approaching to deception. From the same repository she brought forth a night-jacket, in which she also attired herself. Finally, she produced a watchman's coat, which she tied round her neck by the sleeves, so that she became two people; and looked, behind, as if she were in the act of being embraced by one of the old patrol.

All these arrangements made, she lighted the rushlight, coiled herself up on her couch, and went to sleep. Ghostly and dark the room became, and full of lowering shadows. The distant noises in the streets were gradually hushed; the house was quiet as a sepulchre; the dead of night was coffined in the silent city.

> CHARLES DICKENS (1812–70), *The Life and Adventures of Martin Chuzzlewit,* 1844

A Sergeant of the Lawe

No-wher so bisy a man as he ther nas,
And yet he semed bisier than he was.

> GEOFFREY CHAUCER (*c.*1343–1400), 'General Prologue', *The Canterbury Tales, c.*1387, tr. David Wright, 1985

Song—Lord Chancellor

When I went to the Bar as a very young man,
   (Said I to myself—said I),
I'll work on a new and original plan
   (Said I to myself—said I),
I'll never assume that a rogue or a thief
Is a gentleman worthy implicit belief,
Because his attorney has sent me a brief
   (Said I to myself—said I !).

Ere I go into court I will read my brief through
   (Said I to myself—said I),
And I'll never take work I'm unable to do
   (Said I to myself—said I),
My learned profession I'll never disgrace
By taking a fee with a grin on my face,
When I haven't been there to attend to the case
   (Said I to myself—said I !).

I'll never throw dust in a juryman's eyes
   (Said I to myself—said I),
Or hoodwink a judge who is not over-wise
   (Said I to myself—said I),
Or assume that the witnesses summoned in force
In Exchequer, Queen's Bench, Common Pleas, or Divorce,
Have perjured themselves as a matter of course
   (Said I to myself—said I !).

In other professions in which men engage
  (Said I to myself—said I),
The Army, the Navy, the Church, and the Stage
  (Said I to myself—said I),

Professional licence, if carried too far,
Your chance of promotion will certainly mar—
And I fancy the rule might apply to the Bar
  (Said I to myself—said I !).

W. S. GILBERT (1836–1911), *Iolanthe*, 1882

A judge's life, like every other, has in it much of drudgery, senseless bickerings, stupid obstinacies, captious pettifogging, all disguising and obstructing the only sane purpose which can justify the whole endeavor. These take an inordinate part of his time; they harass and befog the unhappy wretch, and at times almost drive him from that bench where like any other workman he must do his work. If that were all, his life would be mere misery, and he a distracted arbiter between irreconcilable extremes. But there is something else that makes it—anyway to those curious creatures who persist in it—a delectable calling. For when the case is all in, and the turmoil stops, and after he is left alone, things begin to take form. From his pen or in his head, slowly or swiftly as his capacities admit, out of the murk the pattern emerges, his pattern, the expression of what he has seen and what he has therefore made, the impress of his self upon the not-self, upon the hitherto formless material of which he was once but a part and over which he has now become the master. That is a pleasure which nobody who has felt it will be likely to underrate.

LEARNED HAND (1872–1961), 'The Preservation of Personality', 1927

Partition

Unbiassed at least he was when he arrived on his mission,
Having never set eyes on this land he was called to partition
Between two peoples fanatically at odds,
With their different diets and incompatible gods.
'Time,' they had briefed him in London, 'is short. It's too late
For mutual reconciliation or rational debate:
The only solution now lies in separation.
The Viceroy thinks, as you will see from his letter,
That the less you are seen in his company the better,
So we've arranged to provide you with other accommodation.
We can give you four judges, two Moslem and two Hindu,
to consult with, but the final decision must rest with you.'

Shut up in a lonely mansion, with police night and day
Patrolling the gardens to keep assassins away,
He got down to work, to the task of settling the fate
Of millions. The maps at his disposal were out of date
And the Census Returns almost certainly incorrect,
But there was no time to check them, no time to inspect
Contested areas. The weather was frightfully hot,
And a bout of dysentery kept him constantly on the trot,
But in seven weeks it was done, the frontiers decided,
A continent for better or worse divided.

The next day he sailed for England, where he quickly forgot
The case, as a good lawyer must. Return he would not,
Afraid, as he told his Club, that he might get shot.

W. H. AUDEN (1907–73), 1966

SCHOOLTEACHERS

... a Schoolmaster's calling is usually but *poor* and very *painful*, requiring much close attendance, but yet it is of so great use to the common good, and alloweth the mind so much leisure and advantage to improve it self in honest studies, that it is fitter to be chosen and delighted in by a well tempered mind, than richer and more honoured employments. It's sweet to be all day doing so much good.

RICHARD BAXTER (1615–91), *A Christian Directory*, 1673

Within a silent Street, and far apart
From Noise of Business, from a Quay or Mart,
Stands an old spacious Building, and the Din
You hear without explains the Work within;
Unlike the whispering of the Nymphs, this noise
Loudly proclaims a 'Boarding-School for Boys:'
The Master heeds it not, for thirty years
Have render'd all familiar to his ears;
He sits in comfort, 'mid the various sound
Of mingled tones for ever flowing round;
Day after day he to his Task attends,—
Unvaried toil, and care that never ends;
Boys in their works proceed; while his employ

Admits no change, or changes but the Boy;
Yet time has made it easy; he beside
Has Power supreme, and Power is sweet to Pride:
But grant him Pleasure;—what can Teachers feel,
Dependent Helpers always at the Wheel?
Their Power despis'd, their Compensation small,
Their Labour dull, their Life laborious all;
Set after set the lower Lads to make
Fit for the Class which their Superiors take;
The Road of Learning for a time to track
In roughest state, and then again go back:
Just the same way on other Troops to wait,—
Attendants fix'd at Learning's lower Gate.

GEORGE CRABBE (1754–1832), *The Borough*, 1810

The Best of School

The blinds are drawn because of the sun,
And the boys and the room in a colourless gloom
Of underwater float: bright ripples run
Across the walls as the blinds are blown
To let the sunlight in; and I,
As I sit on the shores of the class, alone,
Watch the boys in their summer blouses
As they write, their round heads busily bowed:
And one after another rouses
His face to look at me,
To ponder very quietly,
As seeing, he does not see.

And then he turns again, with a little, glad
Thrill of his work he turns again from me,
Having found what he wanted, having got what was to be had.
And very sweet it is, while the sunlight waves
In the ripening morning, to sit alone with the class
And feel the stream of awakening ripple and pass
From me to the boys, whose brightening souls it laves
For this little hour.

       This morning, sweet it is
To feel the lads' looks light on me,
Then back in a swift, bright flutter to work;
Each one darting away with his
Discovery, like birds that steal and flee.

Touch after touch I feel on me
As their eyes glance at me for the grain
Of rigour they taste delightedly.

As tendrils reach out yearningly,
Slowly rotate till they touch the tree
That they cleave unto, and up which they climb
Up to their lives—so they to me.

I feel them cling and cleave to me
As vines going eagerly up; they twine
My life with other leaves, my time
Is hidden in theirs, their thrills are mine.

D. H. LAWRENCE (1885–1930), 1912

Ageing Schoolmaster

And now another autumn morning finds me
    With chalk dust on my sleeve and in my breath,
Preoccupied with vague, habitual speculation
    On the huge inevitability of death.

Not wholly wretched, yet knowing absolutely
    That I shall never reacquaint myself with joy,
I sniff the smell of ink and chalk and my mortality
    And think of when I rolled, a gormless boy,

And rollicked round the playground of my hours,
    And wonder when precisely tolled the bell
Which summoned me from summer liberties
    And brought me to this chill autumnal cell

From which I gaze upon the april faces
    That gleam before me, like apples ranged on shelves,
And yet I feel no pinch or prick of envy
    Nor would I have them know their sentenced selves.

With careful effort I can separate the faces,
    The dull, the clever, the various shapes and sizes,
But in the autumn shades I find I only
    Brood upon death, who carries off all the prizes.

VERNON SCANNELL (1922–), 1962

ACTORS AND ENTERTAINERS

'Travelling Players'

Nor is there lack of Labour—To rehearse,
Day after Day, poor Scraps of Prose and Verse;
To bear each other's Spirit, Pride and Spite;
To hide in Rant the Heart-ache of the Night;
To dress in gaudy Patch-work, and to force
The Mind to think on the appointed Course;—
This is laborious, and may be defin'd
The bootless Labour of the thriftless Mind.

GEORGE CRABBE (1754–1832), *The Borough*, 1810

Concerning *sword swallowing*, I had the subjoined narrative from a fat-faced man, with what may be called a first-rate clown's look, and of grave manners. He and Ramo Samee are, I understand, the only sword swallowers now living—and both are old men. Ramo Samee is the once famous Indian juggler:

'I have been connected with the conjuring and tumbling professions, and every branch of them for 46 years. I lost my mother when a child, and my father was a carpenter, and allowed me to go with the tumblers. I continued tumbling until my feet were knocked up. I tumbled twenty-three or twenty-four years. It was never what you may call a good business, only a living. I got £3 a week certainly, at one time, and sometimes £4; but you had to live up to it, or you were nothing thought of; that is to say, if you kept "good company." Now there's not a living to be made in the trade. Six and twenty years ago I began to practise sword swallowing against the celebrated Ramo Samee, who was then getting £25 and £30 a week. I first practised with a cane, and found it difficult to get the cane down. When I first did it with the cane, I thought I was a dead man. There's an aperture in the chest which opens and shuts; and it keeps opening and shutting, as I understand it; but I know nothing about what they call anatomy, and never thought about such things. Well, if the cane or sword go down upon this aperture when its shut, it can go no further, and the pain is dreadful. If its open, the weapon can go through, the aperture closing on the weapon. The first time I put down the cane, I got it back easily, but put my head on the table and was very sick, vomiting dreadfully. I tried again the same afternoon, however, three or four hours after, and did it without pain. I did it two or three times more, and next day boldly tried it with a sword and succeeded. The sword was blunt, and was 36 inches long, an inch wide, and perhaps a sixth of an inch thick. I felt frightened with the cane, but not with the sword. Before the sword was used, it was rubbed with a handkerchief and made warm by friction. I swallowed swords for 14 years. At one time I used to swallow three swords, a knife and two forks, of course keeping the handles in my mouth, and having all the blades in my stomach together. I felt no pain. No doubt many of the audience felt far more pain at seeing it than I in doing it. I wore a Turkish dress both in the streets and the theatres. I never saw ladies faint at my performance; no, there was no nonsense of that kind. Gentlemen often pulled the swords and knives by their handles out of my mouth, to convince themselves it was real, and they found it real, though people to this day generally believe it's not. I've sometimes seen people shudder at my performance, but I generally had loud applause. I used to hold my head back with the swords in my stomach for two or three minutes. I've had a guinea a day for sword-swallowing. This guinea a day was only for a few days at fair times. I was with old "salt-box" Brown too, and swallowed swords and conjured with him. I swallowed swords with him thirty times a day—more than one each time, sometimes three or four. I had a third of the profits; Brown had two-thirds. We divided after all expenses were paid. My third might have been 30s a week, but it wouldn't be half as much now if I could swallow swords still. If I could swallow a tea-kettle now the people would hardly look at me. Sometimes—indeed a great many times— say twenty—I have brought up oysters out of my stomach after eating them, just as I swallowed them, on the end of the sword. At other times there was blood on the end of the blade. I always felt faint after the blood, and used to take gin or anything I could get at hand to revive me, which it did for a time. At last I injured my health so much that I was obliged to go to the doctor's . . .'

HENRY MAYHEW (1812–87), *Morning Chronicle*, 25 May 1850

Bohemia

Authors and actors and artists and such
Never know nothing, and never know much.
Sculptors and singers and those of their kidney
Tell their affairs from Seattle to Sydney.
Playwrights and poets and such horses' necks
Start off from anywhere, end up at sex.
Diarists, critics, and similar roe
Never say nothing, and never say no.
People Who Do Things exceed my endurance;
God, for a man that solicits insurance!

DOROTHY PARKER (1893–1967), 1928

ARTISTS

When Earth's last picture is painted and the tubes are twisted and dried,
When the oldest colours have faded, and the youngest critic has died,
We shall rest, and, faith, we shall need it—lie down for an æon or two,
Till the Master of All Good Workmen shall put us to work anew.

And those that were good shall be happy: they shall sit in a golden chair;
They shall splash at a ten-league canvas with brushes of comets' hair.
They shall find real saints to draw from—Magdalene, Peter, and Paul;
They shall work for an age at a sitting and never be tired at all!

And only The Master shall praise us, and only The Master shall blame;
And no one shall work for money, and no one shall work for fame,
But each for the joy of the working, and each, in his separate star,
Shall draw the Thing as he sees It for the God of Things as They are!

RUDYARD KIPLING (1865–1936), *The Seven Seas*, 1892

Diderot is so intensely concerned with artists not simply because he loves their paintings or sculptures. The artist is for him an example par excellence of the free man. As a producer he works from inner necessity; art is his life and in this work he appears as his own master, creating from impulse but guided by an ideal of truth, and correcting himself for the perfection of the result and not from fear of others. What Diderot says about the artist's freedom can be applied to the freedom of the citizen, which is a condition of the latter's dignity. In his warmth and spontaneity the artist is a model of the natural, productive, self-fulfilling man. Feeling and thought are equally active in him and joined to a truly social nature. Through this freedom and full individuality he serves others, including a future mankind.

MEYER SCHAPIRO (1904–96), 'Diderot on the Artist and Society', 1964

In general, the men who are employed in the Arts have freely chosen their profession, and suppose themselves to have special faculty for it; yet, as a body, they are not happy men. For which this seems to me the reason,—that they are expected, and themselves expect, to make their bread *by being clever*—not by steady or quiet work; and are, therefore, for the most part, trying to be clever, and so living in an utterly false state of mind and action.

This is the case, to the same extent, in no other profession or employment. A lawyer may indeed suspect that, unless he has more wit than those around him, he is not likely to advance in his profession; but he will not be always thinking how he is to display his wit. He will generally understand, early in his career, that wit must be left to take care of itself, and that it is hard knowledge of law and vigorous examination and collation of the facts of every case entrusted to him, which his clients will mainly demand: this it is which he is to be paid for; and this is healthy and measurable labour, payable by the hour. If he happen to have keen natural perception and quick wit, these will come into play in their due time and place, but he will not think of them as his chief power; and if he have them not, he may still hope that industry and conscientiousness may enable him to rise in his profession without them. Again in the case of clergymen: that they are sorely tempted to display their eloquence or wit, none who know their own hearts will deny, but then they *know* this to *be* a temptation: they never would suppose that cleverness was all that was to be expected from them, or would sit down deliberately to write a clever sermon: even the dullest or vainest of them would throw some veil over their vanity, and pretend to some profitableness of purpose in what they did. They would not openly ask of their hearers—Did you think my sermon ingenious, or my language poetical? They would early understand that they were not paid for being ingenious, nor called to be so, but to preach truth; that if they happened to possess wit, eloquence, or originality, these would appear and be of service in due time, but were not to be continually sought after or exhibited; and if it should happen that they had them not, they might still be serviceable pastors without them.

Not so with the unhappy artist. No one expects any honest or useful work of him; but every one expects him to be ingenious. Originality, dexterity, invention, imagination, everything is asked of him except what alone is to be had for asking—honesty and sound work, and the due discharge of his function as a painter.

JOHN RUSKIN (1819–90), *Pre-Raphaelitism*, 1851

He belonged to the lower ranks of the middle class, to the class of small tradesmen and manual workers, and like others of that class he got up each day before sunrise, worked hard, and wasted no time over his simple meals. He had been brought up without luxuries and he was content to go on living without them. The study and practice of his art was evidently the central fact in his life. He loved his work, it was the 'ruling enthusiasm' of his life, the condition of his happiness. When we realize what his work meant to him, all the details of his life assume their proper proportions. He spoke habitually of his pictures as 'his children'; they were indeed born of his flesh and blood. The joys and pains of their creation dwarfed all other interests and desires. A fine house and establishment, a wife, social importance, all the things the ordinary man values and strives for, had no great attractions for him. After all, they are only means to a possible and hypothetical happiness, while he had found assured and enduring happiness in his work.

A. J. FINBERG (1866–1939), *The Life of J. M. W. Turner*, 1939

No one is idle, who can do any thing. It is conscious inability, or the sense of repeated failure, that prevents us from undertaking, or deters us from the prosecution of any work.

Wilson, the painter, might be mentioned as an exception to this rule; for he was said to be an indolent man. After bestowing a few touches on a picture, he grew tired, and said to any friend who called in, 'Now, let us go somewhere!' But the fact is, that Wilson could not finish his pictures minutely; and that those few masterly touches, carelessly thrown in of a morning, were all that he could do. The rest would have been labour lost. Morland has been referred to as another man of genius, who could only be brought to work by fits and snatches. But his landscapes and figures (whatever degree of merit they might possess) were mere hasty sketches; and he could produce all that he was capable of, in the first half-hour, as well as in twenty years. Why bestow additional pains without additional effect? What he did was from the impulse of the moment, from the lively impression of some coarse, but striking object; and with that impulse his efforts ceased, as they justly ought. There is no use in labouring, *invitâ Minerva*—nor any difficulty in it, when the Muse is not averse.

'The labour we delight in physics pain.'

Denner finished his unmeaning portraits with a microscope, and without being ever weary of his fruitless task; for the essence of his genius was industry. Sir Joshua Reynolds, courted by the Graces and by Fortune, was hardly ever out of his painting-room; and lamented a few days, at any time spent at a friend's house or at a nobleman's seat in the country, as so much time lost. That darkly-illuminated room 'to him a kingdom was:' his pencil was the sceptre that he wielded, and the throne, on which his sitters were placed, a throne for Fame. Here he felt indeed at home; here the current of his ideas flowed full and strong; here he felt most self-possession, most command over others; and the sense of power urged him on to his delightful task with a sort of vernal cheerfulness and vigour, even in the decline of life.

*

Claude Lorraine, in like manner, spent whole mornings on the banks of the Tiber or in his study, eliciting beauty after beauty, adding touch to touch, getting nearer and nearer to perfection, luxuriating in endless felicity—not merely giving the salient points, but filling up the whole intermediate space with continuous grace and beauty! What farther motive was necessary to induce him to persevere, but the bounty of his fate? What greater pleasure could he seek for, than that of seeing the perfect image of his mind reflected in the work of his hand?

WILLIAM HAZLITT (1778–1830), 'On Application to Study', 1826

Wilson] Richard Wilson (1714–82)   *Morland*] George Morland (1763–1804)
Denner] Balthasar Denner (1685–1747)

WRITERS

No laborious occupation has been so much written about as the task of writing itself. Sooner or later, most writers are led to reflect on their motives for writing, the business of getting started, the merits of different working routines, and the spectre of writer's block.

I have met with almost every variety of method among living authors; and almost every variety of view as to the seriousness of their vocation. But I believe the whole fraternity are convinced that the act of authorship is the most laborious effort that men have to make: and in this they are probably right: for I have never met with a physician who did not confirm their conviction by his ready testimony.

HARRIET MARTINEAU (1802–76), *Autobiography*, 1855

Thus, there is no difference between the writer in his garret, and the slave in the mines; but that the former has his situation in the air, and the latter in the bowels of the earth. Both have their tasks assigned them alike; both must drudge and starve; neither can hope for deliverance. The compiler must compile; the composer much compose on; sick or well; in spirit or out; whether furnished with matter or not; till, by the joint pressure of labour, penury, and sorrow, he has worn out his parts, his constitution, and all the little stock of reputation he had acquired among the trade; who were all, perhaps, that ever heard of his name.

JAMES RALPH (1705?–62), *The Case of Authors by Profession or Trade, Stated*, 1758

What the Chairman Told Tom

Poetry? It's a hobby.
I run model trains.
Mr Shaw there breeds pigeons.

It's not work. You dont sweat.
Nobody pays for it.
You *could* advertise soap.

Art, that's opera; or repertory—
The Desert Song.
Nancy was in the chorus.

But to ask for twelve pounds a week—
married, aren't you?—
you've got a nerve.

How could I look a bus conductor
in the face
if I paid you twelve pounds?

Who says it's poetry, anyhow?
My ten year old
can do it *and* rhyme.

I get three thousand and expenses,
a car, vouchers,
but I'm an accountant.

They do what I tell them,
my company.
What do *you* do?

Nasty little words, nasty long words,
it's unhealthy.
I want to wash when I meet a poet.

They're Reds, addicts,
all delinquents.
What you write is rot.

Mr Hines says so, and he's a schoolteacher,
he ought to know.
Go and find *work*.

BASIL BUNTING (1900–85), 1965

Labour on the TECHNIQUE of singable words is honourable labour.

EZRA POUND (1885–1972), *Pavannes and Divagations*, 1958

Having drunk a pint of beer at luncheon—beer is a sedative to the brain, and my afternoons are the least intellectual portion of my life—I would go out for a walk of two or three hours. As I went along, thinking of nothing in particular, only looking at things around me and following the progress of the seasons, there would flow into my mind, with sudden and unaccountable emotion, sometimes a line or two of verse, sometimes a whole stanza at once, accompanied, not preceded, by a vague notion of the poem which they were destined to form part of. Then there would usually be a lull of an hour or so, then perhaps the spring would bubble up again. I say bubble up, because, so far as I could make out, the source of the suggestions thus proffered to the brain was an abyss which I have already had occasion to mention, the pit of the stomach. When I got home I wrote them down, leaving gaps, and hoping that further inspiration might be forthcoming another day. Sometimes it was, if I took my walks in a receptive and expectant frame of mind; but sometimes the poem had to be taken in hand and completed by the brain, which was apt to be a matter of trouble and anxiety, involving trial and disappointment, and sometimes ending in failure. I happen to remember distinctly the genesis of the piece which stands last in my first volume. Two of the stanzas, I do not say which, came into my head, just as they are printed, while I was crossing the corner of Hampstead Heath between the Spaniard's Inn and the footpath to Temple Fortune. A third stanza came with a little coaxing after tea. One more was needed, but it did not come: I had to turn to and compose it myself, and that was a laborious business. I wrote it thirteen times, and it was more than a twelvemonth before I got it right.

A. E. HOUSMAN (1859–1936), *The Name and Nature of Poetry*, 1933

No man but a blockhead ever wrote, except for money.

SAMUEL JOHNSON (1709–84), quoted in James Boswell, *The Life of Samuel Johnson*, 5 Apr. 1776, pub. 1791

Writing, they all say, is the most dreadful chore ever inflicted upon human beings. It is not only exhausting mentally; it is also extremely fatiguing physically. The writer leaves his desk, his day's work done, with his mind empty and the muscles of his back and neck full of a crippling stiffness. He has suffered horribly that the babies may be fed and beauty may not die.

The worst of it is that he must always suffer alone. If authors could work in large, well-ventilated factories, like cigarmakers or garment-workers, with plenty of their mates about and a flow of lively professional gossip to entertain them, their labor would be immensely lighter. But it is essential to their craft that they perform its tedious and vexatious operations *a cappella*, and so the horrors of loneliness are added to its other unpleasantnesses. An author at work is continuously and inescapably in the presence of himself. There is nothing to divert and soothe him. So every time a vagrant regret or sorrow assails him, it has him instantly by the ear, and every time a wandering ache runs down his leg it shakes him like the bite of a tiger. I have yet to meet an author who was not a hypochondriac.

H. L. MENCKEN (1880–1956), 'The Fringes of Lonely Letters', 1926

A man may write at any time, if he will set himself *doggedly* to it.

> SAMUEL JOHNSON (1709–84), quoted in James Boswell, *The Journal of a Tour to the Hebrides, with Samuel Johnson, LL.D.,* 16 Aug. 1773, 1786 edn.

Now in ordinary cases, that is, when I am only stupid, and the thoughts rise heavily and pass gummous through my pen—

Or that I am got, I know not how, into a cold unmetaphorical vein of infamous writing, and cannot take a plumb-lift out of it for my soul; so must be obliged to go on writing like a Dutch commentator to the end of the chapter, unless something be done—

—I never stand conferring with pen and ink one moment; for if a pinch of snuff, or a stride or two across the room will not do the business for me—I take a razor at once; and having tried the edge of it upon the palm of my hand, without further ceremony, except that of first lathering my beard, I shave it off; taking care only if I do leave a hair, that it be not a grey one: this done, I change my shirt—put on a better coat—send for my last wig—put my topaz ring upon my finger; and in a word, dress myself from one end to the other of me, after my best fashion.

Now the devil in hell must be in it, if this does not do: for consider, Sir, as every man chooses to be present at the shaving of his own beard (though there is no rule without an exception), and unavoidably sits over-against himself the whole time it is doing, in case he had a hand in it—the Situation, like all others, has notions of her own to put into the brain.—

—I maintain it, the conceits of a rough-bearded man, are seven years more terse and juvenile for one single operation; and if they did not run a risk of being quite shaved away, might be carried up by continual shavings, to the highest pitch of sublimity—How Homer could write with so long a beard, I don't know—and as it makes against my hypothesis, I as little care—But let us return to the Toilet.

Ludovicus Sorbonensis makes this entirely an affair of the body (ἐξωτερικὴ πρᾶξις) as he calls it—but he is deceived: the soul and body are joint-sharers in every thing they get: A man cannot dress, but his ideas get clothed at the same time; and if he dresses like a gentleman, every one of them stands presented to his imagination, genteelized along with him—so that he has nothing to do, but take his pen, and write like himself.

For this cause, when your honours and reverences would know whether I writ clean and fit to be read, you will be able to judge full as well by looking into my Laundress's bill, as my book; there was one single month in which I can make it appear, that I dirtied one and thirty shirts with clean writing; and after all, was more abused, cursed, criticised, and confounded, and had more mystic heads shaken at me, for what I had wrote in that one month, than in all the other months of that year put together.

—But their honours and reverences had not seen my bills.

> LAURENCE STERNE (1713–68), *The Life and Opinions of Tristram Shandy*,
> 1759–67

Whenever I find myself growing vapourish, I rouse myself, wash and put on a clean shirt brush my hair and clothes, tie my shoestrings neatly and in fact adonize as I were going out—then all clean and comfortable I sit down to write. This I find the greatest relief—

> JOHN KEATS (1795–1821), letter to George and Georgiana Keats, 17–27 Sept. 1819

There is one thing I believe peculiar to me—I work, that is meditate for the purpose of working, best when I have a *quasi* engagement with some other book for example. When I find myself doing ill or like to come to a still stand in writing I take up some slight book, a novel or the like, and usually have not read far ere my difficulties are removed and I am ready to write again. There must be two current[s] of ideas going on in my mind at the same time, or perhaps the slighter occupation serves like a woman's wheel or stocking to ballast the mind as it were by preventing the thoughts from wandering and so give the deeper current the power to flow undisturbd. I always laugh when I hear people say do one thing at once. I have done a dozen things at once all my life.

> SIR WALTER SCOTT (1771–1832), *Journal*, 7 Dec. 1827

I am reading to myself, and therefore slowly, the 'Autobiography of Gibbon,' in English, and with the greatest interest; but I venture to do so only for short intervals. Do not you agree with me that nothing is more interesting than the memoirs of celebrated men when they can be trusted? One always hopes to find the secret of the fine machines which have worked so well. Often one is deceived. Gibbon is evidently sincere. It shows how much may be done by a man with an extraordinary memory, who, in the leisure and the quiet given by a high social position and an independent fortune, passes forty years at work, reads all that has ever been written on an almost boundless subject, retains it, and afterwards quietly, and without hurrying himself, brings together all the results, and finds that, almost without having been aware of what he was doing, he has produced one of the greatest works of modern literature. What was least to be expected is that this man, capable of such patient toil (he gives a list of the readings of a month; in a whole year so employed, he would have done more than would have been done by a whole convent of Benedictines)— that this man, I say, laborious to a degree which generally excludes other great qualities, should, when he came to compose, have proved a concise, nervous, and animated writer. But why am I talking to you of Gibbon? Adieu!

ALEXIS DE TOCQUEVILLE (1805–59), letter to Pierre Freslon, 23 Feb. 1859

Habit also gives promptness; and the soul of dispatch is decision. One man may write a book or paint a picture, while another is deliberating about the plan or the title-page. The great painters were able to do so much, because they knew exactly what they meant to do, and how to set about it. They were thorough-bred workmen, and were not learning their art while they were exercising it. One can do a great deal in a short time if one only knows how. Thus an author may become very voluminous, who only employs an hour or two in a day in study. If he has once obtained, by habit and reflection, a use of his pen with plenty of materials to work upon, the pages vanish before him. The time lost is in beginning, or in stopping after we have begun. If we only go forwards with spirit and confidence, we shall soon arrive at the end of our journey. A practised writer ought never to hesitate for a sentence from the moment he sets pen to paper, or think about the course he is to take. He must trust to his previous knowledge of the subject and to his immediate impulses, and he will get to the close of his task without accidents or loss of time. I can easily understand how the old divines and controversialists produced their folios: I could write folios myself, if I rose early and sat up late at this kind of occupation. But I confess I should be soon tired of it, besides wearying the reader.

In one sense, art is long and life is short. In another sense, this aphorism is not true. The best of us are idle half our time. It is wonderful how much is done in a short space, provided we set about it properly, and give our minds wholly to it. Let any one devote himself to any art or science ever so strenuously, and he will still have leisure to make considerable progress in half a dozen other acquirements. Leonardo da Vinci was a mathematician, a musician, a poet, and an anatomist, besides being one of the greatest painters of his age. The Prince of Painters was a courtier, a lover, and fond of dress and company. Michael Angelo was a prodigy of versatility of talent—a writer of Sonnets (which Wordsworth has thought worth translating) and the admirer of Dante. Salvator was a lutenist and a satirist. Titian was an elegant letter-writer, and a finished gentleman. Sir Joshua Reynolds's Discourses are more polished and classical even than any of his pictures. Let a man do all he can in any one branch of study, he must either exhaust himself and doze over it, or vary his pursuit, or else lie idle. All our real labour lies in a nut-shell. The mind makes, at some period or other, one Herculean effort, and the rest is mechanical. We have to climb a steep and narrow precipice at first; but after that, the way is broad and easy, where we may drive several accomplishments abreast. Men should have one principal pursuit, which may be both agreeably and advantageously diversified with other lighter ones, as the subordinate parts of a picture may be managed so as to give effect to the centre group. It has been observed by a sensible man, that the having a regular occupation or professional duties to attend to is no excuse for putting forth an inelegant or inaccurate work; for a habit of industry braces and strengthens the mind, and enables it to wield its energies with additional ease and steadier purpose.— Were I allowed to instance in myself, if what I write at present is worth nothing, at least it costs me nothing. But it cost me a great deal twenty years ago. I have added little to my stock since then, and taken little from it. I 'unfold the book and volume of the brain,' and transcribe the characters I see there as mechanically as any one might copy the letters in a sampler. I do not say they came there mechanically—I transfer them to the paper mechanically. After eight or ten years' hard study, an author (at least) may go to sleep.

WILLIAM HAZLITT (1778–1830), 'On Application to Study', 1826

Friday night, 2 o'clock

I must love you to write you tonight, for I am *exhausted*. My skull feels encased in an iron helmet. Since two o'clock yesterday afternoon (except for about twenty-five minutes for dinner), I have been writing *Bovary*. I am in full fornication, in the very midst of it: my lovers are sweating and gasping. This has been one of the rare days of my life passed completely in illusion, from beginning to end. At six o'clock tonight, as I was writing the word 'hysterics', I was so swept away, was bellowing so loudly and feeling so deeply what my little Bovary was going through, that I was afraid of having hysterics myself. I got up from my table and opened the window to calm myself. My head was spinning. Now I have great pains in my knees, in my back, and in my head. I feel like a man who has been fucking too much (forgive the expression)—a kind of rapturous lassitude. And since I am in the midst of love it is only proper that I should not fall asleep before sending you a caress, a kiss, and whatever thoughts are left in me.

Will what I have written be good? I have no idea—I am hurrying a little, to be able to show Bouilhet a complete section when he comes. What is certain is that my book has been going at a lively rate for the past week. May it continue so, for I am weary of my usual snail's pace. But I fear the awakening, the disillusion that may come when the pages are copied. No matter: for better or worse, it is a delicious thing to write, to be no longer yourself but to move in an entire universe of your own creating. Today, for instance, as man and woman, both lover and mistress, I rode in a forest on an autumn afternoon under the yellow leaves, and I was also the horses, the leaves, the wind, the words my people uttered, even the red sun that made them almost close their love-drowned eyes.

Is this pride or piety? Is it a foolish overflow of exaggerated self-satisfaction, or is it really a vague and noble religious instinct? But when I brood over these marvellous pleasures I have enjoyed, I would be tempted to offer God a prayer of thanks if I knew he could hear me. Praised may he be for not creating me a cotton merchant, a vaudevillian, a wit, etc.! Let us sing to Apollo as in ancient days, and breathe deeply of the fresh cold air of Parnassus; let us strum our guitars and clash our cymbals, and whirl like dervishes in the eternal hubbub of Forms and Ideas.

> GUSTAVE FLAUBERT (1821–80), letter to Louise Colet, 23 Dec. 1853, tr. Francis Steegmuller, 1980

The work I did during the twelve years that I remained there [at Waltham Cross], from 1859 to 1871, was certainly very great. I feel confident that in amount no other writer contributed so much during that time to English literature. Over and above my novels, I wrote political articles, critical, social, and sporting articles, for periodicals, without number. I did the work of a surveyor of the General Post Office, and so did it as to give the authorities of the department no slightest pretext for fault-finding. I hunted always at least twice a week. I was frequent in the whist-room at the Garrick. I lived much in society in London, and was made happy by the presence of many friends at Waltham Cross. In addition to this we always spent six weeks at least out of England. Few men, I think, ever lived a fuller life. And I attribute the power of doing this altogether to the virtue of early hours. It was my practice to be at my table every morning at 5.30 a.m.; and it was also my practice to allow myself no mercy. An old groom, whose business it was to call me, and to whom I paid £5 a year extra for the duty, allowed himself no mercy. During all those years at Waltham Cross he was never once late with the coffee which it was his duty to bring me. I do not know that I ought not to feel that I owe more to him than to any one else for the success I have had. By beginning at that hour I could complete my literary work before I dressed for breakfast.

All those I think who have lived as literary men,—working daily as literary labourers,—will agree with me that three hours a day will produce as much as a man ought to write. But then he should so have trained himself that he shall be able to work continuously during those three hours,—so have tutored his mind that it shall not be necessary for him to sit nibbling his pen, and gazing at the wall before him, till he shall have found the words with which he wants to express his ideas. It had at this time become my custom,—and it still is my custom, though of late I have become a little lenient to myself,—to write with my watch before me, and to require from myself 250 words every quarter of an hour. I have found that the 250 words have been forthcoming as regularly as my watch went. But my three hours were not devoted entirely to writing. I always began my task by reading the work of the day before, an operation which would take me half an hour, and which consisted chiefly in weighing with my ear the sound of the words and phrases. I would strongly recommend this practice to all tyros in writing. That their work should be read after it has been written is a matter of course,—that it should be read twice at least before it goes to the printers, I take to be a matter of course. But by reading what he has last written, just before he recommences his task, the writer will catch the tone and spirit of what he is then saying, and will avoid the fault of seeming to be unlike himself. This division of time allowed me to produce over ten pages of an ordinary novel volume a day, and if kept up through ten months, would have given as its results three novels of three volumes each in the year;—the precise amount which so greatly acerbated the publisher in Paternoster Row, and which must at any rate be felt to be quite as much as the novel-readers of the world can want from the hands of one man.

ANTHONY TROLLOPE (1815–82), *Autobiography*, wr. 1875–6, pub. 1883

I am not sure it is right to work so hard. But a man must take himself as well as other people when he is in the humour. A man will do twice as much at one time and in half the time and twice as well that he will be able to do in another. People are always crying out about method and in some respects it is good and shows to great advantage among men of business. But I doubt if men of method who can lay aside or take up the pen just at the hour appointed will ever be better than poor creatures. L. L. S—t [Lady Louisa Stewart] used to tell me of Mr Hoole the translator of Tasso and Ariosto, and in that capacity a noble transmuter of gold into lead, that he was a clerk in the India House with long rufles and a snuffcolourd suit of clothes who occasionally visited her father. She sometimes conversed with him and was amused to find that he *did* exactly so many couplets day by day neither more nor less and habit had made it light to him however heavy it might seem to the reader.

SIR WALTER SCOTT (1771–1832), *Journal*, 4 June 1826

I had no table even to myself, much less a room to work in, but sat at the corner of the family table with my writing-book, with everything going on as if I had been making a shirt instead of writing a book. Our rooms in those days were sadly wanting in artistic arrangement. The table was in the middle of the room, the centre round which everybody sat with the candles or lamp upon it. My mother sat always at needle-work of some kind, and talked to whoever might be present, and I took my share in the conversation, going on all the same with my story, the little groups of imaginary persons, these other talks evolving themselves quite undisturbed. It would put me out now to have some one sitting at the same table talking while I worked—at least I would think it put me out, with that sort of conventionalism which grows upon one. But up to this date, 1888, I have never been shut up in a separate room, or hedged off with any observances. My study, all the study I have ever attained to, is the little second drawing-room where all the (feminine) life of the house goes on; and I don't think I have ever had two hours undisturbed (except at night, when everybody is in bed) during my whole literary life. Miss Austen, I believe, wrote in the same way, and very much for the same reason; but at her period the natural flow of life took another form. The family were half ashamed to have it known that she was not just a young lady like the others, doing her embroidery. Mine were quite pleased to magnify me, and to be proud of my work, but always with a hidden sense that it was an admirable joke, and no idea that any special facilities or retirement was necessary. My mother, I believe, would have felt her pride and rapture much checked, almost humiliated, if she had conceived that I stood in need of any artificial aids of that or any other description. That would at once have made the work unnatural to her eyes, and also to mine. I think the first time I ever secluded myself for my work was years after it had become my profession and sole dependence—when I was living after my widowhood in a relation's house, and withdrew with my book and my inkstand from the family drawing-room out of a little conscious ill-temper which made me feel guilty, notwithstanding that the retirement was so very justifiable! But I did not feel it to be so, neither did the companions from whom I withdrew.

MARGARET OLIPHANT (1828–97), *Autobiography*, 1899

One deep and steady conviction, obtained from my own experience and observation, largely qualified any apprehensions I might have, and was earnestly impressed by me upon my remonstrating friends; that enormous loss of strength, energy and time is occasioned by the way in which people go to work in literature, as if its labours were in all respects different from any other kind of toil. I am confident that intellectual industry and intellectual punctuality are as practicable as industry and punctuality in any other direction. I have seen vast misery of conscience and temper arise from the irresolution and delay caused by waiting for congenial moods, favourable circumstances, and so forth. I can speak, after long experience, without any doubt on this matter. I have suffered, like other writers, from indolence, irresolution, distaste to my work, absence of 'inspiration,' and all that: but I have also found that sitting down, however reluctantly, with the pen in my hand, I have never worked for one quarter of an hour without finding myself in full train; so that all the quarter hours, arguings, doubtings, and hesitation as to whether I should work or not which I gave way to in my inexperience, I now regard as so much waste, not only of time but, far worse, of energy. To the best of my belief, I never but once in my life left my work because I could not do it: and that single occasion was on the opening day of an illness. When once experience had taught me that I could work when I chose, and within a quarter of an hour of my determining to do so, I was relieved, in a great measure, from those embarrassments and depressions which I see afflicting many an author who waits for a mood instead of summoning it, and is the sport, instead of the master, of his own impressions and ideas.

> Harriet Martineau (1802–76), *Autobiography*, 1855

I sit down religiously every morning, I sit down for eight hours every day—and the sitting down is all. In the course of that working day of 8 hours I write 3 sentences which I erase before leaving the table in despair . . . I assure you—speaking soberly and on my word of honour—that sometimes it takes all my resolution and power of self control to refrain from butting my head against the wall. I want to howl and foam at the mouth but I daren't do it for fear of waking that baby and alarming my wife.

> Joseph Conrad (1857–1924), letter to Edward Garnett, 29 Mar. 1898

STUDENTS, SCHOLARS, AND SCIENTISTS

But one sort of Children shall not be trained up onely to book learning, and no other imployment, called Schollars, as they are in the Government of Monarchy, for then through idleness, and exercised wit therein, they spend their time to finde out pollicies to advance themselves, to be Lords and Masters above their laboring brethren, as *Simeon* and *Levi* do, which occasions all the trouble in the world.

> Gerrard Winstanley (c.1609–76), *The Law of Freedom in a Platform*, 1652

Vocation

When the gong sounds ten in the morning and I walk to school by our lane,
Every day I meet the hawker crying, 'Bangles, crystal bangles!'
There is nothing to hurry him on, there is no road he must take, no place he must go to, no time when he must come home.
I wish I were a hawker, spending my day in the road, crying, 'Bangles, crystal bangles!'

When at four in the afternoon I come back from the school,
I can see through the gate of that house the gardener digging the ground.
He does what he likes with his spade, he soils his clothes with dust, nobody takes him to task if he gets baked in the sun or gets wet.
I wish I were a gardener digging away at the garden with nobody to stop me from digging.

Just as it gets dark in the evening and my mother sends me to bed,
I can see through my open window the watchman walking up and down.

The lane is dark and lonely, and the street-lamp stands like a giant with one red eye in its head.

The watchman swings his lantern and walks with his shadow at his side, and never once goes to bed in his life.

I wish I were a watchman walking the streets all night, chasing the shadows with my lantern.

RABINDRANATH TAGORE (1861–1941), 1913

> There was a scholar from Oxford as well,
> Not yet an MA, reading Logic still;
> The horse he rode was leaner than a rake,
> And he himself, believe me, none too fat,
> But hollow-cheeked, and grave and serious.
> Threadbare indeed was his short overcoat:
> A man too unworldly for lay office,
> Yet he'd not got himself a benefice.
> For he'd much rather have at his bedside
> A library, bound in black calf or red,
> Of Aristotle and his philosophy,
> Than rich apparel, fiddle, or fine psaltery.
> And though he was a man of science, yet
> He had but little gold in his strongbox;
> But upon books and learning he would spend
> All he was able to obtain from friends;
> He'd pray assiduously for their souls,
> Who gave him wherewith to attend the schools.
> Learning was all he cared for or would heed.
> He never spoke a word more than was need,
> And that was said in form and decorum,
> And brief and terse, and full of deepest meaning.
> Moral virtue was reflected in his speech,
> And gladly would he learn, and gladly teach.

GEOFFREY CHAUCER (*c.*1343–1400), 'General Prologue', *The Canterbury Tales, c.*1387, tr. David Wright, 1985

In my first yeares of logique, I had allmost broken my braine with incessant studyes. I allowed my selfe noe minute of reste. Our very Sabboth . . . was taken up with logical or disputative theology. Our dinners and suppers were the times of our sharpest cumbats in sophistry: The spirite of ambition & pride of Victory forct mee to learne by hearte, & promptly all the logicians, old & newe, Protestants & Romanists, Dominicans & Jesuites, briefe or voluminous, That from Germany, Spaine, Italy or France wee could procure. By this inhumane industry my sleepe was allmost taken from mee, & with this wretched spirit of unquietnesse, I got the habite, or Art to direct that short sleepe that I had, about what kind of busines my dreames should bee imployed: which I did most carefully observe, when I was engaged upon compositions in prose or verse.

JOHN BEALE (c.1613–c.1682), to Samuel Hartlib, 17 Aug. 1657

> So have I wander'd ere those days were past
> Which childhood calls her own. Ah! happy days,
> Days recollection loves, unstain'd with vice,
> Why were ye gone so soon? Did I not joy
> To quit my desk, and ramble in the field,
> To gather austere berries from the bush,
> Or search the coppice for the clust'ring nut?
> Did I not always with a shout applaud
> The voice that welcome holiday announc'd?
> Say, you that knew me, you that saw me oft
> Shut up my book elate, and dance with glee.
> O liberty! how passing sweet art thou
> To him who labours at the constant oar
> Sorely reluctant, to the pining boy
> Who loves enlargement, and abhors his chain.
>
> So on thy banks too, Isis, have I stray'd,
> A tassel'd student. Witness you who shar'd
> My morning walk, my ramble at high noon,
> My evening voyage, an unskilful sail,
> To Godstow bound, or some inferior port,
> For strawberries and cream. What have we found
> In life's austerer hours, delectable
> As the long day so loiter'd? Ye profound
> And serious heads, who guard the twin retreats
> Of British learning, give the studious boy
> His due indulgence. Let him range the field,
> Frequent the public walk, and freely pull
> The yielding oar.

JAMES HURDIS (1763–1801), *The Village Curate*, 1788

Less worrying, but startling for a time, was that the word 'work' meant something dramatically different here. Someone would say 'I must get back to my rooms, I have some work to do'—meaning some reading. For me, work and play had changed places. In the factory, work meant the back-breaking routine of lifting and banging and delicately manoeuvring the eighteen-pound press iron on the garments, so that heat and steam and pressure should fix the layers of cloth and canvas in permanent adhesion and shape, and regularly heaving the cooled iron in an arc at waist height from its steel rest-plate beside the pressing donkey over to the gas-fired heating ovens standing against the bare brick wall behind me, the actions endlessly renewed, my clothes soaked in sweat, the noise and steam, and the drumming of the powered sewing machines enclosing me totally—a hermetic life in hermetic toil. For the rest, in the hours of choice, 'play'—or rather escape—meant going to the Mitchell Library to read. Even though in time I, too, adopting some of the protective colouring of this place, would refer to reading books and essay writing as work, that would not be true, for I never felt it as a burden or a worry—perhaps because, as John Buyers of Glasgow University had said in a report on me, I enjoyed the intellectual chase, a chase of ideas, the lure of new horizons. In truth it was essentially the same quest, now, that drew me to teach myself to sail a dinghy, play tennis and squash, punt straight, dance the waltz and the foxtrot and tango—to explore the Aladdin's Cave that Oxford was, the riches so numerous, the choices exhilarating, where the major burden was choice itself.

RALPH GLASSER (1916–), *Gorbals Boy at Oxford*, 1988

For they that write learnedly to the understanding of a few Scholers , . . . seem to me rather to be pittied than happy, as persons that are ever tormenting themselves; Adding, Changing, Putting in, Blotting out, Revising, Reprinting, showing 't to friends, and nine years in correcting, yet never fully satisfied; at so great a rate do they purchase this vain reward, to wit, Praise, and that too of a very few, with so many watchings, so much sweat, so much vexation and loss of sleep, the most pretious of all things. Add to this the waste of health, spoil of complexion, weakness of eyes or rather blindness, poverty, envie, abstinence from pleasure, over-hasty Old-age, untimely death, and the like; so highly does this Wise man value the approbation of one or two blear-ey'd fellows.

ERASMUS (*c.*1467–1536), *The Praise of Folly*, 1509, tr. John Wilson, 1668

Liddell and Scott

On the Completion of their Lexicon

*(Written after the death of Liddell in 1898.
Scott had died some ten years earlier.)*

'Well, though it seems
Beyond our dreams,'

Liddell and Scott] Henry George Liddell (1811–98) and Robert Scott (1811–87), *A Greek–English Lexicon*, 1843

Said Liddell to Scott,
'We've really got
To the very end,
All inked and penned
Blotless and fair
Without turning a hair,
This sultry summer day, AD
Eighteen hundred and forty-three.

'I've often, I own,
Belched many a moan
At undertaking it,
And dreamt forsaking it.
—Yes, on to Pi,
When the end loomed nigh,
And friends said: "You've as good as done,"
I almost wished we'd not begun.
Even now, if people only knew
My sinkings, as we slowly drew
Along through Kappa, Lambda, Mu,
They'd be concerned at my misgiving,
And how I mused on a College living
Right down to Sigma,
But feared a stigma
If I succumbed, and left old Donnegan
For weary freshmen's eyes to con again:
And how I often, often wondered
What could have led me to have blundered
So far away from sound theology
To dialects and etymology;
Words, accents not to be breathed by men
Of any country ever again!'

'My heart most failed,
Indeed, quite quailed,'
Said Scott to Liddell,
'Long ere the middle! . . .
'Twas one wet dawn
When, slippers on,
And a cold in the head anew,
Gazing at Delta
I turned and felt a
Wish for bed anew,

Donnegan] James Donnegan (*fl.* 1841), compiler of an earlier lexicon

And to let supersedings
Of Passow's readings
In dialects go.
"That German has read
More than we!" I said;
Yea, several times did I feel so! . . .
'O that first morning, smiling bland,
With sheets of foolscap, quills in hand,
To write ἀάατος and ἀαγής,
Followed by fifteen hundred pages,
What nerve was ours
So to back our powers,
Assured that we should reach ὠώδης
While there was breath left in our bodies!'

Liddell replied: 'Well, that's past now;
The job's done, thank God, anyhow.'

'And yet it's not,'
Considered Scott,
'For we've to get
Subscribers yet
We must remember;
Yes; by September.'

'O Lord; dismiss that. We'll succeed.
Dinner is my immediate need.
I feel as hollow as a fiddle,
Working so many hours,' said Liddell.

THOMAS HARDY (1840–1928), 1928

I have had my own anxious moments, of course, in the history of the book. Sometimes—say about 4 o'clock in the morning—I would wake and perplex myself with fears that, from a literary point of view, the work might fail. I was haunted by a dread of inaccuracies. But, on the whole, the work has been very well done and I am very proud of it. I venture to say that no other book involving the same amount of labour and anxiety has ever been published. Nobody who has not been behind the scenes, and witnessed the difficulties we have had to meet, can appreciate the real quality of the work. We have taken infinite pains, we have never grudged toil or expense. We have, of course, met with

Passow's] Franz Ludwig Carl Passow (1786–1833), on whose Greek–German lexicon they based their work

much generous help. Every eminent name in English literature has been, more or less, at our service, and the authorities of the British Museum have helped us in every possible way. There has been notably too a very fine spirit amongst the contributors, a loyalty to the interests of the Dictionary, a zeal to maintain its standard, a generous willingness to take infinite pains in its service. I suppose the sense that they were taking part in a great enterprise acted as some sort of an inspiration. They knew, too, that the Dictionary was not undertaken for commercial ends, nor designed to fill its originator's pockets. They were serving literature when writing for it.

> GEORGE SMITH (1824–1901), publisher of *The Dictionary of National Biography*, 1885–1900

It was down on the shore, tramping along the pebbled terraces of the beach, clambering over the great blocks of fallen conglomerate which broke the white curve with rufous promontories that jutted into the sea, or, finally, bending over those shallow tidal pools in the limestone rocks which were our proper hunting-ground,—it was in such circumstances as these that my Father became most easy, most happy, most human. That hard look across his brows, which it wearied me to see, the look that came from sleepless anxiety of conscience, faded away, and left the dark countenance still always stern indeed, but serene and unupbraiding. Those pools were our mirrors, in which, reflected in the dark hyaline and framed by the sleek and shining fronds of oar-weed there used to appear the shapes of a middle-aged man and a funny little boy, equally eager, and, I almost find the presumption to say, equally well prepared for business.

*

Half a century ago, in many parts of the coast of Devonshire and Cornwall, where the limestone at the water's edge is wrought into crevices and hollows, the tide-line was, like Keats' Grecian vase, 'a still unravished bride of quietness.' These cups and basins were always full, whether the tide was high or low, and the only way in which they were affected was that twice in the twenty-four hours they were replenished by cold streams from the great sea, and then twice were left brimming to be vivified by the temperate movement of the upper air. They were living flower-beds, so exquisite in their perfection, that my Father, in spite of his scientific requirements, used not seldom to pause before he began to rifle them, ejaculating that it was indeed a pity to disturb such congregated beauty. The antiquity of these rock-pools, and the infinite succession of the soft and radiant forms, sea-anemones, sca-weeds, shells, fishes, which had inhabited them, undisturbed since the creation of the

Father] Philip Henry Gosse (1810–88), who was working on his *History of the British Sea-anemones and Corals*, 1860

world, used to occupy my Father's fancy. We burst in, he used to say, where no one had ever thought of intruding before; and if the Garden of Eden had been situate in Devonshire, Adam and Eve, stepping lightly down to bathe in the rainbow-coloured spray, would have seen the identical sights that we now saw,—the great prawns gliding like transparent launches, anthea waving in the twilight its thick white waxen tentacles, and the fronds of the dulse faintly streaming on the water, like huge red banners in some reverted atmosphere.

*

The way in which my Father worked, in his most desperate escapades, was to wade breast-high into one of the huge pools, and examine the worm-eaten surface of the rock above and below the brim. In such remote places—spots where I could never venture, being left, a slightly timorous Andromeda, chained to a safer level of the cliff—in these extreme basins, there used often to lurk a marvellous profusion of animal and vegetable forms. My Father would search for the roughest and most corroded points of rock, those offering the best refuge for a variety of creatures, and would then chisel off fragments as low down in the water as he could. These pieces of rock were instantly plunged in the salt water of jars which we had brought with us for the purpose. When as much had been collected as we could carry away—my Father always dragged about an immense square basket, the creak of whose handles I can still fancy that I hear—we turned to trudge up the long climb home. Then all our prizes were spread out, face upward, in shallow pans of clean sea-water.

EDMUND GOSSE (1849–1928), Father and Son, 1907

That which compels the historian to 'scorn delights and live laborious days' is the ardour of his own curiosity to know what really happened long ago in that land of mystery which we call the past. To peer into that magic mirror and see fresh figures there every day is a burning desire that consumes and satisfies him all his life, that carries him each morning, eager as a lover, to the library and the muniment room. It haunts him like a passion of terrible potency, because it is poetic. The dead were and are not. Their place knows them no more, and is ours today. Yet they were once as real as we, and we shall tomorrow be shadows like them.

G. M. TREVELYAN (1876–1962), 'The Present Position of History', 1927

Even the best and most capable of men may not be wholly exempt from this failing [the fatal disease of 'pottering']. I knew one of them well—I speak of him with all respect for he was a great researcher and almost became a great historian. I mean, of course, Lord Acton [1834–1902]. He started to read history early, he was granted a long life; he had ample leisure and he collected a private library of dimensions which surprised me when I went through it. And he died leaving behind him one good book, some lectures, and an infinite number of reviews and essays scattered about in the back numbers of more or less unattainable periodicals, together with a scheme for a modern history on a great scale, to be written by others, which though excellent in its plan was not carried out precisely on the lines which he had laid down.

This sad paucity of results from a man qualified to accomplish great things proceeded from Lord Acton's resolve to embrace too much, and to master everything before he completed anything. He had a great book hovering before his mind; what exactly it was I have never quite made out. Lord Morley, his literary executor, once told me that he fancied that its subject might have been the growth of the modern idea of Liberty, but I have heard other titles suggested. Whatever it was, its compilation necessitated the accumulation of such a mass of detailed material that no single brain could have formulated it all. I went down into Shropshire to look at that famous library before it was removed to Cambridge. There were shelves on shelves of books on every conceivable subject—Renaissance Sorcery, the Fueros of Aragon, Scholastic Philosophy, the Growth of the French Navy, American Exploration, Church Councils. The owner had read them all, and many of them were full in their margins with cross-references in pencil. There were pigeonholed desks and cabinets with literally thousands of compartments, into each of which were sorted little white slips with references to some particular topic, so drawn up (so far as I could see) that no one but the compiler could easily make out the drift of the section. I turned over one or two from curiosity—one was on early instances of a sympathetic feeling for animals, from Ulysses' old dog in Homer downward. Another seemed to be devoted to a collection of hard words about stepmothers in all national literatures, a third seemed to be about tribal totems.

Arranged in the middle of the long two-storied room was a sort of block or altar composed entirely of unopened parcels of new books from continental publishers. All had arrived since Lord Acton's health began to break up. These volumes were apparently coming in at the rate of ten or so per week, and the purchaser had evidently intended to keep pace with the accumulation, to read them all, and to work their results into his vast thesis—whatever it was. For years, apparently, he had been endeavouring to keep up with everything that was being written—a sisyphean task. Over all there were brown holland sheets, a thin coating of dust, the moths dancing in the pale September sun. There was a faint aroma of mustiness, proceeding from thousands of seventeenth- and eighteenth-century books in a room that had been locked up since the owner's death.

I never saw a sight that more impressed on me the vanity of human life and learning.

SIR CHARLES OMAN (1860–1946), On the Writing of History, 1939

June 15th, 1903. Aston Magna, Gloucestershire
Meanwhile, our big work on local government grows slowly and surely; but still there is a good deal of ground to cover. Since we have been down here— sixteen days—I have mastered the whole of our notes on licensing of public houses by the justices, and the evidence and reports of four parliamentary enquiries, and we have actually written the greater part of the section—some twenty pages of printed matter, I suppose. It reads a straightforward narrative now—but oh! the mental struggle of getting the facts disentangled and mar- shalled one after another! Four hours every morning have we worked either together or separately. I getting the scheme right and Sidney getting the details correct and revising my scheme. We have worked all the harder because we have been absolutely undisturbed and the weather has been bad, so that Sidney has worked on in the afternoon, and I have brooded over the chapters trudging in the rain along the dripping lanes. Some delightful rides we have had together in the few fine days—happy hours of light-hearted companionship, arguing about our book or plotting our little plans.

August 1903
While I spend four whole mornings in mastering the contents of one little book, and rest the whole afternoon and evening in order to work again the next day, Sidney will get through some eight or ten volumes bearing on local government, or likely to contain out of the way references to it . . . The con- tinuous activity of his brain is marvellous: unless he is downright ill, he is never without a book or a pen in his hand. He says that he cannot think with- out reading or writing, and that he cannot brood; if he has nothing before him more absorbing, he finds himself counting the lines or spots on some object. That is why when he is in a street or a bus he sees and reads and often remem- bers the advertisements. If I would let him, he would read through meal times. A woman who wanted a husband to spend hours talking to her, or lis- tening to her chit-chat, would find him a trying husband. As it is, we exactly suit each other's habits. Long hours of solitary brooding is what I am accus- tomed to, and without which I doubt whether I could be productive. It is rest- ful for me to wander off in moor, in lanes and field, or even to sit silently by his side in our tent, or by the fire. I have my thoughts, and he has his book, and both alike go to complete and fulfil our joint task. Of course, it is exactly the eager effort, taken together, the discussion, the planning and the execution, the continuous mutual criticism of each other's ideas and each other's expres- sion of these ideas—all this vigorous co-operation for three or four hours at a

stretch—that makes the silent companionship possible, even when this last is continued, perhaps, for three or four days at a time. Sometimes I am a bit irritated because at some time he will not listen to what seems to me a brilliant suggestion—dismisses it with 'that is not new', or with a slight disparaging 'hmm'. But I generally smile at my own irritation, and take back any idea to clear up or elaborate or correct with other thoughts, or to reject as worthless; sometimes I flare up and scold—then he is all penitence and we kiss away the misunderstanding. Our love gives an atmosphere of quiescent happiness . . . and our work gives us periods of restless or energetic happiness. And when we are alone in the country together there is no other thought or feeling to intrude on this peaceful activity. We have no incompatible desires, either together or apart; our daily existence and our ideal are one and the same—we sail straight to our port over a sunlit sea.

BEATRICE POTTER (later Webb) (1853–1943), *Our Partnership*, 1948

'The Labours of a Great French Historian'

So it was a single-minded life of hard work, extremely hard work. For him, working meant getting through an enormous amount: reading, writing, listening, listening at length, not leaving his work-table until the article or the chapter was finished; rattling through the writing without correcting, so rapidly and sketchily that it was often hardly legible in spite of its clarity; not quitting his table without having dispatched to his friends innumerable letters in which the word 'work' appeared as a refrain in almost every line. 'I have masses of things to do' or 'I am entirely alone: I work' or 'Nothing new here, I am working'; failing that, in the middle of several lines of telegraphese: 'working like a black'. Work which was frenzied, happy, very happy; easy too, very easy, but unending . . .

Is it necessary to add that this work was often a refuge for him, confronted, as he was, by so many hostile circumstances, ordeals, sources of sorrow and distress, public and private? For his generation was not spared. 'Salvation lies in maintaining one's intellect,' he wrote to a friend. 'I experienced this myself at Lyons in the tragic month of July 1940. It required a huge effort to manage to work a little, but when I succeeded in getting back to it, I discovered the benefit of that great sedative, that powerful distraction, which is intellectual labour.'

FERNAND BRAUDEL (1900–85), 'Lucien Febvre [1878–1956]', 1953

Out yonder there was this huge world, which exists independently of us human beings and which stands before us like a great, eternal riddle, at least partially accessible to our inspection and thinking. The contemplation of this world beckoned like a liberation, and I soon noticed that many a man whom I had learned to esteem and to admire had found inner freedom and security in devoted occupation with it. The mental grasp of this extra-personal world within the frame of the given possibilities swam as highest aim half consciously and half unconsciously before my mind's eye. Similarly motivated men of the present and of the past, as well as the insights which they had achieved, were the friends which could not be lost. The road to this paradise was not as comfortable and alluring as the road to the religious paradise; but it has proved itself as trustworthy, and I have never regretted having chosen it.

ALBERT EINSTEIN (1879–1955), *Autobiographical Notes*, 1946, tr. Paul Arthur Schilpp, 1949

Part Three
The Reform of Work

VIII. DISSATISFACTIONS

Although work has afforded mankind many satisfactions, it has also caused an incalculable quantity of unhappiness. Throughout human history most work has been too exhausting, too unhealthy, and too poorly rewarded. Critics and reformers have sought to lessen working hours, to improve the conditions of work, and to increase remuneration. The abolition of slavery was achieved in most parts of the world, but reformers continued to lament a system that permitted 'free' workers to turn themselves into wage slaves. Others have deplored the human consequences of the division of labour and pointed to the boredom and misery of conveyor-belt methods of production. Above all, the inequity of reward for different types of work has never ceased to excite indignation.

PHYSICAL HARDSHIPS

If God (as men say) doth heaven and earth sustayne,
Then why doth not he regarde our dayly payne?
Our greevous labour he justly might devide,
And for us wretches some better life provide.
Some nought doth labour and liveth pleasauntly,
Though all his reason to vices he apply:
But see with what sweat, what business and payne
Our simple living we labour to obtayne:
Behold what illes the shepheardes must endure
For flocke and housholde have living to procure,
In fervent heate we must intende our folde,
And in the winter almost we freze for colde:
Upon the harde ground or on the flintes browne
We slepe, when other lye on a bed of downe.
A thousand illes of daunger and sicknesse,
With divers sores our beastes doth oppresse:
A thousand perils and mo if they were tolde
Dayly and nightly invadeth our poore folde.
Sometime the wolfe our beastes doth devour,
And sometime the thefe awayteth his hour:
Or els the souldiour much worse then wolfe or thefe

Agaynst all our flocke inrageth with mischefe.
See howe my handes are with many a gall,
And stiffe as a borde by worke continuall,
My face all scorvy, my colour pale and wan,
My head all parched and blacke as any pan,
My beard like bristles, so that a pliant leeke
With a little helpe may thrust me throw the cheeke,
And as a stockfish wrinkled is my skinne,
Suche is the profite that I by labour winne.

ALEXANDER BARCLAY, Scottish priest (1475?–1552), *Certaine Eclogues* (*c.*1513–14)

The gentlemen, serving-men and the townsmen of this country are not so unserviceable, but very personable, comely and tall men, which confirms my former assertion that the hard labour, parching of the sun, and starving with cold is a chief cause of the unseemliness of the common people of the country, seeing the gentlemen, serving-men, and those brought up in towns, which are not tormented with these extremities of heat and cold, nor tired with toil, do prove more personable; and of the common people of this country the Welshmen, whom the rest call the mountain men, are found to be the more personable, as people not so cloyed with labour, as those that live by tillage.

GEORGE OWEN OF HENLLYS (1552–1613), *The Description of Pembrokeshire,* 1603

I admit that the great increase of commerce and manufactures hurts the military spirit of a people; because it produces a competition for something else than martial honours,—a competition for riches. It also hurts the bodies of the people; for you will observe, there is no man who works at any particular trade, but you may know him from his appearance to do so. One part or other of his body being more used than the rest, he is in some degree deformed.

SAMUEL JOHNSON (1709–84), quoted in James Boswell, *The Life of Samuel Johnson,* 13 Apr. 1773, pub. 1791

At noon to-day there was sunlight on the Surrey hills; the fields and lanes were fragrant with the first breath of spring, and from the shelter of budding copses many a primrose looked tremblingly up to the vision of blue sky. But of these things Clerkenwell takes no count; here it had been a day like any other, consisting of so many hours, each representing a fraction of the weekly wage. Go where you may in Clerkenwell, on every hand are multiform evidences of toil, intolerable as a nightmare. It is not as in those parts of London where the main thoroughfares consist of shops and warehouses and workrooms, whilst the streets that are hidden away on either hand are devoted in the main to dwellings. Here every alley is thronged with small industries; all but every door and window exhibits the advertisement of a craft that is carried on within. Here you may see how men have multiplied toil for toil's sake, have wrought to devise work superfluous, have worn their lives away in imagining new forms of weariness. The energy, the ingenuity daily put forth in these grimy burrows task the brain's power of wondering. But that those who sit here through the livelong day, through every season, through all the years of the life that is granted them, who strain their eyesight, who overtax their muscles, who nurse disease in their frames, who put resolutely from them the thought of what existence *might* be—that these do it all without prospect or hope of reward save the permission to eat and sleep and bring into the world other creatures to strive with them for bread, surely that thought is yet more marvellous.

GEORGE GISSING (1857–1903), *The Nether World,* 1889

Labour produces works of wonder for the rich, but nakedness for the worker. It produces palaces, but only hovels for the worker; it produces beauty, but cripples the worker; it replaces labour by machines but throws a part of the workers back to a barbaric labour and turns the other part into machines. It produces culture, but also imbecility and cretinism for the worker.

KARL MARX (1818–83), *Economic and Philosophical Manuscripts,* wr. 1844, tr. David McLellan, 1972

Mr Melbury . . . walked up and down looking on the floor—his usual custom when undecided. That stiffness about the arm, hip, and knee-joint which was apparent when he walked was the net product of the divers sprains and over-exertions that had been required of him in handling trees and timber when a young man, for he was of the sort called self-made, and had worked hard. He knew the origin of every one of these cramps: that in his left shoulder had come of carrying a pollard, unassisted, from Tutcombe Bottom home; that in one leg was caused by the crash of an elm against it when they were felling; that in the other was from lifting a bole. On many a morrow after wearying himself by these prodigious muscular efforts, he had risen from his bed fresh as usual; and confident in the recuperative power of his youth, he had repeated the strains anew. But treacherous Time had been only hiding ill results when they could be guarded against for greater effect when they could not. Now in his declining years the store had been unfolded in the form of rheumatisms, pricks, and spasms, in every one of which Melbury recognised some act which, had its consequences been contemporaneously made known, he would have abstained from repeating.

THOMAS HARDY (1840–1928), *The Woodlanders*, 1887

There was another interesting set of statistics that a person might have gathered in Packingtown—those of the various afflictions of the workers. When Jurgis had first inspected the packing plants with Szedvilas, he had marveled while he listened to the tale of all the things that were made out of the carcasses of animals, and of all the lesser industries that were maintained there; now he found that each one of these lesser industries was a separate little inferno, in its way as horrible as the killing beds, the source and fountain of them all. The workers in each of them had their own peculiar diseases. And the wandering visitor might be skeptical about all the swindles, but he could not be skeptical about these, for the worker bore the evidence of them about on his own person—generally he had only to hold out his hand.

There were the men in the pickle rooms, for instance, where old Antanas had gotten his death; scarce a one of these that had not some spot of horror on his person. Let a man so much as scrape his finger pushing a truck in the pickle rooms, and he might have a sore that would put him out of the world; all the joints in his fingers might be eaten by the acid, one by one. Of the butchers and floorsmen, the beef-boners and trimmers, and all those who used knives, you could scarcely find a person who had the use of his thumb; time and time again the base of it had been slashed, till it was a mere lump of flesh against which the man pressed the knife to hold it. The hands of these men would be criss-crossed with cuts, until you could no longer pretend to count them or to trace them. They would have no nails—they had worn them off pulling hides; their knuckles were swollen so that their fingers spread out like a fan. There were men who worked in the cooking rooms, in the midst of steam and sickening odours, by artificial light; in these rooms the germs of tuberculosis might live for two years, but the supply was renewed every hour. There were the beef-luggers, who carried two-hundred-pound quarters into the refrigerator cars—a fearful kind of work, that began at four o'clock in the morning, and that wore out the most powerful men in a few years. There were those who worked in the chilling rooms, and whose special disease was rheumatism; the time limit that a man could work in the chilling rooms was said to be five years. There were the wool-pluckers, whose hands went to pieces even sooner than the hands of the pickle men; for the pelts of the sheep had to be painted with acid to loosen the wool, and then the pluckers had to pull out this wool with their bare hands, till the acid had eaten their fingers off.

There were those who made the tins for the canned meat; and their hands, too, were a maze of cuts, and each cut represented a chance for blood poisoning. Some worked at the stamping machines, and it was seldom that one could work long there at the pace that was set, and not give out and forget himself, and have a part of his hand chopped off. There were the 'hoisters', as they were called, whose task it was to press the lever which lifted the dead cattle off the floor. They ran along upon a rafter, peering down through the damp and the steam; and as old Durham's architects had not built the killing room for the convenience of the hoisters, at every few feet they would have to stoop under a beam, say four feet above the one they ran on; which got them into the habit of stooping, so that in a few years they would be walking like chimpanzees.

UPTON SINCLAIR (1878–1968), *The Jungle*, 1906

Here is what *women's* work was like in Krivoshchekovo. At the brickyard, when they had completed working one section of the clay pit, they used to take down the overhead shelter (before they had mined there, it had been laid out on the surface of the earth). And now it was necessary to hoist wet beams ten to twelve yards up out of a big pit. How was it done? The reader will say: with machines. Of course. A women's brigade looped a cable around each end of a beam, and in two rows like barge haulers, keeping even so as not to let the beam drop and then have to begin over again, pulled one side of each cable and . . . out came the beam. And then a score of them would hoist up one beam on their shoulders to the accompaniment of command oaths from their out-and-out slave driver of a woman brigadier and would carry the beam to its new place and dump it there. A tractor, did you say? But, for pity's sakes, where would you get a tractor in 1948? A crane, you say? But you have forgotten Vyshinsky: 'work, the miracle worker which transforms people from nonexistence and insignificance into heroes'? If there were a crane . . . then what about the miracle worker? If there were a crane . . . then these women would simply wallow in insignificance!

The body becomes worn out at that kind of work, and everything that is feminine in a woman, whether it be constant or whether it be monthly, ceases to be. If she manages to last to the next 'commissioning,' the person who undresses before the physicians will be not at all like the one whom the trusties smacked their lips over in the bath corridor: she has become ageless; her shoulders stick out at sharp angles, her breasts hang down in little dried-out sacs; superfluous folds of skin form wrinkles on her flat buttocks; there is so little flesh above her knees that a big enough gap has opened up for a sheep's head to stick through or even a soccer ball; her voice has become hoarse and rough and her face is tanned by pellagra. (And, as a gynecologist will tell you, several months of logging will suffice for the prolapse and falling out of a more important organ.)

Work—*the miracle worker!*

> ALEKSANDR SOLZHENITSYN (1918–), *The Gulag Archipelago*, 1973–5, tr. Thomas P. Whitney, 1975

THE EFFECTS OF THE DIVISION OF LABOUR

Various arts or operations carried on by the same man, envigorate his mind, because they exercise different faculties; and, as he cannot be equally expert in every art or operation, he is frequently reduced to supply want of skill by thought and invention. Constant application, on the contrary, to a single operation, confines the mind to a single object, and excludes all thought and invention: in such a train of life, the operator becomes dull and stupid, like a beast of burden.

> HENRY HOME, LORD KAMES (1696–1782), *Sketches of the History of Man*, 1774

In the progress of the division of labour, the employment of the far greater part of those who live by labour, that is, of the great body of the people, comes to be confined to a few very simple operations; frequently to one or two. But the understandings of the greater part of men are necessarily formed by their ordinary employments. The man whose whole life is spent in performing a few simple operations, of which the effects too are, perhaps, always the same, or very nearly the same, has no occasion to exert his understanding, or to exercise his invention in finding out expedients for removing difficulties which never occur. He naturally loses, therefore, the habit of such exertion, and generally becomes as stupid and ignorant as it is possible for a human creature to become. The torpor of his mind renders him, not only incapable of relishing or bearing a part in any rational conversation, but of conceiving any generous, noble, or tender sentiment, and consequently of forming any just judgment concerning many even of the ordinary duties of private life. Of the great and extensive interests of his country, he is altogether incapable of judging; and unless very particular pains have been taken to render him otherwise, he is equally incapable of defending his country in war. The uniformity of his stationary life naturally corrupts the courage of his mind, and makes him regard with abhorrence the irregular, uncertain, and adventurous life of a soldier. It corrupts even the activity of his body, and renders him incapable of exerting his strength with vigour and perseverance, in any other employment than that to which he has been bred. His dexterity at his own particular trade seems, in this manner, to be acquired at the expence of his intellectual, social, and martial virtues. But in every improved and civilized society this is the state into which the labouring poor, that is, the great body of the people, must necessarily fall, unless government takes some pains to prevent it.

ADAM SMITH (1723–90), *An Inquiry into the Nature and Causes of the Wealth of Nations*, 1776

My days of labour were days of oblivion. It is impossible to describe to you the state of mind of a human creature, whose incessant office it is from morning to night to watch the evolution of fifty-six threads. The sensorium in man has in it something of the nature of a mill, but it is moved by very different laws from those of a mill contrived for the manufacture of silk threads. The wheels move in swifter rotation than those I was appointed to watch; and to keep this rotation constantly up to a certain pace is one of the great desiderata of human happiness. When the succession of ideas flags, or is violently restrained in its circumvolutions, this produces by degrees weariness, *ennui*, imbecility, and idiotism. Conceive how this progress is impeded by the task of continually watching fifty-six threads! The quantity of thought required in this office is nothing, and yet it shuts out, and embroils, and snaps in pieces, all other thoughts.

Another law which governs the sensorium in man is the law of association. In contemplation and reverie, one thought introduces another perpetually; and it is by similarity, or the hooking of one upon the other, that the process of thinking is carried on. In books and in living discourse the case is the same; there is a constant connection and transition, leading on the chain of the argument. Try the experiment of reading for half an hour a parcel of words thrown together at random, which reflect no light on each other, and produce no combined meaning; and you will have some, though an inadequate, image of the sort of industry to which I was condemned. Numbness and vacancy of mind are the fruits of such an employment. It ultimately transforms the being who is subjected to it, into quite a different class or species of animal.

WILLIAM GODWIN (1756–1836), *Fleetwood*, 1805

When a workman is unceasingly and exclusively engaged in the fabrication of one thing, he ultimately does his work with singular dexterity; but at the same time he loses the general faculty of applying his mind to the direction of the work. He every day becomes more adroit and less industrious; so that it may be said of him that in proportion as the workman improves, the man is degraded. What can be expected of a man who has spent twenty years of his life in making heads for pins? And to what can that mighty human intelligence which has so often stirred the world be applied in him except it be to investigate the best method of making pins' heads? . . .

In proportion as the principle of the division of labor is more extensively applied, the workman becomes more weak, more narrow-minded, and more dependent. The art advances, the artisan recedes.

ALEXIS DE TOCQUEVILLE (1805–59), *Democracy in America*, 1835–40, tr. Henry Reeve, rev. Francis Bowen, rev. Phillips Bradley, 1945

[On 8 January 1850 George Ruby, 'who appeared about fourteen years of age', gave evidence at the Guildhall, London, in a case of assault.]

ALDERMAN HUMPHERY: Well, do you know what you are about? Do you know what an oath is?
BOY: No.
ALDERMAN: Can you read?
BOY: No.
ALDERMAN: Do you ever say your prayers?
BOY: No, never.
ALDERMAN: Do you know what prayers are?
BOY: No.
ALDERMAN: Do you know what God is?
BOY: No.
ALDERMAN: Do you know what the devil is?
BOY: I've heard of the devil, but I don't know him.
ALDERMAN: What do you know?
BOY: I knows how to sweep the crossings.
ALDERMAN: And that's all?
BOY: That's all. I sweeps a crossing.

The Household Narrative of Current Events, Jan. 1850

Some reformers thought that the division of labour could be reversed.

For as soon as labour is distributed, each person has a particular, exclusive area of activity which is imposed on him and from which he cannot escape. He is a hunter, a fisherman, a herdsman, or a critical critic, and he must remain so if he does not want to lose his means of livelihood. In communist society, however, where nobody has an exclusive area of activity and each can train himself in any branch he wishes, society regulates the general production, making it possible for me to do one thing today and another tomorrow, to hunt in the morning, fish in the afternoon, breed cattle in the evening, criticize after dinner, just as I like, without ever becoming a hunter, a fisherman, a herdsman, or a critic.

KARL MARX (1818–83), *The German Ideology*, wr. 1845–6, tr. Loyd D. Easton and Kurt H. Guddat, 1967

When I first knew [William] Morris nothing would content him but being a monk, and getting to Rome, and then he must be an architect, and apprenticed himself to Street, and worked for two years, but when I came to London and began to paint he threw it all up, and must paint too, and then he must give it up and make poems, and then he must give it up and make window hangings and pretty things, and when he had achieved that, he must be a poet again, and then after two or three years of Earthly Paradise time, he must learn dyeing, and lived in a vat, and learned weaving, and knew all about looms, and then made more books, and learned tapestry, and then wanted to smash everything up and begin the world anew, and now it is printing he cares for, and to make wonderful rich-looking books—and all things he does splendidly—and if he lives the printing will have an end—but not I hope, before Chaucer and the *Morte d'Arthur* are done; then he'll do I don't know what, but every minute will be alive.

FRANCES HORNER, *Time Remembered*, 1933

THE TYRANNY OF THE CLOCK

He waits all day beside his little flock
And asks the passing stranger what's o'clock,
But those who often pass his daily tasks
Look at their watch and tell before he asks.
He mutters stories to himself and lies
Where the thick hedge the warmest house supplies,
And when he hears the hunters far and wide
He climbs the highest tree to see them ride—
He climbs till all the fields are blea and bare

And makes the old crow's nest an easy-chair.
And soon his sheep are got in other grounds—
He hastens down and fears his master come,
He stops the gap and keeps them all in bounds
And tends them closely till it's time for home.

JOHN CLARE (1793–1864), 'Farmer's Boy', wr. 1835–7

The operative must be in the mill at half-past five in the morning; if he comes a couple of minutes too late, he is fined; if he comes ten minutes too late, he is not let in until breakfast is over, and a quarter of the day's wages is withheld, though he loses only two and one-half hours' work out of twelve. He must eat, drink, and sleep at command. For satisfying the most imperative needs, he is vouchsafed the least possible time absolutely required by them. Whether his dwelling is a half-hour or a whole one removed from the factory does not concern his employer. The despotic bell calls him from his bed, his breakfast, his dinner.

FRIEDRICH ENGELS (1820–95), *The Condition of the Working Class in England*, 1845, tr. Florence Kelley-Wischnewetsky, 1887

Registration of Time

The Assistants.
1. Except when he has received a day's or part of a day's leave of absence, every Assistant is required to give the library **6 hours' work daily**—in addition to any overtime which may be allowed him.
2. Each Assistant **must enter his times** of commencing and leaving work in the time-register of the building in which he works.
3. These times should be taken at Bodley **from the table-clock** behind the time-register, and **at the Camera from the reading-room clock**.
4. An Assistant doing regular hours of work in both Bodley and the Camera will enter his time **in both books**.
5. An Assistant who obtains **leave to go out on private affairs** during hours of duty will enter the corresponding times of exit and return, and will of course **make up** for the interval of absence.
6. If he should on any occasion, either for the purposes of the library or by accident, **work beyond his regular hours** he can make a corresponding deduction from his hours

of duty at another time. But the reading-room must not be left without an Assistant on duty during the hours when it is open to readers or when boys or the extra staff are at work. Nor must an Assistant deliberately lengthen his hours on one day in order to shorten them on another.

7. **Any disturbance of the ordinary daily amount of work** caused (*e.g.*) by leave of absence or illness, or by deductions for extra time worked on a previous day, should be noted by the Assistant in the column headed 'Notes'.

Boys.

The foregoing regulations will apply equally to boys, except that they will enter their times on one of the **special time-sheets** provided for the purpose; that the entries **must be initialed** by the Janitor, an Assistant, a Sub-Librarian, or the Librarian; and that **time taken under no. 6** can be taken only when no hindrance can be caused to the work of the library. It is absolutely forbidden for one boy to enter another boy's time.

The Extra Staff.

The extra staff have no fixed hours, but **must not stop in Bodley after** the Librarian and Sub-Librarians and any special deputy for Sub-Librarians' attendance, have left it, **or in the Camera when** there is no Assistant in the building.

Each member of the extra staff who is paid by time must, when commencing or leaving work, enter the time on one of the **printed time-certificates**, and at once take it to the Librarian or a Sub-Librarian, or an Assistant, for **initialing. Accounts for payment** must always be accompanied by corresponding time-certificates.

Interruptions during work.

It must be understood that each person after entering his time will proceed straight to work, and **will not spend any part of his hours of duty in private work or private reading. If friends or strangers** should come to see him during those hours on other than Bodleian official business, any time given to them must be made up. It is, of course, desirable that **such visits,** except on emergency, **should only be paid** after or between hours of duty.

Staff Rules, Bodleian Library, Oxford, 1910

In the Shop

Oh, here in the shop the machines roar so wildly, that oft, unaware
That I am, or have been, I sink and am lost in the troubled tumult
And void is my soul . . . I am but a machine.
I work and I work and I work, never ceasing;
Create and create things from morning till e'en;
For what?—and for whom—Oh, I know not!
Oh, ask not!

Who ever has heard of a conscious machine?
No, here is no feeling, no thought and no reason;
This life—crushing labor has ever supprest
Noblest and finest, the truest and richest,
The deepest, the highest and humanly best.
The seconds, the minutes, they pass out forever,
They vanish, swift fleeting like straw in a gale.
I drive the will madly as though to o'ertake them,—
Give chase without wisdom, or weight, or avail.

The Clock in the workshop,—it rests not a moment;
It points on, and ticks on: eternity—time;
And once someone told me the clock had a meaning,—
Its pointing and ticking had reason and rhyme.
And this too he told me,—or had I been dreaming.—
The clock wakened life in one, forces unseen,
And something besides; . . . I forget what; O, ask not!
I know not, I know not, I am a machine.

At times when I listen, I hear the clock plainly;—
The reason of old—the old meaning—is gone!
The maddening pendulum urges me forward
To labor and still labor on.
The tick of the clock is the boss in his anger!
The face of the clock has the eyes of the foe;
The clock—O, I shudder—Dost hear how it draws me?
It calls me 'Machine' and it cries to me 'Sew'!

The sweatshop at midday—I will draw you a picture:
A battlefield bloody; the conflict at rest;
Around and about me the corpses are lying;
The blood cries aloud from the earth's gory breast.
A moment . . . and hark! The loud signal is sounded,
And dead rise again and renewed is the fight . . .
They struggle, these corpses; for strangers, for strangers!
They struggle, they fall, and they sink into night.

MORRIS ROSENFELD (1862–1923), tr. from the Yiddish by Rose Pastor
Stokes and Helen Frank, 1914

SHORTAGE OF TIME

Something Left Undone

Labour with what zeal we will,
  Something still remains undone,
Something uncompleted still
  Waits the rising of the sun.

By the bedside, on the stair,
  At the threshold, near the gates,
With its menace or its prayer,
  Like a mendicant it waits;

Waits, and will not go away;
  Waits, and will not be gainsaid
By the cares of yesterday
  Each to-day is heavier made;

Till at length the burden seems
  Greater than our strength can bear;
Heavy as the weight of dreams,
  Pressing on us everywhere.

And we stand from day to day,
  Like the dwarfs of times gone by,
Who, as Northern legends say,
  On their shoulders held the sky.

HENRY WADSWORTH LONGFELLOW (1807–82), 1863

I have just been travelling. But I like staying at home best. I like day to be like day with no accidents, so that I have just time to write, to work in the garden, to sew and to carry on my established relationships. But in fact nothing like that ever happens, and day is never like day. There is always some reason why Monday has to be consecrated to something, and Tuesday set aside, and on Wednesday it takes one all day to catch up again, like someone who has dropped her knitting stitches, and Thursday is all right, but getting rather near the weekend, and so on. In fact, one scrambles along, a little breathless, both hands full and dropping things, too much furniture in the rooms, too many chances for moth, too many letters unanswered. Christmas, Easter and the birthdays going round and round like a wheel; time to put the tulips in, time to lift the gladioli, and always with the innocent belief that soon there will be some time to spare ahead.

ENID BAGNOLD (1889–1981), in a broadcast interview, *World Books Broadsheet,* Apr. 1953

Dear Friends,

I would have written you a letter instead of a postcard, but I didn't have time.

I wanted to tell you about what's happening in my life, but I didn't have time.

I would have invited you to dinner, but I didn't have time.

I would have done more reading before writing the paper, but I didn't have time.

We never got to cover the end of the novel because we ran out of time.

I would have read your article more carefully, but I didn't have time.

I didn't have time to read your article.

I wanted to call you, but I was afraid it would take too much time.

In haste,
Jane

JANE TOMPKINS (1940–) 'Postcards from the Edge', 1993

THE MACHINE

To the conflict set up by money between buyers and sellers of labour has been added another conflict, set up by the very means of production, between those who have the machine at their disposal and those who are at the disposal of the machine.

SIMONE WEIL (1909–43), *Oppression and Liberty*, 1955, tr. Arthur Wills and John Petrie, 1958

Portrait of a Machine

What nudity is beautiful as this
Obedient monster purring at its toil;
These naked iron muscles dripping oil
And the sure-fingered rods that never miss?
This long and shining flank of metal is
Magic that greasy labour cannot spoil;
While this vast engine that could rend the soil
Conceals its fury with a gentle hiss.

It does not vent its loathing, does not turn
Upon its makers with destroying hate.
It bears a deeper malice; lives to earn

Its master's bread and laughs to see this great
Lord of the earth, who rules but cannot learn
Become the slave of what his slaves create.

LOUIS UNTERMEYER (1885–1977), 1923

Ursula pondered.

'I suppose,' she said, 'there is no *need* for our great works to be so hideous.'

Instantly he broke into motion.

'There you are!' he cried, 'there you are! There is not only *no need* for our places of work to be ugly, but their ugliness ruins the work, in the end. Men will not go on submitting to such intolerable ugliness. In the end it will hurt too much, and they will wither because of it. And this will wither the *work* as well. They will think the work itself is ugly: the machines, the very act of labour. Whereas machinery and the acts of labour are extremely, maddeningly beautiful. But this will be the end of our civilisation, when people will not work because work has become so intolerable to their senses, it nauseates them too much, they would rather starve. *Then* we shall see the hammer used only for smashing, then we shall see it.—Yet here we are—we have the opportunity to make beautiful factories, beautiful machine-houses—we have the opportunity—'

D. H. LAWRENCE (1885–1930), *Women in Love*, 1920

A Worker to His Machine

God! how I hate you!
Every bolt and wheel of you.
Every sound that comes from you,
Hate you so much, Machine,
That you have become human to me,
Fiendishly, devilishly human,
Ever jeering at me,
Leering and mocking at me,
Your slave, your helpless slave.
Well you know you have hold of me,
Ten hours in every day of me,
Working the same steel levers of you;
Two thousand times every day.
You have heard me count them,
You have heard me curse them,
You have listened to my half-mad talk,
And jeered and leered and mocked,

And reminded me of the hills,
The great, free, kindly hills,
My iron master, my tyrant master,
You are my last thought at night,
My first thought at morn,
Thoughts of the bitterest hate.
But sometimes I wonder if I should hate you,
You did not make me a slave,
'Twas those who own you,
The men who never see you,
Who paid for the invention and making of you
Out of gold that they did not earn.
Some day when *I* am your master,
Or my son is your master,
You may sing to us,
You may smile on us,
You may even do more work for us,
And make us as free as the birds of the air,
And the fish of the sea.
For you will make a better slave
Than you do a master, Machine.

JOE CORRIE (1894–1968), 1932

It is the threshing of the last wheat-rick at Flintcomb-Ash Farm. The dawn of the March morning is singularly inexpressive, and there is nothing to show where the eastern horizon lies. Against the twilight rises the trapezoidal top of the stack, which has stood forlornly here through the washing and bleaching of the wintry weather.

When Izz Huett and Tess arrived at the scene of operations only a rustling denoted that others had preceded them; to which, as the light increased, there were presently added the silhouettes of two men on the summit. They were busily 'unhaling' the rick, that is, stripping off the thatch before beginning to throw down the sheaves; and while this was in progress Izz and Tess, with the other women-workers in their whitey-brown pinners, stood waiting and shivering, Farmer Groby having insisted upon their being upon the spot thus early, to get the job over if possible by the end of the day. Close under the eaves of the stack, and as yet barely visible was the red tyrant that the women had come to serve—a timber-framed construction, with straps and wheels appertaining—the threshing-machine, which, whilst it was going, kept up a despotic demand upon the endurance of their muscles and nerves.

A little way off there was another indistinct figure; this one black, with a sustained hiss that spoke of strength very much in reserve. The long chimney running up beside an ash-tree, and the warmth which radiated from the spot, explained without the necessity of much daylight that here was the engine which was to act as the *primum mobile* of this little world. By the engine stood a dark motionless being, a sooty and grimy embodiment of tallness, in a sort of trance, with a heap of coals by his side: it was the engine-man. The isolation of his manner and colour lent him the appearance of a creature from Tophet, who had strayed into the pellucid smokelessness of this region of yellow grain and pale soil, with which he had nothing in common, to amaze and to discompose its aborigines.

What he looked he felt. He was in the agricultural world, but not of it. He served fire and smoke; these denizens of the fields served vegetation, weather, frost, and sun. He travelled with his engine from farm to farm, from county to county, for as yet the steam threshing-machine was itinerant in this part of Wessex. He spoke in a strange northern accent, his thoughts being turned inwards upon himself, his eye on his iron charge; hardly perceiving the scenes around him, and caring for them not at all; holding only strictly necessary intercourse with the natives, as if some ancient doom compelled him to wander here against his will in the service of his Plutonic master. The long strap which ran from the driving-wheel of his engine to the red thresher under the rick was the sole tie-line between agriculture and him.

While they uncovered the sheaves he stood apathetic beside his portable repository of force, round whose hot blackness the morning air quivered. He had nothing to do with preparatory labour. His fire was waiting incandescent, his steam was at high-pressure, in a few seconds he could make the long strap move at an invisible velocity. Beyond its extent the environment might be corn, straw, or chaos; it was all the same to him. If any of the autochthonous idlers asked him what he called himself, he replied shortly 'an engineer.'

The rick was unhaled by full daylight; the men then took their places, the women mounted, and the work began. Farmer Groby—or, as they called him, 'he'—had arrived ere this, and by his orders Tess was placed on the platform of the machine, close to the man who fed it; her business being to untie every sheaf of corn handed on to her by Izz Huett who stood next, but on the rick, so that the feeder could seize it and spread it over the revolving drum which whisked out every grain in one moment.

They were soon in full progress, after a preparatory hitch or two, which rejoiced the hearts of those who hated machinery. The work sped on till breakfast-time, when the thresher was stopped for half-an-hour; and on starting again after the meal the whole supplementary strength of the farm was thrown into the labour of constructing the straw-rick which began to grow beside the stack of corn. A hasty lunch was eaten as they stood, without leaving their positions; and then another couple of hours brought them near to dinner-time; the inexorable wheels continuing to spin, and the penetrating hum of the thresher to thrill to the very marrow all who were near the revolving wire cage.

The old men on the rising straw-rick talked of the past days when they had been accustomed to thresh with flails on the oaken barn-floor; when everything, even to the winnowing, was effected by hand-labour, which to their thinking, though slow, produced better results. Those, too, on the corn-rick, talked a little; but the perspiring ones at the machine, including Tess, could not lighten their duties by the exchange of many words. It was the ceaselessness of the work which tried her so severely, and began to make her wish that she had never come to Flintcomb-Ash. The women on the corn-rick, Marian, who was one of them, in particular, could stop to drink ale or cold tea from the flagon now and then, or to exchange a few gossiping remarks while they wiped their faces or cleared the fragments of straw and husk from their clothing; but for Tess there was no respite; for, as the drum never stopped, the man who fed it could not stop, and she, who had to supply the man with untied sheaves, could not stop either, unless Marian changed places with her, which she sometimes did for half an hour in spite of Groby's objection that she was too slow-handed for a feeder.

THOMAS HARDY (1840–1928), *Tess of the D'Urbervilles*, 1891

As soon as the car has been fitted into the assembly line it begins its half-circle, passing each successive position for soldering or another complementary operation, such as filing, grinding, hammering. As I said, it's a continuous movement and it looks slow: when you first see the line it almost seems to be standing still, and you've got to concentrate on one actual car in order to realize that car is moving, gliding progressively from one position to the next. Since nothing stops, the workers also have to move in order to stay with the car for the time it takes to carry out the work. In this way each man has a well-defined area for the operations he has to make, although the boundaries are invisible: as soon as a car enters a man's territory, he takes down his blow-torch, grabs his soldering iron, takes his hammer or his file, and gets to work. A few knocks, a few sparks, then the soldering's done and the car's already on its way out of the three or four yards of this position. And the next car's already coming into the work area. And the worker starts again. Sometimes, if he's been working fast, he has a few seconds' respite before a new car arrives: either he takes advantage of it to breathe for a moment, or else he intensifies his effort and 'goes up the line' so that he can gain a little time, in other words, he works further ahead, outside his normal area, together with the worker at the preceding position. And after an hour or two he's amassed the incredible capital of two or three minutes in hand, that he'll use up smoking a cigarette, looking on like some comfortable man of means as his car moves past already soldered, keeping his hands in his pockets while the others are working. Short-lived happiness: the next car's already there: he'll have to work on it at his usual position this time, and the race begins again, in the hope of gaining one or two yards, 'moving up' in the hope of another peaceful cigarette. If, on the other hand, the worker's too slow, he 'slips back', that is, he finds himself carried progressively beyond his position, going on with his work when the next laborer has already begun his. Then he has to push on fast trying to catch up. And the slow gliding of the cars, which seems to me so near to not moving at all, looks as relentless as a rushing torrent which you can't manage to dam up: eighteen inches, three feet, thirty seconds certainly behind time, this awkward join, the car followed too far, and the next one already appearing at the usual starting point of the station, coming forward with its mindless regularity and its inert mass. It's already halfway along before you're able to touch it, you're going to start on it when it's nearly passed through and reached the next station: all this loss of time mounts up. It's what they call 'slipping' and sometimes it's as ghastly as drowning.

> ROBERT LINHART (1944–), who became a worker at the Citroën factory at Choisy, France, in 1968, *The Assembly Line*, tr. Margaret Crosland, 1981

JOB INSECURITY

As soon as it becomes known that it is intended to discharge a number of hands considerable anxiety is evidenced by the rank and file, and especially by the unskilled of the shed. They begin to quake and tremble and to be full of apprehension, for it is usually men of their class who are chosen to go, together with any who may be old and feeble, those who are subject to periodical attacks of illness, who have met with an accident at some time or other, those who are awkward and clumsy, dwellers in country places, and those whom the foreman owes a grudge. It can generally be surmised beforehand by the men themselves who will be in the number of unfortunates. Groups of workmen gather and discuss the situation quietly; there is great suspense until the notices are actually issued. Sometimes as many as a hundred men of the same shed have received their notices of dismissal on one day. The notices are written out upon special forms and the clerk of the shed, or the office-boy, carries them round to the men; it is a dramatic moment. Although fully expecting to receive the dreaded 'bit of paper,' the men hope against hope; they are quite dazed when the clerk approaches and hands it to them for they know full well what it means.

*

Great relief is felt in the shed when the discharging is over. A common remark of the workman who is left is, 'Ah well! 'Twill be better for we as be left. 'Tis better to sack a few than to keep us all on short time here.' That is invariably the view of the well-established in the factory. Occasionally, when a workman knows he has been selected for dismissal through spite, or personal malice, he may go to the overseer and 'have it out with him,' but there is no remedy. The foreman has had the whole batch in his eye for some time past. Whatever little indiscretion is committed he records it and the man is marked. The overseer boasts openly that he shall 'get his own back,' sooner or later. 'We don't forget it, mate, you bet, not we! His time'll come all right, some day.' After the last great discharge of hands at the factory, in the year 1909, when a thousand men were dismissed in order to 'reduce expenses,' it was reported that every manager at the works was granted a substantial increase in salary. In less than a month, for some inscrutable reason, a number of new hands, equivalent to those who had been discharged, were put on again.

ALFRED WILLIAMS (1877–1930), *Life in a Railway Factory*, 1915

'I notice there's an account here under the name of Lord Mackworth,' Miss Grig began, having allowed Lilian to stand for a few seconds before looking up from the ledger and other books in which she was apparently absorbed. She spoke with the utmost gentleness, and fixed her oppressive deep eyes on Lilian's.

'Yes, Miss Grig?'

'It hasn't been paid.'

'Oh!' Lilian against an intense volition began to blush.

'Didn't you know?'

'I didn't,' said Lilian.

'But you've been having something to do with the books during my absence.'

'I did a little at first,' Lilian admitted. 'Then Mr Grig saw to them.'

'Miss Merrislate tells me that you had quite a lot to do with them, and I see your handwriting in a number of places here.'

'I've had nothing to do with them for about three weeks—I should think at least three weeks—and of course I expected the bill would be paid by this time.'

'But you never asked?'

'No. It never occurred to me.'

This statement was inaccurate. Lilian had often wondered whether Lord Mackworth had paid his bill, but, from some obscurely caused self-consciousness, she had not dared to make any inquiry . . .

'But can't we send in the account again?' Lilian weakly suggested; she was overthrown by the charge of fast-living against Lord Mackworth, yet she had always in her heart assumed that he was a fast liver.

'I've just telephoned to 6a St James's Street, and I needn't say that Lord Mackworth is no longer there, and they don't know where he is. You see what comes of disobeying rules.'

Lilian lifted her head: 'Well, Miss Grig, the bill isn't so very big, and if you'll please deduct it from my wages on Saturday I hope that will be the end of that.'

It was plain that the bewildered creature had but an excessively imperfect notion of how to be an employee. She had taken to the vocation too late in life.

Miss Grig put her hand to the support of her forehead, and paused.

'I can tolerate many things,' said she, with great benignity, 'but not insolence.'

'I didn't mean to be insolent.'

'You did. And I think you had better accept a week's notice from Saturday. No. On second thoughts, I'll pay your wages up to Saturday week now and you can go at once.' She smiled kindly. 'That will give you time to turn round.'

'Oh! Very well, if it's like that!'

Miss Grig unlocked a drawer; and while she was counting the money Lilian thought despairingly that if Mr Grig, or even if the nice Gertie, had been in the office, the disaster could not have occurred.

Miss Grig shook hands with her and wished her well.

'Where are you going to? It's not one o'clock yet,' asked Millicent in the small room as Lilian silently unhooked her hat and jacket from the clothes-cupboard.

'Out.'

'What for?'

'For Miss G., if you want to know.'

And she left. Except her clothes, not a thing in the office belonged to her. She had no lien, no attachment. The departure was as simple and complete as leaving a Tube train. No word! No good-bye! Merely a disappearance.

ARNOLD BENNETT (1867–1931), *Lilian*, 1922

'Am I just or unjust? I've no idea. All I know is that when I hit hard there are fewer accidents. It isn't the individual that's responsible but a sort of hidden force, and I can't get at it without—getting at every one! If I were merely just, every night flight would mean a risk of death.'

A sort of disgust came over him, that he had given himself so hard a road to follow. Pity is a fine thing, he thought. Lost in his musings, he turned the pages over.

'Roblet, as from this day, is struck off the strength . . .'

He remembered the old fellow and their talk the evening before.

'There's no way out of it, an example must be made.'

'But, sir . . . It was the only time, just once in a way, sir . . . and I've been hard at it all my life!'

'An example must be made.'

'But . . . but, sir. Please see here, sir.'

A tattered pocket-book, a newspaper picture showing young Roblet standing beside an aeroplane. Rivière saw how the old hands were trembling upon this little scrap of fame.

'It was in nineteen ten, sir. That was the first plane in Argentina and I assembled it. I've been in aviation since nineteen ten, think of it, sir! Twenty years! So how can you say . . . ? And the young 'uns, sir, won't they just laugh about it in the shop! Won't they just chuckle!'

'I can't help that.'

'And my kids, sir. I've a family.'

'I told you you could have a job as a fitter.'

'But there's my good name, sir, my name . . . after twenty years' experience. An old employee like me!'

'As a fitter.'

'No, sir, I can't see my way to that. I somehow can't, sir!'

The old hands trembled and Rivière averted his eyes from their plump, creased flesh which had a beauty of its own.

'No, sir, no . . . And there's something more I'd like to say.'

'That will do.'

Not he, thought Rivière, it wasn't he whom I dismissed so brutally, but the mischief for which, perhaps, he was not responsible, though it came to pass through him. For, he mused, we can command events and they obey us; and thus we are creators. These humble men, too, are things and we create them. Or cast them aside when mischief comes about through them.

'There's something more I'd like to say.' What did the poor old fellow want to say? That I was robbing him of all that made life dear? That he loved the clang of tools upon the steel of airplanes, that all the ardent poetry of life would now be lost to him . . . and then, a man must live?

'I am very tired,' Rivière murmured, and his fever rose, insidiously caressing him. 'I liked that old chap's face.' He tapped the sheet of paper with his finger. It came back to him, the look of the old man's hands and he now seemed to see them shape a faltering gesture of thankfulness. 'That's all right,' was all he had to say. 'That's right. Stay!' And then— He pictured the torrent of joy that would flow through those old hands. Nothing in all the world, it seemed to him, could be more beautiful than that joy revealed not on a face, but in those toil-worn hands. Shall I tear up this paper? He imagined the old man's homecoming to his family, his modest pride.

'So they're keeping you on?'

'What do you think! It was I who assembled the first plane in Argentina!'

The old fellow would get back his prestige, the youngsters cease to laugh.

As he was asking himself if he would tear it up, the telephone rang.

There was a long pause, full of the resonance and depth that wind and distance give to voices.

'Landing-ground speaking. Who is there?'

'Rivière.'

'No. 650 is on the tarmac, sir.'

'Good.'

'We've managed to fix it up, but the electric circuit needed overhauling at the last minute, the connections had been bungled.'

'Yes. Who did the wiring?'

'We will enquire and, if you agree, we'll make an example. It's a serious matter when the lights give out on board.'

'You're right.'

If, Rivière was thinking, one doesn't uproot the mischief, whenever and wherever it crops up, the lights fail and it would be criminal to let it pass when, by some chance, it happens to unmask its instrument; Roblet shall go.

ANTOINE DE SAINT-EXUPÉRY (1900–44), *Night Flight,* 1931, tr. Stuart Gilbert, 1932

Caprice

I sat only two tables from the one I was sacked at,
  Just three years ago,
And here was another meringue like the one which I hacked at
  When pride was brought low
And the coffee arrived—the place which she had to use tact at
  For striking the blow.

'I'm making some changes next week in the organisation
  And though I admire
Your work for me, John, yet the need to increase circulation
  Means you must retire:
An outlook more global than yours is the qualification
  I really require.'

Oh sickness of sudden betrayal! Oh purblind Creator!
  Oh friendship denied!
I stood on the pavement and wondered which loss was the greater—
  The cash or the pride.
Explanations to make to subordinates, bills to pay later
  Churned up my inside.

JOHN BETJEMAN (1906–84), 1966

Retirement age in the City has come down so much. There are all the young ambitious people wanting to get into position. Somebody in their late fifties is thrown out now; that seems to be very much 'retirement age' in the City. In terms of the slightly younger people, there's either those in their mid-forties who are working incredibly hard (probably earning a lot of money but, my goodness, probably they deserve that because of what they're sacrificing in terms of family life) or there is the person who is seriously worried about keeping his job.

In fact, I would say all mid-forty-year-olds working in the City are worried about keeping their job. Firms have yet to tackle this. It is piling on more and more pressures on us all without seeing what effect it's having. People are having health problems. It's live by the sword, die by the sword.

> Davina Walter (1954–), quoted in Cathy Courtney and Paul Thompson, *City Lives*, 1996

Dissolve through to Ellroyd's office. Ellroyd at his desk. Lawrence comes through the door near him, from the secretary's office.

LAWRENCE: Sorry, sir. I had some things to attend to.

He stands in front of the desk, a prep school boy.

Ellroyd comes round from behind his desk and sweeps Lawrence before him into the corner of his office, where a black leather banquette along the two walls half surrounds a low, black marble table.

ELLROYD (during this action): What weather! And they say snow tonight. What?

He sits Lawrence down at one end. Lawrence gives an impression of helplessness. Ellroyd sits next to him, rather close. He pushes an open cigarette box between them.

ELLROYD: I shan't beat about the bush, Gurney. Lawrence. Bush! A bird in the hand is worth two in the bush. I always think there's a joke there, but I'm damned if I can find it. Ha ha a ha.

He is putting Lawrence at his ease. He produces a piece of paper on which he has made some notes.

ELLROYD: I don't know how much you know at Management level about the position we are in at this moment?

LAWRENCE (pause): In general terms? Not very much, I'm afraid.

ELLROYD: Our profit figures are still not bad by British standards, but they've been declining very gradually for eight years. A pattern has set in. We've got to reverse it.

As you know, our Chairman Mr Bolton retires in a year. As Vice Chairman I've been put in charge of reversing this pattern.

He stops. Sits back and looks at Lawrence. Change of tone.

ELLROYD: Do you know what I want of this firm Lawrence, what I want this business to be, to *do*?

LAWRENCE: ?

ELLROYD (positively): I want it to sing. I only want singers here. By singers of course I mean those with ambition. Men with fire in their bellies. I want this to be the most ambitious, singing concern in the whole of Europe—and I intend to see that it is. Anyone without ambition—out! Psssst! Kaput!

There are some drops of sweat below Lawrence's nostrils. Ellroyd consults his paper.

ELLROYD: I've already started some reforms, some big, some small. We're after new markets—aggressively. We'll be diversifying. But I've come out at a lot of odd things. Did you know we had an age problem? Age-wise, we're top heavy. Over half the firm are fifty-five or over. With reduced recruiting this will become marked. Old firms don't sing Lawrence. I intend to do something about this. It will be tough on some, but that's the nature of the beast.

Ellroyd pauses. Looks at Lawrence. Change of tone.

ELLROYD: I don't need to tell you what this means. The age problem affects the Board as well. There'll be vacancies. We may need one or two outside people, but I intend to see our boys get a fair crack of the whip. Where there's fire in the belly under forty-five, there's going to be a *very* fair crack of the whip. Of course, it will need a certain ruthlessness. It will mean responsibility. But that's meat and drink to a singer.

Pause. Ellroyd consults his paper.

ELLROYD: Tell me, Lawrence, what's Robert Glenny like?

LAWRENCE (pause): Bob Glenny?

ELLROYD: Does he sing? Has he got it? How does he score?

LAWRENCE (slowly): Bob's not ambitious. He's—what shall I say? Competent. He does a good job. He knows Packaging and Design. But (pause) well, I was promoted over him. He's never appeared to mind. But he's very good.

ELLROYD (decisively): He'll have to go. He's (consults notes) yes, fifty-five. Rising fifty-six. Typical of our problem.

LAWRENCE (shocked): But he's been here years. He's coming up for full pension.

ELLROYD: Precisely. People hanging on for their pension don't sing.

LAWRENCE: But you can't sack him just for that. Can you?

ELLROYD (impatiently): Good heavens, Gurney, where's your fire! I thought I'd explained. It's not sacking. It's redundancy. He won't lose much. He'll get his pension as it stands now. It will be a bit smaller than full pension, of course, smaller than if we'd been able to keep him on. We'll give him a handshake—six months' wages. That's a lump. Skilfully invested it could bring his income practically up to full pension. There'll be others in the same boat I can assure you of that. He'll get another job. What's the market?

LAWRENCE: At fifty-six? I don't know in Packaging and Design. I (pause) I understand it's not too easy in Advertising.

ELLROYD: Competent. Knows his job. He'll find something, perhaps less well paid. He'll have to save. I said it would be tough, but as I said—that's the nature of the beast.

Now, Lawrence, I want you to tell him.

LAWRENCE: Me?

ELLROYD: Yes. As I said, it will mean increased responsibility. It will mean ruthlessness. But the rewards are there.

LAWRENCE: But . . . I mean . . . You want me to tell Bob? To sack him? To make him redundant? Today?

ELLROYD: I don't care when you do it. The sooner the better. Gurney—you have fire in your belly I'm given to understand. You surely don't need time to consider a thing like this? Eh? I thought I'd made it plain. I want singers here. Non-singers—out. Eh?

LAWRENCE: Yes. Of course.

ELLROYD (rising, smiling): Fine. Now, I must get on. Excellent. We'll have more talks, Lawrence. Do you know that terrible army expression? Really vulgar. Stay with me and you'll fart through silk. Awful expression. Now I must get on.

He claps Lawrence on the shoulder and, as it were, serves him like a tennis ball out through the other door of his office. He turns back to his desk.

ELLROYD (calling): Who or what's next?

SECRETARY (from next door): B Division. Sales Manager. Mr Ritson.

ELLROYD: Get him up. We're ahead of schedule.

JONATHAN GATHORNE-HARDY (1933–), *The Office*, 1970

INEQUITY OF CONDITIONS AND REWARDS

Work is of two kinds: first, altering the position of matter at or near the earth's surface relatively to other such matter; second, telling other people to do so. The first kind is unpleasant and ill paid; the second is pleasant and highly paid.

BERTRAND RUSSELL (1872–1970), 'In Praise of Idleness', 1935

Nearly all societies at nearly all times have had a leisure class—a class of persons who were exempt from toil. In modern times and especially in the United States the leisure class, at least in any identifiable phenomenon, has disappeared. To be idle is no longer considered rewarding or even entirely respectable.

But we have barely noticed that the leisure class has been replaced by another and much larger class to which work has none of the older connotation of pain, fatigue, or other mental or physical discomfort. We have failed to appreciate the emergence of this New Class, as it may be simply called, largely as the result of one of the oldest and most effective obfuscations in the field of social science. This is the effort to assert that all work—physical, mental, artistic, or managerial—is essentially the same.

This effort to proclaim the grand homogeneity of work has commanded, for different reasons, the support of remarkably numerous and diverse groups. To economists it has seemed a harmless and, indeed, an indispensable simplification. It has enabled them to deal homogeneously with all of the different kinds of productive effort and to elaborate a general theory of wages applying to all who receive an income for services. Doubts have arisen from time to time, but they have been suppressed or considered to concern special cases. The identity of all classes of labour is one thing on which capitalist and communist doctrine wholly agree. The president of the corporation is pleased to think that his handsomely appointed office is the scene of the same kind of toil as the assembly line and that only the greater demands in talent and intensity justify his wage differential. The communist office-holder cannot afford to have it supposed that his labour differs in any significant respect from that of the comrade at the lathe or on the collective farm with whom he is ideologically one. In both societies it serves the democratic conscience of the more favoured groups to identify themselves with those who do hard physical labour. A lurking sense of guilt over a more pleasant, agreeable, and remunerative life can often be assuaged by the observation 'I am a worker too' or, more audaciously, by the statement that 'mental labour is far more taxing than physical labour'. Since the man who does physical labour is intellectually disqualified from comparing his toil with that of the brainworker, the proposition is uniquely unassailable.

JOHN KENNETH GALBRAITH (1908–   ), *The Affluent Society*, 1958

Watching the Reapers

Tillers of the earth have few idle months;
In the fifth month their toil is double-fold.
A south wind visits the fields at night;
Suddenly the ridges are covered with yellow corn.
Wives and daughters shoulder baskets of rice,
Youths and boys carry flasks of wine,
In a long train, to feed the workers in the field—
The strong reapers toiling on the southern hill,
Whose feet are burned by the hot earth they tread,
Whose backs are scorched by the flames of the shining sky

Tired they toil, caring nothing for the heat,
Grudging the shortness of the long summer day.
A poor woman with a young child at her side
Follows behind, to glean the unwanted grain.
In her right hand she holds the fallen ears,
On her left arm a broken basket hangs.
Listening to what they said as they worked together
I heard something that made me very sad:
They lost in grain-tax the whole of their own crop;
What they glean here is all they will have to eat.

And I to-day—in virtue of what desert
Have I never once tended field or tree?
My government-pay is three hundred 'stones';
At the year's end I have still grain in hand.
Thinking of this, secretly I grew ashamed
And all day the thought lingered in my head.

Po Chü-I (AD 806), tr. Arthur Waley, 1919

The labouring man, that tills the fertile soil,
  And reaps the harvest fruit, hath not in deed
The gain, but pain; and if for all his toil
  He gets the straw, the lord will have the seed.

The manchet fine falls not unto his share;
  On coarsest cheat his hungry stomach feeds.
The landlord doth possess the finest fare;
  He pulls the flowers, the other plucks but weeds.

The mason poor, that builds the lordly halls,
  Dwells not in them; they are for high degree.
His cottage is compact in paper walls,
  And not with brick or stone, as others be.

The idle drone, that labours not at all,
  Sucks up the sweet of honey from the bee.
Who worketh most, to their share least doth fall;
  With due desert reward will never be.

The swiftest hare unto the mastiff slow
  Oft times doth fall to him as for a prey;
The greyhound thereby doth miss his game, we know,
  For which he made such speedy haste away.

manchet] best-quality wheaten bread

So he that takes the pain to pen the book
  Reaps not the gifts of goodly golden Muse;
But those gain that who on the work shall look,
  And from the sour the sweet by skill doth choose.
For he that beats the bush the bird not gets,
But who sits still and holdeth fast the nets.

EDWARD DE VERE, 17TH EARL OF OXFORD (1550–1604), 1573

Such hath it been—shall be—beneath the sun
The many still must labour for the one!

GEORGE GORDON, 6th LORD BYRON (1788–1824), *The Corsair*, 1813

Then the creating Power, or God, gives 2 Commands more. Ver. 27. [28] & Ver. 29.

First, *To subdue the Earth*. And this implies, plowing, digging, and all kind of manuring. So then observe. That bare and simple working in the Earth, according to the freedome of the Creation, though it be in the sweat of mans browes, is not the curse.

But for one part of Mankind to be a Task-master, and to live Idle; and by the Beast-like power of the sword, does force another part of Mankind to worke as a servant and slave, This is the power of the curse, which makes mankind eat his bread in sorrow by the sweat of his browes.

GERRARD WINSTANLEY (*c.*1609–76), *An Humble Request*, 1650

I put a question to him upon a fact in common life, which he could not answer, nor have I found any one else who could. What is the reason that women servants, though obliged to be at the expense of purchasing their own clothes, have much lower wages than men servants, to whom a great proportion of that article is furnished, and when in fact our female house servants work much harder than the male?

JAMES BOSWELL (1740–95), *The Life of Samuel Johnson*, 11 Apr. 1773, pub. 1791

The most obvious Division of Society is into Rich and Poor; and it is no less obvious, that the Number of the former bear a great Disproportion to those of the latter. The whole Business of the Poor is to administer to the

Idleness, Folly, and Luxury of the Rich; and that of the Rich, in return, is to find the best Methods of confirming the Slavery and increasing the Burthens of the Poor. In a State of Nature, it is an invariable Law, that a Man's Acquisition are in proportion to his Labours. In a State of Artificial Society, it is a Law constant and as invariable, that those who labour most, enjoy the fewest Things; and that those who labour not at all, have the greatest Number of Enjoyments . . .

EDMUND BURKE (1729–97), A Vindication of Natural Society, 1756

We labour soon, we labour late,
     To feed the titled knave, man;
And a' the comfort we're to get
     Is that ayont the grave, man.

Attr. to ROBERT BURNS (1759–96), from The Tree of Liberty, 1838

No man of humanity can look at the cottager, and see him meagre, half famished, and worn down with excessive toil; his children naked and uneducated, and at the same time, view the plumpness and healthy appearance of the coach-horse, that drags his Lord in enervating idleness past the humble thatch, and not be ready to allow, that wherever such a wicked disparity between the condition of the human and brutal species exists, the government must be radically wrong, infamous, and little calculated to produce the desirable end for which government was originally instituted.

WILLIAM HODGSON (1745–1851), The Commonwealth of Reason, 1795

Song to the Men of England

I

Men of England, wherefore plough
For the lords who lay ye low?
Wherefore weave with toil and care
The rich robes your tyrants wear?

II

Wherefore feed, and clothe, and save,
From the cradle to the grave,
Those ungrateful drones who would
Drain your sweat—nay, drink your blood?

ayont] beyond

III

Wherefore, Bees of England, forge
Many a weapon, chain, and scourge,
That these stingless drones may spoil
The forced produce of your toil?

IV

Have ye leisure, comfort, calm,
Shelter, food, love's gentle balm?
Or what is it ye buy so dear
With your pain and with your fear?

V

The seed ye sow, another reaps;
The wealth ye find, another keeps;
The robes ye weave, another wears;
The arms ye forge, another bears.

VI

Sow seed,—but let no tyrant reap;
Find wealth,—let no impostor heap;
Weave robes,—let not the idle wear;
Forge arms,—in your defence to bear.

VII

Shrink to your cellars, holes, and cells;
In halls ye deck another dwells.
Why shake the chains ye wrought? Ye see
The steel ye tempered glance on ye.

VIII

With plough and spade, and hoe and loom,
Trace your grave, and build your tomb,
And weave your winding-sheet, till fair
England be your sepulchre.

PERCY BYSSHE SHELLEY (1792–1822), 1819

It is all very well for the business man, the parson, the author, the engineer, the member of Parliament, to abuse the workman as idle, thriftless, and drunken; but let us do the workman justice. Let us remember that his work is neither exciting, pleasing, ennobling, nor remunerative. Often I have heard professional men say, 'Talk about the working classes! what do they know of work? They never work as hard as I do. They have not the worry and strain that mental work involves. I am a manufacturer—a doctor—a lawyer—my work is never done.' All this is true. The doctor's work or the author's work is never done. But remember that he loves it so much that he would not wish it ever done. He is so wrapped up in it, so wedded to it, that if it were done, if he were obliged to take off the harness and to go to grass in the prime of life, he would actually break his heart.

It is very nice for professional men to boast of their industry and love of work. They are doing the work of their choice. But take them away from the theatre or the desk, the pulpit, or the quarter-deck, and set them to carrying bricks up a ladder, stitching slop clothing, or scribbling out invoices, and see how they will enjoy that, and how industrious they will be.

It is easy to tell a workman to be industrious and contented in that walk of life to which Providence has called him. But it would be neither easy nor pleasant to take his place and show him how it should be done; and I tell you frankly I believe that if Providence called a Prime Minister or a Bishop to dig coals or puddle iron, Providence would have to use a long trumpet or the gentlemen would not hear.

ROBERT BLATCHFORD (1851–1943), *Merrie England*, 1894

Those who owned and held the land believed, and acted up to their belief as far as they were able, that the land belonged to the rich man only, that the poor man had no part nor lot in it, and had no sort of claim on society. If a poor man dared to marry and have children, they thought he had no *right* to claim the necessary food wherewith to keep himself and his family alive. They thought, too, every mother's son of them, that, when a labourer could no longer work, he had lost the right to live. Work was all they wanted from him; he was to work and hold his tongue, year in and year out, early and late, and if he could not work, why, what was the use of him? It was what he was made for, to labour and toil for his betters, without complaint, on a starvation wage. When no more work could be squeezed out of him, he was no better than a cumberer of other folk's ground, and the proper place for such as he was the churchyard, where he would be sure to lie quiet under a few feet of earth, and want neither food nor wages any more. A quick death and a cheap burying— that was the motto of those extortioners for the poor man past work.

JOSEPH ARCH (1826–1919), *Joseph Arch: The Story of His Life Told by Himself*, 1898

Here and there with dimes on the eyes walking,
To feed the greed of the belly the brains liberally spooning,
Tickets buying, taking, selling, but in to the feast never once going,
Many sweating, ploughing, thrashing, and then the chaff for payment
    receiving,
A few idly owning, and they the wheat continually claiming.

WALT WHITMAN (1819–92), *Song of Myself*, 1881 edn.

The Silesian Weavers

In somber eyes no tears of grieving;
Grinding their teeth, they sit at their weaving:
'O Germany, at your shroud we sit,
We're weaving a threefold curse in it—
　　We're weaving, we're weaving!

'A curse on the god we prayed to, kneeling
With cold in our bones, with hunger reeling;
We waited and hoped, in vain persevered,
He scorned us and duped us, mocked and jeered—
　　We're weaving, we're weaving!

'A curse on the king of the rich man's nation
Who hardens his heart at our supplication,
Who wrings the last penny out of our hides
And lets us be shot like dogs besides—
　　We're weaving, we're weaving!

'A curse on this false fatherland, teeming
With nothing but shame and dirty scheming,
Where every flower is crushed in a day,
Where worms are regaled on rot and decay —
　　We're weaving, we're weaving!

'The shuttle flies, the loom creaks loud,
Night and day we weave your shroud—
Old Germany, at your shroud we sit,
We're weaving a threefold curse in it,
　　We're weaving, we're weaving!'

HEINRICH HEINE (1797–1856), 1844, tr. Hal Draper, 1982

I met accidentally in Scotland, recently, a lady of the small landlord class, and the conversation turned upon the poverty of the Highland people. 'Yes, they are poor,' she said, 'but they deserve to be poor; they are so dirty. I have no sympathy with women who won't keep their houses neat and their children tidy.'

I suggested that neatness could hardly be expected from women who every day had to trudge for miles with creels of peat and seaweed on their backs.

'Yes,' she said, 'they have to work hard. But that is not so sad as the hard lives of the horses. Did you ever think of the horses? They have to work all their lives—till they can't work any longer. It makes me sad to think of it. There ought to be big farms where horses should be turned out after they had worked some years, so that they might have time to enjoy themselves before they died.'

'But the people?' I interposed. 'They, too, have to work till they can't work longer.'

'Oh yes!' she replied, 'but the people have souls, and even if they have a hard time of it here, they will, if they are good, go to heaven when they die, and be happy hereafter. But the poor beasts have no souls, and if they don't enjoy themselves here they have no chance of enjoying themselves at all. It is too bad!'

The woman was in sober earnest. And I question if she did not fairly represent much that has been taught in Scotland as Christianity. But at last, thank God! the day is breaking, and the blasphemy that has been preached as religion will not be heard much longer.

HENRY GEORGE (1839–97), 'The "Reduction to Iniquity"', 1884

I couldn't touch a stop and turn a screw,
    And set the blooming world a-work for me,
Like such as cut their teeth—I hope, like you—
    On the handle of a skeleton gold key;
I cut mine on a leek, which I eat it every week:
    I'm a clerk at thirty bob as you can see.

But I don't allow it's luck and all a toss;
    There's no such thing as being starred and crossed;
It's just the power of some to be a boss,
    And the bally power of others to be bossed:
I face the music, sir; you bet I ain't a cur;
    Strike me lucky if I don't believe I'm lost!

For like a mole I journey in the dark,
    A-travelling along the underground
From my Pillar'd Halls and broad Suburbean Park,
    To come the daily dull official round;
And home again at night with my pipe all alight,
    A-scheming how to count ten bob a pound.

And it's often very cold and very wet,
    And my missis stitches towels for a hunks;
And the Pillar'd Halls is half of it to let—
    Three rooms about the size of travelling trunks,

hunks] a crusty old miser

And we cough, my wife and I, to dislocate a sigh,
   When the noisy little kids are in their bunks.

But you never hear her do a growl or whine,
   For she's made of flint and roses, very odd;
And I've got to cut my meaning rather fine,
   Or I'd blubber, for I'm made of greens and sod:
So p'r'aps we are in Hell for all that I can tell,
   And lost and damn'd and served up hot to God.

I ain't blaspheming, Mr Silver-tongue;
   I'm saying things a bit beyond your art:
Of all the rummy starts you ever sprung,
   Thirty bob a week's the rummiest start!
With your science and your books and your the' ries about spooks,
   Did you ever hear of looking in your heart?

I didn't mean your pocket, Mr, no:
   I mean that having children and a wife,
With thirty bob on which to come and go,
   Isn't dancing to the tabor and the fife:
When it doesn't make you drink, by Heaven! it makes you think,
   And notice curious items about life.

        JOHN DAVIDSON (1857–1909), from 'Thirty Bob a week', 1894

Riches

A LANDOWNER.
His WIFE.
Their 6-year-old son, VÁSYA.
A TRAMP.

[*The* LANDOWNER *and his* WIFE *are sitting at tea on a balcony with their daughter and* VÁSYA. *A young* TRAMP *approaches.*]

Landowner [*to* TRAMP].   What is it?

Tramp [*bowing*].   You can see what it is, master! Have pity on a workless man! I'm starving and in rags. I've been in Moscow, and am begging my way home. Help a poor man!

Landowner.   Why are you in want?

Tramp.   Because I have no money, master.

Landowner.   If you worked you wouldn't be so poor.

Tramp.   I'd be glad to work, but there's no work to be had nowadays. They're shutting down everywhere.

Landowner.   Other people get work. Why can't you?

Tramp.   Honest, master, I'd be thankful to get a job, but I can't get one. Have pity on me, master! This is the second day I've had nothing to eat.

Landowner [*Looks into his purse. To his* WIFE].   *Avez-vous de la petite monnaie? Je n'ai que des assignats.*

Mistress [*to* VÁSYA].   Go and look in the bag on the little table by my bed, there's a good boy. You'll find a purse there—bring it to me.

Vásya [*Does not hear what his mother has said, but stares at the* TRAMP *without taking his eyes off him*].

Mistress.   Vásya, don't you hear? [*Pulls him by the sleeve.*] Vásya!

Vásya.   What is it, mamma? [*His mother repeats what she had said.* VÁSYA *jumps up.*] All right, mamma. [*Goes out, still looking at the* TRAMP.]

Landowner [*to* TRAMP].   Wait a little—in a minute. [TRAMP *steps aside. To his* WIFE, *in French.*] It's dreadful what a lot of them are going about without work. It's all laziness—but still it's terrible if he's really hungry.

Mistress.   They exaggerate. I hear it's just the same abroad. In New York, I see, there are about a hundred thousand unemployed! Would you like some more tea?

Landowner.   Yes, please, but a little weaker this time. [*He smokes and they are silent.*]

[*The* TRAMP *looks at them, shakes his head, and coughs, evidently wishing to attract their attention.* VÁSYA *runs in with the purse and immediately looks round for the* TRAMP. *He gives the purse to his mother and stares at the man.*]

Landowner [*Taking a threepenny bit from the purse*].   Here you—what's your name—take this!

[TRAMP *takes off his cap, bows, and takes the coin.*]

Tramp.   Thank you for having pity on a poor man.

Landowner.   The chief pity to me is that you don't get work. If you worked you wouldn't go hungry. He who works will not want.

Tramp [*Putting on his cap and turning away*].   It's true what they say:

> 'Work bends your back,
> But fills no sack.'

[*Goes off.*]

Vásya.   What did he say?

Landowner.   Some stupid peasant proverb: 'Work bends your back, but fills no sack.'

Vásya.   What does that mean?

Landowner.   It means that work makes a man bent without his becoming rich.

Vásya.   And is that wrong?

Avez-vous . . . des assignats] 'Have you any small change? I have nothing but paper money.'

Landowner. Of course it is! Those who loaf about like that fellow and don't want to work are always poor. Only those who work get rich.

Vásya. But how is it we are rich? We don't work!

Mistress [*laughing*]. How do you know papa doesn't work?

Vásya. I don't know. But I do know that we are very rich, so papa ought to have a lot of work to do. Does he work very hard?

Landowner. All work is not alike. Perhaps my work couldn't be done by everyone.

Vásya. What is your work?

Landowner. To have you fed, clothed, and taught.

Vásya. But he has to do that, too, for his children. Then why does he have to go about so miserably while we are so . . .

Landowner [*laughing*]. Here's a natural socialist!

Mistress. Yes, indeed: '*Ein Narr kann mehr fragen, als tausend Weise antworten können.*' One fool can ask more than a thousand sages can answer. Only one should say '*ein Kind*' instead of '*ein Narr*'. And it's true of every child.

LEV NIKOLAEVICH TOLSTOY (1828–1910), 'The Wisdom of Children',
1910, tr. Aylmer Maude, 1937

The worker is the slave of capitalist society, the female worker is the slave of that slave.

JAMES CONNOLLY (1865–1916), *The Re-Conquest of Ireland*, 1915

[*This poem was inspired by Millet's painting of the same title, 1860–2.*]

The Man with the Hoe

God made man in his own image,
in the image of God He made him.
—Genesis

Bowed by the weight of centuries he leans
Upon his hoe and gazes on the ground,
The emptiness of ages in his face,
And on his back the burden of the world.
Who made him dead to rapture and despair,
A thing that grieves not and that never hopes,
Stolid and stunned, a brother to the ox?
Who loosened and let down this brutal jaw?

Whose was the hand that slanted back this brow?
Whose breath blew out the light within this brain?

Is this the Thing the Lord God made and gave
To have dominion over sea and land;
To trace the stars and search the heavens for power;
To feel the passion of Eternity?
Is this the dream He dreamed who shaped the suns
And markt their ways upon the ancient deep?
Down all the caverns of Hell to their last gulf
There is no shape more terrible than this—
More tongued with censure of the world's blind greed—
More filled with signs and portents for the soul—
More packt with danger to the universe.

What gulfs between him and the seraphim!
Slave of the wheel of labour, what to him
Are Plato and the swing of Pleiades?
What the long reaches of the peaks of song,
The rift of dawn, the reddening of the rose?
Thru this dread shape the suffering ages look;
Time's tragedy is in that aching stoop;
Thru this dread shape humanity betrayed,
Plundered, profaned and disinherited,
Cries protest to the Powers that made the world,
A protest that is also prophecy.

O masters, lords and rulers in all lands,
Is this the handiwork you give to God,
This monstrous thing distorted and soul-quencht?
How will you ever straighten up this shape;
Touch it again with immortality;
Give back the upward looking and the light;
Rebuild in it the music and the dream;
Make right the immemorial infamies,
Perfidious wrongs, immedicable woes?

O masters, lords and rulers in all lands,
How will the future reckon with this Man?
How answer his brute question in that hour
When whirlwinds of rebellion shake all shores?
How will it be with kingdoms and with kings—
With those who shaped him to the thing he is—
When this dumb Terror shall rise to judge the world,
After the silence of the centuries?

EDWIN MARKHAM (1852–1940), 1899

RESISTANCE: DIRECT AND INDIRECT

Resistance by workers to these injustices could take one of two forms. There was the direct method: wage demands, strikes, trade union activity, political agitation, theft, revolt, and even revolution.

It may please you to understand, that at mine arrival in this town [Dover], it was informed me that certain lewd and naughty persons, working in the King's works here, alleged and said that they would work no longer in the said works except they might have 6d by the day, and that they had named one person amongst them to be a Lord. For the which cause, and also for that I was desirous to see the said works, I thought it convenient to tarry, and spend one day here, as well for the viewing of the said works as to hear what the said unthrifty persons would say or do. And so I did . . . And this morning thirty and more of the said unthrifty persons assembled themselves together by six of the clock, and he whom they named Lord with them, and said that they would not work except they might have 6d by the day; and that he that touched one of them should touch them all. Whereupon, I and my colleagues took some pain to examine and try out the beginnings of the said matter, and found four persons chief movers and doers thereof, whereof he whom they named their Lord and another, which be as seditious and naughty persons as live and sometimes were of the Black Guard of the King's Kitchen, be two of the principals, whom for their seditious dealing in that behalf we have committed unto prison within the Castle of Dover till the King's pleasure may be known of them. And the other two, which be also naught but not so evil as the other be, for as much as it appeared that they were repentant for the offence they had done, we have committed them to the Mayor's prison, there to remain for a week, and then to be discharged.

SIR WILLIAM FITZWILLIAM (d. 1542), letter to Thomas Cromwell, 17 Aug. 1535

The Case for the Miners

Something goes wrong with my synthetic brain
When I defend the Strikers and explain
My reasons for not blackguarding the Miners.
'*What do you know?*' exclaim my fellow-diners
(Peeling their plovers' eggs or lifting glasses
Of mellowed *Château Rentier* from the table),
'*What do you know about the working classes?*'

I strive to hold my own; but I'm unable
To state the case succinctly. Indistinctly
I mumble about World-Emancipation,
Standards of Living, Nationalization
Of Industry; until they get me tangled
In superficial details; goad me on
To unconvincing vagueness. When we've wrangled
From soup to savoury, my temper's gone.

'*Why should a miner earn six pounds a week?*
Leisure! They'd only spend it in a bar!
Standard of life! You'll never teach them Greek,
Or make them more contented than they are!'
That's how my port-flushed friends discuss the Strike.
And that's the reason why I shout and splutter.
And that's the reason why I'd almost like
To see them hawking matches in the gutter.

SIEGFRIED SASSOON (1886–1967), 1926

Care not for work, for we shall have a merrier world shortly; . . . and I will work one day and play the other.

Attr. to BARTHOLOMEW STEERE, one of the leaders of a rising by labourers and tradesmen in Oxfordshire, 1596

To my deare and very loving mother Mrs Winthrop at Boston these be delivered

Deare Mother, my humble dutie remembred to you. It reioyceth me to heare of your recoverie out of your dangerous sicknes, and should be glad to heare how your health is continued to you by a letter from your selfe, for I have not heard from you a long time which troubleth me, though I have sent you three or foure letters to you: I thought it convenient to acquaint you and my father, what a great affliction I have met withal by my maide servant, and how I am like through god his mercie to be freed from it; at her first comminge to me she carried her selfe dutifully as became a servant; but since through mine and my husbands forbearance towards her for small faults, shee hath got such a head and is growen soe insolent, that her carriage towards us especially myselfe is unsufferable. If I bid her doe a thing shee will bid me to doe it my selfe, and she sayes how shee can give content as wel as any servant but shee will not, and sayes if I love not quietnes I was never so fitted in my life, for shee would make me have enough of it. If I should write to you of all the reviling speeches, and filthie language shee hath used towards me I should but greive you. My husband hath used all meanes for to reforme her, reasons and perswasions, but shee doth professe that her heart and her nature will not suffer her to confesse her faults; If I tell my husband of her behaviour towards me, upon examination shee will denie all that shee hath done or spoken: so that we know not how to proceede against her: but my husband now hath hired another maide and is resolved to put her away the next weeke.

Thus with my humble dutie to my father I rest your dutifull and obedient daughter

MARY DUDLEY (1612?–43), letter to Margaret Winthrop, *c.* Jan. 1636

On 23 November 1678 Henry Geeve, a labourer of Biggleswade, Bedfordshire, confessed to the theft of grain from a barn, in the company of one John Blazeden, who had told him:

that if he would be ruled by him and keep his counsel he need never do day's work as long as he lived.

Bedfordshire Assize records

> On Saturday with joy Bill dubs his half,
> And plaits it most exact, then folds it up
> And into wallets puts, then throws it o'er
> His shoulder and, with many an eager stride,
> He gravely stalks along. At warehouse door
> He makes his entrance, takes his wallet down,
> And empties the contents. His master's man
> With poring eye surveys the piece before him,
> And finds no fault. 'Why then,' cries honest Bill,
> 'A shilling more you'll give for work like this.'
> 'Nay,' says the servant. 'Then I'll bring my reed,
> For this has been a most confounded piece,'
> The weaver cries. 'Go call my master, I
> Act only by instruction.' Then appears
> A man dressed like a squire, or justice-like,
> With large white wig and ruffles o'er his hands,
> Enough to daunt a bolder man than Bill.
>
> 'Come, what's the matter, weaver?'—'He demands
> A shilling more, sir, than the common wage.'
> 'No, sure! Does any other master give it?'
> 'I can't say so,' cries Bill.—'Why then should I
> Give more than they? Maid, fetch a jug of ale:

Let's drink together, Bill, to thy good health.'
'I thank you, master.'—'Come, here's to'rds your own,
And all your family.' The matter ends.
But should some surly weaver chance to miss
His stripe, or selvedge mar, the game begins:
'Jack, you must bate for this.'—'Bate! What d'ye mean?'
Then by his G— and by his S— he swears
He never will, but, forced at last, he flings
Out of the warehouse door with dreadful curse:
'Must I, like slave in Turkey, hag and work
My heart's blood out to gratify the pride
Of wanton b——s, flounced and furbelowed
In silk and silver, sipping tea and cream,
Or powder check-men's wigs? No, d—n oppression;
I've brought my hogs t'a pretty market sure,
To slave for upstart gentry. I'll go serve,
With willing mind, his majesty King George.'

ANON., *Gentleman's Magazine*, 1760

Dreams of a Kitchen-maid

My fine gentlemen, today you may see me wash the glasses
And see me make the beds each morning.
And I thank you for your penny and you think I'm pleased as hell
For you only see my ragged frock and this dirty old hotel
And there's no one to give you a warning.
But one fine night there'll be yelling in the harbour
And they'll ask: Who is making all the row?
And they'll see me smiling as I wash my glasses
And they'll say: What's she smiling at, now?
       And a ship with eight sails
       And with fifty big cannon
       Will be moored to the quay.

Someone'll say: Go and dry your glasses, child.
He'll give me a penny, like the rest.
And the penny will be taken
And the bed be made, all right,
But nobody's going to sleep in it that night
And who I really am they still won't have guessed.
And that evening there'll be a din in the harbour
And they'll ask: What is making all that din?
And they'll see me standing watching at the window

And say: Why has she got that nasty grin?
    And the ship with eight sails
    And with fifty big cannon,
    Will shoot at the town.

My fine gentlemen, that'll wipe the smile off your faces,
For the walls will open gaping wide
And the town will tumble down flat to the ground
But a dirty old hotel will stay standing safe and sound
And they'll ask: What big swell lives inside?
All night long there'll be a yelling round about that hotel
And they'll ask: Why is it treated with such care?
And then they'll see me stepping from the door in the morning
And they'll say: What! Did *she* live there?
    And the ship with eight sails
    And with fifty big cannon
    Will beflag her masts.

And at midday there'll be coming a hundred men on land
And the hunt in dark corners will begin
And they'll enter every house, take every soul they see
And throw them into irons and bring them straight to me
And ask: Which of these shall we do in?
And that midday it will be quiet down by the harbour
When they ask who has got to die.
And then they'll hear me answer: All of them!
And as the heads fall I shall cry: Hoppla!
    And the ship with eight sails
    And with fifty big cannon
    Will vanish with me.

        Bertolt Brecht (1898–1956), *Threepenny Novel*, 1934, tr. Christopher
        Isherwood, 1937

Rise Ye! Rise Ye!

Rise ye! rise ye! noble toilers! claim your rights with fire and steel!
Rise ye! for the cursed tyrants crush ye with the hiron 'eel!
They would treat ye worse than sla-a-aves! they would treat ye worse than
    brutes!
  Rise and crush the selfish tyrants! ker-r-rush with your hobnailed boots!
  Rise ye! rise ye! glorious toilers!
  Rise ye! rise ye! noble toilers!
    Erwake! er-rise!

Rise ye! rise ye! noble toilers! tyrants come across the waves!
Will ye yield the Rights of Labour, will ye? *will* ye still be sla-a-aves?
Rise ye! rise ye! mighty toilers and revoke the rotten laws!
Lo, your wives go out a-washing while ye battle for the caws!
   Rise ye! rise ye! glorious toilers!
   Rise ye! rise ye! noble toilers!
     Erwake! er-rise!

Our gerlorious dawn is breaking! Lo, the tyrant trembles now!
He shall star-r-rve us here no longer! toilers will not bend or bow!
Rise ye! rise ye! noble toilers! Rise! behold, revenge is near;
See the Leaders of the People! Come an' 'ave a pint o' beer!
   Rise ye! rise ye! glorious toilers!
   Rise ye! rise ye! noble toilers!
     Erwake! er-rise!

Lo, the poor are starved, my brothers! Lo, our wives and children weep!
Lo, our women toil to keep us while the toilers are asleep!
Rise ye! rise ye! noble toilers! rise and break the tyrant's chain!
March ye! march ye! mighty toilers! even to the battle-plain!
   Rise ye! rise ye! glorious toilers!
   Rise ye! rise ye! noble toilers!
     Erwake! er-rrise!

HENRY LAWSON (1867–1922), 1892

My wife was mending, and did not look up when I came in. How differently she behaved at home. She not only used to look up when I came in, she got up, and got up quickly too, hastening at the first sound of my return to meet me in the passage, and greeting me with the smiles of a dutiful and accordingly contented wife.

Shutting the Elsa's windows I drew her attention to this.

'But there isn't a passage,' said she, still with her head bent over a sock.

Really Edelgard should take care to be specially feminine, for she certainly will never shine on the strength of her brains.

'Dear wife,' I began—and then the complete futility of trying to thresh any single subject out in that airy, sound-carrying dwelling stopped me. I sat down on the yellow box instead, and remarked that I was extremely fatigued.

'So am I,' said she.

'My feet ache so,' I said, 'that I fear there may be something serious the matter with them.'

'So do mine,' said she.

This, I may observe, was a new and irritating habit she had got into: whatever I complained of in the way of unaccountable symptoms in divers portions of my frame, instead of sympathising and suggesting remedies she said hers (whatever it was) did it too.

'Your feet cannot possibly,' said I, 'be in the terrible condition mine are in. In the first place mine are bigger, and accordingly afford more scope for disorders. I have shooting pains in them resembling neuralgia, and no doubt traceable to some nervous source.'

'So have I,' said she.

'I think bathing might do them good,' I said, determined not to become angry. 'Will you get me some hot water please?'

'Why?' said she.

She had never said such a thing to me before. I could only gaze at her in a profound surprise.

'Why?' I repeated at length, keeping studiously calm. 'What an extraordinary question. I could give you a thousand reasons if I chose, such as that I desire to bathe them; that hot water—rather luckily for itself—has no feet, and therefore has to be fetched; and that a wife has to do as she is told. But I will, my dear Edelgard, confine myself to the counter inquiry, and ask why not?'

'I too, my dear Otto,' said she—and she spoke with great composure, her head bent over her mending, 'could give you a thousand answers to that if I chose, such as that I desire to get this sock finished—yours, by the way—that I have walked exactly as far as you have, that I see no reason why you should not as there are no servants here fetch your own hot water, and that your wishing or not wishing to bathe your feet has really if you come to think of it nothing to do with me. But I will confine myself just to saying that I prefer not to go.'

It can be imagined with what feelings—not mixed but unmitigated— I listened to this. And after five years! Five years of patience and guidance.

'Is this my Edelgard?' I managed to say, recovering speech enough for those four words but otherwise struck dumb.

'Your Edelgard?' she repeated musingly as she continued to mend, and not even looking at me. 'Your boots, your handkerchief, your gloves, your socks— yes—'

I confess I could not follow, and could only listen amazed.

'But not your Edelgard. At least, not more than you are my Otto.'

'But—my boots?' I repeated, really dazed.

'Yes,' she said, folding up the finished sock, 'they really are yours. Your property. But you should not suppose that I am a kind of living boot, made to be trodden on. I, my dear Otto, am a human being, and no human being is another human being's property.'

ELIZABETH VON ARNIM (1866–1941), *The Caravaners*, 1909

The more subtle method of resistance was that of quiet subversion.

I heard a servant asked what hee coulde doe, whoe made this answeare: 'I can sowe, I can mowe, and I can stacke, and I can doe my Master too, when my Master turns his backe.'

HENRY BEST, Yorkshire farmer (*c*.1592–1647), *Farming Book*, 1642

And bycause that servauntes customarily doe loyter in theire woorke it is necessarie to lye in a wayte against their frawde.

WALTER OF HENLEY, *Husbandry*, *c*.1276–90, tr. William Lambarde, 1577

> A worthy manciple of the Middle Temple
> Was there; he might have served as an example
> To all provision-buyers for his thrift
> In making purchase, whether on credit
> Or for cash down: he kept an eye on prices,
> So always got in first and did good business.
> Now isn't it an instance of God's grace,
> Such an unlettered man should so outpace
> The wisdom of a pack of learned men?
> He'd more than thirty masters over him,
> All of them proficient experts in law,
> More than a dozen of them with the power
> To manage rents and land for any peer
> So that—unless the man were off his head—
> He could live honourably, free of debt,
> Or sparingly, if that were his desire;
> And able to look after a whole shire
> In whatever emergency might befall;
> And yet this manciple could hoodwink them all.

GEOFFREY CHAUCER (*c*.1343–1400), 'General Prologue', *The Canterbury Tales*, *c*.1387, tr. David Wright, 1985

When your master or lady calls a servant by name, if that servant be not in the way, none of you are to answer, for then there will be no end of your drudgery: and masters themselves allow, that if a servant comes when he is called, it is sufficient.

When you have done a fault, be always pert and insolent, and behave yourself as if you were the injured person; this will immediately put your master or lady off their mettle.

If you see your master wronged by any of your fellow-servants, be sure to conceal it, for fear of being called a tell-tale. However, there is one exception, in case of a favourite servant, who is justly hated by the whole family; who therefore are bound, in prudence, to lay all the faults they can upon the favourite.

*

It often happens, that servants sent on messages are apt to stay out somewhat longer than the message requires, perhaps two, four, six, or eight hours, or some such trifle, for the temptation to be sure was great, and flesh and blood cannot always resist. When you return, the master storms, the lady scolds; stripping, cudgelling, and turning off is the word. But here you ought to be provided with a set of excuses, enough to serve on all occasions. For instance, your uncle came fourscore miles to town this morning, on purpose to see you, and goes back by break of day tomorrow; a brother-servant, that borrowed money of you when he was out of place, was running away to Ireland; you were taking leave of an old fellow-servant, who was shipping for Barbados: your father sent a cow for you to sell, and you could not find a chapman till nine at night; you were taking leave of a dear cousin who is to be hanged next Saturday; you wrenched your foot against a stone, and were forced to stay three hours in a shop before you could stir a step; some nastiness was thrown on you out of a garret-window, and you were ashamed to come home before you were cleaned, and the smell went off; you were pressed for the sea-service, and carried before a justice of peace, who kept you three hours before he examined you, and you got off with much a-do; a bailiff, by mistake, seized you for a debtor, and kept you the whole evening in a sponging-house; you were told your master had gone to a tavern, and came to some mischance, and your grief was so great, that you inquired for his honour in a hundred taverns between Pall Mall and Temple Bar.

Take all tradesmen's parts against your master, and when you are sent to buy any thing, never offer to cheapen it, but generously pay the full demand. This is highly for your master's honour; and may be some shillings in your pocket; and you are to consider, if your master hath paid too much, he can better afford the loss than a poor tradesman.

Never submit to stir a finger in any business, but that for which you were particularly hired. For example, if the groom be drunk or absent, and the butler be ordered to shut the stable door, the answer is ready, 'An please your honour, I don't understand horses.' If a corner of the hanging wants a single nail to fasten it, and the footman be directed to tack it up, he may say he doth not understand that sort of work, but his honour may send for the upholsterer.

Masters and ladies are usually quarrelling with the servants for not shutting the doors after them; but neither masters nor ladies consider that those doors must be open before they can be shut, and that the labour is double to open and shut the doors; therefore the best, the shortest, and easiest way is to do neither. But if you are so often teased to shut the door, that you cannot easily forget it, then give the door such a clap at your going out, as will shake the whole room, and make everything rattle in it, to put your master and lady in mind that you observe their directions . . .

I could never endure to see maid-servants so ungenteel as to walk the streets with their petticoats pinned up; it is a foolish excuse to allege their petticoats will be dirty, when they have so easy a remedy as to walk three or four times down a clean pair of stairs after they come home.

When you step to tattle with some crony servant in the same street, leave your own street-door open, that you may get in without knocking when you come back; otherwise your mistress may know you are gone out, and you will be chidden.

I do most earnestly exhort you all to unanimity and concord. But mistake me not: you may quarrel with each other as much as you please, only bear in mind that you have a common enemy, which is your master and lady, and you have a common cause to defend. Believe an old practitioner; whoever, out of malice to a fellow-servant, carries a tale to his master, should be ruined by a general confederacy against him.

The general place of rendezvous for all servants, both in winter and summer, is the kitchen; there the grand affairs of the family ought to be consulted, whether they concern the stable, the dairy, the pantry, the laundry, the cellar, the nursery, the dining-room, or my lady's chamber: there, as in your own proper element, you can laugh, and squall, and romp, in full security . . .

When you want proper instruments for any work you are about, use all expedients you can invent rather than leave your work undone. For instance, if the poker be out of the way, or broken, stir up the fire with the tongs; if the tongs be not at hand, use the muzzle of the bellows, the wrong end of the fire-shovel, the handle of the fire-brush, the end of a mop, or your master's cane. If you want paper to singe a fowl, tear the first book you see about the house. Wipe your shoes, for want of a clout, with the bottom of a curtain, or a damask napkin. Strip your livery lace for garters. If the butler wants a jordan, in case of need he may use the great silver cup.

JONATHAN SWIFT (1667–1745), from *Directions to Servants*, 1745

I am the boy at Mugby. That's about what *I* am.

You don't know what I mean? What a pity! But I think you do. I think you must. Look here. I am the boy at what is called The Refreshment Room at Mugby Junction, and what's proudest boast is, that it never yet refreshed a mortal being.

Up in a corner of the Down Refreshment Room at Mugby Junction, in the height of twenty-seven cross draughts (I've often counted 'em while they brush the First-Class hair twenty-seven ways), behind the bottles, among the glasses, bounded on the nor'west by the beer, stood pretty far to the right of a metallic object that's at times the tea-urn and at times the soup-tureen, according to the nature of the last twang imparted to its contents which are the same groundwork, fended off from the traveller by a barrier of stale sponge-cakes erected atop of the counter, and lastly exposed sideways to the glare of Our Missis's eye—you ask a Boy so sitiwated, next time you stop in a hurry at Mugby, for anything to drink; you take particular notice that he'll try to seem not to hear you, that he'll appear in a absent manner to survey the Line through a transparent medium composed of your head and body, and that he won't serve you as long as you can possibly bear it. That's me.

What a lark it is! We are the Model Establishment, we are, at Mugby. Other Refreshment Rooms send their imperfect young ladies up to be finished off by Our Missis. For some of the young ladies, when they're new to the business, come into it mild! Ah! Our Missis, she soon takes that out of 'em. Why, I originally come into the business meek myself. But Our Missis, she soon took that out of *me* . . .

You should see our Bandolining Room at Mugby Junction. It's led to by the door behind the counter, which you'll notice usually stands ajar, and it's the room where Our Missis and our young ladies Bandolines their hair. You should see 'em at it, betwixt trains, Bandolining away, as if they was anointing themselves for the combat. When you're telegraphed, you should see their noses all a-going up with scorn, as if it was a part of the working of the same Cooke and Wheatstone electrical machinery. You should hear Our Missis give the word, 'Here comes the Beast to be Fed!' and then you should see 'em indignantly skipping across the Line, from the Up to the Down, or Wicer Warsaw, and begin to pitch the stale pastry into the plates, and chuck the sawdust sangwiches under the glass covers, and get out the—ha, ha, ha!—the sherry,—O my eye, my eye!—for your Refreshment.

It's only in the Isle of the Brave and Land of the Free (by which, of course, I mean to say Britannia) that Refreshmenting is so effective, so 'olesome, so constitutional a check upon the public. There was a Foreigner, which having politely, with his hat off, beseeched our young ladies and Our Missis for 'a leetel gloss hoff prarndee,' and having had the Line surveyed through him by all and no other acknowledgment, was a-proceeding at last to help himself, as seems to be the custom in his own country, when Our Missis, with her hair almost a-coming un-Bandolined with rage, and her eyes omitting sparks, flew at him, cotched the decanter out of his hand, and said, 'Put it down! I won't allow that!' The foreigner turned pale, stepped back with his arms stretched out in front of him, his hands clasped, and his shoulders riz, and exclaimed: 'Ah! Is it possible, this! That these disdaineous females and this ferocious old woman are placed here by the administration, not only to empoison the voyagers, but to affront them! Great Heaven! How arrives it? The English people. Or is he then a slave? Or idiot?' Another time, a merry, wideawake American gent had tried the sawdust and spit it out, and had tried the Sherry and spit that out, and had tried in vain to sustain exhausted natur upon Butter-Scotch, and had been rather extra Bandolined and Line-surveyed through, when, as the bell was ringing and he paid Our Missis, he says, very loud and good-tempered: 'I tell Yew what 'tis, ma'arm. I la'af. Theer! I la'af. I Dew. I oughter ha'seen most things, for I hail from the Onlimited side of the Atlantic Ocean. and I haive travelled right slick over the Limited, head on through Jeerusalemm and the East, and likeways France and Italy, Europe Old World, and am now upon the track to the Chief Europian Village; but such an Institution as Yew, and Yewer young ladies, and Yewer fixin's solid and liquid, afore the glorious Tarnal I never did see yet! And if I hain't found the eighth wonder of monarchical Creation, in finding Yew, and Yewer young ladies, and Yewer fixin's solid and liquid, all as aforesaid, established in a country where the people air not absolute Loo-naticks, I am Extra Double Darned with a Nip and Frizzle to the innermostest grit! Wheerfur—Theer!—I la'af! I Dew, ma'arm. I la'af!' And so he went, stamping and shaking his sides, along the platform all the way to his own compartment.

I think it was her standing up agin the Foreigner as giv' Our Missis the idea of going over to France, and droring a comparison betwixt Refreshmenting as followed among the frog-eaters, and Refreshmenting as triumphant in the Isle of the Brave and Land of the Free (by which, of course, I mean to say agin, Britannia). Our young ladies, Miss Whiff, Miss Piff, and Mrs Sniff, was unanimous opposed to her going; for, as they says to Our Missis one and all, it is well beknown to the hends of the herth as no other nation except Britain has a idea of anythink, but above all of business. Why then should you tire yourself to prove what is already proved? Our Missis, however (being a teazer at all pints) stood out grim obstinate, and got a return pass by South-eastern Tidal, to go right through, if such should be her dispositions, to Marseilles.

Sniff is husband to Mrs Sniff, and is a regular insignificant cove. He looks arter the sawdust department in a back room, and is sometimes, when we are very hard put to it, let behind the counter with a corkscrew; but never when it can be helped, his demeanour towards the public being disgusting servile. How Mrs Sniff ever come so far to lower herself as to marry him, I don't know; but I suppose *he* does, and I should think he wished he didn't, for he leads a awful life. Mrs Sniff couldn't be much harder with him if he was public. Similarly, Miss Whiff and Miss Piff, taking the tone of Mrs Sniff, they shoulder Sniff about when he *is* let in with a corkscrew, and they whisk things out of his hands when in his servility he is a-going to let the public have 'em, and they snap him up when in the crawling baseness of his spirit he is a-going to answer a public question, and they drore more tears into his eyes than ever the mustard does which he all day long lays on to the sawdust. (But it ain't strong.) Once, when Sniff had the repulsiveness to reach across to get the milk-pot to hand over for a baby, I see Our Missis in her rage catch him by both his shoulders, and spin him out into the Bandolining Room.

But Mrs Sniff,—how different! She's the one! She's the one as you'll notice to be always looking another way from you, when you look at her. She's the one with the small waist buckled in tight in front, and with the lace cuffs at her wrists, which she puts on the edge of the counter before her, and stands a-smoothing while the public foams. This smoothing the cuffs and looking another way while the public foams is the last accomplishment taught to the young ladies as come to Mugby to be finished by Our Missis; and it's always taught by Mrs Sniff.

When Our Missis went away upon her journey, Mrs Sniff was left in charge. She did hold the public in check most beautiful! In all my time, I never see half so many cups of tea given without milk to people as wanted it with, nor half so many cups of tea with milk given to people as wanted it without. When foaming ensued. Mrs Sniff would say: 'Then you'd better settle it among your-selves, and change with one another.' It was a most highly delicious lark. I enjoyed the Refreshmenting business more than ever, and was so glad I had took to it when young.

CHARLES DICKENS (1812–70), *Mugby Junction,* 1866

When an apprentice enters a shop, he will in all probability be taught to 'keep nix' before he is told the names of the tools; and though the apprentice, every-thing around him being novel, would prefer being enlightened regarding the elementary mysteries of his trade to being put to keep nix, this merely shows his want of wisdom. Keeping nix is a really important job, and one the efficient discharge of which is supposed to imply the possession of consider-able ability on the part of the apprentice, and which elevates him in the esti-mation of those who are to bring him up in the way he should go. Keeping nix, consists in keeping a bright look-out for the approach of managers or fore-men, so as to be able to give prompt and timely notice to men who may be skulking, or having a sly read or smoke, or who are engaged on 'corporation work'—that is, work of their own. The boy who can keep nix well—who can detect the approach of those in authority, while they are yet afar off, and give warning to those over whose safety he has been watching, without betraying any agitation, or making any movement that might excite the suspicion of the enemy—will win the respect of his mates; he will be regarded by them as a treasure, a youth of promise. But should he be so slow or so unfortunate as to allow his mates to be 'dropped on' while he is upon guard, then woe to him! Curses loud and deep will be heaped upon his thick head; a stout stick and his back will probably be made acquainted; and from that time forth, until he has redeemed his tarnished reputation by doing something specially meritorious in the nix keeping way, he will be regarded as one concerning whose capacity to learn his trade there are grave doubts.

A JOURNEYMAN ENGINEER (Thomas Wright) (*fl.* 1867), *Some Habits and Customs of the Working Classes,* 1867

Wangling was the art of obtaining one's just due by unfair means. For instance, every officer and man of the BEF had his allotted daily rations, his camp or billet, his turn for leave. In practice, to get these necessities, it was well to know the man who provided them and do him some small service—a bottle of whisky, the loan of transport (if you had any) or of a fatigue party. Wangling extended to the lowest ranks. Men wangled from the NCOs the better sorts of jam and extra turns off duty. The main stream of wangling flowed from the enormous and growing number of small units, like Uncle's, the apportionment of whose daily subsistence was at once a nuisance and an opportunity to the Supply Officers and the Railhead Panjandrums—for the bigger units, battalions, batteries, Head-quarters had to be and could be more easily provided for. But Wangling was by no means confined to troops in the field. As the War grew and grew—the contracts for supplying steel helmets to Americans, the command of smaller Allied Armies, the very sovereignty of nations all became subject to the Wangle, so remote had become the chances of justly obtaining bare justice.

To return to the unit in the field, when its Wangle was completed, behold it housed, fed and allowed some leave. But life was still very hard—almost insupportable—to bear it, men, those fathers of invention, evolved the art of Scrounging.

Scrounging could be defined as obtaining that to which one had not a shadow of a claim by unfair means. It was more insidious than the Wangle, but just as necessary—men scrounged the best dug-outs off one another, or off neighbouring sections. NCOs scrounged rum by keeping a thumb in the dipper while doling it out. Officers scrounged the best horse-lines from other units. Colonials scrounged telephone wire to snare rabbits. Nations scrounged territory or trade. It was simply done. You walked about whistling, with your hands in your pockets and a cigarette in your mouth, until you saw what you wanted, and then took it. The main stream of Scrounging was for wood. The armies were provided with coal and coke and presumably intended to ignite it by holding a match to it. In result, millions of men during the five winters of the War, burnt a colossal cubage of wood. It was easy to obtain. Vast quantities were being cut by an entire Forestry Corps that had rights over several Picard and Norman forests and did nothing else but provide the timber required for dug-outs, railways, roads and gunpits. No great percentage ever reached its proper destination. A little was built into huts, horselines or billets. The bulk was burnt. From the timber dumps in the great cold of January, 1917, whole stacks disappeared. If any high authority went into the matter, a dumb, putty-faced sentry was produced who had heard nothing, seen nothing, knew nothing. But even the enormous quantity taken from dumps was not enough. Farms, houses, public buildings were ransacked. Shelving, forms, ladders, carts, partitions disappeared. In the Belgian hop-fields the British Army alone is said to have destroyed 1,000,000 hop-poles. Who shall blame them? Shall a soldier die of cold as well as of other things?

Wangling is known in peace-time. It is a necessity of civilization, where violence is difficult and costly. Scrounging was a necessity of war, for men must live. There was another Art that was more truly an Art than either of these. For it did not rest upon necessity, but was an ornament, a superfluity, a creative effort of the mind. This was the Art of Winning. It may be defined as Stealing. More fully, it was the Art of obtaining that which one had no right to, for the sake of obtaining it, for the joy of possession.

Some say that it arose from taking millions of decent civilian people and planking them down upon battlefields from which the last sign of decency had disappeared, in a war so bloody and so endlessly long that the issue of it was beyond imagining. Some say it was simply the primeval joy of loot, ever present in man, and bursting out from time to time in Tudor or Elizabethan Filibuster, in Georgian Colonists, or Victorian Journalists.

As the War went on the contagion spread. Decent Flemish and Picard girls, with no particular tenderness for any one man, possessed glazed cases containing the badges of every unit in the BEF. Decent English boys conveyed or sent home every sort of appliance, equipment, projectile, arm—not one of which they had obtained by personal combat, but which they had found lying about and appropriated.

R. H. MOTTRAM (1883–1971), Sixty-Four, Ninety-Four!, 1925

IN DEFENCE OF IDLENESS

Some observers rejected the work ethic altogether. Questioning whether so much labour was desirable, leave alone necessary, they praised the life of idleness.

Consider the lilies of the field, how they grow; they toil not, neither do they spin.

And yet I say unto you, That even Solomon in all his glory was not arrayed like one of these.

Matthew 7: 28–9

Work, I imagine, is not a good in itself. There is nothing laudable in work for work's sake. To work voluntarily for a worthy object is laudable; but what constitutes a worthy object? On this matter, the oracle of which your contributor [Thomas Carlyle] is the prophet has never yet been prevailed on to declare itself. He revolves in an eternal circle round the idea of work, as if turning up the earth, or driving a shuttle or a quill, were ends in themselves, and the ends of human existence.

JOHN STUART MILL (1806–73), 'The Negro Question', 1850

'The blessing of work' is an ennobling phrase for slaves.

FRIEDRICH NIETZSCHE (1844–1900), *The Will to Power*, wr. 1883–9, tr. Anthony M. Ludovici, 1910

The Sleepers

As I walked down the waterside
    This silent morning, wet and dark;
Before the cocks in farmyards crowed,
    Before the dogs began to bark;
Before the hour of five was struck
By old Westminster's mighty clock:

As I walked down the waterside
    This morning, in the cold damp air,
I saw a hundred women and men
    Huddled in rags and sleeping there:
These people have no work, thought I,
And long before their time they die.

That moment, on the waterside,
    A lighted car came at a bound;
I looked inside, and saw a score
    Of pale and weary men that frowned;
Each man sat in a huddled heap,
Carried to work while fast asleep.

Ten cars rushed down the waterside
    Like lighted coffins in the dark;
With twenty dead men in each car,
    That must be brought alive by work:
These people work too hard, thought I,
And long before their time they die.

W. H. DAVIES (1871–1940), 1911

I have read many novels in which the chief characters have been unemployed, but I cannot say that I have been impressed. They always seem to make their characters either totally miserable or totally unconcerned about their unemployment. Whilst it is true that there is much more misery than joy, it is also true that one finds happiness in things which one had never noticed before. One hoards pleasant little incidents in the mind, incidents which would never be noticed if one was at work. Often in the summer I have been starting off for a long walk through the woods just as the men have been going to the pits, and I frankly admit that I have been glad that I was free to go where I wished. Many a drowsy July afternoon I have laid for hours under the hedgerows listening to the puffing of the pit winding-engine in the distance. I have actually found it in me to pity those who were sweating in the darkness beneath me. I would think to myself on such occasions—not in order to console myself, but because I was myself happy about it—'Well if I have lost my job I have also lost a hard master.'

Even after four years of unemployment I get a thrill out of ignoring the pit buzzer.

G. A. W. Tomlinson, Nottinghamshire miner, *Coal-Miner*, 1937

Sing care away with sport and play,
    Pastime is all our pleasure;
If well we fare for nought we care,
    In mirth consists our treasure.

Let snudges lurk and drudges work,
    We do defy their slavery;
He is but a fool that goes to school,
    All we delight in bravery.

What doth avail far hence to sail
    And lead our life in toiling;
Or to what end should we here spend
    Our days in irksome moiling?

It is the best to live at rest,
    And take't as God doth send it,
To haunt each wake and mirth to make,
    And with good fellows spend it.

Nothing is worse than a full purse
    To niggards and to pinchers;
They always spare and live in care,
    There's no man loves such flinchers.

The merry man with cup and can
    Lives longer than doth twenty;
The miser's wealth doth hurt his health,
    Examples we have plenty.

Anon., *Misogonus*, c.1564–5

Song

What man in his wits had not rather be poor,
    Than for lucre his freedom to give?
Ever busy the means of his life to secure,
    And so ever neglecting to live?

Environed from morning to night in a crowd,
  Not a moment unbent or alone;
Constrain'd to be abject, though never so proud,
  And at everyone's call but his own.

Still repining, and longing for quiet, each hour,
  Yet studiously flying it still;
With the means of enjoying his wish, in his power;
  But accursed with his wanting the will.

For a year must be pass'd, or a day must be come,
  Before he has leisure to rest;
He must add to his store this or that pretty sum,
  And then he will have time to be blessed.

But his gains, more bewitching the more they increase,
  Only swell the desire of his eye.
Such a wretch, let mine enemy live, if he please,
  Let not even mine enemy die.

SAMUEL WESLEY (1691–1739), 1736

In a moral view, the industrious mechanic is a more pleasing object than the loitering peasant. But in a picturesque light, it is otherwise. The arts of industry are rejected; and even idleness, if I may so speak, adds dignity to a character.

WILLIAM GILPIN (1724–1804), *Observations, Relative Chiefly to Picturesque Beauty, Made in the Year 1772, on Several Parts of England; Particularly the Mountains and Lakes of Cumberland, and Westmorland,* 1786

'I could wish it done as soon as it *can* be done, Wickfield,' said Doctor Strong, 'for Jack Maldon is needy, and idle; and of those two bad things, worse things sometimes come. What does Doctor Watts say,' he added, looking at me, and moving his head to the time of his quotation, ' "Satan finds some mischief still, for idle hands to do." '

'Egad, Doctor,' returned Mr Wickfield, 'if Doctor Watts knew mankind, he might have written, with as much truth, "Satan finds some mischief still, for busy hands to do." The busy people achieve their full share of mischief in the world, you may rely upon it. What have the people been about, who have been the busiest in getting money, and in getting power, this century or two? No mischief?'

CHARLES DICKENS (1812–70), *David Copperfield,* 1850

Death is the end of life; ah, why
Should life all labour be?

ALFRED, LORD TENNYSON (1809–92), from 'The Lotos-Eaters', 1832

I did not read books the first summer; I hoed beans. Nay, I often did better than this. There were times when I could not afford to sacrifice the bloom of the present moment to any work, whether of the head or hands. I love a broad margin to my life. Sometimes, in a summer morning, having taken my accustomed bath, I sat in my sunny doorway from sunrise till noon, rapt in a reverie, amidst the pines and hickories and sumachs, in undisturbed solitude and stillness, while the birds sang around or flitted noiselessly through the house, until by the sun falling in at my west window, or the noise of some traveller's waggon on the distant highway, I was reminded of the lapse of time. I grew in those seasons like corn in the night, and they were far better than any work of the hands would have been. They were not time subtracted from my life, but so much over and above my usual allowance. I realised what the Orientals mean by contemplation and the forsaking of works. For the most part I minded not how the hours went. The day advanced as if to light some work of mine; it was morning and lo! now it is evening, and nothing memorable is accomplished. Instead of singing like the birds, I silently smiled at my incessant good fortune. As the sparrow had its trill, sitting on the hickory before my door, so had I my chuckle or suppressed warble which he might hear out of my nest. My days were not days of the week, bearing the stamp of any heathen deity, nor were they minced into hours and fretted by the ticking of a clock; for I lived like the Puri Indians, of whom it is said that 'for yesterday, to-day and to-morrow they have only one word, and they express the variety of meaning by pointing backward for yesterday, forward for to-morrow, and overhead for the passing day.' This was sheer idleness to my fellow-townsmen, no doubt; but if the birds and flowers had tried me by their standard, I should not have been found wanting.

HENRY DAVID THOREAU (1817–62), *Walden, or Life in the Woods*, 1854

'We must love work,' say our sages. Well! How can we? What is lovable about work in civilization? For nine-tenths of all men work procures nothing but profitless boredom. Rich men, consequently, find work loathsome and do only the easiest and most lucrative kinds of work such as managing companies.

FRANÇOIS MARIE CHARLES FOURIER (1772–1837), *La Théorie de l'Unité Universelle*, 2nd edn. 1841–3, tr. Jonathan Beecher and Richard Bienvenu, 1972

Idleness

God, you've so much to do,
To think of, watch and listen to,
That I will let all else go by
And lending ear and eye
Help you to watch how in the combe
Winds sweep dead leaves without a broom;
And rooks in the spring-reddened trees
Restore their villages,
Nest by dark nest
Swaying at rest on the trees' frail unrest;
Or on this limestone wall,
Leaning at ease, with you recall
How once these heavy stones
Swam in the sea as shells and bones;
And hear that owl snore in a tree
Till it grows dark enough for him to see;
In fact, will learn to shirk
No idleness that I may share your work.

ANDREW YOUNG (1885–1971), 1939

I asked him, What do you do?

He smiled patiently, The typical American question.
In Europe they would ask, What are you doing? Or,
What are you doing now?

What do I do? I listen, to the water falling. (No
sound of it here but with the wind!) This is my entire
occupation.

WILLIAM CARLOS WILLIAMS (1883–1963), *Paterson*, 1948

. . . if a person cannot be happy without remaining idle, idle he should
remain. It is a revolutionary precept; but, thanks to hunger and the workhouse, one not easily to be abused; and within practical limits, it is one of the
most incontestable truths in the whole Body of Morality. Look at one of your
industrious fellows for a moment, I beseech you. He sows hurry and reaps
indigestion; he puts a vast deal of activity out to interest, and receives a large
measure of nervous derangement in return. Either he absents himself entirely
from all fellowship, and lives a recluse in a garret, with carpet slippers and a

leaden inkpot; or he comes among people swiftly and bitterly, in a contraction of his whole nervous system, to discharge some temper before he returns to work. I do not care how much or how well he works, this fellow is an evil feature in other people's lives. They would be happier if he were dead. They could easier do without his services in the Circumlocution Office, than they can tolerate his fractious spirits. He poisons life at the well-head. It is better to be beggared out of hand by a scapegrace nephew, than daily hag-ridden by a peevish uncle.

And what, in God's name, is all this pother about? For what cause do they embitter their own and other people's lives? That a man should publish three or thirty articles a year, that he should finish or not finish his great allegorical picture, are questions of little interest to the world. The ranks of life are full; and although a thousand fall, there are always some to go into the breach. When they told Joan of Arc she should be at home minding women's work, she answered there were plenty to spin and wash. And so, even with your own rare gifts! When nature is 'so careless of the single life', why should we coddle ourselves into the fancy that our own is of exceptional importance? Suppose Shakespeare had been knocked on the head some dark night in Sir Thomas Lucy's preserves, the world would have wagged on better or worse, the pitcher gone to the well, the scythe to the corn, and the student to his book; and no one been any the wiser of the loss.

Robert Louis Stevenson (1850–94), 'An Apology for Idlers', 1881

During his relatively short life, Stevenson wrote some eighty books. He was immensely hard-working and productive. The same can be said of Aldous Huxley and Bertrand Russell, whose praises of idleness follow below.

There are many, I know, who can see no virtues in a leisured class. And, indeed, it is certainly easier to see the vices of such a class than its virtues. In every society the majority of the leisured people do, in point of fact, waste their opportunities in a fashion that is positively astonishing. Not knowing how better to occupy their endless spare time, they indulge in every kind of stupidity, silliness and vice. By a routine of what is technically known as pleasure, they brutalise themselves as effectively as the sweated labourer does by his routine of work. In some countries the leisured class has consisted almost exclusively of these people. But in other countries there has been a minority—and sometimes an influential minority—of leisured people who have devoted their leisure to the cultivation of their intelligences, their tastes, their sensibilities.

It would be absurd to claim for such leisured societies that they ever produced anything of epoch-making importance. La Rochefoucauld, and Madame de Lafayette, Shaftesbury, Chesterfield and Walpole—these are the fine flowers of the leisured class. They are the best that such a class can produce, but they are also typical of it. The ideal leisured society—and it is an ideal which has not infrequently been realised—is one which cultivates the graces of the spirit, which is at home in the world of thought, which is not shocked by unfamiliar ideas and which protects the propounders of such new notions from the effects of popular prejudice. Leisured society, at its best, is detached and unprejudiced, has good taste, and an open mind; it may, it is true, regard the arts and the philosophies with insufficient seriousness—as mere pastimes—but, at any rate, it admits their existence; it interests itself in them, and in their practitioners. And it is able to do so because it is leisured.

Infatuated by a generous democratic enthusiasm, or, more often, intimidated by public opinion, our men of leisure have almost all abandoned their hereditary right to do nothing at all, and have plunged into the vortex of money-making labour. The results seem to me, on the whole, deplorable. For if a good many imbeciles who would otherwise have spent all their time drinking, love-making, and playing games are now compelled, for a certain number of hours each day, to think soberly of the best way of making money out of their neighbours, a few intelligent men, who might otherwise have cultivated a taste for spiritual amusements, are caught up into the machine of business and made to devote their wits to purely practical and immediate ends. Honest work thus tends to rob society of its genial and unprejudiced sceptics, its refined appreciators, its setters of elegant standards. It can be no mere coincidence that the absorption of the old leisured class in practical and immediately profitable work should have been going on at the same time as the break-up of literary and artistic tradition and the general decay of taste.

ALDOUS HUXLEY (1894–1963), 'The Dangers of Work', 1924

I think that there is far too much work done in the world, that immense harm is caused by the belief that work is virtuous, and that what needs to be preached in modern industrial countries is quite different from what always has been preached. Everyone knows the story of the traveller in Naples who saw twelve beggars lying in the sun (it was before the days of Mussolini), and offered a lira to the laziest of them. Eleven of them jumped up to claim it, so he gave it to the twelfth. This traveller was on the right lines. But in countries which do not enjoy Mediterranean sunshine idleness is more difficult, and a great public propaganda will be required to inaugurate it . . .

I want to say, in all seriousness, that a great deal of harm is being done in the modern world by belief in the virtuousness of WORK, and that the road to happiness and prosperity lies in an organized diminution of work.

*

If the ordinary wage-earner worked four hours a day, there would be enough for everybody, and no unemployment—assuming a certain very moderate amount of sensible organization. This idea shocks the well-to-do, because they are convinced that the poor would not know how to use so much leisure. In America, men often work long hours even when they are already well off; such men, naturally, are indignant at the idea of leisure for wage-earners, except as the grim punishment of unemployment; in fact, they dislike leisure even for their sons. Oddly enough, while they wish their sons to work so hard as to have no time to be civilized, they do not mind their wives and daughters having no work at all. The snobbish admiration of uselessness, which, in an aristocratic society, extends to both sexes, is, under a plutocracy, confined to women; this, however, does not make it any more in agreement with common sense.

The wise use of leisure, it must be conceded, is a product of civilization and education. A man who has worked long hours all his life will be bored if he becomes suddenly idle. But without a considerable amount of leisure a man is cut off from many of the best things. There is no longer any reason why the bulk of the population should suffer this deprivation; only a foolish asceticism, usually vicarious, makes us continue to insist on work in excessive quantities now that the need no longer exists.

BERTRAND RUSSELL (1872–1970), 'In Praise of Idleness', 1932

TOWARDS UTOPIA

For most people, total idleness was not an option. Yet many Utopian thinkers envisaged an ideal society in which the hours of labour would be reduced and work made pleasant for all. A Second Coming would lift the curse laid on mankind at the Fall; or a regime of personal austerity would reduce the demand for goods and thus for the labour necessary to produce them.

'Utopia'

This commodity they have also above other, that in the most part of necessary occupations they need not so much work, as other nations do. For first of all the building or repairing of houses asketh everywhere so many men's continual labour, because that the unthrifty heir suffereth the houses that his father builded in continuance of time to fall in decay. So that which he might have upholden with little cost, his successor is constrained to build it again anew, to his great charge. Yea many times also the house that stood one man in much money, another is of so nice and so delicate a mind, that he setteth nothing by it. And it being neglected, and therefore shortly falling into ruin, he buildeth up another in another place with no less cost and charge. But among the Utopians, where all things be set in good order, and the commonwealth in a good stay, it very seldom chanceth, that they choose a new plot to build an house upon. And they do not only find speedy and quick remedies for present faults: but also prevent them that be like to fall. And by this means their houses continue and last very long with little labour and small reparations: insomuch that this kind of workmen sometimes have almost nothing to do. But that they be commanded to hew timber at home, and to square and trim up stones, to the intent that if any work chance, it may the speedier rise. Now, sir, in their apparel, mark (I pray you) how few workmen they need. First of all, whilst they be at work, they be covered homely with leather or skins, that will last seven years. When they go forth they cast upon them a cloak, which hideth the other homely apparel. These cloaks throughout the whole island be all of one colour, and that is the natural colour of the wool. They therefore do not only spend much less woollen cloth than is spent in other countries, but also the same standeth them in much less cost. But linen cloth is made with less labour, and is therefore had more in use. But in linen cloth only whiteness, in woollen only cleanliness is regarded. As for the smallness or fineness of the thread, that is nothing passed for. And this is the cause wherefore in other places four or five cloth gowns of divers colours, and as many silk coats be not enough for one man. Yea and if he be of the delicate and nice sort ten be too few: whereas there one garment will serve a man most commonly two years. For why should he desire more? Seeing if he had them, he should not be the better wrapped or covered from cold, neither in his apparel any whit the comelier. Wherefore, seeing they be all exercised in profitable occupations, and that few artificers in the same crafts be sufficient, this is the cause that plenty of all things being among them, they do sometimes bring forth an innumerable company of people to amend the highways, if any be broken. Many times also, when they have no such work to be occupied about, an open proclamation is made, that they shall bestow fewer hours in work. For the magistrates do not exercise their citizens against their wills in unneedful labours. For why in the institution of that weal public, this end is only and chiefly pretended and minded, that what time may possibly be spared from the necessary occupations and affairs of the commonwealth, all that the citizens should withdraw from the bodily service to the free liberty of the mind, and garnishing of the same. For herein they suppose the felicity of this life to consist.

THOMAS MORE (1477?–1535), *Utopia*, 1516, tr. Ralph Robinson, 1551

> *Gonzalo.*   I'th' commonwealth I would by contraries
>   Execute all things, for no kind of traffic
>   Would I admit; no name of magistrate;

Letters should not be known; riches, poverty,
And use of service, none; contract, succession,
Bourn, bound of land, tilth, vineyard, none;
No use of metal, corn, or wine, or oil;
No occupation, all men idle, all,
And women too, but innocent and pure;
No sovereignty—

*

All things in common nature should produce
Without sweat or endeavour. Treason, felony,
Sword, pike, knife, gun, or need of any engine
Would I not have, but nature should bring forth
Of it own kind all foison, all abundance
To feed my innocent people.

WILLIAM SHAKESPEARE (1564–1616), *The Tempest*, wr. 1611

There is no want of any thing necessary for the use of man.

Food groweth every where without labour, and that of all sorts to be desired.

For rayment, howsing, or any thing else that you may imagine possible for a man to want, or desire, it is provided by the command of Superiors, though not without labour, yet so little, as they doe nothing but as it were playing, and with pleasure.

FRANCIS GODWIN (1562–1633), *The Man in the Moon*, 1638

'Work under the Rule of the Saints'

But . . . it may be queried, whether, when the Saints shall enjoy all these things, they shall not follow their several employments and vocations as now they do.

To which I answer, yes: it is clear they shall follow several employments as now they do; but doubtless in a more regular, and more excellent and comfortable way than many now do: i.e. some shall not labour and toil day and night (scarce allowing themselves any time to spend in the performance of holy duties or for lawful and convenient recreations) to maintain others that live viciously, in idleness, drunkenness and other evil practices . . .

So that all of them, by their labours and employments, not toilsome and burdensome employments, but by their employments which shall be as recreation to them, as some employments are to ingenious men now, for it is irksome to them to be always idle: I say all of them by their pleasant, easy and well-regulated employments shall get a plentiful store of all those outward things which shall tend to the comfortable subsistence of them and theirs, with which they shall have no grief or vexation at all, but sorrow and sighing shall flee away, and everlasting joy shall be unto them.

> MARY CARY, Fifth Monarchist (*fl.* 1653), *The Little Horns Doom and Downfall . . . and a More Exact Mappe or Description of the New Ierusalems Glory,* 1651

'It is clear from all that we hear and read, that in the last age of civilisation men had got into a vicious circle in the matter of production of wares. They had reached a wonderful facility of production, and in order to make the most of that facility they had gradually created (or allowed to grow, rather) a most elaborate system of buying and selling, which has been called the World-Market; and that World-Market, once set a-going, forced them to go on making more and more of these wares, whether they needed them or not. So that while (of course) they could not free themselves from the toil of making real necessaries, they created in a never-ending series sham or artificial necessaries, which became, under the iron rule of the aforesaid World-Market, of equal importance to them with the real necessaries which supported life. By all this they burdened themselves with a prodigious mass of work merely for the sake of keeping their wretched system going.'

'Yes—and then?' said I.

'Why, then, since they had forced themselves to stagger along under this horrible burden of unnecessary production, it became impossible for them to look upon labour and its results from any other point of view than one—to wit, the ceaseless endeavour to expend the least possible amount of labour on any article made, and yet at the same time to make as many articles as possible. To this "cheapening of production," as it was called, everything was sacrificed: the happiness of the workman at his work, nay, his most elementary comfort and bare health, his food, his clothes, his dwelling, his leisure, his amusement, his education—his life, in short—did not weigh a grain of sand in the balance against this dire necessity of "cheap production" of things, a great part of which were not worth producing at all. Nay, we are told, and we must believe it, so overwhelming is the evidence, though many of our people scarcely *can* believe it, that even rich and powerful men, the masters of the poor devils aforesaid, submitted to live amidst sights and sounds and smells which it is in the very nature of man to abhor and flee from, in order that their riches might bolster up this supreme folly. The whole community, in fact, was cast into the jaws of this ravening monster, "the cheap production" forced upon it by the World-Market.'

'I think I do understand,' said I: 'but now, as it seems, you have reversed all this?'

'Pretty much so,' said he. 'The wares which we make are made because they are needed: men make for their neighbours' use as if they were making for themselves, not for a vague market of which they know nothing, and over which they have no control: as there is no buying and selling, it would be mere insanity to make goods on the chance of their being wanted; for there is no longer any one who can be *compelled* to buy them. So that whatever is made is good, and thoroughly fit for its purpose. Nothing *can* be made except for genuine use; therefore no inferior goods are made. Moreover, as aforesaid, we have now found out what we want, so we make no more than we want; and as we are not driven to make a vast quantity of useless things, we have time and resources enough to consider our pleasure in making them. All work which would be irksome to do by hand is done by immensely improved machinery; and in all work which it is a pleasure to do by hand machinery is done without. There is no difficulty in finding work which suits the special turn of mind of everybody; so that no man is sacrificed to the wants of another. From time to time, when we have found out that some piece of work was too disagreeable or troublesome, we have given it up and done altogether without the thing produced by it. Now, surely you can see that under these circumstances all the work that we do is an exercise of the mind and body more or less pleasant to be done: so that instead of avoiding work everybody seeks it: and, since people have got defter in doing the work generation after generation, it has become so easy to do, that it seems as if there were less done, though probably more is produced. I suppose this explains that fear, which I hinted at just now, of a possible scarcity in work, which perhaps you have already noticed, and which is a feeling on the increase, and has been for a score of years.'

WILLIAM MORRIS (1834–96), *News from Nowhere*, 1890

This argument will be strengthened if we reflect on the amount of labour that a state of equality will require. What is this quantity of exertion from which the objection supposes many individuals to shrink? It is so light as rather to assume the guise of agreeable relaxation and gentle exercise than of labour. In such a community, scarcely anyone can be expected, in consequence of his situation or avocations, to consider himself as exempted from the obligation to manual industry. There will be no rich man to recline in indolence, and fatten upon the labour of his fellows. The mathematician, the poet and the philosopher will derive a new stock of cheerfulness and energy from the recurring labour that makes them feel they are men. There will be no persons devoted to the manufacture of trinkets and luxuries; and none whose office it should be to keep in motion the complicated machine of government, tax-gatherers, beadles, excise-men, tide-waiters, clerks and secretaries. There will be neither fleets nor armies, neither courtiers nor lacqueys. It is the unnecessary employments that, at present, occupy the great mass of every civilized nation, while the peasant labours incessantly to maintain them in a state more pernicious than idleness . . .

From the sketch which has been given, it seems by no means impossible that the labour of every twentieth man in the community would be sufficient to supply to the rest all the absolute necessaries of life. If then this labour, instead of being performed by so small a number, were amicably divided among the whole, it would occupy the twentieth part of every man's time. Let us compute that the industry of a labouring man engrosses ten hours in every day, which, when we have deducted his hours of rest, recreation and meals, seems an ample allowance. It follows that half an hour a day employed in manual labour by every member of the community would sufficiently supply the whole with necessaries.

WILLIAM GODWIN (1756–1836), *Political Justice*, 1793

Socialists are often asked how work of the rougher and more repulsive kind could be carried out in the new condition of things. To attempt to answer such questions fully or authoritatively would be attempting the impossibility of constructing a scheme of a new society out of the materials of the old, before we knew which of those materials would disappear and which endure through the evolution which is leading us to the great change. Yet it is not difficult to conceive of some arrangement whereby those who did the roughest work should work for the shortest spells. And again, what is said above of the variety of work applies specially here. Once more I say, that for a man to be the whole of his life hopelessly engaged in performing one repulsive and never-ending task, is an arrangement fit enough for the hell imagined by theologians, but scarcely fit for any other form of society. Lastly, if this rougher work were of any special kind, we may suppose that special volunteers would be called on to perform it, who would surely be forthcoming, unless men in a state of freedom should lose the sparks of manliness which they possessed as slaves.

And yet if there be any work which cannot be made other than repulsive, either by the shortness of its duration or the intermittency of its recurrence, or by the sense of special and peculiar usefulness (and therefore honour) in the mind of the man who performs it freely—if there be any work which cannot be but a torment to the worker, what then? Well, then, let us see if the heavens will fall on us if we leave it undone, for it were better that they should. The produce of such work cannot be worth the price of it.

WILLIAM MORRIS (1834–96), 'Useful Work versus Useless Toil', 1885

If, uprooting from its heart the vice which dominates it and degrades its nature, the working class were to arise in terrible strength, not to demand the Rights of Man, which are but the rights of capitalist exploitation, not to demand the Right to Work, which is but the right to misery, but to forge a brazen law forbidding any man to work more than three hours a day, the earth, the old earth, trembling with joy would feel a new universe leaping within her.

PAUL LAFARGUE (1842–1911), *The Right to be Lazy and Other Studies*, tr. Charles H. Kerr, 1907

Report from Paradise

In paradise the work week is fixed at thirty hours
salaries are higher prices steadily go down
manual labour is not tiring (because of reduced gravity)
chopping wood is no harder than typing
the social system is stable and the rulers are wise
really in paradise one is better off than in whatever country

At first it was to have been different
luminous circles choirs and degrees of abstraction
but they were not able to separate exactly
the soul from the flesh and so it would come here
with a drop of fat a thread of muscle
it was necessary to face the consequences
to mix a grain of the absolute with a grain of clay
one more departure from doctrine the last departure
only John foresaw it: you will be resurrected in the flesh

not many behold God
he is only for those of 100 per cent pneuma
the rest listen to communiqués about miracles and floods
some day God will be seen by all
when it will happen nobody knows

As it is now every Saturday at noon
sirens sweetly bellow
and from the factories go the heavenly proletarians
awkwardly under their arms they carry their wings like violins

ZBIGNIEW HERBERT (1924–98), tr. Peter Dale Scott, 1968

Not everyone was convinced by the utopians.

Some reformers have hoped to reach a social system under which all work should be in itself a source of satisfaction. It is probable that such persons are made optimistic by the nature of their own doings. They are writers, schemers, reformers; they are usually of strongly altruistic character, and the performance of any duty or set task brings to them the approval of an exacting conscience; and they believe that all mankind can be brought to labor in their own spirit. The world would be a much happier place if their state of mind could be made universal. But the great mass of men are of a humdrum sort, not born with any marked bent or any loftiness of character. Moreover, most of the world's work for the satisfaction of our primary wants must be of a humdrum sort, and often of a rough and coarse sort. There must be ditching and delving, sowing and reaping, hammering and sawing, and all the severe physical exertion which, however lightened by tools and machinery, yet can never be other than labor in the ordinary sense of the term.

F. W. TAUSSIG (1859–1940), *Principles of Economics*, 1911

Dobson.   Have you ever taken your ideas to their logical conclusion? Well, have you? Hasn't a worker in a factory ever looked at you as though you were mad—a little potty, you know? Would you have the world do without cars, planes, electricity, houses, roads? Because *that's* the logical conclusion. If no man should be tied to turning out screws all his life, then that's what it means. No screws—no transport! No labourers—no roads! No banks or offices—no commercial market! No humdrum jobs, then no anything! There you are, solve it! Go on. Think about it. Reorganize the world so's everyone's doing a job he enjoys, so everyone's 'expressing' himself. Go on. Universal happiness? Get it!

ARNOLD WESKER (1932–), *I'm Talking about Jerusalem*, 1960

Closely associated with these utopian dreams were schemes for the establishment of communes in which rewards would be equal and manual labour no longer despised. Russian and Chinese Communism owed something to this tradition, as do the kibbutzim of Israel.

[In 1841 Nathaniel Hawthorne spent several months at Brook Farm, a co-operative community at West Roxbury, Massachusetts, strongly influenced by the ideas of the French utopian Charles Fourier, 1772–1837.]

After a reasonable training, the yeoman-life throve well with us. Our faces took the sunburn kindly; our chests gained in compass, and our shoulders in breadth and squareness; our great brown fists looked as if they had never been capable of kid gloves. The plough, the hoe, the scythe, and the hay-fork, grew familiar to our grasp. The oxen responded to our voices. We could do almost as fair a day's work as Silas Foster himself, sleep dreamlessly after it, and awake at daybreak with only a little stiffness of the joints, which was usually quite gone by breakfast-time.

To be sure, our next neighbors pretended to be incredulous as to our real proficiency in the business which we had taken in hand. They told slanderous fables about our inability to yoke our own oxen, or to drive them afield, when yoked, or to release the poor brutes from their conjugal bond at nightfall. They had the face to say, too, that the cows laughed at our awkwardness at milking-time, and invariably kicked over the pails; partly in consequence of our putting the stool on the wrong side, and partly because, taking offence at the whisking of their tails, we were in the habit of holding these natural flyflappers with one hand, and milking with the other. They further averred, that we hoed up whole acres of Indian corn and other crops, and drew the earth carefully about the weeds; and that we raised five hundred tufts of burdock, mistaking them for cabbages; and that, by dint of unskilful planting, few of our seeds ever came up at all, or if they did come up, it was stern foremost, and that we spent the better part of the month of June in reversing a field of beans, which had thrust themselves out of the ground in this unseemly way. They quoted it as nothing more than an ordinary occurrence for one or other of us to crop off two or three fingers, of a morning, by our clumsy use of the hay-cutter. Finally, and as an ultimate catastrophe, these mendacious rogues circulated a report that we Communitarians were exterminated, to the last man, by severing ourselves asunder with the sweep of our own scythes!—and that the world had lost nothing by this little accident.

But this was pure envy and malice on the part of the neighboring farmers. The peril of our new way of life was not lest we should fail in becoming practical agriculturalists, but that we should probably cease to be anything else. While our enterprise lay all in theory, we had pleased ourselves with delectable visions of the spiritualization of labor. It was to be our form of prayer, and ceremonial of worship. Each stroke of the hoe was to uncover some aromatic root of wisdom, heretofore hidden from the sun. Pausing in the field, to let the wind exhale the moisture from our foreheads, we were to look upward, and catch glimpses into the far-off soul of truth. In this point of view, matters did not turn out quite so well as we anticipated. It is very true, that, sometimes, gazing casually around me, out of the midst of my toil, I used to discern a richer picturesqueness in the visible scene of earth and sky. There was, at such moments, a novelty, an unwonted aspect on the face of Nature, as if she had been taken by surprise and seen at unawares, with no opportunity to put off her real look, and assume the mask with which she mysteriously hides herself from mortals. But this was all. The clods of earth, which we so constantly belabored and turned over and over, were never etherealized into thought. Our thoughts, on the contrary, were fast becoming cloddish. Our labor symbolized nothing, and left us mentally sluggish in the dusk of the evening. Intellectual activity is incompatible with any large amount of bodily exercise. The yeoman and the scholar—the yeoman and the man of finest moral culture, though not the man of sturdiest sense and integrity—are two distinct individuals, and can never be melted or welded into one substance.

NATHANIEL HAWTHORNE (1804–64), *The Blithedale Romance*, 1852

Then another stroke of genius on Fourier's part was the restoration of work to a position of honour, by making it the public function, the pride, health, gaiety, and very law of life. It would suffice to reorganise work in order to re-organise the whole of society, of which work would be the one civic obliga-tion, the vital rule. There would be no further question of brutally imposing work on vanquished men, mercenaries crushed down and treated like fam-ished beasts of burden; on the contrary, work would be freely accepted by all, allotted according to tastes and natures, performed during the few hours that might be indispensable, and constantly varied according to the choice of the voluntary toilers. A town would become an immense hive in which there would not be one idler, and in which each citizen would contribute his share towards the general sum of labour which might be necessary for the town to live. The tendency towards unity and final harmony would draw the inhabi-tants together and compel them to group themselves among the various series of workers. And the whole mechanism would rest in that: the workman choosing the task which he could perform most joyously, not riveted for ever to one and the same calling, but passing from one form of work to another. Moreover, the world would not be revolutionised all of a sudden, the begin-nings would be small, the system being tried first of all in some township of a few thousand souls. The dream would then approach fulfilment, the pha-lange, the unit at the base of the great human army would be created; the pha-lanstery, the common house, would be built. At first, too, one would simply appeal to willing men, and link them together in such wise as to form an asso-ciation of capital, work, and talent. Those who now possessed money, those whose arms were strong, and those who had brains would be asked to come to an understanding and combine, putting their various means together. They would produce with an energy and an abundance far greater than now, and they would divide the profits they reaped as equitably as possible, until the day came when capital, work, and talent might be blended together and form the common patrimony of a free brotherhood, in which everything would belong to everybody amidst general harmony.

ÉMILE ZOLA (1840–1902), *Travail*, 1901, tr. E. A. Vizetelly, 1900

[The Swedish socialist Nicholas Schliemann outlines his vision of the future.]

'I have pointed out some of the negative wastes of competition,' answered the other. 'I have hardly mentioned the positive economies of cooperation. Allowing five to a family, there are fifteen million families in this country; and at least ten million of these live separately, the domestic drudge being either the wife or a wage-slave. Now, set aside the modern system of pneumatic house-cleaning, and the economies of cooperative cooking, and consider one single item, the washing of dishes. Surely it is moderate to say that the dish-washing for a family of five takes half an hour a day; with ten hours as a day's work, it takes, therefore, half a million able-bodied persons—mostly women—to do the dish-washing of the country. And note that this is most filthy and deadening and brutalizing work; that it is a cause of anemia, nervousness, ugliness, and ill temper; of prostitution, suicide, and insanity; of drunken husbands and degenerate children—for all of which things the community has naturally to pay. And now consider that in each of my little free communities there would be a machine which would wash and dry the dishes, and do it, not merely to the eye and the touch, but scientifically— sterilizing them—and do it at a saving of all of the drudgery and nine tenths of the time!

UPTON SINCLAIR (1878–1968), *The Jungle*, 1906

Automation offered another route to the elimination of painful labour, a prospect that had been contemplated since the days of ancient Greece.

Each article of furniture will come to him when he calls it. Place yourself here, table! Get yourself ready for dinner! Get to work, my little kneading-trough. Fill up, ladle. Where's the cup got to? Get yourself washed, while you're about it. Over here, barley-cake. The pot ought to be serving up the beets. Get a move on, fish. 'But I'm not yet done properly on the other side.' Then be so good as to turn yourself over. With oil, please, and salt.

CRATES OF ATHENS (*fl.* 450 BC), *Wild Animals*, tr. Thomas Wiedemann, 1974

We can imagine a situation in which each instrument could do its own work, at the word of command or by intelligent anticipation, like the statues of Daedalus or the tripods made by Hephaestus, of which the poet relates that

Of their own motion they entered the conclave of Gods on Olympus

A shuttle would then weave of itself, and a plectrum would do its own harp-playing. In this situation managers would not need subordinates and masters would not need slaves.

ARISTOTLE (384–322 BC), *Politics*, c.335–322 BC, tr. Ernest Barker, rev. R. F. Stalley, 1995

The abstraction of one man's production from another's makes work more and more mechanical, until finally man is able to step aside and install machines.

GEORG WILHELM FRIEDRICH HEGEL (1770–1831), *Philosophy of Right*, 1821, tr. T. M. Knox, 1942

The Steam Threshing-machine

With the Straw Carrier

Flush with the pond the lurid furnace burn'd
At eve, while smoke and vapour fill'd the yard;
The gloomy winter sky was dimly starr'd,
The fly-wheel with a mellow murmur turn'd;
While, ever rising on its mystic stair
In the dim light, from secret chambers borne,
The straw of harvest, sever'd from the corn,
Climb'd, and fell over, in the murky air.
I thought of mind and matter, will and law,
And then of him, who set his stately seal
Of Roman words on all the forms he saw
Of old-world husbandry: *I* could but feel
With what a rich precision *he* would draw
The endless ladder, and the booming wheel!

Did any seer of ancient time forebode
This mighty engine, which we daily see
Accepting our full harvests, like a god,
With clouds about his shoulders,—it might be
Some poet-husbandman, some lord of verse,
Old Hesiod, or the wizard Mantuan
Who catalogued in rich hexameters
The Rake, the Roller, and the mystic Van:
Or else some priest of Ceres, it might seem,
Who witness'd, as he trod the silent fane,
The notes and auguries of coming change,
Of other ministrants in shrine and grange,—
The sweating statue, and her sacred wain
Low-booming with the prophecy of steam!

CHARLES TENNYSON-TURNER (1808–79), 1868

Goujet, meanwhile, had stopped in front of one of the rivet machines. He stood there deep in thought, hanging his head, staring. The machine was forging forty-millimetre rivets with the placid ease of a giant. And in truth nothing could have been simpler. The stoker took the piece of iron from the furnace; the hammer-man placed it in the heading frame which a stream of water kept permanently wet so the steel would remain tempered; and that was that, the screw came down and the bolt fell out with its head as round as if it had been cast in a mould. In twelve hours this infernal machine produced hundreds of kilos of them. Goujet was not at all vindictive, but there were times when he'd gladly have picked up Fifine and bashed that iron contraption to bits, out of fury because its arms were stronger than his own. It filled him with real anguish which he was unable to reason away by telling himself that human flesh couldn't fight against iron. Certainly someday the machine would be the death of the manual worker; wages had already dropped from twelve to nine francs a day, and there was talk of further cuts; in fact, they weren't at all funny, these great brutes that turned out rivets and bolts as if they were making sausages. He gazed at this one in silence for a good three minutes with his brow furrowed and his handsome golden beard bristling threateningly. Then an expression of sweetness and resignation gradually softened his features. He turned to Gervaise who was close beside him, saying with a sad smile:

'That's got us beat alright, hasn't it! But perhaps one day it'll serve to bring happiness to everybody.'

ÉMILE ZOLA (1840–1902), *L'Assommoir*, 1877, tr. Margaret Mauldon, 1995

All unintellectual labour, all monotonous, dull labour, all labour that deals with dreadful things, and involves unpleasant conditions, must be done by machinery. Machinery must work for us in coal mines, and do all sanitary services, and be the stoker of steamers, and clean the streets, and run messages on wet days, and do anything that is tedious or distressing. At present machinery competes against man. Under proper conditions machinery will serve man. There is no doubt at all that this is the future of machinery; and just as trees grow while the country gentleman is asleep, so while Humanity will be amusing itself, or enjoying cultivated leisure—which, and not labour, is the aim of man—or making beautiful things, or reading beautiful things, or simply contemplating the world with admiration and delight, machinery will be doing all the necessary and unpleasant work. The fact is, that civilisation requires slaves. The Greeks were quite right there. Unless there are slaves to do the ugly, horrible, uninteresting work, culture and contemplation become almost impossible. Human slavery is wrong, insecure, and demoralising. On mechanical slavery, on the slavery of the machine, the future of the world depends.

OSCAR WILDE (1854–1900), 'The Soul of Man under Socialism', 1891

In the nineteenth and twentieth centuries most Western countries passed legislation restricting the hours worked by employees and regulating the conditions in which their work was carried out. Mechanization and automation further reduced the hours of labour required. Even before the revolution brought by information technology, it became possible to envisage a time when very little work would be required of anyone. The problem of work would be replaced by the problem of leisure.

The desirable medium is one which mankind have not often known how to hit: when they labour, to do it with all their might, and especially with all their mind; but to devote to labour, for mere pecuniary gain, fewer hours in the day, fewer days in the year, and fewer years of life.

JOHN STUART MILL (1806–73), *The Principles of Political Economy*, 1848

The chief model . . . in which labor is likely to be made less irksome is not by a change in its character or its intrinsic attractiveness, but by a diminution in its severity. It will probably be lightened by the increasing perfection of tools and the increasing use of machinery; though on the other hand, it may be that from this cause its monotony will become no less, perhaps greater. More important is the prospect that the hours of labor are likely to be shortened, and the hours for recreation and variety correspondingly lengthened. The weariness of labor is by no means in proportion to the number of hours spent on it. For a healthy and well-nourished person, the first hours of work are not a source of fatigue. Some writers have indeed maintained that during these earlier hours—barring perhaps a brief initial period of stiffness—there is a sense of pleasure rather than of pain. This may be the case in intellectual activity, and in some handicraft occupations; and the experience is a familiar one in holiday jaunts. But little direct consciousness of pleasure comes at any stage from the stated work of the great majority of men. The difference between the earlier parts of their day and the later is not so much that the former are pleasant and the latter unpleasant, as that fatigue does not begin until some hours have passed, and then becomes increasingly severe with each of the later hours. When indeed the hours of labor are unduly prolonged, fatigue becomes so great and so deep-seated that the period of rest and sleep does not suffice to remove it. The next day begins again with fatigue, and worse succeeds worse. Such was the effect of the factory system in its early stages in England; such is still the situation in backward countries like Russia. Under these wretched conditions, the work of the day has covered eleven, twelve, even fourteen, hours. In the United States, in our own day, some of the steel-making industries, whose operations go on night and day, have had two shifts, in each of which the men worked twelve hours. To cut off one, two, three hours, from such a day's labor is to cut off a much larger proportion of the weariness of labor.

The movement for shorter hours has been one of the most beneficent aspects of the betterment of material conditions in civilized countries during the last two or three generations. The day's labor was first cut down to eleven and ten, partly from the pressure of workmen's organizations and partly from legislation restricting the hours of women and children employed in factories. It is still in process of being reduced.

F. W. TAUSSIG (1859–1940), *Principles of Economics*, 1911

When I had seen as much as I wanted to see of this imposing industrial organisation, we lingered at the outer door, three or four of us, and began discussing the mechanical and monotonous work imposed by this mass production. There was no putting back the clock, they said; and I did not remind them that we would all be putting back the clock on the following Saturday night, at the end of summer-time. There was general agreement that we are committed to these industrial methods. The only thing to do now was to keep on cutting down the hours of this monotonous employment. Which meant much more leisure, said one of them, and that meant that this leisure would have to be organised. The whole point about leisure, another objected, is that it should not be organised. A third said that most of the men working under his management did not really want more leisure and did not know what to do with themselves when some accident thrust it on them. The danger is, of course, that this robot employment will alternate with robot leisure, passive amusement as standardised and impersonal as the tasks at the machines. If within these next few years, the hours are cut down in these highly organised factories, then the people who work their five or six hours a day in them should be encouraged to be as active and individual and freely creative as possible in their spare time; though I cannot help suspecting that if that encouragement is successful and these people are active and individual and freely creative in their leisure, they will soon want to make a full-time job of being active and individual and may take it into their heads to blow up the factories. The trouble is that a man does not want to work at something he despises in order to enjoy his ample periods of leisure; he would much rather work like blazes at something that expresses him and shows his skill and resource.

J. B. PRIESTLEY (1894–1984), *English Journey*, 1934

After this, how would men spend the remainder of their time? Not probably in idleness, not all men, and the whole of their time, in the pursuit of intellectual attainments. There are many things, the fruit of human industry, which, though not to be classed among the necessaries of life, are highly conducive to our well being. The criterion of these things will appear when we have ascertained what those accommodations are which will give us real pleasure, after the insinuations of vanity and ostentation shall have been dismissed. A considerable portion of time would probably be dedicated, in an enlightened community, to the production of such accommodations. A labour of this sort is perhaps not inconsistent with the most desirable state of human existence. Laborious employment is a calamity now, because it is imperiously prescribed upon men as the condition of their existence, and because it shuts them out from a fair participation in the means of knowledge and improvement. When it shall be rendered in the strictest sense voluntary, when it shall cease to interfere with our improvement, and rather become a part of it, or at worst be converted into a source of amusement and variety, it may then be no longer a calamity, but a benefit.

WILLIAM GODWIN (1756–1836), *Political Justice*, 1793

Now for my conclusion, which you will find, I think, to become more and more startling to the imagination the longer you think about it.

I draw the conclusion that, assuming no important wars and no important increase in population, the *economic problem* may be solved, or be at least within sight of solution, within a hundred years. This means that the economic problem is not—if we look into the future—*the permanent problem of the human race.*

Why, you may ask, is this so startling? It is startling because—if, instead of looking into the future, we look into the past—we find that the economic problem, the struggle for subsistence, always has been hitherto the primary, most pressing problem of the human race—not only of the human race, but of the whole of the biological kingdom from the beginnings of life in its most primitive forms.

Thus we have been expressly evolved by nature—with all our impulses and deepest instincts—for the purpose of solving the economic problem. If the economic problem is solved, mankind will be deprived of its traditional purpose.

Will this be a benefit? If one believes at all in the real values of life, the prospect at least opens up the possibility of benefit. Yet I think with dread of the readjustment of the habits and instincts of the ordinary man, bred into him for countless generations, which he may be asked to discard within a few decades.

To use the language of today—must we not expect a general 'nervous breakdown'? We already have a little experience of what I mean—a nervous breakdown of the sort which is already common enough in England and the United States amongst the wives of the well-to-do classes, unfortunate women, many of them, who have been deprived by their wealth of their traditional tasks and occupations—who cannot find it sufficiently amusing, when deprived of the spur of economic necessity, to cook and clean and mend, yet are quite unable to find anything more amusing.

To those who sweat for their daily bread leisure is a longed-for sweet—until they get it . . .

Thus for the first time since his creation man will be faced with his real, his permanent problem—how to use his freedom from pressing economic cares, how to occupy the leisure, which science and compound interest will have won for him, to live wisely and agreeably and well.

The strenuous purposeful money-makers may carry all of us along with them into the lap of economic abundance. But it will be those peoples, who can keep alive, and cultivate into a fuller perfection, the art of life itself and do not sell themselves for the means of life, who will be able to enjoy the abundance when it comes.

Yet there is no country and no people, I think, who can look forward to the age of leisure and of abundance without a dread. For we have been trained too long to strive and not to enjoy. It is a fearful problem for the ordinary person, with no special talents, to occupy himself, especially if he no longer has roots in the soil or in custom or in the beloved conventions of a traditional society. To judge from the behaviour and the achievements of the wealthy classes today in any quarter of the world, the outlook is very depressing! For these are, so to speak, our advance guard—those who are spying out the promised land for the rest of us and pitching their camp there. For they have most of them failed disastrously, so it seems to me—those who have an independent income but no associations or duties or ties—to solve the problem which has been set them.

I feel sure that with a little more experience we shall use the new-found bounty of nature quite differently from the way in which the rich use it today, and will map out for ourselves a plan of life quite otherwise than theirs.

For many ages to come the old Adam will be so strong in us that everybody will need to do *some* work if he is to be contented. We shall do more things for ourselves than is usual with the rich today, only too glad to have small duties and tasks and routines. But beyond this, we shall endeavour to spread the bread thin on the butter—to make what work there is still to be done to be as widely shared as possible. Three-hour shifts or a fifteen-hour week may put off the problem for a great while. For three hours a day is quite enough to satisfy the old Adam in most of us!

JOHN MAYNARD KEYNES (1883–1946), 'Economic Possibilities for Our Grandchildren', 1930

Epilogue

IX. LIFE AFTER WORK

Compulsory retirement is a relatively modern invention. In 1900 nearly two thirds of the men over sixty-five in Britain were still in full employment. In the past it was usual for some of those who could afford to do so to withdraw from active work as they grew older, while others were forced into penurious retirement by incapacity or ill-health. Many continued working until they died. Only in the twentieth century has the development of state and private pension schemes made customary the practice of mandatory retirement at a fixed numerical age.

This abrupt transition from full-time work to enforced idleness has created almost as many problems as it has solved.

Lyarde is an Olde Horse

Lyarde is an olde horse and may nought wel drawe;
He shall be put into the park holyn for to gnawe.
Barefoot withouten shone there shall he go,
For he is an old horse and may no more do.
Whiles that Lyarde might drawe, the whiles was he loved,
They put him to provande, and therewith he proved.
Now he may nought do his dede as he might beforn,
They lig before him pese-straw, and beres away the corn.
They lede him to the smethy to pull off his shone
And puttes him to greenswoode, ther for to gone.
Who-so may nought do his dede, he shall to parke,
Barefoot withouten shone, and go with Lyarde.

ANON., 15th c.

Give even a dunce the employment he desires,
And he soon finds the talents it requires;
A business with an income at its heels
Furnishes always oil for its own wheels.
But in his arduous enterprise to close
His active years with indolent repose,

---

holyn] holly   *provande*] fodder   *proved*] throve

He finds the labours of that state exceed
His utmost faculties, severe indeed.
'Tis easy to resign a toilsome place,
But not to manage leisure with a grace;
Absence of occupation is not rest,
A mind quite vacant is a mind distressed.
The veteran steed, excused his task at length,
In kind compassion of his failing strength,
And turned into the park or mead to graze,
Exempt from future service all his days,
There feels a pleasure perfect in its kind,
Ranges at liberty, and snuffs the wind.
But when his lord would quit the busy road,
To taste a joy like that he has bestowed,
He proves, less happy than his favoured brute,
A life of ease a difficult pursuit.

WILLIAM COWPER (1731–1800), from 'Retirement', 1782

[John Bale, an indomitable Protestant controversialist, died in 1563, aged 68.]

To Doctor Bale

Good aged Bale,
That with thy hoary hairs
    Dost yet persist
To turn the painful book,
    O happy man
That hast obtained such years,
    And leav'st not yet
On papers pale to look,
    Give over now
To beat thy wearied brain,
    And rest thy pen
That long hath laboured sore;
    For aged men
Unfit sure is such pain,
    And thee beseems
To labour now no more.
    But thou, I think,
Don Plato's part will play,

With book in hand
To have thy dying day.

BARNABE GOOGE (1540–94), 1563

[Zachary Pearce (1690–1774), Bishop of Rochester and Dean of Westminster, entreats King George III to allow him to retire, 1763.]

He there made known his request to his Majesty, and acquainted him with the grounds of it, telling him, that he had no motive for resigning his Bishopric and Deanery from dislikes which he had to any thing in the Church or State; that being of the age before mentioned [73], he found the business belonging to those two stations too much for him, and that he was afraid, that it would still grow much more so, as he advanced in years; that he was desirous to retire for the opportunity of spending more time in his devotions and studies, and that he was in the same way of thinking with a General Officer of the Emperor Charles the Fifth, who, when he desired a dismission from that Monarch's service, and the Emperor asking the reason of it, answered, 'Sir, every wise man would, at the latter end of life, wish to have an interval between the fatigues of business and eternity.'

The Life of Dr Zachary Pearce by Himself, 1777

In all my wand'rings round this world of care,
In all my griefs—and God has giv'n my share—
I still had hopes, my latest hours to crown,
Amidst these humble bow'rs to lay me down;
To husband out life's taper at the close,
And keep the flame from wasting by repose:

OLIVER GOLDSMITH (1730–74), *The Deserted Village,* 1770

There is a certain time of life, when almost every man wishes to escape from the hurry and bustle of the world, and to taste the sweets of retirement and repose; but how few are there, who, when they have arrived at that period which they fixed for this retreat, and have put their designs in execution, meet with that enjoyment which they looked for! Instead of pleasure, they find satiety, weariness, and disgust; time becomes a heavy burden upon them, and in what way they may kill the tedious hours, grows, at length, their only object. But had these men received a good education, they would never be at a loss how to fill up their time; rich fields of entertainment would open to them from various sources. Company and conversation would receive a finer relish; books would give perpetual enjoyments; the gay prospects of the country, the romantic scenes which it affords, the adorning and beautifying those scenes, and the culture of all the elegant arts, would make that fortune, which many possess without knowing how to use, the minister of every thing that can afford delight.

I believe it may be true, that neither learning, nor a taste for the elegant arts, is requisite, to enable a person engaged in the ordinary business of life, to succeed in his profession; and, while so engaged, the occupations of that profession will prevent his feeling any vacuity or suffering any inconvenience from his ignorance, and want of refinement. But when such a person has acquired a fortune, and given up business, I have often observed, that, from this uncultivated state of mind, he is at a loss how to enjoy himself or his riches. He either becomes a prey to chagrin and *ennui*, or he gives himself up to the coarsest intemperance; or, should he wish to figure as a man of taste or fashion, he receives but little entertainment himself, and his attempts are so absurd and preposterous, as to make him the object of scoff and ridicule to others.

WILLIAM, LORD CRAIG (1745–1813), *The Mirror*, 13 May 1780

A great statesman, whom many of us remember, after having long filled a high official situation with honour and ability, began at length impatiently to look forward to the happy period when he should be exonerated from the toils of office. He pathetically lamented the incessant interruptions which distracted him, even in the intervals of public business. He repeatedly expressed to a friend of the author, how ardently he longed to be discharged from the oppressive weight of his situation, and to consecrate his remaining days to repose and literature. At length one of those revolutions in party, which so many desire, and by which so few are satisfied, transferred him to the scene of his wishes. He flew to his rural seat, but he soon found that the sources to which he had so long looked, failed in their power of conferring the promised enjoyment; his ample park yielded him no gratification but what it had yielded him in town, without the present drawback; there he had partaken of its venison, without the incumbrance of its solitude. His Hamadryads, having no despatches to present, and no votes to offer, soon grew insipid. The stillness of retreat became insupportable; and he frankly declared to the friend above alluded to, that such was to him the blank of life, that the only relief he ever felt was to hear a rap at the door. Though he had before gladly snatched the little leisure of a hurried life for reading, yet when life became all leisure, books had lost their power to interest. Study could not fill a mind long kept on the stretch by great concerns in which he himself had been a prime mover.

The history of other times could not animate a spirit habitually quickened by a strong personal interest in actual events.—There is a quality in our nature strongly indicative that we were formed for active and useful purposes.

HANNAH MORE (1745–1833), *Christian Morals*, 1813

Here
Lye the Remains of
ELIZABETH GAY
who after a Service of
Forty Years
finding her strength diminished
with unparalleled disinterestedness
Requested that her wages might
be proportionably lessened
She died July 7th 1789.
As a testimony of their Gratitude for the care she
took of them in their tender years this Stone is
Erected by the surviving Daughters of her late
Master and Mistress Christopher and Elizabeth
Warrick of Park in this Parish.

Epitaph, place unknown, in Arthur Joseph Munby, *Faithful Servants*, 1891

You know that one of my first opinions is that life has no period of rest; that external and, still more, internal exertion is as necessary in age as in youth— no, even more necessary. Man is a traveller towards a colder and colder region, and the higher his latitude, the faster ought to be his walk. *The great malady of the soul is cold.* In order to combat this formidable evil, it is necessary not only to keep one's mind active through work, but through contact with other men and with the affairs of this world. It is especially at this age that one cannot survive on what one has already learned but must attempt to learn more.

ALEXIS DE TOCQUEVILLE (1805–59), letter to Louis de Kergurlay, 3 Feb. 1857, tr. Larry Siedentop, 1994

[The narrator has fallen asleep in 1887 and wakes up in the year 2000.]

That evening I sat up for some time after the ladies had retired, talking with Dr Leete about the effect of the plan of exempting men from further service to the nation after the age of forty-five, a point brought up by his account of the part taken by the retired citizens in the government.

'At forty-five,' said I, 'a man still has ten years of good manual labour in him, and twice ten years of good intellectual service. To be superannuated at that age and laid on the shelf must be regarded rather as a hardship than a favour by men of energetic dispositions.'

'My dear Mr West,' exclaimed Dr Leete, beaming upon me. 'You cannot have any idea of the piquancy your nineteenth century ideas have for us of this day, the rare quaintness of their effect. Know, oh child of another race and yet the same, that the labour we have to render as our part in securing for the nation the means of a comfortable physical existence, is by no means regarded as the most important, the most interesting, or the most dignified employment of our powers. We look upon it as a necessary duty to be discharged before we can fully devote ourselves to the higher exercise of our faculties, the intellectual and spiritual employment and pursuits which alone mean life. Everything possible is indeed done by the just distribution of burdens, and by all manner of special attractions and incentives to relieve our labour of irksomeness, and, except in a comparative sense, it is not usually irksome, and is often inspiring. But it is not our labour, but the higher and larger activities which the performance of our task will leave us free to enter upon, that are considered the main business of existence.

'Of course not all, nor the majority, have those scientific, artistic, literary, or scholarly interests which make leisure the one thing valuable to their possessors. Many look upon the last half of life chiefly as a period for enjoyment of other sorts; for travel, for social relaxation in the company of their lifetime friends; a time for the cultivation of all manners of personal idiosyncracies and special tastes, and the pursuit of every imaginable form of recreation; in a word a time for the leisurely and unperturbed appreciations of the good things of the world which they have helped to create. But whatever the differences between our individual tastes as to the use we shall put our leisure to, we all agree in looking forward to the date of our discharge as the time when we shall first enter upon the full enjoyment of our birthright, the period when we shall first really attain our majority and become enfranchised from discipline and control, with the fee of our lives vested in ourselves. As eager boys in your day anticipated twenty-one, so men nowadays look forward to forty-five. At twenty-one we become men, but at forty-five we renew youth. Middle age, and what you would have called old age, are considered, rather than youth, the enviable time of life. Thanks to the better conditions of existence nowadays, and above all the freedom of every one from care, old age approaches many years later and has an aspect far more benign than in past times. Persons of average constitutions usually live to eighty-five or ninety, and at forty-five we are physically and mentally younger, I fancy, than you were at thirty-five. It is a strange reflection that at forty-five, when we are just entering upon the most enjoyable period of life, you already began to think of growing old and to look backward. With you it was the forenoon, but with us it is the afternoon which is the brighter half of life.'

EDWARD BELLAMY (1850–98), *Looking Backward: 2000–1887*, 1888

Mr Craigan had gone to work when he was nine and every day he had worked through most of daylight till now, when he was going to get old age pension. So you will hear men who have worked like this talk of monotony of their lives, but when they grow to be old they are more glad to have work and this monotony has grown so great that they have forgotten it. Like on a train which goes through night smoothly and at an even pace—so monotony of noise made by the wheels bumping over joints between the rails becomes rhythm—so this monotony of hours grows to be the habit and regulation on which we grow old. And as women who have had nits in their hair over a long period collapse when these are killed, feeling so badly removal of that violent irritation which has become stimulus for them, so when men who have worked these regular hours are now deprived of work, so, often, their lives come to be like puddles on the beach where tide no longer reaches.

HENRY GREEN (1905–73), *Living*, 1929

Ages of compulsory retirement are fixed at points varying from 55 to 75, all being equally arbitrary and unscientific. Whatever age has been decreed by accident and custom can be defended by the same argument. Where the retirement age is fixed at 65 the defenders of this system will always have found, by experience, that the mental powers and energy show signs of flagging at the age of 62. This would be a most useful conclusion to have reached had not a different phenomenon been observed in organizations where the age of retirement has been fixed at 60. There, we are told, people are found to lose their grip, in some degree, at the age of 57. As against that, men whose retiring age is 55 are known to be past their best at 52. It would seem, in short, that efficiency declines at the age of R minus 3, irrespective of the age at which R has been fixed.

C. NORTHCOTE PARKINSON (1909–93), *Parkinson's Law, or the Pursuit of Progress*, 1958

Going out to work is much easier than staying at home. Your life is far more clearly defined and you're not so much at everyone's beck and call. Here everyone says, 'Oh she's not working, she can do such and such.' Particularly it's my husband's attitude: if things went wrong and you were working it was excusable, but if you weren't he just couldn't understand that not having a job can be as much of a strain and as tiring as a full-time job.

MRS BRUCE, a retired woman, quoted in Michael Young and Tom Schuller, *Life after Work*, 1991

'There's a last time for everything.'
    It was not his habit to talk to himself, he was rounding up and tidying away a sickness of heart, some universal heart of the matter. He hoped his own feelings had not become distorted, this was supposed to be a happy occasion.

This, he remembered, putting his key into the lock, was a moment people cherished. He himself was marking the occasion with thought, certainly he did not feel one way or the other.

The habit of a lifetime was about to be broken. He could say so, but the habit would not break now, nor tomorrow, nor next week. It would scarcely break at all, it would wither and starve and hang on in shreds. The human spirit being what it was, he must from time to time expect to find himself ready to go through the hoops.

Trying, he thought, that will be very trying. He would have preferred a clean finish on the other side of the door mat. From then on he might say he was his own master, he was free—which he had never been before. Before, it was all to do, he owed a living. Now he was paid up and the living was his own. What was left of it.

The time of day prompted that last thought, he was tired, therefore he was inclined to pessimism. When the daylight ran out it took a long wick of youth to burn up against the dark.

He wiped his feet on the mat. As far as he was concerned it was finished and if any of it went on it must be regarded as reflex action, a nervous twitch. The sickness was not in his heart.

Habit suffered its first fracture: he did not hang up his bowler and his umbrella, he lifted the lid of the hall chest and laid them away. He then took out an old grey felt and put it on the peg which his City hat had always occupied.

Charlotte, coming from the kitchen, saw the grey felt and her prepared face, not prepared for that, pursed, then brightened defensively. 'Oh, it's you,' she said, thus making her distinction because it would hardly be anyone else and because she always at this time said, 'Hallo, dear.' 'Hallo, dear,' at five past seven, for going on forty years, with one break—one small break it seemed now—of the war years. She looked at him—with pride, was it, compunction, or disquiet?—before she reached up to kiss his cheek bone. 'I thought you would be later.'

'Why?' He knew, but sensed more preparation, a going-gently, against possible disappointment, snub, hurt, or even something enough to corrode and undermine the forty years. 'We did have a bit of a gathering. Colonel Rayburn is off to the States tonight so it had to be early.'

'Why, that was nice!' She sounded relieved.

'One or two people came in to say goodbye.' At five o'clock, when they all had the week's work to wind up and leave ready coiled for Monday, cutting out of the legitimate day an aimless and uncomfortable hour of holding glasses, cigarettes and sweet French biscuits and trying not to catch, let alone hold, anyone's glance. 'Sherry doesn't agree with me.'

'And Colonel Rayburn was there—and Langley? Did Langley come?'

'And Cyril Ford and Miss Endicott.'

'Even Miss Endicott!'

'Cody's office took it in turns to go down and man the phone.'

'Then it was quite a party, quite a send-off?'

'I'm not going anywhere,' he said, 'unless you count Edensea.' He unstrapped his wrist-watch, as always, to lay aside on his dressing-table when he changed into his house jacket. 'They gave me a clock.'

'A clock?'

'With an inscription. As far as I can remember it reads: "Presented to John Henry Agar by his friends and colleagues on the occasion of his retirement from the Solomon Rayburn Company"!'

'But how nice of them!'

'Eight-day Westminster chime, walnut case, Arabic gold figures, a dignified and reliable piece,' he said, winding his watch. 'They should have given it to me forty years ago, I had more need of time then.'

'Where is it?' Charlotte peered round his shoulder. 'Where's the clock?'

'Cody's bringing it tomorrow in his car. I didn't want it chiming on the Underground.'

'It was a nice gesture, but no more than you deserve.'

She was being too careful, as if he had suffered a bereavement. 'There's a last time for everything,' he said, 'only we don't always know when it's come.'

Charlotte had always known what to do with her hands, she fastened them warmly round his wrists. 'You'll feel it at first, of course. You're bound to. But that will pass—'

'I don't feel it. Why should I? I've done my job, I organised and ran an efficient department and now it's all theirs.' He did not say, as he thought, that now it would go to pieces. 'I'm an old man. I ceased to be useful at 5.30 this p.m.' Watching her face disarrange and crumple, he thought so here was the sickness in her heart, being nursed and softly handled because she thought it must be in his. 'If they were honest they would have told me so at 5.31 instead of pretending it was the end of an era.'

A. L. Barker (1918–   ), 'A Question of Identity', 1964

The organisation where Letty and Marcia worked regarded it as a duty to provide some kind of a retirement party for them, when the time came for them to give up working. Their status as ageing unskilled women did not entitle them to an evening party, but it was felt that a lunchtime gathering, leading only to more than usual drowsiness in the afternoon, would be entirely appropriate. The other advantage of a lunchtime party was that only medium Cyprus sherry need be provided, whereas the evening called for more exotic and expensive drinks, wines and even the occasional carefully concealed bottle of whisky or gin—'the hard stuff', as Norman called it, in his bitterness at being denied access to it. Also at lunchtime sandwiches could be eaten, so that there was no need to have lunch and it was felt by some that at a time like this it was 'better' to be eating—it gave one something to do.

Retirement was a serious business, to be regarded with respect, though the idea of it was incomprehensible to most of the staff. It was a condition that must be studied and prepared for, certainly—'researched' they would have said—indeed it had already been the subject of a seminar, though the conclusions reached and the recommendations drawn up had no real bearing on the retirement of Letty and Marcia, which seemed as inevitable as the falling of the leaves in autumn, for which no kind of preparation needed to be made. If the two women feared that the coming of this date might give some clue to their ages, it was not an occasion for embarrassment because nobody else had been in the least interested, both of them having long ago reached ages beyond any kind of speculation. Each would be given a small golden handshake, but the State would provide for their basic needs which could not be all that great. Elderly women did not need much to eat, warmth was more necessary than food, and people like Letty and Marcia probably had either private means or savings, a nest-egg in the Post Office or a Building Society. It was comforting to think on these lines, and even if they had nothing extra, the social services were so much better now, there was no need for anyone to starve or freeze. And if governments failed in their duty there were always the media—continual goadings on television programmes, upsetting articles in the Sunday papers and disturbing pictures in the colour supplements. There was no need to worry about Miss Crowe and Miss Ivory.

The (acting) deputy assistant director, who had been commanded to make the presentation speech, wasn't quite sure what it was that Miss Crowe and Miss Ivory did or had done during their working life. The activities of their department seemed to be shrouded in mystery—something to do with records or filing, it was thought, nobody knew for certain, but it was evidently 'women's work', the kind of thing that could easily be replaced by a computer. The most significant thing about it was that nobody was replacing them, indeed the whole department was being phased out and only being kept on until the men working in it reached retirement age. Yet under the influence of a quick swig of sherry, even this unpromising material could be used to good effect.

The deputy assistant director stepped into the middle of the room and began to speak.

'The point about Miss Crowe and Miss Ivory, whom we are met together to honour today, is that nobody knows exactly, or has ever known exactly, what it is that they do,' he declared boldly. 'They have been—they *are*—the kind of people who work quietly and secretly, doing good by stealth, as it were. *Good*, do I hear you ask? Yes, good, I repeat, and good I mean. In these days of industrial unrest it is people like Miss Ivory and Miss Crowe'—the names seemed to have got reversed, but presumably it didn't matter—'who are an example to us all. We shall miss them very much, so much so that nobody has been found to replace them, but we would be the last to deny them the rewards of a well earned retirement. It gives me much pleasure on behalf of the company and staff to present each of these ladies with a small token of our appreciation of their long and devoted service, which carries with it our best wishes for their future.'

Letty and Marcia then came forward, each to receive an envelope containing a cheque and a suitably inscribed card, the presenter remembered a luncheon engagement and slipped away, glasses were refilled and a buzz of talk broke out. Conversation had to be made and it did not come very easily once the obvious topics had been exhausted.

BARBARA PYM (1913–80), *Quartet in Autumn*, 1977

Epitaph for a Tired Housewife

Here lies a poor woman who was always tired,
She lived in a house where help wasn't hired:
Her last words on earth were: 'Dear friends, I am going
To where there's no cooking, or washing, or sewing,
For everything there is exact to my wishes,
For where they don't eat there's no washing of dishes.
I'll be where loud anthems will always be ringing,
But having no voice I'll be quit of the singing.
Don't mourn for me now, don't mourn for me never,
I am going to do nothing for ever and ever.'

ANON.

On the evening of the 12th of April, just as I was about quitting my desk to go home (it might be about eight o'clock), I received an awful summons to attend the presence of the whole assembled firm in the formidable back parlour. I thought, now my time is surely come, I have done for myself, I am going to be told that they have no longer occasion for me. L——, I could see, smiled at the terror I was in, which was a little relief to me,—when to my utter astonishment B——, the eldest partner, began a formal harangue to me on the length of my services, my very meritorious conduct during the whole of the time (the deuce, thought I, how did he find out that? I protest I never had the confidence to think as much). He went on to descant on the expediency of retiring at a certain time of life (how my heart panted!), and asking me a few questions as to the amount of my own property, of which I have a little, ended with a proposal, to which his three partners nodded a grave assent, that

I should accept from the house, which I had served so well, a pension for life to the amount of two-thirds of my accustomed salary—a magnificent offer! I do not know what I answered between surprise and gratitude, but it was understood that I accepted their proposal, and I was told that I was free from that hour to leave their service. I stammered out a bow, and at just ten minutes after eight I went home—for ever. This noble benefit—gratitude forbids me to conceal their names—I owe to the kindness of the most munificent firm in the world—the house of Boldero, Merryweather, Bosanquet and Lacy.

Esto perpetua!

For the first day or two I felt stunned, overwhelmed. I could only apprehend my felicity; I was too confused to taste it sincerely. I wandered about, thinking I was happy, and knowing that I was not. I was in the condition of a prisoner in the old Bastile, suddenly let loose after a forty years' confinement. I could scarce trust myself with myself. It was like passing out of Time into Eternity—for it is a sort of Eternity for a man to have his Time all to himself. It seemed to me that I had more time on my hands than I could ever manage. From a poor man, poor in Time, I was suddenly lifted up into a vast revenue; I could see no end of my possessions; I wanted some steward, or judicious bailiff, to manage my estates in Time for me. And here let me caution persons grown old in active business, not lightly, nor without weighing their own resources, to forego their customary employment all at once, for there may be danger in it. I feel it by myself, but I know that my resources are sufficient; and now that those first giddy raptures have subsided, I have a quiet home-feeling of the blessedness of my condition. I am in no hurry. Having all holidays, I am as though I had none. If Time hung heavy upon me, I could walk it away; but I do *not* walk all day long, as I used to do in those old transient holidays, thirty miles a day, to make the most of them. If Time were troublesome, I could read it away; but I do *not* read in that violent measure, with which, having no Time my own but candle-light Time, I used to weary out my head and eyesight in by-gone winters. I walk, read, or scribble (as now) just when the fit seizes me. I no longer hunt after pleasure; I let it come to me. I am like the man

——that's born, and has his years come to him
In some green desart.

'Years!' you will say! 'what is this superannuated simpleton calculating upon? He has already told us, he is past fifty.'

I have indeed lived nominally fifty years, but deduct out of them the hours which I have lived to other people, and not to myself, and you will find me still a young fellow. For *that* is the only true Time, which a man can properly call his own, that which he has all to himself; the rest, though in some sense he may be said to live it, is other people's time, not his. The remnant of my poor days, long or short, is at least multiplied for me three-fold. My ten next years, if I stretch so far, will be as long as any preceding thirty. 'Tis a fair rule-of-three sum.

Among the strange fantasies which beset me at the commencement of my freedom, and of which all traces are not yet gone, one was, that a vast tract of time had intervened since I quitted the Counting House. I could not conceive of it as an affair of yesterday. The partners, and the clerks, with whom I had for so many years, and for so many hours in each day of the year, been closely associated—being suddenly removed from them—they seemed as dead to me. There is a fine passage, which may serve to illustrate this fancy, in a Tragedy by Sir Robert Howard, speaking of a friend's death:

> ——'Twas but just now he went away;
> I have not since had time to shed a tear;
> And yet the distance does the same appear
> As if he had been a thousand years from me.
> Time takes no measure in Eternity.

To dissipate this awkward feeling, I have been fain to go among them once or twice since; to visit my old desk-fellows—my co-brethren of the quill—that I had left below in the state militant. Not all the kindness with which they received me could quite restore to me that pleasant familiarity, which I had heretofore enjoyed among them. We cracked some of our old jokes, but methought they went off but faintly. My old desk; the peg where I hung my hat, were appropriated to another. I knew it must be, but I could not take it kindly. D——l take me, if I did not feel some remorse—beast, if I had not,— at quitting my old compeers, the faithful partners of my toils for six-and-thirty years, that smoothed for me with their jokes and conundrums the ruggedness of my professional road. Had it been so rugged, then, after all? or was I a coward simply? Well, it is too late to repent; and I also know, that these suggestions are a common fallacy of the mind on such occasions. But my heart smote me. I had violently broken the bands betwixt us. It was at least not courteous. I shall be some time before I get quite reconciled to the separation. Farewell, old cronies, yet not for long, for again and again I will come among ye, if I shall have your leave. Farewell, Ch——, dry, sarcastic, and friendly!— Do——, mild, slow to move, and gentlemanly! Pl——, officious to do, and to volunteer, good services!—and thou, thou dreary pile, fit mansion for a Gresham or a Whittington of old, stately House of Merchants; with thy labyrinthine passages, and light-excluding, pent-up offices, where candles for one half the year supplied the place of the sun's light; unhealthy contributor to my weal, stern fosterer of my living, farewell! In thee remain, and not in the obscure collection of some wandering bookseller, my 'works!' There let them rest, as I do from my labours, piled on thy massy shelves, more MSS. in folio than ever Aquinas left, and full as useful! My mantle I bequeath among ye.

A fortnight has passed since the date of my first communication. At that period I was approaching to tranquillity, but had not reached it. I boasted of a calm indeed, but it was comparative only. Something of the first flutter was left; an unsettling sense of novelty; the dazzle to weak eyes of unaccustomed light. I missed my old chains, forsooth, as if they had been some necessary part of my apparel. I was a poor Carthusian, from strict cellular discipline suddenly by some revolution returned upon the world. I am now as if I had never been other than my own master. It is natural to me to go where I please, to do what I please. I find myself at eleven o'clock in the day in Bond street, and it seems to me that I have been sauntering there at that very hour for years past. I digress into Soho, to explore a book-stall. Methinks I have been thirty years a collector. There is nothing strange nor new in it. I find myself before a fine picture in the morning. Was it ever otherwise? What is become of Fish-street Hill? Where is Fenchurch-street? Stones of old Mincing-lane, which I have worn with my daily pilgrimage for six-and-thirty years, to the footsteps of what toil-worn clerk are your everlasting flints now vocal? I indent the gayer flags of Pall Mall. It is 'Change time, and I am strangely among the Elgin marbles. It was no hyperbole when I ventured to compare the change in my condition to a passing into another world. Time stands still in a manner to me. I have lost all distinction of season. I do not know the day of the week, or of the month. Each day used to be individually felt by me in its reference to the foreign post days; in its distance from, or propinquity to, the next Sunday. I had my Wednesday feelings, my Saturday nights' sensations. The genius of each day was upon me distinctly during the whole of it, affecting my appetite, spirits, &c. The phantom of the next day, with the dreary five to follow, sate as a load upon my poor Sabbath recreations. What charm has washed that Ethiop white? What is gone of Black Monday? All days are the same. Sunday itself—that unfortunate failure of a holyday, as it too often proved, what with my sense of its fugitiveness, of it—is melted down into a week-day. I can spare to go to church now, without grudging the huge cantle which it used to seem to cut out of the holyday. I have Time for everything. I can visit a sick friend. I can interrupt the man of much occupation when he is busiest. I can insult over him with an invitation to take a day's pleasure with me to Windsor this fine May-morning. It is Lucretian pleasure to behold the poor drudges, whom I have left behind in the world, carking and caring; like horses in a mill, drudging on in the same eternal round—and what is it all for? A man can never have too much Time to himself, nor too little to do. Had I a little son, I would christen him NOTHING-TO-DO; he should do nothing. Man, I verily believe, is out of his element as long as he is operative. I am altogether for the life contemplative. Will no kindly earthquake come and swallow up those accursed cotton mills? Take me that lumber of a desk there, and bowl it down

As low as to the fiends.

I am no longer * * * * * *, clerk to the Firm of, &c. I am Retired Leisure. I am to be met with in trim gardens. I am already come to be known by my vacant face and careless gesture, perambulating at no fixed pace, nor with any settled purpose. I walk about: not to and from. They tell me, a certain *cum dignitate* air, that has been buried so long with my other good parts, has begun to shoot forth in my person. I grow into gentility perceptibly. When I take up a newspaper, it is to read the state of the opera. *Opus operatum est.* I have done all that I came into this world to do. I have worked task work, and have the rest of the day to myself.

CHARLES LAMB (1775–1834), 'The Superannuated Man', 1825

It's not too bad, but I rather miss the vacations.

Oxford don, on being asked how he was enjoying his retirement

Acknowledgements

The editor and publisher gratefully acknowledge permission to include the following copyright material:

Extracts from the *Authorized Version of the Bible* (*The King James Bible*), the rights of which are vested in the Crown, are reproduced by permission of the Crown's Patentee, Cambridge University Press.

Claude Colleer Abbott, 'Hedgers' and 'Harvest-End' from *Collected Poems* (Sidgwick & Jackson, 1963), copyright holder not traced.

Aelfric, 'Colloquy' translated by Kevin Crossley-Holland in *The Anglo-Saxon World* (Boydell & Brewer, 1982), copyright © 1982 Kevin Crossley-Holland, by permission of Rogers Coleridge & White Ltd. 20 Powis Mews, London W11 1JN.

Aristotle, from *Politics*, translated by Ernest Barker, revised by R. F. Stalley (Oxford World's Classics, 1995), by permission of Oxford University Press.

Kenneth H. Ashley, 'Out of Work' from *Up Hill and Down Dale* (Bodley Head, 1924), by permission of Random House UK Ltd.

W. H. Auden, 'The Managers', copyright © 1955 by W. H. Auden, and lines from 'Horae Canonicae, 3. Sext', copyright © 1949 by W. H. Auden, both from *Collected Poems* (Faber, 1961, 1966), by permission of the publishers, Faber & Faber Ltd., and Random House, Inc.

Enid Bagnold, from a broadcast interview, 1953, by permission of the Comtesse Laurian d'Harcourt.

A. L. Barker, from 'A Question of Identity' in *Lost Upon the Roundabouts* (Hogarth Press, 1964), by permission of MBA Literary Agents on behalf of the author.

Charles Baudelaire, from *Selected Writings on Art and Artists* translated by P. E. Charvet (1981), by permission of the publishers, Cambridge University Press.

Hilaire Belloc, lines from 'Peter Goole, Who Ruined His Father and Mother by Extravagance' from *New Cautionary Tales* (Duckworth, 1930); and from 'The mowing of a field' in *Hills and the Sea* (Methuen, 1906), © as printed in the original volumes, by permission of The Peters Fraser & Dunlop Group Limited on behalf of The Estate of Hilaire Belloc.

Saint Benedict, from *Rule for Monks* translated by Justin McCann (Sheed & Ward, 1970), by permission of the publishers.

Lord Benson, quoted in Cathy Courtney and Paul Thompson, *City Lives* (Methuen, National Life Story Collection, 1996).

Francis Berry, 'Closed Works' from *Morant Bay and Other Poems* (Routledge & Kegan Paul, 1961), by permission of the publisher.

Sir John Betjeman, 'Executive' and 'Caprice' from *The Collected Poems*, by permission of John Murray (Publishers) Ltd.

Edmund Blunden, 'The Waggoner' and 'Mole Catcher' from *The Poems of Edmund Blunden* (Cobden-Sanderson, 1980), © as printed in the original volume, by permission of The Peters Fraser & Dunlop Group Limited.

James Boswell, from *The Life of Samuel Johnson* edited by G. B. Hill and L. F. Powell, (OUP, 1934), by permission of Oxford University Press.

Nicole Bozon, from *Metaphors of Brother Bozon* translated by John Rose (Constable & Co, 1913), copyright holder not traced.

Fernand Braudel, from *Hommage à Lucien Febvre* (Armand Colin Editeur, Paris, 1953), this translation by Keith Thomas.

Bertolt Brecht, 'Moscow Workers' translated by Edith Anderson, and 'Questions from a Worker who reads' translated by Michael Hamburger from J. Willett and R. Manheim (eds.), *Poems* (1976), by permission of Methuen Publishing Ltd.

Basil Bunting, 'What the Chairman Told Tom' from *The Complete Poems* edited by Richard Caddel (OUP, 1994), by permission of Oxford University Press.

Mrs Burrows, quoted in Margaret Llewelyn-Davies (ed.), 'A Childhood in the Fens about 1850–60' from *Life as We Have Known It* (Hogarth 1931), copyright holder not traced.

Geoffrey Chaucer, from 'The General Prologue' to *The Canterbury Tales* translated by David Wright (Oxford World's Classics, OUP, 1985), by permission of The Peters Fraser & Dunlop Group Limited.

Anton Chekhov, from *The Three Sisters* translated by Ronald Hingley in *Five Plays* (Oxford World's Classics, 1980), by permission of Oxford University Press.

Chrétien de Troyes, from *Yvain: The Knight of the Lion* translated by Burton Raffel (New Haven, 1987), by permission of Yale University Press.

Winston S. Churchill, from a letter to his son Randolph Churchill, in *His Father's Son: The Life of Randolph Churchill* (Weidenfeld & Nicolson, 1996), Copyright © Winston S. Churchill, by permission of Curtis Brown Ltd., London, on behalf of the Estate of Winston S. Churchill.

Marcus Tullius Cicero, from *Philosophical Treatises,* vol. xviii, translated by J. E. King (Harvard University Press, 1945), by permission of the publishers and the Loeb Classical Library.

John Clare, from Eric Robinson (ed.), *John Clare's Autobiographical Writings* (OUP, 1983); 'Farmer's Boy' from Eric Robinson and David Powell (eds.), *John Clare: The Oxford Authors* (OUP, 1984); 'The Foddering Boy' and lines from 'The Woodman' from Eric Robinson and David Powell (eds.), *The Early Poems of John Clare* (OUP, 1989); and lines from 'The Shepherd's Calendar' from Eric Robinson, David Powell, and Paul Dawson (eds.), *John Clare: Poems of the Middle Period 1822–1837* (OUP, 1996); Copyright © Eric Robinson 1983, 1984, 1989, 1996, by permission of Curtis Brown Ltd., London, on behalf of Eric Robinson.

Leonard Clark, 'Bell Ringer', first published in Maurice Wollman (ed.), *Seven Themes in Modern Verse* (Harrap, 1968). By permission of Robert Clark, the literary executor of Leonard Clark.

Richard Cobb, from *Still Life* (Hogarth Press, 1992), by permission of Random House UK Ltd.

Tony Connor, 'Elegy for Alfred Hubbard' from *New and Selected Poems* (Anvil Press Poetry, 1982), by permission of the publishers.

Joseph Conrad, from Frederick R. Karl and Laurence Davis (eds.), *The Collected Letters of Joseph Conrad,* ii (1986), by permission of the publishers, Cambridge University Press.

Joe Corrie, 'A Worker to His Machine' from *Rebel Poems* (1932), by permission of Morag Corrie.

Hannah Cullwick, from *The Diaries of Hannah Cullwick* edited by Liz Stanley (Virago, 1984), by permission of the publishers; also from *Diaries*, a MS held at Trinity College, Cambridge.

H. E. Dale, from *The Higher Civil Service of Great Britain* (OUP, 1941), by permission of Oxford University Press.

R. T. Davies, lines from his translation of 'Smoke-blackened smiths' from R. T. Davies (ed.), *Medieval English Lyrics* (Faber, 1963), by permission of the publishers, Faber & Faber Ltd.

Simone de Beauvoir, from *The Second Sex* translated by H. M. Parshley (Jonathan Cape, 1953), by permission of Random House UK Ltd.

Diodorus Siculus, from *The Library of History* translated by C. H. Oldfather (Harvard University Press, 1939), by permission of the publishers and the Loeb Classical Library.

Clifford Dyment, 'The Carpenter' from *Experiences and Places* (J. M. Dent, 1955), by permission of Classic Presentations Ltd. (Martin Starkie), on behalf of Irene Dyment.

Ifan Edwards, from *No Gold on My Shovel* (Porcupine Press, 1947), copyright holder not traced.

Egyptian texts, from Egyptian school book, 'Papyrus Lansing', in volume i and from 'The Satire of the Trades' in volume ii of *Ancient Egyptian Literature*, 3 volumes, translated by Miriam Lichtheim (University of California Press, 1976), copyright © 1973–1980 the Regents of the University of California, by permission of University of California Press.

Albert Einstein, from *Autobiographical Notes* translated by Paul Arthur Schlipp in *Albert Einstein: Philosopher Scientist* (Library of Living Philosophers, 1949), by permission of the Albert Einstein Archives, The Jewish National and University Library, The Hebrew University of Jerusalem, Israel.

T. S. Eliot, lines from 'The Waste Land' from *Collected Poems* (1963), by permission of the publishers, Faber & Faber Ltd.

H. F. Ellis, 'Advice to Men in Aprons' first published in *Punch*, 13 February 1946, by permission of the author.

Aleksandr Nikolaevich Engelhardt, from *Letters from the Country* translated by Cathy Frierson (OUP, 1993), translation copyright © 1993 by Oxford University Press, Inc., by permission of Oxford University Press, Inc.

Gavin Ewart, 'Office Friendships' from *The Collected Ewart* (Hutchinson, 1980), by permission of Mrs Margot Ewart.

Nissim Ezekiel, 'The Railway Clerk' from *Collected Poems* (OUP, Delhi, 1989), by permission of Oxford University Press, India.

Geoffrey Faber, from *Jowett* (1957), by permission of the publishers, Faber & Faber Ltd.

U. A. Fanthorpe, 'You will be hearing from us shortly' from *Standing To* (Peterloo, 1982), and 'Washing-up' from *A Watching Brief* (Peterloo, 1987), by permission of the publishers.

Blessed Simone Fidati, from *Rich and Poor in Christian Thought* translated by Walter Shewring, by permission of Burns & Oates Ltd.

A. J. Finberg, from *The Life of J. M. W. Turner* (OUP, 1939), by permission of Oxford University Press.

F. Scott Fitzgerald, from *The Last Tycoon* (Penguin, 1960), by permission of Simon & Schuster Inc.

Gustave Flaubert, from *The Letters of Gustave Flaubert 1830–1857*, selected, edited, and translated by Francis Steegmuller (Harvard University Press, 1980), Copyright © 1979 by the President and Fellows of Harvard College, by permission of the publisher.

Robin Flower, 'Pangur Bán', translated from the Gaelic, from *Poems and Translations* (The Lilliput Press, Dublin, 1995), by permission of the publishers.

Henry Ford [in collaboration with Samuel Crowther], from *My Life and Work* (Wm. Heinemann, 1922), copyright holder not traced.

François Marie Charles Fourier, from *The Utopian Vision of Charles Fourier* edited and translated by J. Beecher and R. Bienvenu (Cape, 1972), copyright © 1972 by Beecher and Bienvenu, by permission of Random House UK Ltd. and Beacon Press, Boston.

Anne Frank, from *The Diary of a Young Girl* original translation by B. M. Mooyaart-Doubledoay (Vallentine, Mitchell & Co., 1952), by permission of the Anne Frank Fonds, Basle.

Maureen Freely, from *What about Us? An Open Letter to the Mothers Feminism Forgot* (Bloomsbury, 1995).

Sigmund Freud, from *Civilization and its Discontents* translated by Joan Riviere (Hogarth, 1957), from *The Standard Edition of the Complete Psychological Works of Sigmund Freud* translated and edited by James Strachey, translation copyright © 1961 by James Strachey, renewed 1989 by Alix Strachey, by permission of the publishers, The Hogarth Press, Random House UK Ltd. and W. W. Norton & Company, Inc., Sigmund Freud Copyrights, and The Institute of Psycho-Analysis.

Robert Frost, 'Line-Gang' and 'After Apple-picking' from *The Poetry of Robert Frost* edited by Edward Connery Lathem (Jonathan Cape/Henry Holt), Copyright 1942, 1944, 1951, © 1962 by Robert Frost, © 1970 by Lesley Frost Ballantine, Copyright 1916, 1923, 1934, © 1969 by Henry Holt and Company, Inc., by permission of Henry Holt and Company, Inc. and Random House UK Ltd. on behalf of the Estate of Robert Frost.

John Fuller, 'Alex at the Barber's' from *Fairground Music* (Chatto & Windus, 1961), by permission of the author.

John Kenneth Galbraith, from *The Affluent Society* (Hamish Hamilton, 1958), by permission of Penguin Books Ltd.

Ernest Gambier-Parry, from *The Spirit of the Old Folk* (Smith, Elder, 1913), copyright holder not traced.

Jonathan Gathorne-Hardy, from *The Office* (Hodder & Stoughton, 1970), Copyright © Jonathan Gathorne-Hardy 1970, by permission of Curtis Brown Ltd., London, on behalf of the author.

Wilfrid Gibson, 'The Plough' and 'The Release' from *Collected Poems* (Macmillan, 1926), by permission of the publisher.

Ralph Glasser, from *Gorbals Boy in Oxford* (Chatto & Windus, 1988), by permission of David Higham Associates.

Richard Gordon, from *Doctor in the House* (Michael Joseph 1952), Copyright © Richard Gordon 1952, by permission of Curtis Brown Ltd., London, on behalf of the author.

Maxim Gorky, from *My Universities* translated by Ronald Wilks (Penguin, 1979), by permission of Penguin Books Ltd.

Robert Graves, from *Goodbye to All That* (Cape, 1929), by permission of A. P. Watt Ltd. on behalf of The Trustees of the Robert Graves Copyright Trust.

Henry Green, from *Living* (first published in Great Britain by The Hogarth Press, 1929 and by Harvill, 1991), by permission of The Harvill Press.

Walter Greenwood, from *Love on the Dole* (Jonathan Cape, 1933), by permission of Random House UK Ltd.

Thom Gunn, 'Waitress' from *Passages of Joy* (1982), and 'Round and Round' from *Fighting Terms* (1954), by permission of the publishers, Faber & Faber Ltd.

Learned Hand, from 'The Preservation of Personality' in *The Spirit of Liberty: Essays and Addresses* edited by I. Dilliard (Alfred Knopf, 1954), by permission of the publisher.

Heinrich Heine, 'The Silesian Weavers' from *Poems*, translated by Hal Draper (OUP, 1982), by permission of Oxford University Press.

Zbigniew Herbert, 'Report from Paradise' from *Selected Poems* translated by Peter Dale Scott (Penguin, 1968), by permission of Penguin Books Ltd.

Herodotus, from *The Histories* translated by H. Carter (Oxford, 1958) by permission of Oxford University Press.

Hesiod, from *Works and Days* translated and edited by M. L. West (Oxford World's Classics, 1988), by permission of Oxford University Press.

Thomas Hobbes, from *Man and Citizen* (*De Homine*) translated by C. T. Wood, T. S. K. Scott-Craig, and Bernard Gert (Doubleday Anchor, 1972).

Homer, from *The Iliad* translated by Martin Hammond (Penguin, 1987), by permission of Penguin Books Ltd.

Frances Horner, from *Time Remembered* (Heinemann, 1923), copyright holder not traced.

A. E. Housman, from *The Name and Nature of Poetry* (Cambridge, 1933), by permission of the Society of Authors as the Literary Representative of the Estate of A. E. Housman.

Aldous Huxley, from 'The Dangers of Work' first published in *Vogue*, April 1924, by permission of the Reece Halsey Agency.

Christopher Isherwood, 'Dreams of a Kitchen-Maid' translated from Bertolt Brecht, *Dreigroschenroman* (*The Threepenny Novel*), Copyright © the Estate of Christopher Isherwood by permission of Curtis Brown Ltd., London, on behalf of the Estate of Christopher Isherwood.

K. Ishwaran: from *Shivapur: A South Indian Village* (Routledge & Kegan Paul, 1968), by permission of the publisher.

Bruce Jackson (ed.), *Wake-up Dead Man: Afro-American Worksongs from Texas Prisons* (Harvard, 1972), from interview with anonymous Texas prisoner by permission of Bruce Jackson.

Geoffrey Johnson, from 'Hobbs' in Maurice Wollman (ed.), *Seven Themes in Modern Verse* (Harrap, 1968), copyright holder not traced.

Ernest Jones, from *Sigmund Freud—Life and Works* (Hogarth Press, 1955), by permission of Random House UK Ltd.

Sir Lawrence Jones, from *Georgian Afternoon* (Hart-Davis, 1958), by permission of HarperCollins Publishers Ltd.

Satoshi Kamata, extract from *Japan in the Passing Lane* translated by Tatsuru Akimoto (Allen & Unwin, 1983), by permission of HarperCollins Publishers Ltd. and Pantheon Books, a division of Random House, Inc.

John Maynard Keynes, from 'Economic Possibilities for our Grandchildren' (1930) from *The Collected Writings of John Maynard Keynes*, vol. ix (Macmillan, for the Royal Economic Society), Copyright © The Royal Economic Society, 1972, by permission of Macmillan Ltd.

Sunil Khilnani, from *The Idea of India* (Hamish Hamilton, 1977), reprinted by permission of Penguin Books Ltd.

James Kirkup, 'A Correct Comparison' from *Collected Longer Poems*, i: *An Extended Breath* (University of Salzburg Press, 1996), by permission of the author.

Verlyn Klinkenborg, from *The Last Fine Time* (Martin Secker & Warburg, 1991), by permission of Random House UK Ltd.

William Langland, from *The Vision of Piers Plowman* translated by Henry W. Wells (Sheed & Ward, 1938), by permission of the publishers.

Philip Larkin, 'Toads' from *The Less Deceived* (1955), by permission of The Marvell Press, England and Australia; 'Toads Revisited' from *The Whitsun Weddings* (1964), and lines from 'Livings' from *High Windows* (1974) by permission of the publishers, Faber & Faber Ltd.; from a letter to Winifred Bradshaw, in *Selected Letters of Philip Larkin 1940–1985* edited by Anthony Thwaite (1992) by permission of the publishers, Faber & Faber Ltd.

Primo Levi, from *The Wrench* (*La chiave a stella*) translated by William Weaver (Michael Joseph, 1984), by permission of Penguin Books Ltd. and the Blake Friedman Agency.

Jeremy Lewis, from *The Chatto Book of Office Life* (Chatto & Windus, 1992), copyright © 1992 Jeremy Lewis, by permission of Gillon Aitken Associates Ltd.

Sinclair Lewis, from *The Job* (Cape, 1933).

Robert Linhart, from *The Assembly Line* translated by Margaret Crosland (John Calder/University of Massachusetts Press, 1981), copyright © 1981 by John Calder Ltd., by permission of The Calder Educational Trust, London and the University of Massachusetts Press.

David Lodge, from *Ginger, You're Barmy* (Penguin, 1984), Copyright © David Lodge 1962, and from *Nice Work* (Secker & Warburg, 1988), Copyright © David Lodge 1988, both by permission of Curtis Brown Ltd., London, on behalf of the author.

Thomas Lynch, from *The Undertaking* (Jonathan Cape, 1997), by permission of Random House UK Ltd. and Richard P. McDonough, Literary Agent.

Sylvia Lynd, 'The Mower' from *Collected Poems* (Macmillan, 1945), copyright holder not traced.

Phyllis McGinley, 'Office Party' from *Times Three* (Martin Secker & Warburg, 1961), by permission of Random House UK Ltd. on behalf of the author and Viking Penguin, a division of Penguin Putnam, Inc.

Geoffrey Marshall, from *Oxford Magazine* (1987), by permission of the author.

Karl Marx, from *Theories of Surplus Value* (Part 1) translated by G. A. Bonner and Emile Burns (Lawrence & Wishart, 1969), by permission of the publishers; from *Economic and Philosophical Manuscripts* translated by David McLellan in *Early Works* (Blackwell, 1972), by permission of the publishers; from *The German Ideology* edited and translated by Loyd D. Easton and Kurt H. Guddat (Doubleday

Anchor, 1967; reprinted with corrections by Hackett Publishing Co. Inc., 1997), by permission of L. D. Easton and the publishers; and from *Grundrisse* translated by Martin Nicolaus (Penguin, 1973), copyright holder not traced.

John Masefield, 'The Everlasting Mercy' from *Collected Poems* (Heinemann, 1932), by permission of The Society of Authors as the Literary Representative of the Estate of John Masefield.

Mass-Observation, from Tom Harrisson (ed.), *War Factory: Mass Observation Report* (1943), Copyright © the Trustees of the Mass-Observation Archive at the University of Sussex, by permission of Curtis Brown Ltd., London.

Edgar Lee Masters, 'Editor Whedon' from *Spoon River Anthology* (Macmillan New York, 1966).

Peter Medawar, from *Pluto's Republic* (OUP, 1982), by permission of Oxford University Press.

H. L. Mencken, from *Selected Prejudices, First Series* (Capo, 1926-1935), by permission of Random House, Inc. and the Enoch Pratt Free Library, Baltimore, Maryland, in accordance with the terms of the will of H. L. Mencken.

C. Wright Mills, from *White Collar: The American Middle Class* (OUP, 1953), copyright © 1951 by C. Wright Mills, by permission of Oxford University Press, Inc.

Elma Mitchell, 'Thoughts after Ruskin' from *The Man in the Flesh* (Peterloo Poets, 1976), by permission of the publisher.

Sydney Moseley, from *Private Diaries* (Max Parrish in association with Outspoken Press, Bournemouth, 1960), copyright holder not traced.

R. H. Mottram, from *Sixty-Four, Ninety Four* (Chatto & Windus), by permission of A. P. Watt on behalf of the Estate of R. H. Mottram.

Ogden Nash, 'Will Consider Situation' from *Collected Verse* (J. M. Dent, 1961).

Friedriche Nietzsche, from *The Gay Science* translated by Walter Kaufmann (Vintage, 1974); from *Beyond Good and Evil* translated by Walter Kaufmann (Modern Library, 1966), by permission of Random House, Inc.

Sir Charles Oman, from *On the Writing of History* (Methuen, 1939), copyright holder not traced.

George Orwell, from 'Looking Back on the Spanish War' from *Such, Such Were the Joys*, copyright 1953 by the Estate of Sonia B. Orwell; from *Down and Out in Paris and London* (1933), copyright © George Orwell 1933 and renewed 1961 by Sonia Pitt-Rivers; and from *The Road to Wigan Pier* (1937), copyright © George Orwell 1937, copyright © 1958 by the Estate of Sonia B. Orwell; all by permission of A. M. Heath & Company Limited on behalf of Mark Hamilton as the Literary Executor of the Estate of the Late Sonia Brownell Orwell, Martin Secker & Warburg Ltd. (publishers), and Harcourt Brace & Company.

Dorothy Parker, 'Bohemia' from *The Collected Dorothy Parker* (1973), by permission of the publishers, Gerald Duckworth & Co, Ltd., and Viking Penguin, a division of Penguin Putnam Inc.

Tony Parker and Robert Henry Allerton, from *The Courage of His Convictions* (Hutchinson, 1962).

C. Northcote Parkinson, from *Parkinson's Law or the Pursuit of Progress* (Murray, 1957), and *Parkinson's Law or the Rising Pyramid* (Murray, 1958), by permission of John Murray (Publishers) Ltd.

Tara Patel, 'In Bombay' from Eunice de Souza (ed.), *Nine Indian Women Poets* (OUP Delhi, 1997), by permission of Oxford University Press, New Delhi.

J. G. Patterson, from *Industrial Welfare* (1934), copyright holder not traced.

Okot p'Bitek, 'Woman of Africa' from *Song of Lawino and Song of Ocol* (Heinemann Educational, 1984), by permission of East African Educational Publishers Ltd.

Samuel Pepys, from *The Diary of Samuel Pepys*, edited by Robert Latham and William Matthews (HarperCollins), Copyright © The Master, Fellows and Scholars of Magdalene College, Cambridge, Robert Latham and the Executors of William Matthews, 1983, by permission of the Peters Fraser & Dunlop Group Limited.

Pliny the Younger, from *Letters and Panegyricus* translated by Betty Radice (Harvard University Press, 1969), by permission of the publishers and the Loeb Classical Library.

Po Chü-I, 'Watching the Reapers' and 'Lazy Man's Song' translated from the Chinese by Arthur Waley in *Chinese Poems* (Allen & Unwin, 1949), by permission of John Robinson for the Arthur Waley Estate.

Eileen Power, from her translation of *The Goodman of Paris* (The Broadway Translations, Routledge, 1928), by permission of the publisher.

J. B. Priestley, from *English Journey* (Wm. Heinemann, in association with Gollancz, 1934), by permission of Random House UK Ltd. on behalf of the author; from *Angel Pavement* (Wm. Heinemann, 1930), by permission of Random House UK Ltd. and of The Peters Fraser & Dunlop Group Limited.

V. S. Pritchett, from *Cab at the Door* (Chatto & Windus, 1968), and from *It May Never Happen* (Chatto & Windus, 1945), © as printed in the original volumes, by permission of The Peters Fraser & Dunlop Group Limited.

Libby Purves, 'Hard at Work, Off and On', © Libby Purves, first published in *The Times*, 9 March 1992, by permission of the author and The Lisa Eveleigh Literary Agency.

Barbara Pym, from *Quartet in Autumn* (Macmillan, 1977), by permission of the publishers.

Tracy Quan, Letter to *New York Review of Books*, 5 November 1992, Copyright © 1992 NYREV, Inc., by permission of *The New York Review of Books*.

Rabanus Maurus, translated by Siegfried Wenzel from *The Sin of Sloth [De Ecclesiastica Disciplina]* (University of California Press, 1967), by permission of the publishers.

Kathryn Allen Rabuzzi, from *The Sacred and the Feminine: Toward a Theology of Work* (Seabury Press, 1982) by permission of the author.

Craig Raine, 'The Grocer' from *The Onion, Memory* (OUP, 1978), by permission of Oxford University Press.

Henry Handel Richardson, from *The Getting of Wisdom* (Wm. Heinemann, 1910), by permission of Random House UK Ltd.

Lillian B. Rubin, trucker quoted in *Words of Pain* (Basic Books, 1972).

Carol Rumens, 'Gifts and Loans' from *Unplayed Music* (Chatto, 1981), also in *Selected Poems* (1987), by permission of The Peters Fraser & Dunlop Group Ltd. on behalf of the author.

Bertrand Russell, from 'In Praise of Idleness', first published in *Harper's Magazine* (October 1932), reprinted in *In Praise of Idleness and Other Essays* (1935), by permission of Routledge on behalf of the Bertrand Russell Peace Foundation.

Vita Sackville-West, 'Honour the Gardener' from *The Garden* (Michael Joseph, 1946), Copyright © Vita Sackville-West 1946; and 'The Yeoman' from *The Land*

(Heinemann, 1926), Copyright © Vita Sackville-West 1926; both by permission of Curtis Brown Ltd., London.

Antoine de Saint-Exupéry, from *Night Flight* translated by Stuart Gilbert (Harmsworth, 1932), copyright holder not traced.

Raphael Samuel, from 'The Workshop of the World' in *History Workshop Journal*, 3 (1977), by permission of Oxford University Press.

Carl Sandburg, 'Psalm of Those Who Go Forth Before Daylight' from *Cornhuskers*, copyright 1918 by Holt, Rinehart & Winston and renewed 1946 by Carl Sandburg, by permission of Harcourt Brace & Company.

Siegfried Sassoon, 'The Case for the Miners' from *Collected Poems of Siegfried Sassoon* (Faber, 1984), copyright 1918, 1920 by E. P. Dutton, copyright 1936, 1946, 1947, 1948 by Siegfried Sassoon, by permission of George Sassoon and Viking Penguin, a division of Penguin Putnam Inc.

Vernon Scannell, 'The Old Books' and 'Ageing Schoolmaster' from *Collected Poems 1950–1993* (Robson Books, 1993), by permission of the author.

Meyer Schapiro, from 'Diderot as Artist' in *Theory and Philosophy of Art* (George Braziller, 1944).

Margaret Scott, 'Housework' from *The Black Swans*, by permission of the publishers, HarperCollins Publishers, Australia.

Vikram Seth, 'Work and Freedom' from *All You Who Sleep Tonight*, Copyright Vikram Seth, 1990, by permission of Curtis Brown Ltd., London, on behalf of the author.

Upton Sinclair, from *The Jungle* (Penguin Classics, 1985), copyright 1905, 1906 by Upton Sinclair, by permission of Laurence Pollinger Ltd. on behalf of the Estate of Upton Sinclair and Viking Penguin, a division of Penguin Putnam Inc.

Gary Snyder, 'Hay for the Horses' from *Riprap and Cold Mountain Poems* (City Lights Books, 1965).

Aleksandr Solzhenitsyn, from *The Gulag Archipelago* published by Harvill in three volumes under the following titles: *The Gulag Archipelago: 1918–1956, I–II*, copyright © Aleksandr I. Solzhenitsyn, copyright © English translation Harper & Row Publishers, Inc. 1973, 1974; *The Gulag Archipelago: 1918–1956, III–IV*, copyright © Aleksandr I. Solzhenitsyn 1974, copyright © English translation Harper & Row Publishers, Inc. 1975; and *The Gulag Archipelago: 1918–1956, V–VII*, copyright © the Russian Social Fund for Persecuted Persons and Their Families 1976, copyright © English translation Harper & Row Publishers, Inc. 1978; by permission of The Harvill Press and HarperCollins Publishers, Inc.

Statius, from *Silvae* translated by K. D. White in K. D. White, *Greek and Roman Technology* (Thames & Hudson, 1984), by permission of the publishers.

John Steinbeck, from *Cannery Row* (Wm. Heinemann, 1954), Copyright 1945 by John Steinbeck, renewed © 1973 by Elaine Steinbeck, John Steinbeck IV, and Thom Steinbeck, by permission of Random House UK Ltd.; from *The Grapes of Wrath*, copyright 1939, renewed © 1967 by John Steinbeck, by permission of Viking Penguin, a division of Penguin Putnam Inc.

Brian Stone, translation of anonymous poem 'I've waited longing for today,' from *Medieval English Verse* (Penguin, 1964), by permission of Penguin Books Ltd.

A. G. Street, from *Farmer's Glory* (1932), copyright holder not traced.

Laurie Taylor, from 'The Timetable' from *Professor Lapping Sends His Apologies* (Trentham Books, 1986), by permission of the publishers.

A. S. J. Tessimond, 'The Man in the Bowler Hat' from *Voices in a Giant City* (Wm. Heinemann, 1947).

R. S. Thomas, 'The Labourer' and 'Cynddylan on a Tractor' from *Song of the Year's Turning* (Hart-Davis, 1955), by permission of the author.

Flora Thompson, from *Lark Rise to Candleford* (OUP, 1945), by permission of Oxford University Press.

Lev Nikolaevich Tolstoy, from 'Letter on Education' translated by Aylmer Maude (OUP, 1903); from 'The Cossacks' in *Tales of Army Life* translated by Louise and Aylmer Maude (OUP, 1935); from 'The Wisdom of Children' in *Recollections and Essays* translated by Aylmer Maude (OUP, 1937); and from *Anna Karenina* translated by Louise and Aylmer Maude (OUP, 1918, 1949); all by permission of Oxford University Press.

G. A. W. Tomlinson, from *Coal Miner* (Hutchinson, 1937), copyright holder not traced.

Jane Tompkins, 'postcard 14' from *A Life in School*, copyright © 1996 by Jane Tompkins, by permission of Addison Wesley Longman, USA.

Alexis de Tocqueville, from Larry Siedentop, *Tocqueville* (Past Masters) (OUP, 1994), by permission of Oxford University Press.

Polly Toynbee, from *A Working Life* (Hodder & Stoughton, 1971), by permission of the author.

G. M. Trevelyan, from *Clio—A Muse, and Other Essays* (1913) by permission of George Trevelyan and the publishers, Addison Wesley Longman.

Louis Untermeyer, 'Portrait of a Machine' from *Portrait of a Machine* (Chatto & Windus), copyright holder not traced.

David Verey, quoted in Cathy Courtney and Paul Thompson, *City Lives* (Methuen, National Life Story Collection, 1996).

Voltaire, from 'Candide' from *Candide and Other Stories* translated and edited by Roger Pearson (Oxford World's Classics, 1990), by permission of Oxford University Press.

Margaret Walker, 'Lineage' from *This is My Century* (University of Georgia Press, 1989), copyright © 1989 by Margaret Walker Alexander.

Davina Walter, quoted in Cathy Courtney and Paul Thompson, *City Lives* (Methuen, National Life Story Collection, 1996).

Keith Waterhouse, from 'How Long, O Lord . . .? in *Waterhouse at Large* (1985), by permission of David Higham Associates.

Simone Weil, from *Oppression and Liberty*, translated by Arthur Wills and John Petrie (Routledge & Kegan Paul, 1958), by permission of Routledge.

H. G. Wells, from *Kipps* (Collins) by permission of A. P. Watt Ltd. on behalf of the Literary Executors of the Estate of H. G. Wells.

Arnold Wesker, from *I'm Talking About Jerusalem* in *The Wesker Trilogy* (Jonathan Cape, 1960), by permission of Random House UK Ltd.

Margaret Wheeler, extract from letter to George Bernard Shaw, 29 March 1950, from *Letter from Margaret* edited by Rebecca Swift (Chatto & Windus, 1992), by permission of Random House UK Ltd. on behalf of the author.

William Carlos Williams, lines from 'Pictures from Brueghel, vii, The Corn Harvest' from *Collected Poems 1939–1962*, vol. ii (Carcanet), Copyright © 1962 by William Carlos Williams; and from 'Paterson: Book Two' from *Selected Poems* (Penguin), Copyright © 1948 by William Carlos Williams by permission of Laurence Pollinger Ltd. and New Directions Publishing Corp.

Sloan Wilson, from *The Man in the Grey Flannel Suit* (London, Cassell & Co. Ltd., 1956), Copyright © 1955 by Sloan Wilson, renewed 1983 by Sloan Wilson, by permission of Simon & Schuster.

Hope Wise, from 'The Signalwoman' quoted in Ronald Fraser, *Work* (Penguin, 1968), by permission of Penguin Books Ltd.

P. G. Wodehouse, from *Heavy Weather* (1933) by permission of A. P. Watt Ltd. on behalf of The Trustees of the Wodehouse Estate, and of Random House UK Ltd.

Tom Wolfe, from *The Bonfire of the Vanities* (Jonathan Cape, 1987), Copyright © 1987, 1988 by Tom Wolfe, by permission of Random House UK Ltd. on behalf of the author.

Glyn Wright, 'Where the Sexes Meet' from *Could Have Been Funny* (Spike, 1995), by permission of the publishers on behalf of the author.

Andrew Young, 'Idleness' from *Selected Poems*, by permission of the publishers, Carcanet Press Limited.

Michael Young and Tom Schuller, *Life After Work* (quoting Mrs Bruce) (HarperCollins, 1991), by permission of the publishers.

Émile Zola, from *L'Assommoir* translated by Margaret Mauldon (Oxford World's Classics, 1995); from *Germinal* translated and edited by Peter Collier (Oxford World's Classics, 1993); from *The Masterpiece* translated by Thomas Walton, revised by Roger Pearson (Oxford World's Classics, 1993); all by permission of Oxford University Press.

Index of Authors and Sources Quoted